펴낸이 김기훈 I 김진희

펴낸곳 (주)쎄듀 I 서울특별시 강남구 논현로 305 (역삼동)

발행일 2022년 4월 30일 제1개정판 1쇄

내용문의 www.cedubook.com

구입문의 콘텐츠 마케팅 사업본부

　　　　　Tel. 02-6241-2007

　　　　　Fax. 02-2058-0209

등록번호 제 22-2472호

ISBN 978-89-6806-261-2

첫단추

듣기유형편

BUTTON

저자

김기훈　現 ㈜ 쎄듀 대표이사

現 메가스터디 영어영역 대표강사

前 서울특별시 교육청 외국어 교육정책자문위원회 위원

　　　저서　천일문 / 천일문 Training Book / 천일문 GRAMMAR

첫단추 BASIC / 쎄듀 본영어 / 어휘끝 / 어법끝 / 문법의 골든룰 101

절대평가 PLAN A / 리딩 플랫폼 / ALL씀 서술형

Reading Relay / The 리딩플레이어 / 빈칸백서 / 오답백서

첫단추 / 파워업 / 수능영어 절대유형 / 수능실감 등

쎄듀 영어교육연구센터

쎄듀 영어교육센터는 영어 콘텐츠에 대한 전문지식과 경험을 바탕으로
최고의 교육 콘텐츠를 만들고사 최선의 노력을 나하는 전문가 집단입니다.

장정문 선임연구원 · **김진경** 전임연구원

마케팅	콘텐츠 마케팅 사업본부
제작	정승호
영업	문병구
인디자인 편집	올댓에디팅
디자인	쎄듀 디자인팀
영문교열	Eric Scheusner · Stephen Daniel White

●● 이 책을 내며

어떻게 하면 영어를 잘할 수 있을까 고민하고 있는 당신에게 이렇게 말하고 싶습니다.
"영어를 많이 접하세요."

어떻게 하면 영어 듣기를 잘할 수 있을까 고민하고 있는 당신에게 이렇게 말하고 싶습니다.
"일단 들어보세요."

영어 듣기 능력이 나아지지 않는다고 조급해하는 당신에게 묻고 싶습니다.
"들릴 때까지 반복해서 들어보셨나요?"

아무리 듣기 문제를 많이 풀어도 실력이 향상되지 않는다며 고민하는 당신에게 묻고 싶습니다.
"혹시 문제만 풀고 바로 책을 덮어버리지는 않으셨나요?"

지금 이 순간에도 수능 영어 듣기 시험이 걱정되는 당신에게 힘주어 말합니다.
"들으면 들립니다!"

수능 영어의 듣기 시험은 듣기의 형태로 의사소통 능력을 테스트합니다.
수능 영어의 듣기 실력을 기르려면, 다음 학습 과제들을 효과적으로 수행해야 합니다.

1 수능 영어 듣기 평가의 '유형'을 파악하고 해결 전략을 학습한다.
2 문제를 풀고 나서 '딕테이션'으로 듣기 실력과 정확도를 높인다.
3 실제 시험을 보듯 듣기 모의고사를 풀어보면서 실전 적용력을 키운다.

쎄듀 첫단추 듣기 유형편은 위의 과제를 무리 없이 효율적으로 수행할 수 있도록
각 단계를 세분화하여 구성하였습니다.
학습자들의 영어 듣기 실력 향상에 이 책이 도움이 되길 기원합니다.

저자

목차

Contents

● PART Ⅰ ┊ 유형편

● PART Ⅱ | 실전편

[별책] 정답 및 해설

구성과 특징

About This Book

• PART I 유형편

12개의 수능 듣기 유형을 분석하고, 해결 전략을 제시합니다.
4단계의 듣기 연습을 통해 문제 풀이 능력을 향상할 수 있습니다.

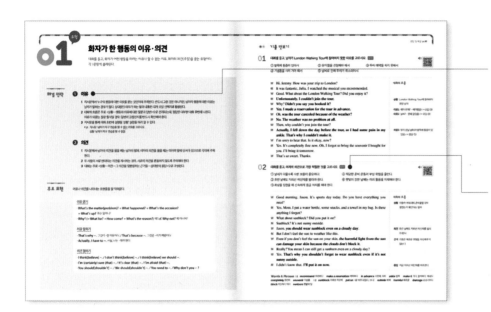

유형 소개 및 해결 전략

출제 유형을 탐구하고 문제 풀이에
핵심이 되는 해결 전략과 주요 표현을
학습합니다.

기출 맛보기

기출 문제 분석을 통해 출제 경향을
확인합니다.

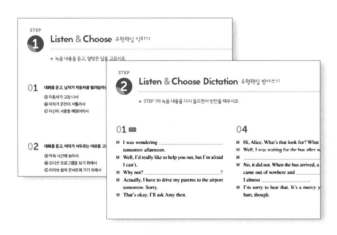

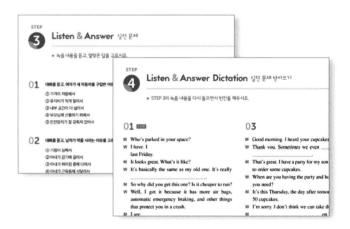

Step 1·2 Listen & Choose

유형별 연습 문제를 풀어보고
받아쓰기로 듣기 자신감을 키웁니다.

Step 3·4 Listen & Answer

유형별 실전 문제를 풀어보고
받아쓰기로 청취력을 향상시킵니다.

딕테이션 방법

녹음을 들으며 딕테이션 빈칸을 채워 봅니다. → 들리지 않는 부분이 있다면 두세 번 연속해서 듣습니다. → 스크립트를 보며 정답을 확인하고 틀린 이유를 파악합니다. → 모르는 어휘나 표현은 암기하고, 잘 들리지 않았던 발음을 학습합니다. → 다시 녹음을 들으며 내용을 확인합니다.

PART Ⅱ · 실전편

유형편에서 쌓은 실력을 10회분의 실전 모의고사로 점검할 수 있습니다.

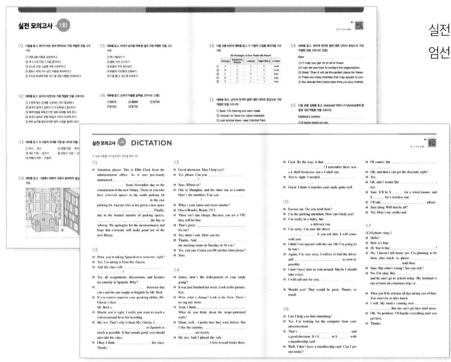

실전과 꼭 같은 유형 배치와
엄선된 문제로 실전에 완벽히 대비합니다.

정답 근거, 주요 표현, 연음을 위주로
받아쓰기 연습을 할 수 있는 딕테이션을
매 회 수록했습니다.

정답 및 해설

스크립트 및 해석은 물론 상세한 해설이 있어,
혼자서도 충분한 학습이 가능합니다.

온라인 무료 부가서비스 www.cedubook.com

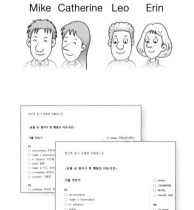

Mike Catherine Leo Erin

듣기 MP3 파일

다양한 원어민들의 목소리와
억양에 익숙해질 수 있도록
총 4명의 남/여 성우가 녹음했습니다.

어휘리스트, 어휘테스트

중요 어휘를 정리한
어휘리스트로 단어를 암기하고,
어휘테스트로 확인합니다.

수능 모의고사 첫단추 Q&A

Q 모의고사는 언제 보나요?

A 모의고사는 수능(대학수학능력시험)을 준비하기 위한 연습 시험입니다. 각 학교마다 모의고사를 치르는 횟수는 모두 다르지만 3월, 6월, 9월, 11월에는 전국 모든 고등학생을 대상으로 하는 전국연합학력평가가 실시됩니다. 그러므로 같은 학년의 학생들과 비교하여 자신의 실력을 점검해볼 수 있는 좋은 기회이며, 이때 출제되는 문제 유형은 지난해의 대학수학능력시험과 거의 유사하게 출제되므로 수능이 무엇인지 미리 경험해볼 수 있는 중요한 시험입니다.

Q 내신이 중요한가요, 수능 모의고사가 중요한가요?

A 각 대학에서는 수능, 내신, 대학별 고사 등 다양한 기준을 마련하고 있습니다. 그중에서 반영 비율이 가장 높은 것은 단연 수능입니다. 현재, 고등학교 교육 정상화를 위한 대입 전형 간소화 추세에 따라 논술, 적성 고사, 구술면접 등 기타 전형요소들이 줄어들고 있어, 수능의 영향력은 더 커질 것으로 예상됩니다. 각 대학에서는 수능의 영향력이 막강한 정시모집 비율을 늘릴 가능성도 있습니다. 수능은 단기간에 준비할 수 있는 것이 아니므로 학교 수업을 차분히 따라가면서 내신 기간에는 내신 대비를, 그 외의 기간에는 꾸준히 수능 모의고사를 준비하는 것이 좋습니다.

Q 첫 모의고사 점수가 끝까지 유지되나요?

A 고등학교 첫 모의고사 점수가 수능 점수가 되어버린다는 이야기를 종종 듣게 됩니다. 그러나 처음의 실력이 그대로 유지될 확률이 높다는 것일 뿐입니다. 처음에 아무리 실력이 좋은 학생이라도 공부를 게을리하면 낮은 점수를 받게 되고, 꾸준히 노력하는 학생은 좋은 성적을 거둘 수 있습니다. 다만, 첫 모의고사에서 좋은 성적을 기둔다면 좀 더 자신감을 가지고 고등학교 생활을 시작할 수 있을 것입니다.

Q 첫 모의고사 범위는 어떻게 되나요?

A 공식적으로는 고1 첫 모의고사는 중학교에서 배운 모든 내용이 시험 범위라고 나와 있습니다. 그러나 영어 영역의 경우에는 영어 실력 전반을 측정하므로 범위를 나누는 것은 무의미합니다. 다만, 중학교 과정을 마쳤다면 알 수 있는 어휘, 어법을 포함한 지문이 출제되므로 고1 난이도에 알맞은 문제를 풀어보며 유형을 익히는 것이 좋습니다.

Q **모의고사는 어떻게 준비해야 하나요?**

A 모의고사는 어디까지나 자신의 실력을 점검하기 위한 시험입니다. 내신처럼 성적이 기록되어 대학 입시에 바로 반영되는 시험은 아니지만, 수능에 대비하고 실력을 점검하기 위해 꾸준히 다양한 문제를 풀어보면서 차분히 준비하는 것이 좋습니다.

1 **기출 문제 및 다양한 문제를 풀어봅니다.**

많은 문제를 풀어보는 것만큼 좋은 시험 대비 방법은 없습니다. 특히 기출 문제는 실제 수능이나 전국연합학력 평가가 어떻게 출제되는지 보여주는 가장 정확한 자료입니다. 모든 문제는 EBSi 사이트의 '기출문제'란에서 무료로 다운받을 수 있으며(www.ebsi.co.kr), 수능 출제기관인 한국교육과정평가원에서 시행하는 시험은 평가원 사이트 (kice.re.kr)에서도 다운받을 수 있습니다. 쎄듀 첫단추 시리즈는 이 중 가장 대표적인 기출 문제를 엄선하여 유형별로 자세한 해결 전략을 제시하고 있습니다.

2 **틀린 문제들을 중점적으로 공부합니다.**

문제를 많이 풀어보는 것보다 한 번 풀어본 문제를 확실히 이해하고 넘어가는 것이 더 중요합니다. 모든 문제를 다시 살펴보면서 몰랐던 어휘나 해석하기 어려운 구문 등을 표시해두고 해설과 해석을 참고하여 확실히 암기하고 이해하도록 합니다. 적어도, 틀린 문제와 헷갈리는 문제는 따로 표시를 해두고 반드시 다시 풀어보면서 자신이 부족한 점을 보완하도록 합니다.

Q **곧 모의고사를 봅니다. 주의할 점은 없나요?**

A 모의고사는 실제 수능처럼 하루 동안 전 영역의 시험을 보게 되므로 긴 시간 동안 집중력을 유지하면서 많은 문제를 풀 수 있어야 합니다. 또한, 실제로 모의고사를 보게 되면 시간이 모자라 당황하는 경우가 많습니다. 영어 영역은 70분간 총 45문제를 풀게 되는데, 검토와 답안지 작성을 위해서 3~5분의 시간이 필요하므로 평소에도 실제 모의고사를 보는 것처럼 시간 관리 연습을 하는 것이 좋습니다.

수능 영어 듣기 **출제 경향 및 대책**

수능 영어 듣기의 유형별 출제 빈도 및 경향

유형		2019 수능	2020~23 수능	2024 수능
사실적 이해 Ⅰ (특정 정보 파악)	이유	1	1	1
	의견	1	1	1
	할 일·부탁한 일	1 (부탁한 일)	1 (할 일)	1 (할 일)
사실적 이해 Ⅱ (세부 내용 파악)	금액	1	1	1
	그림 불일치	1	1	1
	표의 내용	1	1	1
	미언급	1	1	1
	불일치	1	1	1
추론적·종합적 이해	관계	1	1	0
	목적·요지	1	1	2
	세트형 문항	2 (주제·미언급)	2 (주제·미언급)	2 (주제·미언급)
적응력 (말하기 영역)	짧은 대화에 이어질 응답	2	2	2
	긴 대화에 이어질 응답	2	2	2
	담화 상황	1	1	1
계		17	17	17

수능 영어 듣기의 출제 경향 분석

- **출제 유형 및 문항 수** : 2019학년도 수능 이후로 거의 유사한 유형의 문제들이 출제되고 있다. 배점은 2점 14문항, 3점 3문항으로 **총점 100점**에 듣기가 37점을 차지한다.

- **길이** : 수능 평균 단어 수는 약 110~145개를 유지하고 있다. (단, 세트형 문항은 제외. 세트형 문항 단어 수는 약 160~185개다.)

- **속도** : 원어민의 자연스러운 말하기 속도는 1분당 170~190단어 정도인 데 비해, 수능은 평균 140~150단어로 다소 느린 편이다. 하지만 속도는 조금씩 빨라지고 있는 추세이다.

- **내용** : 수능 듣기의 대화문 또는 담화문은 수험생의 삶과 밀접히 연관되어 있거나(가정, 학교, 교우관계 등), 사회 구성원이라면 누구든지 겪게 되는 일상적인 상황 또는 소재(의식주, 일, 쇼핑, 이동, 방송, 여가 생활 등)를 활용하여 실제로 있을 법한 진정성(authenticity) 있는 내용을 다루고 있다. 최근 모의고사에서는 실용 소재가 70~80%, 기초 학술 소재가 20~30% 출제되었다.

• 난이도 : 속도, 내용 등은 평이한 수준에 속한다. 하지만 아래 여러 가지 요인에 의해 전반적으로 난이도는 상승 추세이고, 앞으로도 지속적으로 상향 조정될 것으로 예상된다.

① 소재의 범위가 넓어지고 있으며, 실용 소재뿐 아니라 기초 학술 소재도 다뤄지고 있다.
② 대화 또는 담화의 전개 구조가 다소 복잡해지고 있다.
③ 특정한 구어체 표현을 알아야 풀 수 있는 문제도 출제되고 있어 실용영어 학습의 강화라는 영어 학습의 방향을 따르고 있다.
④ 과거에는 정답의 단서가 두세 번 반복되어 노출되었지만, 최근에는 한 번만 언급되는 경향이 늘고 있다. 순간적으로 이를 놓치면 정답을 맞힐 수 없으므로 집중력이 더욱 요구된다.
⑤ 세트형 문항의 출현을 들 수 있다. 세트형 문항이란, 하나의 담화나 대화를 듣고 그에 관련된 문제를 두 개 푸는 것인데, 들으면서 머릿속으로 처리해야 할 문제 수가 늘어나므로 난이도가 자연히 상승하게 된다.

3
수능 영어 듣기를 위한 다섯 가지 조언

첫째, 들으면 들린다.
언어 학습은 특별한 재능을 필요로 하지 않는다. 그 언어에 대한 노출량을 늘리는 것이 최선의 방법이다. 듣기를 잘하려면, 무엇보다도 듣는 양을 늘려야 한다.

둘째, 안 들리는 원인을 제거하라.
듣기는 들었는데 무슨 말인지 이해가 되지 않는 것은 주로 영어의 특정한 발음 현상 때문이거나, 어휘 또는 표현을 몰라서인 경우가 많다. 수능 듣기의 녹음 속도는 실제 발화 속도보다 느리기 때문에 몇 가지 발음 현상만 익히면 대부분 해결될 수 있다. 어휘 및 표현은 듣기 대본을 통해서 꾸준히 습득해 나가야 한다.

셋째, 직독직해 · 직청직해를 연습하라.
평소에 영어 지문을 읽을 때 우리말 어순대로 번역하는 습관을 가지고 있다면, 지금 당장 버려야 한다. 영어 문장을 영어의 어순 그대로 읽고 바로 이해하는 직독직해의 습관을 들여야 한다. 그래야만 청취할 때에도 의미 단위별로 직청직해하기가 훨씬 수월해진다.

넷째, 받아쓰기를 하라.
듣기 문제를 풀고 채점하는 것만으로는 실력이 늘지 않는다. 의사소통에 긴요한 대화문 또는 담화문을 받아쓰는 연습을 함으로써, 청취가 안 되는 부분을 확인하고 이를 보완하는 과정이 필요하다. 받아쓰기를 하며 잘 안 들리는 부분은 반복 청취하므로 자신에게 부족한 부분의 학습이 저절로 강화되는 효과가 있다.

다섯째, 핵심 정보의 청취에 집중하라.
문제를 풀 때는 모든 정보를 다 들으려고 욕심을 내서는 안 된다. 듣지 못한 것에 대한 미련은 현재 들리는 것을 청취하는 데 방해가 될 뿐이다. 녹음 내용을 듣기 전에 문제의 지시문과 선택지를 잘 읽고, 문제 유형에 따라 그 문제 해결에 필요한 핵심 정보의 청취에 집중해야 한다.

PART

I

유형편

수능의 듣기 유형은 변화 없이 거의 정해져 있다.
각 유형별로 문제 해결의 핵심이 되는 아래 세 가지 사항들을 목표로 학습해나가도록 하자.

☑ 목표 Check!

1 빈출되는 표현들을 잘 익힌다.
2 주로 정답을 이끄는 표현이 무엇인지를 알아둔다.
3 대화나 담화의 공통된 내용 흐름과 그 흐름상 정답이 주로 위치하는 부분을 알아둔다.

첫단추
듣기 모의고사

유형편

CHAPTER

1

사실적 이해 I
(특정 정보 파악)

대화에서 지시문이 요구하는 특정한 정보를 잘 듣고 답하면 된다.
흔히 대화마다 공통적인 흐름이 있고 정답이 주로 드러나는 위치가
있으므로 이들을 잘 알아두는 것이 좋다. 남, 여의 말을 혼동하지 않는
것도 중요하다. 비교적 쉽게 정답을 맞힐 수 있는 유형이다.

화자가 한 행동의 이유·의견

대화를 듣고, 화자가 어떤 행동을 한 이유나 할 수 없는 이유, 화자의 의견(주장)을 묻는 유형이다.
각 1문항씩 출제된다.

해결 전략

❶ 이유

1 지시문에서 누구의 행동에 대한 이유를 묻는 것인지에 주목한다. 반드시 그런 것은 아니지만, 남자의 행동에 대한 이유는
남자가 말하는 경우가 많다. 상대방인 여자가 하는 말의 내용은 대개 오답 선택지로 활용된다.

2 대화의 흐름은 주로 <상황―행동의 이유에 대한 질문과 답변>으로 전개되는데, 정답은 대부분 대화 후반에 나온다.
이유가 되묻는 질문 형식일 경우, 답변이 긍정인지를 반드시 확인해야 한다.

3 지시문을 통해 대화 초반에 설명될 '상황' 설정을 미리 알 수 있다.

    e.g. 지시문: 남자가 탁구 연습을 할 수 <u>없는</u> 이유를 고르시오.
            상황: 남자가 탁구 연습을 할 수 없음

❷ 의견

1 지시문에서 남자의 의견을 물을 때는 남자의 말에, 여자의 의견을 물을 때는 여자의 말에 단서가 있으므로 각각에 주목
한다.

2 두 사람이 서로 반대되는 의견을 제시하는 경우, 서로의 의견을 혼동하지 않도록 주의해야 한다.

3 대화는 주로 <상황―의견―그 의견을 뒷받침하는 근거들―상대방의 응답>으로 구성된다.

주요 표현

이유나 의견을 나타내는 표현들을 잘 익혀둔다.

이유 묻기

• What's the matter[problem]? = What happened? = What's the occasion?
  = What's up? 무슨 일이니?

• Why? (= What for? = How come? = What's the reason?) 왜? *cf.* Why not? 왜 아니야?

이유 말하기

• That's why ~. 그것이 ~한 이유이다. / That's because ~. 그것은 ~이기 때문이다.

• Actually, I have to ~. 사실, 나는 ~해야 한다.

의견 말하기

• I think[believe] ~. / I don't think[believe] ~. / I think[believe] we should ~.

• I'm (certainly) sure (that) ~. / It's clear (that) ~.

• I'm afraid (that) ~.

• You should[shouldn't] ~. / We should[shouldn't] ~. / You need to ~. / Why don't you ~ ?

✻✻ **기출 맛보기**

01 대화를 듣고, 남자가 London Walking Tour에 참여하지 못한 이유를 고르시오. 모의

① 발목에 통증이 있어서　　　　② 뮤지컬을 관람해야 해서　　　　③ 투어 예약을 하지 못해서

④ 기념품을 사러 가야 해서　　　　⑤ 날씨로 인해 투어가 취소되어서

		대화의 흐름
W	Hi, Jeremy. How was your trip to London?	
M	It was fantastic, Julia. I watched the musical you recommended.	
W	Good. What about the London Walking Tour? Did you enjoy it?	
M	Unfortunately, I couldn't join the tour.	• **상황**: London Walking Tour에 참여하지 못한 남자
W	Why? Didn't you say you booked it?	
M	Yes. I made a reservation for the tour in advance.	• **이유1**: 예약 문제? - 예약했음 (→ 오답 ③)
W	Oh, was the tour canceled because of the weather?	• **이유2**: 날씨? - 문제 없었음 (→ 오답 ⑤)
M	No. The weather was no problem at all.	
W	Then, why couldn't you join the tour?	
M	Actually, I fell down the day before the tour, so I had some pain in my ankle. That's why I couldn't make it.	• **이유3**: 투어 전날 넘어져 발목에 통증이 있었음 (→ 정답 ①)
W	I'm sorry to hear that. Is it okay, now?	
M	Yes. It's completely fine now. Oh, I forgot to bring the souvenir I bought for you. I'll bring it tomorrow.	
W	That's so sweet. Thanks.	

02 대화를 듣고, 여자의 의견으로 가장 적절한 것을 고르시오. 모의

① 날씨가 더울수록 수분 보충이 중요하다.　　　　② 적당한 준비 운동이 부상 위험을 줄인다.

③ 흐린 날에도 자외선 차단제를 발라야 한다.　　　　④ 햇빛이 강한 날에는 야외 활동을 자제해야 한다.

⑤ 화상을 입었을 때 신속하게 응급 처치를 해야 한다.

		대화의 흐름
W	Good morning, Jason. It's sports day today. Do you have everything you need?	• **상황**: 아들이 체육 대회 준비물을 모두 챙겼는지 확인하는 엄마
M	Yes, Mom. I put a water bottle, some snacks, and a towel in my bag. Is there anything I forgot?	
W	What about sunblock? Did you put it on?	
M	Sunblock? It's not sunny outside.	
W	Jason, you should wear sunblock even on a cloudy day.	• **의견**: 흐린 날에도 자외선 차단제를 발라야 한다.
M	But I don't feel the sun in weather like this.	
W	Even if you don't feel the sun on your skin, the harmful light from the sun can damage your skin because the clouds don't block it.	• **근거**: 구름은 해로운 햇빛을 차단해주지 않는다.
M	Really? You mean I can still get a sunburn even on a cloudy day?	
W	Yes. That's why you shouldn't forget to wear sunblock even if it's not sunny outside.	
M	I didn't know that. I'll put it on now.	• **응답**: 지금 자외선 차단제를 바르겠다.

Words & Phrases 01 recommend 추천하다　**make a reservation** 예약하다　**in advance** 사전에, 미리　**ankle** 발목　**make it** 가다, 참석하다; 해내다
completely 완전히　**souvenir** 기념품　**02** sunblock 자외선 차단제　**put on** ~을 바르다[입다, 쓰다]　**outside** 밖에　**harmful** 해로운　**damage** 손상시키다
block 차단하다, 막다　**sunburn** 햇볕에 탐

Listen & Choose 유형핵심 익히기

＊ 녹음 내용을 듣고, 알맞은 답을 고르시오.

01 대화를 듣고, 남자가 자동차를 빌려달라는 여자의 요청을 거절한 이유를 고르시오. 모의

ⓐ 자동차가 고장 나서
ⓑ 여자가 운전이 서툴러서
ⓒ 자신이 사용할 예정이어서

02 대화를 듣고, 여자가 서두르는 이유를 고르시오.

ⓐ 약속 시간에 늦어서
ⓑ 오디션 프로그램을 보기 위해서
ⓒ 라이브 음악 콘서트에 가기 위해서

03 대화를 듣고, 남자가 회사를 그만둔 이유를 고르시오.

ⓐ 급여가 적어서
ⓑ 근무 시간이 길어서
ⓒ 출퇴근이 오래 걸려서

04 대화를 듣고, 여자의 표정이 좋지 <u>않은</u> 이유를 고르시오.

ⓐ 버스가 너무 붐벼서
ⓑ 버스가 늦게 도착해서
ⓒ 새치기를 당해 넘어질 뻔해서

05 대화를 듣고, 남자가 헬스장 회원권을 연장하지 <u>않은</u> 이유를 고르시오. 모의

ⓐ 어깨 부상이 회복되지 않아서
ⓑ 샤워 시설이 낡고 좁아서
ⓒ 운동에 흥미를 잃어서

유형 01 화자가 한 행동의 이유·의견

06 대화를 듣고, 여자의 의견으로 가장 적절한 것을 고르시오.

ⓐ 예상 시간보다 일찍 출발해야 한다.
ⓑ 약속에 늦을 때는 미리 연락해야 한다.
ⓒ 혼잡 시간대에는 지하철을 이용하는 것이 낫다.

07 대화를 듣고, 남자의 의견으로 가장 적절한 것을 고르시오. 모의

ⓐ 운동 전 음식 섭취가 운동을 위한 힘을 준다.
ⓑ 운동 전에 준비 운동을 해야 한다.
ⓒ 운동은 꾸준히 해야 효과가 있다.

08 대화를 듣고, 여자의 의견으로 가장 적절한 것을 고르시오.

ⓐ 영화관 좌석은 편안해야 한다.
ⓑ 영화관에서는 휴대 전화를 꺼야 한다.
ⓒ 조용한 영화 상영 중에 음식 섭취는 부적절하다.

09 대화를 듣고, 남자의 의견으로 가장 적절한 것을 고르시오.

ⓐ 판매자는 상세한 제품 정보를 제공해야 한다.
ⓑ 제품 구매 시 제품의 용도를 먼저 고려해야 한다.
ⓒ 구매를 결정하기 전에 여러 브랜드를 비교해야 한다.

10 대화를 듣고, 여자의 의견으로 가장 적절한 것을 고르시오. 모의

ⓐ 무리한 계획은 여행을 망칠 수 있다.
ⓑ 여행을 가면 현지 음식을 먹어보는 것이 좋다.
ⓒ 남들이 추천하는 음식점에 꼭 가볼 필요는 없다.

Listen & Choose Dictation 유형핵심 받아쓰기

✳ STEP 1의 녹음 내용을 다시 들으면서 빈칸을 채우시오.

01 모의

W I was wondering _____ tomorrow afternoon.

M Well, I'd really like to help you out, but I'm afraid I can't.

W Why not? _____?

M Actually, I have to drive my parents to the airport tomorrow. Sorry.

W That's okay. I'll ask Amy then.

02

M Hi, Emma! Why are you in such a hurry?

W I must go home right away. There's a TV program _____.

M A TV program? You mean the live music concert?

W No, that's not it. It's a new audition program _____.

03

M I _____ last month.

W Why? I thought you were quite satisfied with your job. Weren't you making good money?

M Yes, but I quit it _____ _____. I was working up to 70 hours a week.

04

M Hi, Alice. What's that look for? What happened?

W Well, I was waiting for the bus after work.

M _____?

W No, it did not. When the bus arrived, a young man came out of nowhere and _____. I almost _____.

M I'm sorry to hear that. It's a mercy you weren't hurt, though.

05 모의

M Mom, I'm home.

W Hi. Did you go to the gym?

M Yes. My membership ended today, but _____ _____.

W Why? Does your shoulder still hurt?

M No, my shoulder _____.

W So, what's the problem?

M Well, the shower facilities at the gym are too old, and _____ in the shower stalls.

06

W Have you heard anything from Nancy? She's late.

M I got a text message from her. She said she left her house on time, but she's _____.

W _____. There are many variables on the road and even in the subway.

M _____.

07 모의

W Hello, Chris. Why are you sweating like that?

M Hi, Helen. I've just jogged for an hour.

W For an hour? But, _____.

M That's because I had a banana before jogging. If you eat something before running, you _____ _____.

W Really? I should try it.

08

M How did you like the movie?

W The movie was good, but I couldn't enjoy it.

M Why not? Was your seat uncomfortable?

W No, the girls right next to me _____ _____ the whole time.

M Well, _____ in the theater.

W But I don't think it's appropriate during quiet movies!

M You might be right.

09

W Hey, what's wrong? You look annoyed.

M Well, I recently bought a smartphone, but it doesn't have enough memory.

W Didn't the clerk explain the features of the phone?

M He did, but not well enough. Don't you think that _____ of their products?

W I agree. Customers _____ about products.

10 모의

W Hey, Daniel. How are the preparations for your trip to Seoul going?

M Hi, Claire. Everything is going great, but _____ _____.

W Why?

M I heard that Korean food is very hot and spicy. I think I should bring some food with me.

W But _____. It's the best way to get to the heart of the culture.

M Maybe you're right. _____ during my trip.

Listen & Answer 실전 문제

* 녹음 내용을 듣고, 알맞은 답을 고르시오.

01 대화를 듣고, 여자가 새 자동차를 구입한 이유를 고르시오. 고난도

① 가격이 저렴해서
② 유지비가 적게 들어서
③ 내부 공간이 더 넓어서
④ 부모님께 선물하기 위해서
⑤ 안전장치가 잘 갖춰져 있어서

02 대화를 듣고, 남자가 약을 사려는 이유를 고르시오.

① 기침이 심해서
② 아내가 감기에 걸려서
③ 꽃가루 알레르기가 있어서
④ 아내가 근육통에 시달려서
⑤ 아내가 하이킹 중에 다쳐서

03 대화를 듣고, 여자가 컵케이크 주문을 받을 수 <u>없는</u> 이유를 고르시오.

① 주문이 너무 많아서
② 재료가 다 떨어져서
③ 오븐에 문제가 생겨서
④ 제빵사가 휴가를 가서
⑤ 목요일에는 문을 닫아서

04 대화를 듣고, 남자가 여자의 파티에 갈 수 <u>없는</u> 이유를 고르시오.

① 몸이 좋지 않아서
② 집을 비울 수가 없어서
③ 해야 할 과제가 있어서
④ 가족 모임 행사가 있어서
⑤ 동창회에 참석할 예정이어서

05 대화를 듣고, 여자가 Alan의 가게를 이용하지 <u>않는</u> 이유를 고르시오.

① 가격이 비싸서
② 물건 배송이 느려서
③ 서비스가 좋지 않아서
④ 교환을 해주지 않아서
⑤ 상품이 다양하지 않아서

06 대화를 듣고, 남자의 의견으로 가장 적절한 것을 고르시오.

① 보안을 위해 온라인 비밀번호를 자주 바꿔야 한다.
② 비밀번호를 온라인상에 기록해두는 것은 위험하다.
③ 개인 정보가 도용되었는지 수시로 확인하는 것이 좋다.
④ 인터넷 뱅킹 로그인 시 보안 프로그램을 설치해야 한다.
⑤ 컴퓨터 백신 프로그램을 정기적으로 업데이트해야 한다.

07 대화를 듣고, 여자의 의견으로 가장 적절한 것을 고르시오. 고난도

① 개를 기르면 일거리가 많아진다.
② 다른 사람의 개를 돌보는 것은 쉽지 않다.
③ 집안일은 가족 구성원 모두가 분담해야 한다.
④ 아이는 개를 기르면서 책임감을 배울 수 있다.
⑤ 개를 입양하기 전에 돌보는 방법부터 배워야 한다.

08 대화를 듣고, 남자의 의견으로 가장 적절한 것을 고르시오.

① 도서관에서는 정숙해야 한다.
② 도서 반납 기일을 지켜야 한다.
③ 대출 도서는 깨끗이 이용해야 한다.
④ 도서 대출 규정은 개정될 필요가 있다.
⑤ 무인 도서 대출 서비스를 시행해야 한다.

09 대화를 듣고, 여자의 의견으로 가장 적절한 것을 고르시오.

① 학교 우유 급식은 무상으로 제공되어야 한다.
② 우유를 고를 때에는 영양 성분을 잘 살펴봐야 한다.
③ 학교 우유 급식 여부는 학생의 자율에 맡겨야 한다.
④ 맛이 첨가된 우유보다는 흰 우유를 마시는 것이 건강에 좋다.
⑤ 학교는 학생들이 급식 우유의 종류를 선택할 수 있게 해야 한다.

10 대화를 듣고, 남자의 의견으로 가장 적절한 것을 고르시오.

① 적절한 보상이 자녀에게 학습 동기를 부여한다.
② 자녀가 실수했을 때 질책보다는 격려를 해야 한다.
③ 자녀에게는 결과보다 노력에 대한 칭찬이 도움이 된다.
④ 자녀의 성적에 지나치게 관여하면 역효과를 낼 수 있다.
⑤ 자녀의 학업 성적에 대해서는 즉각적인 피드백이 필요하다.

Listen & Answer Dictation 실전 문제 받아쓰기

✳ STEP 3의 녹음 내용을 다시 들으면서 빈칸을 채우시오.

01 고난도

M Who's parked in your space?

W I have. I _____
last Friday.

M It looks great. What's it like?

W It's basically the same as my old one. It's really
_____.

M So why did you get this one? Is it cheaper to run?

W Well, I got it because it has more air bags,
automatic emergency braking, and other things
that protect you in a crash.

M I see. _____
of all. I'd like to see your new car more closely.

W If you're interested, we can go for a drive at lunch
time.

M Oh, thanks. See you then.

02

W Can I help you, sir?

M Yes, do you have some cold medicine?

W Oh, _____. Do you
have a sore throat and a fever, too?

M No, it's just a pollen allergy I suffer from every
spring.

W Then, why do you need cold medicine?

M It's for my wife. _____
_____ during a hiking trip and
both got really wet. So she is pretty sick now.

W Okay, just a moment. But, are you sure you don't
need anything for yourself? Some medicine
_____.

M I think I just need some rest. _____
_____ if I can.

03

M Good morning. I heard your cupcakes are great.

W Thank you. Sometimes we even _____
_____.

M That's great. I have a party for my son and I'd like
to order some cupcakes.

W When are you having the party and how many do
you need?

M It's this Thursday, the day after tomorrow. I need
50 cupcakes.

W I'm sorry. I don't think we can take the order.

M _____ on Thursdays?

W No, we close on Mondays. There is another
problem.

M Do you already have too many orders?

W It's not that. _____
_____ and the repairman is coming
on Thursday. We're only selling drinks until then.

M That's too bad.

04

W I'm having a dinner party this Saturday night.
Can you come?

M Oh, I'd love to, but I'm afraid I can't.

W What's the matter? Do you _____
_____?

M No, I finished it already.

W Oh, then I guess you're not in good condition.

M Actually, _____
for the weekend.

W Really? Isn't there any way _____
_____?

M Well, I would if I could, but I've already booked
a flight.

W Where are you going?

M I am going to Miami _____
_____.

W That sounds like fun.

05

W Where are you off to, Ross?

M I'm going to Alan's Store to look at toasters. They sell small appliances there, don't they?

W They do, but I wouldn't shop there.

M Why not? Did they charge you too much?

W No, I thought _____.

M Then, did they not have a good selection of products?

W Well, actually, the last time I went _____
_____. I bought a drill there, and it broke the first time I used it!

M Couldn't you just return it?

W That's what I thought, but when I showed it to the shop assistant, he was terribly rude.

M So _____?

W Finally, the manager agreed to _____
_____ for another one, but I'll never go back.

06

W Honey, I can't log in to our banking website.

M Oh, sorry. I changed the password yesterday and forgot to tell you.

W Again? Was that really necessary?

M Well, the experts _____
_____ as often as possible.

W But it's really annoying to have to constantly change our passwords.

M Maybe, but some sites are less secure than others. So _____.

W Hmm, I didn't think of that.

M I think it wouldn't hurt to be careful. Imagine _____ if someone got your online passwords.

W I can't even imagine that situation. I'll be more careful about my passwords from now on.

M Thank you for understanding.

07 고난도

M Honey, Nate really wants a puppy. I think _____
_____.

W I'm afraid he is too young. Besides, what about the mess it will make? Who will clean that up?

M It will be Nate's job to clean up after it. It _____
_____.

W I don't think he can handle all of that. That means we'll have to do it. On top of that, where will it go when we travel?

M Hmm.... It could stay with one of my friends.

W But we travel a lot and we would always be asking someone to take care of it. We _____
_____.

M Okay. Let's think it over for a few weeks and talk again, then.

08

M Olivia, did you return your library books? I reminded you about it last week.

W Not yet. But don't worry, I'll return them tomorrow.

M Not yet? _____.

W Yeah, but the books took longer than expected to read.

M Then _____ for another week. You always _____ _____ because you don't think overdue books are a big deal.

W You're right. I have nothing to say.

M A late fee is just one of the problems. The library might also limit the number of books you can check out. Besides, there could be people _____ _____.

W I hadn't thought about that. I'll try to do better next time.

M I hope so.

09

W Dad, would you like some milk with your bread?

M Thanks for offering, but I finished all the milk this morning.

W This is milk that I brought from school. You know I rarely drink plain milk.

M It might not be tasty, but _____ _____ than flavored ones.

W But _____ that my school doesn't even give us any other choice.

M There must be some kind of policy on school milk, I guess. They are just trying to _____ _____ which has more nutrients and less sugar.

W But I learned in health class that both flavored and plain milk have the nutrients that teenagers need.

M I guess I can see your point there.

10

W Honey, I'm home.

M Oh, Vera. I have good news.

W What is it?

M Well, you know how hard Miles worked on his math test.

W Oh, did he get an A in math finally?

M Yes, he did. He _____.

W Wow! I'm very proud of him. Where is he?

M He went to his taekwondo lesson. Uh, Vera, as I'm sure you know, when you talk to him about this, _____.

W Of course. But I'm also proud of his grade.

M Well, I think we need to _____ _____. It will be much more useful in helping our child grow.

W You're right. _____.

발음이 잘 안 들리는 이유 ❶

발음이 생략되는 어구

1 약한 모음

강세가 주어지지 않는 모음 발음 부분은 자음만 스치듯이 빠르게 발음된다. 우리말의 '어'나 '으'와 같은 명료함이 없다. 즉, today를 '투데이'가 아니라 'ㅌ데이'로, come in은 'ㅋ민'으로 발음하는 식이다. 아래 밑줄 부분의 발음에 주의하면서 듣고 따라 말해보자.

a**gain**	fav**o**rite	t**o**morrow
diff**e**rent	eas**i**ly	foc**u**s
to the store	C**a**n you do **it**?	Give **it to** me.

2 자음 탈락 /d/, /t/

자음+d/t+자음의 구성일 때 중간의 d/t는 발음이 생략된다.

frien**d**ly	san**d**wich	perfec**t**ly
exac**t**ly	bes**t** seller	nex**t** night

02 화자가 할 일·부탁한 일

대화를 듣고, 화자가 할 일 또는 부탁한 일 등의 특정 정보를 파악하는 유형이다.
두 유형 중 1문항이 출제되는데 최근에는 주로 화자가 할 일이 출제된다.

해결 전략

❶ 화자가 할 일

1 어떤 일을 하게 되는 상황이 먼저 제시된다.
2 오답 선택지의 내용들은 대부분 대화에 등장하기는 하지만 다음과 같은 이유로 정답이 아니다.
   e.g. ① 할 일이 아니라 이미 과거에 한 일
       ② 화자가 아니라 상대방이나 제3자가 했거나 할 일
       ③ 화자가 하려고 하지만 상대방이 그럴 필요가 없다고 응답한 일
   또한, 대화에서 등장한 어휘를 포함하여 그럴 듯한 오답을 만들기도 하므로 주의해야 한다.
3 화자가 할 일은 화자가 자발적으로 제안할 수도 있고, 상대방이 부탁[요청, 제안]하여 화자가 응낙할 수도 있다.
   대화에 나오는 여러 일들 중에서 다른 누가 아닌 화자가 할 일과 이를 상대방이 긍정적으로 응답하는지 여부까지 반드시 확인해야 한다. 정답은 대화의 후반부에 나오는 경우가 많다.

❷ 화자가 부탁한 일

1 지시문을 잘 읽고 누가 누구에게 부탁한 일을 묻는 것인지를 유념하며 대화를 들어야 한다. 예를 들어, 남자가 여자에게 부탁한 일은 남자의 말에 단서가 있다. 단, 부탁한 일에 대한 긍정적인 응답 표현을 확인해야 한다.
2 화자가 부탁하기 전에 상대방이 먼저 일을 하겠다고 제안하는 경우도 있다. 그러나 화자가 이를 거절하고 대신 다른 일을 부탁하는 내용이 이어질 수도 있으므로 상대방의 제안에 대한 화자의 응답을 정확하게 파악해야 한다.
3 대화의 흐름은 주로 <상황—(제안—응답—)부탁>으로 전개되며, 선택지는 영어로 나오기도 한다.

주요 표현

부탁, 요청 및 제안과 관련된 표현들을 잘 익혀둔다.

부탁·요청하기

• Could[Can, Would, Will] you ~? ~해주시겠습니까?
• Can[May] I ask you a favor? = Will[Would, Could] you do me a favor? 부탁 좀 들어주시겠습니까?
• I need to ask you a favor. = I have a favor to ask you. 한 가지 부탁할 것이 있습니다.
• I want you to-v ~. 나는 당신이 v해주기를 원합니다.
• I wonder if you could ~. ~해주실 수 있는지 궁금합니다.
• I would be grateful if you could ~. = I'd appreciate it if you could ~. ~해주시면 감사하겠습니다.
• If you don't[wouldn't] mind ~. 괜찮으시다면 ~.

제안하기

• What can I do for you? = Is there anything I can do for you? = Can I give you a hand?
  제가 도와드릴까요?
• Do you want[need] any help v-ing ~? v하는 것을 도와드릴까요?
• I can do that for you. = Let me do that for you. 제가 그것을 해드리겠습니다.

✳✳ 기출 맛보기

01 대화를 듣고, 여자가 할 일로 가장 적절한 것을 고르시오. [모의]

① 모금함 만들기   ② 물품 배치하기   ③ 가격표 붙이기
④ 스피커 점검하기   ⑤ 동영상 제작하기

W	Simon, **I think we're ready for the fundraising event.**
M	Right. Let's do one last check.
W	Okay. We're going to play a short video clip for the event. Is the screen working?
M	Yes. **I checked the screen** and there's no problem at all.
W	Great. **What about the speakers?**
M	**I already tried using them**, and they worked fine. **Did you bring the donation box?**
W	**Yes. Look. I made it by myself.**
M	Wow! It looks nice.
W	Thanks. **All the items we're going to sell are nicely set up on the table.**
M	Okay. The only thing left is to put the price tags on. I'll do that later because **I have to go to my part-time job now.**
W	Oh, don't worry. **I'll put the price tags on.**
M	Really? Thanks.

대화의 흐름

• **상황**: 모금 행사의 준비 상황을 최종 점검 하는 남녀

• **완료된 일**:
1. 스크린 확인하기
2. 스피커 점검하기 (→ 오답 ④)
3. 모금함 만들기 (→ 오답 ①)
4. 물품 배치하기 (→ 오답 ②)

• **할 일**:
- 남자: 아르바이트 가기
- 여자: 가격표 붙이기 (→ 정답 ③)

---

02 대화를 듣고, 남자가 여자에게 부탁한 일로 가장 적절한 것을 고르시오. [모의]

① 회의실 예약 확인하기   ② 일정 알림 문자 보내기   ③ 차에서 간식 가져오기
④ 참석자 이름표 만들기   ⑤ 회의 자료 출력하기

W	David, **how are the preparations going for your meeting tomorrow**?
M	Hi, Jennifer. They're almost done. I'm about to check if everything is ready.
W	Sounds good. Since I finished my own work today, I can help you.
M	That's very kind of you. I confirmed the reservation for the meeting room and sent text messages informing the participants of tomorrow's schedule.
W	What about the snacks for the meeting?
M	They're in my car. I'll get them tomorrow morning.
W	And, is there anything else left to do?
M	Let me see... **I need to make name tags to give to the participants.**
W	**Do you want me to help you with that?**
M	**No, thanks. I can handle it. Could you print out some materials for the meeting instead?**
W	**Sure.** I'll do that for you.
M	I'll send you the file to print out right now. Thank you.

대화의 흐름

• **상황**: 내일 있을 회의를 준비 중인 남자

• **제안**: 여자가 남자에게 참석자 이름표를 만드는 데 도움이 필요한지 물음
• **응답**: 남자가 거절
• **부탁**: 남자가 여자에게 회의 자료를 출력 해줄 것을 부탁함
• **응답**: 여자가 수락

Words & Phrases 01 fundraising event 자선 모금 행사   **work** (기계가) 작동하다   **try v-ing** 시험 삼아 한번 v해보다   **donation box** 모금함   **price tag** 가격표   **put A on** A를 붙이다[달다]   **02** preparation 준비   **be about to-v** 막 v하려는 참이다   **confirm** 확인하다   **reservation** 예약   **inform A of B** A에게 B에 대해 알리다   **participant** 참석자   **name tag** 이름표   **print out** (프린트로) 출력하다   **material** 자료

Listen & Choose 유형핵심 익히기

✳ 녹음 내용을 듣고, 알맞은 답을 고르시오.

정답 및 해설 **p.10**

01 대화를 듣고, 남자가 할 일로 가장 적절한 것을 고르시오.

ⓐ 파일 찾기 ⓑ 보고서 제출하기 ⓒ 이메일 보내기

02 대화를 듣고, 여자가 할 일로 가장 적절한 것을 고르시오. 모의

ⓐ 사진 앨범 만들기 ⓑ 생일 케이크 만들기 ⓒ 풍선으로 거실 장식하기

03 대화를 듣고, 남자가 여자를 위해 할 일로 가장 적절한 것을 고르시오. 모의

ⓐ 점심 준비하기 ⓑ 딸 데리러 가기 ⓒ 부엌 청소하기

04 대화를 듣고, 여자가 할 일로 가장 적절한 것을 고르시오. 모의

ⓐ 배지 가져오기 ⓑ 동영상 편집하기 ⓒ 스크린 점검하기

05 대화를 듣고, 남자가 여자를 위해 할 일로 가장 적절한 것을 고르시오.

ⓐ 세차 도와주기 ⓑ 휴대 전화 수리 맡기기 ⓒ 버스 기사에게 전화하기

06 대화를 듣고, 여자가 할 일로 가장 적절한 것을 고르시오. 모의

ⓐ 악기 점검하기 ⓑ 콘서트 포스터 붙이기 ⓒ 콘서트 포스터 디자인하기

07 대화를 듣고, 남자가 여자에게 부탁한 일로 가장 적절한 것을 고르시오. 모의

ⓐ 꽃 사러 가기 ⓑ 거실 청소하기 ⓒ 식료품 구입하기

08 대화를 듣고, 여자가 남자에게 부탁한 일로 가장 적절한 것을 고르시오. 모의

ⓐ 손님 마중 나가기 ⓑ 선물 구입하기 ⓒ 호텔 예약하기

09 대화를 듣고, 남자가 여자에게 부탁한 일로 가장 적절한 것을 고르시오.

ⓐ to sell the products ⓑ to visit a flea market ⓒ to post a photo on her blog

10 대화를 듣고, 여자가 남자에게 부탁한 일로 가장 적절한 것을 고르시오.

ⓐ to prepare dinner for her ⓑ to make an appointment with the client
ⓒ to postpone their reservation to tomorrow

＊ STEP 1의 녹음 내용을 다시 들으면서 빈칸을 채우시오.

정답 및 해설 **p.10**

01

W Alex! Thank goodness I've got hold of you. I've been trying to reach you all day.

M I _____ too. Did you get my email?

W Yes, but for some reason I couldn't open _____ _____.

M Really? Then, I'll _____.

W Thank you.

02 모의

M Honey, Nathan's birthday is tomorrow.

W Yeah, I made a digital photo album for his birthday party.

M Sounds good. _____?

W Every birthday party needs balloons and a cake.

M Okay. _____ with balloons.

W Then _____.

03 모의

W Smells nice, Daniel. What did you make for lunch?

M Creamy pasta. I found the recipe online.

W Fantastic.

M By the way, do you remember _____ _____ from the library this afternoon?

W Oh, my! I totally forgot. What should I do? My friend Amy is coming in an hour.

M Don't worry. I'll pick up Betty instead.

W Thanks, honey. Then _____.

04 모의

M Grace, I _____ about plastic waste.

W Then, I'm going to check the screen that we'll use for the video.

M No worries. _____. By the way, where are the badges you ordered for visitors?

W Oh, I left the badges in my car. _____ _____.

05

W I took a bus from Busan and I left my cell phone on the bus. I really _____.

M Well, since your bus arrived half an hour ago, _____ to the car wash.

W Is there any chance that the bus driver is still around?

M He may be at the drivers' lounge. _____ _____.

06 모의

M Ellie, the school orchestra's concert is just three days away. _____?

W Of course. Everything sounded fine in practice today.

M Great. And I heard the posters were ready.

W Yes. Here they are. _____ _____.

M They look pretty nice. When are you going to _____ in the hallway?

W I'm going to do that now.

07 모의

W Dad, where are you going?

M I'm going to the grocery store. We're having a surprise party because Mom was promoted at work.

W Good. I also want to help. _____ _____ for the dinner table?

M No. I'll do that. _____ instead?

W Sure. _____ before you come back.

08 모의

M Hi, Jenny. I've heard you're preparing for our buyers visiting our company. How's it going?

W Hi, Nick. I'm almost done. I _____ _____ for hotel rooms and _____ _____ for them.

M Is there anything I can help you with?

W Actually, I need someone to pick up the buyers at the airport. _____?

M Of course!

09

M I'm going to _____ this Saturday. I was wondering _____ _____.

W How can I help you?

M You _____ on your blog to promote our products.

W Sure. No problem.

10

M Hello?

W Honey, it's me. Do you remember our plan for dinner tonight?

M Yes, _____?

W My client came _____, so I have to go to a meeting now. If you don't mind, could you _____ _____?

M All right. I'll see you at home.

✽ 녹음 내용을 듣고, 알맞은 답을 고르시오.

정답 및 해설 **p.12**

유형 02 화자가 할 일·부탁한 일

01 대화를 듣고, 여자가 남자를 위해 할 일로 가장 적절한 것을 고르시오.

① 상자 옮기기
② 이사 도와주기
③ 저녁 식사 준비하기
④ 엘리베이터 잡아주기
⑤ 소파 버리는 것 도와주기

02 대화를 듣고, 남자가 할 일로 가장 적절한 것을 고르시오. 고난도

① 보고서 작성하기
② 콘택트렌즈 찾기
③ 리조트에 전화하기
④ 셔틀버스 시간표 확인하기
⑤ 인터넷에서 정보 검색하기

03 대화를 듣고, 여자가 할 일로 가장 적절한 것을 고르시오.

① 창고에 사람 보내기
② 서평 읽어보기
③ 책 주문하기
④ 재고 확인하기
⑤ 베스트셀러 추천하기

04 대화를 듣고, 남자가 여자를 위해 할 일로 가장 적절한 것을 고르시오.

① 택시 부르기
② 초콜릿 사오기
③ 관광지 추천하기
④ 차로 데려다주기
⑤ 맛집 링크 보내주기

05 대화를 듣고, 여자가 할 일로 가장 적절한 것을 고르시오.

① 음식 주문하기
② 회의 참석하기
③ 식당에 전화하기
④ 영화표 취소하기
⑤ 내비게이션 검색하기

06 대화를 듣고, 남자가 할 일로 가장 적절한 것을 고르시오.

① 책 빌려주기
② 점심 주문하기
③ 식당에서 줄 서기
④ 오렌지 주스 만들기
⑤ ATM에서 현금 인출하기

07 대화를 듣고, 여자가 남자에게 부탁한 일로 가장 적절한 것을 고르시오.

① 자동차 대여하기
② 관광 가이드 구하기
③ 관광 팸플릿 설명하기
④ 관광 상품 예약하기
⑤ 편의 시설 안내하기

08 대화를 듣고, 남자가 여자에게 부탁한 일로 가장 적절한 것을 고르시오. 고난도

① to introduce him to her friend
② to help him do his assignment
③ to give advice on writing a journal
④ to give back the book she borrowed
⑤ to borrow a textbook from her friend

09 대화를 듣고, 여자가 남자에게 부탁한 일로 가장 적절한 것을 고르시오.

① 식료품 쇼핑하기
② 생일 파티 계획하기
③ 버터 가지러 다녀오기
④ 계산대 줄에서 기다리기
⑤ 차로 집까지 바래다주기

10 대화를 듣고, 남자가 여자에게 부탁한 일로 가장 적절한 것을 고르시오.

① to lend him a book
② to help him train a dog
③ to take his dog to the vet
④ to buy him some dog food
⑤ to give him the title of the book

01

W Hi, Steve! I see you finally bought a new couch.

M Yes, now I just have to get it upstairs.

W Do you want some help getting it in the elevator?

M _____. Mark and Kyle are coming to help me carry it up the stairs.

W Can the three of you do it by yourselves?

M I hope so.... By the way, do you know _____ _____ on the stairs?

W Sharon's. She's moving out. _____ _____ for you.

M Really? That'd be very helpful. Afterwards, _____ _____ for all of us. You are welcome to come.

W Sounds good. I'll just go change clothes quickly.

02 고난도

M Hi, honey. Still on the computer?

W Yes. I have some reports to finish before we leave on our trip tomorrow.

M Oh, that reminds me, I _____ some more contact lenses!

W It's too late now, and the stores _____ _____. It's a holiday.

M That's true. Maybe I can get some near the resort.

W I'm not sure. I _____ for you after I finish what I'm doing.

M That's okay. _____.

W Good idea. Can you also ask about the schedule for the shuttle from the airport to the resort?

M I already did and they sent it to my email. The shuttle _____.

W Thank you, sweetheart.

03

W May I help you?

M Yes, I'm looking for the new book by Sarah Parker.

W It's in the best-seller display in the next aisle, right next to the travel-guide section.

M Well, I just checked there, but _____ _____.

W Oh, sorry. Then _____. Let me check on the computer first. We don't have it here, but _____ in the warehouse.

M Really? That's great. Can I get one now?

W Sure, _____.

M That would be great. Will I have to wait long?

W Not really. The warehouse is just behind this building.

M Okay, then I'll read some book reviews while I wait.

04

M Hi, Alice. Looks like you are in a hurry.

W Oh, hi, Bill. I'm really late. _____ _____ in 40 minutes.

M Stay calm. I'll give you a ride.

W Thanks. But I _____.

M Where are you going, anyway?

W I'm going to Jeju Island with my friends.

M Oh, there're so many good restaurants in Jeju Island. You should definitely try black pork!

W I _____. Do you know some good restaurants there?

M Yes. _____.

W That would be great. I'll get you a box of chocolate on my way back. Thanks.

05

M Susan, are you on your way here?

W Peter, _____. I don't think I can make it there on time.

M Well.... Let's just forget about the movie, then.

W I'm so sorry. Should I cancel the tickets?

M It's okay. _____.

W Thanks. And Instead of a movie, how about dinner at Chang's restaurant?

M Sounds good. _____ to get there?

W About 15 minutes. I'll call the restaurant and check _____ there now.

M Great. My navigation says it's only 10 minutes away by car from here.

W Good. See you at the restaurant.

06

W I can't believe I still have to study half of the book and the test is tomorrow.

M Me neither. And it's already about lunch time.

W Yeah... but I _____.

M Oh, come on. Eating something will help keep up our energy.

W Hmm... then, let's _____ at the cafeteria. But I should stop by somewhere before.

M Where do you need to go?

W I need to get some money out of an ATM.

M Then _____. Are you having the usual?

W Yes, with a bottle of orange juice.

M OK, you can _____ later.

W Thanks. I'll catch up to you soon.

07

W Excuse me, but can you tell us about the things we can do here?

M Well, there are lots of things to do at the hotel. We have a swimming pool, a sauna, a PC game room, and tennis courts.

W Oh, I meant _____ _____.

M Ah! Sorry. Here are some brochures.

W Great! Do you have any maps of the island?

M Of course. Here's one _____ _____. I can help arrange a car rental if you'd like.

W No, thanks. But _____?

M Certainly. Just look at the brochures and let me know _____.

W OK. We'll be back again after we look through them.

08 고난도

W Hey, Scott. Where are you going?

M Emily! So glad to see you! I need to _____ _____ for Mr. Baker's class.

W I'm sorry, but I took it home for the journal assignment and left it there.

M Oh, no.... What should I do? You know that Mr. Baker is really strict about students _____ _____.

W Yeah.... Oh! I know that Martin has that class this afternoon.

M Really? Hmm... but I don't know him well.... I'm so sorry, but if you don't mind, _____ _____?

W I can do that for you if you promise to return it before lunch time.

M I promise I will. Thank you so much.

W That's _____!

09

W We got everything on the list. Let's head for the cashier.

M Okay, I'll push the cart. Wow, we really have a lot of groceries.

W Yes, it's not going to be cheap. But Jane wants a big birthday party.

M _____, I don't mind. But I see a long line at the checkout counter.

W Yeah, but we have _____.

M After we pay and drive home, let's prepare everything together.

W Okay, great. Uh oh, we forgot butter. I can't cook without it.

M _____?

W No, I'll do that. I know exactly where it is. _____ _____? I'll be right back.

M Sure. Please make it quick. It'll soon be our turn.

10

W Hi, Steven. Are you okay? You look really tired.

M I'm exhausted. It's my roommate's new dog. It _____!

W I thought the two of you were going to train it together. What happened?

M It's much harder than we thought. How did you come to have _____?

W Cubert? He was a very active puppy. But I bought a great book _____. Shall I tell you the title?

M If you don't mind, maybe _____ _____?

W Sure. I'll bring it to work tomorrow. I'll also bring _____. It'll be very helpful when you're training the dog.

M You're so thoughtful! Thank you.

첫단추
듣기 모의고사

CHAPTER

2

사실적 이해 Ⅱ
(세부 내용 파악)

대화나 담화를 들으면서 여러 세부 내용들을 확인해야 하는 것으로,
Chapter 1보다 난이도가 높다. '금액'을 묻는 유형을 제외하고는 대부분
선택지 순서대로 대화나 담화가 진행되므로 선택지를 차례대로 보면서
판단하면 된다.

유형 **03** 금액

요금, 가격 등이 등장하는 대화를 듣고, 화자가 지불할 금액을 파악하는 유형이다.
정답 금액이 그대로 제시되는 경우는 거의 없고, 대부분 대화에 언급된 정보들을 이용하여 간단한 계산을
해야 한다.

해결 전략

1 대화는 대개 <상황―구입하려는 물품의 금액―최종 구입 물품 및 수량 결정―금액에 변동을 주는 요소(쿠폰 등)>로 구성된다.

2 원하는 물품 등의 총 수량에 해당하는 금액에서 할인, 추가 항목, 쿠폰, 회원 카드, 적립금, 할부 구매 등의 금액에 변동을 주는
요소들을 고려해서 계산하도록 한다. 이들 요소를 고려하지 않은 금액은 오답 선택지로 등장한다.
   e.g. two bags of dog food($20 × 2) + one brush($10)
   → $50 - $5(10% 할인권) = $45 (오답 선택지: $50)

3 여러 개의 수치와 금액이 제시되므로, 필요한 정보와 혼동을 유발하는 정보를 구분하여 재빨리 메모하면서 듣는 것이 좋다.

4 선택지는 적은 금액에서 큰 금액 순서로 제시된다.

주요 표현

금액과 관련된 표현들을 잘 익혀둔다.

- **bill** 지폐; 계산서 • **cash** 현금 • **check** 수표 • **change** 거스름돈 • **tax** 세금
- **exchange** 교환 • **total** 합계, 총액 • **receipt** 영수증 • **difference** 차액
- **on sale** 할인 판매 중인 • **for sale** 판매 중인 • **sold out** 매진된 • **service charge** 봉사료
- **half price** 반값 • **$5 each** 개당 5달러 • **$3 a meter** 미터당 3달러 • **for free** 무료로
- **reasonable price** 적절한 가격 • **good bargain** 싸게 사는 물건 • **discount coupon** 할인 쿠폰
- **25% off** 25% 할인 • **extra[additional] charge** 추가 요금 • **standard fare** 표준 요금
- **monthly fee** 월 이용료 • **special promotion** 특별 판촉 활동 • **membership card** 회원 카드
- **membership points** 적립금 • **out of one's budget** 예산을 초과하는

✳✳ 기출 맛보기

01 대화를 듣고, 여자가 지불할 금액을 고르시오. 모의

① $45   ② $50   ③ $54   ④ $55   ⑤ $60

M	Welcome to Kids' Clothing Club. How may I help you?
W	**I'm looking for a muffler for my son.** He's 5 years old.
M	Okay. Follow me. *[pause]* This red muffler is one of the best sellers in our shop.
W	I love the color. **How much is it?**
M	**It's $50.** This one is popular because of the cartoon character here.
W	Oh, that's my son's favorite character. I'll buy one red muffler, then.
M	Great. Anything else?
W	**How much are these winter socks?**
M	**A pair of socks is $5.**
W	All right. **I'll buy two pairs.**
M	So, **one red muffler and two pairs of winter socks**, right?
W	Yes. **Can I use this discount coupon?**
M	Of course. **With that coupon, you can get 10% off the total price.**
W	Good. Here's my credit card.

대화의 흐름

· **상황**: 아들을 위해 목도리를 사러 가게에 간 엄마

· **구입하려는 물품의 금액**:
  - 빨간색 목도리: $50
  - 겨울 양말(한 켤레당): $5

· **최종 구입 물품 및 수량**:
  빨간색 목도리 1개+겨울 양말 2켤레

· **금액에 변동을 주는 요소**:
  10% 할인 쿠폰

Words & Phrases **muffler** 목도리 **best seller** 베스트셀러, 가장 잘 나가는 상품 **cartoon** 만화 (영화) **a pair of** 한 켤레[짝, 벌] **discount** 할인(의) **total** 총, 전체의 **credit card** 신용 카드

Listen & Choose 유형핵심 익히기

✴ 녹음 내용을 듣고, 알맞은 답을 고르시오.

정답 및 해설 p.16

01 대화를 듣고, 여자가 지불할 금액을 고르시오. 모의

ⓐ $25   ⓑ $30   ⓒ $60

02 대화를 듣고, 남자가 지불할 금액을 고르시오. 모의

ⓐ $20   ⓑ $25   ⓒ $35

03 대화를 듣고, 여자가 지불할 금액을 고르시오. 모의

ⓐ $63   ⓑ $72   ⓒ $80

04 대화를 듣고, 남자가 지불할 금액을 고르시오. 모의

ⓐ $20   ⓑ $30   ⓒ $50

05 대화를 듣고, 여자가 지불할 금액을 고르시오. 모의

ⓐ $36   ⓑ $38   ⓒ $40

06 대화를 듣고, 남자가 지불할 금액을 고르시오.

ⓐ $13   ⓑ $28   ⓒ $38

07 대화를 듣고, 여자가 지불할 금액을 고르시오.

ⓐ $128   ⓑ $160   ⓒ $200

08 대화를 듣고, 남자가 지불할 금액을 고르시오. 모의

ⓐ $61   ⓑ $120   ⓒ $122

09 대화를 듣고, 두 사람이 지불할 금액을 고르시오. 모의

ⓐ $30   ⓑ $70   ⓒ $100

10 대화를 듣고, 여자가 지불할 금액을 고르시오. 수능

ⓐ $30   ⓑ $40   ⓒ $50

✳ STEP 1의 녹음 내용을 다시 들으면서 빈칸을 채우시오.

정답 및 해설 **p.16**

01 모의

M Good afternoon. May I help you?

W Yes, please. I want to buy a bag for my laptop.

M How about this one? It's _____.
The original price was $_____.

W Wow, more than 50% off? I'll take it.

M Here it is.

02 모의

W Hello. How can I help you?

M Hi, how much is the ice cream?

W _____. The small cup
is $_____, the medium is $_____, and the
large is $_____. What size would you like?

M I'll take _____ smalls and _____
medium.

W Okay.

03 모의

W Hi, I'm looking for camping chairs. Can you
recommend one?

M Good morning. This is our bestselling chair.
They're $_____ each.

W That sounds good. I need _____.
Do you offer any discounts?

M Yes. _____,
we'll give you a 10% discount on the total amount.

04 모의

M Hello. I'm looking for a teapot for my mother.

W Okay. How about this teapot with a classic
design?

M I think she'll like it. How much is it?

W It's $_____. But if you like this design, we also
have this teapot set _____.
It's only $_____.

M Great! I'll take the set.

05 모의

W Hello. I'm looking for a cushion for my dog.

M Okay, these are _____.

W The pink one looks cute. How much is it?

M Originally, it was $_____. But _____
_____, you can get
a 10% discount on cushions.

W Excellent! I'll buy one cushion, then.

06

M Excuse me. I'd like to purchase one-way tickets
for _____ adults and _____ child.

W It's $_____ for adults and $_____ for
children.

M Can I get a discount using my membership
points? Here is my membership card.

W Yes, I'll check it. It says you have 1,000 points,
worth $_____.

M Okay. I'd like to use them all.

07

W I'd like to reserve seats for the musical *Lion King*. How much are the tickets?

M $_____ on weekdays and $_____ on weekends.

W I'd like to _____.
Do you offer a student discount?

M Yes. If you have a student ID card, you can get a _____% discount each.

W Terrific. These are our student ID cards, and I'll pay with cash. Here.

08 모의

W Good afternoon. What I can I do for you?

M How much is this pair of wireless earphones?

W It's $_____ for a pair.

M Great. I'll take _____ for my children.

W Would you like them gift-wrapped? It's _____.

M Yes, please. Here's my credit card.

09 모의

M Honey, I think Paul needs new shoes.

W You're right. His shoes are getting too tight for his feet.

M Let's buy a pair online. I know a good store. Have a look.

W Oh, how about these shoes? They're originally $_____ a pair, but they're _____% off now.

M _____. Let's buy a pair.

W Okay.

10 수능

M Welcome to Daisy Valley Restaurant.

W Hi. I'd like to _____.
How much is the shrimp pasta and the chicken salad?

M The shrimp pasta is $_____, and the chicken salad is $_____.

W I'll take _____ shrimp pastas and _____ chicken salad, please.

M Sure.

Listen & Answer 실전 문제

✳ 녹음 내용을 듣고, 알맞은 답을 고르시오.

정답 및 해설 **p.18**

01 대화를 듣고, 여자가 지불할 금액을 고르시오.
① $60   ② $65   ③ $75   ④ $100   ⑤ $105

02 대화를 듣고, 남자가 지불할 금액을 고르시오.
① $550   ② $570   ③ $590   ④ $600   ⑤ $610

03 대화를 듣고, 여자가 지불할 금액을 고르시오. 고난도
① $45   ② $50   ③ $60   ④ $65   ⑤ $70

04 대화를 듣고, 남자가 지불할 금액을 고르시오.
① $80   ② $90   ③ $95   ④ $100   ⑤ $105

05 대화를 듣고, 여자가 지불할 금액을 고르시오.
① $32   ② $36   ③ $44   ④ $56   ⑤ $63

06 대화를 듣고, 남자가 지불할 금액을 고르시오.
① $342   ② $350   ③ $405   ④ $420   ⑤ $450

07 대화를 듣고, 여자가 지불할 금액을 고르시오.
① $30   ② $40   ③ $50   ④ $60   ⑤ $80

08 대화를 듣고, 남자가 지불할 금액을 고르시오.
① $120   ② $135   ③ $150   ④ $360   ⑤ $432

09 대화를 듣고, 여자가 지불할 금액을 고르시오.
① $55   ② $60   ③ $65   ④ $70   ⑤ $75

10 대화를 듣고, 남자가 지불할 금액을 고르시오. 고난도
① $65   ② $69   ③ $75   ④ $79   ⑤ $84

✳ STEP 3의 녹음 내용을 다시 들으면서 빈칸을 채우시오.

01

M Hello. How can I help you today?

W I want to send this package to Germany.

M Sure. Let me weigh it for you first. _____ kilograms. When would you like it to arrive?

W As soon as possible.

M It is $_____ per kilogram _____ _____. That will guarantee that it arrives tomorrow.

W That's a bit too expensive....

M Normal shipping will save you _____%, but it will take two or three extra days.

W That sounds better for me. And _____ _____, too.

M That will be an additional $_____. Is that alright?

W Yes. Here is my credit card.

M Thank you. Here is your receipt.

02

W Hello, welcome to Discount Mart. How may I help you?

M I would like to order the 50-inch flat screen TV, the one _____.

W Okay. It is $_____ with the discount, for the standing model.

M Oh, but I would like to fix it to my wall.

W Then, there will be an extra $_____ for installation.

M That's fine. And how much is delivery?

W Delivery is $_____, but _____ for gold card members and _____ for silver card members.

M I have a gold card, and I'll take the TV, with installation and delivery.

W Great. Can I have your name and address?

M Certainly.

03 고난도

M Hello. Is there anything I can help you with?

W Hi, I'd like to buy some doughnuts. How much are they?

M The plain ones are $_____ and the chocolate ones are $_____.

W I'll have _____. And do you sell this music box as well?

M Yes, as a promotion, any customer _____ _____ can buy this music box for $_____. Its original price was $_____.

W I'll take one. My daughter will love it.

M Great. Do you have a store membership?

W Yes, here's my membership card. Can I _____ _____?

M Sure. Let me check. You can get $_____ off with your points.

W Good. Here's my credit card.

04

W Good afternoon. What can I help you with?

M Hi, I'd like to send a flower basket to my wife.

W Sure. The prices start from $35. The small basket is $_____, the medium is $_____, and the large is $_____.

M I'll take _____.

W Great. Would you like to leave a message card? It's _____.

M Yes, please write "Happy Anniversary" on it.

W Congratulations! Do you need anything else?

M Well, how much is this flower pot?

W It's $_____. And if you buy two, you _____ _____.

M That sounds nice. I'll take _____. Please deliver them with the flower basket. Here's my credit card.

W Thank you. Please write your address in this form.

05

W Hello, one ticket to Seoul, please.

M I'm sorry, but the one o'clock train is almost full. We only have first class seats for $_____.

W That's okay. I have this membership card. So I can get a _____% discount, right?

M Normally, yes. But today is a holiday, so the discount is only _____%.

W Oh, really? When is the next train?

M Two o'clock. Regular seats are $_____. But the train makes two extra stops.

W How much longer will it take?

M An extra _____ minutes.

W That's fine. I'll _____ and use my membership card.

M Alright, here you are. Have a good trip.

06

W Hello, sir. How was your meal?

M It was great. I really enjoyed the main dish, a lamb steak.

W I'm glad you enjoyed it. So, you had the 6-course menu for seven people, correct?

M Yes, it costs $_____ per person, right?

W Well, the price _____ last month.

M Wow, that's huge. And there must be _____ _____.

W Yes, that costs an extra $_____.

M Okay. Can I get a 10% discount for _____ _____?

W Let me check. Yes, you can get a 10% discount from the total amount. Would you like to pay with your credit card?

M Yes, here you are.

07

M Hi, what can I do for you?

W Well, I'm thinking of planting a garden, but I don't know what kind of sprinkler to buy.

M We have _____. This one here, for instance, is great for small gardens. It's $_____.

W Hmm.... What about this one? It looks good.

M It's an automatic sprinkler. It uses a timer, and it costs $_____.

W I travel a lot, so that's the one I want. _____ _____ a hose?

M No, those are sold separately. A short hose is $_____, and a longer one is $_____.

W _____.

Oh, I also have this coupon I downloaded from the Internet. It's for a free hose. Can I use it?

M Certainly. It _____ the hose you want.

W Great.

08

W Welcome to Paradise Fitness. How can I help you?

M Hi. _____ a membership.

W We offer monthly membership and yearly membership. Which one do you want?

M How much is the monthly membership?

W The fee is $_____ per month. The yearly membership fee is $_____, so _____ _____ $120.

M I'm a college student. Is there a discount for students?

W Yes. You can get a 10% discount _____ _____ if you have a student ID.

M Okay. I'll pay for a monthly membership _____ _____. Here's my student ID.

W All right. Can you _____?

M Sure.

09

W Excuse me. I'm looking for a Halloween costume for my daughter.

M Come this way. How old is she?

W She's 7 years old and she wants to _____ _____.

M We have _____ here. How about this white dress?

W It's pretty! How much is it?

M It was originally $_____, but it's 20% off now.

W That sounds great. Wait, this dress _____ _____.

M It does. Look here! It has beautiful white wings on the back.

W Good, I'll take it. I also like these gold sandals.

M You made a good choice. The sandals _____ _____ for the dress, and they're only $_____.

W Perfect. I'll take them as well. Here's my credit card.

10 고난도

W Hello. How can I help you?

M I'm looking for a nice gift for my friend. _____ _____ a new house.

W You've come to the right place. We have _____ _____.

M Those glasses look nice. How much are they?

W These hand-painted glasses are very popular these days. The set costs $_____.

M It's too expensive. I'd like to stay under $_____.

W Then I have something you'll like. How about this tray? It's $_____.

M Hmm, I don't think she likes black. Is there _____?

W We also have green and silver. The green tray is the same price as the black one, but the silver tray is $_____ cheaper.

M Perfect. I'll take a silver one. Could I have it gift-wrapped?

W Yes, but there's a $_____ charge for that. Is that alright with you?

M No problem. Here's my credit card.

발음이 잘 안 들리는 이유 ❷

발음기호와 다르게 발음되는 어구

1 중간에 오는 자음 /d/, /t/

우리말 ㄹ에 가까운 소리가 난다.

rea**d**y	da**dd**y	clou**d**y
me**d**al	mi**dd**le	me**d**ia
me**d**icine	au**d**io	au**d**ience
a lo**t** of	check i**t** out	ge**t** ou**t** of

2 자음 /l/

L이 단어 끝이나 모음과 자음 사이에 끼면 우리가 흔히 알고 있는 [엘]과는 다른 발음이 들린다. school을 [스쿨]이 아니라 [스꾸어]와 유사하게 발음하는 식이다.

he**l**p	hee**l**	poo**l**	fi**l**m
gir**l**	smi**l**e	fa**ll**	bubb**l**e
fee**l**	fee**l** it	a**ll**	a**ll** over
wi**ll**	wi**ll** you	rea**l**	we**ll**
possib**l**e	peop**l**e		

유형 04 그림과 불일치하는 내용

한 장소에 여러 사물이 있는 그림에서 대화 내용과 일치하지 않는 사물(모양, 무늬, 개수, 위치 등)을 판별하는 문제이다. 1문항 출제된다.

해결 전략

1 선택지 순서대로 그림의 사물이 대화에서 언급되므로 선택지를 차례대로 짚어가면서 대화 내용과 일치 여부를 판단한다. 문제 시작 전에 그림을 보며 앞으로 나올 표현을 미리 예상해 보는 것도 도움이 된다.

2 최근에는 이미 그림에 나와 있는 사물이 아니라 앞으로 추가될 사물을 말하는 내용을 언급해 혼동을 주기도 하므로 주의해야 한다.

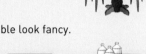
→ two chairs
→ a round table

e.g. **M** I like the striped tablecloth on the table. It makes the table look fancy.
W Yeah, I'm going to put water bottles on it.'

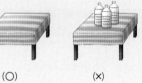

(O) (×)

주요 표현

외형적 특징 및 위치를 나타내는 표현들을 잘 익혀둔다.

모양

- **heart-shaped** 하트 모양의(♡) • **arched** 아치 모양의(∩) • **rectangular** 직사각형의(▭)
- **square** 정사각형의(□) • **circular** 원형의(○) • **semicircular** 반원(형)의(◠)
- **oval** 타원형의(⬭) • **round** 둥근(○) • **triangular** 삼각형의(△)
- **cube** 정육면체(⬡) • **diamond-shaped** 다이아몬드 모양의, 마름모꼴의(◇)
- **wide** 넓은 (↔ **narrow** 좁은) • **vertical** 수직의 (↔ **horizontal** 수평의)

무늬

- **plain** 무늬가 없는 • **striped/stripe-patterned** 줄무늬의 • **flowered** 꽃무늬의
- **checked/checkered** 체크무늬의 • **polka dot/polka-dotted** 물방울무늬(의)

위치

- **in** 안에 • **on** 위에 • **above/over** ~보다 위에 • **below/beneath/under** 아래에
- **bottom** 맨 아래 (↔ **top** 맨 위) • **in front of** 앞에 • **behind** 뒤에 • **next to/beside/by** 옆에
- **between** 사이에 • **around** 주위에 • **near** ~에서 가까이 • **in the center[middle] of** ~의 가운데에
- **on the left[right] side** 왼쪽[오른쪽]에 • **in the corner** 구석에 • **opposite** 맞은편에
- **across** ~을 가로질러 • **inside** 안에 (↔ **outside** 밖에)

cf.

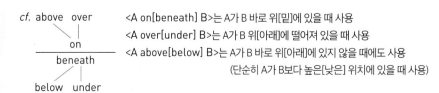

<A on[beneath] B>는 A가 B 바로 위[밑]에 있을 때 사용
<A over[under] B>는 A가 B 위[아래]에 떨어져 있을 때 사용
<A above[below] B>는 A가 B 바로 위[아래]에 있지 않을 때에도 사용
　　　　　　　　(단순히 A가 B보다 높은[낮은] 위치에 있을 때 사용)

✳✳ 기출 맛보기

01 대화를 듣고, 그림에서 대화의 내용과 일치하지 <u>않는</u> 것을 고르시오. 모의

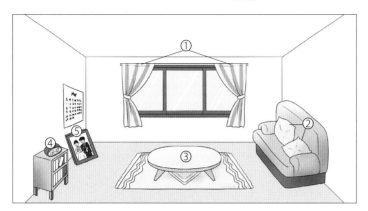

W	Hi, Harry. Congratulations on your wedding. Did you finish decorating the new house?
M	I just finished the living room. Look at this picture, Linda.
W	Wow. **I love the striped curtains on the window.**
M	Thanks. **Do you see those two cushions on the sofa?** My sister made them as wedding gifts.
W	That's lovely. Oh, **you put a round table on the rug.**
M	Yeah. We spend time reading books around the table. **What do you think of the clock on the bookshelf?**
W	It looks good in that room. By the way, **is that a plant under the calendar**?
M	**Yes.** I placed it there because the plant helps to clean the air.
W	You decorated your house really well.
M	Thanks. I'll invite you over when we have the housewarming party.

대화의 흐름

그림 속 사물에 대한 설명:
① 창문에 줄무늬 커튼
② 소파 위에 쿠션 두 개
③ 깔개 위에 원형 탁자
④ 책꽂이 위에 시계
⑤ 달력 아래에 식물(→ 정답)

Words & Phrases decorate 꾸미다, 장식하다 striped 줄무늬의 rug 깔개, 러그 bookshelf 책꽂이 calendar 달력 invite A over A를 집으로 초대하다 housewarming party 집들이

Listen & Choose 유형핵심 익히기

* 녹음 내용을 듣고, 알맞은 답을 고르시오.

01 대화를 듣고, 남자가 구입할 우산을 고르시오.

ⓐ  ⓑ  ⓒ

02 대화를 듣고, 여자가 구입할 쓰레기통을 고르시오.

ⓐ   ⓑ   ⓒ

03 대화를 듣고, 두 사람이 선택한 그릇을 고르시오.

ⓐ  ⓑ 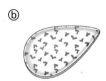 ⓒ

04 대화를 듣고, 남자가 찾고 있는 가방을 고르시오.

ⓐ  ⓑ 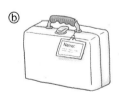 ⓒ

05 대화를 듣고, 두 사람이 선택한 연을 고르시오.

ⓐ  ⓑ  ⓒ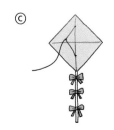

06 대화를 듣고, 대화의 내용과 일치하는 그림을 고르시오. 모의

ⓐ

ⓑ

ⓒ

07 대화를 듣고, 그림에서 대화의 내용과 일치하지 <u>않는</u> 것을 고르시오. 모의

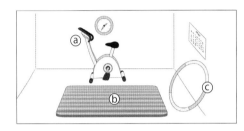

08 대화를 듣고, 그림에서 대화의 내용과 일치하지 <u>않는</u> 것을 고르시오. 모의

09 대화를 듣고, 그림에서 대화의 내용과 일치하지 <u>않는</u> 것을 고르시오. 모의

10 대화를 듣고, 그림에서 대화의 내용과 일치하지 <u>않는</u> 것을 고르시오. 모의

Listen & Choose Dictation 유형핵심 받아쓰기

∗ STEP 1의 녹음 내용을 다시 들으면서 빈칸을 채우시오.

01

M These umbrellas are on sale! Which ones do you like?

W Well, _____ better than the plain ones. How about you?

M I _____. I'll take one of them.

02

M There are several kinds of trash cans, ma'am. Do you want _____ with a lid or the round one without a lid?

W I don't like either. I want _____ _____.

M You made a good choice. It also has _____ _____.

03

M Honey, what about _____? It has a heart pattern on it.

W I don't like the shape. I want to choose _____ _____. What do you think?

M In that case, _____.

04

M Oh, no! One of my bags is missing.

W What does it look like? Is it a backpack?

M No, _____. It has a name tag where my name and address are written. It's square _____.

05

M I think Bridget would love the kite that _____ _____.

W Well, I thought it looked quite scary.... How about _____?

M I think it's too simple. But the same shape _____ _____ would be good for her.

W I like that one, too. Let's get it.

06 모의

M Grace, let me show you my new desk.

W Wow, Jake! It's so cool.

M Look at _____. I changed my old monitor for this new one.

W Looks nice. But isn't your desk _____ _____ on it?

M It's fine with me. I find it convenient there.

07 모의

W Henry. I set up an exercise room in my house.

M Cool! _____ looks nice.

W Thanks. What do you think of _____ _____ on the floor?

M Oh, it looks great! Is that a hula-hoop _____ _____?

W Yes. I exercise with it every day.

08 모의

W Honey, Sally sent me a picture of the new community park near her house.

M Let me see it. Oh, I can see _____ _____.

W Yeah, there are also swings _____. Our son would like this park, too.

M He sure would. Oh, and there is a see-saw _____ _____, too.

W Wow, this park has everything a child could want.

09 모의

W Austin, _____ on our poster.

M Okay. Let me take a look.

W First of all, I wrote _____ _____, Magic Show.

M Nice choice. It's more eye-catching. Oh, you _____, instead of the square one.

W Yes. And as you suggested, I drew a magician _____.

M Nice. I think it's perfect now.

10 모의

M Mom, this is a picture from Science Day.

W Let me see. _____ must be your science teacher.

M Yes, she is. Do you see the rocket _____ _____? I made it myself.

W Oh, it looks fantastic! Good job. By the way, _____?

M They are pictures of great scientists.

Listen & Answer 실전 문제

＊ 녹음 내용을 듣고, 알맞은 답을 고르시오.

01 대화를 듣고, 그림에서 대화의 내용과 일치하지 <u>않는</u> 것을 고르시오.

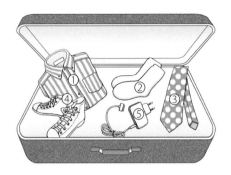

02 대화를 듣고, 그림에서 대화의 내용과 일치하지 <u>않는</u> 것을 고르시오.

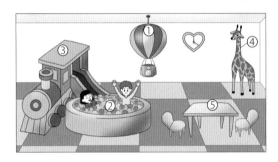

03 대화를 듣고, 그림에서 대화의 내용과 일치하지 <u>않는</u> 것을 고르시오.

04 대화를 듣고, 그림에서 대화의 내용과 일치하지 <u>않는</u> 것을 고르시오. 고난도

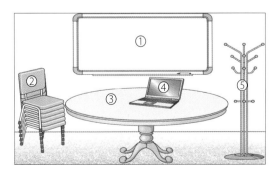

05 대화를 듣고, 그림에서 대화의 내용과 일치하지 <u>않는</u> 것을 고르시오. 고난도

06 대화를 듣고, 그림에서 대화의 내용과 일치하지 <u>않는</u> 것을 고르시오.

07 대화를 듣고, 그림에서 대화의 내용과 일치하지 <u>않는</u> 것을 고르시오.

08 대화를 듣고, 그림에서 대화의 내용과 일치하지 <u>않는</u> 것을 고르시오.

09 대화를 듣고, 그림에서 대화의 내용과 일치하지 <u>않는</u> 것을 고르시오.

10 대화를 듣고, 그림에서 대화의 내용과 일치하지 <u>않는</u> 것을 고르시오. 고난도

STEP 4 Listen & Answer Dictation 실전 문제 받아쓰기

✳ STEP 3의 녹음 내용을 다시 들으면서 빈칸을 채우시오.

정답 및 해설 p.24

01

W Honey, did you finish packing your suitcase for your business trip?

M Yes, I _____ you bought me for my birthday.

W Good. You'll also need a pair of socks since you'll stay overnight.

M I've already packed _____.

W What about your tie? Did you find the one with polka dots?

M No, I looked everywhere but I couldn't find it. I _____.

W All right. Oh, I think _____ _____ just in case.

M Yeah, I'm taking my high-top sneakers with me.

W Okay. And you didn't forget the charger for your cell phone, did you?

M Of course not. It's in my suitcase.

W Good. I think you're ready. Travel safe.

M Thanks.

02

M Rachel, what are you looking at?

W It's a photo of the new kids' cafe that opened up last month. I'm going to take James there.

M He must be excited. Wow! Look at the hot air balloon _____.

W Isn't it fantastic? Also, check out the ball pool on the left.

M _____ and it even has a slide that's shaped like a train.

W Yeah, James loves trains, so he'll probably enjoy sliding down there.

M I'm sure he will. There's also a giant teddy bear _____.

W Yes, it's a great place for kids. I really like the square table on the right of the photo.

M I know why. You can rest there while watching James play.

W You bet! And we can also _____ _____.

M That sounds good.

03

W Honey, I downloaded a free invitation card for Chloe's birthday party.

M Wow! I can't believe it's free. There's a smiling sun in the upper right corner.

W Look at the swing below it. There's a little bird _____.

M How cute! And you wrote the message "Chloe is turning 5!" in the square frame.

W Yes. And I also wrote the date and location of the party there.

M Good job. I also like the slide _____. I'm sure Chloe will love it.

W Can you see the three balloons _____ _____?

M Well, since Chloe will be turning 5, how about having 5 balloons?

W I'd love to, but I _____. I can only change or add the things in the box.

M Okay. Then, let's print it like this.

04 고난도

W Hi, Tom. Have you prepared everything for the meeting?

M I think so, Ms. Stuart. First of all, I _____ _____ as you asked.

W Good. And I'm sure you set up some chairs.

M Yes, _____.

W Oh, did you get a round table?

M Yes, I _____.

W Great. And I hope you remembered the laptop we use for meetings.

M Of course. I placed it on the table.

W Perfect. We also need somewhere to hang coats.

M I _____.

W All right. Thanks, Tom.

05

M Mom! I organized my desk just like you asked me to. Look at this!

W Wow! Good job! You placed a lamp on the left side. Since you're right-handed, this will help you _____.

M Thanks, but it was your idea.

W I can see you also put a picture frame next to the lamp. It _____ to your desk.

M Also, Mom, look at my new mouse pad.

W _____ a soccer field. The previous one looked like a soccer ball, right?

M Yeah! You have a really good memory.

W There is a nice cup near your monitor. Is it for your pens?

M No, I'm going to put some flowers in it. Can you see the tray on the right side?

W Oh, you are going to _____ on it! Am I right?

M Yes. That way I will be able to find them easily, but they won't be messy.

W What a brilliant idea!

06

W Dad, I've finally finished my homework. It's a newspaper article about our family trip to Jeju Island.

M OK. Let me have a look at it. Wow, I love _____ _____.

W Thanks. I put the newspaper's name, "My Family News," _____.

M It looks good. And the headline under it, "The Emersons Travel in Style!" sounds wonderful.

W What about our family picture on the beach? I _____ at Mt. Halla.

M Good choice. And I see that the article is _____ _____ of the picture.

W Yes, I wrote about the first day of our trip. Can you check it for me?

M I'd be happy to.

07

W Welcome to the Starplus publishing company. I'm Monica, your senior.

M Oh, hello. I'm Sean. It's a pleasure to work with you.

W Me, too. _____.

M Thanks. I can see a round table by the window.

W That's for our meetings. And the man _____ _____ near the table is our sales manager, Steve.

M You mean the man who is talking on the phone? I met him at my job interview.

W Good. And the woman standing next to the plant pot is Alice.

M The woman _____? I also met her at my interview.

W Great. Did you meet Simon, who is working on a laptop at the desk?

M No, I didn't.

W Your desk is _____. Can you see _____? That's a welcome gift for you.

M Wow! Thanks a lot.

08

W Ethan, how's it going with the preparation for our Jazz Night?

M I'm all finished. This is a picture of _____ _____.

W Let me see. You set up a microphone on the left side as I asked.

M Yes. And I placed a grand piano and its chair behind it.

W Great. I like the banner that says "Jazz Night" on the wall. It's _____.

M Thanks. What do you think of the drums under the banner?

W I think they look good.

M And _____, I put two chairs on the right. Are they for the singers?

W No, those are for the guitarists. I think _____ _____. Nice work!

M Thank you.

09

M Grandma, come and see what I drew in art class. It's a picture of your house on Christmas!

W Oh, it's wonderful! There's a snowman _____ _____.

M I drew a sled beside the snowman, too. What do you think of the house?

W I love _____.

M Good. And then I put a sign that says "Merry Christmas" in front of the house.

W Great. Oh, I _____.

M Yes, just like in your yard. I _____ _____, too! Aren't they beautiful?

W They are!

M I'm so glad you think so, Grandma, because it's for you!

10 고난도

M Before the play begins, why don't you check the stage?

W Okay. It looks good! Especially the poster on the wall.

M I agree. The woman's smiling face will contrast nicely with her loneliness.

W How about the window? Shouldn't it show a full moon?

M No, _____. It turns into a full moon later in the play, but it doesn't start out like that.

W Now I remember. Well, _____ _____ is perfect.

M Yes, it's good _____ of the stage.

W And there's a chair beside the table. I remember you prepared two chairs before.

M Since it's a solo performance that is focusing on loneliness, a single chair will be better.

W Good idea. Oh, and is that _____ _____ on top of the drawers?

M Yes, it turned out well.

05

표의 내용

각종 표(안내표, 가격표, 광고표, 시간표, 메뉴 등)를 보면서 대화를 듣고, 지시문에서 요구하는 것을
고르는 유형이다. 다양한 소재를 이용하여 1문항 출제되고 있다.

해결 전략

1 제시된 표의 제목 및 항목과 지시문을 미리 보고 무엇에 관한 대화인지, 어떤 부분에 주목해서 들어야 하는지를 생각한다.

2 대화의 진행은 대개 표에 있는 항목의 순서를 따른다. 대화를 들으면서 각 항목에서 선택되지 않은 것을 표에서 지워나가며 듣
는 것이 좋다.

e.g. 아래 표가 제시될 경우 대화의 진행은 Capacity—Available Times—Price—Projector의 순서이다.

Study Rooms

	Room	Capacity (persons)	Available Times	Price (per hour)	Projector
①	A	2-3	9 a.m. – 11 a.m.	$10	×
②	B	4-6	9 a.m. – 11 a.m.	$16	○
③	C	4-6	2 p.m. – 4 p.m.	$14	×
④	D	6-8	2 p.m. – 4 p.m.	$19	○
⑤	E	6-9	4 p.m. – 6 p.m.	$21	×

3 대화 후반부에는 대개 두 개의 선택지가 남게 되는데, 대화 마지막 부분의 '최종 선택 요건(위의 표에서는 Projector)'에 해당
하는 부분을 잘 듣고 정답을 골라야 한다.

✳✳ 기출 맛보기

01 다음 표를 보면서 대화를 듣고, 여자가 구입할 휴대용 선풍기를 고르시오. 모의

Handheld Fans

	Model	Price	Battery Run Time	Fan Speed Level	Foldable
①	A	$20	6 hours	2	×
②	B	$23	9 hours	3	×
③	C	$25	9 hours	3	○
④	D	$28	12 hours	4	○
⑤	E	$33	12 hours	4	○

M Julie, what are you looking at?

W I'm thinking of buying a new handheld fan. Can you help me pick one?

M Sure. Hmm, how about this one?

W It looks good, but **I don't want to spend more than $30**.

M Okay. And **I think you should get one with a battery that lasts more than 8 hours.**

W **I think so, too.** I usually spend more than 8 hours outside.

M What about the fan speed levels? **Do you need a fan with four levels?**

W **No. Three levels will be enough for me.**

M Then you have two models left. **I recommend the foldable one.**

W What's special about it?

M If you fold the handle, it'll easily fit into your handbag. It can also stand up on your desk.

W That sounds convenient. **I'll buy that one.**

대화의 흐름

<선택 요건>

· **가격**: $30 미만 (→ ⑤ 제외)

· **배터리 지속 시간**: 8시간 이상 (→ ① 제외)

· **선풍기 속도 단계**: 3단계 (→ ④ 제외)

· **접이식 기능**: ○ (→ ② 제외, ③ 정답)

Words & Phrases handheld 휴대용인, 손에 들고 쓰는; (손에 들고 조작할 수 있을 정도의) 소형 기기 last 지속되다 recommend 추천하다 foldable 접을 수 있는, 접혀지는 *cf.* fold 접다 fit into ~에 꼭 들어맞다 convenient 편리한

Listen & Choose 유형핵심 익히기

* 녹음 내용을 듣고, 알맞은 답을 고르시오.

01 다음 표를 보면서 대화를 듣고, 두 사람이 시청할 프로그램을 고르시오.

TV Timetable

Time	Channel	Programs
7:00 - 7:50	7	World News
	9	ⓐ The History of Gold
8:00 - 8:50	7	ⓑ Fashion Today
	9	ⓒ The Vampire

02 다음 표를 보면서 대화를 듣고, 남자가 예약할 캠핑장을 고르시오. 모의

Best Campsites

	Campsite	Location	Price (per night)
ⓐ	A	Seaside	$65
ⓑ	B	Jungle Hut	$70
ⓒ	C	Rose Valley	$85

03 다음 표를 보면서 대화를 듣고, 여자가 구입할 운동 매트를 고르시오. 모의

Exercise Mats

	Model	Thickness	Non-slip Surface
ⓐ	A	4 mm	○
ⓑ	B	6 mm	○
ⓒ	C	8 mm	×

04 다음 표를 보면서 대화를 듣고, 두 사람이 예약할 방을 고르시오. 모의

Wayne Hotel Rooms

	Room	View	Breakfast
ⓐ	A	Mountain	×
ⓑ	B	Ocean	○
ⓒ	C	Ocean	×

05 다음 표를 보면서 대화를 듣고, 두 사람이 볼 영화를 고르시오.

Movies

	Title	Time
ⓐ	Deep Ocean	12:30 - 2:00
ⓑ	Family Troubles	2:30 - 4:30
ⓒ	The Tree	3:00 - 4:50

06 다음 표를 보면서 대화를 듣고, 남자가 구입할 모델을 고르시오. 모의

Selfie Sticks

	Model	Weight	Bluetooth Remote Control
ⓐ	A	220 g	○
ⓑ	B	190 g	×
ⓒ	C	180 g	○

07 다음 표를 보면서 대화를 듣고, 여자가 구매할 스마트 워치를 고르시오. 모의

Smartwatches

	Model	Warranty	Price
ⓐ	A	1 year	$90
ⓑ	B	3 years	$110
ⓒ	C	4 years	$125

08 다음 표를 보면서 대화를 듣고, 남자가 지원할 직종을 고르시오. 모의

Part-time Jobs at Royal Theater

	Job	Days	Time	Pay (per hour)
ⓐ	Ticket office	Sat. & Sun.	1:00 - 5:00 p.m.	$10
ⓑ	Information desk	Mon. - Fri.	1:00 - 5:00 p.m.	$10
ⓒ	Coat check	Sat. & Sun.	5:00 - 10:00 p.m.	$11

09 다음 표를 보면서 대화를 듣고, 여자가 구입할 미술용품을 고르시오. 모의

Art Supplies Set for Children

	Model	Coloring Tool	Number of Colors
ⓐ	A	Crayons	32
ⓑ	B	Watercolors	28
ⓒ	C	Markers	25

10 다음 표를 보면서 대화를 듣고, 두 사람이 수강할 운동 강좌를 고르시오.

Classes

Time	Tue.	Wed.	Thu.
6:00 p.m. - 7:00 p.m.	ⓐ Yoga		
7:00 p.m. - 8:00 p.m.	ⓑ Taekwondo	ⓒ Aerobics	Yoga
8:00 p.m. - 9:00 p.m.		Weight Training	

✴ STEP 1의 녹음 내용을 다시 들으면서 빈칸을 채우시오.

01

M It's 8:05. _____ TV?

W The documentary *The History of Gold* has finished, and a fashion program and the soap opera *The Vampire* are on.

M Well, _____ fashion.

W Then, _____.

02 모의

M Honey, how about _____ on the list next week?

W Sounds great. There are three different campsites.

M Yeah. Since we went to Seaside campsite last time, let's _____.

W Good. Hmm, I don't want _____ _____ per night. It's too expensive.

M I agree with that. I'll reserve this one right now.

03 모의

W Excuse me. Are thicker mats better for home training?

M Not really. But I think _____ _____ for home trainers.

W I see. Then I have to choose between these two.

M Right. _____ with a non-slip surface. It _____ _____.

W Okay. Safety is important. I'll take it.

04 모의

W Let's book a hotel room for our vacation.

M Okay. _____?

W I was hoping to get _____ _____.

W Me too. Shall we have breakfast in the hotel?

M _____. I heard there are some good restaurants near the hotel.

05

M Jeff's party will begin at 5 o'clock. What shall we do before the party?

W We can _____ to the party. Here, look at this listing.

M Well, if we leave now, we can get to the cinema _____.

W _____ to get to Jeff's house, so that leaves only one choice.

06 모의

M Hello, I'm looking for a selfie stick. And _____ _____.

W Then I don't recommend _____ _____.

M Okay. I also want a bluetooth remote control. I heard _____.

07 모의

W Do you think a one-year warranty is too short for a smartwatch?

M Yes. I recommend one _____ _____.

W Okay. That leaves me with these two options.

M _____ because it's as good as the other one.

W Okay. I'll take your advice.

08 모의

W Working at the information desk seems easy, doesn't it?

M Yeah, but I _____.

W I see. Then, how about this job?

M The pay is pretty good, but _____ _____ I need some time to do my homework.

W Then, that _____.

09 모의

W I'm searching for an art supplies set for children.

M Let me see. Watercolors _____ _____. The kids would need extra things like brushes.

W I agree. How about the number of colors?

M _____ to express what they want.

10

W Lucas, _____ at the health center this week?

M I have to work after school on Wednesday.

W How about taking the yoga class then?

M _____.

W Then, we have no choice except one.

Listen & Answer 실전 문제

※ 녹음 내용을 듣고, 알맞은 답을 고르시오.

01 다음 표를 보면서 대화를 듣고, 두 사람이 선택한 프로그램을 고르시오.

Family Arts Festival Programs

	Program	Day	Time	Price
①	Postcard Drawing	Friday	2 p.m.	$12
②	Mini Concert	Saturday	7 p.m.	$13
③	Mask Decorating	Thursday	7 p.m.	$19
④	Self-portraits	Saturday	2 p.m.	$15
⑤	Candle Making	Saturday	7 p.m.	$23

02 다음 표를 보면서 대화를 듣고, 여자가 선택한 아파트를 고르시오.

Apartments

	Apartment	Location	Bedroom	Monthly Rent	Security Guard
①	A	Downtown	1	$650	○
②	B	East Side	1	$500	×
③	C	Downtown	2	$800	○
④	D	Downtown	2	$700	×
⑤	E	Downtown	2	$1,050	○

03 다음 표를 보면서 대화를 듣고, 두 사람이 구매할 물뿌리개를 고르시오.

Watering Cans

	Model	Material	Capacity (liters)	Price	Color
①	A	Plastic	2	$32	Blue
②	B	Plastic	3	$17	Red
③	C	Metal	2	$26	Silver
④	D	Plastic	1	$19	Red
⑤	E	Plastic	2.5	$15	Black

04 다음 표를 보면서 대화를 듣고, 남자가 지원할 인턴십 프로그램을 고르시오. 고난도

Summer Internship Programs

	Job	Paid	In State	Start Date	End Date	Schedule
①	hotel receptionist	○	×	May 1	September 1	full-time
②	computer programmer	×	○	June 15	August 31	full-time
③	copy editor	○	○	July 1	August 20	part-time
④	hospital coordinator	○	○	June 1	September 15	full-time
⑤	software engineer	×	×	July 10	October 15	part-time

05 다음 표를 보면서 대화를 듣고, 여자가 구매할 휴대폰 케이스를 고르시오.

Phone Cases

	Model	Material	Color	Price	Customer Rating
①	A	Leather	Brown	$15	★★★☆☆
②	B	Plastic	Blue	$12	★★★☆☆
③	C	Silicone	Pink	$23	★★★★☆
④	D	Silicone	Green	$19	★★★★★
⑤	E	Plastic	Black	$10	★★★★☆

06 다음 표를 보면서 대화를 듣고, 두 사람이 선택할 여행 상품을 고르시오. 고난도

Tour Packages

	Tour	Days	Day of Departure	Guide	Countries
①	Sunny Holiday	15	Tues. & Thurs. & Sat.	×	4
②	Exotic Island	16	Tues. & Thurs. & Sat.	○	5
③	Ultimate Adventure	18	Tues. & Thurs. & Sat.	×	6
④	Historic Monument	10	Wed. & Fri.	○	3
⑤	Dream Vacation	25	Wed. & Fri.	○	8

07 다음 표를 보면서 대화를 듣고, 남자가 주문할 무선 진공청소기를 고르시오.

Cordless Vacuum Cleaners

	Brand	Type	Cost	Battery Life (min.)	Second Battery
①	Hover	Handheld	$150	40	×
②	Erica	Stick	$490	60	×
③	Carlson	Stick	$780	80	○
④	Somerset	Stick	$430	50	○
⑤	Vex	Stick	$320	30	○

08 다음 표를 보면서 대화를 듣고, 두 사람이 선택한 도서관 강좌를 고르시오.

Children's Programs at Bloomfield County Libraries

	Library	Program	Ages	Class Time	Driving Time
①	Central	Tails and Tales	5-7	Tue. 11 a.m.	30 min.
②	Westville	Book Bingo	4-7	Wed. 2 p.m.	20 min.
③	Belmont	Coloring Books	4-6	Fri. 3 p.m.	40 min.
④	Logan Lake	Storytime in the Park	3-5	Tue. 2 p.m.	60 min.
⑤	Woodstock	Art of Words	5-6	Wed. 3 p.m.	50 min.

09 다음 표를 보면서 대화를 듣고, 여자가 선택할 강좌를 고르시오.

Astrid Dance Studio

	Class	Age Limit	Day & Time	Price (per month)	Class Size
①	Salsa	17 and up	Tuesday 4 p.m.	$70	8
②	Hip Hop	13 and up	Saturday 11 a.m.	$60	10
③	Jazz	13 and up	Friday 4 p.m.	$95	4
④	K-Pop	10 and up	Friday 5 p.m.	$65	8
⑤	Ballet	7 and up	Thursday 4 p.m.	$65	10

10 다음 표를 보면서 대화를 듣고, 남자가 선택한 태블릿을 고르시오.

Tablets

	Model	Price	Screen Size (inches)	Battery Life (hours)	Weight (pounds)
①	A	$314	10	9	1.7
②	B	$699	12	12	1.2
③	C	$475	11	10	1.0
④	D	$225	10	5	1.1
⑤	E	$184	7	4	1.0

✻ STEP 3의 녹음 내용을 다시 들으면서 빈칸을 채우시오.

01

W Honey, our kids want to participate in one of the Family Arts Festival programs next week.

M Great! It will be nice _____ _____.

W Let's decide which program to take from this list.

M Let me see. Our kids _____ _____ the concert. They're not that into music.

W Got it. This seems interesting and it's on Thursday evening.

M It seems good, but I have an appointment with my client at that time.

W I see. Since we both work during the day, we should pick something in the evening or on Saturdays.

M Yeah, we _____ _____. That leaves us with these two options. How about this one?

W That sounds cool but _____ _____. I don't want to spend that much money on a program.

M Okay. Let's sign up for this one, then. I think it'll be a lot of fun.

02

M I see you are still looking for apartments. Can't find anything you like?

W _____ to five, but it's still confusing.

M Do you care about the location?

W I don't want _____. That would be inconvenient.

M Okay, so not the east side. And you want two bedrooms, right?

W I really do, but I _____ _____ a month.

M Well, that only leaves two. _____ _____ for your budget. What do you think?

W That's important, but I also need a security guard for safety.

M Then I guess it's settled.

W I think you're right. I'll call and set up a time to view that one.

03

W Felix, we need to get a watering can for the garden.

M Why don't we buy one online? Look at this website.

W Let me see. First, we _____ _____.

M How about the metal one? It looks more durable.

W I think plastic would be better _____ _____.

M You're right. And which size of can do you want?

W Between 2 to 3 liters _____.

M Okay. What about the price?

W _____ more than $20.

M Then it's between these two. Which color do you prefer?

W I like the red one better.

M Good choice. I'll order it now.

04 고난도

W Hi, John. What are you doing?

M I'm choosing an internship for the summer.

W Can I look at your options?

M Sure. Ideally I want to do _____ _____.

W So, one of these two then?

M Right. But _____. I can't take a position that isn't paid, because of my financial situation.

W I understand. Do you care about the location?

M I _____.

W And what about the start date? Some start sooner than others.

M I _____. And I need to be back in school in September.

W Well, there is still one that could work for you. Are you okay with working part-time?

M I wouldn't mind. I'll apply for that one.

05

W Oliver, I'm thinking of buying one of these smartphone cases. Can you help me choose one?

M Sure. What do you think of this leather case? This is the one I have.

W Well, _____ about the material, but I think leather is hard to clean.

M Okay. What about the color?

W It's difficult to choose, but I definitely don't like black.

M _____ on it?

W No more than 20 dollars.

M Then you have to choose from these two. How about _____?

W Actually, I'll choose the other one. It's more expensive, but it has _____.

M Good choice.

06 고난도

M Honey, we should decide on our honeymoon destination. Do you have a place in mind?

W I want to visit Europe. Here is a brochure about tour packages. Let's pick one.

M Okay. Let's see.... My work schedule won't allow me _____.

W Oh, that's right. Maybe we should try one of these four.

M Well, our wedding is on Friday afternoon, so it would be better _____.

W Okay, then do you think we need a guide?

M I _____. Wouldn't you?

W That does sound like more fun. And I want to _____.

M Then I think we have made our choice.

07

M I need a cordless vacuum cleaner. Can you help me choose a good one?

W Sure. First, we have to choose either a handheld or a stick model. Which one do you want?

M I'd prefer a stick one since _____ _____.

W Next, how much can you spend on it?

M I'd better not spend more than 500 dollars. What else should I consider?

W As a rule of thumb, battery life is the most important. I think _____ _____.

M I see. Then, it looks like I have two choices left. I'll choose the one with longer run time.

W Wait a minute! The other one includes a second battery. _____, I'd get this one.

M Right, its second battery can _____ _____.

W Definitely. Moreover, the difference in run time between these two is only 10 minutes.

M Got it! I'll take it.

08

W Honey, I want to sign Anna up for a library program.

M What kind of program?

W Take a look at this site. Local libraries _____ _____ for children.

M They look great. One of them offers a coloring book class. Anna already took the class last year, didn't she?

W Yes, so I don't think she needs to take it again.

M Okay. Since Anna is 6 years old, _____ _____ take this class.

W That's right. A morning class is also not possible since she comes home from kindergarten at 1 p.m.

M Then, we have two choices left.

W I think this library is _____. Anna won't be happy if she has to be in the car for a long time.

M Exactly. It'd be better to choose the library _____.

W I hope Anna will enjoy this class!

09

M Penny, you said you wanted to take a dance class, right? I've brought the brochure of Astrid Dance Studio here.

W How nice of you! Let me see.... I'd like to take this class.

M I don't think you can. Its age limit is seventeen,

and you're only fifteen.

W Oh, you're right. And I have volleyball practice after school every Thursday.

M Then you _____. What does your budget look like?

W Well, _____ a month.

M You have these two classes in that price range. Which class are you interested in?

W They both sound good, but I prefer the class _____.

M That's a good idea. The studio _____ _____.

W Yes, I'll sign up for it.

10

M Layla. Can you help me? I'm looking for a tablet online.

W Sure. How much _____?

M I'd prefer not to spend more than $500.

W Okay. What screen size would you like? There are many different sizes.

M I have no idea. What do you think?

W I recommend a screen size of 10 inches or more if you want to use it for online classes.

M All right. And I should get a tablet with a long battery life, right?

W Definitely. The battery life should be _____ _____.

M Now I have two options left. What else should I consider?

W Well, they're both good tablets. This one is lighter but more expensive. Which one do you think _____?

M Since I'll carry the tablet around a lot, _____ _____. Thanks, Layla.

발음이 잘 안 들리는 이유 ❸

실제 발음을 잘못 알기 쉬운 단어

외래어 표기 또는 발음기호 상으로는 아래 우리말 발음과 같지만, 실제 원어민들의 발음을 들어보면 차이가 크므로 주의해야 한다.

amateur	[아마추어] ✕	basic	[베이직] ✕
brother	[브라더] ✕	buffet	[뷔페] ✕
caffeine	[카페인] ✕	chaos	[카오스] ✕
charisma	[카리스마] ✕	cocoa	[코코아] ✕
elite	[엘리트] ✕	lettuce	[레터스] ✕
label	[라벨] ✕	mobile	[모바일] ✕
oasis	[오아시스] ✕	realm	[렐름] ✕
sauna	[사우나] ✕		

언급되지 않은 내용 · 불일치하는 내용

대화를 듣고 지시문에 제시된 대상에 대한 여러 세부 사항 중에서 언급되지 않은 것을 고르거나,
담화를 듣고 내용과 일치하지 않는 것을 파악하는 문제이다. 각 1문항씩 출제된다.

해결 전략

❶ 언급되지 않은 내용

1 지시문과 선택지를 미리 확인하고 나올 내용을 예상하면서 듣는 것이 좋다. 선택지 다섯 개 중 네 개는 언급되므로 대략
어떤 내용들이 나올 것인지를 파악할 수 있어 도움이 된다.
e.g. 대화를 듣고, Tour of Liberty University에 관해 언급되지 <u>않은</u> 것을 고르시오.
① 날짜 ② 활동 내용 ③ 참가 가능 인원수 ④ 기념품 ⑤ 신청 방법
2 선택지는 보통 대화 순서대로 언급되지만 반드시 그렇지는 않다. 이 유형은 비교적 선택지 길이가 짧으므로 대화 순서
와 다르더라도 들으면서 충분히 판단해낼 수 있다.

❷ 불일치하는 내용

주요 소재로는 경연 대회, 프로그램, 관광 상품, 행사, 공연, 강좌, 시설, 상(award) 등에 관한 안내 또는 공지사항이 있다.
1 지시문에서 얻을 수 있는 정보로 소재 및 내용을 예측해본다.
e.g. Mascot Design Contest에 관한 다음 내용을 듣고, 일치하지 <u>않는</u> 것을 고르시오.
(→ 디자인 경연 대회에 대한 안내)
2 담화의 진행은 대개 선택지와 같은 순서이고 선택지는 짧은 우리말 문장으로 구성된다. 그러므로 선택지를 재빨리
훑어보고 나올 내용을 예상하면서 듣는 것이 좋다.
3 담화에 나온 문장 중 일부 단어만 바꾸어 정답 선택지로 출제하므로 이에 주의해야 한다.
e.g. And the winner will receive **a team uniform** as a prize.
정답: 수상자는 상으로 **시즌 티켓**을 받을 것이다.
The prize for the winner **will be delivered** by October 11th.
정답: 우승 상품은 10월 11일까지 **직접 찾아가야 한다**.

✳✴ 기출 맛보기

01 대화를 듣고, Winter Lake Festival에 관해 언급되지 <u>않은</u> 것을 고르시오. 모의

① 기간   ② 장소   ③ 입장료
④ 기념품   ⑤ 활동 종류

M What are you doing, Laura?	**대화의 흐름**
W Hi, Tim. I'm looking for winter festivals to visit during vacation.	
M Is there anything good?	
W Yes, look at this. There is a new local event called the Winter Lake Festival.	
M Awesome. **When does it start?**	
W **It starts on December 18th, and it'll be held for two weeks.**	① **기간**: 12월 18일부터 2주간
M Cool. Oh, **it'll take place in Stevenson Park.**	② **장소**: 스티븐슨 공원
W Great. It's near our school. If you don't have any plans during vacation, let's go together.	
M Of course. **Is there an entrance fee?**	③ **입장료**: $3
W **Yes. Here, it says $3.** It's not expensive.	④ **기념품**: 언급 X (➔ 정답)
M Good. Look! **There are so many kinds of activities to enjoy.**	⑤ **활동 종류**: 아이스 스케이팅, 얼음낚시, 눈싸움
W **Yeah, there is ice skating, ice fishing, and a snowball fight.**	
M They all sound exciting. Let's have fun there.	

02 Sharing Friday Movement에 관한 다음 내용을 듣고, 일치하지 <u>않는</u> 것을 고르시오. 모의

① 매주 금요일에 2달러씩 기부하는 운동이다.
② 2001년 핀란드에서 시작되었다.
③ 기부금은 가난한 지역에 깨끗한 물을 공급하는 데 쓰인다.
④ 올해 20명의 학생에게 장학금을 지급했다.
⑤ 추가 정보는 홈페이지를 통해 얻을 수 있다.

W Good afternoon, listeners. Why don't you join the Sharing Friday Movement and **donate two dollars to our fund every Friday**? **This movement started in 2001 in Finland** as an idea to encourage people to do good. Since then, this idea has grown into a global movement. **Most of the donations go to poor areas across the world and help people get clean water. This year, scholarships were given to 100 students** in these areas to celebrate our 20th anniversary. Please join us, and help make a difference. **If you want to get more information, visit our homepage.**	**대화의 흐름** ① **운동 소개**: 매주 금요일에 2달러씩 기부하는 운동 ② **운동의 유래**: 2001년 핀란드에서 시작 ③ **기부금의 용도**: 가난한 지역에 깨끗한 물 공급 ④ **올해 장학금을 받은 학생 수**: 100명 (➔ 정답) ⑤ **추가 정보**: 홈페이지 방문

Words & Phrases 01 hold (행사 등을) 열다   **take place** 개최되다, 열리다   **entrance fee** 입장료   **activity** 활동   **02** movement (사회적·정치적) 운동   **donate** 기부하다 *cf.* donation 기부   **encourage** 장려하다; 격려하다   **scholarship** 장학금   **celebrate** 기념[축하]하다   **anniversary** 기념일   **make a difference** 변화를 가져오다

✳ 녹음 내용을 듣고, 알맞은 답을 고르시오.

정답 및 해설 **p.36**

01 대화를 듣고, 캐비아에 관해 언급되지 <u>않은</u> 것을 고르시오.

ⓐ 색깔   ⓑ 원산지   ⓒ 보관 방법

02 대화를 듣고, Madagascar에 관해 언급되지 <u>않은</u> 것을 고르시오.

ⓐ 기후   ⓑ 크기   ⓒ 사용 언어

03 대화를 듣고, Madison House에 관해 언급되지 <u>않은</u> 것을 고르시오.

ⓐ 건축 시기   ⓑ 천장 높이   ⓒ 가구 품질

04 대화를 듣고, 강아지 키우기에 관해 언급되지 <u>않은</u> 것을 고르시오. 모의

ⓐ 산책시키기   ⓑ 목욕시키기   ⓒ 배변 훈련시키기

05 대화를 듣고, World Dinosaur Exhibition에 관해 언급되지 않은 것을 고르시오. 모의

ⓐ 운영 시간   ⓑ 입장료   ⓒ 교통편

06 Greenville Animation Film Festival에 관한 다음 내용을 듣고, 일치하지 <u>않는</u> 것을 고르시오. 모의

ⓐ 일주일 동안 열린다.   ⓑ 올해의 주제는 우정이다.   ⓒ 근처에 주차장이 있다.

07 Show Me Your Creativity에 관한 다음 내용을 듣고, 일치하지 <u>않는</u> 것을 고르시오. 모의

ⓐ 고등학생과 대학생을 대상으로 한다.   ⓑ 참가자는 환경 관련 프로젝트를 만들어야 한다.
ⓒ 신청 마감일은 6월 30일이다.

08 Family Night at the Museum에 관한 다음 내용을 듣고, 일치하지 <u>않는</u> 것을 고르시오. 모의

ⓐ 박물관 정규 운영 시간 종료 후에 열린다.   ⓑ 행성과 별 모형 아래에서 잠을 잔다.
ⓒ 사전 등록 없이 현장에서 참가할 수 있다.

09 Green Action Photo Contest에 관한 다음 내용을 듣고, 일치하지 <u>않는</u> 것을 고르시오. 모의

ⓐ 10월 한 달간 사진을 올릴 수 있다.   ⓑ 정해진 해시태그를 붙이면 자동으로 참가하게 된다.
ⓒ 우승 사진은 연말까지 마을 웹사이트에 게시된다.

10 Magic Show에 관한 다음 내용을 듣고, 일치하지 <u>않는</u> 것을 고르시오. 모의

ⓐ Fantasia Gallery 개관 기념으로 열린다.   ⓑ 카드 마술사가 출연할 예정이다.
ⓒ Fantasia Gallery 방문객은 공연 관람료가 할인된다.

2 Listen & Choose Dictation 유형핵심 받아쓰기

✳ STEP 1의 녹음 내용을 다시 들으면서 빈칸을 채우시오.

정답 및 해설 **p.36**

01

M Have you tried the caviar over there?

W Not yet, but I've seen it. _____ _____?

M Yeah, red and black. The black is usually expensive and strong.

W Really? Then I'll try the black caviar. Do you know _____?

M Probably Russia, but there are other possibilities.

02

W Tom, _____ Madagascar, haven't you? I heard that the island is huge.

M Right. It's _____ island in the world.

W Wow! I didn't know that. _____ _____?

M They speak both French and Madagascar's native language.

03

M Welcome to Madison House. This historical building _____.

W Wow, the ceilings are amazing! And the furniture is very impressive.

M The furniture that you see represents _____ _____ at the time.

W It certainly looks great.

04 모의

W Dad, I want to have a puppy. I will name my puppy Toby.

M Okay. But _____ Toby every day?

W That'll be easy.

M Also, _____ Toby, too.

W Really? Hmm... Dad, you'll help me, right?

M Sometimes. But remember _____ _____.

05 모의

W There will be a World Dinosaur Exhibition this Saturday. Why don't we take the kids?

M That sounds great! _____?

W Since _____ from 10 a.m. to 5 p.m., how about going there in the afternoon?

M Okay. _____?

W It's $10 for an adult and $5 for a child.

06 모의

W Hello, listeners! Are you excited for the Greenville Animation Film Festival? This year, it'll start on December 5th and _____. Throughout the festival, visitors can watch different animation movies _____ _____ of this year, friendship, every night. Remember, _____ _____. So, please use public transportation.

07 모의

M Are you full of creative thoughts? Then our annual science contest, Show Me Your Creativity, is the perfect place _____ _____. This competition _____ all high school and university students. Students that wish to participate _____ _____ about this year's theme of space exploration. _____ is June 30th.

08 모의

W We are starting a special program — Family Night at the Museum. When _____ _____, you and your children get to walk around the museum with a flashlight. After your adventure is complete, you _____ _____ of planets and stars. All those who want to join _____ _____. On-site registration is not accepted.

09 모의

M Why don't you join our Green Action Photo Contest? From September 1st until September 30th, you can upload photos of your _____ _____ on social media. By tagging your photos with the hash tag #GreenAction, you can _____ _____. The winning photos will be posted on the town's website until _____ _____.

10 모의

W May I have your attention, please? As manager of Fantasia Gallery, I am pleased to announce _____ a Magic Show to celebrate our grand opening. John Potter, who _____, will perform in the show. The show is _____ _____ for everyone visiting our gallery today. Seats are limited!

✻ 녹음 내용을 듣고, 알맞은 답을 고르시오.

정답 및 해설 **p.38**

01 대화를 듣고, Bollywood 영화에 관해 언급되지 <u>않은</u> 것을 고르시오.

① 제작 지역   ② 대표작   ③ 연간 제작 편 수
④ 평균 상영 시간   ⑤ 흥행 조건

02 대화를 듣고, Camp John Hay에 관해 언급되지 <u>않은</u> 것을 고르시오.

① 보유 시설   ② 숲의 면적   ③ 여름 기온
④ 위치   ⑤ 교통편 제공 여부

03 대화를 듣고, Arendal Annual Flea Market에 관해 언급되지 <u>않은</u> 것을 고르시오.

① 개최 요일   ② 개최 장소   ③ 등록 방법
④ 판매 참가자 수   ⑤ 수익금 용도

04 대화를 듣고, Maria Arroyo-Diamond에 관해 언급되지 <u>않은</u> 것을 고르시오.

① 출신 국가   ② 결혼 시기   ③ 대표작
④ 화풍   ⑤ 작품 가격

05 대화를 듣고, Ellis Island에 관해 언급되지 <u>않은</u> 것을 고르시오.

① 용도   ② 면적   ③ 시설 사용 기간
④ 시설 개관 시기   ⑤ 위치

06 Spring Swim Lesson Program에 관한 다음 내용을 듣고, 일치하지 <u>않는</u> 것을 고르시오.

① 커뮤니티 센터에서 4월에 시작될 예정이다.
② 수영 실력에 따라 반이 나뉜다.
③ 총 8주 과정으로 이루어져 있다.
④ 수강료에는 물안경과 수영모가 포함되어 있다.
⑤ 수업은 평일 오후 및 토요일 오전에 있다.

07 Wharf Amusement Park에 관한 다음 내용을 듣고, 일치하지 <u>않는</u> 것을 고르시오. `고난도`

① Macau 최초의 테마 놀이공원이다.
② 2005년 12월에 개장했다.
③ 놀이 기구 이용권이 무료이다.
④ 세 가지 테마 구역으로 나뉘어 있다.
⑤ 세계 각지의 음식을 파는 레스토랑이 있다.

08 Carson Electronics 채용 공고에 관한 다음 내용을 듣고, 일치하지 <u>않는</u> 것을 고르시오.

① Dallas 지점의 판매사원을 모집한다.
② 관련 업무 경력이 요구된다.
③ 학력 제한 없이 지원이 가능하다.
④ 지원서는 웹사이트에서 구할 수 있다.
⑤ 서류 접수는 9월 16일에 마감한다.

09 The Great Welsh Walk에 관한 다음 내용을 듣고, 일치하지 <u>않는</u> 것을 고르시오.

① 10월 9일 일요일에 개최될 예정이다.
② 성별 제한 없이 참가할 수 있다.
③ 유방암 퇴치 기금 마련을 목적으로 한다.
④ 참가자들은 개와 함께 참가할 수 있다.
⑤ 에어로빅 준비 운동 시간이 있다.

10 Bulwer-Lytton Fiction Contest에 관한 다음 내용을 듣고, 일치하지 <u>않는</u> 것을 고르시오. `고난도`

① San José 주립 대학 영문학과가 후원한다.
② 참가자들은 소설의 첫 문장을 쓴다.
③ 대회명은 한 작가의 이름을 따서 지어졌다.
④ 대회 첫해에 만여 개의 작품이 출품되었다.
⑤ 소설을 여러 하위 부문으로 나눠 진행하고 있다.

01

M I want to watch a movie. What about you?

W Me too. There's a new one from Bollywood that you might like.

M What's Bollywood?

W It's the Indian film industry, which is based in Mumbai. Mumbai _____ Bombay, so it's a combination of Bombay and Hollywood.

M Oh, then I think *3 Idiots* is a well-known Bollywood movie.

W Right. That's one of its most famous movies. They produce nearly a thousand films each year, and _____.

M That's amazing. What are Bollywood films like?

W There is a lot of singing and dancing, so a film's success often _____ _____.

02

W Nick, did you get a chance to look at this brochure for Camp John Hay?

M I did, and it looks great! They have a fitness gym, a golf course, and horses for horseback riding.

W Look, they have _____ 246 hectares.

M Yes. There are over 250,000 pine trees. It sounds beautiful.

W The trees also _____ during the summer there, between 15 to 23 degrees. I just wish it wasn't so far away.

M Yes, _____ Baguio City. That's a long way from here, but I think the trip

would be fun.

W Yeah, let's take our car. _____ the wildlife in the forest.

M All right, then it's settled. We're going.

03

W James, would you like to go to the Arendal Annual Flea Market with me?

M I'm not sure. It opens this Saturday, right?

W Yes. _____ of Arendal High School.

M _____ this time. There was not much to look around last year.

W It will be a lot bigger than the last time. I heard _____ this year.

M Oh, really? I might be able to find the board games I've been looking for.

W Probably. And _____ for student scholarships and activities as usual.

M That's great. Then I'd like to join you.

W Okay. Let's go together.

04

M Diane, did you hear about the Maria Arroyo-Diamond exhibition?

W I did! Most of her work is _____. We should go together.

M I was hoping you would say that. She's one of my favorite artists.

W She's from Mexico, isn't she?

M Right. She moved to Italy _____ _____, but I think

Mexico is where she developed her painting style.

W Her work _____. I could see that coming from Mexican culture.

M Right, and she's become quite famous in Italy.

W Oh, I know. _____ for $80,000 in an auction.

M Wow! I think she'll be even more popular in the future.

05

M Welcome to Ellis Island! I'll be your guide for today. This island _____ _____. Please look around.

W How long was it in operation?

M Good question. For more than sixty years.

W I see, _____?

M Unfortunately, yes. It opened in 1892 and closed in 1954. Now it's a popular tourist attraction, as you can see.

W Then _____ during its history?

M Because of its location, New York City, and the fact that _____ to get from Europe to America, it received millions of immigrants.

W That's interesting. It has such a rich history.

06

M Good afternoon, Oak Ridge residents! If you can't swim, or just want to improve your technique, Spring Swim Lesson Program is the chance you've been waiting for. Applications are now being accepted for the program, _____ _____, at the Community Center. _____ _____ for ages 8 to 12, ages 13 to 18, and ages over 18. Classes are offered in eight-week sessions. _____, which includes swimming goggles and a cap. Classes are offered on weekday afternoons and Saturday mornings, so you can choose a time that suits you. For more information please contact the Community Center at 786-7110.

07 고난도

W Hello, visitors! Welcome to the Wharf Amusement Park. It is Macau's _____ and offers recreation, retail stores, a convention center, hotels, and more, all in one place. _____ _____, the park is locally managed. It opens year-round with no admission fee, but you must purchase tickets for the rides. The park _____, namely Dynasty Wharf, East Meets West, and Legend Wharf. Also, you can enjoy many fine restaurants _____ _____. Whether your travel is for business or pleasure, you are sure to enjoy your trip to this fascinating world-class amusement complex.

08

M Are you looking for an exciting job opportunity? Carson Electronics is now inviting applications for enthusiastic sales people for our Dallas office. Relevant work experience is a bonus, but _____ _____. We are accepting all applications _____. Please note that we will only accept applications that are complete. The application form is available on our website, www.carsonelectronics. com, and applications in other formats _____ _____. All documents must be sent to our recruiter, David Johnson, by September 16th. Thank you for your interest in Carson Electronics!

09

W Hello, supporters! The Great Welsh Walk will take place next month on Sunday, October 9th. The Walk is _____ over a 5 km, 10 km, or half-marathon distance. The goal of the event is _____ _____ for the fight against breast cancer. _____ _____ or babies in strollers. The event will start at the Llanelli Discovery Center, and _____ a special aerobics warm-up session. Why not take part and encourage those around you to do the same?

10 고난도

M The Bulwer-Lytton Fiction Contest is _____ _____ the English Department of San José State University. Participants _____ the worst possible opening line to a novel, and the most awful is crowned the winner. The contest _____ English writer Edward George Bulwer-Lytton, author of the much-quoted first line "It was a dark and stormy night." The first year of the competition _____ _____, but it was widely advertised the next year and attracted around 10,000 entries. There are also now several subcategories including fiction, romance novels, and others.

첫단추
듣기 모의고사

유형편

CHAPTER

3

추론적·종합적 이해

대화나 담화에서 직접적으로 언급되지 않지만 여러 정보들로 미루어
짐작하거나 정보들을 종합하여 판단해야 하는 문제들이다. 대개 혼동을
주는 정보들이 같이 등장하여 오답 선택지로도 활용되기 때문에 이들을
잘 구별하여 듣는 것도 중요하다.

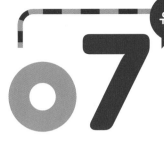

화자의 관계

대화를 듣고, 누구와 누구 사이에서 일어나는 대화인지 추론하는 유형이다. 의사와 환자, 점원과 손님같이 전형적인 관계 외에도 다양한 관계의 화자들이 등장한다. 1문항 출제된다.

해결 전략

1 대화 속에서 화자의 직업과 밀접한 관계가 있는 표현들이 정답 단서로 자주 등장하므로 잘 알아둔다.

e.g. **약사(pharmacist)**: prescription, drug, medicine, dose

의사(doctor): surgery, operation, treatment, hospital, give a prescription

비행기 승무원(flight attendant): fasten your seat belt, take-off, landing, boarding pass

호텔 프런트 직원(hotel receptionist): reservation, book a room, check in[out], stay, room service

요리사(chef): recipe, flavor, dish, restaurant, kitchen, cook, ingredient, menu

성우(voice actor): record, audio book, voice acting, script, recording booth, microphone

기자(reporter): interview, article, magazine, newspaper, reader, subscriber, feature story, press conference

코치(coach), 운동선수(athlete): match, opponent, training program, win the first prize, trophy

감독(director), 배우(actor): scene, scenario, film, shoot, direct, act, play a role, performance

패션모델(fashion model): stage, fashion show, rehearsal, pose, photo, runway

옷가게 직원(clothing store staff): look for, try on, suit, fit, style, go well with, in a different color[size]

세탁소 주인(dry cleaner owner): pick up, clothes, remove, get cleaned, stain, steaming machine, dry-cleaned

작가(author), 출판사 직원(publishing company employee): edit(or), publish, book, novel, be released, first[final] draft

2 정답 단서들 외에 오답을 유도하는 혼동 어구들도 등장하므로, 대화를 전체적인 맥락에서 이해해야 한다.
(→ p. 87 기출 맛보기 혼동 어구 1~4)

✳✳ 기출 맛보기

01 대화를 듣고, 두 사람의 관계를 가장 잘 나타낸 것을 고르시오. 모의

① 호텔 직원 — 투숙객　　　　　　② 열쇠 수리공 — 집주인
③ 경비원 — 입주민　　　　　　　　④ 은행원 — 고객
⑤ 치과의사 — 환자

[Telephone rings.] **M** Hello. This is G-Solution. How may I help you? **W** Hello. *I'm locked out of my home.* **The keypad on my door isn't responding.** **M** It might be an electric problem. **It's probably a simple fix and it won't cost much.** **W** How much is it? **M** It's 30 dollars including *the service charge.* But you'll have to pay extra if there are any additional problems. **W** I got it. Can you come over right away? **M** I'm afraid not. I'm doing a job at *the Capital Bank.* **W** How long will it take you to finish? **M** Just one hour. I'll call you as soon as I'm done. Address, please? **W** 705 Cozy Street near *Lee's Dental Clinic.* **M** Okay. See you soon.	**대화의 흐름** ·**정답 단서 1**: 여자의 현관 키패드가 작동을 안 함 ·**정답 단서 2**: 남자가 키패드를 쉽게 고칠 수 있다고 함 ·**혼동 어구 1**: I'm locked out of my home. (→ 오답 ③) ·**혼동 어구 2**: the service charge (→ 오답 ①) ·**혼동 어구 3**: the Capital Bank (→ 오답 ④) ·**혼동 어구 4**: Lee's Dental Clinic (→ 오답 ⑤)

Words & Phrases **be locked out of** (문이 잠겨) ~에 못 들어가다　**respond** 반응하다　**electric** 전기의　**cost** (비용이) 들다　**including** ~을 포함하여
service charge 서비스 비용　**extra** 추가 요금; 추가의　**additional** 추가적인

✳ 녹음 내용을 듣고, 알맞은 답을 고르시오.

정답 및 해설 **p.42**

01 대화를 듣고, 두 사람의 관계를 가장 잘 나타낸 것을 고르시오.
ⓐ 세입자 — 집주인　　　　ⓑ 탑승객 — 항공사 직원　　　　ⓒ 투숙객 — 호텔 프런트 직원

02 대화를 듣고, 두 사람의 관계를 가장 잘 나타낸 것을 고르시오. 모의
ⓐ 배우 — 방송 작가　　　　ⓑ 소설가 — 영화감독　　　　ⓒ 서점 직원 — 출판업자

03 대화를 듣고, 두 사람의 관계를 가장 잘 나타낸 것을 고르시오. 모의
ⓐ 우체국 직원 — 손님　　　　ⓑ 여행 가이드 — 관광객　　　　ⓒ 고속버스 운전기사 — 승객

04 대화를 듣고, 두 사람의 관계를 가장 잘 나타낸 것을 고르시오. 모의
ⓐ 호텔 직원 — 투숙객　　　　ⓑ 박람회장 안내원 — 방문객　　　　ⓒ 가구 제작자 — 의뢰인

05 대화를 듣고, 두 사람의 관계를 가장 잘 나타낸 것을 고르시오.
ⓐ 팬 — 배우　　　　ⓑ 독자 — 작가　　　　ⓒ 청취자 — 라디오 진행자

06 대화를 듣고, 두 사람의 관계를 가장 잘 나타낸 것을 고르시오.
ⓐ 고객 — 렌터카 직원　　　　ⓑ 차 주인 — 자동차 정비사　　　　ⓒ 손님 — 주유소 직원

07 대화를 듣고, 두 사람의 관계를 가장 잘 나타낸 것을 고르시오. 모의
ⓐ 화장품 판매원 — 손님　　　　ⓑ 피부과 의사 — 환자　　　　ⓒ 제약 회사 직원 — 약사

08 대화를 듣고, 두 사람의 관계를 가장 잘 나타낸 것을 고르시오. 모의
ⓐ 손님 — 의류매장 직원　　　　ⓑ 의상 디자이너 — 패션모델　　　　ⓒ 무대 연출가 — 안무가

09 대화를 듣고, 두 사람의 관계를 가장 잘 나타낸 것을 고르시오. 모의
ⓐ 신문 기자 — 영화배우　　　　ⓑ 매니저 — 가수　　　　ⓒ 녹음 기사 — 성우

10 대화를 듣고, 두 사람의 관계를 가장 잘 나타낸 것을 고르시오. 모의
ⓐ 파티 주최자 — 요리사　　　　ⓑ 슈퍼마켓 점원 — 손님　　　　ⓒ 배달 기사 — 음식점 주인

✳ STEP 1의 녹음 내용을 다시 들으면서 빈칸을 채우시오.

정답 및 해설 **p.42**

01

W I'd like to _____. My name is Monica Scott.

M Ms. Scott? Here's your final bill.

W Hmm.... This is strange. I didn't order anything _____.

M Really? Let me check. I'm so sorry, there was a mistake. _____ right away.

02 모의

W Hello, Mr. Johnson. Have you thought about _____?

M Yes. You said you wanted to _____, right?

W That's right. I loved your novel, and it would make a great movie.

M I'm glad to hear that. And _____ the movie, it would be a great honor for me.

03 모의

M Hello. What can I do for you?

W Hi, I'd like to _____ to Seoul, South Korea.

M Put it on the scale, please. All right. You can _____ within a week using Express Mail Service for $15.

W That sounds good. _____.

04 모의

M Hi, I made an online reservation. Do I get the tickets here?

W You don't have to get tickets if you have a reservation number. Just _____ _____ and you can enjoy the whole camping expo.

M That's great. I heard _____ for camping tables and chairs. Where can I find it?

W When you go inside, _____.

05

W I think _____ on TV. Aren't you Brad Johnson?

M Yes, I am.

W Wow! I never thought _____ _____ like you in person. I really enjoy reading your books. Could I get your autograph?

M Certainly.

06

M Should I _____ before I return the car?

W Yes, you should.

M I see. And _____ on Saturday by 11 a.m., right?

W Yes. Please bring it back on time, or you'll have to pay _____.

07 모의

W Hello, Mr. Cooper. You came here last week because of a sunburn. _____ now?

M Much better.

W Great. Let me look at the sunburn. The redness _____.

M Yeah. The cream _____ was really helpful.

08 모의

M I'm honored to have you on my stage.

W My pleasure. The dresses you made are gorgeous.

M Thank you. The theme of today's show is "Nature", so _____ with only natural materials.

W I see. Is there _____ I should use on the runway?

M I asked the other models _____ the soft lines of the dress.

09 모의

W Did you hear about one of the audio books _____ _____ in this studio last year?

M You mean "The Dreaming Tree?" I heard it was the bestselling audio book of the year.

W It was. The sound effects you added _____ _____.

M Thank you. Most of all, your voice acting was great _____.

10 모의

M Welcome, Ms. Jones. Mr. Harvey told me you're coming.

W Thanks. I hear that _____ at your house in two weeks.

M That's right. I'm hoping you _____ _____ for my party.

W Sure. _____ the party food from start to finish.

✳ 녹음 내용을 듣고, 알맞은 답을 고르시오.

정답 및 해설 **p.44**

01 대화를 듣고, 두 사람의 관계를 가장 잘 나타낸 것을 고르시오.

① 비서 — 직장 상사
② 판매원 — 손님
③ 음식 평론가 — 잡지 편집자
④ 식당 종업원 — 고객
⑤ 프로그램 진행자 — 요리사

02 대화를 듣고, 두 사람의 관계를 가장 잘 나타낸 것을 고르시오.

① 부동산 중개인 — 집주인
② 가구점 사장 — 직원
③ 택배 기사 — 경비원
④ 피아노 조율사 — 의뢰인
⑤ 이삿짐센터 직원 — 고객

03 대화를 듣고, 두 사람의 관계를 가장 잘 나타낸 것을 고르시오.

① 손님 — 약사
② 환자 보호자 — 의사
③ 학부모 — 교사
④ 야구팀 감독 — 물리치료사
⑤ 고객 — 보험사 직원

04 대화를 듣고, 두 사람의 관계를 가장 잘 나타낸 것을 고르시오.

① 아버지 — 딸
② 상담 교사 — 학부모
③ 대학 입학처 직원 — 수험생
④ 교사 — 학생
⑤ 형사 — 용의자

05 대화를 듣고, 두 사람의 관계를 가장 잘 나타낸 것을 고르시오.

① 코치 — 운동선수
② 작곡가 — 가수
③ 신입사원 — 직장 상사
④ 면접관 — 구직자
⑤ 음향 감독 — 성우

06 대화를 듣고, 두 사람의 관계를 가장 잘 나타낸 것을 고르시오.

① 야생 동물 보호가 — 기자
② 매표소 직원 — 손님
③ 호텔 관리인 — 투숙객
④ 항공기 승무원 — 탑승객
⑤ 여행사 직원 — 고객

07 대화를 듣고, 두 사람의 관계를 가장 잘 나타낸 것을 고르시오.

① 뉴스 진행자 — 현지 기자
② 강연자 — 방청객
③ 기상 캐스터 — 방송작가
④ 구조대원 — 조난자
⑤ 다큐멘터리 제작자 — 지역 주민

08 대화를 듣고, 두 사람의 관계를 가장 잘 나타낸 것을 고르시오.

① 집주인 — 세입자
② 건물 관리인 — 입주민
③ 부동산 중개인 — 고객
④ 신문사 직원 — 광고주
⑤ 인테리어 디자이너 — 의뢰인

09 대화를 듣고, 두 사람의 관계를 가장 잘 나타낸 것을 고르시오. 고난도

① 배우 — 감독
② 성우 — 방송 작가
③ 정신과 의사 — 환자
④ 소설가 — 연극 연출가
⑤ 신문 기자 — 시나리오 작가

10 대화를 듣고, 두 사람의 관계를 가장 잘 나타낸 것을 고르시오. 고난도

① 항공사 직원 — 여행객
② 택시 운전사 — 휴대폰 주인
③ 휴대폰 판매원 — 고객
④ 분실물 보관소 직원 — 관광객
⑤ 경찰관 — 신고자

✳ STEP 3의 녹음 내용을 다시 들으면서 빈칸을 채우시오.

정답 및 해설 **p.44**

01

W This is a new brand of chocolate. It's called *Moira*.

M *Moira*?

W Yes, the filling _____ fresh cream and _____ dark chocolate.

M Well, it looks beautiful. It's a very unusual shape.

W Yes, this chocolate looks beautiful _____ _____. Why don't you taste it?

M Mmm.... Oh, it's wonderful... absolutely delicious.

W If you buy *Moira* _____, you can get two packs for the price of one.

M OK. I'll buy two packs.

02

M Hello, Ms. Palmer.

W Hi, Mr. Watts! Come on in.

M Thanks. Well, you said _____ is in Fairfax County.

W Yes, it's 3481 Green Street.

M It takes an hour to get there from here. Can I look around the rooms and kitchen?

W Go ahead. Oh, I have a piano. How _____ _____?

M We have movers _____ all kinds of pianos. We use the appropriate padded wrapping to protect them.

W Good. Do you also _____?

M Sure. When are you planning to move?

W November 4th.

M Okay. I think a 5-ton truck will be enough for you.

03

W Hello, I'm Erin Taylor, Aidan's mother.

M Oh, hello, Mrs. Taylor. Everything went well.

W Thanks. How's Aidan?

M He is in the recovery room, and he will recover soon.

W That's a relief. So will he be all right?

M Yes, it was a simple surgery. But _____ _____ after he gets home.

W What should I do?

M _____ for him. Give him the medicine _____.

W My son likes to play baseball. _____ _____ again?

M Well, he can't play baseball for 3 months after the surgery. But after 3 months, it will be all right.

W I see. Thanks a lot.

04

M Monica, you seem very tired these days. What's the matter?

W Well, actually, I've been playing mobile games until late at night.

M That's not good. If you do that, then you _____ _____ the next day.

W I know. I'm sorry, Mr. Taylor.

M Your performance in class _____ _____, and that can actually hurt your chances of going to university.

W Yes, you're right. I have to stop.

M If this happens again, I'll have no choice but _____.

W Yes, I understand.

M And you must stay after class to clean _____ _____ since you were sleeping during my lesson.

W Okay. I'm really sorry.

05

M Let's see. Your name is....

W Jennifer Winslot.

M So, why do you think _____, Jennifer?

W Well, for one thing, I've got all the qualifications you mentioned in the ad.

M Oh, so do you have experience in the recording industry?

W Yes. I was a producer in a small recording company for three years.

M _____ the company?

W Well, I worked on most of their major projects, but in the end they _____ _____. So I decided _____ _____.

M I see. We ensure that our employees are paid fairly.

W That's great.

M All right. I'll contact you in the next week.

06

M Good morning, can I help you?

W Yes, please. I'd like some information about the special trips to the Amazon rain forest.

M Well, can you tell me more about _____ _____ first? When will you be going, and how long do you plan to stay?

W Well, I'd like to leave next month, and I'll be staying there for a week.

M OK. _____ would you like?

W Oh, a good hotel. I don't like to be uncomfortable.

M Well, I think we have something here _____ _____. I guarantee, with this tour, you'll see plenty of wildlife and amazing landscapes.

W That sounds good. Thanks. I'll take that brochure and _____ tonight.

M After that, please contact us as soon as possible since these trips _____.

07

M Now, for the very latest on the hurricane which _____ the southeastern United States, we cross live to Nancy Hilton in Miami. OK, Nancy. What's happening right now?

W Well, we're expecting hurricane Charlie in the next 24 hours. The state weather agency is warning people _____.

M What are people doing?

W Well, lots of people are leaving. The roads are full and others are packing up and getting ready to leave.

M Nancy, _____ these extremely strong hurricanes?

W Too often it seems this year! It's the third one.

M Well, good luck. _____ about you.

W Thanks. We'll need it.

M And we'll hear more from Miami later this evening.

08

M Can I help you?

W Yes, _____ in the paper. I'd like to rent the advertised apartment on Square Garden Road.

M Oh, I'm sorry. That one's _____ _____.

W Umm. My current lease expires next month. I want to move into a new place by the end of next month.

M OK, _____? I mean, how much do you want to spend on rent?

W About $750 a month, if possible.

M Ah, there is another apartment at that price _____ _____.

W Is it on Square Garden Road?

M Yes. It has two bedrooms, a living room, and a kitchen. Would you like to see it?

W Yeah, I would.

09 고난도

M "Here, sit down for a cup of tea. I'm sorry about what happened."

W That was good. Just remember _____ _____ for her as you say the line.

M Should I say it in a more friendly tone, since I'm trying to comfort her?

W No. Your character has _____ _____.

M So... I care, but I'm not showing that I care?

W Exactly. It's hard, but you're doing a great job so far.

M Thanks. Should I _____ for the next few lines?

W Perfect. You're really good at _____ _____. We'll start shooting in 5 minutes.

10 고난도

M Hello, Peter Jones speaking.

W Hi, umm, this is Erica Lee.

M Are you the person who owns this cell phone?

W Yes, I am! I lost it last night, but _____ _____ until this morning.

M Well, a passenger I picked up at the airport found it on my back seat.

W Really? I thought I lost it somewhere in the airport.

M Where are you calling from? I'm driving down Burwood Street. _____ if you are somewhere around here.

W Actually, I'm in Sydney now, and _____ _____ in Melbourne until next week.

M I see. Just call again when you get back, and _____ to you.

W You are so kind! Thank you!

08 담화의 목적

안내 방송, 공지 사항, 광고, 연설 등 다양한 종류의 담화를 듣고, 목적이 무엇인지를 파악하는 유형이다.
1문항 출제된다.

해결 전략

1 담화를 듣기 전에 선택지를 미리 읽어보고 소재 및 내용을 예측해본다.

2 담화의 시작은 대개 인사말과 자기소개이다.

3 담화의 여러 정보를 종합하거나 중심 내용을 파악하여 목적을 판단해야 한다. 일부 내용만을 근거로 판단하면 오답을 선택할
수 있으므로 주의한다.

4 오답 선택지는 주로 담화에서 반복되는 핵심 단어와 연관되거나 그 단어로 연상되는 것들을 이용한다. 담화에 나온 단어를
이용하여 오답을 만들기도 한다.

   e.g. 아래에서 정답은 ⑤인데 나머지 오답들도 모두 '개'나 '훈련'이라는 단어와 연관되거나 이들 단어들로 연상되는 표현들을 포함한다.

   ① **조련사** 자격증 취득 방법을 설명하려고
   ② **동물 병원** 확장 이전을 공지하려고
   ③ 새로 출시된 **개 사료**를 소개하려고
   ④ **반려동물 입양 절차**를 안내하려고
   ⑤ **개 훈련** 센터를 홍보하려고

주요 표현

선택지에는 대개 아래와 같은 말이 포함되는데, 각각 담화에 자주 나오는 표현들을 잘 알아두자.

공지[안내]하려고

• I'd like to announce that ~. / This is an announcement that ~. / As it was previously announced, ~.

• I'm happy to inform you that ~.

• Please keep in mind this information about ~. / I'd like to let you know about ~.

권장하려고

• I'd like to encourage you to ~. / I'd recommend you to ~.

홍보하려고

• I'd like to tell you about ~. / I'd like to introduce ~. / I'd like to invite you to ~.

• 연락처 / 웹사이트 주소

광고하려고

• 제품의 장점을 나열하므로 긍정적인 표현이 많이 등장한다.

   e.g. 진공청소기 광고: really good, perfect, powerful and quiet

요청하려고

• We'd like to ask you to ~. / We kindly request that ~. / Please ~.

• We really appreciate your help. / Thank you for your cooperation.

당부하려고

• I'd like to remind you ~. / I urge you to ~.

독려하려고

• 명령문 / Please ~. / It's time to ~. / We encourage everyone to ~.

✳✳ 기출 맛보기

01 다음을 듣고, 남자가 하는 말의 목적으로 가장 적절한 것을 고르시오. 모의

① 시민 자율 방범 단원을 모집하려고
② 어린이 안전 교육 장소를 안내하려고
③ 초등학교 개교 기념행사를 홍보하려고
④ 학교 주변 제한 속도 준수를 독려하려고
⑤ 시청에서 열리는 공청회 일정을 공지하려고

M Hello, citizens of Portland. This is Jerry Wilson, your Mayor. As you know, Port Elementary School has opened, and it is so nice to hear the kids playing. **To ensure the safety of the students at the school, we've been communicating with the New Jersey State Police and requested that they enforce speed limits in the area around the school.** This is in response to the many complaints City Hall has received regarding excessive speeding, especially in front of the school. **Please obey the speed limits for the safety of the kids and your fellow citizens.** Thank you for your cooperation. Stay safe and healthy.

대화의 흐름

- **정보 1**: 뉴저지주 경찰에게 학교 주변 속도 제한을 시행할 것을 요청
- **정보 2**: 학교 앞 과속운전에 대한 민원에 따른 조치임
- **목적**: 제한 속도를 준수할 것을 독려

Words & Phrases citizen 시민　　mayor 시장　　ensure 확실하게 하다　　request 요청하다　　enforce 시행하다　　speed limit 속도 제한
in response to ~에 응하여　　complaint 항의, 불평　　regarding ~에 대하여　　excessive 과도한　　obey (법을) 준수하다　　cooperation 협조, 협동

＊ 녹음 내용을 듣고, 알맞은 답을 고르시오.   정답 및 해설 **p.48**

01 다음을 듣고, 남자가 하는 말의 목적으로 가장 적절한 것을 고르시오.

ⓐ 비상 대피 방법을 안내하려고   ⓑ 건물 이용 수칙을 설명하려고   ⓒ 화재 예방의 중요성을 강조하려고

02 다음을 듣고, 여자가 하는 말의 목적으로 가장 적절한 것을 고르시오.

ⓐ 여진의 위험성을 경고하려고   ⓑ 지진 대피 장소를 안내하려고   ⓒ 지진 피해자들을 위한 기부를 요청하려고

03 다음을 듣고, 남자가 하는 말의 목적으로 가장 적절한 것을 고르시오.

ⓐ 새 동물원 개장을 홍보하려고   ⓑ 야생 동물 보호를 호소하려고   ⓒ 동물원의 깨끗한 이용을 당부하려고

04 다음을 듣고, 여자가 하는 말의 목적으로 가장 적절한 것을 고르시오. 모의

ⓐ 건강 검진 일정을 공지하려고   ⓑ 독감 예방 접종을 권장하려고   ⓒ 독감 백신의 부작용을 경고하려고

05 다음을 듣고, 남자가 하는 말의 목적으로 가장 적절한 것을 고르시오.

ⓐ 차량 도난 사건을 알리려고   ⓑ 주차장 보수 공사를 공지하려고   ⓒ 목격자에게 신고할 것을 요청하려고

06 다음을 듣고, 여자가 하는 말의 목적으로 가장 적절한 것을 고르시오. 모의

ⓐ 지하철 연장 운행을 안내하려고   ⓑ 지하철 앱 출시를 홍보하려고   ⓒ 지하철 운행 지연에 대해 사과하려고

07 다음을 듣고, 남자가 하는 말의 목적으로 가장 적절한 것을 고르시오.

ⓐ 질의 방식을 안내하려고   ⓑ 세미나 주제를 소개하려고   ⓒ 세미나 참가 신청을 독려하려고

08 다음을 듣고, 여자가 하는 말의 목적으로 가장 적절한 것을 고르시오.

ⓐ 비행기 도착 시간을 안내하려고   ⓑ 안전벨트 착용을 요청하려고   ⓒ 비행기 출발 지연을 사과하려고

09 다음을 듣고, 남자가 하는 말의 목적으로 가장 적절한 것을 고르시오. 모의

ⓐ 교내 청소 일정을 공지하려고   ⓑ 하교 시 교실 창문을 닫을 것을 요청하려고
ⓒ 교내의 젖은 바닥을 걸을 때 조심하도록 당부하려고

10 다음을 듣고, 여자가 하는 말의 목적으로 가장 적절한 것을 고르시오. 모의

ⓐ 사물함을 반드시 잠그고 다녀야 함을 강조하려고   ⓑ 사물함 교체를 위해 사물함을 비울 것을 당부하려고
ⓒ 사물함 사용에 대한 학생 설문 조사 참여를 요청하려고

✱ STEP 1의 녹음 내용을 다시 들으면서 빈칸을 채우시오.

정답 및 해설 **p.48**

01

M Attention please. This is Brandon Harrison, the manager of this building. There has been a report of an emergency. _____ in the restaurant on the seventh floor. _____ _____ and leave the building immediately. Do not use the elevators. Use the stairways.

02

W Hello. I'm Angela, leader of World Peace Unity. _____ in Chile last week, hundreds of people have died and over 20,000 people are now homeless. Now _____ _____ who are in need. Please _____ for the victims.

03

M Hello, everyone. Thank you for visiting Rainbow Zoo. It's a great place _____ in the animal kingdom, and we know you will have a great time visiting them. Please help us _____. We urge you not to _____ around the cages, on the pavement, or on the lawn.

04 모의

W Hello, students. This is Alisa, your school nurse. Many students get sick with seasonal influenza, so I would _____. A flu shot can _____ _____. Please get a flu shot offered in doctors' offices or health departments by the end of this month. Thank you.

05

M Good afternoon. This is Adam Smith from the security office. This morning in the parking lot, one of our tenants found that her car _____ _____ overnight. We reported the damage to the police and an investigation is underway. If there's anyone _____ _____ last night, _____ _____ to the police.

06 모의

W Hello, passengers. I'm Jane Walker from the Greenville Subway System. This is an announcement that we _____ _____ since an international film festival _____ in our city next month. You can easily check _____ _____ using the Greenville Subway App. Thank you.

07

M Hello, everyone. I'm the host of this seminar, Eric Bolton. Before we _____, let me say that we welcome questions from the audience. But we kindly request that _____ _____ until all speakers have finished their presentations. Then, please step to the microphone in the center of the room so that everyone _____.

08

W Attention, please. This is captain Amy Johnson. Please notice that _____ _____. We expect to experience moderate turbulence for about 5 or 10 minutes. Please make sure that your seat belts _____ _____ and that your seats _____. Thank you.

09 모의

M Good morning, students. This is Mr. Lewis from the school administration office. _____ _____ the first floor hallway and the central stairway _____. Please be extra careful when _____ _____. You could get seriously hurt if you slip on the wet floor.

10 모의

W Hello, students. This is your vice principal, Rachel Brown. As the student lockers are getting old, _____ _____ over the weekend. We ask that you _____ _____ by this Friday. Make sure to take all the items from your lockers and _____ _____.

Listen & Answer 실전 문제

✻ 녹음 내용을 듣고, 알맞은 답을 고르시오.

정답 및 해설 p.50

01 다음을 듣고, 여자가 하는 말의 목적으로 가장 적절한 것을 고르시오.

① 독자들에게 감사를 표하려고
② 작가 초청 행사를 홍보하려고
③ 독서 모임 일정을 안내하려고
④ 이달의 베스트셀러를 발표하려고
⑤ 새로 나온 판타지 소설을 소개하려고

02 다음을 듣고, 남자가 하는 말의 목적으로 가장 적절한 것을 고르시오.

① 야외 활동 취미를 권장하려고
② 열기구 체험 활동을 홍보하려고
③ 깨끗한 캠프장 사용을 당부하려고
④ 휴양지의 다양한 즐길 거리를 소개하려고
⑤ 레저 스포츠에 필요한 장비를 안내하려고

03 다음을 듣고, 여자가 하는 말의 목적으로 가장 적절한 것을 고르시오.

① 시청 견학 일정을 안내하려고
② 과제 제출 방법을 설명하려고
③ 미술 대회 수상자를 발표하려고
④ 시의 새 마스코트를 소개하려고
⑤ 디자인 공모전 참가를 독려하려고

04 다음을 듣고, 남자가 하는 말의 목적으로 가장 적절한 것을 고르시오. 고난도

① 아파트 청소 직원을 모집하려고
② 쓰레기를 줄이는 방법을 설명하려고
③ 쓰레기 종량제 봉투 사용을 권장하려고
④ 쓰레기 분리수거 요일 변경을 공지하려고
⑤ 올바른 쓰레기 배출에 대한 협조를 요청하려고

05 다음을 듣고, 여자가 하는 말의 목적으로 가장 적절한 것을 고르시오.

① 축제 참가를 독려하려고
② 티셔츠 판매를 홍보하려고
③ 축제 개최 성공에 감사하려고
④ 축제 자원봉사 지원을 요청하려고
⑤ 자원봉사자에게 유의 사항을 안내하려고

06 다음을 듣고, 남자가 하는 말의 목적으로 가장 적절한 것을 고르시오.

① 사이버 범죄 예방법을 알려주려고
② 소셜 네트워크 서비스를 소개하려고
③ 인터넷 사기 유형에 대해 설명하려고
④ 개인 정보 유출시 대처법을 안내하려고
⑤ 웹사이트의 비밀번호 변경을 요청하려고

07 다음을 듣고, 여자가 하는 말의 목적으로 가장 적절한 것을 고르시오.

① 야영이 가능한 장소들을 소개하려고
② 화재 예방을 위한 협조를 당부하려고
③ 산불로 인한 환경 파괴에 대해 알리려고
④ 여름철 산행 시 주의 사항을 안내하려고
⑤ 야영장에서의 화기 사용 자제를 부탁하려고

08 다음을 듣고, 남자가 하는 말의 목적으로 가장 적절한 것을 고르시오.

① 신장개업한 병원을 홍보하려고
② 교통사고의 후유증의 사례를 소개하려고
③ 다이어트에 효과적인 걷기 운동을 추천하려고
④ 보행 중 스마트폰 사용의 위험성을 경고하려고
⑤ 스마트폰을 이용한 건강 관리 방법을 안내하려고

09 다음을 듣고, 여자가 하는 말의 목적으로 가장 적절한 것을 고르시오.

① 라디오 프로그램 개편을 공지하려고
② 새로운 사회자로서 인사를 하려고
③ 시상식에서 수상자를 발표하려고
④ 새로운 프로그램을 홍보하려고
⑤ 프로그램의 수상을 축하하려고

10 다음을 듣고, 남자가 하는 말의 목적으로 가장 적절한 것을 고르시오. 고난도

① 방문객 전용 주차장을 안내하려고
② 주차장의 안전 문제를 제기하려고
③ 주차장 확장 공사에 대해 알리려고
④ 주차장 이용 시 주의 사항을 당부하려고
⑤ 최근 접수된 주민 불편 사항을 보고하려고

Listen & Answer Dictation 실전 문제 받아쓰기

* STEP 3의 녹음 내용을 다시 들으면서 빈칸을 채우시오.

정답 및 해설 **p.50**

01

W Attention, please. This is the store manager of Blackwell Books. We _____ _____ that the best-selling author, Veronica Keys, will be coming to our bookstore this Saturday. Fans of the *Never-ending Wizardry* series _____ to meet Ms. Keys in person. She will do a short reading followed by a question-and-answer session, and then a book signing. As you may know, Ms. Keys has announced that her latest book will be the final novel in this series. So we are very lucky to have this event in our bookstore, and we'd like _____ _____.

02

M Hello, listeners! I'm Paul Larson from Sunny Tours. _____ of the perfect vacation? With over 300 sunny days a year and many outdoor activities, Colorado Springs is a popular camping and family destination. _____ magnificent rock formations and shady mountain forests are perfect for hiking, biking, and horseback riding. Or you _____ _____: a hot air balloon ride up into the big Colorado sky, or a historic train ride through Cripple Creek, or a visit to the Colorado Springs Arts Center. There is something for everyone. Come see for yourself!

03

W Good morning, students. This is your art teacher, Ms. Woods. This is an announcement about a wonderful opportunity _____.
Our school is participating in a citywide design contest sponsored by the city government. _____ _____ a new town mascot in a fresh style. I encourage all students to participate. If you are interested, _____ _____ to your homeroom teacher by the end of the month. The winner will get gift certificates. I hope that all of you _____ _____. Good luck!

04 고난도

M May I have your attention, please? This message concerns all residents of this apartment complex. Recently, there has been _____ around the waste disposal area. Many people are using incorrect garbage bags, misplacing their garbage, and generally _____ _____. This is a huge inconvenience for the staff and other residents. Please be careful with your waste. Take the time _____ _____. We thank those of you who already do this, and remind those who are not careful that there are fines _____ _____. Thank you.

05

W Hello! Thank you for applying to help us! You are essential to the Churchill Book Festival's success this year. _____ author assistants, festival guides, and sales assistants in the merchandise area. Please arrive at least 20 minutes _____. This will give you enough time to sign in and get ready. You need to be prepared to stand or walk since _____. Due to this, comfortable shoes are a must. Also, _____ a volunteer's T-shirt. We'll give you the T-shirts after the orientation. Thanks again and please be polite and helpful to all participants.

06

M Hello, listeners. This is Michael Andrews from the Cyber Crime Investigation Unit. Internet usage continues to increase, and _____ _____. However, if you are a little more careful in your daily Internet use, you can _____. Here are a few simple steps that you can take to protect yourself. First, don't give more information than is absolutely necessary. Keep your personal details to a minimum, even on social networking sites. Second, _____ _____. Don't use the same password repeatedly, and don't pick something simple like your birthday. Finally, _____ if an advertisement sounds too good to be true, it probably is (too good to be true).

07

W Good afternoon, campers. This announcement is from the management office of Hancock Campground. Summer is here once again. _____ and enjoy nature. But, just like every other year, the summer sun has dried out the forests and killed the grass. This means that even the smallest spark can start a huge forest fire. So please _____ and avoid building them near tents, vehicles, or trees. Make sure that all fires are completely out before leaving your campsite. And report anyone who violates these rules. If we all work together, we may be able to _____ this year. We appreciate your cooperation.

08

M Hello, listeners. This is Dr. Michael Davis from the Fogville Health Center. I've been working as a doctor in this town for many years now, and recently I've started to see _____ _____. Each year, more and more people are getting hurt when using a smartphone while walking. Several people have been hit by cars, and one unlucky woman even fell into an open manhole. It may sound highly unlikely to happen, but the fact is that _____ _____ is really dangerous. It doesn't matter who you're texting. You should stop for a moment _____. Please pay attention to traffic and other people _____. I hope you keep this in mind and stay safe.

09

W Good evening, everyone! I'm Mindy Kang, and I just want to start by saying _____ _____ to have this opportunity. There is _____ here, and so many great hosts have sat in this chair before me. _____ working alongside the Emmy Award winning Mark Johnson, who I spent so much time watching as a child. To be honest, I'm a bit nervous, but I know that we are going to have a lot of fun and cover some amazing stories _____ _____. Please support us and enjoy our show.

10 고난도

M Attention please. I'm Paul Larson, your building manager. We are sorry to interrupt you, but there _____ about the use of the parking lot. So, we have several requests. First, we would like to remind everyone that the use of the parking lot _____ _____. Visitors must park in the nearby lot. Second, please be considerate. _____ or block another car, even if it is only for a few minutes. Finally, we _____ the parking lot's speed limit. Many children live here, and this is a huge safety issue. Thank you for your cooperation.

세트형 문항

담화를 듣고 두 개의 문제에 답하는 유형이다. 다른 유형과 달리, 유일하게 두 번 반복해서 들려준다.

해결 전략

1 첫 번째 문제는 대부분 '주제'를 묻는 유형이며, 모의고사에서는 간혹 '목적'을 묻기도 한다.

두 번째 문제는 '언급되지 않은 것'을 묻는 세부 내용 파악 문제이다.

2 '주제'는 담화를 시작하면서 인사말 등의 뒤에 언급되므로 초반부를 집중하여 듣는 것이 좋다. 주제를 이끄는 어구는 다음과 같다.

e.g. Today, we'll learn ~. / So, we're talking about ~.

정답 선택지는 종종 담화에 나온 어구와는 다른 말로 바꿔 표현된다. 이와 반대로 오답 선택지는 담화에 반복되어 나온 핵심 어구를 그대로 포함하여 선택을 유도하는 경우가 많으므로 주의해야 한다.

3 '언급되지 않은 것'은 선택지 순서대로 담화에 언급되므로, 들으면서 차례대로 언급 여부를 판단하면 된다.

서수(*e.g.* first, second, third 등) 또는 부사(*e.g.* also, next, finally 등)를 사용하여 내용이 나열되는 경우가 많다.

4 세트형 문항은 두 번 들려주므로, 이를 전략적으로 잘 활용하는 것이 중요하다.

① 처음 들려줄 때 첫 번째 문제를 해결하고 다시 들려줄 때 두 번째 문제를 해결하는 방식

② 처음 들려줄 때 두 문제를 다 해결하고 다시 들으면서 이를 검증하는 방식

어느 한 가지 방식이 다른 것에 비해 절대적으로 낫다고 할 수 없으며, 어떤 방식이 자신에게 더 수월하고 정답률이 높은지를 판단해야 한다. 문제를 접하면서 자신에게 효과적인 방식을 파악한 뒤, 실전 문제를 많이 풀며 연습하도록 한다.

✳✳ 기출 맛보기

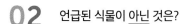

[01-02] 다음을 듣고, 물음에 답하시오. 모의

01 여자가 하는 말의 주제로 가장 적절한 것은?

① ways to prevent plant diseases
② factors that affect plant growth
③ benefits of growing plants at home
④ plants that can grow in shaded areas
⑤ materials that help plants grow in shade

02 언급된 식물이 <u>아닌</u> 것은?

① lemon balm   ② ivy   ③ mint
④ camellia   ⑤ lavender

W   Hello, students. Previously, we discussed why gardening is a great hobby. But not everyone has a sunny front yard. **So, today we'll learn about plants that grow even in shade. First, lemon balm survives in full shade.** So if your place is sunless, it's the plant you should choose. **Next, ivy is the ultimate shade-loving plant.** Its ability to grow in shade makes it survive under trees where most plants can't. **Also, there's mint.** It lives well under low-light conditions, so you can grow it in a small pot indoors. **Lastly, camellia grows better in partial shade.** Especially when it's a young plant, it needs protection from the sun. Many plants like these can live even in the shade. Isn't it fascinating? Now, let's watch a video clip about how to grow these plants.

대화의 흐름

· 주제:
그늘에서도 자라는 식물들(➡01-④)

· 예시:
1. 레몬밤(➡02-①)
2. 담쟁이덩굴(➡02-②)
3. 민트(➡02-③)
4. 동백나무(➡02-④)

Words & Phrases   **previously** 이전에   **gardening** 원예   **front yard** 앞마당   **shade** 그늘   **survive** 살아남다   **ultimate** 최고의   **pot** 화분   **indoors** 실내에서   **partial** 부분적인   **protection** 보호   **fascinating** 대단히 흥미로운

Listen & Choose 유형핵심 익히기

* 녹음 내용을 듣고, 알맞은 답을 고르시오.

[01-02] 다음을 듣고, 물음에 답하시오. 모의

01 여자가 하는 말의 주제로 가장 적절한 것은?

ⓐ benefits of using LEDs
ⓑ how the LED was invented
ⓒ ways to advance LED technology

02 언급된 물건이 <u>아닌</u> 것은?

ⓐ lamps   ⓑ televisions   ⓒ a computer keyboard

[03~04] 다음을 듣고, 물음에 답하시오. 모의

03 남자가 하는 말의 주제로 가장 적절한 것은?

ⓐ various aerobic workouts for losing weight
ⓑ effective exercises for reducing back pain
ⓒ activities to make your body flexible

04 언급된 운동이 <u>아닌</u> 것은?

ⓐ yoga   ⓑ walking   ⓒ swimming

[05-06] 다음을 듣고, 물음에 답하시오.

05 여자가 하는 말의 주제로 가장 적절한 것은?

ⓐ facts about negative-calorie foods
ⓑ effects of diet foods on your body
ⓒ differences between various negative-calorie foods

06 언급된 음식이 <u>아닌</u> 것은?

ⓐ a cucumber   ⓑ celery   ⓒ an apple

정답 및 해설 **p.54**

[07-08] 다음을 듣고, 물음에 답하시오.

07 남자가 하는 말의 주제로 가장 적절한 것은?

ⓐ how plants live and grow in Antarctica
ⓑ beneficial seeds that will help Antarctica
ⓒ why the Antarctic ecosystem is under threat

08 언급된 씨앗의 이동 수단이 <u>아닌</u> 것은?

ⓐ wind   ⓑ insects   ⓒ people

[09-10] 다음을 듣고, 물음에 답하시오.

09 여자가 하는 말의 주제로 가장 적절한 것은?

ⓐ ways to respect animal welfare
ⓑ endangered animals in the world
ⓒ the necessity of establishing animal shelters

10 언급된 동물의 고통이 <u>아닌</u> 것은?

ⓐ fear   ⓑ hunger   ⓒ discomfort

＊ STEP 1의 녹음 내용을 다시 들으면서 빈칸을 채우시오.

01-02 모의

W Hello, class! Last time we learned about LED technology. I hope all of you have a clear idea of what an LED is now. Today, I'll talk about how LEDs _____. First, one of the advantages of LEDs is the long lifespan. LED bulbs are used in lamps and last for over 17 years before you need to change them. Also, thanks to their small size, LEDs can be used in _____. Any light you see on a computer keyboard is an LED light, and they can be used to show functions or _____ _____ in low-light environments. Now, let's think about other products that use LEDs.

03-04 모의

M Good morning, listeners. This is Dr. Cooper of Daily Health Line Radio. These days, you can see many people around you _____ _____. Any incorrect positioning of your body or lifting of heavy objects may cause it. So, today, I'll _____ _____ to help reduce your own back pain. As you probably know, yoga is a helpful way to stretch safely and strengthen your back. Doing the appropriate poses for even a few minutes a day _____ and give your back some relief. Also, walking is the easiest exercise to keep your spine in a natural position to avoid back pain. When you walk, your back muscles are activated and stretched. I hope this will be helpful information for you and _____.

05-06

W Today I'd like to talk about a dieting myth. Some people say certain foods _____ _____ than they provide. These foods are called "negative-calorie foods." In theory, the more of them that we eat, the more weight _____. These "negative-calorie foods" are mainly fruits and vegetables. Among them, celery is perhaps the most famous for burning lots of calories, but in fact, only about 10% of its calories _____ _____. Just like with other foods, the more celery that we eat, the more weight we will gain. Another example is an apple. It can promote fullness because it's high in water and fiber. But even with these qualities, _____ _____ by eating one because only about 5% of its calories are burned in the process of digestion. In reality, there are no shortcuts for dieting, and everything _____ _____.

07-08

M Some of you may already know that there is a small amount of plant life in Antarctica. Only 1% of Antarctica is free from ice, but plants do grow there. Unfortunately, there is growing concern that the Antarctic ecosystem _____ _____. This is mostly due to _____ _____, which come to Antarctica in various ways. First, _____ _____, carried by wind, water, or birds. Next, more and more people are visiting Antarctica for tourism and to do scientific research, and some seeds can stick to their socks or backpacks. It turns out that each person that visits Antarctica accidentally _____ _____ with them. Efforts should be made to remove non-native seeds before they dominate the native ecosystem of Antarctica. Now, let's watch a video that explains this in detail.

09-10

W Before we start, I want to thank everyone for attending this class on the well-being of animals. Like people, animals have the right to be happy and healthy. Today, I'd like to talk about _____ _____. This is mainly about _____ _____. First of all, there is the issue of hunger and thirst. It is crucial that animals always have access to fresh water and food that keeps them healthy. Also, freedom from discomfort is important. We should provide animals with _____ _____. This includes a comfortable resting area that has suitable bedding, low noise levels, and natural light. Now I'd like you to come up with other examples of animal rights.

Listen & Answer 실전 문제

✳ 녹음 내용을 듣고, 알맞은 답을 고르시오.

[01-02] 다음을 듣고, 물음에 답하시오.

01 남자가 하는 말의 주제로 가장 적절한 것은?

① importance of making a list
② positive effects of healthy snacks
③ effective activities for losing weight
④ how to prevent unnecessary eating
⑤ the harmful effect of TV on eating habits

02 언급된 활동이 <u>아닌</u> 것은?

① knitting   ② writing letters   ③ talking to a friend
④ washing a car   ⑤ walking a dog

[03-04] 다음을 듣고, 물음에 답하시오.

03 여자가 하는 말의 주제로 가장 적절한 것은?

① reasons why plants need sunlight
② how to water plants for healthy growth
③ various factors that pose a threat to plants
④ endangered species in a desert environment
⑤ different types of plants that survive in the desert

04 언급된 식물이 <u>아닌</u> 것은?

① cactuses   ② aloes   ③ acacias
④ mulberries   ⑤ sagebrushes

[05-06] 다음을 듣고, 물음에 답하시오.

05 남자가 하는 말의 주제로 가장 적절한 것은?

① what we can learn from animal language
② how language evolved in humans and animals
③ difficulties in understanding the grammar of animal language
④ the differences between human and animal language
⑤ ways human language continues to develop

06 언급된 동물이 <u>아닌</u> 것은?

① monkeys　　　　　② wolves　　　　　③ skunks
④ peacocks　　　　　⑤ cats

[07-08] 다음을 듣고, 물음에 답하시오.

07 여자가 하는 말의 주제로 가장 적절한 것은?

① the advantages of regular exercise
② the effects of music on human minds
③ how to recover from physical burnout
④ the use of music for effective exercise
⑤ selecting the right exercise for an individual

08 언급된 음악이 <u>아닌</u> 것은?

① hip hop　　　　　② rock music　　　　　③ classical music
④ jazz　　　　　⑤ electronic dance music

[09-10] 다음을 듣고, 물음에 답하시오. 고난도

09 남자가 하는 말의 주제로 가장 적절한 것은?

① health benefits of outdoor play for children
② effective physical activities for treating obesity
③ various types of outdoor recreation for children
④ the necessity of expanding outdoor play spaces
⑤ considerations when choosing the right outdoor location

10 언급된 야외 활동이 <u>아닌</u> 것은?

① hiking　　　　　② rafting　　　　　③ jogging
④ canoeing　　　　　⑤ biking

＊ STEP 3의 녹음 내용을 다시 들으면서 빈칸을 채우시오.

01-02

M What is hunger? Hunger is the natural feeling you experience about four or five hours after a meal. But even when you're not hungry, many things can trick you into thinking you are — the aroma of food, the sight of a favorite dish, or a commercial on television. _____ _____ is the first step in controlling your eating. To start with, keeping a food diary can help you notice when you feel hungry. If you find that sitting in front of the television makes you hungry, _____. Take up knitting or write letters when you are watching television. On the other hand, if _____ _____, make a list of alternate activities to do instead, such as talking to a friend or washing a car. The key is to learn what makes you hungry and then to set up an action plan _____. Any healthy eating plan must include ways to deal with hunger in a sensible manner. Now, let's talk about how to plan a healthy diet.

03-04

W Hello, students. Last class, we learned about different kinds of animals that live in the desert. Today, we'll talk about desert plants _____ _____ to their environment. First, cactuses have sharp spines _____, keeping them cool. Next, some plants are equipped with fleshy leaves that contain much of their water supply. For example, aloes store large volumes of water with thick leaves _____

_____ a waterproof coating. Also, plants such as acacias _____ _____ to lose less water. They shed their leaves during the hot season and grow them back as soon as the weather improves. Finally, there are plants with light-colored leaves which _____ _____ by reflecting sunlight. A good example of this is sagebrushes which have very light green to almost white leaves. Now, we'll look at some photos of these incredible plants.

05-06

M Good afternoon, class! What do you think is the greatest achievement of human evolution? Most of you would say it is language. Of course, all animal species have evolved systems of communication. Some monkeys, for example, use alarm calls _____ _____. Other natural forms of animal communication include scents for wolves marking their areas, visual signals like male peacocks _____ mates, and touch like cats rubbing heads with other cats to greet. Yet, animal communication doesn't have the one thing _____ _____. That thing is grammar, the fixed patterns and rules of word order that enable speakers of the same language _____. Furthermore, human language is able to change easily. And its speed is incredible. During normal speech, humans _____ 25 different sounds per second. And listeners can understand all of those signals immediately. Now, let's search the Internet for information on how human language evolved.

07-08

W Hello, everyone. Today, I want to talk about how music affects people doing exercise. Music and exercise go hand in hand, just like chocolate and peanut butter. Music does more than _____ _____ of a workout. Research conducted at Brunel University has confirmed that listening to music while you exercise _____. In the experiment, thirty participants exercised on a treadmill while listening to a selection of music. They _____ with the music. The findings show that when carefully selected, music can enhance endurance by 15% and improve the 'feeling states' of exercisers. The most interesting point is that exercise is much more beneficial when working out with music _____. For instance, the right tempo can help your body move more efficiently. If you are just walking, the tempo of hip hop can _____ _____. Likewise, rock music may be good for running. The relaxing tempo of classical music and jazz can also help increase endurance levels during exercise. Music leads to less physical burnout, more time spent exercising, and more calories burned.

09-10 고난도

M Hello, listeners. This is Mike Wilson and I'm here to talk about the health of your children. Children _____ _____ are active and have lots of fun. Playing outside is a great idea, and it has a lot to offer. A recent study revealed that children who participate in outdoor play for several hours daily had significantly _____, like sore eyes, than those who spent shorter periods of time outdoors. Outdoor recreation such as hiking or rafting offers various physical benefits, like muscular and aerobic fitness. Health experts believe that children who explore and play outside are more likely to _____ _____. In addition, outdoor play gives children a great opportunity to exercise their bodies in an enjoyable way. _____ _____ among the young generation, outdoor play, like jogging, biking, or swimming, offers a good remedy for this issue. Children who take part in outdoor play also laugh a lot, _____. Now, how about taking your children outside for some fun in the sun?

첫단추
듣기 모의고사

유형편

CHAPTER

4

적용력
(말하기 영역)

말하기 영역이라고 하지만 실제 말하는 것이 아니라 선택지를 읽고 그중에서 가장 적절한 응답을 고르는 것이므로, <듣기+독해>라 할 수 있다. 대화나 담화의 전체적인 흐름을 파악하여 어떤 말을 해야 할지 추론해야하고 선택지들의 길이도 다소 긴 경우가 많아, 비교적 정답률이 낮은 편이므로 충분한 양의 연습이 필요하다.

짧은 대화에 이어질 응답

A-B-A로 이어진 짧은 대화를 듣고 마지막 A의 말에 대한 B의 응답으로 가장 적절한 것을 고르는 유형이다.
마지막 A의 말이 의문문인 것과 평서문인 것 각각 1문항씩 출제된다.

해결 전략

❶ 마지막 A의 말이 의문문

1 when과 where의 발음을 혼동하지 않도록 주의한다.
  Q. **Where** is the new exhibition being shown? 새 전시회가 어디서 열리죠?
    ① From Tuesday through Sunday. 화요일부터 일요일까지요.
    ② **It's at the National Art Museum.** 국립 미술관에서요.

2 의문사 의문문이더라도 그에 대한 구체적 정보가 나와야만 정답인 것은 아니다.
  Q. **What** is the overseas shipping rate? 해외 운송 요금이 어떻게 되죠? → '가격'을 묻는 질문이지만, ②, ③도 가능한 응답
    ① **A dollar seventy per kilo.** 1킬로당 1달러 70센트예요.
    ② **It depends on the distance.** 운송 거리에 따라 달라요.
    ③ **Sorry, I don't know.** 죄송하지만, 모르겠어요.

3 부정의문문, 부가의문문의 응답은 어렵게 생각하지 말고 그냥 긍정의문문이라 생각하면 쉽다.
  Q. **Isn't** it chilly in here? 여기 춥지 않나요? → Is it chilly in here? 여기 춥죠?
    ① **Yes, I'll close all the windows.** 네, 제가 창문을 다 닫을게요.
    ② **Not really, I like it this way.** 아뇨, 전 이대로가 좋아요.

4 <Do you know+의문사>는 yes나 no로 응답을 시작할 수도 있다는 점 외에는 의문사 의문문과 유사하다.
  Q. *Do you know* **why** she left the company? 그녀가 왜 퇴사했는지 아시나요?
    – **She took a job in Seoul.** 서울에 직장을 구했거든요.

5 <Do[Would] you mind if I ~? / Do[Would] you mind v-ing?> 질문에 대답하는 방법은 아래와 같다.
  • 긍정 대답: Of course not. / Not at all. / No, I don't mind. / No, go ahead. / No problem.
      (괜찮다는 대답, 꺼리지 않는다는 뜻)
  • 부정 대답: Yes, I'm Sorry. / Yes, I do. / I mind. (괜찮지 않다는 대답, 꺼린다는 뜻)

❷ 마지막 A의 말이 평서문

1 대화의 흐름을 잘 파악하면서 마지막 A의 말을 놓치지 않아야 한다.

2 오답은 주로 대화에 등장한 단어들을 그대로 이용하여 만들어지므로, 단지 대화에서 들렸던 단어가 포함되었다고 해서 정답으로 잘못 판단하지 않도록 주의해야 한다. 대화에 나온 단어와 연관된 단어를 이용하여 오답이 만들어지기도 한다.
  e.g. **M** Hello, this is Bob's Camera Shop.
    W Hi, this is Clara Patterson. I'm calling to see if I can pick up my camera today.
    M Let me check. Yes. I've finished repairing your camera. It's ready to go.
    W _____
    ① Excellent. I like the camera you bought for me. (대화에 나온 camera를 이용한 오답)
    ② Good. I'll stop by and get it on my way home. (정답)
    ③ Never mind. I'll drop off the camera tomorrow. (대화에 나온 camera를 이용한 오답)
    ④ I see. Thanks for taking those pictures of me. (camera와 연관된 pictures를 이용한 오답)
    ⑤ No way. That's too expensive for the repair. (대화에 나온 repair를 이용한 오답)

✳✳ **기출 맛보기**

01

대화를 듣고, 여자의 마지막 말에 대한 남자의 응답으로 가장 적절한 것을 고르시오. 모의

① Really? I should have seen her.
② No way. I'm going to miss you a lot.
③ No. I didn't go to the bookstore that day.
④ I'm sorry. I'm not interested in her writing.
⑤ Yes. I can't believe I'm going to see her in person.

W Did you hear that **Golden Bookstore will hold a book signing event for Lora Johnson**?	**대화의 흐름** 남자가 좋아하는 작가의 책 사인회가 서점에서 열릴 예정
M Oh, she is one of my favorite writers. I've read all of her novels. When is it?	
W This Sunday afternoon. **Do you want to come with me?**	**여자의 마지막 말**: 남자에게 사인회에 같이 갈지 질문
M _____	

02

대화를 듣고, 남자의 마지막 말에 대한 여자의 응답으로 가장 적절한 것을 고르시오. 모의

① Again? You've lost your bag twice.
② You're right. I'll take a warm jacket.
③ Why? I know you prefer cold weather.
④ What? I finished packing a present for you.
⑤ Sorry. But you can't join the trip at this point.

M **Have you finished packing your bags for your trip to Mount Jiri?**	**대화의 흐름** 지리산 여행을 위한 짐을 다 쌌는지 확인 중
W I think so. Look! What else do I need?	
M **You'd better prepare for the cold weather at night.**	**남자의 마지막 말**: 밤의 추위를 대비하는 것이 좋겠다고 함
W _____	

Words & Phrases 01 **hold** (행사 등을) 열다[개최하다]   **book signing event** 책 사인회   **02** **pack** (짐을) 싸다   **had better+동사원형** ~하는 것이 좋을 것이다, ~해야 한다   **prepare for** ~을 대비하다

Listen & Choose 유형핵심 익히기

* 녹음 내용을 듣고, 알맞은 답을 고르시오.

01 대화를 듣고, 여자의 마지막 말에 대한 남자의 응답으로 가장 적절한 것을 고르시오.

ⓐ No, I'm still scared of flying.
ⓑ Yes, it will be warm in Brazil.
ⓒ I guess, but it doesn't bother me.

02 대화를 듣고, 남자의 마지막 말에 대한 여자의 응답으로 가장 적절한 것을 고르시오.

ⓐ Great. Then, I'll make some sandwiches.
ⓑ I had a perfect picnic yesterday.
ⓒ The park is near here.

03 대화를 듣고, 여자의 마지막 말에 대한 남자의 응답으로 가장 적절한 것을 고르시오.

ⓐ The library is closed today.
ⓑ Of course not. Let's go together.
ⓒ Let's join the book club tomorrow.

04 대화를 듣고, 남자의 마지막 말에 대한 여자의 응답으로 가장 적절한 것을 고르시오. 모의

ⓐ Sure. I'll order a shirt for you.
ⓑ Oh, I should get it exchanged.
ⓒ Well, it's too expensive for me.

05 대화를 듣고, 여자의 마지막 말에 대한 남자의 응답으로 가장 적절한 것을 고르시오.

ⓐ She has an upset stomach.
ⓑ You should go to the doctor.
ⓒ She got better after resting at home.

06 대화를 듣고, 남자의 마지막 말에 대한 여자의 응답으로 가장 적절한 것을 고르시오. 모의

ⓐ Of course. You can borrow my tent.
ⓑ Okay. I'll bring you the speakers now.
ⓒ No problem. Your car has been repaired.

07 대화를 듣고, 여자의 마지막 말에 대한 남자의 응답으로 가장 적절한 것을 고르시오. 모의

ⓐ It takes an hour by bus.
ⓑ You should've left home earlier.
ⓒ The company moved last month.

08 대화를 듣고, 남자의 마지막 말에 대한 여자의 응답으로 가장 적절한 것을 고르시오. 모의

ⓐ Great. I'll book for five people at six.
ⓑ Okay. I'll set a place and time for the meeting.
ⓒ Sorry to hear that. I'll cancel the reservation now.

09 대화를 듣고, 여자의 마지막 말에 대한 남자의 응답으로 가장 적절한 것을 고르시오.

ⓐ You should read more books.
ⓑ I threw them out this morning.
ⓒ I heard the city library collects them.

10 대화를 듣고, 남자의 마지막 말에 대한 여자의 응답으로 가장 적절한 것을 고르시오. 모의

ⓐ Actually, I couldn't find your essay.
ⓑ Don't worry. I can make a copy for you.
ⓒ Too bad. I can't remember the deadline.

01

W Nick, _____ for Christmas?

M I'm going to Brazil to stay with my grandma.

W Wow, isn't _____?

02

M Honey, it's great weather outside today.

W You can say that again! How about _____ to the Richmond Park?

M Good idea. _____ and drinks.

03

W Liam, do you want _____ with me tomorrow?

M Actually, Jessica and I are going there right now.

W Then _____?

04 모의

M Blair, how did _____?

W It was good, Dad. I got this shirt _____.

M It looks nice. Wait! _____ a button.

05

W Where is Shelly? _____ today.

M She's really sick, so she's resting at home.

W Do you know _____?

06 모의

M Honey, _____ we used when we went camping?

W Oh, I just left them in my car.

M Really? I _____ tomorrow.

07 모의

W I heard your company moved to a new office. How is it?

M It's all good except one thing. _____ my house.

W Oh, really? _____ to get there?

08 모의

M Honey, _____ this evening.

W Why not? _____ at the restaurant.

M I'm sorry. I have an important business meeting at that time.

09

W I think I'm going to _____. I don't read them any more.

M Really? Wait! How about _____?

W Oh, that's a great idea. Where should I take them?

10 모의

M Mrs. Smith, can you give me advice _____ _____?

W Sure. First, _____ the handout I gave you last class. It has helpful examples.

M Really? Oh, I'm sorry. _____.

Listen & Answer 실전 문제

✽ 녹음 내용을 듣고, 알맞은 답을 고르시오.

정답 및 해설 p.61

01 대화를 듣고, 여자의 마지막 말에 대한 남자의 응답으로 가장 적절한 것을 고르시오.

① It's hung on my chair.
② I'll meet you after class.
③ I left there at three o'clock.
④ It's the third room on the left.
⑤ My sweater is brown and red.

02 대화를 듣고, 남자의 마지막 말에 대한 여자의 응답으로 가장 적절한 것을 고르시오.

① Your notebook was very helpful.
② I'll let you know as soon as I finish it.
③ Sorry, I'll make sure to bring it tomorrow.
④ There is a history exam tomorrow.
⑤ I'll help you find your notebook.

03 대화를 듣고, 여자의 마지막 말에 대한 남자의 응답으로 가장 적절한 것을 고르시오.

① No worries, it's not that expensive.
② I think there's still plenty of time.
③ All of our friends will be there.
④ Last year's camp was great.
⑤ I'll show you how to apply.

04 대화를 듣고, 남자의 마지막 말에 대한 여자의 응답으로 가장 적절한 것을 고르시오.

① That would be great.
② It's really far from here.
③ Let's wait for the next bus.
④ The concert is too late at night.
⑤ Thanks for driving me such a long way.

05 대화를 듣고, 여자의 마지막 말에 대한 남자의 응답으로 가장 적절한 것을 고르시오.

① The bus has already left.
② I prefer to take a bus from here.
③ Yes, I've been here since six o'clock.
④ No, the bus stop is really close.
⑤ It leaves in twenty minutes.

06 대화를 듣고, 남자의 마지막 말에 대한 여자의 응답으로 가장 적절한 것을 고르시오.

① I enjoyed that action movie.
② Let's go to the downtown theater.
③ A comedy sounds like more fun to me.
④ I booked the tickets online yesterday.
⑤ I don't think I have time for a movie.

07 대화를 듣고, 여자의 마지막 말에 대한 남자의 응답으로 가장 적절한 것을 고르시오. 고난도

① I left my report at home.
② I'll turn it in before it is due.
③ I've been working on it all week.
④ The due date is next Wednesday.
⑤ It took me a while to pick a topic.

08 대화를 듣고, 남자의 마지막 말에 대한 여자의 응답으로 가장 적절한 것을 고르시오.

① I'd like to have some local food.
② We're having a party on Saturday.
③ Certainly. I'll be right back with them.
④ All right. Your reservation has been made.
⑤ I think you'll have to wait for about 20 minutes.

09 대화를 듣고, 여자의 마지막 말에 대한 남자의 응답으로 가장 적절한 것을 고르시오. 고난도

① This is my favorite song.
② He certainly deserves to.
③ The singer you like already lost.
④ There are many audition participants.
⑤ Listening to this song makes me happy.

10 대화를 듣고, 남자의 마지막 말에 대한 여자의 응답으로 가장 적절한 것을 고르시오.

① We need to finish this report.
② I can introduce you to my friends.
③ I couldn't complete my report alone.
④ You have to be a responsible partner.
⑤ Good. I should go and ask him right away.

✳ STEP 3의 녹음 내용을 다시 들으면서 빈칸을 채우시오.

정답 및 해설 **p.61**

01

W Jake, Mr. Harrison _____ to the classroom. Will you wait here for me?

M Sure. Actually, I left my sweater there. _____ _____ for me?

W No problem. Where did you leave it?

02

M Tonya, _____ my history notebook?

W Yeah, but _____.

M That's okay, but I need it for the history class tomorrow.

03

W I don't know _____ this summer vacation. Do you have any plans?

M Sure. I'm going to soccer camp. Why don't you sign up, too?

W That's an idea. But _____ _____, hasn't it?

04

M Are you going to the concert tonight?

W Of course, but I'm not sure _____.

M Steve and I are planning to share a taxi. _____ _____ if you like.

05

W Sam, _____ yet? It's so late.

M _____ to catch the last bus. It comes at 11:30.

W Really? It's 11:20 now! Don't you have to hurry?

06

M _____ a movie tonight?

W Sounds good. What movies are playing now?

M A comedy and an action movie _____ _____.

07 고난도

W Eden, your report _____. Do you have it?

M I'm sorry, Ms. Taylor, but I'm not finished yet. Can I have more time?

W Oh, _____?

08

M I don't have a reservation. _____ _____ now?

W How many are there _____?

M There are four of us.

09 고난도

W Hey, what are you watching?

M It's a TV audition show. _____ _____ is singing right now.

W Wow, he's really good. Do you think _____ _____?

10

M Cindy, are you going to do your report with Danny?

W No, I worked with him last time. I _____ _____.

M I think Kevin _____, too.

11 긴 대화에 이어질 응답

긴 대화를 듣고, 남자 혹은 여자의 마지막 말에 이어질 상대방의 응답을 고르는 유형이다. 2문항씩 출제되며 대개 둘 중 하나는 배점이 3점이다. 정답률이 가장 낮은 유형 중 하나이다.

해결 전략

1 대화의 주제와 장소, 화자들의 관계와 같은 종합적 이해를 바탕으로 문제를 해결해야 하는 경우가 대부분이다. 마지막 말은 평서문인 경우가 많으며, 대화의 흐름을 통해 그 마지막 말의 의미나 의도를 잘 파악해야 한다.

2 선택지의 길이가 긴 편이므로 주어진 시간 내에 선택지 내용을 빠르고 정확하게 파악하는 능력이 요구된다.

3 대화의 주제와 관련은 있지만 대화에서 언급된 내용과는 다르거나, 마지막 말에 이어질 상대방의 응답이 아니라 마지막 말을 한 화자가 할 수 있는 말을 내용으로 하는 오답 선택지에 주의한다.

주요 표현

상황별로 대화에 자주 등장하는 표현들을 잘 익혀두자.

칭찬	(Very) Good (for you)! / (You did a) Good[Nice] job. / Well done! / Terrific! / Excellent! / That's neat. / Way to go. 잘했어.
격려	Don't worry. / No worries. / Never mind. / Cheer up. / I'm sure you will do better next time. / Don't take it so hard. 너무 상심하지 마. / Look on the bright side. 긍정적으로 생각해. / There's no rush. 서두를 것 없어. / You can do it. / I believe in you.
기원	Good luck! / Keep it up! / All the best! / I wish you well. / I'll keep my fingers crossed (for you)! 행운을 빌게! / I hope everything goes well.
수정	That's not quite right. 그렇지만은 않아. / You've made a mistake. / I'm afraid you are wrong. / Sorry, you're mistaken. 미안하지만, 네가 잘못 생각하고 있어.
동의	Me, too. (긍정에 동의) / Me neither. (부정에 동의) / Same here. / You said it. 그렇긴 해. / You can say that again. 정말 그래. / I couldn't agree more[less]. / I completely agree with what you say. 전적으로 동의해. / That's just what I was thinking. / That's a good idea. / I'm with you all the way. 난 언제나 네 편이야. / That's right[true]. / In my opinion, you are right[correct]. / That's my opinion, too.
반대	I don't think so. / I can't agree with you. / I'm afraid I can't accept that. / I disagree with what you're saying. / I don't see it that way. 난 그렇게 생각하지 않아. / I couldn't disagree more. 전적으로 반대해.

✳✳ 기출 맛보기

01 대화를 듣고, 남자의 마지막 말에 대한 여자의 응답으로 가장 적절한 것을 고르시오. 모의

Woman: _____

① Oh, no! I can come over today to help you clear it out.
② Never mind. Everyone needs time to make a decision.
③ Okay. We can go to the basement if we're in danger.
④ Yes. Why don't you water your trees more often?
⑤ Sorry. I don't know how to change a light bulb.

W Hi, James. Is everything okay? **I heard there was a huge storm in your area last night.**

M Yeah, we had some really intense thunderstorms throughout the night. There was some damage.

W Did anyone get hurt?

M Thankfully, no, but there were a lot of fallen trees, and the roads were blocked.

W Oh, my! That must have been scary!

M Yeah, it was. Then the electricity went out while the roads were being cleared.

W So, you didn't have any power last night?

M No, I couldn't turn on any lights or use any electronic devices, but it's okay now.

W That must have been so frustrating. **Is there anything you need help with?**

M **Well, my basement is a mess. The water is up to my knees and all of my stuff down there is wet.**

W _____

대화의 흐름

지난밤에 남자가 사는 지역에 큰 폭풍이 몰아침

여자가 남자에게 도울 일이 있는지 물음

남자의 마지막 말: 지하실에 물이 무릎까지 차올라서 물건이 다 젖었음

Words & Phrases **intense** 강렬한 **thunderstorm** 폭풍우, 뇌우 **throughout** ~동안 죽 **fallen** 쓰러진 **block** 막다 **electricity** 전기 **go out** (불·전기 등이) 나가다 **electronic device** 전자기기 **frustrating** 답답하게 하는, 불만스러운 **basement** 지하실 **mess** 엉망인 상태

＊ 녹음 내용을 듣고, 알맞은 답을 고르시오.

01 대화를 듣고, 여자의 마지막 말에 대한 남자의 응답으로 가장 적절한 것을 고르시오.

Man: _____

ⓐ I don't have time to read it.

ⓑ Someone has already checked it out.

ⓒ It must be returned two weeks from today.

02 대화를 듣고, 남자의 마지막 말에 대한 여자의 응답으로 가장 적절한 것을 고르시오.

Woman: _____

ⓐ I'm sorry, that model is sold out.

ⓑ Oh dear. You really ought to have kept it.

ⓒ That's strange. The hair dryer worked well.

03 대화를 듣고, 여자의 마지막 말에 대한 남자의 응답으로 가장 적절한 것을 고르시오.

Man: _____

ⓐ Well, good luck, then.

ⓑ OK, I'll consider it once more.

ⓒ I appreciate your sincere hospitality.

04 대화를 듣고, 남자의 마지막 말에 대한 여자의 응답으로 가장 적절한 것을 고르시오.

Woman: _____

ⓐ Sorry, the promotion ended yesterday.

ⓑ You'd better hurry. They'll be gone soon.

ⓒ You got a good deal. The scarf looks good on you.

05 대화를 듣고, 여자의 마지막 말에 대한 남자의 응답으로 가장 적절한 것을 고르시오. 모의

Man: _____

ⓐ I have enough money to get a new bike.

ⓑ You really need one for your own safety.

ⓒ Luckily, I didn't get hurt in the accident.

06 대화를 듣고, 남자의 마지막 말에 대한 여자의 응답으로 가장 적절한 것을 고르시오.

Woman: _____

ⓐ No, thanks. I've already found it.

ⓑ It's very kind of you to keep my wallet.

ⓒ Would you? That would be a great help.

07 대화를 듣고, 여자의 마지막 말에 대한 남자의 응답으로 가장 적절한 것을 고르시오.

Man: _____

ⓐ No rush. It is due next Monday morning.

ⓑ Well, you have to practice harder to be perfect.

ⓒ Sure, but there will be a penalty for late submission.

08 대화를 듣고, 남자의 마지막 말에 대한 여자의 응답으로 가장 적절한 것을 고르시오. 모의

Woman: _____

ⓐ I have, but she didn't take it seriously.

ⓑ Don't worry. I have no problem with her.

ⓒ Sorry. I delayed moving out of the apartment.

09 대화를 듣고, 여자의 마지막 말에 대한 남자의 응답으로 가장 적절한 것을 고르시오. 모의

Man: _____

ⓐ Well, you'd better buy new clothes.

ⓑ Then, you should sell them using this app.

ⓒ Good. Let's buy a sweater in the marketplace.

10 대화를 듣고, 남자의 마지막 말에 대한 여자의 응답으로 가장 적절한 것을 고르시오. 모의

Woman: _____

ⓐ You're right. I think I need to see a doctor.

ⓑ That's why I'm telling you not to miss his class again.

ⓒ Don't worry. I'll take good notes and lend them to you.

✳ STEP 1의 녹음 내용을 다시 들으면서 빈칸을 채우시오.

01

W I want to check these two books out, please.

M You can _____, but that English dictionary _____.

W Oh, I didn't know that. _____ _____ this book?

02

M I bought this hair dryer here yesterday, but _____ _____.

W Let me see. Oh, there seems to be a problem with the wire. May I _____?

M I don't have it. I _____.

03

W Hey, Jack. I don't think you can afford _____ _____ to work abroad.

M Maybe you're right, but I've got a lot on my mind.

W I _____. Then, later, you can always move back home if you don't like it.

04

M What do you want to buy _____?

W A scarf. I saw a good one last week. It was $_____, but we can save 25% today.

M Wow! 25% off! That's a really good buy. _____ _____ for my mom, too.

05 모의

M Kathy! Let's ride our bikes to school together.

W Sounds nice. But _____ _____.

M It's okay. We can go slowly. Also, _____ _____ your helmet.

W But I don't have a helmet yet.

06

W Excuse me. After I left the restaurant, _____ _____ on the table?

M Do you remember where you sat?

W Yes, it was the table _____.

M I've just cleaned up that table, but I didn't see anything. _____ at the counter.

07

W Professor Jones, I'm sorry I _____
_____ on time.

M Did you have any problems? You never miss due dates.

W I _____ yesterday, so I'm wondering _____ now.

08 모의

M Alice, aren't you sharing an apartment with Jane?

W Yeah, but I'm thinking about moving out.

M Why? I thought you two _____
_____.

W There have been a lot of problems between us. Actually, _____.
The kitchen and the bathroom are always messy.

M That's awful. _____ this issue with her?

09 모의

W Paul, what are you doing?

M _____ my old sweater using the Local Market app.

W Interesting! How do you use it?

M _____ of my sweater, somebody who needs a sweater will see and buy it.

W That's great. I also _____
_____.

10 모의

W Chris, you don't look well. Why don't you _____
_____?

M I'd like to, but I don't want to miss biology class. The exam is _____.

W But you need to get better first.

M I know, but a lot of the questions on the exam _____.

✱ 녹음 내용을 듣고, 알맞은 답을 고르시오.

01 대화를 듣고, 남자의 마지막 말에 대한 여자의 응답으로 가장 적절한 것을 고르시오.

Woman: _____

① I know. Trust me. I won't let you down.
② Don't be silly. You'll do better next time.
③ Same here. I nearly failed two subjects, too.
④ I have a good idea. Why don't we try it again?
⑤ I'm sorry, but I can't finish the report this week.

02 대화를 듣고, 여자의 마지막 말에 대한 남자의 응답으로 가장 적절한 것을 고르시오.

Man: _____

① That's fine. Here is my credit card for the tickets.
② That's OK. Even if they are poor seats I want them.
③ This is unacceptable! I want to speak to your manager.
④ Can I get a discount with my membership card?
⑤ Oh no, I should have reserved a seat earlier.

03 대화를 듣고, 남자의 마지막 말에 대한 여자의 응답으로 가장 적절한 것을 고르시오. 고난도

Woman: _____

① Yes, I do. We could go by my car.
② OK. Let's leave here in 30 minutes.
③ Why don't we buy some presents together?
④ Sorry, but I can't make it to the party tonight.
⑤ No problem. See you there in the evening, then.

04 대화를 듣고, 여자의 마지막 말에 대한 남자의 응답으로 가장 적절한 것을 고르시오.

Man: _____

① I don't feel like jogging today.
② Take your time. I'll wait for you.
③ OK, and you can choose when to exercise.
④ Don't hurry. Slow and steady wins the race.
⑤ I'd like to, but I have to go to the office right now.

05 대화를 듣고, 남자의 마지막 말에 대한 여자의 응답으로 가장 적절한 것을 고르시오.

Woman: _____

① I envy you. You are good at everything.

② Yeah, I don't think jet-skiing is dangerous.

③ Sounds good. I have to learn to swim this week.

④ No, I don't. Instead let's go jet-skiing this weekend.

⑤ No, I'd better not. I don't even know how to ride a bike.

06 대화를 듣고, 여자의 마지막 말에 대한 남자의 응답으로 가장 적절한 것을 고르시오.

Man: _____

① What a great idea! Thanks for letting me know.

② I work until 6 p.m., so I can't be there until 7 p.m.

③ Then I'll call and let them know that I'm not coming.

④ I'm not sure if I'll be there tonight, but I'll give it a try.

⑤ I must leave now. I have to get an early start tomorrow.

07 대화를 듣고, 남자의 마지막 말에 대한 여자의 응답으로 가장 적절한 것을 고르시오.

Woman: _____

① I don't want to work for either company.

② Oh, that's too bad. I hope you'll get a good job soon.

③ That's nonsense! I think you are qualified more than anyone.

④ I'm sorry to hear that, but thank you for the opportunity.

⑤ Don't be silly. You are amazing just the way you are.

08 대화를 듣고, 여자의 마지막 말에 대한 남자의 응답으로 가장 적절한 것을 고르시오.

Man: _____

① I feel bad for our neighbor next door.

② I had a very good time with my parents.

③ My dog is feeling better now thanks to you.

④ You should have called me about being late.

⑤ I'm terribly sorry. I'll make sure that never happens again.

09 대화를 듣고, 남자의 마지막 말에 대한 여자의 응답으로 가장 적절한 것을 고르시오. 고난도

Woman: _____

① Let's go to see a comedy this weekend.

② Well, we don't have anything in common.

③ You're into the same kind of films as me.

④ What is the romance movie that made you cry?

⑤ Me, too. I spend lots of time reading love stories.

10 대화를 듣고, 여자의 마지막 말에 대한 남자의 응답으로 가장 적절한 것을 고르시오.

Man: _____

① Really? I'd love to join your car pool.

② Oh, that's too bad. Traffic will only get worse.

③ Good. I'm glad public transportation will be cheaper.

④ OK. I'll give you a ride if you've left your car at home.

⑤ That's good to hear. What else are you guys doing?

※ STEP 3의 녹음 내용을 다시 들으면서 빈칸을 채우시오.

정답 및 해설 **p.67**

01

M Susan, did you finish the survey?

W Sorry, not yet.

M You told me _____ on Wednesday, but it's now Friday and you still haven't finished it.

W Well, I'm sorry, but there has been a lot of other work to finish this week. You know _____ _____.

M But you did promise. Look, the point is that the deadline for our team's report _____ _____ and if the survey isn't ready, we can't finish the report.

W I'm really sorry. It'll be in your hands first thing tomorrow. I promise.

M Please don't forget. If we can't hand the report in, four of us, including you and me, _____ _____.

02

W Welcome. May I help you?

M Yes, I made a reservation online, and _____ _____ my tickets.

W What sort of reservation was it?

M It was for today's 7 p.m. concert.

W And what is your name?

M Brown... John Brown.

W Yes, Mr. Brown. Here's your ticket.

M But I ordered two tickets. _____ my wife.

W Are you sure you ordered two?

M Of course. It was just yesterday. I _____ _____ two.

W I'm terribly sorry, but our records show a reservation for one, and the concert is now sold out. I'm afraid _____ _____.

03

M I hope _____ for dinner at Pat's house. I'm starving.

W Don't worry about that. Pat always prepares a lot of food. I bought some chocolates for her. What are you bringing?

M A bottle of white wine.

W Why did you get white wine? Do you know _____?

M I think she said she was going to cook fish.

W Oh, that sounds good. Let's see. Do you want me to _____?

M Well, what time did she say the dinner was, six-thirty or seven o'clock?

W Seven.

M Then I have time to walk, so let's just meet at her house. But _____ after dinner?

04

W Hi, Jason. Going out for a run?

M Yes.

W I see _____ these days.

M _____ a few extra kilograms.

W Well, you have put on just a little weight over the last year.

M A little? Three years ago, I was 10 kilograms lighter than I am now.

W Oh, really?

M Yeah. I _____ I bought last year.

W That's nothing to complain about. I got these pants only last month. At that time, they were very comfortable to wear. Now, they're _____ _____.

M Then you should be getting some exercise, too. Why don't you join me?

W Great idea. I'll go and change my clothes quickly and be right back.

05

W Hey, Alan, what are you going to do this Saturday?

M I'm going jet-skiing on the Han River.

W Jet-skiing?

M Yeah. _____?

W No. How long have you been jet-skiing?

M About a month. It is really exciting.

W But jet-skiing _____.

M Absolutely not. Anyone can learn it easily.

W Isn't it scary?

M No, not at all. It's just like riding a bike. _____ _____ in no time. Do you want to come along?

06

W Where are you going at this late hour?

M Mom, some friends and I are going to watch the Super Bowl at Bill's house.

W _____ the game here?

M It's more fun to watch it together.

W Isn't Bill's house on Cedar Street?

M Yes. It's not that far.

W Well, _____ anyway. I don't think it's a good idea to go at this time of night.

M Why not? I'll drive safely.

W I heard there's a big snow storm _____ _____. The streets _____ _____ when you're on your way back.

M Really? Let me check the weather forecast. Oh, you're right.

W Yes. Look at the sky. It's very cloudy.

07

W Lucas, what did you say _____?

M Well, I'm currently out of work.

W Oh, are you?

M Yes. Only last week I had two jobs, but now _____.

W What did you do?

M I was a part-time lecturer at two different universities, but both universities said they _____ _____.

W What subject do you teach?

M Sociology. But _____ full-time university teaching jobs.

W Are you looking for other jobs?

M Yes. I had two different interviews today, but they _____. They said I was overqualified.

08

M Hi, Hailey. I haven't seen you around for a while, even though we live next door to each other.

W Hi, Andy. Actually, I'm here to ask you something.

M What is it?

W Well, I want to know what happened last night.

M What do you mean?

W Your dog was barking all night long. I thought _____.

M Sorry about that. I wasn't at home last night. I _____ at my parent's house.

W I could hear him very clearly from my house! Why did you _____?

M Because my parents don't like dogs, and I thought he would be okay.

W Well, I _____, and I almost missed work this morning.

09

W So what do you feel like doing tonight? Any ideas?

M Well, I'd like to see a film or maybe see if there are any good bands playing around town, _____ _____.

W Yes, that's a good idea. What kind of music do you like, then?

M Oh, all sorts really, you know, but mainly I like blues and jazz.

W Oh, really? I'm more into dance music myself, so maybe....

M Well, we could always go and see a film. I really like movies. And _____ _____, you know, car chases, guns, bombs,

anything that's fast and exciting.

W Oh, right. _____, I'm not really into violent films. I like romantic comedies better. Do you like that kind of movie?

M I don't like _____. They are so boring.

10

M Hi, April! What a pleasant surprise. How are you and your family?

W We're all fine, thanks. And you?

M I'm fine too. I haven't seen you in ages. _____ _____?

W I've been busy. I've been getting advice from the mayor's office on a project.

M What kind of project?

W We're starting a neighborhood association _____ _____ in this community.

M This is the first I've heard of it. Is it a lot of work?

W Yeah, but it's also interesting.

M Well, I wish _____ about the traffic, especially during rush hour.

W Actually, that's one of our projects. We're encouraging people _____ _____ and to use public transport.

유형 12 담화 상황에 적절한 표현

주어진 상황 설명을 듣고, 그 상황에 처한 사람 중의 한 명이 할 말로 가장 적절한 것을 고르는 유형이다. 1문항 출제된다.

해결 전략

1 우선 지시문을 통해 누가 누구에게 할 말인지를 파악한다. 담화의 마지막 말은 지시문과 같은 내용으로서 In this situation 으로 시작한다.

2 담화 초중반에는 대개 두 사람의 관계, 벌어진 문제나 상황 등이 설명되고, 담화 후반에는 상황을 정리해 결론짓는 문장이 나오는데 이것이 정답과 연결되므로 놓치지 말아야 한다.

e.g. 다음 상황 설명을 듣고, Jason이 Sarah에게 할 말로 가장 적절한 것을 고르시오.

~ So, Jason wants to tell Sarah that he can finish it in time and that she doesn't have to be concerned. In this situation, what would Jason most likely say to Sarah?

① Good luck. I hope you finish your work in time.

② Okay. Let's meet to discuss the changes to the sculpture.

③ That's terrible. I'm sorry that the reopening was postponed.

④ Hurry up. You have to send the final design immediately.

⑤ Don't worry. I can get the job done before the deadline.

주요 표현

상황을 결론짓는 문장에 자주 등장하는 표현들을 잘 익혀두자.

· So[Thus, Therefore] ~ / Now ~

· A wants[would like] to tell[suggest to] B that ~

· A wants[would like] to tell[ask, persuade, advise] B to ~

· A doesn't want B to ~ / A doesn't think that ~

· A decides to tell[ask, persuade] ~

· A is going to talk about ~

· A thinks[realizes] ~ and wants to ~

✳✳ **기출 맛보기**

01 다음 상황 설명을 듣고, Amy가 Terry에게 할 말로 가장 적절한 것을 고르시오. 모의

Amy: _____

① How about using a colorful font on the poster?
② You'd better inform your friends of the concert.
③ Can you make the letter size bigger on the poster?
④ Why don't we hold a concert in the school festival?
⑤ You should put important information on the poster.

W **Amy is the leader of a high school band and Terry is one of the band members.** The band is going to hold a mini concert in the school festival, and Terry is in charge of making a concert poster. When he completes the poster, he shows it to the band members. Even though the poster has all the necessary information, **it's hard to read it because the size of the letters is too small.** Amy thinks if Terry changes the font size to a larger one, it could be easier to notice. **So, Amy wants to suggest that Terry increase the size of the letters on the poster.** In this situation, what would Amy most likely say to Terry?

대화의 흐름

· **두 사람의 관계**:
  학교 밴드 리더(Amy) - 밴드 멤버(Terry)

· **상황**:
  Terry가 준비한 콘서트 포스터의 글씨가
  너무 작아서 읽기 힘듦

· **결론**:
  Amy는 Terry에게 글씨 크기를 키울 것을
  제안하고 싶어 함 (→ 정답 ③)

Words & Phrases **hold** (행사 등을) 열다 **in charge of** ~을 담당하는 **complete** 완성하다 **necessary** 필수적인 **notice** 알아차리다 **suggest** 제안하다 **increase** 늘리다, 증가시키다

Listen & Choose 유형핵심 익히기

* 녹음 내용을 듣고, 알맞은 답을 고르시오.

01 다음 상황 설명을 듣고, Yumi가 교수님에게 할 말로 가장 적절한 것을 고르시오. 모의

Yumi: _____

ⓐ Is it possible for me to take the exam on another day?

ⓑ Could you tell me what I did wrong in the examination?

ⓒ I wish my team had done better in the dance competition.

02 다음 상황 설명을 듣고, Cathy가 Brian에게 할 말로 가장 적절한 것을 고르시오. 모의

Cathy: _____

ⓐ You should practice more after school.

ⓑ You need to follow the doctor's instructions.

ⓒ Why don't you try yoga for your back pain?

03 다음 상황 설명을 듣고, Tony가 Jessica에게 할 말로 가장 적절한 것을 고르시오.

Tony: _____

ⓐ There's a mistake in the bill.

ⓑ Let's pay separately today.

ⓒ Let me treat you this time.

04 다음 상황 설명을 듣고, Jasper가 Mary에게 할 말로 가장 적절한 것을 고르시오. 모의

Jasper: _____

ⓐ Let's play a different song this time.

ⓑ I think you should be our lead singer.

ⓒ Don't you think we need more practice?

05 다음 상황 설명을 듣고, Alex가 Emma에게 할 말로 가장 적절한 것을 고르시오. 모의

Alex: _____

ⓐ Let's keep in touch even after we part.

ⓑ I hope you'll get used to your new city.

ⓒ I was deeply touched by your kind words.

06 다음 상황 설명을 듣고, Olivia가 온라인 쇼핑몰 고객센터 직원에게 할 말로 가장 적절한 것을 고르시오. 모의

Olivia: _____

ⓐ Can I exchange them for other pants?

ⓑ Could you deliver the pants by tomorrow?

ⓒ I'd like to send the pants back and get a refund.

07 다음 상황 설명을 듣고, Sophia가 노인에게 할 말로 가장 적절한 것을 고르시오.

Sophia: _____

ⓐ Please hold on to me. I'll guide you.

ⓑ May I help you? Where do you want to go?

ⓒ What's your destination? I can drive you there.

08 다음 상황 설명을 듣고, Kevin의 어머니가 Kevin에게 할 말로 가장 적절한 것을 고르시오. 모의

Kevin's mother: _____

ⓐ I'm so proud that you won the race.

ⓑ You shouldn't go out before you're completely healed.

ⓒ Why don't you invite your friends to the sports competition?

09 다음 상황 설명을 듣고, Becky가 Clara에게 할 말로 가장 적절한 것을 고르시오. 모의

Becky: _____

ⓐ Why don't we find a camp on different dates?

ⓑ You should check the camp dates on this flyer first.

ⓒ You need your parents' permission to join the camp.

10 다음 상황 설명을 듣고, Amy가 택시 운전사에게 할 말로 가장 적절한 것을 고르시오. 수능

Amy: _____

ⓐ Could you let me off here, please?

ⓑ How long does it take to get to the market?

ⓒ Can you recommend a place to visit in Seoul?

Listen & Choose Dictation 유형핵심 받아쓰기

＊ STEP 1의 녹음 내용을 다시 들으면서 빈칸을 채우시오.

01 모의

M Yumi is a member of her college dance team. Her team _____ the city dance competition. However, there is a midterm exam on the day of the competition. She does not _____. Thus, she decides to ask her professor _____ _____. In this situation, what would Yumi most likely say to her professor?

02 모의

W Cathy and Brian are members of the same orchestra. _____ preparing for the upcoming concert, Brian _____ _____. Cathy had the same problem last year, but her pain disappeared after starting yoga. Therefore, she wants to suggest to Brian _____ _____. In this situation, what would Cathy most likely say to Brian?

03

M When Tony _____ by his manager, his co-worker Jessica helped him with it. Today _____ Jessica a nice dinner, so he takes her to a famous restaurant in town. After dinner, Jessica is about to pay the bill, but Tony _____. In this situation, what would Tony most likely say to Jessica?

04 모의

W Jasper and Mary are _____ _____. Since they don't have a singer yet, the guitarist Mary sings instead in their first practice. Hearing her sing, _____ _____ that she has a perfect voice for rock music! So, Jasper wants to tell Mary _____ for their band. In this situation, what would Jasper most likely say to Mary?

05 모의

M Alex and Emma have been close friends since they were children. One day, Alex tells Emma that _____ to another city. But he really hopes to _____ _____ with her. So, Alex wants to suggest that _____ even after he leaves the city. In this situation, what would Alex most likely say to Emma?

06 모의

W Olivia _____ from an online shopping mall. When they are delivered, she finds out that _____ _____. So, she decides to call the customer service center to return the pants and _____. In this situation what would Olivia most likely say to the customer service employee?

07

M While Sophia is waiting for the bus, she sees an old man at the bus stop. He's _____ _____ on the bus stop sign. He _____ the sign. So, she wants to _____. In this situation, what would Sophia most likely say to the old man?

09 모의

M Today Clara gets a flyer for an interesting camp and asks Becky _____ together. However, Becky has a family vacation _____. So, Becky wants to suggest to Clara _____ _____. In this situation, what would Becky most likely say to Clara?

08 모의

W Kevin _____ as the class representative on the school sports day. But he sprained his ankle, so he needed to be careful for a couple of weeks. One week later, Kevin _____ for the race. However, his mother thinks he is not fully recovered yet and _____. In this situation, what would Kevin's mother most likely say to Kevin?

10 수능

W Amy is visiting Seoul for the first time. Today, she wants to go to a place where she can see a view of the entire city. She _____ _____ N Seoul Tower. As the taxi gets near the destination, she sees some people _____ leading up to the tower. She suddenly feels like _____ _____. So, she wants to ask the driver _____. In this situation, what would Amy most likely say to the taxi driver?

Listen & Answer 실전 문제

* 녹음 내용을 듣고, 알맞은 답을 고르시오.

01 다음 상황 설명을 듣고, Michael이 요리사에게 할 말로 가장 적절한 것을 고르시오.

Michael: _____

① Thank you for such an incredible experience.
② We don't have anything available at this time.
③ I'd like to order a well-done steak. Is it too late?
④ A customer wants to change her order. Is that OK?
⑤ Sorry, I got the order wrong. Can you cook it more?

02 다음 상황 설명을 듣고, Ms. Thompson이 John에게 할 말로 가장 적절한 것을 고르시오.

Ms. Thompson: _____

① Don't worry. Practice makes perfect.
② It's entirely up to you. I don't mind it at all.
③ If there's anything you need, don't hesitate to ask.
④ You're doing all right so far. I'm very proud of you.
⑤ You should work harder to study what you want later.

03 다음 상황 설명을 듣고, David가 Mark에게 할 말로 가장 적절한 것을 고르시오.

David: _____

① I'm afraid I can't tell you who he is.
② When did you drink the last of the milk?
③ I've forgotten that it's my turn to buy milk.
④ I'm really sorry, I should have believed you.
⑤ You promised that it wouldn't happen again.

04 다음 상황 설명을 듣고, Theresa가 Hena에게 할 말로 가장 적절한 것을 고르시오.

Theresa: _____

① Can you turn down the volume a little?
② Is there any way I can join the jazz club?
③ Please help me find the name of this song.
④ Do you know any other jazz songs like this?
⑤ Would you come with me to the jazz concert?

05 다음 상황 설명을 듣고, Charlie의 어머니가 Charlie에게 할 말로 가장 적절한 것을 고르시오. 고난도

Charlie's mother: _____

① I forgot to buy milk. Can you go and get some?

② Thank you, Charlie! You can keep the change!

③ Go back and ask if they made a mistake.

④ The items were on sale until yesterday.

⑤ Why did you spend so much money?

06 다음 상황 설명을 듣고, Ben이 Susan에게 할 말로 가장 적절한 것을 고르시오.

Ben: _____

① It's my pleasure to help you get a refund.

② I'm sorry. The policy shouldn't be violated.

③ All right. I'll let you exchange it just this once.

④ Thanks. I am grateful you've changed your mind.

⑤ You're being unreasonable. There's nothing I can help you with.

07 다음 상황 설명을 듣고, Lucy가 Steven에게 할 말로 가장 적절한 것을 고르시오. 고난도

Lucy: _____

① Why didn't you ask for my help in advance?

② What do we need to do next for the project?

③ I'm glad I get to work with you on this project.

④ I heard you were very sick. Are you feeling alright?

⑤ I can't stand it any longer. You should do your part!

08 다음 상황 설명을 듣고, Linda가 Beth에게 할 말로 가장 적절한 것을 고르시오.

Linda: _____

① We'd better try to rest on the weekend.

② How about visiting more palaces next week?

③ Be sure not to forget our plans for the weekend.

④ Why don't we skip shopping and go to a festival?

⑤ I heard that there're several festivals on the weekend.

09 다음 상황 설명을 듣고, Alex가 손님에게 할 말로 가장 적절한 것을 고르시오.

Alex: _____

① I'm sorry, but delivery on Sunday is not available.

② Right. We promise to deliver them within 24 hours.

③ Your furniture will be delivered on the date specified.

④ Yes, but you have to pay an extra charge for delivery.

⑤ The price includes tax, so no additional cost will be added.

10 다음 상황 설명을 듣고, Dick이 남자에게 할 말로 가장 적절한 것을 고르시오.

Dick: _____

① Is this seat taken?

② Do you mind if I sit down?

③ Is it possible to move over one seat?

④ Will you be getting off the subway soon?

⑤ Are you going to the exhibition at the Arts Center, too?

01

M Michael started a new job as a waiter in a steak restaurant today. His first night as a waiter is almost over. It is nearly 10 o'clock and the last table _____. Michael is walking around the dining room and a customer _____. The customer says the steak which Michael brought her is rare, but she _____. So, Michael says sorry and takes the steak off the table and walks into the kitchen. He wants to ask the chef _____. In this situation, what would Michael most likely say to the chef?

02

W John is a high-school student. He took a math exam last week but _____. Since his math grade was bad, his math teacher, Ms. Thompson, asks him what's going on with him these days. John says he couldn't study much because he is a member of the school dance club and _____ for a contest before the test. She asks John _____ _____ after high school. John says he wants to study computer science in college. Ms. Thompson knows that he needs a high grade in math to get into the computer science department. So, Ms. Thompson wants to persuade John _____. In this situation, what would Ms. Thompson most likely say to John?

03

M David and Mark are roommates. Last week, Mark ate a sandwich that belonged to David. When David talked to Mark about this, Mark promised that _____. However, this morning David finds that the milk he bought yesterday is empty. David asks Mark if he finished it, but Mark _____ _____. He says that actually one of David's friends drank the milk. David doesn't believe him and leaves angrily. A few hours later, David runs into that friend and learns that Mark was telling the truth. So David wants to apologize to Mark _____. In this situation, what would David most likely say to Mark?

04

W Theresa and Hena are sisters. While Hena enjoys listening to jazz music, Theresa doesn't like it much. She considers jazz too complicated. One day, Theresa hears a jazz song at a coffee shop while waiting for a friend. Unlike the jazz songs _____, she finds the song calm and relaxing. _____, she listens to the song again with Hena. Hena says it is one of her favorite jazz songs, too. Now, Theresa wants to know if Hena _____ _____. In this situation, what would Theresa most likely say to Hena?

05 고난도

M Marie, the mother of two teenage boys, has always emphasized _____ to her sons. She absolutely _____ _____ lying or stealing and has taught these values to her children since they were little boys. She's a loving and kind mother, but very strict _____. One day she gave Charlie, her youngest son, 20 dollars to go on a shopping errand for her. She knows that the items she needs — milk, butter, eggs, flour, and salt — cost around 15 dollars. Charlie comes back from the shop and hands his mom 10 dollars in change, which is _____ _____. She thinks the cashier made a mistake and wants Charlie _____ _____. In this situation, what would Charlie's mother most likely say to Charlie?

06

W Last week Susan received a music CD by the singer MOA as a birthday present from her brother. She, unfortunately, _____ _____. Today she takes the CD to the music store where her brother bought it. She doesn't have the receipt. But she hopes the store will _____ for one by the Lee Lee Band. After entering the store, she explains the situation to the store manager, Ben. He says the store's policy is _____ _____. However, after a lot of pleading, Ben finally decides _____ _____ just this time. In this situation, what would Ben most likely say to Susan?

07 고난도

M Lucy is working on an important group project with one of her classmates, Steven. Lucy _____ _____ than Steven, and recently she has discovered that Steven hardly cares about the project. Because they are friends, Lucy _____. But when Lucy was sick last weekend, she asked Steven to do a few things for the project by Monday, and Steven promised that he would. However, when Monday comes, Lucy finds that _____ _____. Now, Lucy decides to tell Steven that she _____ anymore. In this situation, what would Lucy most likely say to Steven?

08

W Linda and Beth are cousins, and they are on vacation together for the first time. They have similar interests and generally enjoy the same activities. This weekend they _____ _____ and do some shopping downtown. While surfing the Internet, Linda finds an advertisement for a street food festival. The festival _____ this weekend. She thinks that it will be something _____ _____. So, Linda wants to suggest to Beth that _____ _____ for the weekend. In this situation, what would Linda most likely say to Beth?

09

M Alex works for a furniture store. Today, one woman visits the store to buy a table. She _____ _____, but when she sees a beautiful antique dresser, she wants to buy it, too. She asks Alex about the price of the dresser. Alex says that there is a 10% off sale on all furniture. She decides to buy the dresser and the table. After paying for her things, she _____. But her car is too small and _____ _____. She asks Alex if the store can deliver them to her house. The store's delivery service _____. So, Alex wants to explain to her that there is a delivery fee. In this situation, what would Alex most likely say to the customer?

10

W Dick and Jane have just gotten on the subway. They are heading to the Arts Center downtown _____. They are searching for a seat on the subway. On one of the benches there are two empty seats. But the two empty seats are not together. A man is sitting _____. They stand in front of the man for a moment. The man is reading a review of the new exhibition at the Arts Center in the newspaper. Dick and Jane really want to sit together, so Dick decides to ask the man _____ _____. In this situation, what would Dick most likely say to the man?

II
실전편

실전 모의고사 1~10회

01 다음을 듣고, 여자가 하는 말의 목적으로 가장 적절한 것을 고르시오.

① 대중교통 이용을 권장하려고
② 새 도서관 건립 소식을 알리려고
③ 공사로 인한 소음에 대해 사과하려고
④ 캠퍼스 밖의 주차 공간 이용을 독려하려고
⑤ 주차장 폐쇄에 따른 조치 및 권장 사항을 안내하려고

02 대화를 듣고, 남자의 의견으로 가장 적절한 것을 고르시오.

① 수준에 맞는 강의를 수강하는 것이 중요하다.
② 외국어 말하기 능력이 쓰기 능력보다 중요하다.
③ 해외여행을 위해 간단한 회화 공부를 해야 한다.
④ 외국어 습득은 문법 학습이 기반이 되어야 한다.
⑤ 회화 능력을 향상하려면 원어 수업을 들어야 한다.

03 대화를 듣고, 두 사람의 관계를 가장 잘 나타낸 것을 고르시오.

① 비서 — 상사
② 호텔 직원 — 투숙객
③ 세관 직원 — 입국자
④ 문방구 직원 — 손님
⑤ 여행사 직원 — 여행객

04 대화를 듣고, 그림에서 대화의 내용과 일치하지 않는 것을 고르시오.

05 대화를 듣고, 여자가 남자를 위해 할 일로 가장 적절한 것을 고르시오.

① 택시 불러주기
② 불법 주차 신고하기
③ 화물차 주인 찾아보기
④ 화물차 주인에게 전화하기
⑤ 차를 뺄 수 있도록 도와주기

06 대화를 듣고, 남자가 지불할 금액을 고르시오. [3점]

① $670
② $690
③ $700
④ $720
⑤ $770

07 대화를 듣고, 여자가 회사에 늦게 출근하는 이유를 고르시오.

① 교통 체증이 심해서
② 심한 감기에 걸려서
③ 출장에서 늦게 돌아와서
④ 아픈 아들을 돌봐야 해서
⑤ 어머니를 병원에 모시고 가야 해서

08 대화를 듣고, tepee에 관해 언급되지 않은 것을 고르시오.

① 용도
② 설치 소요 시간
③ 내구성
④ 소재
⑤ 그림 장식

09 Francis Rivera에 관한 다음 내용을 듣고, 일치하지 않는 것을 고르시오.

① Puerto Rico 태생이다.
② 무명 축구 선수였다.
③ 의과 대학에 진학했다.
④ 학업과 일을 병행했다.
⑤ 무료 의료 프로그램을 만들었다.

10 다음 표를 보면서 대화를 듣고, 두 사람이 구입할 패키지를 고르시오.

Ski Packages at Sun Peaks Ski Resort

	Package	Equipment Rentals	Lessons	Night Skiing	Lockers
①	A	×	○	○	small
②	B	○	×	○	small
③	C	○	○	×	large
④	D	○	×	○	large
⑤	E	○	×	×	large

11 대화를 듣고, 남자의 마지막 말에 대한 여자의 응답으로 가장 적절한 것을 고르시오.

① Sure. I'm moving out next week.
② I expect to have my cable installed.
③ Just across town, near Central Park.
④ I wonder if there's a cancellation fee.
⑤ Thanks so much for helping me move.

12 대화를 듣고, 여자의 마지막 말에 대한 남자의 응답으로 가장 적절한 것을 고르시오.

① Yes, my boss canceled the meeting.
② Well, we could still meet later at night.
③ No, I'm waiting for you near your office.
④ Great! I can join you for lunch tomorrow.
⑤ I need to ask for more time off from work.

13 대화를 듣고, 남자의 마지막 말에 대한 여자의 응답으로 가장 적절한 것을 고르시오.

Woman: _____

① Are you sure you don't want to come?
② I don't like soccer as much as basketball.
③ You would? Great! I'll ask Sara right away.
④ Cindy and Mark had birthdays last month.
⑤ I want to make friends with more of our class-mates.

14 대화를 듣고, 여자의 마지막 말에 대한 남자의 응답으로 가장 적절한 것을 고르시오. [3점]

Man: _____

① I'll help you get rid of all of these.
② I can tell you how to contact the organization.
③ Great. Then it will be the perfect place for these.
④ There are many charities that may appeal to you.
⑤ You should think twice next time you buy clothes.

15 다음 상황 설명을 듣고, Matilda의 어머니가 Matilda에게 할 말로 가장 적절한 것을 고르시오.

Matilda's mother: _____

① It looks good on you.
② You shouldn't run here.
③ Don't let go of my hand.
④ Let's go to the store over there.
⑤ It's your aunt's wedding next week.

[16-17] 다음을 듣고, 물음에 답하시오.

16 남자가 하는 말의 주제로 가장 적절한 것은? [3점]

① various hobbies for mental health
② advantages of expressing feelings
③ psychological benefits of gardening
④ ways to keep a vegetable garden healthy
⑤ profitable plants for your vegetable garden

17 언급된 식물이 <u>아닌</u> 것은?

① carrots   ② cucumbers
③ strawberry   ④ lettuce
⑤ watermelon

✳ 녹음 내용을 다시 들으면서 빈칸을 채우시오.

01

W Attention, please. This is Ellie Clark from the administration office. As it was previously announced, _____ _____ from November due to the construction of the new library. Those of you who have reserved spaces in the north parking lot _____ in the east parking lot. Anyone who is not given a new space _____. Finally, due to the limited number of parking spaces, _____ the bus or subway. We apologize for the inconvenience and hope that everyone will make good use of the new library.

02

W Peter, you're taking Spanish next semester, right?

M Yes, I'm taking it from Ms. Garcia.

W And the class will _____ _____?

M Yes, all assignments, discussions, and lectures are entirely in Spanish. Why?

W _____ between that class and the one taught in English by Mr. Berk.

M If you want to improve your speaking ability, Ms. Garcia's class _____ Mr. Berk's.

W Maybe you're right. I really just want to reach a conversational level for traveling.

M Me, too. That's why I chose Ms. Garcia. I _____ _____ in Spanish as much as possible. If that sounds good, you should also take her class.

W Okay, I think _____ her class. Thanks.

03

W Good afternoon. May I help you?

M Yes, please. Can you _____ _____?

W Sure. Where to?

M One to Shanghai, and the other one to London. Here are the numbers. Can you _____ _____?

W What's your name and room number?

M Owen Brooks, Room 1512.

W There isn't any charge. Because you are a VIP, they will be free.

M That's great. _____ for me?

W Yes, there's one. Here you are.

M Thanks. And _____ the meeting room on Tuesday at 10 a.m.?

W Yes, you can. Could you fill out this form please?

M Sure.

04

M Janice, how's the redecoration of your study going?

W It was just finished last week. Look at this picture, Eric.

M Wow, what a change! Look at the floor. There's no rug any more.

W Yeah, I think _____. What do you think about the stripe-patterned walls?

M Hmm, well... I prefer how they were before. But I like the curtains. _____ _____ are lovely.

W Me too. And I placed the sofa _____ _____. I love to read books there.

M Cool. By the way, is that _____ _____? I remember there was a 4-shelf bookcase, not a 5-shelf one.

W You're right. I needed _____ _____.

M Great. I think it matches your study quite well.

05

M Excuse me. Do you work here?

W I'm the parking attendant. How can I help you?

M I'm really in a hurry, but _____ _____ a delivery van.

W I'm sorry. I'm sure the driver _____ _____ if you ask him. I will come with you.

M I didn't see anyone with the van. Oh, I'm going to be late!

W Again, I'm very sorry. I will try to find the driver and _____ as soon as possible.

M I don't have time to wait around. Maybe I should take a taxi.

W I will call one for you. _____ _____.

M Would you? That would be great. Thanks so much.

06

W Can I help you find something?

M Yes, I'm looking for the computer from your advertisement.

W That's _____ and a good decision. It's $_____ or $_____ with a membership card.

M Well, I don't have a membership card. Can I get one today?

W Of course, but _____ _____.

M OK, and then I can get the discount, right?

W Yes.

M Oh, and I would like _____, too.

W Sure. It'll be $_____ for a wired mouse, and $_____ for a wireless one.

M I'll take _____, please.

W Sure thing. Will that be all?

M Yes. Here's my credit card.

07

M Hello?

W Bob, it's Jane.

M Hi. You're late. _____?

W No, I haven't left home yet. I'm planning to be there after lunch, so please _____ _____ until then.

M Sure. But what's wrong? Are you sick?

W No, I'm okay. But _____ and he can't go to school today. My husband is out of town on a business trip, so _____ _____.

M Then you'll be at home all day taking care of him. You won't be in after lunch.

W I will. My mom's coming over _____ _____. But she can't get here until noon.

M OK. No problem. I'll handle everything until you get here.

W Thanks.

08

W The next exhibit shows several different types of Native American tepees.

M They look like tents. Were they really _____ _____?

W Yes, many Native Americans lived in tepees. And they brought these tepees with them _____ _____.

M That must have been very difficult.

W Actually, _____ a tepee because of the simple construction. Two people could put up a tepee in under an hour.

M What are they made from?

W All of the tepees you see here _____ _____ buffalo skin.

M That one is really colorful! I thought tepees would be more plain.

W Most tepees were plain. But some tepees used for religious ceremonies _____ _____, such as pictures of animals.

M Oh, I see.

09

M Hello, subscribers! Francis Rivera was chosen as the Person of the Year by News Weekly. Francis Rivera traveled _____.
Born in Puerto Rico, he had lived in Mexico, Texas, California, and Colorado by the time he was fourteen. At high school in Colorado _____ _____. But rather than pursuing a career in sports, _____ medical school. In order to make his living while at college, he _____ _____. Despite this, he graduated at the top of his class. For the next twenty years, Francis traveled with little money, but _____ _____ in many poor countries.

10

M Here we are! I can't wait to start skiing.

W Me too. I can't remember the last time we came here.

M I know. Let's get our tickets and go have fun.

W You know, we _____. Maybe we should get one of these packages.

M Sounds good. It's been a while, but _____ _____.

W Me neither. What about night skiing?

M I came to ski as much as possible!

W Hmm.... _____, but it sounds more fun!

M Absolutely. Lastly, do we need a large locker?

W I think _____ to keep our shoes in.

M OK then, it's settled. I'll pay for that package.

11

M Hello. This is Cable Center. How may I help you?

W Hi. I'm calling _____ because I'm moving houses.

M I think I can help you. Could you let me know _____?

12

W Hi, Philip. It's me. Are we still meeting tomorrow?

M My boss _____. We're too busy.

W Oh, no! I'm _____ this week.

13

W Jim! I'm so glad to have run into you here.

M Hi, Karen. What's new?

W You know I'm playing on the soccer team this year. I was actually hoping _____ _____ this Saturday.

M Oh, you know I'm not a big fan of sports.

W I remember. But this game is really important to me. And _____.

M Really? Who?

W John, Cindy, Mark, Jeff, Dan, and Sara.

M Oh, Sara? Is she really coming? Because she said this Saturday is her birthday.

W Right, after the game we will _____ _____.

M I would be happy to come to the game _____ _____ afterward.

14

W Sean, why are all of your clothes in boxes?

M That's just some of my old stuff _____ _____. I'm throwing all of it out.

W Some of these are _____! You are really throwing them away?

M Well, I don't need them anymore, and just keeping them is wasting space.

W _____ to Helping Hand?

M Helping Hand? I don't know what that is.

W It's a place that accepts old clothes and things.

M What happens to the clothes?

W They _____, and then given away to needy families.

15

W Matilda is a six-year-old girl. Matilda and her mother _____ next Saturday. Matilda's mother would like to buy Matilda a pretty pink dress for the wedding. So today, Matilda's mother _____ _____ with Matilda. Since it is near the holiday season, there are a lot of people at the department store. Matilda's mother

_____.

She doesn't want to lose her daughter in the crowd. In this situation, what would Matilda's mother most likely say to Matilda?

16-17

M The term "gardening" itself brings to our mind feelings that relax the body and mind. If the word alone can give us peace of mind, imagine _____

_____.

Did you know that a few minutes of gardening every day can not only relax your body but also

_____?

This is just the beginning. The benefits that gardening can bring are beyond boundaries. Various mental health organizations, over the last few years, _____ of gardening to mental health. Are you convinced, but not sure how to start? Try planting vegetables in an attractive design which _____ _____. Plant seeds for carrots and cucumbers early in the spring. After that, complete your garden with some flowers, like sunflowers, red roses, or tulips. Then add in some strawberry or watermelon seeds. As you water, weed, and loosen the soil in your garden each day, you will come to see its relaxing and stress-relieving benefits.

실전 모의고사 2회

01 다음을 듣고, 남자가 하는 말의 목적으로 가장 적절한 것을 고르시오.

① 독서회 가입을 권유하려고
② 독서의 중요성을 강조하려고
③ 책을 고르는 방법을 소개하려고
④ 새로 출판된 서적을 홍보하려고
⑤ 효과적인 독서법을 안내하려고

02 대화를 듣고, 여자의 의견으로 가장 적절한 것을 고르시오.

① 선물을 살 때는 미리 예산을 정해야 한다.
② 선물을 줄 때는 손 편지를 같이 주는 것이 좋다.
③ 아무리 작은 선물도 받는 사람에게는 행복을 준다.
④ 기프트 카드를 선물로 주는 것은 성의 없어 보일 수 있다.
⑤ 기프트 카드를 선물하는 것이 받는 사람에게 더 유용하다.

03 대화를 듣고, 두 사람의 관계를 가장 잘 나타낸 것을 고르시오.

① 의사 — 환자   ② 정치인 — 기자
③ 영화감독 — 배우   ④ 면접관 — 지원자
⑤ 프로듀서 — 쇼 진행자

04 대화를 듣고, 그림에서 대화의 내용과 일치하지 <u>않는</u> 것을 고르시오.

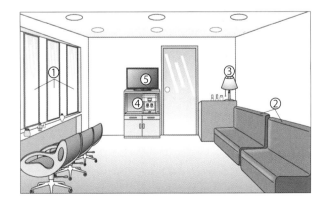

05 대화를 듣고, 남자가 여자에게 부탁한 일로 가장 적절한 것을 고르시오.

① to buy some salt
② to give her mother a call
③ to help him with cooking
④ to find some cold medicine
⑤ to take the food to her mother

06 대화를 듣고, 여자가 지불할 금액을 고르시오. [3점]

① $35   ② $38   ③ $48
④ $75   ⑤ $78

07 대화를 듣고, 남자가 독서 클럽 모임에 갈 수 <u>없는</u> 이유를 고르시오.

① 몸이 피곤해서
② 동생을 돌봐야 해서
③ 집안일을 도와야 해서
④ 책을 읽어두지 않아서
⑤ 시험공부를 해야 해서

08 대화를 듣고, 회사 야유회에 관해 언급되지 <u>않은</u> 것을 고르시오.

① 가족 동반 가능 여부   ② 날짜
③ 참가 비용   ④ 식사 제공 여부
⑤ 모이는 장소

09 Outstanding Achievement Scholarship에 관한 다음 내용을 듣고, 일치하지 <u>않는</u> 것을 고르시오.

① 장학금으로 만 달러가 수여된다.
② 지원자는 교육 관련 분야를 전공해야 한다.
③ 지원서 마감일은 2월 16이다.
④ 추천서 제출은 선택 사항이다.
⑤ 결과는 5월에 발표된다.

10 다음 표를 보면서 대화를 듣고, 두 사람이 선택할 캠프를 고르시오.

Summer Camps

	Camp	Dates	Hiking	Water Activities	Fee
①	Green Camp	July 4 - 15	×	○	$300
②	Bubbles and Fun	July 11 - 22	○	○	$500
③	Mountain Meadow	July 18 - 29	○	×	$300
④	Forest Camp	August 1 - 12	○	×	$400
⑤	Super Camp	August 14 - 25	×	○	$380

11 대화를 듣고, 남자의 마지막 말에 대한 여자의 응답으로 가장 적절한 것을 고르시오.

① No, I even forgot to bring it.
② Yes, I have a pretty bad sunburn.
③ Maybe we should go back inside.
④ No, you don't need to do that for me.
⑤ Yes, I don't feel like sitting in the sand.

12 대화를 듣고, 여자의 마지막 말에 대한 남자의 응답으로 가장 적절한 것을 고르시오.

① I just did, but the line was busy.
② Oh, okay. I'll hang up and call again.
③ I'm sorry to bother you again with this.
④ I'm sure you've got the wrong number.
⑤ Let me think about it and call you back.

13 대화를 듣고, 남자의 마지막 말에 대한 여자의 응답으로 가장 적절한 것을 고르시오. [3점]

Woman: _____

① The water quality is fine in this area.
② I don't think it's my fault that all the fish died.
③ That's why I insisted we feed the fish more often.
④ I guess we'll find out what the cause was soon enough.
⑤ You can't find information like that anywhere on the web.

14 대화를 듣고, 여자의 마지막 말에 대한 남자의 응답으로 가장 적절한 것을 고르시오.

Man: _____

① I'm not sure whether I chose the right job.
② You can do it. Good luck with your new life.
③ I think I'll apply to be an exchange student as well.
④ I'll lend you my book. You can find some ideas in it.
⑤ I recommend that you book early to avoid disappointment.

15 다음 상황 설명을 듣고, Jacob이 David에게 할 말로 가장 적절한 것을 고르시오.

Jacob: _____

① Did you have your computer fixed?
② Can you send your copy of the data to me?
③ The report is gone and we have to start over.
④ I don't think we can finish the report on time.
⑤ I'm sorry. I shouldn't have turned the computer off.

[16-17] 다음을 듣고, 물음에 답하시오.

16 여자가 하는 말의 주제로 가장 적절한 것은? [3점]

① pros and cons of independent living communities
② importance of fitness for seniors living independently
③ how seniors can live a healthy life with their children
④ problems of growing number of seniors living alone
⑤ why seniors should move to independent living communities

17 노인들의 건강한 삶을 위한 활동으로 언급되지 <u>않은</u> 것은?

① 일찍 일어나기   ② 여유롭게 산책하기
③ 균형 잡힌 식사하기   ④ 다양한 사교 활동하기
⑤ 스트레스 피하기

✳ 녹음 내용을 다시 들으면서 빈칸을 채우시오.

01

M How many times has this happened to you? You plan a trip to the library or bookstore, but once there, you _____. You know you can't read every book that comes out. So, how can we choose one? Let me suggest _____. First, look at what your friends are reading. Ask them for recommendations. Next, join a book club. Book clubs usually _____ _____ to discuss books. Each week, they choose a new book and discuss the previous book. Third, find bestseller lists. Many online bookstores have _____ _____. Finally, when you find a book online, you _____ for other books you might like.

02

M Okay, the last thing to buy is a gift for your mother.

W I've already decided to _____.

M But a gift card doesn't show that we care.

W With a gift card, she can choose anything she wants. What could be better than that?

M Choosing a gift shows _____ _____ about her.

W I do care. I just don't want to _____ _____ that she might not like.

M You shouldn't focus on money. The important thing is your mother's happiness.

W I agree. That's why I _____ _____.

M Alright, but let's at least attach a personal message.

03

W This week Anderson Smith _____ _____. Remember, your job is to ask the hard questions _____ _____.

M Don't worry. I've prepared a list of difficult questions.

W Which topics will you discuss?

M Mainly, the future of his company, but also his involvement in politics.

W I don't know _____ about that, but you should give it a try.

M Of course.

W And next week _____ Dr. Romney.

M Isn't he the doctor who found a new cure for heart disease?

W Yes. It will be his first TV interview, so _____ _____.

M I always am.

04

M Madison, congratulations on the opening of your hair salon.

W Thank you! So, what do you think?

M It looks great! The interior design is very cozy.

W Due to the small space, I was only able to _____ _____.

M I also like these two long sofas _____ _____.

W So do I! My parents bought them for me as a gift.

M Cool! Oh, there's a counter by the door.

W Yes, I put a plant on it. It _____.

M It looks great there! Is that a cabinet you made on the left side of the door?

W Yes, I made it so I could put a water purifier there. I _____ because I had to place the TV on it.

M Well done! It's very compact and well-designed.

05

W Dad, I'm home!

M Hi, Emma. Did you talk to your mother today?

W No, not yet. Is everything okay?

M I talked to her on the phone a couple of hours ago, and _____.

W What's wrong with her?

M It sounds like she has the flu, and _____ _____. So, I made some chicken noodle soup.

W That's so sweet of you. I _____ _____ after I change clothes.

M Oh, thanks, but I'll do that. _____ _____ instead? I need more salt, but we're almost out of it.

W Sure. Can I have some money?

M Here's a five-dollar bill. You can keep the change.

06

W Hello, I want to send these presents to Australia in time for Christmas.

M It's $_____ per kilogram for ordinary airmail service. It _____.

W Oh, no. Christmas is only four days away. _____ _____?

M There is a faster service. Express Post takes a maximum of three days, guaranteed.

W Great. How much does that cost?

M It's a bit expensive: $_____ per kilogram. And you'll need a size 3 box, _____ _____.

W I see, and my parcel weighs _____ kilograms. That's going to be really expensive!

M I'm afraid there's no other way to get the presents to Australia by Christmas Day.

W Okay. _____ Express Post. Here's my credit card.

07

M Hi, Lucy. Can you talk?

W Sure. Are you all right? You don't look good.

M I'm just tired. I had a math test this morning, so I studied late last night.

W You must be tired. Did you read the book for our book club meeting?

M Of course. But it looks like _____ _____ today.

W What's wrong? Do you have more exams to prepare for?

M No, I don't. My mom just called and _____ _____ today.

W Why? Do you need to help her with housework?

M No, actually my little sister has a bad cold, but my mom _____.

W Oh, you have to take care of her, then.

M Yeah. I won't miss the meeting next time.

W I understand. I hope _____.

08

M Hi, Rachel, are you coming to the annual company trip?

W Hi, Kyle. Yes, I heard we will be hiking up Mt. Cornwall this year.

M Oh, is your family coming? You know, family _____.

W Sure, my husband and son will be there. It's _____, May 18th, right?

M Yes. Do we need to prepare anything?

W I don't think so. They will provide water, snacks, and lunch.

M Excellent. Are you taking the shuttle bus from the office?

W _____ with my family. I'll meet you there.

M Okay, _____ at 9 a.m. Make sure to be there on time.

W I will.

09

W Good afternoon, students. This is professor Angela Hawkins. Today, I'm glad to introduce the Outstanding Achievement Scholarship to you. This is a scholarship given to students who work to improve the lives of children. Those _____ will get $10,000 to be used for tuition and school expenses. _____ in the field of education and maintain excellent grades. All students applying for this scholarship _____ by February 16th. Applicants must write an essay of around 5 pages, detailing their work with children. A letter of recommendation should also be included in the application. Results _____ _____. Good luck!

10

W Honey, the kids have been begging to go to summer camp this year. I think we should send them.

M I agree. Let's look at some of the options.

W Firstly, _____ August 5th to 10th because of our family vacation.

M Oh, that's right. Hmm.... This one looks nice. They offer hiking.

W Well, the kids _____ _____.

M Right. Then, what about this one? They offer both.

W It's also the most expensive. We _____ _____ over $350.

M Then, I guess we're left with this camp.

W Yeah, let's sign up for this one.

11

M Look at the sandy beach! It's so beautiful.

W Yeah, but the sun is so strong that _____ _____.

M Don't worry. You _____, didn't you?

12

W Hello? Adam?

M Hi, Debbie! _____ all morning.

W Hello? Adam? Can you hear me? Hello? I _____ _____. I think the connection is very bad.

13

M I can't believe all of our fish died. Our business is really in trouble now.

W Do you think it could have been the food we gave them? Or maybe it was _____ _____.

M It's hard to know at this point. It _____ _____.

W Maybe it was the water quality?

M What do you mean?

W Well, _____ can affect the fish.

M I don't know, but I've called an expert. He will come and _____. Hopefully we can fix this situation soon.

W When is he coming?

M He'll be here in an hour.

14

M What have you been up to, Tammy?

W Oh, the same old stuff. What about you, Simon?

M I'm planning _____ as an exchange student in Germany.

W Really? How did you decide to do that?

M I read a book, _____ a newly found appreciation for different cultures, people, and places.

W Can you speak German?

M A little, but I'm studying it so hard now.

W Wow... _____. I don't know if I could do it.

M I know it's going to be hard, but I think it will be a great opportunity for me.

W What's your secret? I want to be _____ _____.

15

M Jacob is in the lab finishing a report that he and his partner, David, worked very hard to complete. Suddenly _____. When Jacob turns it on again, he finds that most of the report, _____, is gone. He wouldn't finish it on time if he _____. He is worried, but then remembers that David has a copy of the data on his computer. So, Jacob wants to ask David _____. Jacob calls David and he answers on the phone. In this situation, what would Jacob most likely say to David?

16-17

W Today I'd like to introduce a solution for seniors who would like to live independently. Many seniors _____ when they need assistance in their daily lives. If you are in this position, I have some good news for you. Simply by moving to an independent living community, you can receive the care that you need. At an independent living community, there are _____ for you to enjoy. There are walking paths, biking areas, miniature golf courses, swimming pools, and much more. Plus, independent living communities _____ for seniors. You can remain in good health _____. Wake up early, take long lazy walks, eat a balanced diet, and avoid stress. These things will help you live a healthy life. If you are _____ _____ in your home, consider moving to one of the many independent living communities near you.

실전 모의고사 3회

01 다음을 듣고, 여자가 하는 말의 목적으로 가장 적절한 것을 고르시오.

① 게임 참가자들을 소개하려고
② 대회의 우승자를 발표하려고
③ 학생들에게 식사 예절을 가르치려고
④ 참가자들에게 게임 방법을 설명하려고
⑤ 게임에 참가할 지원자들을 모집하려고

02 대화를 듣고, 남자의 의견으로 가장 적절한 것을 고르시오.

① 최신 컴퓨터일수록 제조 공정이 복잡하다.
② 환경을 위해 컴퓨터 부품을 재활용해야 한다.
③ 재활용 전자제품 사용에는 많은 이점이 있다.
④ 컴퓨터 제조사는 폐기물 처리 규칙을 지켜야 한다.
⑤ 소비자는 환경을 위해 친환경 제품을 구매해야 한다.

03 대화를 듣고, 두 사람의 관계를 가장 잘 나타낸 것을 고르시오.

① 선수 ─ 심판
② 택시 운전사 ─ 승객
③ 보행자 ─ 경찰관
④ 운전자 ─ 정비공
⑤ 보험 청구인 ─ 보험사 직원

04 대화를 듣고, 그림에서 대화의 내용과 일치하지 않는 것을 고르시오.

05 대화를 듣고, 여자가 할 일로 가장 적절한 것을 고르시오.

① 의상 수선하기
② 야구 코치와 이야기하기
③ 대사 외우기
④ 야구 훈련하기
⑤ 최종 리허설 준비하기

06 대화를 듣고, 남자가 지불할 금액을 고르시오. [3점]

① $19
② $27
③ $33
④ $34
⑤ $41

07 대화를 듣고, 여자가 남자를 마중하러 갈 수 없는 이유를 고르시오.

① 차가 정비 중이어서
② 진료 예약이 있어서
③ 아이가 사고를 당해서
④ 식사 준비를 해야 해서
⑤ 학부모 면담에 가야 해서

08 대화를 듣고, Greater Flamingo에 관해 언급되지 않은 것을 고르시오.

① 서식지
② 평균 수명
③ 알의 부화 기간
④ 키
⑤ 주식

09 Coconut milk에 관한 다음 내용을 듣고, 일치하지 않는 것을 고르시오.

① 기름 함유량이 많다.
② 신선할수록 독특한 향이 강하다.
③ 열대 지방 요리에 흔히 쓰인다.
④ 센 불로 가열하면 크림 성분이 기름과 분리된다.
⑤ 달콤하게 만들어 음료로 마시기도 한다.

10 다음 표를 보면서 대화를 듣고, 두 사람이 선택할 음악 밴드를 고르시오.

Music Bands

	Genre	Price (for 3 hours)		Singer
		Weekday	Weekend	
①	Rock	$600	$720	×
②	Jazz	$800	$900	×
③	Blues	$900	$1,050	×
④	Jazz	$950	$1,200	○
⑤	Blues	$650	$750	○

11 대화를 듣고, 남자의 마지막 말에 대한 여자의 응답으로 가장 적절한 것을 고르시오.

① I knew that I failed the exam.
② I'm afraid it won't be like the last time.
③ I was relieved that the exam was cancelled.
④ Right, you shouldn't worry about the marks.
⑤ I'm looking forward to seeing the exam results.

12 대화를 듣고, 여자의 마지막 말에 대한 남자의 응답으로 가장 적절한 것을 고르시오.

① It's her last day of work.
② It was decided last month.
③ Because of the farewell party.
④ I want to take a trip to Canada.
⑤ She's going to live with her parents.

13 대화를 듣고, 남자의 마지막 말에 대한 여자의 응답으로 가장 적절한 것을 고르시오. [3점]

Woman: _____

① I really enjoy living by myself.
② I should have stayed with the Smiths.
③ But Serena has been cleaner recently.
④ I want to thank you for letting me move out.
⑤ I'm so happy the Smiths will be my homestay family.

14 대화를 듣고, 여자의 마지막 말에 대한 남자의 응답으로 가장 적절한 것을 고르시오.

Man: _____

① I've thought about it too much already.
② Oh, no. I wish it hadn't been decided yet.
③ Well, then I'll put some more thought into it.
④ Yeah, I completely agree with your suggestion.
⑤ Sure, I'd love to sing a song like other classes.

15 다음 상황 설명을 듣고, Tim이 부모님에게 할 말로 가장 적절한 것을 고르시오.

Tim: Mom, Dad, _____

① let me pay for that.
② I appreciate all your support.
③ this graduation party is great.
④ I'm so grateful that I could help you.
⑤ you've really fixed up the store nicely.

[16-17] 다음을 듣고, 물음에 답하시오.

16 남자가 하는 말의 주제로 가장 적절한 것은? [3점]

① how to use art for therapy
② positive effects of art on health
③ reasons why humans create art
④ different types of art classes for patients
⑤ relationships between paintings and music

17 언급된 예술 분야가 <u>아닌</u> 것은?

① ballet   ② poem
③ opera   ④ sculpture
⑤ photography

✳ 녹음 내용을 다시 들으면서 빈칸을 채우시오.

01

W Hello, students. This is Kayla Wood, your P.E. teacher. Now, we're ready for the final game. After this game the points will be totaled and the winner announced. So, let me tell you _____ _____. All the members of your team put straws in their mouths. And the boy at the end of the line puts one of these snacks called an onion ring on his straw. The onion ring _____ from straw to straw down the line. When the boy at the other end of the line has the onion ring on his straw, his team _____. If the team gets it right, it gets one point. _____ _____ your team is out. Now, are you ready to start?

02

W It seems that no one can live without computers these days.

M Very true. Unfortunately, we have _____ _____.

W What do you mean?

M Because so many people want the latest computers, _____ _____ every day.

W That's a problem.

M About 12 million computers _____ _____ every year in America.

W There must be something we can do.

M I think the manufacturers need to rethink the way they build computers.

W In what way?

M They _____ all the computer parts.

W Oh, right. Isn't that called electronic recycling? I read about it somewhere.

M Yes, by recycling the parts, we _____ _____ in a big way.

W I agree.

03

W The accident wasn't my fault. The light was green.

M Uh-huh.

W The guy in the other car _____ _____ when he shouldn't have.

M That's too bad. But your car _____ _____.

W And his car _____. So he suggested we avoid the insurance company.

M So you're not making an insurance claim?

W No. We didn't call the police either. I just want you to tell me _____ to fix my front bumper.

M OK. Well, after I repair it, I will have to _____ _____.

W I know that. But the other driver will be paying for it. So just tell me the cost.

M Just a minute.

04

W Hello?

M Hi, Jenny. It's me. I just called to see how setting up the stage is going.

W It's almost done. First of all, I hung the curtains _____ for the window.

M Great. Did you find _____ _____?

W Yes, and I put a portrait of a woman in it.

M What about the coffee table?

W I placed _____ as you said.

M Good. And did you find that two-armed candlestick I was talking about?

W Yes, I put it on the table. It _____ the three-armed one. And I _____ of the stage.

M Then it sounds like everything's ready!

05

W Brad, how did you feel about the rehearsal today?

M Um, pretty good. And _____ _____ with my character.

W Yeah, it looked nice. How about the lines?

M Well, I _____.

W I know Shakespeare is difficult, but you are Hamlet and you must memorize all your lines.

M I know.

W Final rehearsal is Friday night. Until then you are _____ your lines.

M But what about my baseball practice? Our coach _____ if I don't go.

W I'll talk to him. Don't worry.

M Okay, then I'll do it.

06

W Good Morning. How can I help you?

M Hello. I'm looking for some shampoo for dry hair.

W How about this? It coats your hair, _____ _____.

M Sounds good. How much is it?

W It's $_____.

M That's very expensive. How is this _____ -dollar shampoo?

W That's good, too. But if you color your hair, I recommend the other shampoo.

M I don't dye my hair, so _____ _____. What conditioners do you have?

W I have a nice conditioner for $_____ and a deep hydrating hair mask for $_____.

M I'll take both of them. My hair tends to be very dry.

W If you use the hair mask, you won't need the conditioner. Would you _____?

M Oh, really? Then I'll just take the hair mask. Here's my credit card.

07

W Oh, honey. I was waiting for your phone call. How was your business trip?

M It was a success. _____.

W That's great. When are you coming home?

M I'll be home tomorrow. Do you think you can pick me up at 3 p.m. at the airport?

W 3 p.m.? I'm afraid I can't.

M Oh, is that because _____ _____ tomorrow?

W No, that's next week. Actually, I have a parent-teacher meeting with Lily's teacher at that time.

M Did something happen to Lily?

W No, everything is fine. But I'm afraid _____ _____.

M That's okay. I'll just take a taxi home.

W I'm sorry. I'll make _____ _____ tomorrow.

M That'd be great. See you at home.

08

W Welcome to the San Diego Zoo. I'm your guide, Mary.

M Mary, is that a flamingo on the pond?

W Yes. Technically, it is a Greater Flamingo. _____ Africa, Asia, and Europe.

M I heard they live for twenty years on average.

W That's true. And they _____ when cared for by humans.

M Oh, I see. _____?

W They lay only one egg at a time, and the eggs _____.

M I didn't know that. So that one is an adult?

W Yes, it's about 120 centimeters tall, which is _____.

M It sure is beautiful.

09

M Coconut milk is a liquid that comes from coconut fruit. As the name suggests, it is white and has the rich taste of milk. The color and taste are _____ it contains. Coconut milk has a very unique smell, but when it's fresh, the smell is not strong. It is _____, such as the curries of Southeast Asia. To make these curry sauces, the milk is first cooked over high heat _____. In southern China, sweetened coconut milk _____ as a drink. In all cases, unused coconut milk is usually stored frozen, as this _____.

10

M Planning this event has been really difficult!

W Yes, but now we only need to make a final choice about the band.

M Right. I like rock, but I'm not sure _____.

W I agree. Jazz or blues would be better. What do you think?

M You're right. We also have to consider that _____.

W Okay, and we obviously need them for 3 hours on Saturday night.

M Do you think it would be better to have a singer?

W I think _____ would be nice, since we only need background music during the event.

M I agree. And, if we really need a singer, _____, right?

W You must be kidding! Okay, then I guess we've decided.

11

M Kate, did you hear that the exam results came out already?

W Really? Oh, _____ about mine.

M I don't think you need to worry. You _____ in the last exam.

12

W Jim, _____ today?

M I'm going to Jenny's farewell party. She's moving to Canada.

W Oh, really? _____ to Canada?

13

M Hyunjeong, I'm really sorry you're not happy with your roommate. But I can't do much about the problem now.

W But Serena is too dirty. She doesn't wash her dishes and _____.

M I talked to her and she promised _____.

W She hasn't changed.

M I'll talk to her again.

W Can I _____ the Smiths, the homestay family I had when I first came to America?

M No, someone else is staying with them now.

W That's too bad. _____ a new roommate?

M I don't have _____ for another 4 months.

14

W Jinho, have you thought about _____ _____ for the school festival?

M Let's do a play.

W I'd rather do a dance. Many classes are doing special dances.

M I know everyone loves to dance. But not me!

W Well, how about _____?

M No, I don't like that either. I _____ _____. But I do like to act. I want to do a short play.

W About what? What's the title?

M Hmm... I don't know.

W Well, you have to _____ _____ to the class. Subin has suggested doing a Nanta-style drumming show.

M Really?

W And Sue has suggested _____ _____.

15

W Tim graduated from law school and got a job in New York City. He is successful, but so busy that _____ very often. This Sunday, however, he is free. So he drives his new car to his hometown. He parks and walks into the small convenience store _____ _____. When he was a child, the store seemed special. Now he realizes it's tiny and simple. He watches his parents for a minute. They

_____. He feels more grateful than ever for their efforts to help him graduate. Thus, Tim would like to tell them _____. In this situation, what would Tim most likely say to his parents?

16-17

M Hello, everyone. Today, I want to talk about art. "Wait a minute," you might say, "this is a broadcast about health. What does that _____ _____?" Let me explain. The fact is that art is closely connected to staying healthy. Do you know that just by listening to Mozart for 10 minutes, you can improve your health? It can _____.

You can gain the same benefits by watching ballet. Additionally, art simply makes you feel better. Reading a poem or classic novel takes you to another world. Those activities _____ _____ during periods of stress. Furthermore, art helps your mind to be active. Exploring an art gallery with paintings and sculptures _____ _____, which help to keep your brain healthy. Lastly, studies have also shown that art can help sick people get well. That's why some doctors advise their patients to draw or paint. So find your joy through the arts. Join dance lessons or sign up for a photography course; let your mind wander into the creative space.

실전 모의고사 4회

01 다음을 듣고, 남자가 하는 말의 목적으로 가장 적절한 것을 고르시오.

① 세금 신고 방법을 알려주려고
② 세금 상담 프로그램을 홍보하려고
③ 퀴즈 프로그램 참가를 권유하려고
④ 체납된 세금의 납부를 독촉하려고
⑤ 세금에 관한 전화 상담을 신청하려고

02 대화를 듣고, 여자의 의견으로 가장 적절한 것을 고르시오.

① 학생은 과도한 화장을 삼가야 한다.
② 상황에 맞는 옷차림을 하는 것이 중요하다.
③ 겉모습으로 사람을 판단하는 것은 부당하다.
④ 해외 생활 경험은 견문을 넓히는 데 도움이 된다.
⑤ 어린 시절의 경험이 개인의 취향에 큰 영향을 미친다.

03 대화를 듣고, 두 사람의 관계를 가장 잘 나타낸 것을 고르시오.

① 댄서 — 가수　　　　② 사진작가 — 모델
③ 환자 — 의사　　　　④ 고객 — 구두 수선공
⑤ 수강생 — 댄스 강사

04 대화를 듣고, 그림에서 대화의 내용과 일치하지 않는 것을 고르시오.

05 대화를 듣고, 남자가 여자에게 부탁한 일로 가장 적절한 것을 고르시오.

① to phone his teacher
② to call Bob right away
③ to bring him his homework
④ to give his homework to Bob
⑤ to put his notebook on his desk

06 대화를 듣고, 여자가 지불할 금액을 고르시오. [3점]

① $95　　　　② $100　　　　③ $162
④ $171　　　　⑤ $180

07 대화를 듣고, 남자가 여행 기간을 연장하려는 이유를 고르시오.

① 여행 경비가 남아서
② 요리 강좌를 듣고 싶어서
③ 비행기 예약이 잘못되어서
④ 다른 도시를 방문하고 싶어서
⑤ 둘러보지 못한 관광지가 있어서

08 대화를 듣고, National Student Leadership Conference 에 관해 언급되지 않은 것을 고르시오.

① 개최 장소　　② 개최 기간　　③ 선발 기준
④ 지원 자격　　⑤ 모집 인원

09 The Beethoven Summer Music Camp에 관한 다음 내용을 듣고, 일치하지 않는 것을 고르시오.

① 7세에서 15세까지의 아이들을 대상으로 한다.
② 교사 한 명이 아이들 10명까지 지도한다.
③ 성악과 현악기 및 피아노를 배울 수 있다.
④ 오전반과 오후반으로 나누어 수업을 한다.
⑤ 일주일 수업료가 400달러이다.

10 다음 표를 보면서 대화를 듣고, 남자가 예약할 박물관을 고르시오.

Museum Group Tours in Arbor County

	Museum	Day	Maximum Participants	Recommended Age (yrs.)	Group Discount
①	War Museum	Thurs.	20	8 - 12	20%
②	Toy Museum	Wed.	20	5 - 9	10%
③	Science Museum	Fri.	15	6 - 12	5%
④	Museum of Natural History	Wed.	17	10 - 18	none
⑤	Auto Museum	Tues. & Fri.	10	over 16	none

11 대화를 듣고, 여자의 마지막 말에 대한 남자의 응답으로 가장 적절한 것을 고르시오.

① I'll let her know soon.
② Oh, her wedding was amazing.
③ Adele is going to be a beautiful bride.
④ Really? I'll send it to your phone, then.
⑤ I have the date written down somewhere.

12 대화를 듣고, 남자의 마지막 말에 대한 여자의 응답으로 가장 적절한 것을 고르시오.

① I want to try the new Chinese restaurant.
② It's three blocks away from my house.
③ Next time, I'll have lunch with you.
④ I've had too much pizza recently.
⑤ Let's meet at two o'clock.

13 대화를 듣고, 여자의 마지막 말에 대한 남자의 응답으로 가장 적절한 것을 고르시오.

Man: _____

① May I speak to your supervisor?
② That sounds expensive for a chip.
③ I'll bring it in right away, thank you.
④ Where can I buy a disposable camera?
⑤ The repair shop is just around the corner.

14 대화를 듣고, 남자의 마지막 말에 대한 여자의 응답으로 가장 적절한 것을 고르시오. [3점]

Woman: _____

① You can have the clothes machine washed.
② Read the instruction tag first before laundering.
③ You should put your laundry in the laundry bag.
④ All right. I'll keep that in mind when I buy clothes.
⑤ That's right. We'd better buy a new washing machine.

15 다음 상황 설명을 듣고, Emily가 호텔 직원에게 할 말로 가장 적절한 것을 고르시오. [3점]

Emily: _____

① Please get me a taxi while I get ready.
② Can I rent a laptop for my presentation?
③ I received scrambled eggs instead of the omelet.
④ I'd like to cancel the breakfast order I made earlier.
⑤ Could you tell me the fastest way to my destination?

[16-17] 다음을 듣고, 물음에 답하시오.

16 여자가 하는 말의 주제로 가장 적절한 것은?

① necessity of recycling old stuff
② how to keep a house organized
③ pros and cons of well-kept houses
④ ways of preventing unplanned spending
⑤ things to consider when buying a household goods

17 언급된 물품이 아닌 것은?

① T-shirt　　　② vase　　　③ coffee table
④ chair　　　⑤ watch

※ 녹음 내용을 다시 들으면서 빈칸을 채우시오.

01

M You're listening to KLOS radio, and we have a special announcement. It's the time of year _____. If you're afraid of having to pay more tax, worry no more. That's because _____ _____ with Mr. Stephen Collins, an expert tax lawyer at Barnes Law Firm. He'll be at our studio for any questions from 2 p.m. to 4 p.m. tomorrow. He'll also give you useful tips to help you file your own taxes and _____ _____. So if there's anything you'd like to know about taxes, _____ _____. We're sure you'll greatly benefit from this consultation, so join us tomorrow. Our toll-free number is 1-800-552-8255.

02

M Hey, Catherine. Where have you been?

W I was in the cafeteria talking to Karen. She has great stories from when she lived in Germany.

M Karen? You mean that new girl? Well, _____ _____.

W What do you mean? She's really nice.

M She always _____ and she wears so much make-up.

W But, _____, isn't it?

M Hmm... I suppose you're right. On second thought, I _____ because people thought I looked unkind.

W Yeah, it was hard to start talking to you at first. I think we _____ their clothing or appearance.

M Right. I kind of regret what I said now.

W Don't worry about it. Come with me and I'll introduce you to her.

03

W Carlos? Do you mind if we stop for a little while? I just _____.

M Sure. Your rhythm and timing weren't so good in the partner waltz today. What's the matter?

W Actually, _____. They've given me blisters.

M I'll get some Band-Aids for you. Do you have another pair of shoes?

W Only the sandals I had on when I came to the studio.

M They'll be fine today.

W OK. I'll go and get them.

M I'm going to show you some basic salsa and mambo steps next. Don't worry. I _____ _____.

W I don't mind. I love the Latin style. If I change my shoes, _____.

04

M Ann, I finished designing the poster for this year's summer camp. What do you think?

W It looks great. You _____ _____, Elm High School Summer Camp.

M Yes. I want them to stand out.

W They really do. I can see two native American tents on the left. I love them.

M I'm glad you like them.

W I also like _____. Sitting around a campfire is an enjoyable part of the camping experience.

M Absolutely! And I put a camping car on the right side.

W Well, since it's a school camp, how about _____ _____?

M You're right. I'll make the change right away. What do you think about _____ _____?

W It goes well with everything else. Good job!

05

W Hello?

M Hi, Mom. It's Jerry.

W Hi. Are you OK? Is something wrong?

M I left my homework at home.

W Do you _____?

M No, you don't need to.

W Will your teacher _____?

M No. I phoned my friend Bob. He hasn't left for school yet.

W Bob?

M Yes. I _____ our apartment and get it. Can you give him the blue notebook on my desk?

W OK. _____ school?

M He'll be here in time. I came here way too early today.

06

W Do you still have tickets to the Dream Concert?

M We have a couple of seats left in the front section and a few in the back.

W How much are the seats in the front?

M Those are $_____ per seat. They're the best seats we have.

W And the ones in the back?

M Those are $_____ per seat.

W Okay, then I'll buy _____ _____. Also, are you offering student discounts?

M Yes. _____ if you show your student identification.

W Okay, here's my ID and two one-hundred-dollar bills.

M Actually, we only offer the discount to people _____.

W Oh, if I had known that, _____ _____. But I understand.

M Thank you, and here's your change.

07

M Mom! It's me, Jacob.

W Jacob! How is your trip going?

M Rome is just amazing! There's so much to do and see.

W I wish I was there with you. So, you are coming home next Monday, right?

M Well, I was thinking of _____ _____.

W Really? Are you going to visit other cities in Italy?

M No, I'll stay in Rome for the rest of my trip.

W Then, do you _____ in the city?

M No, _____ in Rome. Actually, I signed up for a week-long cooking class here run by an Italian master chef.

W Good idea! Let me know if you need help to change your flight schedule.

M It's okay. I _____.

W Alright. Always be safe and have fun!

08

M Sally, have you heard about the National Student Leadership Conference?

W Yes, I heard it's pretty amazing.

M Then, let's go together this year. _____ _____ Heritage Oak University.

W When's the conference?

M From July 18th to the 23rd.

W I would love to, but isn't it _____ _____?

M Yeah, but you can apply _____ _____ in college, and have a recommendation letter.

W I guess we could try. When are applications due?

M They're due on the 25th of next month. And since today's only the beginning of May, we still have time to get _____.

W Okay, let's go for it.

09

W The Beethoven Summer Music Camp is offering a variety of music programs to keep your kids busy this summer. The camp will provide a wonderful opportunity _____ _____ to receive classical music education. We have some of the best music teachers _____ _____, and each of them will be in charge of up to 10 children. Our camp includes voice, string, and piano lessons. All classes _____ so that students are free to enjoy various recreational activities in the afternoon. You _____ _____ a one-week program to a four-week program. The tuition cost for each week is $400. Space is limited, so please sign up today.

10

M Clara, I have to reserve a museum field trip for our school students. I made a list of museums around here. Could you help me choose?

W Sure. Let me see. Firstly, _____ _____ the trip?

M Anytime Wednesday or Friday is available.

W Okay. How many students _____ _____?

M I'll take 12 students there.

W You have these three options. Oh, there is an age recommendation. How old are your students?

M Most of them are 10 years old, but some are 11 years old.

W Then I guess that leaves these two. Which one would you like?

M Well, I'd go with this one. It _____ _____.

W That's good. Have a nice field trip!

M Thanks for helping me.

11

W Mark, _____ of Kelly's wedding?

M I'm not sure, but Adele definitely knows. Why don't you _____?

W Good idea, but I don't have her number.

12

M Vanessa, do you _____ at Pizza King?

W I'd love to, but I had pizza last night. _____ _____?

M That's fine with me. Where would you like to go?

13

W Thank you for calling Camera World. What can I do for you?

M My digital camera's screen is blinking and the shutter doesn't work.

W Alright. _____ with the main chip.

M What do you mean?

W The chip inside your camera _____ _____.

M Let me see. I _____ without a small screwdriver.

W When you find a tool, call back and ask for extension 51.

M I don't know much about cameras. I don't think _____.

W Well, we have five locations in the city you can visit for a repair.

M _____ to my place? I live on King's Road.

W We have one on Third Street. It probably takes about ten minutes to get there from your place.

14

W Andy, don't put those clothes in the washing machine.

M Why? I think we can wash these clothes in the washing machine.

W No, we can't. These are 100% silk. We _____ _____.

M How much does it cost to dry clean a shirt?

W A shirt costs $10.

M Really? It's very expensive.

W Well, _____ by machine washing them. It's cheaper in the end.

M Why did you buy clothes _____ _____? Think about the money we spend to dry clean them.

W So _____ I put these in the machine?

M No, but you should buy clothes that can be machine washed next time.

15

M Emily is _____ on a business trip. She has an important presentation this afternoon and wants to start the day with a nice breakfast. Emily _____ and orders an omelet and toast. However, soon after she hangs up, Emily _____ _____ telling her that the time of the meeting has been moved forward. She leaves immediately, and takes a taxi to her destination. On the way, Emily suddenly remembers the room service she ordered. So, Emily _____ _____. In this situation, what would Emily most likely say to the hotel staff?

16-17

W Hello, everyone. Do you feel you have too many things in your house? Sometimes, it's a good idea _____. Today, I'd like to share some tips to make your home tidy. Firstly, every month, take a good look at your closet. When did you wear that T-shirt last? If it's been hanging in your closet for over a year _____, it's a sign to let it go. You may think you will wear it someday. I can tell you, you won't. Say goodbye. Keep your closet only 80 percent full, and always put your things back in the same place. Another idea is to think hard before you buy something. Ask yourself, "Do I really need this vase or do I just want it?" Also, think carefully about _____ _____ in your house. For example, suppose you want a coffee table, but you don't have a good place for it. Then you don't need it. Lastly, when you do buy something new, throw out something old. If a chair is too old, buy a new one and throw the old one out. Free yourself from too many things, and _____ _____.

실전 모의고사 5회

01 다음을 듣고, 여자가 하는 말의 목적으로 가장 적절한 것을 고르시오.

① 저축을 장려하려고
② 보험 약관 변경을 알리려고
③ 보험 상품 가입을 권유하려고
④ 자녀의 교육비 지원을 공지하려고
⑤ 올바른 소비 습관에 대해 설명하려고

02 대화를 듣고, 남자의 의견으로 가장 적절한 것을 고르시오.

① 주말은 아이들과 시간을 보내는 것이 좋다.
② 부모는 아이들의 TV 시청을 감독해야 한다.
③ TV 시청보다 신체 활동이 아이 발달에 좋다.
④ 연령별로 아이의 TV 시청 시간을 조절해야 한다.
⑤ 아이가 스스로 TV 시청 규칙을 정하도록 해야 한다.

03 대화를 듣고, 두 사람의 관계를 가장 잘 나타낸 것을 고르시오.

① 의사 — 환자
② 상담사 — 학생
③ 남편 — 아내
④ 면접관 — 지원자
⑤ 교사 — 학부모

04 대화를 듣고, 그림에서 대화의 내용과 일치하지 <u>않는</u> 것을 고르시오.

05 대화를 듣고, 여자가 할 일로 가장 적절한 것을 고르시오.

① 날씨 알아보기
② 렌터카 예약하기
③ 남자와 하이킹 가기
④ 별장 사용 허락받기
⑤ 주말에 친구들 초대하기

06 대화를 듣고, 남자가 지불할 금액을 고르시오. [3점]

① $11
② $14
③ $18
④ $20
⑤ $22

07 대화를 듣고, 여자가 연어를 사지 <u>않은</u> 이유를 고르시오.

① 신선하지 않아서
② 가격이 많이 올라서
③ 남아 있는 것이 없어서
④ 구매할 것을 잊어버려서
⑤ 스테이크가 할인 중이어서

08 대화를 듣고, Baby Love Diapers에 관해 언급되지 <u>않은</u> 것을 고르시오.

① 재질
② 가격
③ 묶음당 수량
④ 발송 예정일
⑤ 사은품

09 Crystal Lake Park에 관한 다음 내용을 듣고, 일치하지 <u>않는</u> 것을 고르시오.

① 평일보다 주말의 보트 대여 운영 시간이 더 길다.
② 쿠폰이 있으면 보트 대여료를 할인받는다.
③ 보트 탑승객 중 적어도 한 명은 20세 이상이어야 한다.
④ 월요일에는 식당 메뉴의 일부 품목이 할인된다.
⑤ 6월 1일부터 10월 말까지 개장한다.

10 다음 표를 보면서 대화를 듣고, 두 사람이 예약할 캠핑장을 고르시오.

Camping Sites

	Camp	Opening Dates	Location	Facilities	Pets
①	A	All year round	near the beach	Free WiFi	×
②	B	May - September	mountain	Free WiFi	○
③	C	All year round	mountain	Hot Shower	○
④	D	March - October	near a lake	Free WiFi	○
⑤	E	All year round	near the beach	Hot Shower	×

11 대화를 듣고, 남자의 마지막 말에 대한 여자의 응답으로 가장 적절한 것을 고르시오.

① Let me call you tomorrow morning.
② We can finish if we work together.
③ We'll meet to work on it tonight.
④ I'll make sure to be on time.
⑤ Our project is almost due.

12 대화를 듣고, 여자의 마지막 말에 대한 남자의 응답으로 가장 적절한 것을 고르시오.

① I did, but I don't really care.
② Yes, there isn't much time left.
③ No, I heard the news yesterday.
④ Monday's test was harder than usual.
⑤ That means I can study over the weekend.

13 대화를 듣고, 남자의 마지막 말에 대한 여자의 응답으로 가장 적절한 것을 고르시오.

Woman: _____

① Sorry, sir. We are out of french fries.
② I'll take your order when you're ready.
③ That's a good suggestion. I'll have that.
④ Sure. We offer a discount on set menus.
⑤ Certainly. I will take care of the problem right away.

14 대화를 듣고, 여자의 마지막 말에 대한 남자의 응답으로 가장 적절한 것을 고르시오.

Man: _____

① As you know, I'm not a persuasive person.
② More people will join us later, so don't worry.
③ I'll tell her that you want to go instead of her.
④ What if I promise to help with her assignment?
⑤ Well, do you think that I should talk to her about our plan?

15 다음 상황 설명을 듣고, Tony가 Calvin에게 할 말로 가장 적절한 것을 고르시오. [3점]

Tony: _____

① When will you buy me a new hat?
② I have a pair of gloves that match it.
③ Don't let your friends borrow your clothes.
④ Can I borrow your leather jacket tomorrow?
⑤ Please don't take my things without asking.

[16-17] 다음을 듣고, 물음에 답하시오.

16 남자가 하는 말의 주제로 가장 적절한 것은? [3점]

① elements of a good coach
② science behind good coaching
③ various roles of sports coaches
④ importance of personal training
⑤ challenges facing modern coaches

17 새로운 훈련 기법을 개발하는 방법으로 언급되지 <u>않은</u> 것은?

① 최신 연구 동향 살피기
② 코칭 강습 참가하기
③ 선수들과 함께 연구하기
④ 다른 코치들에게 조언 구하기
⑤ 대학 수업 듣기

✽ 녹음 내용을 다시 들으면서 빈칸을 채우시오.

01

W If suddenly you could not support your family, would they continue to live comfortably? Would they have the money for food, shelter, clothing, and education? _____ _____, they will be in a big trouble. But most people don't know how much insurance is adequate. That is why Acme Insurance Co. _____ for you. We will analyze your current spending habits and lifestyle, and your family's needs, such as university costs for your children. _____ _____ to discuss your insurance requirements today.

02

M Honey, our kids are watching too much television these days. Some steps must be taken.

W I know. _____, and sometimes watch things that they shouldn't.

M Right. I think parents _____ _____.

W Can you tell me more about it?

M It is about letting kids watch certain programs rather than _____. My friend, Matthew, is a great example of this.

W What does he do?

M Every Sunday, he sits down with the kids and decides _____.

W I see. That's a great idea.

M They can turn on the TV when it's time to watch the program. After the end of the program, the TV is turned off.

W That sounds good. Let's give it a try.

03

M Billy _____ in class.

W I wasn't aware of that. He never said a thing about it.

M That's why I wanted you to come in here. We need to _____ _____.

W Oh my. That would really break Billy's heart.

M It _____ so he can move back into this class.

W Well, if this is what you think is best, I'll tell my husband and we will explain it to our son.

M Thank you. This is really the best thing for him.

W I know it is. I'm just worried about Billy. He is very sensitive.

M I _____ on his progress.

W Thank you.

04

M Hey, Sally. What are you looking at?

W Hi, Harry. It's a photo I took at the picnic I went on with my family.

M You're a good photographer. Oh, I like that checkered-patterned mat.

W Thanks. It was a free gift I got from the ice cream store.

M It seems perfect for a picnic. Oh, there're _____ _____. They are so cute!

W I agree. And do you recognize my sister, Amelia? She _____ playing the guitar.

M Yes, I remember her. By the way, who is the boy wearing a T-shirt _____?

W He is my brother, Daniel.

M And these people playing badminton must be your parents, right?

W Yes, _____.

M I'm sure your family had a wonderful time.

05

M Amy, some of my friends from college are visiting this weekend. Let's hang out together.

W Sounds great! Oh, _____ over the weekend?

M No, I've already checked the weather, and it is going to be sunny.

W Great. So, what shall we do this weekend?

M I know _____.

W That would be nice, but if it's hot, we should go somewhere to cool off.

M Do you have _____?

W How about going to my family's lake house? Then we could go hiking and swimming there!

M That sounds like a great idea. _____ _____ over the weekend.

W Good. I'll find out if it's OK with my parents.

M Let me know. I'll call the guys and tell them about our idea.

06

W What kind of sandwich do you want?

M I think I'll get a ham and cheese sandwich.

W Okay, I think I'll just have a classic one. I only have $_____. A ham and cheese sandwich costs $_____.

M _____ today. We're celebrating!

W Celebrating what? Did you get the promotion?

M Yes, plus I _____ than I expected. Eat and drink whatever you want.

W Wow, that's great! Congratulations! I guess I will have _____. And I'll order an americano. I can pay for that. It's only $_____.

M No way. _____. I'll also have an americano.

W Thanks. You _____.

M My pleasure. Let's order now.

07

M Here, Annie. Let me help you with those shopping bags.

W Thanks.

M I think _____ a baked salmon dish. You bought salmon, didn't you?

W Actually, I didn't get any salmon.

M Was the store _____?

W No, they had some.

M Then, _____?

W No, they looked fresh. But then I saw that _____ _____, so I changed my mind. Maybe we can have salmon another time.

M OK. Then, let's barbecue the steaks in the yard. _____ the grill.

W Thanks. I'll get the salad and potatoes ready.

08

M Plus Home Shopping. How can I help you?

W I'd like to ask you about the diapers _____ _____.

M Okay, you're talking about the Baby Love Diapers, right?

W Yes. Is it silky? My baby has a sensitive skin.

M Certainly. _____ 100% cotton.

W Right. How many diapers are in one pack?

M Hold on, please. There are fifty in a pack.

W If I order now, can I receive them by this week?

M Of course. As soon as you purchase them, we'll send them out _____.

W Okay. Can I pay with my credit card?

M Certainly. And _____,
we'll give you a toddler's toy for free.

W Great. I'd like to order 10 packs.

09

M Hello, visitors! Welcome to Crystal Lake Park in Urbana. Please come and _____ _____ here. We offer boat rentals, such as rowboats and canoes, from Monday to Friday from 1 p.m. to 8 p.m., and Saturday and Sunday from 10 a.m. to 8 p.m. If you have one of our coupons, you _____ _____ on a boat rental. For any boat rental, at least one member of the group _____. You can also relax at our cafe and enjoy your choice of sandwiches, salads, and snacks. We offer a 10% discount on _____.
Our doors will be open from June 1 all throughout summer and into fall until October 31. So please stop by for a tasty sandwich or a lovely boat ride on the lake.

10

M Honey, I want to talk to you about our camping trip this autumn.

W I almost forgot about it. Did you make a reservation?

M Not yet, but I made a list of camping sites. Let's choose one together.

W Good! Oh, we can't choose this one because I have _____.

M Okay. Let's leave this one out.

W Since we usually _____ _____, I want to go camping on the beach or a lake this time.

M I'd also like that.

W _____ with a free WiFi connection. We probably need to get Internet while camping.

M That's right. Now we have only two options left.

W Oh, we forgot the most important thing! We have to bring our dog, Max.

M Right! Let's choose this one.

11

M We need to _____ soon. When do you want to meet?

W I think I'll have some time tomorrow, but I'm not sure when.

M Should I _____ later?

12

W What's wrong, Chris? You look really stressed out.

M I'm worried that I'm going to fail today's test. I _____.

W Didn't you hear the news? The test _____ _____ until Monday.

13

M Excuse me! Can you come here, please?

W What seems to be the problem here, sir? You don't look very happy.

M Well, for starters, my steak _____. And I asked for a baked potato, but you gave me french fries.

W I am sorry, sir. That is _____ _____ at our restaurant.

M But I asked for medium.

W I wrote down your order on my pad here. Let me take a look.

M Yes, please check.

W Yes, sir. I actually wrote down an "M" for medium. I think _____ _____ in the kitchen.

M So, I would like _____. Is that OK?

14

M So how far away is the amusement park we're going to tomorrow?

W It's about two and a half hours away.

M Wow! That's really far. Is it worth visiting?

W Trust me. This new place _____ _____.

M I hope so.

W Anyway, it would be nice _____ _____ of people going tomorrow. Then nobody would have to sit alone on a ride.

M Well, there'll be five including the two of us.

W I wish Cindy could join us. It's too bad she's busy with her assignment.

M You're right. Hmm.... Why don't I _____ _____ with us to the amusement park?

W Really? What will you say _____?

15

W Tony's best friend, Calvin, always borrows his things _____. Sometimes, when Calvin returns what he has borrowed, it is _____. One time, he even lost Tony's favorite baseball cap. Although he said he was sorry for losing the hat, he _____. Now, Calvin is about to leave Tony's house, and he is wearing Tony's new leather jacket. Tony _____ _____. So, Tony decides to tell Calvin that he should ask for his permission before using his stuff. In this situation, what would Tony most likely say to Calvin?

16-17

M Hello, everyone. Today, I want to talk a bit about sports. In my opinion, all sports are good. But the truth is that good coaches are needed to make a sport truly great. Sports and fitness coaching is _____. First of all, coaches must have an understanding of the sport. Coaches must plan for the season, know the rules, and provide _____ _____. While most coaches already know a great deal about a sport, they must also continue to learn and develop new training techniques. For example, staying up-to-date on new research, as well as attending coaching clinics, and _____ from other coaches are all good methods. Also, watching videos and reading books can also be helpful. Finally, attending university classes is a great idea for any coach _____ _____.

01 다음을 듣고, 남자가 하는 말의 목적으로 가장 적절한 것을 고르시오.

① 정기 건강 검진의 중요성을 알리려고
② 약물 과다 복용의 위험성을 경고하려고
③ 콜레스테롤 신약의 부작용을 설명하려고
④ 콜레스테롤을 낮추는 식이요법을 소개하려고
⑤ 콜레스테롤 수치 관리의 중요성을 강조하려고

02 대화를 듣고, 여자의 의견으로 가장 적절한 것을 고르시오.

① 환경 보호를 위한 아이디어를 모아야 한다.
② 안 입는 옷은 정기적으로 정리해 버려야 한다.
③ 환경을 위해 안 입는 옷을 재사용하는 게 좋다.
④ 환경 보존을 위해 오래 입을 옷을 구매해야 한다.
⑤ 안 입는 옷은 기부해서 재활용하는 것이 바람직하다.

03 대화를 듣고, 두 사람의 관계를 가장 잘 나타낸 것을 고르시오.

① 자동차 판매원 — 고객
② 경찰 — 운전자
③ 택시 운전사 — 승객
④ 운전 강사 — 운전 연수생
⑤ 인테리어 디자이너 — 집주인

04 대화를 듣고, 그림에서 대화의 내용과 일치하지 않는 것을 고르시오.

05 대화를 듣고, 남자가 여자에게 부탁한 일로 가장 적절한 것을 고르시오.

① 딸 돌봐주기
② 동물병원에 전화하기
③ 잃어버린 개 찾기
④ 병원에 데려다주기
⑤ 빨래 세탁하기

06 대화를 듣고, 여자가 지불할 금액을 고르시오. [3점]

① $210
② $220
③ $225
④ $230
⑤ $250

07 대화를 듣고, 남자가 소개받은 아파트를 선택하지 않은 이유를 고르시오.

① 부엌이 작아서
② 임대료가 비싸서
③ 방 개수가 적어서
④ 채광이 좋지 않아서
⑤ 동네가 안전하지 않아서

08 The Greatest Cake Master에 관한 다음 내용을 듣고, 언급되지 않은 것을 고르시오.

① 참가자 수
② 경연 시간
③ 경연 방식
④ 우승 혜택
⑤ 첫 회 방영일

09 퀘벡의 Ice Hotel에 관한 다음 내용을 듣고, 일치하지 않는 것을 고르시오.

① 특수 제작된 얼음으로 지어졌다.
② 내부 평균 온도는 섭씨 영하 4도이다.
③ 실내에 온수 욕조가 있다.
④ 얼음 미끄럼틀이 있다.
⑤ 투어가 일주일 내내 있다.

10 다음 표를 보면서 대화를 듣고, 두 사람이 구입할 식물을 고르시오.

Plants

	Plant	Width (cm)	Height (cm)	Sunlight Needed	When to Water
①	Lavender	24	60	Full sunlight	Once a week
②	Scindapsus	30	45	Partial sunlight	Twice a week
③	Lily	14	30	Full sunlight	Every other week
④	Hydrangea	55	80	Partial sunlight	Twice a week
⑤	Succulent	15	20	Partial sunlight	Once a month

11 대화를 듣고, 여자의 마지막 말에 대한 남자의 응답으로 가장 적절한 것을 고르시오.

① They are on a red key chain.
② I'm going to need them tonight.
③ I'm afraid that's my last spare key.
④ Maybe you should check your locker.
⑤ I locked my house this morning with them.

12 대화를 듣고, 남자의 마지막 말에 대한 여자의 응답으로 가장 적절한 것을 고르시오.

① What a shame. I was out of town.
② I think so. I hope you have a great time.
③ Sorry. I think I'd better stay in bed today.
④ Thanks for coming today. Enjoy the party.
⑤ You should have taken some cold medicine.

13 대화를 듣고, 여자의 마지막 말에 대한 남자의 응답으로 가장 적절한 것을 고르시오.

Man: _____

① Not at all. I'm not picky about food.
② Got it. Let me find a good Thai restaurant.
③ I'd appreciate it. Dinner is on me next time.
④ Thank you for inviting me. I'm looking forward to it.
⑤ Okay. Frankly, I didn't feel like having leftovers, either.

14 대화를 듣고, 남자의 마지막 말에 대한 여자의 응답으로 가장 적절한 것을 고르시오.

Woman: _____

① Are you sure? I thought the game was this week.
② You had better make peace with them right away.
③ You're right. I envy you for having such good friends.
④ That's a great idea. Maybe the coach will listen to you.
⑤ Good thinking! I hope you can solve this situation.

15 다음 상황 설명을 듣고, Sally가 종업원에게 할 말로 가장 적절한 것을 고르시오. [3점]

Sally: _____

① How long does it take to cook the pasta?
② Can I get what he's having at the next table?
③ My friend would like to get what I'm getting.
④ Could you tell me the chef's specials for today?
⑤ I've read very good reviews about your restaurant.

[16-17] 다음을 듣고, 물음에 답하시오.

16 여자가 하는 말의 주제로 가장 적절한 것은? [3점]

① teaching teamwork in schools
② the benefits of playing team sports
③ causes of students' improved health
④ the necessity of a balanced education
⑤ importance of Physical Education in school

17 팀 스포츠 활동을 통해 얻을 수 있는 것으로 언급되지 <u>않은</u> 것은?

① confidence　　　② positive attitude
③ teamwork　　　④ school spirit
⑤ friendship

* 녹음 내용을 다시 들으면서 빈칸을 채우시오.

01

M Hello. Welcome back to my channel, *Dr. Harris' office*. Today we are going to talk about _____ _____ named Lenochol. It is designed for people who have high cholesterol. According to its instructions, it helps to reduce cholesterol levels if used daily. However, before you take this prescription medication, there are _____ _____. You may experience unexplained muscle pain or weakness while you're on it, and in that case call your doctor right away. Any allergic reaction to this medication _____. Common side effects include sleepiness, dizziness, and rashes on the skin.

02

W Elliot, what are all these clothes in this box?

M They're old clothes I don't wear anymore, so I want to throw them away.

W Why? Some of them _____.

M They're not good enough to sell or give away. And _____ in a year.

W Why don't you reuse these clothes? We _____ _____.

M Then what can I do with the clothes I don't wear anymore?

W You can make an apron out of your old shirt. Look! I made this bag out of my old jeans.

M It looks great! But I don't think I can do that.

W You can learn _____ _____ online. This is a great way to help the environment.

M Okay. I'll give it a try.

03

M If you go straight and then make a right at the light, we will be back at the lot.

W You mean this light?

M Yes. That's it. And then you can park _____ _____.

W Okay.

M Great. So, what do you think?

W Well, I like _____, and the interior is very nice. I like it a lot, but frankly, I'm not sure _____.

M I'll make sure you get a good deal.

W Even so, _____ a bit more.

M Here's my business card. When you're ready, please give me a call.

W I will. Thanks for all your help today.

04

M Rachel, you don't need me to read the book for you?

W It's okay, Daddy. I already know the story. It's about a small mouse that's looking for a home.

M Hmm.... You're talking about the mouse _____ _____, right?

W Yes, and the mother bird sitting in the nest is asking the mouse if she wants to live there.

M Oh, you really do know the story. How many chicks does the mother bird have?

W Three. They _____ and singing.

M I see. What's this clinging to the left side of the tree?

W That's a squirrel. He _____.

M Oh, you're right. _____ from the hole in the tree?

W It's an owl. He asks the mouse if she wants to live in there.

M You really impress me, Rachel. Shall we turn to the next page?

05

M Laura, it's me, Noah, your next-door neighbor.

W Oh, hi, Noah.

M Sorry to bother you, but are you busy?

W No, not really. I _____. What's up?

M Well, I think my dog, Rocky, is ill.

W What happened to him?

M I think he _____. I need to rush him to the hospital.

W Oh, dear. Do you want a ride to the hospital?

M No, but I was wondering _____ _____ my little daughter, Claire.

W Don't worry. I'll come over right now.

M Thank you so much. I may be late.

W Not a problem. _____?

06

M Good morning. May I help you?

W I noticed the sale sign outside. Is everything really 10% off?

M Yes. We're _____.

W That's great. Do you still have the Norman 8 Coffee Machine?

M Let me check.... No, I'm afraid _____ _____.

W I see. Then how much is this one?

M It's normally $_____, but today you can get a 10% discount on everything here.

W Okay, I'll take it. Do you _____ _____ on espresso capsules?

M Well, normally, a pack of 20 capsules costs $_____. But I can give you an additional 10% discount _____.

W Then I'll _____. Here's my credit card.

07

M Hello, I'm David Nelson. You showed me an apartment yesterday.

W Hello, Mr. Nelson. I was waiting for you to call. Did you _____?

M Well, I loved the apartment, but I decided not to rent it.

W You asked for an apartment with two bedrooms and a large kitchen. Is that correct?

M Yes, the apartment _____.

W Then, you didn't like the neighborhood?

M No, I quite liked the neighborhood. It's quiet and safe.

W Was the rent _____?

M No, I thought $1,200 a month including water and electricity was reasonable.

W Then, what seems to be the problem?

M Actually, the apartment _____ _____.

W Oh, I get that. Shall I arrange some other apartments to show you then?

M Yes, please.

08

W _____ the TV show, The Greatest Cake Master.

M Is it the TV program you mentioned before?

W Yes. 20 cake masters from around the world _____.

M That sounds interesting. How will they choose the winner?

W Well, competitors make a cake according to the theme of the week and judges _____ _____ until there is only one baker remaining.

M I bet the winner will receive a special award.

W Right. The winner _____ The Greatest Cake Master, and receive a grand prize of $50,000.

M Wow, that's huge. I think it is going to be very popular.

W Let's watch the first episode together. It will be on this Thursday at 8 p.m.

09

W Good afternoon, listeners. Why don't you plan a visit to the Ice Hotel in Quebec this winter? It is North America's first ice hotel. The hotel _____ _____ that is specially produced for construction. Temperatures inside the hotel stay around minus 4 degrees Celsius on average, and guests sleep in special sleeping bags on beds made of snow and ice. However, there are heated washrooms and _____ _____ to warm up in. Each year, thousands of families come to tour the hotel, _____ for kids. Tours are available in French or English, seven days a week.

10

M Hazel, could you help me _____ _____ under the window?

W Sure, what are you looking at?

M I have this list of five plants. How about this one?

W The space is only 50 cm wide. It won't fit.

M Then, what about this plant? It's only 24 cm wide.

W Hmm... wait. Isn't it too tall? It _____ _____.

M You're right, then it should be under 50 cm high.

W Yes, and _____. It has to be able to live with less than full sunlight.

M Then that leaves us with these two.

W You know, we _____ the plants. With this one, we don't have to water it every week.

M Okay. Then let's get it.

11

W What's wrong, Jack? Did you lose something?

M Yeah, I lost my keys. _____, but I can't find them.

W I'll help you look. When was the last time _____ _____?

12

M Hi, Karen. It's me. Are you feeling better today?

W Yes, I _____ and I'm feeling much better.

M Oh, then you _____ tonight.

13

W I'm a bit hungry. What should we have for dinner?

M We have a lot of leftovers from the party. Let's eat those.

W _____ the leftovers. We had them for dinner last night and breakfast this morning.

M Well, I can make you pasta if you want.

W Hmm, I _____ now. Do you remember that Thai food we had with Lillian?

M Oh, _____ the shrimp and seafood dish at the Thai Market?

W Yes, it was pretty great. _____ _____ for dinner tonight?

M What about the leftovers?

W We'll have them tomorrow.

14

W Max, have you heard? There was a problem during practice _____.

M What happened?

W George and Travis got into an argument. It was _____.

M I hope _____ soon. There's a soccer game next week.

W Well, I overheard the coach saying that unless George and Travis make up, he won't let them in the game.

M So, they _____ next week? But they're the best players on the team!

W I know, but what can we do?

M I know both of them well, so I'll go and talk to them.

15

M Sally is at a restaurant with her friend Oliver. The two have met _____ that Sally has read about. After looking at the menu, Sally decides on a pasta dish, and _____ _____. The waiter comes to take their order. However, just then she looks over at the next table, and _____ _____. She doesn't know what it is but it looks delicious, and she wants to _____. In this situation, what would Sally most likely say to the waiter?

16-17

W Hello, everyone. I'm Mavis Clark, a P.E. teacher at Arlington High School. People sometimes think that Physical Education, or P.E., costs too much money. So I want to explain to you _____ _____. An education is about creating opportunities to try new things and discover gifts. _____ P.E., many people wouldn't find out that they have a talent for a sport, or even that they enjoy it. Once experienced, sport can be enjoyed for life. For some _____ of a college scholarship or even a career. Furthermore, playing team sports has lots of advantages. It builds positive attitudes and encourages students to use teamwork in order to win. It also builds _____ _____ with other institutions. It is often the experience of playing on a team together that builds the strongest friendships at school. And many of those friendships _____ _____ afterwards.

실전 모의고사 7회

01 다음을 듣고, 여자가 하는 말의 목적으로 가장 적절한 것을 고르시오.

① 다양한 맛의 소스를 소개하려고
② 신제품 판촉 행사를 홍보하려고
③ 오늘의 특선 요리를 공지하려고
④ 이탈리아 요리 수업을 안내하려고
⑤ 전자레인지를 이용한 요리법을 설명하려고

02 대화를 듣고, 남자의 의견으로 가장 적절한 것을 고르시오.

① 규모가 작은 학원이 학습 환경이 좋다.
② 정부는 교육 부문의 지원을 확대해야 한다.
③ 인기 있는 강좌의 수강 인원을 늘려야 한다.
④ 선생님은 학생과 관계를 쌓는 것이 중요하다.
⑤ 여러 사람들과 공부하는 것이 학습 효과가 좋다.

03 대화를 듣고, 두 사람의 관계를 가장 잘 나타낸 것을 고르시오.

① 승객 — 선원
② 손님 — 약사
③ 사장 — 비서
④ 관광객 — 여행 가이드
⑤ 배 주인 — 정비사

04 대화를 듣고, 그림에서 대화의 내용과 일치하지 않는 것을 고르시오.

05 대화를 듣고, 여자가 남자를 위해 할 일로 가장 적절한 것을 고르시오.

① 일자리 소개해주기
② 무료 법률 상담해주기
③ 박물관 위치 알려주기
④ 주문한 커피 가져다주기
⑤ 문자로 연락처 보내주기

06 대화를 듣고, 남자가 지불할 금액을 고르시오. [3점]

① $90
② $115
③ $140
④ $155
⑤ $180

07 대화를 듣고, 여자가 바이올린 강좌를 수강하지 못하는 이유를 고르시오.

① 악기가 없어서
② 거리가 멀어서
③ 수강료가 비싸서
④ 봉사 활동을 가야 해서
⑤ 수강 신청 인원이 다 차서

08 대화를 듣고, Diamond Valley Baseball Team에 관해 언급되지 않은 것을 고르시오.

① 선발 인원
② 지원 자격
③ 선발전 날짜
④ 선발전 장소
⑤ 지원 방법

09 Crestmont's Summer Safety Program에 관한 다음 내용을 듣고, 일치하지 않는 것을 고르시오.

① 이틀간 실시하는 안전 교육이다.
② 12세부터 17세까지의 학생을 대상으로 한다.
③ 참가비는 무료이나 점심은 제공하지 않는다.
④ 강좌의 인원은 최대 30명이고 선착순 마감된다.
⑤ 등록은 소방서에서 하거나 온라인으로 할 수 있다.

10 다음 표를 보면서 대화를 듣고, 두 사람이 선택할 항공편을 고르시오.

Flights to Orlando

	Airline	Departure Time	Arrival Time	Direct Flight	Ticket Price (per person)
①	Horizon	5 A.M.	4 P.M.	×	$450
②	Jet Express	10 A.M.	6 P.M.	×	$500
③	Skyline	11 A.M.	3 P.M.	○	$700
④	Americana	5 P.M.	10 P.M.	○	$650
⑤	Tropicana	6 P.M.	3 A.M.	×	$550

11 대화를 듣고, 여자의 마지막 말에 대한 남자의 응답으로 가장 적절한 것을 고르시오.

① I'm not used to hiking this far.
② It's less than a kilometer to the top.
③ Let's get home as soon as possible.
④ This mountain is the best in summer.
⑤ I'm really looking forward to the peak.

12 대화를 듣고, 남자의 마지막 말에 대한 여자의 응답으로 가장 적절한 것을 고르시오.

① Help yourself! There is much left.
② Take your time. There's no hurry.
③ No, thanks. I can bring it myself.
④ I really appreciate your help.
⑤ Of course. I'd be glad to.

13 대화를 듣고, 여자의 마지막 말에 대한 남자의 응답으로 가장 적절한 것을 고르시오. [3점]

Man: _____

① Then we'll just have to call a mechanic.
② The trunk is locked, and I can't open it.
③ Let me help you take out the suitcases.
④ Thanks. I couldn't have done it without you.
⑤ The instruction manual is under the front seat.

14 대화를 듣고, 남자의 마지막 말에 대한 여자의 응답으로 가장 적절한 것을 고르시오.

Woman: _____

① I can't believe you bought it again!
② You shouldn't work out late at night.
③ Awesome. What a great way to exercise!
④ That's why the newer model is better.
⑤ Well, I don't think you should buy it.

15 다음 상황 설명을 듣고, Ian이 Science Buzz 회원들에게 할 말로 가장 적절한 것을 고르시오. [3점]

Ian: _____

① Why don't we celebrate together?
② I think we have to try another method to win.
③ We're doing such a great job. Let's keep it up!
④ I can't believe we won the competition this year.
⑤ Can we cancel our meeting today and meet tomorrow?

[16-17] 다음을 듣고, 물음에 답하시오.

16 남자가 하는 말의 주제로 가장 적절한 것은?

① architecture inspired by nature
② principles of building with nature
③ ways to make buildings eco-friendly
④ impact of architecture on the environment
⑤ reasons why shapes found in nature are artistic

17 언급된 도시가 <u>아닌</u> 것은?

① Beijing　　　　② Barcelona
③ Taipei　　　　④ Chicago
⑤ Cape Town

✱ 녹음 내용을 다시 들으면서 빈칸을 채우시오.

01

W Shoppers, may I have your attention please? _____ what to have for dinner this evening, how about trying these delicious new microwavable dinners? They ____ _____: Roasted Garlic, Spicy Barbecue, and Creamy Italian. I guarantee that you will love all these flavors, but the best part is _____. Simply unwrap them, microwave them for 5 minutes, and then mix in the special sauce that is included. They _____ $8 each, but today we are giving out coupons for 50% off. If you are interested, please come up and try a free sample.

02

W Andy, are you doing well at your academy?

M Yes, I'm very satisfied with it.

W That's good. You _____ _____ between a larger academy and a smaller one.

M Yes, but now I'm sure that a smaller one _____ _____.

W What do you think is the biggest advantage?

M I think they have a better learning environment.

W What's so good about it?

M Well, in big, highly regarded academies, the class sizes are very large. So the teachers _____ _____ to have a close relationship with their students.

W It does sound better for students who want a relatively close relationship with their teachers to attend smaller academies.

M Sure. And students can study _____ _____.

03

M I noticed that you have a boat ride _____ _____, but I don't think I can go.

W Why not?

M I get really seasick. The last time I was on a boat, I was throwing up the whole time. I don't want to try again.

W _____ for it?

M Yes, but it didn't help.

W That's too bad. The island is _____ _____.

M What can I do instead?

W You can come with us in the morning. There are _____. I'll give you a brochure.

M Thanks. When will the group return?

W We'll be back around noon.

04

W Here we are. This is my house.

M It looks wonderful! There's a swing chair hung on the left side of the porch.

W That's my favorite part of the house. It's nice to sit on it and relax.

M Sounds great! You hung two plant baskets _____ _____.

W Yes. I think they _____ _____.

M Right. Look! There's a mail box by the porch stairs.

W I made it myself. _____, "384 Scott Street," on it.

M Lovely! Oh, I like the bench below the window.

W My husband and I love to sit there and drink tea. That's why we _____ _____.

M It looks romantic!

05

M May I take your order?

W A large coffee, please. Oh, is that you George? It's me, Laurie!

M Laurie? I _____! How have you been?

W Pretty good. I'm working for a law firm now.

M I always knew _____.

W Thanks. So, what are you up to these days?

M I graduated about six months ago, but it's been hard _____. So I'm working here part-time until I can find _____ _____.

W What was your major?

M History.

W Really? I know the manager of a museum downtown. He's planning to recruit more staff. I _____ if you'd like.

M Really? You would do that for me?

W Of course. Just text me your information. Here's my number.

06

W Hello. May I help you?

M Yes, I like this blue sweater very much. Is this _____?

W Yes. The regular price on this sweater is $_____, but...

M Oh, _____, but this black jacket is nice, too.

W It's the most popular one in our store. It's $_____. But all the jackets are _____% off this week.

M Hmm... it's a great deal. I'll get one.

W Okay. And I was going to tell you that if you buy two sweaters of the same type, you'll _____ _____.

M Oh, really? Blue and green are my favorite colors. _____ then.

W All right. Is that all?

M Yes. Here is my credit card.

07

W Hi, John, what are you looking at?

M Hi, Scarlett. It's a catalogue of classes at the community center. _____ a violin class on Saturdays.

W Cool! I took violin lessons when I was little, but now _____.

M Really? Then why don't we take the class together? The tuition fee is only $80 a month.

W Oh, that's a good price, but I can't.

M Why not? Is it because the community center is _____?

W No, it only takes half an hour by bus.

M Then, maybe you don't have a violin to practice with?

W No, actually, I visit an animal shelter every Saturday _____.

M Oh, I see. Well, I'll play the violin for you when I finish the course.

W That sounds nice! I'm already looking forward to it.

08

M Hello, Ms. Green. Did you want to see me?

W Yes, Jonathan. You've heard about Diamond Valley Baseball Team, haven't you?

M Of course I have.

W Apparently, they _____ _____ for the upcoming season. Why don't you apply to the team?

M Oh, I'd love to. But I'm not sure I'm qualified.

W It _____ at least a B average and get permission from your parents.

M That won't be a problem.

W Good. If you qualify, you will have _____ _____ your baseball skills. Trials will be held on May 16th.

M I got it. How can I apply then?

W You need to submit your application to Mr. Thomas' office, _____.

M Okay. Thank you for telling me, Ms. Green.

09

M I'm happy to inform you of Crestmont's Summer Safety Program. _____ for anyone who wants to prepare for possible accidents over the summer. The course will be held from 10 a.m. to 4 p.m. on June 9th and 10th. And _____ between the ages 12 and 17. The course is free of charge and _____. The class will hold up to 30 students, and enrollment will be _____. You can stop by the Crestmont Fire Department to enroll or do it online. Our website address is www.crestmontfire.com.

10

W Honey, _____ our plane tickets to Orlando?

M Yeah, the cheapest one leaves at 5 a.m.

W That's way too early. I think it's better to take the plane which leaves after 9 a.m.

M Okay. Does the hotel's shuttle bus _____ _____?

W No, it operates from 7 a.m. to 11 p.m. So, we need to arrive before 11 p.m.

M Right. And are you okay to take an indirect flight?

W Not really. I _____.

M Then, there are two options left, and both are over $600.

W Oh, _____.

M You know, an indirect flight won't be that bad.

W Alright.... Since we're already spending $650 on the hotel, I guess _____ on the plane tickets.

M Okay, then we're going with that one.

11

W Nick, are you planning to _____ _____?

M Yeah, _____. Do you want to rest?

W Actually, I really do. _____ do we need to go?

12

M _____ an eraser you could lend me?

W Sure, I do. Here it is.

M Thanks a lot. _____.

13

W There's something wrong with our car. I think _____.

M There's an auto mechanic's shop a couple of miles down the road. _____?

W I don't think we can go any farther. Maybe I can fix it by myself.

M Have you changed a tire before?

W _____ a few times. I think I know what to do.

M OK. I'll help you. What do we do first?

W We need to _____.

M Check the trunk. I'll find the instruction manual.

W OK. Oh, I took out the tools to make room for the suitcases.

14

W Can you change the channel, please? My favorite TV show _____.

M Oh, wait. I want to watch this program.

W What is it about?

M They're introducing their brand-new model. It _____.

W Not this again!

M That guy _____ in just 2 weeks by using it.

W Don't you _____?

M Yes, but this is the newest model. If I use this, I'll be able to have stronger muscles.

W You've only used the one you have now a few times!

M I know, but I'm pretty sure I'm going to use this one every day.

15

W Ian is part of a school club called the Science Buzz. It is made up of 15 members _____ and, most importantly, practice for the yearly National Science Competition. The Science Buzz _____ last year. This year, they are aiming to win first place. The members have been practicing daily for the upcoming competition, but Ian feels that _____ _____. He has already thought of a better method that _____. So, he wants to suggest to club members that they use the new method. In this situation, what would Ian most likely say to his club members?

16-17

M Good morning, class! Previously, we learned about eco-friendly architecture around the world. Those structures _____ _____. Today, we are going to learn about architectural masterpieces _____ _____. First, the national stadium in Beijing, which hosted numerous sports events during the Beijing Olympics in 2008, _____. Next, a cathedral in Barcelona, La Sagrada Familia, was designed to look like a forest. Also, Taipei 101, the 101-story skyscraper opened in Taipei in 2004, was modeled after bamboo, _____. Lastly, a museum of modern art in Cape Town has windows that look like a beehive at night when they glow with a warm yellow light. Now, let's search for other examples of this kind of architecture on the Internet.

01 다음을 듣고, 남자가 하는 말의 목적으로 가장 적절한 것을 고르시오.

① 자원봉사 참여를 권장하려고
② 기금 마련 바자회를 홍보하려고
③ 교내 추수 감사절 파티를 안내하려고
④ 양로원 방문 일정 변경을 공지하려고
⑤ 자원봉사 운영 위원회 신설을 알리려고

02 대화를 듣고, 여자의 의견으로 가장 적절한 것을 고르시오.

① 자동차 운행을 줄여 환경을 보호해야 한다.
② 건강을 위해 가까운 거리는 걸어 다녀야 한다.
③ 운동은 정기적으로 꾸준히 해야 효과를 볼 수 있다.
④ 살을 빼려면 식이 요법과 운동을 병행해야 한다.
⑤ 다이어트를 하려면 디저트를 줄여야 한다.

03 대화를 듣고, 두 사람의 관계를 가장 잘 나타낸 것을 고르시오.

① 연출가 — 배우
② 변호사 — 판사
③ 운동선수 — 기자
④ 식당 지배인 — 고객
⑤ 스포츠팀 감독 — 심판

04 대화를 듣고, 그림에서 대화의 내용과 일치하지 않는 것을 고르시오.

05 대화를 듣고, 남자가 여자에게 부탁한 일로 가장 적절한 것을 고르시오.

① to help him complete a paper
② to install an anti-virus program
③ to save his data onto her computer
④ to call someone to repair his computer
⑤ to show him how to reformat his hard drive

06 대화를 듣고, 여자가 지불할 금액을 고르시오. [3점]

① $60　　　② $72　　　③ $96
④ $120　　　⑤ $240

07 대화를 듣고, 남자가 생물학 강의를 신청하지 않은 이유를 고르시오.

① 수강 인원이 다 차서
② 필수 과목이 아니라서
③ 아르바이트 시간과 겹쳐서
④ 수강 신청 기간을 착각해서
⑤ 지난 학기에 수강한 과목이라서

08 대화를 듣고, coral reefs에 관해 언급되지 않은 것을 고르시오.

① 구성 물질
② 평균 수명
③ 생성되는 기간
④ 성장 원리
⑤ 단단한 이유

09 power nap에 관한 다음 내용을 듣고, 일치하지 않는 것을 고르시오.

① James Maas가 붙인 이름이다.
② 30분 이내의 낮잠이다.
③ 창의력과 수행력을 향상시킨다고 밝혀졌다.
④ 여러 유명인이 실천했다.
⑤ 오후 3시 이후에 가장 효과적이다.

10 다음 표를 보면서 대화를 듣고, 남자가 렌트할 차를 고르시오.

Rental Cars

	Cars	Type	Fuel	Rental Fee (per day)	GPS Navigation System
①	A	compact	electric	$55	×
②	B	SUV	gas	$92	○
③	C	SUV	electric	$75	○
④	D	full-size	gas	$68	○
⑤	E	full-size	gas	$63	×

11 대화를 듣고, 여자의 마지막 말에 대한 남자의 응답으로 가장 적절한 것을 고르시오.

① I'll call you every week.
② I'll be back in two months.
③ It's kind of you to help me pack.
④ There are five plants in my house.
⑤ About twice a week would be perfect.

12 대화를 듣고, 남자의 마지막 말에 대한 여자의 응답으로 가장 적절한 것을 고르시오.

① Your paper is due by Friday.
② I'm sorry, but this is unacceptable.
③ I'm planning to visit Egypt this summer.
④ I'll give you a list of some helpful books.
⑤ Go over your paper before you hand it in.

13 대화를 듣고, 여자의 마지막 말에 대한 남자의 응답으로 가장 적절한 것을 고르시오.

Man: _____

① I'd like to take a break from school.
② I think we should go grab a bite to eat.
③ Can you tell me the places you liked best, first?
④ I need to go to the university's enrollment office.
⑤ There's really no place like home, don't you agree?

14 대화를 듣고, 남자의 마지막 말에 대한 여자의 응답으로 가장 적절한 것을 고르시오.

Woman: _____

① It's just because I practiced really hard.
② You need to learn the rules of the game.
③ Well, you know I always look on the bright side.
④ I wanted to say thank you for letting me join you.
⑤ You're right. I think we had better give up this time.

15 다음 상황 설명을 듣고, Alex가 전 집주인에게 할 말로 가장 적절한 것을 고르시오. [3점]

Alex: _____

① I hope everything is fixed before we move in.
② Do you think we could move in anytime soon?
③ Could you let me know the number of a plumber?
④ I appreciate that you have already repaired the house.
⑤ I'd like to know why you haven't kept your promise.

[16-17] 다음을 듣고, 물음에 답하시오.

16 여자가 하는 말의 주제로 가장 적절한 것은? [3점]

① common symptoms of jet lag
② things to pack on a long flight
③ reasons why everyone dislikes long flights
④ tips for improving a long flight experience
⑤ activities that make your long flight shorter

17 jet lag를 줄이는 방법으로 언급되지 <u>않은</u> 것은?

① 물 마시기　　　　　② 편안한 옷 입기
③ 스트레칭하기　　　④ 현지 시간에 맞춰 식사하기
⑤ 햇볕 쬐기

✳ 녹음 내용을 다시 들으면서 빈칸을 채우시오.

01

M Attention, students. This is your vice principal, Liam Moore. Our school has formed a committee _____ senior citizens. Volunteers will go to the local nursing home on November 18th. We will host a Thanksgiving party there from 3 p.m. to 8 p.m. People who volunteer _____ to have conversations with them and provide assistance throughout the party. Many of the elderly living at the nursing home _____ _____, so I'd like to encourage you to come and spend some time with them.

02

W Felix, we're out of butter. Can you get some at the grocery store?

M Butter? Are you baking cookies?

W Yes, I'm going to make your favorite chocolate chip cookies.

M Okay, I'll go right now. Where is the car key, Mom?

W _____? It only takes about 15 minutes.

M But it will take less than 5 minutes by car.

W You usually drive everywhere _____ _____. That isn't good for your health.

M I regularly go to the gym and exercise.

W You don't need to go on a diet or join a gym when you walk a lot. Walking is a free and easy way _____.

M Got it. I'm going to _____ _____.

W Great! Here's the card.

03

W Wait a minute! This is ridiculous. I object! Ashley and Melanie from our team clearly blocked that ball.

M Please _____.

W How could you call "out" when the ball _____ on the other side of the court?

M That's for me to decide, not you.

W This is so unfair. I can't believe this!

M You have no say in this matter. I _____ _____. Now, get back to the bench.

W This is not the first time _____ _____. I'm going to report this to the association.

M This is my final warning to you.

W Fine! I'm going to do something about this. You wait and see.

M Final warning!

04

W Let's talk about some stage details for our puppet show.

M Okay. I brought a picture of a puppet show that I was part of. Take a look.

W Hmm.... The stage _____.

M Isn't that a good idea? Look at the sun on top, in the middle. We should do that, too.

W Sure. Let's also place two huge rocks _____ _____ of the top stage.

M Yes, they are important symbols in this puppet show.

W Right. And there's _____ of the top stage.

M Yeah. What do you think about the house on the left side of the lower stage?

W I think it's cool. Do you see that _____ _____ on each side?

M Aren't they beautiful! I heard this puppet show is based on a Mexican folk tale.

W Oh, I see.

05

W Hey Justin, did you finish your paper?

M No, I need to call someone _____ _____.

W What's wrong with it?

M It keeps turning off.

W Did you _____?

M I'm not very good with computers.

W Maybe you just need to reformat your hard drive. Just don't forget to save all the data first on an external drive.

M Could you please _____? I don't think I can do it by myself.

W Sure. But could you save all the data first? It _____.

M Okay, I can do that.

W Then, I'll come over around six today and _____.

M Thanks so much.

06

W Hello?

M Hello. This is Tom Ford calling from World Geographic. I was wondering if you'd be interested in _____.

W Well, I do read your magazine regularly.

M Great, because we are currently offering a one-year subscription, that's _____ magazines, for only $_____.

W That sounds okay.

M Actually, it's a great deal! That's 40% off the regular price of $_____ per magazine. And the two-year subscription _____.

W How much is that?

M You can get 24 magazines at 60% off the regular price.

W 60% off the regular price? That's $_____ per magazine.

M Exactly. _____ a lot of money if you read our magazine regularly.

W I'll sign up for the two-year subscription then.

07

W Hey, Mark. I just bought my textbooks, and I'm definitely going to need your help with biology.

M Oh, I'm sorry to tell you this, but _____ _____ this semester.

W Why not? Was the course already full? You didn't miss the registration, did you?

M No, _____ my part-time job. I didn't have a choice.

W But biology _____ _____. What are you going to do?

M Well, I think I can still take it next year.

W It certainly won't be easy to take several requirements at once.

M I know, but I'm still _____ _____ at university.

W That's good. Well, I'm sure you will do well.

08

M Clara, how was your trip to Jeju Island?

W Great! I saw some amazing coral reefs!

M Sounds exciting. You know, I was surprised to learn that coral reefs _____ _____ of tiny marine animals.

W Right. They are called polyps. It takes hundreds of years _____.

M Wow, that's quite long. Does a coral reef keep growing?

W Sure. It gets bigger as new polyps are born and _____.

M Interesting. It's also strange that coral reefs are so hard. They're the bodies of animals!

W I heard it's because polyps _____ _____ from calcium that they find in the water.

M That's really amazing.

09

W Hello, listeners! I'm Susan Cruz from Austin Sleeping Clinic. Drinking a cup of coffee is a common way to refresh yourself, but a power nap _____. The term "power nap" was created by James Maas. _____ _____ a nap taken during the day of less than thirty minutes. Many studies demonstrate that power naps _____ _____. There are several examples of famous people who have practiced power napping regularly, including John F. Kennedy and Albert Einstein. But power napping _____ _____ later in the day, especially past three o'clock in the afternoon.

10

W Hello, Luke. What are you doing?

M I'm looking at a rental car website. I want to rent a car for my trip to San Francisco, but I'm not sure which one to choose from this list.

W Let me help you. First, _____ _____?

M I'll be traveling with my two friends, so the total number of people is three.

W Then I don't think a compact car _____ _____. You need a larger car.

M I see. What do you think of this electric car? It's the newest model.

W I don't recommend it because _____ _____.

M Oh, I didn't think about that.

W Do you have a budget for the rental?

M I'd like to stay under $70 a day.

W Now _____. Would you like a GPS navigation system?

M Definitely. It's my first visit to San Francisco, so GPS is a must-have. I'll reserve this one now.

11

W I bet you are excited about your trip! Are you all packed?

M Yes, I'm almost ready. But _____ _____ about my plants.

W _____ while you are gone. How often should I water them?

12

M Mrs. Gardner, I'm not sure _____ _____.

W Well, what about the history of Egypt? It's very interesting.

M I think that's good. But I don't know _____ _____.

13

M Soyeon! Long time no see! What _____ _____?

W Actually I just got back to Korea last week.

M Really? How long were you away?

W I was away for almost a year.

M _____?

W No, I was backpacking all over the world.

M That's awesome. But I thought you were studying to be a doctor.

W I _____. I'm re-enrolling

today. That's why I'm here.

M My parents _____.
So, I plan to travel after I graduate.

W Really? That's great. Have you thought about a destination?

14

W Hi, Jake. I just got here. So, how's the game going?

M Not so good. We were doing well until halftime, but after that, _____.

W What happened?

M The players made a lot of mistakes. I'm sure _____ if you had seen it.

W Well, I'm positive that we'll win this time.

M _____ last time, but we lost. Remember?

W Yes, but I have a good feeling today.

M Our team _____ in the next five minutes to win.

W I know, but I still think we can win.

M Seriously, I wonder _____ _____.

15

M Alex has recently purchased a house that is a little old and _____. Some of the repairs that he will immediately have to work on are a broken door, a cracked wall, and a leak in the kitchen sink. Fortunately, when he first purchased the house, _____ _____ that she would fix the leak in the kitchen before Alex and his family moved in. On the day of the move, however, he finds that _____. So, Alex calls the previous owner and she picks up. He wants to ask her _____.
In this situation, what would Alex most likely say to her?

16-17

W Hello, listeners. A long flight can often ruin a pleasant holiday or business trip. So, what can you do _____?
First of all, reduce your carry-on luggage as much as possible. One small backpack is good for the plane because _____ under your seat. If you plan on trying to sleep, bring a travel pillow. Also, consider bringing something to entertain yourself with, as well as your own food. Finally, remember that _____ _____ jet lag after a long flight. The symptoms of jet lag may include headaches, fatigue, irregular sleep patterns, and mild depression. To minimize the effects of jet lag, try matching your sleeping hours on the plane with your destination's time zone. Drink a lot of water and _____.
Upon arrival, adapt to the local time and eat accordingly. Also, it helps _____ _____ if possible.

실전 모의고사 9회

01 다음을 듣고, 여자가 하는 말의 목적으로 가장 적절한 것을 고르시오.

① 자녀와의 대화의 중요성을 알리려고
② 교내 포스터 전시회 일정을 안내하려고
③ 사이버 괴롭힘 반대 캠페인을 설명하려고
④ 학교 폭력 피해자 상담 센터를 소개하려고
⑤ 집단 따돌림 문제에 대한 해결책을 논의하려고

02 대화를 듣고, 남자의 의견으로 가장 적절한 것을 고르시오.

① 어릴 때부터 창의력 교육을 실시해야 한다.
② 모바일 게임은 재미있지만 중독성이 강하다.
③ 적당한 양의 게임은 아이들에게 도움이 된다.
④ 좀 더 다양한 교육용 게임이 개발되어야 한다.
⑤ 부모는 아이에게 적정 게임 시간을 정해주어야 한다.

03 대화를 듣고, 두 사람의 관계를 가장 잘 나타낸 것을 고르시오.

① 교장 — 교사
② 서점 주인 — 직원
③ 의사 — 환자 보호자
④ 의사 — 간호사
⑤ 부모 — 베이비시터

04 대화를 듣고, 그림에서 대화의 내용과 일치하지 <u>않는</u> 것을 고르시오.

05 대화를 듣고, 여자가 할 일로 가장 적절한 것을 고르시오.

① 전화로 길 안내하기
② 음식 주문하기
③ 친구들 마중 나가기
④ 레스토랑 장식하기
⑤ 파티 참석하기

06 대화를 듣고, 남자가 지불할 금액을 고르시오. [3점]

① $65
② $70
③ $75
④ $85
⑤ $90

07 대화를 듣고, 여자가 International Student Night 행사를 돕지 <u>못하는</u> 이유를 고르시오.

① 요리를 잘하지 못해서
② 연구 과제를 끝내야 해서
③ 휴가 여행 계획이 있어서
④ 할머니를 찾아뵈어야 해서
⑤ 식당 아르바이트를 가야 해서

08 대화를 듣고, Historic Richmond Town에 관해 언급되지 <u>않은</u> 것을 고르시오.

① 소재지
② 건물의 재건축 여부
③ 투어 비용
④ 건물 수
⑤ 사적지로 지정된 연도

09 AFB Chess Tournament에 관한 다음 내용을 듣고, 일치하지 <u>않는</u> 것을 고르시오.

① 2009년부터 매년 열리는 대회이다.
② 지원에는 나이 제한이 없다.
③ 대회는 세 부문으로 나뉜다.
④ 각 부문 우승자들은 상금 5천 달러를 받는다.
⑤ 호텔 숙박료는 참가자가 별도로 부담해야 한다.

10 다음 표를 보면서 대화를 듣고, 두 사람이 선택한 자전거 투어를 고르시오.

City Bike Tours

	Tour	Starting Time	Duration	Bike Type	Price
①	A	9 a.m.	5 hours	City	$25
②	B	1 p.m.	4 hours	Electric	$40
③	C	4 p.m.	3 hours	City	$18
④	D	11 a.m.	2 hours	Electric	$30
⑤	E	2 p.m.	2 hours	City	$15

11 대화를 듣고, 여자의 마지막 말에 대한 남자의 응답으로 가장 적절한 것을 고르시오.

① Do you mind if I close the trunk?
② Do you know if we can park here?
③ Why don't you put it in the back seat?
④ Fortunately your car has a spacious trunk.
⑤ How about waiting for the next traffic signal?

12 대화를 듣고, 남자의 마지막 말에 대한 여자의 응답으로 가장 적절한 것을 고르시오.

① Anything with a yellow tag.
② You will get a 10% discount.
③ The sale ends next Tuesday.
④ Your order has been shipped.
⑤ We accept either cash or credit cards.

13 대화를 듣고, 여자의 마지막 말에 대한 남자의 응답으로 가장 적절한 것을 고르시오.

Man: _____

① Hopefully, everything will be done by tomorrow.
② White and black complement each other very nicely.
③ The desk will look great over there by the window.
④ I'm sorry, but it doesn't go well with the new furniture.
⑤ I'm not satisfied with the size of the new book-cases.

14 대화를 듣고, 남자의 마지막 말에 대한 여자의 응답으로 가장 적절한 것을 고르시오. [3점]

Woman: _____

① You're right. I'll follow your example and work harder.
② That's good advice. I'm going to start enjoying my life.
③ Well, I'd rather go to the beach during the summer.
④ Thank you. I'm excited about graduating this May, too.
⑤ Thanks a lot. The class you had recommended was really helpful.

15 다음 상황 설명을 듣고, Michael이 Asher에게 할 말로 가장 적절한 것을 고르시오.

Michael: _____

① You should apologize to the customers.
② I'm sorry, but I'm going to have to let you go.
③ You've delivered this package to the wrong address.
④ You're going to start working in a different position.
⑤ I'd like to hire someone with experience in this business.

[16-17] 다음을 듣고, 물음에 답하시오.

16 남자가 하는 말의 주제로 가장 적절한 것은? [3점]

① solar energy today and in the future
② the undeniable strengths of solar energy
③ the latest advancements in solar technology
④ reasons for calling attention to clean energy
⑤ how solar energy has changed the world

17 solar energy 이용 상 불리한 점으로 언급되지 않은 것은?

① 설치에 필요한 면적　　　② 연간 에너지 생산량
③ 사용되는 재료의 가격　　④ 대기 오염과 날씨의 영향
⑤ 충전 시간의 제약

✳ 녹음 내용을 다시 들으면서 빈칸을 채우시오.

01

W Welcome, parents. Thank you for making the time to come for this meeting. As you may know, our school _____ _____ cyber-bullying. Students have been creating posters to display around the school. They will have messages written on them _____ of this growing problem. Our main goal is to make everyone in the community aware, and to _____ they are not alone. We also want to let students know that bullying online is wrong. We hope this campaign _____ cyber-bullying problems in our school. Thank you again for coming this evening.

02

W Honey, where's our son?

M Darren is in his room playing mobile games.

W Again? He plays mobile games too much these days. I'm worried about him.

M Half an hour a day is not that much. Also, _____ at his age.

W I know most children want to play them, but they are just for fun. Darren _____ what is more important.

M Maybe you should try some of the games that Darren plays _____.

W Why would I want to play them?

M They might not appeal to you, but they _____ _____. They teach creativity.

W He may be learning something, but it _____ _____.

M Actually, a moderate amount of play is perfect for a growing brain.

03

M Penelope's already asleep, so just listen _____ _____.

W Okay, no problem.

M She was sick last week. I think she is fine now, but if she starts crying, _____ _____.

W Of course. I'll remember to do that.

M And here's _____ _____ just in case.

W Is this the number of your family doctor?

M Yes. Do you have any questions before we leave?

W Just one. Is there _____ Penelope if she can't sleep?

M You can read her this book. It's her favorite.

W Okay. _____ and don't worry about anything.

M Thank you. We'll be back by ten o'clock.

04

M Mom, come take a look! This is a picture from our field trip to the Space Center.

W Nice picture. There is a huge rocket at the back. Is it a real rocket?

M No, it's just a model. But I was told that _____ _____ of the real one.

W Oh, there is a spaceman next to the rocket. Is it a model as well?

M No, he is a real person. He walks around the center and _____.

W I see. And there's a fountain in the center. It looks like the earth.

M It's _____. My friends and I waited for a long time to take a picture there.

W The three of you look great! And there is a table _____ on the right side.

M Yes, we had our lunch there. Your sandwich was so delicious. Thanks, Mom.

W I'm glad you had a great time!

05

W Wow! You did an amazing job with these decorations.

M I'm glad you think so. Did you just arrive?

W Yes. Is everyone already here?

M No, I'm still waiting for David and Sue. They're having _____.

W Where are they now?

M They're _____, but the restaurant's kind of difficult to see from the main street.

W I'll give them a call _____.

M You don't have to. I just talked to them.

W Then, _____ and meet them?

M That would be wonderful. While you do that, _____.

W Sounds good. I'll be back soon.

M Thanks, Kayla.

06

M How much are these flowerpots? They're beautiful and lovely.

W They're $2 each.

M _____ on a windowsill.

W Absolutely. It would also look nice if you put a few of these in a basket and _____ _____.

M I'd like to get about thirty of them. Can you give me a little discount?

W If you buy thirty, _____.

M Okay, I'll take them. How much is this basket?

W It's $15.

M I'll take two baskets, please. Can I get a discount on these, too?

W I'm sorry, _____.

M That's okay. I'll take them. Here's my card.

07

W How is your preparation for International Student Night this Saturday going?

M _____. I don't have many friends to help me out.

W That's too bad. What do you need help with?

M We need people _____. Can you help?

W Oh, I'd love to, but I can't.

M Why not? Is it because of your part-time job at the restaurant?

W No, that's not it. I _____.

M Then do you have a group project to finish?

W No. Actually, I'm going to New York this Friday. _____.

M Oh, are you going to New York on holiday?

W No, I'm visiting my grandmother. It's her 70th birthday.

M I see. I hope you have a good time.

08

W I'm so excited about our trip to New York City this weekend!

M Me, too. What do you want to do first, honey?

W I want to go to Historic Richmond Town in Staten Island.

M Oh, that's the historic village _____ _____ from the past.

W Yes. They _____. All of the buildings are original.

M That sounds interesting. How many buildings are there?

W _____ over 30 historic buildings and sites. The oldest building is nearly 350 years old.

M Wow, I really want to see that one. By the way, do you know when Historic Richmond Town was named _____?

W I heard that happened in 1958.

M _____ the lives of Americans from the past.

09

M Hello, listeners. I'm Eric Bolton, the organizer of the AFB Chess Tournament. I'm pleased to announce that the 15th AFB Chess Tournament will be at the Midway Hotel. This competition _____ which has been held since 2009. There are _____ _____ on applications. The competition _____ three categories. Category A will consist of competitors who are under 15. Those between the ages of 15 and 20 will belong to Category B, and competitors 21 and older will belong to Category C. Category winners will receive $5,000 and _____ _____ the grand prize of $15,000. Hotel accommodations _____ _____ of $250.

10

W Owen, look at this flyer. It's about bike tours in the city. Why don't we go on one of these tomorrow?

M Great idea. Hmm, 9 a.m. seems _____ _____ a tour.

W I agree. Let's choose one of the remaining four tours.

M Okay. How much time can we spend on the tour?

W 3 hours is the maximum for me. If we ride more than that, _____.

M Okay. Which type of bike do you think we should choose, city or electric?

W I don't like electric bicycles. _____ _____ and they're too fast.

M Then there are two choices left. Which one do you want?

W I'd like to _____.

M Sounds good. Let's book this tour.

11

W Hi, James! Here!

M Hi, Debbie! Get in the car! Parking _____ _____.

W Okay, but first I need to _____ _____.

12

M I'd like to buy these five shirts. They are $100 at a discount, right?

W I'm sorry, but these items _____ _____.

M Oh, I didn't know that. Then _____ _____?

13

M I'm so excited about having our own home library.

W Me too. We just need to _____ _____.

M Great! Did the desk and bookcases arrive?

W Yes. I chose black instead of white. What do you think?

M Hmm... I like them. I think _____ _____.

W I'm glad. I was afraid you wouldn't like them.

M Well, I do. And _____?

W Open the door and take a look. What do you think?

M Oh, I don't think I like it. I'm afraid we're going to have to paint the whole room again.

W But you're the one _____.

14

W Congratulations, Evan! I heard you're graduating in May.

M Thanks. How about you? Are you close to finishing your studies?

W No. I have a lot more to do. How did you _____?

M I was determined, so I took summer classes.

W Wow, I _____.

M Well, you can always start now.

W True, but I have a long way to go. Two years ago I took some time off, but I now realize that was a mistake.

M I'm sure _____.

W No, _____ and change my decision.

M Well, it's your choices now that _____.

15

W Michael is the owner of a small delivery company. He started the business alone, _____ the office work and the deliveries by himself. Now, he has 10 employees working for him, and _____. Recently, Michael has hired a new employee, Asher, to help with deliveries. Unfortunately, Asher _____, and has already delivered 6 packages to the wrong addresses. Michael is concerned, and finally decides to tell Asher _____ from now on. In this situation, what would Michael most likely say to Asher?

16-17

M Good afternoon, everyone! Today, we'll talk about saving the Earth with solar energy. Solar energy is _____. If you install solar panels on your roof, they will produce most of the electricity that your house needs. Of course, there are some disadvantages to using solar energy. Most solar panels _____. The silicon used in the panels is also very expensive. Air pollution and weather can have _____. Also, solar energy _____ while the sun is shining. During the night, your expensive solar-energy equipment will be useless. Still, there are many more advantages than disadvantages of solar energy. The high initial cost _____. Other renewable sources, wind and water power, are noisy, expensive, and _____ solar-energy systems. Hence, economically, using solar energy still makes good sense. And most of all, it's the right thing to do. If no one switches to cleaner power sources, environmental problems _____.

실전 모의고사 10회

01 다음을 듣고, 남자가 하는 말의 목적으로 가장 적절한 것을 고르시오.

① 새로 생긴 놀이 기구를 홍보하려고
② 무료입장권 신청 방법을 안내하려고
③ 놀이공원 폐장 시간 변경을 공지하려고
④ 놀이 기구 탑승 시 주의사항을 설명하려고
⑤ 특정 놀이 기구의 운행 임시 중단을 알리려고

02 대화를 듣고, 여자의 의견으로 가장 적절한 것을 고르시오.

① 유산소 운동과 근력 운동을 병행해야 한다.
② 근력 운동 시 낮은 중량부터 시작해야 한다.
③ 운동 전 스트레칭은 부상 예방에 도움이 된다.
④ 어떤 운동이든 무리하면 건강을 해칠 수 있다.
⑤ 운동은 질병 예방뿐 아니라 치료 효과도 있다.

03 대화를 듣고, 두 사람의 관계를 가장 잘 나타낸 것을 고르시오.

① 기차 차장 — 탑승객
② 형사 — 용의자
③ 손님 — 서점 직원
④ 영화감독 — 배우
⑤ 작가 — 편집자

04 대화를 듣고, 그림에서 대화의 내용과 일치하지 않는 것을 고르시오.

05 대화를 듣고, 남자가 여자에게 부탁한 일로 가장 적절한 것을 고르시오.

① to tell him where the files are
② to make copies of the contracts
③ to make sure his office gets cleaned
④ to finish preparing the files for tomorrow
⑤ to stay in the office until he comes back

06 대화를 듣고, 여자가 지불할 금액을 고르시오. [3점]

① $155   ② $170   ③ $180
④ $340   ⑤ $360

07 대화를 듣고, 남자가 가족여행을 갈 수 <u>없는</u> 이유를 고르시오.

① 비가 올 예정이라서
② 엄마가 내일 출근해야 해서
③ 남동생이 숙제가 너무 많아서
④ 남자가 스케이트장에 가길 원해서
⑤ 남동생이 깁스를 한 주 더 해야 해서

08 대화를 듣고, Hoover Dam에 관해 언급되지 <u>않은</u> 것을 고르시오. [3점]

① 건축 자재
② 발전량
③ 설계자
④ 연간 방문객 수
⑤ 건축 양식

09 Discovery Tour Bus에 관한 다음 내용을 듣고, 일치하지 <u>않는</u> 것을 고르시오.

① 첫 번째 정거장은 National Mall이다.
② 총 9개의 관광 명소에 정차한다.
③ 정거장 중 원하는 곳에서 내릴 수 있다.
④ 버스는 1시간 간격으로 운행한다.
⑤ 버스에 탑승하려면 관광 패스가 필요하다.

10 다음 표를 보면서 대화를 듣고, 여자가 선택한 아파트를 고르시오.

Apartments for Rent

	Apartment	Monthly Rent	Floor	Number of Bathrooms	Apartment Age
①	A	$1,100	8	1	12 years
②	B	$1,200	2	1	25 years
③	C	$1,300	3	2	32 years
④	D	$1,400	4	2	15 years
⑤	E	$1,800	5	3	7 years

11 대화를 듣고, 남자의 마지막 말에 대한 여자의 응답으로 가장 적절한 것을 고르시오.

① I don't know if I can afford it.
② There is a car waiting for you.
③ You sound like an advertisement.
④ I'm sorry that you have to sell your car.
⑤ Your father must be happy to buy a new car.

12 대화를 듣고, 여자의 마지막 말에 대한 남자의 응답으로 가장 적절한 것을 고르시오.

① I don't have time to sign up.
② They take a trip every month.
③ We should start our own club.
④ They love going to the Folk Village.
⑤ Mr. Beckman is in charge of the club.

13 대화를 듣고, 남자의 마지막 말에 대한 여자의 응답으로 가장 적절한 것을 고르시오.

Woman: _____

① Fine. I'll help you prepare from now on.
② That's not true. I love eating canned food.
③ Sure. Let's go buy the camping supplies today.
④ Calm down. You can go to the store tomorrow.
⑤ Don't get me wrong. I just want to prepare in advance.

14 대화를 듣고, 여자의 마지막 말에 대한 남자의 응답으로 가장 적절한 것을 고르시오.

Man: _____

① Success is often won at a great cost.
② When you find it, you need to seize it.
③ My advice would be to focus on your health.
④ It was a once-in-a-lifetime opportunity for me.
⑤ I'm glad you're so motivated about donations.

15 다음 상황 설명을 듣고, Juliet이 직원에게 할 말로 가장 적절한 것을 고르시오. [3점]

Juliet: _____

① Is it okay if I pay with my credit card?
② Who should I thank for the free car wash?
③ Why did it take so long time to fix my car?
④ How do I get to the department store from here?
⑤ Why did I get charged for a service I didn't request?

[16-17] 다음을 듣고, 물음에 답하시오.

16 여자가 하는 말의 주제로 가장 적절한 것은?

① benefits of warming up for exercise
② tips for staying safe while exercising
③ reasons to exercise and be physically active
④ types of exercise that can keep people healthy
⑤ ways of choosing the right exercise equipment

17 언급된 운동이 <u>아닌</u> 것은?

① hockey   ② swimming
③ hiking   ④ skateboarding
⑤ inline skating

* 녹음 내용을 다시 들으면서 빈칸을 채우시오.

01

M May I have your attention, please? The Dominator will be closed this afternoon _____ _____. The last rides will be given at 3 p.m. If you are unable to get on the ride before then, we will be giving out tickets, _____ _____, at the ticket office. These tickets can be used anytime before September. We sincerely apologize for any disappointment, and hope that you _____ _____ the many other thrilling attractions available at Coaster City. Thank you.

02

W Ah! We missed the bus.

M Hold on. I need to catch my breath. _____ _____?

W Well, I'm combining two different kinds of exercises. I lift weights and go jogging.

M Two different kinds? Anyway, I lift weights every day, too.

W Then you _____. For your lungs and heart, you also need aerobic activities like cycling, running, or jumping rope.

M Hmm... so what do you suggest?

W I think you _____ aerobic exercise and weight lifting.

M Sounds tiring. My muscles _____ _____ after lifting weights.

W If you have sore muscles, you need to stretch, too. Stretching _____.

M All right. It'll be hard at first, but I'll try.

03

M What did you think about the work I emailed you?

W I liked it overall, _____.

M Oh, like which ones?

W I didn't get why the train conductor suddenly changed clothes. It _____ _____.

M Actually, I'm glad you noticed that detail. It might be puzzling, but _____ _____.

W So, we should keep it then?

M Yes. It's an important clue.

W I see. Also, I made _____ _____ here and there.

M Okay. What did you think about the ending of the chapter?

W It was perfect. I think this is going to be a best seller.

04

W Louis, how's the stage setting for the student drama going?

M It's finished, Ms. Wyatt. I've got a picture of the stage. Can you check it out?

W Okay. There is _____ on the left side of the stage.

M And I put a diamond-shaped clock on the wall next to the door.

W Good. And you placed a sofa _____ _____. I like the two cushions on it.

M I'm glad you like them. Is _____ _____ okay with you?

W It looks perfect to me.

M What do you think about the windows on the right side?

W They're good. I especially like the heart-patterned curtains.

M Thanks. I chose them _____ _____.

W Good job!

05

M Helen, you're still here? Why haven't you left?

W I still have a lot of work to do.

M Well, _____. I'm taking off.

W Oh, before you go, could you tell me _____ _____ of last year's contracts?

M The files are in the cabinet behind my desk.

W Thanks.

M By the way, are you staying until 9?

W Yeah, I think so.

M Sorry, but when the cleaning people come, could you make sure _____?

W Sure, no problem.

M Great. _____ recently. It's a bit of a mess.

W OK. Don't worry. See you tomorrow!

06

W Paul, _____ for the trip last week?

M Let's see... the car rental was $_____ per day.

W We only rented the car for two days, right?

M Yes. And it cost $_____ to fill up the tank. We drove about 450 miles, so we _____ _____.

W What about food?

M I remember we only ate out for lunch and dinner.

W Right. Thanks to the free breakfast from the hotel, we didn't have to spend much money on food.

M Yeah. According to my credit card statement, we spent $_____ in total for food.

W Oh, you need to add an extra $_____ for snacks and coffee. _____ at the convenience store.

M Right. I forgot about it. I think that's all. Please _____.

07

M Alright, Mom, I'm all packed for the hot springs tomorrow.

W I'm sorry, Benjamin, but we should cancel our family trip.

M Oh, no! I thought you _____ _____ from work.

W It's not that. It's your little brother.

M But it's spring break! He can't possibly have school work!

W Well, his doctor said _____ _____ for another week.

M So we're going to stay home? _____ _____ all week, and there's nothing to do!

W Actually, since _____ _____, I am planning to take you to an indoor skating rink.

M Really? Can I bring my friend Kelly?

W Sure. Just check with her parents first.

08

M Monica, look over there. It's the Hoover Dam.

W Oh, wow! It's _____.

M Would you like to stop and take a look?

W That sounds fun. In fact, I was just reading about it this morning.

M I remember. You said _____ _____ concrete and bigger than the Great Pyramid of Giza.

W That's right. And _____ 4 billion kWh per year.

M It sure is an impressive structure.

W That's the work of the architect, Gordon Kaufmann. He wanted the dam to _____ _____.

M He certainly succeeded. I've never seen anything like it.

W Kaufmann's work, including the Hoover Dam, was heavily influenced by the Art Deco movement of the 1930s. That's _____ _____.

M I see. Let's take some pictures!

09

W Welcome to the Discovery Tour Bus. Our first stop is the National Mall, where you can see the Lincoln and Jefferson Memorials. This tour bus _____ _____ including the White House and Georgetown. You _____, or take a look around at any of the 9 stops and wait for the next bus. It is exactly 11:00 right now, and _____ _____. Also, please remember to show your tour pass _____ _____. I hope you enjoy the tour and have a great day!

10

W Hello, Mr. Cromwell. I'm Miranda Wilson. I called you yesterday about renting a 3-bedroom apartment.

M Hello, Ms. Wilson. Could you tell me _____ _____?

W I don't want to spend more than $1,500 a month.

M Is there anything else you want?

W I like lower floors since I _____ _____ with my kids. I'd like it to be not higher than the 5th floor.

M Okay. How many bathrooms would you like?

W I need at least two bathrooms since we are a family of five.

M Now you can choose between these two. Which one do you prefer?

W I'll choose _____. I'm worried that an older apartment would have too many problems.

M All right. _____ to see this apartment tomorrow.

11

M You know, I bought a compact car. It runs well, and it's so easy to park.

W Is it _____ that larger model you used to have?

M Definitely. I was astonished at _____ _____. I really like the car. It's a pleasure to drive.

12

W I heard Mary and Tom are going to the Folk Village this afternoon. It sounds like fun.

M Yes, they're in the history club. They _____ _____.

W I'd like to join them. _____ about signing up?

13

W Honey, what's all this canned food in the kitchen cabinet?

M I bought those yesterday for emergencies.

W Emergencies?

M Well, after the last earthquake, I realized that _____.

W I guess it _____.

M My thoughts exactly. So, I made a list of things to buy. We still need whistles, batteries, blankets, masks, and so on.

W Don't you think that's too much?

M Of course not! You just don't understand _____ _____.

W Okay, okay. You _____.

M Well, it feels like I'm the only one who is taking this seriously.

14

W Thank you _____, Mr. Johnson.

M It's my pleasure, Miss...?

W Smith, but you can call me Judy.

M It's nice to meet you, Judy. I often read your magazine.

W I'm glad to hear that. You know, I've read about _____. What motivated you?

M I think my children _____ in that.

W I see. And do you have any advice for those _____ in business?

M I have two pieces of advice. First, always be looking for opportunities. People _____ _____.

W Okay.

M My second piece of advice also _____ _____.

W And what is that?

15

M Juliet is driving to the department store when she hears an awful screeching noise coming from her car. Worried, she pulls into the nearest repair shop. They tell her that she needs to _____ _____. About one hour later, her car comes out and she sees that they have not only fixed the brakes, _____ _____. Feeling satisfied with a free car wash, Juliet goes to pay. She reviews her bill, but sees _____ for a car wash. Now, she wants to _____ _____. In this situation, what would Juliet most likely say to the employee?

16-17

W Good afternoon, everyone. We all know that frequent physical activity is good for us, and there are many activities to choose from. You can play hockey or baseball. You can take yoga classes. But _____, do it carefully. First of all, do not exercise if you are sick. If you do get an injury, stop what you are doing immediately. Wait _____ _____. Next, make sure to warm up. If you are swimming, start off slowly. Give your muscles a chance to move before working them too hard. Before playing a sport, do some easy jogging or walking, followed by stretching. Third, wear pads _____ of your body for activities such as skateboarding. Also, wear footwear that is comfortable and gives you the necessary support. Finally, follow the rules of the game you are playing. _____ _____ and protect the people playing. Likewise, follow the rules of the road if you are inline skating or riding your bike. Keep these in mind, and you can fully enjoy working out.

ANSWER PART Ⅱ 실전편

01회

01 ⑤ 02 ⑤ 03 ② 04 ⑤ 05 ① 06 ④ 07 ④ 08 ③ 09 ② 10 ② 11 ③ 12 ② 13 ③ 14 ③ 15 ③ 16 ③ 17 ④

02회

01 ③ 02 ⑤ 03 ⑤ 04 ③ 05 ① 06 ⑤ 07 ② 08 ③ 09 ④ 10 ① 11 ① 12 ② 13 ④ 14 ④ 15 ② 16 ⑤ 17 ④

03회

01 ④ 02 ② 03 ④ 04 ④ 05 ② 06 ② 07 ⑤ 08 ⑤ 09 ② 10 ② 11 ② 12 ⑤ 13 ② 14 ② 15 ② 16 ② 17 ③

04회

01 ② 02 ③ 03 ⑤ 04 ④ 05 ④ 06 ④ 07 ② 08 ③ 09 ④ 10 ③ 11 ④ 12 ① 13 ③ 14 ④ 15 ④ 16 ② 17 ⑤

05회

01 ③ 02 ② 03 ⑤ 04 ③ 05 ④ 06 ⑤ 07 ⑤ 08 ② 09 ④ 10 ④ 11 ① 12 ⑤ 13 ⑤ 14 ④ 15 ⑤ 16 ① 17 ③

06회

01 ③ 02 ③ 03 ① 04 ③ 05 ① 06 ② 07 ④ 08 ② 09 ③ 10 ⑤ 11 ⑤ 12 ③ 13 ⑤ 14 ⑤ 15 ② 16 ⑤ 17 ①

07회

01 ② 02 ① 03 ④ 04 ③ 05 ① 06 ② 07 ④ 08 ④ 09 ③ 10 ② 11 ② 12 ② 13 ① 14 ⑤ 15 ② 16 ① 17 ④

08회

01 ① 02 ② 03 ⑤ 04 ② 05 ⑤ 06 ③ 07 ③ 08 ② 09 ⑤ 10 ④ 11 ⑤ 12 ④ 13 ③ 14 ③ 15 ⑤ 16 ④ 17 ②

09회

01 ③ 02 ③ 03 ⑤ 04 ④ 05 ③ 06 ④ 07 ④ 08 ③ 09 ⑤ 10 ⑤ 11 ③ 12 ① 13 ④ 14 ① 15 ④ 16 ② 17 ②

10회

01 ⑤ 02 ① 03 ⑤ 04 ⑤ 05 ③ 06 ③ 07 ⑤ 08 ④ 09 ④ 10 ④ 11 ③ 12 ⑤ 13 ① 14 ② 15 ⑤ 16 ② 17 ③

① 구문　　판매 1위 '천일문' 콘텐츠를 활용하여 정확하고 다양한 구문 학습

(끊어읽기)　(해석하기)　(문장 구조 분석)　(해설·해석 제공)　(단어 스크램블링)　(영작하기)

② 문법·서술형　　쎄듀의 모든 문법 문항을 활용하여 내신까지 해결하는 정교한 문법 유형 제공

(객관식과 주관식의 결합)　(문법 포인트별 학습)　(보기를 활용한 집합 문항)　(내신대비 서술형)　(어법+서술형 문제)

③ 어휘　　초·중·고·공무원까지 방대한 어휘량을 제공하며 오프라인 TEST 인쇄도 가능

(영단어 카드 학습)　(단어 ↔ 뜻 유형)　(예문 활용 유형)　(단어 매칭 게임)

④ 선생님 보유 문항 이용

(Online Test)　(OMR Test)

쎈쓰업 듣기 모의고사 **개정판**

S SENSE UP

쎈쓰업
듣기 모의고사
30회

1
최신 경향 반영 실전 대비
듣기 모의고사 30회 수록

2
STUDY DIARY
계획적인 학습 제공

3
MP3 QR CODE
PLAYER 무료 제공

4
자세한 정답·해설과
다양한 부가서비스 제공

쎄듀북닷컴(www.cedubook.com)에서 부가 자료를 무료로 다운로드할 수 있습니다.

쎄듀

POWER UP

파워업
듣기 모의고사
40회

1

최신 경향 반영 실전 대비
듣기 모의고사 40회 수록

2

총 4명의 남/여 원어민
성우 참여로 살아있는
회화체 표현

3

MP3 QR CODE
PLAYER 무료 제공

4

핵심표현 DICTATION과
다양한 부가서비스 제공

쎄듀 초·중등 커리큘럼

	예비초	초1	초2	초3	초4	초5	초6
구문		천일문 365 일력 |초1-3| 교육부 지정 초등 필수 영어 문장		초등코치 천일문 SENTENCE 1001개 통문장 암기로 완성하는 초등 영어의 기초			
문법				초등코치 천일문 GRAMMAR 1001개 예문으로 배우는 초등 영문법			
			왓츠 Grammar		Start (초등 기초 영문법) / Plus (초등 영문법 마무리)		
독해				왓츠 리딩 70 / 80 / 90 / 100 A / B 쉽고 재미있게 완성되는 영어 독해력			
어휘			초등코치 천일문 VOCA&STORY 1001개의 초등 필수 어휘와 짧은 스토리				
		패턴으로 말하는 초등 필수 영단어 1 / 2		문장 패턴으로 완성하는 초등 필수 영단어			
ELT	Oh! My PHONICS 1 / 2 / 3 / 4		유·초등학생을 위한 첫 영어 파닉스				
		Oh! My SPEAKING 1 / 2 / 3 / 4 / 5 / 6 핵심 문장 패턴으로 더욱 쉬운 영어 말하기					
		Oh! My GRAMMAR 1 / 2 / 3 쓰기로 완성하는 첫 초등 영문법					

	예비중	중1	중2	중3
구문	천일문 STARTER 1 / 2			중등 필수 구문 & 문법 총정리
문법	천일문 GRAMMAR LEVEL 1 / 2 / 3			예문 중심 문법 기본서
	GRAMMAR Q Starter 1, 2 / Intermediate 1, 2 / Advanced 1, 2			학기별 문법 기본서
	잘 풀리는 영문법 1 / 2 / 3			문제 중심 문법 적용서
	GRAMMAR PIC 1 / 2 / 3 / 4			이해가 쉬운 도식화된 문법서
			1센치 영문법	1권으로 핵심 문법 정리
문법+어법		첫단추 BASIC 문법·어법편 1 / 2		문법·어법의 기초
문법+쓰기	EGU 영단어&품사 / 문장 형식 / 동사 써먹기 / 문법 써먹기 / 구문 써먹기			서술형 기초 세우기와 문법 다지기
			올씀 1 기본 문장 PATTERN	내신 서술형 기본 문장 학습
쓰기	거침없이 Writing LEVEL 1 / 2 / 3			중등 교과서 내신 기출 서술형
	중학 영어 쓰작 1 / 2 / 3			중등 교과서 패턴 드릴 서술형
어휘	천일문 VOCA 중등 스타트/필수/마스터			2800개 중등 3개년 필수 어휘
	어휘끝 중학 필수편		중학 필수어휘 1000개 · 어휘끝 중학 마스터편	고난도 중학어휘 +고등기초 어휘 1000개
독해	ReadingGraphy LEVEL 1 / 2 / 3 / 4			중등 필수 구문까지 잡는 흥미로운 소재 독해
	Reading Relay Starter 1, 2 / Challenger 1, 2 / Master 1, 2			타교과 연계 배경 지식 독해
	READING Q Starter 1, 2 / Intermediate 1, 2 / Advanced 1, 2			예측/추론/요약 사고력 독해
독해전략			리딩 플랫폼 1 / 2 / 3	논픽션 지문 독해
독해유형			Reading 16 LEVEL 1 / 2 / 3	수능 유형 맛보기 + 내신 대비
		첫단추 BASIC 독해편 1 / 2		수능 유형 독해 입문
듣기	Listening Q 유형편 / 1 / 2 / 3			유형별 듣기 전략 및 실전 대비
		쎄듀 빠르게 중학영어듣기 모의고사 1 / 2 / 3		교육청 듣기평가 대비

쎄듀 고등 커리큘럼

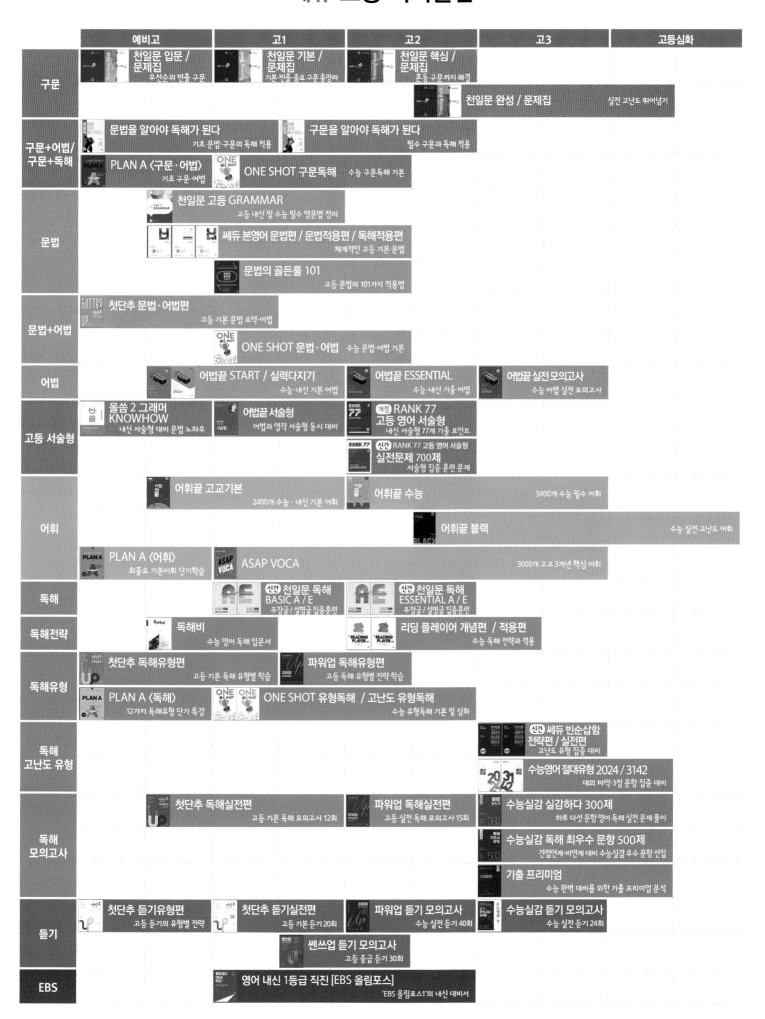

	예비고	고1	고2	고3	고등심화
구문	천일문 입문 / 문제집 우선순위 빈출 구문	천일문 기본 / 문제집 기본·빈출·중요 구문 총망라	천일문 핵심 / 문제집 혼동 구문까지 해결		
			천일문 완성 / 문제집	실전 고난도 뛰어넘기	
구문+어법/ 구문+독해	문법을 알아야 독해가 된다 기초 문법·구문의 독해 적용		구문을 알아야 독해가 된다 필수 구문과 독해 적용		
	PLAN A 〈구문·어법〉 기초 구문·어법	ONE SHOT 구문독해 수능 구문독해 기본			
문법		천일문 고등 GRAMMAR 고등 내신 및 수능 필수 영문법 정리			
		쎄듀 본영어 문법편 / 문법적용편 / 독해적용편 체계적인 고등 기본 문법			
		문법의 골든룰 101 고등 문법의 101가지 적용법			
문법+어법	첫단추 문법·어법편 고등 기본 문법 요약·어법				
		ONE SHOT 문법·어법 수능 문법·어법 기본			
어법		어법끝 START / 실력다지기 수능·내신 기본·어법	어법끝 ESSENTIAL 수능·내신 기출 어법	어법끝 실전모의고사 수능·어법 실전 모의고사	
고등 서술형		올씀 2 그래머 KNOWHOW 내신 서술형 대비 문법 노하우	어법끝 서술형 어법과 영작 서술형 동시 대비	RANK 77 고등 영어 서술형 내신 서술형 77개 기출 포인트	
				신간 RANK 77 고등 영어 서술형 실전문제 700제 서술형 집중 훈련 문제	
어휘		어휘끝 고교기본 2400개 수능·내신 기본 어휘	어휘끝 수능	3400개 수능 필수 어휘	
			어휘끝 블랙		수능 실전·고난도 어휘
	PLAN A 〈어휘〉 최중요 기본어휘 단기학습	ASAP VOCA		3000개 교교 3개년 핵심 어휘	
독해		신간 천일문 독해 BASIC A / E 주장글 / 설명글 집중훈련	신간 천일문 독해 ESSENTIAL A / E 주장글 / 설명글 집중훈련		
독해전략		독해비 수능 영어 독해 입문서	리딩 플레이어 개념편 / 적용편 수능 독해 전략과 적용		
독해유형	첫단추 독해유형편 고등 기본 독해 유형별 학습	파워업 독해유형편 고등 독해 유형별 전략 학습			
	PLAN A 〈독해〉 12가지 독해유형 단기 특강	ONE SHOT 유형독해 / 고난도 유형독해 수능 유형독해 기본 및 심화			
독해 고난도 유형				신간 쎄듀 빈순삽함 전략편 / 실전편 고난도 유형 집중 대비	
				수능영어 절대유형 2024 / 3142 대의 파악·3점 문항 집중 대비	
독해 모의고사		첫단추 독해실전편 고등 기본 독해 모의고사 12회	파워업 독해실전편 고등 실전 독해 모의고사 15회	수능실감 실감하다 300제 하루 다섯 문항 영어 독해 실전 문제 풀이	
				수능실감 독해 최우수 문항 500제 간접연계·비연계 대비 수능실감 우수 문항 선집	
				기출 프리미엄 수능 완벽 대비를 위한 기출 프리미엄 분석	
듣기	첫단추 듣기유형편 고등 듣기의 유형별 전략	첫단추 듣기실전편 고등 기본 듣기 20회	파워업 듣기 모의고사 수능 실전 듣기 40회	수능실감 듣기 모의고사 수능 실전 듣기 24회	
		쎈쓰업 듣기 모의고사 고등 중급 듣기 30회			
EBS		영어 내신 1등급 직진 [EBS 올림포스] 'EBS 올림포스'의 내신 대비서			

첫단추 BUTTON UP

내신·수능 준비는 첫단추 시리즈로!

첫단추 문법·어법편

40가지 어법 포인트로
내신·수능 영어 완벽 대비

첫단추 독해유형편

수능 독해 유형별
확실한 해결전략 제시

첫단추 독해실전편

최신 경향을 반영한
실전 대비 독해 모의고사 12회

첫단추 듣기유형편

수능 듣기 유형별 학습 &
실전 대비 듣기 모의고사 10회

첫단추 듣기실전편

최신 경향을 반영한
실전 듣기 모의고사 20회

수능과 모의고사의 첫단추를 잘 끼우려는

모든 수험생을 위한
필수 교재

01 수능 듣기에 대한 완벽한 이해를 할 수 있습니다.

02 문제풀이에 꼭 필요한 전략과 기본기를 쌓을 수 있습니다.

03 충분한 양의 예상문제를 통해 실전 적용력이 자연스럽게 배양됩니다.

정가 **19,000**원

MP3 파일·어휘리스트·어휘테스트 무료 제공

www.cedubook.com

문의사항은 지역총판 또는 book@ceduenglish.com

ISBN 978-89-6806-261-2

제1개정판 7쇄

53740

9 788968 062612

ISBN 978-89-6806-261-2

첫단추
듣기유형편

BUTTON

정답 및 해설

쎄듀

첫단추

듣기유형편

BUTTON

정답 및 해설

01 화자가 한 행동의 이유·의견

※※ 기출 맛보기   본문 p.17

01 ①

해설 남자는 투어 전날 넘어져서 발목이 아파 런던 워킹 투어에 참여하지 못했다.

어휘 recommend 추천하다
make a reservation 예약하다
in advance 사전에, 미리
ankle 발목
make it 가다, 참석하다; 해내다
completely 완전히
souvenir 기념품

W Hi, Jeremy. How was your trip to London?
M It was fantastic, Julia. I watched the musical you recommended.
W Good. What about the London Walking Tour? Did you enjoy it?
M Unfortunately, I couldn't join the tour.
W Why? Didn't you say you booked it?
M Yes. I made a reservation for the tour in advance.
W Oh, was the tour canceled because of the weather?
M No. The weather was no problem at all.
W Then, why couldn't you join the tour?
M Actually, I fell down the day before the tour, so I had some pain in my ankle. That's why I couldn't make it.
W I'm sorry to hear that. Is it okay, now?
M Yes. It's completely fine now. Oh, I forgot to bring the souvenir I bought for you. I'll bring it tomorrow.
W That's so sweet. Thanks.

여 안녕, 제레미. 런던 여행은 어땠어?
남 환상적이었어, 줄리아. 난 네가 추천한 뮤지컬을 봤어.
여 좋네. 런던 워킹 투어는 어땠어? 즐거웠어?
남 안타깝게도, 나는 그 투어에 참가할 수 없었어.
여 왜? 예약했다고 하지 않았어?
남 응, 나는 그 투어를 사전에 예약했어.
여 아, 날씨 때문에 투어가 취소됐니?
남 아니. 날씨는 전혀 문제없었어.
여 그럼, 왜 투어에 참가하지 못했니?
남 사실, 내가 투어 전날 넘어져서 발목이 좀 아팠어. 그것이 내가 못 간 이유야.
여 그 말을 들으니 유감이야. 이제 괜찮아?
남 응. 이제 완전히 괜찮아. 아, 내가 너를 위해 산 기념품을 깜빡하고 안 가져왔네. 내일 가지고 올게.
여 정말 다정하구나. 고마워.

02 ③

해설 여자는 구름이 해로운 햇빛을 차단해주지 않으므로 흐린 날에도 자외선 차단제를 발라야 한다고 말하고 있다.

어휘 sunblock 자외선 차단제
put on ~을 바르다[입다, 쓰다]
outside 밖에
harmful 해로운
damage 손상시키다
block 차단하다, 막다
sunburn 햇볕에 탐

W Good morning, Jason. It's sports day today. Do you have everything you need?
M Yes, Mom. I put a water bottle, some snacks, and a towel in my bag. Is there anything I forgot?
W What about sunblock? Did you put it on?
M Sunblock? It's not sunny outside.
W Jason, you should wear sunblock even on a cloudy day.
M But I don't feel the sun in weather like this.
W Even if you don't feel the sun on your skin, the harmful light from the sun can damage your skin because the clouds don't block it.
M Really? You mean I can still get a sunburn even on a cloudy day?
W Yes. That's why you shouldn't forget to wear sunblock even if it's not sunny outside.
M I didn't know that. I'll put it on now.

여 좋은 아침이야, 제이슨. 오늘 체육 대회네. 필요한 건 다 챙겼니?
남 네, 엄마. 제 가방에 물병, 약간의 간식, 수건을 넣었어요. 제가 잊은 게 있을까요?
여 선크림은? 선크림 발랐니?
남 선크림이요? 밖이 화창하지 않은 걸요.
여 제이슨, 흐린 날이라도 선크림을 발라야 해.
남 하지만 이런 날씨에는 햇빛이 느껴지지 않아요.
여 햇빛이 피부로 느껴지지 않는다 하더라도, 태양에서 오는 해로운 빛은 구름이 차단해주지 않기 때문에 네 피부를 손상시킬 수 있단다.
남 정말요? 흐린 날에도 여전히 햇볕에 탈 수 있다는 말씀이세요?
여 맞아. 그게 밖이 화창하지 않더라도 선크림을 바르는 것을 잊으면 안 되는 이유야.
남 전 그걸 몰랐어요. 지금 바를게요.

01 ⓒ **02** ⓑ **03** ⓑ **04** ⓒ **05** ⓑ **06** ⓐ **07** ⓐ **08** ⓒ **09** ⓐ **10** ⓑ

01 ⓒ

해설 남자는 내일 부모님을 공항까지 태워다드리기 위해 자신이 차를 사용할 예정이므로 여자의 요청을 거절했다.

어휘 wonder 궁금하다
borrow 빌리다
help out 도와주다
drive 태워다주다

W I was wondering if I could borrow your car tomorrow afternoon.
M Well, I'd really like to help you out, but I'm afraid I can't.
W Why not? Is your car broken down?
M Actually, I have to drive my parents to the airport tomorrow. Sorry.
W That's okay. I'll ask Amy then.

여 내일 오후에 네 차를 빌릴 수 있을지 궁금해.
남 글쎄, 정말 널 도와주고 싶지만, 그럴 수 없을 것 같아.
여 왜 안 돼? 네 차가 고장 났니?
남 사실, 내일 부모님을 공항까지 태워다드려야 해. 미안.
여 괜찮아. 그럼 에이미한테 물어볼게.

02 ⓑ

해설 여자는 새로 시작하는 오디션 프로그램을 보기 위해 서둘러 집에 가야 한다고 했다.

어휘 be in a hurry 서두르다
miss 놓치다

M Hi, Emma! Why are you in such a hurry?
W I must go home right away. There's a TV program I shouldn't miss.
M A TV program? You mean the live music concert?
W No, that's not it. It's a new audition program starting today.

남 안녕, 엠마! 왜 그렇게 서두르는 거야?
여 나 지금 당장 집에 가야 해. 놓치면 안 되는 TV 프로그램이 있거든.
남 TV 프로그램? 라이브 음악 콘서트 말하는 거야?
여 아니, 그게 아니야. 그건 오늘부터 시작하는 새 오디션 프로그램이야.

03 ⓑ

해설 남자는 급여는 많지만 근무 시간이 길어서 회사를 그만뒀다.

어휘 be satisfied with ~에 만족하다
quit 그만두다
up to ~까지

M I left my job last month.
W Why? I thought you were quite satisfied with your job. Weren't you making good money?
M Yes, but I quit it because of the long hours. I was working up to 70 hours a week.

남 나는 지난달에 직장을 그만뒀어.
여 왜? 난 네가 직업에 꽤 만족한다고 생각했는데. 돈을 잘 벌고 있지 않았어?
남 맞아, 하지만 장시간 근무 때문에 그만뒀어. 일주일에 70시간까지 일하고 있었거든.

04 ⓒ

해설 여자는 버스를 기다리던 중에 새치기를 당해 넘어질 뻔해서 표정이 좋지 않았다.

어휘 come out of nowhere 불쑥 나오다
cut in line 새치기하다
fall over 넘어지다
It's a mercy. 다행이다.
cf. mercy 자비; 다행스러운 일

M Hi, Alice. What's that look for? What happened?
W Well, I was waiting for the bus after work.
M Did the bus arrive late?
W No, it did not. When the bus arrived, a young man came out of nowhere and cut in line. I almost fell over.
M I'm sorry to hear that. It's a mercy you weren't hurt, though.

남 안녕, 앨리스. 표정이 왜 그래? 무슨 일이야?
여 음, 내가 퇴근하고 버스를 기다리고 있었거든.
남 버스가 늦게 도착했어?
여 아니, 그렇지 않았어. 버스가 도착했을 때 한 젊은 남자가 불쑥 나와서 새치기했어. 난 거의 넘어질 뻔했어.
남 그 말을 들으니 유감이야. 그래도 네가 다치지 않아서 다행이야.

05 ⓑ

해설 남자는 헬스장 샤워 시설이 낡고 좁아서 회원권을 연장하지 않았다.

어휘 membership 회원권
renew 연장[갱신]하다
completely 완전히, 전적으로
facility ((보통 복수형)) 시설
shower stall 샤워실

M Mom, I'm home.
W Hi. Did you go to the gym?
M Yes. My membership ended today, but I didn't renew it.
W Why? Does your shoulder still hurt?
M No, my shoulder feels completely fine.
W So, what's the problem?

남 엄마, 저 왔어요.
여 안녕. 헬스장 다녀왔니?
남 네. 오늘 제 회원권이 만료됐는데, 연장하지 않았어요.
여 왜? 어깨가 아직도 아프니?
남 아뇨, 제 어깨는 완전히 괜찮아요.
여 그럼 뭐가 문제니?

| M | Well, the shower facilities at the gym are too old, and there's not enough space in the shower stalls. | 남 | 음, 헬스장 샤워 시설이 너무 낡았고, 샤워실에 공간이 충분하지 않아요. |

06 ⓐ

해설 여자는 교통 상황에 여러 변수가 있을 수 있으므로 예상 시간보다 일찍 출발해야 한다고 했다.

어휘 on time 정시에
be stuck in traffic 교통 체증으로 막히다
variable 변수

W	Have you heard anything from Nancy? She's late.	여	낸시한테 얘기 들은 게 있니? 그 애가 늦네.
M	I got a text message from her. She said she left her house on time, but she's stuck in traffic.	남	그 애한테 문자를 받았어. 집에서 정시에 나왔는데, 교통 체증으로 막힌다고 했어.
W	We should always leave early. There are many variables on the road and even in the subway.	여	우리는 항상 일찍 출발해야 해. 도로, 심지어 지하철에도 많은 변수가 있거든.
M	I couldn't agree more.	남	아주 동감이야.

07 ⓐ

해설 남자는 달리기 전에 음식을 섭취하는 것이 더 많은 에너지를 준다고 말하고 있다.

어휘 sweat 땀을 흘리다; 땀
jog 조깅하다

W	Hello, Chris. Why are you sweating like that?	여	안녕, 크리스. 왜 그렇게 땀을 흘려?
M	Hi, Helen. I've just jogged for an hour.	남	안녕, 헬렌. 나는 방금 한 시간 동안 조깅했거든.
W	For an hour? But, you don't look that tired.	여	한 시간 동안? 근데 넌 그렇게 지쳐 보이지 않아.
M	That's because I had a banana before jogging. If you eat something before running, you get more energy.	남	그건 내가 조깅하기 전에 바나나를 먹었기 때문이야. 달리기 전에 무언가를 먹으면, 더 많은 에너지를 얻게 돼.
W	Really? I should try it.	여	진짜? 나도 해봐야겠다.

08 ⓒ

해설 여자는 조용한 영화 상영 중에는 음식을 먹는 것이 적절하지 않다고 주장하고 있다.

어휘 uncomfortable 불편한
crunchy 바삭거리는
permit 허용[허락]하다
appropriate 적절한

M	How did you like the movie?	남	영화 어땠어?
W	The movie was good, but I couldn't enjoy it.	여	영화는 좋았는데 나는 그것을 즐길 수 없었어.
M	Why not? Was your seat uncomfortable?	남	왜? 네 좌석이 불편했니?
W	No, the girls right next to me were eating crunchy snacks the whole time.	여	아니, 내 바로 옆에 앉은 여자애들이 내내 바삭거리는 간식을 먹고 있었거든.
M	Well, eating is permitted in the theater.	남	음, 영화관에서 먹는 건 허용되는걸.
W	But I don't think it's appropriate during quiet movies!	여	하지만 조용한 영화 상영 중에는 적절하지 않다고 생각해!
M	You might be right.	남	네 말이 맞을 수도 있겠다.

09 ⓐ

해설 남자는 판매자가 제품 판매 시 모든 세부 사항을 고객에게 제공해야 한다고 주장하고 있다.

어휘 annoyed 짜증이 난
recently 최근에
clerk 점원
feature 특징
detail 세부 사항
deserve ~을 받을 자격이 있다
exact 정확한

W	Hey, what's wrong? You look annoyed.	여	저기, 무슨 일이야? 너 짜증 나 보여.
M	Well, I recently bought a smartphone, but it doesn't have enough memory.	남	음, 내가 최근에 스마트폰을 샀는데, 메모리가 충분하지 않아.
W	Didn't the clerk explain the features of the phone?	여	점원이 전화기 특징을 설명해주지 않았어?
M	He did, but not well enough. Don't you think that they should explain every detail of their products?	남	해주긴 했지만 충분하지 않았어. 너는 점원들이 제품의 모든 세부 사항을 설명해야 한다고 생각하지 않니?
W	I agree. Customers deserve exact information about products.	여	나도 그렇게 생각해. 고객은 제품에 대한 정확한 정보를 얻을 자격이 있어.

10 ⓑ

해설 여자는 현지 음식을 먹어보는 것이 여행의 묘미라고 말하고 있다.

어휘 preparation 준비, 채비
spicy 양념 맛이 강한
bring 가져가다

W	Hey, Daniel. How are the preparations for your trip to Seoul going?	여	이봐, 다니엘. 서울 여행 준비는 어떻게 되고 있니?
M	Hi, Claire. Everything is going great, but I'm worried about the food.	남	안녕, 클레어. 모든 게 잘되고 있지만, 난 음식이 걱정돼.
W	Why?	여	왜?

	M I heard that Korean food is very hot and spicy. I think I should bring some food with me.	남 난 한국 음식이 매우 맵고 양념 맛이 강하다고 들었어. 나는 음식을 좀 가져가야 할 것 같아.

local 현지의
give it a try 한번 해보다

M I heard that Korean food is very hot and spicy. I think I should bring some food with me.

W But trying local food is the beauty of travel. It's the best way to get to the heart of the culture.

M Maybe you're right. I'll give it a try during my trip.

남 난 한국 음식이 매우 맵고 양념 맛이 강하다고 들었어. 나는 음식을 좀 가져가야 할 것 같아.

여 그렇지만 현지 음식을 먹어보는 것이 여행의 묘미잖아. 그게 그 문화의 중심에 도달하는 가장 좋은 방법이야.

남 네 말이 맞을 수도 있겠다. 여행 동안 한번 시도해볼게.

STEP ③ · ④ Listen & Answer

본문 p.22

01 ⑤ **02** ② **03** ③ **04** ⑤ **05** ③ **06** ① **07** ① **08** ② **09** ⑤ **10** ③

01 ⑤

해설 여자는 새 자동차가 이전 것과 비슷하지만 많은 안전장치를 갖추고 있어서 구입했다.

어휘 deliver 배달하다; 인계하다
basically 기본적으로
run (차를) 몰다
automatic 자동의
emergency 비상
crash 충돌
safety 안전
closely 자세히; 가까이

M Who's parked in your space?

W I have. I had my new car delivered last Friday.

M It looks great. What's it like?

W It's basically the same as my old one. It's really comfortable and quiet.

M So why did you get this one? Is it cheaper to run?

W Well, I got it because it has more air bags, automatic emergency braking, and other things that protect you in a crash.

M I see. Safety is the most important thing of all. I'd like to see your new car more closely.

W If you're interested, we can go for a drive at lunch time.

M Oh, thanks. See you then.

남 네 자리에 누가 주차했지?

여 내가 했어. 지난주 금요일에 새 차를 받았거든.

남 멋져 보이네. 차는 어때?

여 기본적으로 예전 것과 같아. 정말 편하고 조용해.

남 그럼 왜 이걸 샀어? 차량 운행에 돈이 더 적게 들어?

여 음, 이게 더 많은 에어백, 자동 비상 제동 장치, 그리고 충돌 시 보호해주는 다른 것들이 있어서 샀어.

남 그렇구나. 안전이 무엇보다 가장 중요하지. 네 새 차를 좀 더 자세히 보고 싶어.

여 관심 있으면, 점심시간에 드라이브하러 가도 돼.

남 오, 고마워. 그때 보자.

02 ②

해설 남자는 비를 맞고 감기에 걸린 아내를 위해 약을 산다고 했다.

어휘 cough (헛)기침; 기침하다
badly 심하게, 몹시
sore throat 인후통
fever 열
pollen 꽃가루
suffer from ~을 겪다, ~로 고통받다
ease 완화시키다
symptom 증상
treat 치료하다; 다루다
naturally 자연적으로, 저절로

W Can I help you, sir?

M Yes, do you have some cold medicine? *[cough, cough]*

W Oh, you're coughing so badly. Do you have a sore throat and a fever, too?

M No, it's just a pollen allergy I suffer from every spring.

W Then, why do you need cold medicine?

M It's for my wife. We were caught out in the rain during a hiking trip and both got really wet. So she is pretty sick now.

W Okay, just a moment. *[pause]* But, are you sure you don't need anything for yourself? Some medicine may help ease your symptoms.

M I think I just need some rest. I prefer to treat myself naturally if I can.

여 도와드릴까요, 손님?

남 네, 감기약 있나요? *[콜록, 콜록]*

여 오, 기침이 너무 심하시네요. 인후통과 열도 있으신가요?

남 아뇨, 이건 그냥 제가 봄철마다 겪는 꽃가루 알레르기예요.

여 그럼 감기약은 왜 필요하시나요?

남 제 아내를 위한 거예요. 저희는 하이킹 여행 중에 비를 맞아서 둘 다 흠뻑 젖었거든요. 그래서 아내가 지금 많이 아파요.

여 알겠습니다, 잠시만요. *[잠시 후]* 그런데 손님을 위해선 정말 아무것도 필요 없으신가요? 몇몇 약이 손님의 증상을 완화시키는 데 도움이 될 수 있어요.

남 전 그냥 휴식이 좀 필요한 것 같아요. 가능하면 저는 자연적으로 치료하는 걸 선호하거든요.

03 ③

해설 여자는 오븐에 문제가 생겼는데 수리 기사가 목요일에나 와서 컵케이크 주문을 받을 수 없다고 했다.

M Good morning. I heard your cupcakes are great.

W Thank you. Sometimes we even run out of ingredients early.

남 안녕하세요. 여기 컵케이크가 훌륭하다고 들었어요.

여 고맙습니다. 저희는 가끔 재료가 일찍 떨어지기도 한답니다.

어휘 run out of 떨어지다, 다 써버리다

ingredient (요리의) 재료

order 주문(하다)

repairman 수리 기사

M That's great. I have a party for my son and I'd like to order some cupcakes.

W When are you having the party and how many do you need?

M It's this Thursday, the day after tomorrow. I need 50 cupcakes.

W I'm sorry. I don't think we can take the order.

M Is your store closed on Thursdays?

W No, we close on Mondays. There is another problem.

M Do you already have too many orders?

W It's not that. We're having problems with our oven and the repairman is coming on Thursday. We're only selling drinks until then.

M That's too bad.

남 굉장하군요. 아들을 위한 파티가 있는데 컵케이크를 주문하고 싶어요.

여 파티를 언제 하고 얼마나 필요하세요?

남 모레인 이번 목요일이에요. 컵케이크 50개가 필요해요.

여 죄송합니다. 그 주문을 받을 수가 없을 것 같군요.

남 가게가 목요일에는 문을 닫나요?

여 아니요, 저희는 월요일에 문을 닫습니다. 다른 문제가 있어서요.

남 벌써 주문이 너무 많은가요?

여 그게 아닙니다. 오븐에 문제가 생겼는데 수리 기사가 목요일에 올 거예요. 그때까지는 음료만 판매할 겁니다.

남 유감이군요.

---

04 ⑤

해설 남자는 고등학교 동창회에 참석하러 마이애미로 떠나기 때문에 여자의 저녁 식사 파티에 갈 수 없다.

어휘 assignment 과제

condition (건강) 상태

arrange 계획[준비]하다; 정리하다

go away (멀리) 떠나다

put off 미루다

reunion 동창회

W I'm having a dinner party this Saturday night. Can you come?

M Oh, I'd love to, but I'm afraid I can't.

W What's the matter? Do you have an assignment to do?

M No, I finished it already.

W Oh, then I guess you're not in good condition.

M Actually, I've arranged to go away for the weekend.

W Really? Isn't there any way you could put it off?

M Well, I would if I could, but I've already booked a flight.

W Where are you going?

M I am going to Miami to attend a high school reunion.

W That sounds like fun.

여 이번 주 토요일 밤에 저녁 식사 파티를 하려고 해. 너 올 수 있니?

남 오, 그러고 싶지만, 안될 것 같아.

여 뭐가 문제야? 해야 할 과제가 있니?

남 아니, 난 이미 과제를 끝냈어.

여 아, 그럼 몸 상태가 안 좋은가 보구나.

남 사실, 주말에 멀리 갈 계획이 있어.

여 정말? 그걸 미룰 수 있는 방법은 없을까?

남 글쎄, 할 수 있다면 하겠지만, 이미 항공편을 예매해놨어.

여 어디로 가는데?

남 난 고등학교 동창회에 참석하기 위해 마이애미에 갈 거야.

여 재미있겠다.

---

05 ③

해설 여자는 이전에 앨런의 가게를 이용했을 때 서비스가 좋지 않았기 때문에 다시는 이용하지 않을 거라고 했다.

어휘 be off to ~로 가다[떠나다]

appliance 가전제품

charge 청구하다

reasonable 합리적인

selection 선택 가능한 것들(의 집합); 선발

shop assistant 점원

terribly 아주, 몹시

rude 무례한

manage to-v (어떻게든, 간신히) v해내다

refund 환불(하다)

exchange A for B A를 B와 교환하다

W Where are you off to, Ross?

M I'm going to Alan's Store to look at toasters. They sell small appliances there, don't they?

W They do, but I wouldn't shop there.

M Why not? Did they charge you too much?

W No, I thought their prices were quite reasonable.

M Then, did they not have a good selection of products?

W Well, actually, the last time I went I thought the service was terrible. I bought a drill there, and it broke the first time I used it!

M Couldn't you just return it?

W That's what I thought, but when I showed it to the shop assistant, he was terribly rude.

M So did you manage to get a refund?

W Finally, the manager agreed to let me exchange the drill for another one, but I'll never go back.

여 어디 가니, 로스?

남 난 앨런의 가게에 토스터를 보러 가는 중이야. 거기서 소형 가전제품을 팔잖아, 그렇지 않니?

여 그렇긴 한데, 나라면 거기서 쇼핑하지 않을 거야.

남 왜? 거기서 너에게 비싸게 팔았어?

여 아니, 난 거기 가격이 꽤 합리적이라고 생각했어.

남 그럼 선택 가능한 다양한 상품들을 갖추지 않았니?

여 음, 사실 내가 지난번에 갔을 때 서비스가 형편없다고 생각했어. 거기서 드릴을 샀는데, 내가 처음 사용했을 때 고장이 난 거야!

남 그냥 반품할 수는 없었니?

여 나도 그렇게 생각했는데 내가 점원에게 그걸 보여줬을 때 그가 아주 무례했어.

남 그래서 환불은 받았어?

여 결국 점장이 그 드릴을 다른 것과 교환하는 것에 합의했지만, 나는 다시는 가지 않을 거야.

---

06 ①

해설 남자는 보안이 취약한 사이트들도 있으므로 온라인 비밀번호는 자주 바꿔야 한다고 말하고 있다.

어휘 log in 로그인하다
necessary 필요한
expert 전문가
recommend 권장하다
constantly 계속해서
secure 안전한
expose 노출시키다

W Honey, I can't log in to our banking website.
M Oh, sorry. I changed the password yesterday and forgot to tell you.
W Again? Was that really necessary?
M Well, the experts recommend changing your password as often as possible.
W But it's really annoying to have to constantly change our passwords.
M Maybe, but some sites are less secure than others. So your password could be exposed.
W Hmm, I didn't think of that.
M I think it wouldn't hurt to be careful. Imagine how horrible it would be if someone got your online passwords.
W I can't even imagine that situation. I'll be more careful about my passwords from now on.
M Thank you for understanding.

여 여보, 우리 은행 사이트에 로그인이 안 돼요.
남 아, 미안해요. 내가 어제 비밀번호를 바꿨는데 당신한테 말해주는 걸 잊었네요.
여 또요? 꼭 그럴 필요가 있었나요?
남 음, 전문가들은 비밀번호를 가능한 한 자주 바꾸도록 권장해요.
여 하지만 비밀번호를 계속 바꿔야 하는 것은 정말 귀찮아요.
남 그럴지도 모르지만, 어떤 사이트들은 다른 사이트들보다 덜 안전해요. 그래서 비밀번호가 노출될 수 있어요.
여 음, 그건 생각 못했네요.
남 조심해서 나쁠 건 없다고 생각해요. 누군가가 당신의 온라인 비밀번호를 알아낸다면 얼마나 끔찍할지 생각해봐요.
여 그런 상황은 상상조차 못하겠네요. 이제부터 내 비밀번호에 좀 더 주의할게요.
남 이해해줘서 고마워요.

07 ①

해설 여자는 강아지를 기르면 해야 할 일이 많아질 거라고 말하고 있다.

어휘 adopt 입양하다
besides 게다가
make a mess 어지르다
clean up after A A가 어지럽힌 것을 치우다
responsibility 책임감
handle 처리하다
on top of ~뿐 아니라
take care of ~을 돌보다
reconsider 재고하다
think over ~을 심사숙고하다

M Honey, Nate really wants a puppy. I think we should adopt one.
W I'm afraid he is too young. Besides, what about the mess it will make? Who will clean that up?
M It will be Nate's job to clean up after it. It will teach him responsibility.
W I don't think he can handle all of that. That means we'll have to do it. On top of that, where will it go when we travel?
M Hmm.... It could stay with one of my friends.
W But we travel a lot and we would always be asking someone to take care of it. We should reconsider having a dog.
M Okay. Let's think it over for a few weeks and talk again, then.

남 여보, 네이트가 강아지를 정말 원해요. 우리가 한 마리 입양해야 할 것 같아요.
여 네이트는 너무 어려요. 게다가, 강아지가 어지르는 건 어쩌고요? 누가 그걸 치울 거죠?
남 강아지가 어지럽힌 것을 치우는 건 네이트의 일이 되겠지요. 그것은 아이에게 책임감을 가르쳐줄 거예요.
여 아이가 그걸 다 처리할 수 있을 거라고 생각하지 않아요. 그건 우리가 해야 할 거란 뜻이죠. 그뿐만 아니라, 우리가 여행할 때 강아지는 어디에 두죠?
남 음…. 내 친구 중 한 명과 지낼 수 있잖아요.
여 하지만 우리는 여행을 많이 다녀서 항상 누군가에게 강아지를 돌봐달라고 부탁하게 될 거예요. 우리는 강아지를 기르는 것을 다시 생각해봐야 해요.
남 알겠어요. 그럼 몇 주 더 심사숙고하고 다시 얘기해요.

08 ②

해설 남자는 연체료, 도서 대출 권수의 제한, 책을 기다리는 사람들을 이유로 들어 도서 반납 기일을 지켜야 한다고 말하고 있다.

어휘 remind A about[of] B A에게 B를 다시 한 번 알려주다
end up v-ing 결국 v하다
overdue 기한이 지난
late fee 연체료
limit 제한하다
check out (책 등을) 빌리다

M Olivia, did you return your library books? I reminded you about it last week.
W Not yet. But don't worry, I'll return them tomorrow.
M Not yet? You have to return them on time.
W Yeah, but the books took longer than expected to read.
M Then you should have renewed them for another week. You always end up paying a late fee because you don't think overdue books are a big deal.
W You're right. I have nothing to say.
M A late fee is just one of the problems. The library might also limit the number of books you can check out. Besides, there could be people waiting for the books you haven't returned.

남 올리비아, 도서관 책들은 반납했니? 내가 지난주에 다시 한 번 알려줬잖아.
여 아직 못 했어. 하지만 걱정 마, 내일 반납할 거야.
남 아직 못 했다고? 넌 그것들을 제때 반납해야 해.
여 응, 하지만 그 책들은 예상했던 것보다 읽는 데 오래 걸렸어.
남 그럼 한 주 더 연장했어야지. 네가 연체된 책이 큰 문제라고 생각하지 않으니까 항상 결국 연체료를 내는 거야.
여 네 말이 맞아. 할 말이 없네.
남 연체료는 단지 문제들 중 하나일 뿐이야. 도서관은 또한 네가 빌릴 수 있는 책 권수를 제한할지 몰라. 게다가, 네가 반납하지 않은 책들을 기다리고 있는 사람들이 있을 수도 있어.

W I hadn't thought about that. I'll try to do better next time.

M I hope so.

여 그건 생각하지 못했어. 다음번엔 더 잘하도록 노력할게.

남 그러길 바라.

09 ⑤

해설 여자는 모든 우유에 청소년에게 필요한 영양소가 충분하다는 것을 근거로, 학교가 학생들에게 우유 종류를 선택할 수 있는 권리를 줘야 한다고 주장하고 있다.

어휘 rarely 좀처럼 ~하지 않는
plain 보통의, 평범한
nutritional value 영양가
cf. nutrient 영양소
flavored ~한 맛[향]이 첨가된
unfair 불공평한
policy (on) (~에 대한) 방침, 정책
encourage A to-v A가 v하도록 권장[장려]하다

W Dad, would you like some milk with your bread?

M Thanks for offering, but I finished all the milk this morning.

W This is milk that I brought from school. You know I rarely drink plain milk.

M It might not be tasty, but plain milk is higher in nutritional value than flavored ones.

W But I think it's unfair that my school doesn't even give us any other choice.

M There must be some kind of policy on school milk, I guess. They are just trying to encourage you to drink the milk which has more nutrients and less sugar.

W But I learned in health class that both flavored and plain milk have the nutrients that teenagers need.

M I guess I can see your point there.

여 아빠, 빵과 같이 드실 우유 좀 드릴까요?

남 권해줘서 고맙다만, 내가 오늘 아침에 우유를 다 마셨단다.

여 이건 제가 학교에서 가져온 우유예요. 제가 흰 우유를 잘 안 마시는 거 아시잖아요.

남 그게 맛이 없을 수도 있지만, 맛이 첨가된 우유보다 흰 우유가 영양가가 더 높단다.

여 하지만 학교가 우리에게 다른 어떤 선택권도 주지 않는 것은 불공평한 것 같아요.

남 내 생각에는, 분명 학교 우유에 대한 어떤 방침이 있을 거란다. 학교에서는 단지 너희들이 더 많은 영양소와 더 적은 설탕을 함유한 우유를 마시도록 권장하려는 것뿐이야.

여 하지만 저는 보건 수업에서 맛이 첨가된 우유와 흰 우유 모두 십대들이 필요한 영양소를 가지고 있다고 배웠어요.

남 네 말에도 일리가 있는 것 같구나.

10 ③

해설 아이가 수학 시험에서 A를 받았다는 소식을 전하는 상황에서 남자는 여자에게 아이의 노력을 칭찬해달라고 당부하면서 결과보다 과정에 초점을 맞추는 것이 자녀의 성장을 도울 것이라고 말하고 있다.

어휘 finally 마침내, 결국
praise 칭찬하다
hard work 노력, 노고
focus on ~에 초점을 맞추다, 중점을 두다
process 과정
result 결과
follow 따르다

W Honey, I'm home.

M Oh, Vera. I have good news.

W What is it?

M Well, you know how hard Miles worked on his math test.

W Oh, did he get an A in math finally?

M Yes, he did. He was very pleased.

W Wow! I'm very proud of him. Where is he?

M He went to his taekwondo lesson. Uh, Vera, as I'm sure you know, when you talk to him about this, please praise him for his hard work.

W Of course. But I'm also proud of his grade.

M Well, I think we need to focus on the process rather than the result. It will be much more useful in helping our child grow.

W You're right. I'll follow your advice.

여 여보, 나 왔어요.

남 오, 베라. 좋은 소식이 있어요.

여 뭔가요?

남 저, 마일스가 수학 시험공부를 얼마나 열심히 했는지 알잖아요.

여 아, 그 애가 드디어 수학에서 A를 받았어요?

남 네, 그랬어요. 그 애가 아주 기뻐했어요.

여 우와! 그가 매우 자랑스러워요. 어디 있죠?

남 태권도 수업에 갔어요. 어, 베라, 당신이 알 거라고 믿지만 그 애에게 이 일에 대해 이야기할 때 부디 그의 노력을 칭찬해줘요.

여 물론이죠. 하지만 나는 그의 성적도 자랑스러워요.

남 음, 나는 우리가 결과보다는 과정에 초점을 맞추어야 한다고 생각해요. 그것이 우리 자녀가 성장하게 돕는 데 훨씬 더 유용할 거예요.

여 당신 말이 맞아요. 당신 충고를 따를게요.

01 ③

해설 아르바이트를 가야 하는 남자를 대신해서 여자가 가격표를 붙이겠다고 말했다.

어휘 fundraising event 자선 모금 행사
work (기계가) 작동하다
try v-ing 시험 삼아 한번 v해보다
donation box 모금함
price tag 가격표
put A on A를 붙이다[달다]

W Simon, I think we're ready for the fundraising event.
M Right. Let's do one last check.
W Okay. We're going to play a short video clip for the event. Is the screen working?
M Yes. I checked the screen and there's no problem at all.
W Great. What about the speakers?
M I already tried using them, and they worked fine. Did you bring the donation box?
W Yes. Look. I made it by myself.
M Wow! It looks nice.
W Thanks. All the items we're going to sell are nicely set up on the table.
M Okay. The only thing left is to put the price tags on. I'll do that later because I have to go to my part-time job now.
W Oh, don't worry. I'll put the price tags on.
M Really? Thanks.

여 사이먼, 우리 자선 모금 행사를 위한 준비가 다 된 것 같아.
남 맞아. 마지막으로 한 번 확인해보자.
여 그래. 우리는 행사를 위해 짧은 동영상을 틀 거야. 스크린은 잘 작동되고 있니?
남 응. 내가 스크린을 확인했는데 전혀 문제없었어.
여 좋아. 스피커는 어때?
남 내가 이미 그것들을 한번 써봤는데 잘 작동했어. 모금함은 가져왔어?
여 응. 봐봐. 내가 직접 만들었어.
남 와! 멋져 보인다.
여 고마워. 우리가 판매할 물건들은 모두 테이블 위에 잘 배치되어 있어.
남 그래. 가격표를 붙이는 일만 남았네. 나는 지금 아르바이트를 하러 가야 해서 그건 내가 나중에 할게.
여 아, 걱정 마. 내가 가격표를 붙일게.
남 정말? 고마워.

02 ⑤

해설 남자는 회의 준비를 도와주려는 여자에게 회의에 필요한 자료를 출력해달라고 부탁했다.

어휘 preparation 준비
be about to-v 막 v하려는 참이다
confirm 확인하다
reservation 예약
inform A of B A에게 B에 대해 알리다
participant 참석자
name tag 이름표
print out (프린트로) 출력하다
material 자료

W David, how are the preparations going for your meeting tomorrow?
M Hi, Jennifer. They're almost done. I'm about to check if everything is ready.
W Sounds good. Since I finished my own work today, I can help you.
M That's very kind of you. I confirmed the reservation for the meeting room and sent text messages informing the participants of tomorrow's schedule.
W What about the snacks for the meeting?
M They're in my car. I'll get them tomorrow morning.
W And, is there anything else left to do?
M Let me see... I need to make name tags to give to the participants.
W Do you want me to help you with that?
M No, thanks. I can handle it. Could you print out some materials for the meeting instead?
W Sure. I'll do that for you.
M I'll send you the file to print out right now. Thank you.

여 데이비드, 내일 회의 준비는 어떻게 되어가고 있나요?
남 안녕하세요, 제니퍼. 거의 다 됐어요. 모두 준비됐는지 막 확인하려는 참이에요.
여 좋네요. 오늘 제 일이 끝났으니 제가 도와 드릴 수 있어요.
남 정말 친절하시네요. 저는 회의실 예약을 확인했고 참석자들에게 내일 일정을 알리는 문자 메시지를 보냈어요.
여 회의 때 먹을 간식은요?
남 제 차 안에 있어요. 제가 내일 아침에 가져올 거예요.
여 그리고, 또 다른 해야 할 남아 있는 일이 있나요?
남 잠시만요… 참석자들에게 줄 이름표를 만들어야 해요.
여 제가 도와드릴까요?
남 아뇨, 괜찮아요. 제가 할 수 있어요. 대신 회의를 위한 자료를 출력해주실 수 있나요?
여 물론이죠. 제가 그것을 해드릴게요.
남 제가 지금 바로 출력할 파일을 보내드릴게요. 고마워요.

01 ⓒ **02** ⓑ **03** ⓑ **04** ⓐ **05** ⓒ **06** ⓑ **07** ⓑ **08** ⓐ **09** ⓒ **10** ⓒ

01 ⓒ

해설 여자가 남자에게 이메일의 첨부 파일을 열 수 없다고 하자 남자가 다시 보내주겠다고 했다.

어휘 get hold of ~와 연락하다 (= reach)
attached file 첨부 파일

[Cell phone rings.]

W Alex! Thank goodness I've got hold of you. I've been trying to reach you all day.

M I was just about to call you too. Did you get my email?

W Yes, but for some reason I couldn't open the attached file.

M Really? Then, I'll send it again right away.

W Thank you.

[휴대전화벨이 울린다.]

여 알렉스! 너와 연락이 되어서 다행이다. 하루 종일 너에게 연락하려고 했거든.

남 나도 막 너에게 전화하려던 참이었어. 내 이메일 받았니?

여 응, 그런데 무슨 이유인지 첨부 파일을 열 수 없었어.

남 정말? 그럼 내가 지금 바로 다시 보내줄게.

여 고마워.

02 ⓑ

해설 네이선의 생일 파티를 위해 남자는 거실을 풍선으로 꾸미겠다고 했고 여자는 케이크를 만들겠다고 했다.

어휘 balloon 풍선
decorate 꾸미다

M Honey, Nathan's birthday is tomorrow.

W Yeah, I made a digital photo album for his birthday party.

M Sounds good. What else do we need?

W Every birthday party needs balloons and a cake.

M Okay. I'll decorate the living room with balloons.

W Then I'll bake the cake.

남 여보, 네이선의 생일이 내일이에요.

여 네, 내가 네이선의 생일 파티를 위해 디지털 사진 앨범을 만들었어요.

남 좋네요. 또 뭐가 필요하죠?

여 모든 생일 파티에는 풍선과 케이크가 필요해요.

남 알겠어요. 내가 거실을 풍선으로 꾸밀게요.

여 그럼 내가 케이크를 구울게요.

03 ⓑ

해설 도서관에 딸을 데리러 가야 하는 것을 잊은 여자를 위해 남자가 대신 가겠다고 했다.

어휘 recipe 요리법
pick up 데리러 가다

W Smells nice, Daniel. What did you make for lunch?

M Creamy pasta. I found the recipe online.

W Fantastic.

M By the way, do you remember you have to pick up our daughter from the library this afternoon?

W Oh, my! I totally forgot. What should I do? My friend Amy is coming in an hour.

M Don't worry. I'll pick up Betty instead.

W Thanks, honey. Then I'll clean the kitchen.

여 냄새가 좋네요, 다니엘. 점심으로 뭘 만들었나요?

남 크림 파스타요. 인터넷에서 요리법을 찾았어요.

여 멋지네요.

남 그런데, 당신 오늘 오후 도서관에 우리 딸을 데리러 가야 하는 것을 기억하죠?

여 이런! 완전히 깜빡했어요. 어떻게 해야 하죠? 내 친구 에이미가 한 시간 후에 올 거예요.

남 걱정 말아요. 내가 대신 베티를 데리러 갈게요.

여 고마워요, 여보. 그럼 내가 주방을 치울게요.

04 ⓐ

해설 여자가 방문객들을 위한 배지를 자신의 차에 두고 왔다며 지금 가지고 오겠다고 했다.

어휘 edit 편집하다
waste 쓰레기
badge 배지, 휘장
order 주문하다

M Grace, I just finished editing a video clip about plastic waste.

W Then, I'm going to check the screen that we'll use for the video.

M No worries. I've already done it. By the way, where are the badges you ordered for visitors?

W Oh, I left the badges in my car. I'll bring them right away.

남 그레이스, 저는 플라스틱 쓰레기에 관한 동영상 편집을 막 끝냈어요.

여 그럼, 저는 영상을 위해 사용할 스크린을 확인할게요.

남 걱정 마세요. 그건 제가 이미 했어요. 그런데, 당신이 방문객들을 위해 주문한 배지는 어디 있나요?

여 아, 제 차에 배지를 두고 왔어요. 제가 지금 바로 가져올게요.

05 ⓒ

해설 버스 기사가 근처에 있을 가능성은 없냐는 여자의 질문에 남자가 기사에게 전화해보겠다고 했다.

어휘 on one's way to ~로 가는 길에

W I took a bus from Busan and I left my cell phone on the bus. I really need to find my phone.

M Well, since your bus arrived half an hour ago, it should be on its way to the car wash.

W Is there any chance that the bus driver is still around?

여 제가 부산에서 버스를 탔는데 그 버스에 핸드폰을 두고 내렸어요. 저는 제 핸드폰을 꼭 찾아야 해요.

남 음, 손님이 타신 버스가 30분 전에 도착했으니까 아마 버스는 세차장으로 가는 길일 거예요.

여 버스 기사분이 아직 근처에 계실 가능성은 없나요?

lounge 휴게실

| M | He may be at the drivers' lounge. <u>Let me give him a call</u>. | 남 | 아마 운전기사 휴게실에 있을 수도 있어요. 제가 그에게 전화해볼게요. |

06 ⓑ

해설 포스터를 언제 복도에 붙일 거냐는 남자의 질문에 여자는 지금 할 것이라고 대답했다.

어휘 orchestra 오케스트라
instrument 악기
design 디자인하다
put up ~을 붙이다[게시하다]
hallway 복도

M	Ellie, the school orchestra's concert is just three days away. <u>Did everyone check their instruments?</u>	남	엘리, 학교 오케스트라 콘서트가 3일밖에 안 남았구나. 다들 악기를 점검했니?
W	Of course. Everything sounded fine in practice today.	여	물론이죠. 오늘 연습에서 모두 괜찮게 들렸어요.
M	Great. And I heard the posters were ready.	남	좋아. 그리고 포스터가 준비됐다고 들었어.
W	Yes. Here they are. <u>One of the orchestra members designed them.</u>	여	네. 여기 있어요. 오케스트라 단원 중 한 명이 디자인했어요.
M	They look pretty nice. When are you going to <u>put the posters up</u> in the hallway?	남	꽤 멋져 보이는구나. 포스터를 언제 복도에 붙일 예정이니?
W	I'm going to do that now.	여	지금 할 거예요.

07 ⓑ

해설 엄마를 위한 깜짝 파티를 위해 남자는 여자에게 거실을 청소해달라고 부탁했다.

어휘 grocery store 식료품점
promote 승진시키다; 홍보하다
neat 깔끔한, 정돈된 (= tidy)

W	Dad, where are you going?	여	아빠, 어디 가세요?
M	I'm going to the grocery store. We're having a surprise party because Mom was promoted at work.	남	식료품점에 가려고 해. 엄마가 직장에서 승진하셔서 깜짝 파티를 열 거야.
W	Good. I also want to help. <u>Shall I go buy some flowers</u> for the dinner table?	여	좋아요. 저도 돕고 싶어요. 제가 가서 식탁에 올릴 꽃을 살까요?
M	No. I'll do that. <u>Can you clean the living room</u> instead?	남	아니. 그건 내가 하마. 대신 거실을 청소해 줄 수 있겠니?
W	Sure. <u>I'll make it neat and tidy</u> before you come back.	여	물론이죠. 아빠가 돌아오시기 전까지 깔끔하게 정리해 놓을게요.

08 ⓐ

해설 여자는 공항에 바이어들을 데리러 갈 사람이 필요하다며 남자에게 도와달라고 부탁했다.

어휘 buyer 바이어, 구매자
make a reservation 예약하다

M	Hi, Jenny. I've heard you're preparing for our buyers visiting our company. How's it going?	남	안녕하세요, 제니. 바이어들이 우리 회사를 방문하는 것을 당신이 준비하고 있다고 들었어요. 어떻게 돼가고 있나요?
W	Hi, Nick. I'm almost done. I <u>made reservations</u> for hotel rooms and <u>bought some gifts</u> for them.	여	안녕하세요, 닉. 거의 다 했어요. 그들을 위해 호텔 객실을 예약하고 선물을 샀어요.
M	Is there anything I can help you with?	남	제가 도와드릴 일이 있나요?
W	Actually, I need someone to pick up the buyers at the airport. <u>Could you do that for me?</u>	여	사실, 공항에 바이어들을 데리러 갈 사람이 필요해요. 저를 위해 그것을 해주실 수 있나요?
M	Of course!	남	물론이죠!

09 ⓒ

해설 남자는 여자에게 제품 홍보를 위해 블로그에 사진을 올려달라고 부탁했다.
ⓐ 상품 판매하기
ⓑ 벼룩시장 방문하기
ⓒ 블로그에 사진 올리기

어휘 flea market 벼룩시장
participate in ~에 참여하다
post (웹사이트에) 올리다, 게시하다

M	I'm going to <u>participate in a flea market</u> this Saturday. I was wondering if <u>you could give me a hand</u>.	남	난 이번 주 토요일에 벼룩시장에 참여할 예정이야. 혹시 네가 나를 도와줄 수 있는지 궁금해.
W	How can I help you?	여	어떻게 도와주면 될까?
M	You <u>can start by posting a photo</u> on your blog to promote our products.	남	네 블로그에 우리 제품을 홍보하기 위해 사진을 올려주는 것부터 시작할 수 있어.
W	Sure. No problem.	여	좋아. 문제없어.

10 ⓒ

해설 여자는 갑자기 회의에 들어가게 되어 남자에게 저녁 예약을 내일로 미뤄달라고 부탁했다.
ⓐ 여자를 위해 저녁 식사 준비하기
ⓑ 고객과 약속 정하기
ⓒ 예약을 내일로 미루기

어휘 appointment (업무 관련) 약속; 예약
postpone 미루다, 연기하다

[Cell phone rings.]
M Hello?
W Honey, it's me. Do you remember our plan for dinner tonight?
M Yes, is there something wrong?
W My client came without an appointment, so I have to go to a meeting now. If you don't mind, could you postpone our reservation to tomorrow?
M All right. I'll see you at home.

[휴대전화벨이 울린다.]
남 여보세요?
여 여보, 나예요. 오늘 저녁 식사 약속 기억해요?
남 그럼요, 무슨 일 있어요?
여 고객이 약속도 없이 와서 지금 회의에 들어가봐야 해요. 괜찮다면 우리 예약을 내일로 미뤄줄래요?
남 알겠어요. 집에서 봐요.

STEP ③·④ Listen & Answer

본문 p.33

01 ① **02** ③ **03** ① **04** ⑤ **05** ③ **06** ② **07** ④ **08** ⑤ **09** ④ **10** ①

---

01 ①

해설 여자는 계단으로 소파를 옮기려는 남자를 위해 계단에 있는 상자들을 옮겨주겠다고 했다.

어휘 couch 소파
upstairs 위층(으로)
fit (크기가) 맞다
carry 옮기다
afterwards 나중에, 그 후

W Hi, Steve! I see you finally bought a new couch.
M Yes, now I just have to get it upstairs.
W Do you want some help getting it in the elevator?
M It doesn't fit. Mark and Kyle are coming to help me carry it up the stairs.
W Can the three of you do it by yourselves?
M I hope so.... By the way, do you know whose boxes those are on the stairs?
W Sharon's. She's moving out. I'd be happy to move them for you.
M Really? That'd be very helpful. Afterwards, I'm going to make dinner for all of us. You are welcome to come.
W Sounds good. I'll just go change clothes quickly.

여 안녕, 스티브! 드디어 새 소파를 샀구나.
남 응, 이제 이걸 위층으로 올리기만 하면 돼.
여 엘리베이터에 싣는 것을 도와줄까?
남 이건 들어가질 않아. 마크와 카일이 계단으로 옮기는 걸 도와주러 올 거야.
여 너희 셋이서만 할 수 있겠어?
남 그러기를 바라지…. 그런데, 계단에 있는 저 상자들이 누구 건지 아니?
여 샤론 거야. 그녀가 이사를 가거든. 널 위해 내가 기꺼이 그것들을 옮겨줄게.
남 정말? 그럼 정말 도움이 될 거야. 나중에 내가 우리 모두를 위해 저녁을 만들 거야. 너도 와.
여 좋아. 가서 빨리 옷 좀 갈아입을게.

---

02 ③

해설 남자가 리조트 근처에서 콘택트렌즈를 살 수 있을지 리조트에 전화해서 확인하겠다고 했다.

어휘 leave on a trip 여행을 떠나다
remind 생각나게 하다, 상기시키다
resort 리조트, 휴양지
look up 찾아보다
shuttle 정기 왕복 버스[기차, 항공기]

M Hi, honey. Still on the computer?
W Yes. I have some reports to finish before we leave on our trip tomorrow.
M Oh, that reminds me, I forgot to get some more contact lenses!
W It's too late now, and the stores might be closed tomorrow. It's a holiday.
M That's true. Maybe I can get some near the resort.
W I'm not sure. I will look it up online for you after I finish what I'm doing.
M That's okay. I'll call the resort and check.
W Good idea. Can you also ask about the schedule for the shuttle from the airport to the resort?
M I already did and they sent it to my email. The shuttle leaves every hour.
W Thank you, sweetheart.

남 안녕, 여보. 아직 컴퓨터 하고 있어?
여 응. 내일 우리가 여행을 떠나기 전에 끝내야 할 보고서가 좀 있거든.
남 아, 그러고 보니 생각났는데, 콘택트렌즈를 몇 개 더 사는 걸 깜빡했네!
여 지금은 너무 늦었고, 내일은 가게들이 아마 문을 닫을 거야. 휴일이잖아.
남 맞아. 어쩌면 리조트 근처에서 살 수 있을 거야.
여 잘 모르겠어. 내가 하고 있는 일을 끝내고 온라인으로 찾아봐줄게.
남 괜찮아. 내가 리조트에 전화해서 확인해볼게.
여 좋은 생각이야. 공항에서 리조트까지 가는 셔틀버스 시간표도 물어봐 줄래?
남 내가 이미 물어봐서 리조트에서 그걸 내 이메일로 보내줬어. 셔틀버스는 매시간 출발해.
여 고마워, 여보.

03 ①

해설 여자는 창고에 사람을 보내 남자가 찾고 있는 책을 가져오게 하겠다고 했다.

어휘 display 진열대
aisle 통로
section 코너, 구간
sold out 다 팔린, 매진된
copy (책·잡지 등의) 1권; 사본
warehouse 창고
book review 서평, 후기

W May I help you?
M Yes, I'm looking for the new book by Sarah Parker.
W It's in the best-seller display in the next aisle, right next to the travel-guide section.
M Well, I just checked there, but I couldn't find it.
W Oh, sorry. Then maybe it's sold out. Let me check on the computer first. *[pause]* We don't have it here, but we do have several in the warehouse.
M Really? That's great. Can I get one now?
W Sure, I'll send someone to bring a copy.
M That would be great. Will I have to wait long?
W Not really. The warehouse is just behind this building.
M Okay, then I'll read some book reviews while I wait.

여 도와드릴까요?
남 네, 저는 사라 파커의 신간을 찾고 있어요.
여 그건 다음 통로의 베스트셀러 진열대에 있습니다. 여행 가이드 코너 바로 옆이에요.
남 음, 방금 거길 확인해봤는데 찾을 수가 없었어요.
여 아, 죄송합니다. 그럼 다 팔렸나 봅니다. 먼저 컴퓨터로 확인해볼게요. *[잠시 후]* 여기에는 없지만, 창고에는 몇 권 있습니다.
남 정말요? 잘됐네요. 지금 하나 살 수 있을까요?
여 물론이죠, 제가 책을 가지고 오도록 사람을 보내겠습니다.
남 그래주시면 좋겠어요. 오래 기다려야 할까요?
여 아닙니다. 창고는 이 건물 바로 뒤에 있거든요.
남 알겠어요, 그럼 기다리는 동안 서평을 읽고 있을게요.

04 ⑤

해설 제주도에 있는 식당을 많이 알아보지 못한 여자를 위해 남자가 관련 링크를 보내주겠다고 했다.

어휘 in a hurry 바쁜
give A a ride A를 태워주다
definitely 반드시

M Hi, Alice. Looks like you are in a hurry.
W Oh, hi, Bill. I'm really late. I have a flight to catch in 40 minutes.
M Stay calm. I'll give you a ride.
W Thanks. But I already called a taxi.
M Where are you going, anyway?
W I'm going to Jeju Island with my friends.
M Oh, there're so many good restaurants in Jeju Island. You should definitely try black pork!
W I haven't done much research on that. Do you know some good restaurants there?
M Yes. I'll send you the link.
W That would be great. I'll get you a box of chocolate on my way back. Thanks.

남 안녕, 앨리스. 바빠 보이네.
여 어, 안녕, 빌. 나 정말 늦었어. 40분 후에 비행기를 타야 하거든.
남 진정해. 내가 태워줄게.
여 고마워. 하지만 내가 이미 택시를 불렀어.
남 그나저나 어디에 가는 건데?
여 친구들과 제주도에 가는 거야.
남 오, 제주도에는 맛있는 식당들이 정말 많아. 넌 흑돼지를 반드시 먹어봐야 해!
여 그건 많이 알아보지 못했어. 거기에 있는 좋은 식당들을 알고 있니?
남 응. 내가 링크 보내줄게.
여 그러면 좋지. 돌아오는 길에 내가 초콜릿 한 박스 사다줄게. 고마워.

05 ③

해설 회의 때문에 늦어져서 영화를 볼 수 없게 되자 여자는 남자에게 저녁을 먹자고 하며 식당에 자리가 있는지 전화해서 확인해보겠다고 했다.

어휘 get tied up in ~에 붙잡혀 있다
on time 제시간에
cancel 취소하다
take care of ~을 처리하다
navigation 내비게이션

[Cell phone rings.]
M Susan, are you on your way here?
W Peter, I've got tied up in a meeting. I don't think I can make it there on time.
M Well.... Let's just forget about the movie, then.
W I'm so sorry. Should I cancel the tickets?
M It's okay. I'll take care of it.
W Thanks. And Instead of a movie, how about dinner at Chang's restaurant?
M Sounds good. How long will it take you to get there?
W About 15 minutes. I'll call the restaurant and check whether we can get a table there now.
M Great. My navigation says it's only 10 minutes away by car from here.
W Good. See you at the restaurant.

[휴대전화벨이 울린다.]
남 수잔, 여기 오는 길이야?
여 피터, 나 회의에 붙잡혀 있었어. 제시간에 그곳에 도착할 수 없을 것 같아.
남 음…. 그럼 영화는 그냥 없던 일로 하자.
여 정말 미안해. 내가 표를 취소할까?
남 괜찮아. 내가 처리할게.
여 고마워. 그리고 영화 대신 챙 식당에서 저녁 먹는 게 어때?
남 좋아. 네가 거기까지 가는 데 얼마나 걸릴까?
여 약 15분. 내가 식당에 전화해서 지금 거기에 자리가 있는지 확인해볼게.
남 좋아. 내 내비게이션에 따르면 여기서 차로 10분밖에 안 걸린데.
여 잘됐다. 식당에서 보자.

06 ②

해설 남자는 현금 인출기에 잠시 들르는 여자를 대신해서 먼저 점심을 주문해주기로 했다.

어휘 half 절반
keep up ~을 유지하다
grab a bite to eat 간단히 먹다
stop by ~에 잠시 들르다
ATM (= Automated Teller Machine) 현금 자동 인출기
catch up to ~을 따라잡다

W I can't believe I still have to study half of the book and the test is tomorrow.
M Me neither. And it's already about lunch time.
W Yeah... but I don't feel like eating anything.
M Oh, come on. Eating something will help keep up our energy.
W Hmm... then, let's grab a bite to eat at the cafeteria. But I should stop by somewhere before.
M Where do you need to go?
W I need to get some money out of an ATM.
M Then I'll go ahead and order our lunch. Are you having the usual?
W Yes, with a bottle of orange juice.
M OK, you can pay me back later.
W Thanks. I'll catch up to you soon.

여 아직도 책의 절반을 공부해야 하는데 시험이 내일이라니 믿을 수 없어.
남 나도 그래. 그리고 벌써 점심때가 다 됐어.
여 그러게… 하지만 난 아무것도 먹고 싶지 않아.
남 에이, 그러지 마. 뭔가 먹는 게 에너지를 유지하는 데 도움이 될 거야.
여 음… 그럼, 구내식당에서 간단히 먹자. 그런데 난 그전에 어디 잠시 들러야 해.
남 어디에 가야 하는데?
여 현금 자동 인출기에서 돈을 좀 찾아야 하거든.
남 그럼 내가 먼저 가서 우리 점심을 주문할게. 늘 먹던 걸로 먹을 거야?
여 응, 오렌지 주스 한 병도 같이.
남 알겠어, 돈은 나중에 줘도 돼.
여 고마워. 곧 따라갈게.

07 ④

해설 여자는 남자에게 관광 예약하는 것을 도와달라고 부탁했다.

어휘 sight ((복수형)) 명소, 관광지
surrounding 주위의
brochure 팸플릿
label 표를 붙이다
arrange 주선[마련]하다
book 예약하다
look through 살펴보다

W Excuse me, but can you tell us about the things we can do here?
M Well, there are lots of things to do at the hotel. We have a swimming pool, a sauna, a PC game room, and tennis courts.
W Oh, I meant tours and sights to see in the surrounding area.
M Ah! Sorry. Here are some brochures.
W Great! Do you have any maps of the island?
M Of course. Here's one with all the major landmarks labeled. I can help arrange a car rental if you'd like.
W No, thanks. But can you help us book tours?
M Certainly. Just look at the brochures and let me know what tours you are interested in.
W OK. We'll be back again after we look through them.

여 실례합니다만, 저희가 여기서 할 수 있는 것들을 알려주시겠어요?
남 음, 호텔에서 할 수 있는 일들이 많이 있습니다. 수영장, 사우나, PC방, 그리고 테니스 코트가 있습니다.
여 아, 저는 관광이나 인근 지역에서 볼 만한 명소를 말한 거였어요.
남 아! 죄송합니다. 여기 팸플릿이 몇 개 있어요.
여 잘됐네요! 섬의 지도를 가지고 있으신가요?
남 물론이죠. 여기 모든 주요 명소가 표시되어 있는 지도가 있습니다. 원하시면 자동차 대여를 알선해 드릴 수 있어요.
여 아니에요, 괜찮습니다. 하지만 저희가 관광을 예약하는 것을 도와주실 수 있나요?
남 물론이죠. 팸플릿을 보시고 관심이 있는 관광을 제게 알려주시면 됩니다.
여 알겠어요. 저희가 그것들을 살펴보고 나서 다시 올게요.

08 ⑤

해설 남자는 마틴을 잘 모르기 때문에 여자에게 그의 책을 대신 빌려다 줄 것을 부탁했다.

① 남자를 여자의 친구에게 소개해주기
② 남자가 숙제하는 것을 도와주기
③ 저널 쓰기에 대해 조언해주기
④ 여자가 빌려간 책 돌려주기
⑤ 여자의 친구에게서 교과서 빌려다 주기

어휘 journal (특정 주제나 전문 분야를 다루는) 저널, 학술지
assignment 과제, 숙제
strict 엄격한
textbook 교과서
lend 빌려주다

W Hey, Scott. Where are you going?
M Emily! So glad to see you! I need to borrow your book for Mr. Baker's class.
W I'm sorry, but I took it home for the journal assignment and left it there.
M Oh, no.... What should I do? You know that Mr. Baker is really strict about students not bringing their textbook.
W Yeah.... Oh! I know that Martin has that class this afternoon.
M Really? Hmm... but I don't know him well.... I'm so sorry, but if you don't mind, can you ask him to lend it to me?
W I can do that for you if you promise to return it before lunch time.

여 이봐, 스콧. 어디 가니?
남 에밀리! 만나서 정말 반갑다! 나 너한테 베이커 선생님 수업 교재를 빌려야 해.
여 미안한데, 내가 저널 과제 때문에 집에 가져가서 두고 왔어.
남 이런…. 어떻게 해야 하지? 베이커 선생님께서 교과서를 안 가져오는 학생들에 대해서 아주 엄격하신 거 알잖아.
여 그렇지…. 아! 마틴이 오늘 오후에 그 수업이 있는 걸로 알고 있어.
남 정말? 음… 하지만 난 그 아이를 잘 몰라…. 정말 미안한데, 너만 괜찮다면 책을 내게 빌려주라고 그에게 부탁해줄래?
여 네가 점심시간 전에 돌려주겠다고 약속하면 그렇게 해줄 수 있어.

promise to-v v할 것을 약속하다

| M | I promise I will. Thank you so much. |
| W | That's what friends are for! |

남 그러겠다고 약속할게. 정말 고마워.
여 친구 좋다는 게 이런 거지!

09 ④

해설 여자는 버터를 가져오기 위해 자리를 떠나면서 남자에게 계산대 줄에서 기다려 달라고 부탁했다.

어휘 head for ~로 향하다
cashier 계산대 (점원)
(= checkout counter)
grocery 식료품
as long as ~하기만 하면, ~하는 한
have no choice but to-v
v할 수 밖에 없다, v하지 않을 수 없다
exactly 정확히
turn 차례

W We got everything on the list. Let's head for the cashier.
M Okay, I'll push the cart. Wow, we really have a lot of groceries.
W Yes, it's not going to be cheap. But Jane wants a big birthday party.
M As long as it makes her happy, I don't mind. But I see a long line at the checkout counter.
W Yeah, but we have no choice but to wait.
M After we pay and drive home, let's prepare everything together.
W Okay, great. Uh oh, we forgot butter. I can't cook without it.
M Shall I go and grab some?
W No, I'll do that. I know exactly where it is. Can you wait in the line instead? I'll be right back.
M Sure. Please make it quick. It'll soon be our turn.

여 목록에 있는 거 다 담았어요. 계산대로 가요.
남 알겠어요. 내가 카트를 밀게요. 와, 우리 식료품이 정말 많네요.
여 네, 물건 값이 적게 나오진 않을 거예요. 그래도 제인이 성대한 생일 파티를 원하잖아요.
남 제인을 기쁘게 할 수 있기만 하면, 난 상관없어요. 그런데 계산대 줄이 길어 보이네요.
여 그러네요, 그래도 기다리는 수밖에 없죠.
남 계산하고 집에 가면, 함께 준비해요.
여 좋아요, 잘됐네요. 어, 버터를 깜빡했어요. 그게 없으면 요리할 수 없어요.
남 내가 가서 좀 가져올까요?
여 아니에요, 내가 할게요. 난 그게 어디 있는지 정확히 알아요. 대신 줄에서 기다려 줄래요? 금방 돌아올게요.
남 그럼요. 서둘러요. 곧 우리 차례가 올 거예요.

10 ①

해설 남자가 반려견 훈련을 어려워하자 여자는 훈련에 관한 좋은 책을 샀다고 했고, 남자는 그 책을 빌려달라고 부탁했다.
① 책 빌려주기
② 개 훈련 도와주기
③ 개를 수의사에게 데려가기
④ 개 사료 사주기
⑤ 책 제목 알려주기

어휘 exhausted 매우 지친
bark 짖다
train 훈련하다
well-behaved 얌전한; 품행이 바른
active 활동적인, 활발한
thoughtful 사려 깊은

W Hi, Steven. Are you okay? You look really tired.
M I'm exhausted. It's my roommate's new dog. It never stops barking!
W I thought the two of you were going to train it together. What happened?
M It's much harder than we thought. How did you come to have such a well-behaved dog?
W Cubert? He was a very active puppy. But I bought a great book about training dogs. Shall I tell you the title?
M If you don't mind, maybe I could just borrow the book?
W Sure. I'll bring it to work tomorrow. I'll also bring some extra dog food. It'll be very helpful when you're training the dog.
M You're so thoughtful! Thank you.

여 안녕하세요, 스티븐. 괜찮아요? 아주 피곤해 보여요.
남 전 매우 지쳤어요. 제 룸메이트의 새 반려견 때문이에요. 짖는 걸 절대 멈추지 않아요!
여 저는 두 분이 함께 그 개를 훈련할 거라고 생각했어요. 무슨 일이 있었나요?
남 저희가 생각했던 것보다 훨씬 더 어려워요. 당신은 어떻게 그렇게 얌전한 개를 가지게 된 거죠?
여 큐버트 말이에요? 걔도 아주 활동적인 강아지였어요. 하지만 제가 개 훈련에 관한 아주 좋은 책을 한 권 샀거든요. 제목을 알려줄까요?
남 괜찮다면, 그냥 그 책 좀 빌려볼 수 있을까요?
여 물론이죠. 내일 회사에 가져올게요. 여분의 개 사료도 좀 가져올게요. 개를 훈련할 때 매우 도움이 될 거예요.
남 정말 사려 깊군요! 고마워요.

---

03 유형 금액

🌟 기출 맛보기

본문 p.41

01 ③

해설 여자는 빨간색 목도리($50) 하나와 겨울 양말($5) 두 켤레를 산다고 했으므로 총 60달러이다. 여기서 할인 쿠폰을 이용해 10%를 할인받으므로 지불할 금액은 54달러이다.

M Welcome to Kids' Clothing Club. How may I help you?
W I'm looking for a muffler for my son. He's 5 years old.

남 아동복 클럽에 오신 것을 환영합니다. 어떻게 도와드릴까요?
여 제 아들에게 줄 목도리를 찾고 있어요. 다섯 살이에요.

어휘 muffler 목도리
best seller 베스트셀러, 가장 잘 나가
는 상품
cartoon 만화 (영화)
a pair of 한 켤레[짝, 벌]
discount 할인(의)
total 총, 전체의
credit card 신용 카드

M Okay. Follow me. [pause] This red muffler is one of the best sellers in our shop.
W I love the color. How much is it?
M It's $50. This one is popular because of the cartoon character here.
W Oh, that's my son's favorite character. I'll buy one red muffler, then.
M Great. Anything else?
W How much are these winter socks?
M A pair of socks is $5.
W All right. I'll buy two pairs.
M So, one red muffler and two pairs of winter socks, right?
W Yes. Can I use this discount coupon?
M Of course. With that coupon, you can get 10% off the total price.
W Good. Here's my credit card.

남 네. 절 따라오세요. [잠시 후] 이 빨간 목도리는 저희 가게에서 가장 잘 팔리는 목도리 중 하나입니다.
여 색깔이 마음에 드네요. 얼마인가요?
남 50달러입니다. 이건 여기 있는 만화 캐릭터 때문에 인기가 많아요.
여 아, 그건 우리 아들이 제일 좋아하는 캐릭터예요. 그럼 빨간색 목도리 하나 살게요.
남 좋습니다. 또 다른 건 없으신가요?
여 이 겨울 양말들은 얼마인가요?
남 양말 한 켤레에 5달러입니다.
여 좋아요. 두 켤레 살게요.
남 그럼, 빨간 목도리 하나와 겨울 양말 두 켤레 맞으시죠?
여 네. 이 할인 쿠폰을 사용할 수 있나요?
남 물론입니다. 그 쿠폰으로, 총 금액의 10%를 할인받으실 수 있습니다.
여 잘됐군요. 여기 제 신용카드요.

STEP ① · ② Listen & Choose

본문 p.42

01 ⓐ **02** ⓐ **03** ⓑ **04** ⓑ **05** ⓐ **06** ⓑ **07** ⓑ **08** ⓒ **09** ⓑ **10** ⓒ

01 ⓐ

해설 여자가 사려는 노트북 가방은 세일해서 25달러이다.

어휘 laptop 노트북
original 원래의

M Good afternoon. May I help you?
W Yes, please. I want to buy a bag for my laptop.
M How about this one? It's on sale for only $25. The original price was $60.
W Wow, more than 50% off? I'll take it.
M Here it is.

남 안녕하세요. 도와드릴까요?
여 네. 제 노트북을 위한 가방을 사고 싶어요.
남 이건 어떠신가요? 세일해서 25달러밖에 안 해요. 원래 가격은 60달러였어요.
여 와, 50% 넘는 할인이네요? 그걸로 살게요.
남 여기 있습니다.

02 ⓐ

해설 남자는 작은 컵($5) 두 개와 중간 컵($10) 한 개를 산다고 했으므로 지불할 금액은 20달러이다.

어휘 depend on ~에 따라 다르다

W Hello. How can I help you?
M Hi, how much is the ice cream?
W It depends on the size. The small cup is $5, the medium is $10, and the large is $15. What size would you like?
M I'll take two smalls and one medium.
W Okay.

여 안녕하세요. 어떻게 도와드릴까요?
남 안녕하세요, 아이스크림은 얼마인가요?
여 크기에 따라 다릅니다. 작은 컵은 5달러, 중간 컵은 10달러, 그리고 큰 컵은 15달러입니다. 어떤 사이즈를 원하세요?
남 작은 컵 두 개와 중간 컵 한 개 주세요.
여 알겠습니다.

03 ⓑ

해설 여자는 캠핑 의자($20) 4개를 구매할 예정이고, 총 금액에서 10% 할인을 받을 수 있으므로 지불할 금액은 72달러이다.

어휘 recommend 추천하다
bestselling 베스트셀러의, 가장 잘 팔리는
offer 제공하다

W Hi, I'm looking for camping chairs. Can you recommend one?
M Good morning. This is our bestselling chair. They're $20 each.
W That sounds good. I need four chairs. Do you offer any discounts?
M Yes. Since your total purchase is over $70, we'll give you a 10% discount on the total amount.

여 안녕하세요, 캠핑 의자를 찾고 있는데요. 하나 추천해주실 수 있나요?
남 안녕하세요. 이것이 가장 잘 팔리는 의자입니다. 개당 20달러입니다.
여 좋은 것 같네요. 의자 4개가 필요해요. 할인해주실 수 있나요?
남 네. 총 구매 금액이 70달러가 넘기 때문에 총액에서 10%를 할인해드리겠습니다.

04 ⓑ

해설 남자는 컵이 포함된 찻주전자 세트를 사기로 했으므로 지불할 금액은 30달러이다.

어휘 teapot 찻주전자
come with ~이 딸려 있다

M Hello. I'm looking for a teapot for my mother.
W Okay. How about this teapot with a classic design?
M I think she'll like it. How much is it?
W It's $20. But if you like this design, we also have this teapot set that comes with the cups. It's only $30.
M Great! I'll take the set.

남 안녕하세요. 저는 어머니께 드릴 찻주전자를 찾고 있어요.
여 네. 클래식한 디자인의 이 찻주전자는 어떠신가요?
남 어머니가 좋아하실 것 같아요. 얼마죠?
여 20달러입니다. 하지만 이 디자인이 마음에 드신다면 컵이 포함된 찻주전자 세트도 있습니다. 30달러밖에 안 합니다.
남 좋네요! 세트로 사겠습니다.

05 ⓐ

해설 여자는 강아지 쿠션($40) 한 개를 구매할 예정이고, 특별 판촉 행사로 10% 할인이 적용되므로 지불할 금액은 36달러이다.

어휘 originally 원래
promotion 판촉[홍보]

W Hello. I'm looking for a cushion for my dog.
M Okay, these are the most popular models.
W The pink one looks cute. How much is it?
M Originally, it was $40. But due to a special promotion, you can get a 10% discount on cushions.
W Excellent! I'll buy one cushion, then.

여 안녕하세요. 저희 강아지를 위한 쿠션을 찾고 있어요.
남 네, 이것들이 가장 인기 있는 모델이에요.
여 핑크색 쿠션이 귀엽네요. 얼마인가요?
남 원래 그건 40달러였어요. 하지만 특별 판촉 행사로 쿠션들에 대해 10% 할인 받으실 수 있어요.
여 좋네요! 그럼 쿠션을 하나 살게요.

06 ⓑ

해설 남자는 어린이 승차권($8) 한 장, 어른 승차권($15) 두 장을 구매할 예정이다. 남자의 멤버십 포인트가 10달러의 가치가 있으므로 지불할 금액은 28달러이다.

어휘 one-way 편도의
worth ~의 가치가 있는

M Excuse me. I'd like to purchase one-way tickets for two adults and one child.
W It's $15 for adults and $8 for children.
M Can I get a discount using my membership points? Here is my membership card.
W Yes, I'll check it. [pause] It says you have 1,000 points, worth $10.
M Okay. I'd like to use them all.

남 실례합니다. 어른 두 명과 어린이 한 명의 편도 승차권을 구매하고 싶습니다.
여 어른은 15달러, 어린이는 8달러입니다.
남 제 멤버십 포인트를 사용해서 할인을 받을 수 있나요? 여기 제 멤버십 카드예요.
여 네, 확인해보겠습니다. [잠시 후] 10달러의 가치가 있는 1,000포인트가 있다고 나오네요.
남 네. 포인트를 전부 사용하겠습니다.

07 ⓑ

해설 여자는 토요일 좌석($100) 두 자리를 예약하는데 20%의 학생 할인을 받을 수 있으므로 지불할 금액은 160달러이다.

어휘 reserve 예약하다
weekday 평일
weekend 주말

W I'd like to reserve seats for the musical *Lion King*. How much are the tickets?
M $80 on weekdays and $100 on weekends.
W I'd like to reserve two tickets for this Saturday. Do you offer a student discount?
M Yes. If you have a student ID card, you can get a 20% discount each.
W Terrific. These are our student ID cards, and I'll pay with cash. Here.

여 뮤지컬 <라이언 킹>의 좌석을 예약하고 싶습니다. 표는 얼마인가요?
남 평일에는 80달러, 주말에는 100달러입니다.
여 이번 주 토요일 표 두 장을 예매하고 싶습니다. 학생 할인이 되나요?
남 네. 학생증이 있으면 각각 20% 할인 받으실 수 있습니다.
여 잘됐네요. 이건 저희 학생증이고요, 현금으로 계산할게요. 여기 있습니다.

08 ⓒ

해설 남자는 무선 이어폰($60) 두 쌍을 구매하고, 각각 선물 포장($1) 비용이 추가되므로 지불할 금액은 122달러이다.

어휘 wireless 무선의
gift-wrapped 선물용으로 포장된
extra 추가되는 것; 추가의

W Good afternoon. What I can I do for you?
M How much is this pair of wireless earphones?
W It's $60 for a pair.
M Great. I'll take two pairs for my children.
W Would you like them gift-wrapped? It's $1 extra for each item.
M Yes, please. Here's my credit card.

여 안녕하세요. 무엇을 도와드릴까요?
남 이 무선 이어폰은 얼마인가요?
여 한 쌍에 60달러입니다.
남 좋아요. 제 아이들을 위해 두 쌍 살게요.
여 선물용으로 포장해 드릴까요? 각 물품에 1달러씩 추가됩니다.
남 네, 부탁드려요. 여기 제 신용카드입니다.

09 ⓑ

M Honey, I think Paul needs new shoes.
W You're right. His shoes are getting too tight for his feet.
M Let's buy a pair online. I know a good store. [clicking sound] Have a look.
W Oh, how about these shoes? They're originally $100 a pair, but they're 30% off now.
M That's a good deal. Let's buy a pair.
W Okay.

남 여보, 폴에게 새 신발이 필요한 것 같아요.
여 당신 말이 맞아요. 신발이 아이 발에 너무 꽉 끼고 있어요.
남 온라인으로 한 켤레 삽시다. 내가 좋은 가게를 알고 있어요. [클릭하는 소리] 봐요.
여 오, 이 신발은 어때요? 원래는 한 켤레에 100달러인데, 지금 30% 할인 중이에요.
남 가격이 좋네요. 한 켤레 삽시다.
여 좋아요.

10 ⓒ

M Welcome to Daisy Valley Restaurant.
W Hi. I'd like to order some food to go. How much is the shrimp pasta and the chicken salad?
M The shrimp pasta is $20, and the chicken salad is $10.
W I'll take two shrimp pastas and one chicken salad, please.
M Sure.

남 데이지 밸리 레스토랑에 오신 것을 환영합니다.
여 안녕하세요. 포장 음식을 주문하고 싶은데요. 새우 파스타와 치킨 샐러드는 얼마인가요?
남 새우 파스타는 20달러이고, 치킨 샐러드는 10달러입니다.
여 새우 파스타 두 개랑 치킨 샐러드 하나 주세요.
남 알겠습니다.

STEP ③·④ Listen & Answer

본문 p.45

01 ③   **02** ③   **03** ②   **04** ③   **05** ②   **06** ③   **07** ④   **08** ②   **09** ③   **10** ②

01 ③

M Hello. How can I help you today?
W I want to send this package to Germany.
M Sure. Let me weigh it for you first. [pause] 5 kilograms. When would you like it to arrive?
W As soon as possible.
M It is $20 per kilogram for express delivery. That will guarantee that it arrives tomorrow.
W That's a bit too expensive....
M Normal shipping will save you 30%, but it will take two or three extra days.
W That sounds better for me. And I would like insurance, too.
M That will be an additional $5. Is that alright?
W Yes. Here is my credit card.
M Thank you. Here is your receipt.

남 안녕하세요. 오늘 어떻게 도와드릴까요?
여 이 소포를 독일로 보내고 싶어요.
남 네. 제가 먼저 무게를 달아보겠습니다. [잠시 후] 5킬로그램이네요. 언제 도착하기를 원하시나요?
여 가능한 한 빨리요.
남 속달 우편은 킬로그램당 20달러입니다. 그것은 소포가 내일 도착하는 것을 보장합니다.
여 그건 좀 너무 비싸네요….
남 일반 배송은 30% 절약되지만, 추가로 2~3일이 더 소요됩니다.
여 그게 더 좋을 것 같아요. 그리고 보험도 들고 싶어요.
남 그건 5달러가 추가됩니다. 괜찮으신가요?
여 네. 여기 제 신용카드요.
남 감사합니다. 여기 영수증입니다.

02 ③

W Hello, welcome to Discount Mart. How may I help you?
M I would like to order the 50-inch flat screen TV, the one on sale.
W Okay. It is $550 with the discount, for the standing model.
M Oh, but I would like to fix it to my wall.

여 안녕하세요, 디스카운트 마트에 오신 것을 환영합니다. 어떻게 도와드릴까요?
남 50인치 평면 TV를 주문하고 싶습니다. 할인 판매 중인 것으로요.
여 알겠습니다. 세워놓는 모델은 할인해서 550달러입니다.
남 아, 하지만 저는 벽에 고정시키고 싶어요.

어휘 **flat** 평평한
on sale 할인 판매 중인
installation 설치
delivery 배송
free 무료의
address 주소

W Then, there will be an extra $40 for installation.
M That's fine. And how much is delivery?
W Delivery is $20, but it is free for gold card members and half price for silver card members.
M I have a gold card, and I'll take the TV, with installation and delivery.
W Great. Can I have your name and address?
M Certainly.

여 그러면 설치하는 데 40달러가 추가됩니다.
남 괜찮아요. 그리고 배송비는 얼마인가요?
여 배송비는 20달러이지만, 골드카드 회원은 무료이고 실버카드 회원은 반값입니다.
남 저는 골드카드를 가지고 있고, 설치와 배송을 같이 해서 TV를 살게요.
여 좋습니다. 고객님의 성함과 주소를 말씀해주시겠어요?
남 물론이죠.

03 ②

해설 여자는 기본 도넛($2)과 초콜릿 도넛($3)을 각각 10개씩 구매한다고 했으므로 총 50달러이다. 또한, 판촉 활동으로 5달러에 뮤직 박스를 구매하고, 멤버십 적립 포인트로 5달러를 할인 받으므로 지불할 금액은 50달러이다.

어휘 **plain** 보통의, 평범한
promotion 판촉[홍보]
save 모으다; 절약하다

M Hello. Is there anything I can help you with?
W Hi, I'd like to buy some doughnuts. How much are they?
M The plain ones are $2 and the chocolate ones are $3.
W I'll have ten of each. And do you sell this music box as well?
M Yes, as a promotion, any customer who spends more than $30 can buy this music box for $5. Its original price was $10.
W I'll take one. My daughter will love it.
M Great. Do you have a store membership?
W Yes, here's my membership card. Can I use the points I saved?
M Sure. Let me check. [pause] You can get $5 off with your points.
W Good. Here's my credit card.

남 안녕하세요. 제가 뭐 도와드릴 일이 있을까요?
여 안녕하세요, 도넛을 좀 사고 싶은데요. 이것들은 얼마인가요?
남 기본 도넛은 2달러이고 초콜릿 도넛은 3달러입니다.
여 각각 10개씩 주세요. 그리고 이 뮤직 박스도 판매하시나요?
남 네, 판촉 활동으로 30달러 넘게 구매하신 모든 고객님들은 이 뮤직 박스를 5달러에 구매하실 수 있습니다. 그것의 원래 가격은 10달러였어요.
여 하나 살게요. 제 딸이 좋아할 거예요.
남 알겠습니다. 매장 회원권을 가지고 계신가요?
여 네, 여기 제 멤버십 카드입니다. 적립한 포인트를 사용할 수 있나요?
남 물론입니다. 확인해볼게요. [잠시 후] 포인트로 5달러 할인 받으실 수 있습니다.
여 좋아요. 여기 제 신용카드요.

04 ③

해설 남자는 큰 꽃바구니($65) 한 개를 구매할 예정이다. 그리고 화분($20) 두 개 중 하나는 반값($10)에 살 수 있으므로 지불할 금액은 95달러이다.

어휘 **free of charge** 무료의
anniversary 기념일
flower pot 화분
form 양식

W Good afternoon. What can I help you with?
M Hi, I'd like to send a flower basket to my wife.
W Sure. The prices start from $35. The small basket is $35, the medium is $50, and the large is $65.
M I'll take the large one.
W Great. Would you like to leave a message card? It's free of charge.
M Yes, please write "Happy Anniversary" on it.
W Congratulations! Do you need anything else?
M Well, how much is this flower pot?
W It's $20. And if you buy two, you get the second one at half price.
M That sounds nice. I'll take two. Please deliver them with the flower basket. Here's my credit card.
W Thank you. Please write your address in this form.

여 안녕하세요. 무엇을 도와드릴까요?
남 안녕하세요. 아내에게 꽃바구니를 보내고 싶은데요.
여 네. 가격은 35달러부터 시작합니다. 작은 바구니는 35달러, 중간 바구니는 50달러, 큰 바구니는 65달러입니다.
남 큰 것으로 하겠습니다.
여 알겠습니다. 메시지 카드를 남기시겠어요? 그것은 무료예요.
남 네, '기념일 축하해'라고 써주세요.
여 축하드려요! 그 밖에 필요한 것은 없으신가요?
남 음, 이 화분은 얼마인가요?
여 20달러입니다. 그리고 두 개를 사시면 두 번째 것은 반값에 드려요.
남 괜찮네요. 두 개 살게요. 꽃바구니와 함께 배달해주세요. 여기 제 신용카드요.
여 감사합니다. 이 양식에 주소를 적어주세요.

05 ②

해설 여자는 2시 기차의 일반석($40)을 탈 예정이고, 휴일에 받을 수 있는 멤버십 할인은 10%이므로 지불할 금액은 36달러이다.

W Hello, one ticket to Seoul, please.
M I'm sorry, but the one o'clock train is almost full. We only have first class seats for $70.

여 안녕하세요, 서울행 표 한 장 주세요.
남 죄송하지만, 1시 기차는 거의 만석입니다. 70달러의 일등석 좌석만 있습니다.

어휘 **first class** 일등석[칸]
normally 보통은; 정상적으로
holiday 휴일
regular 일반적인, 보통의; 정기적인
extra 추가의

W That's okay. I have this membership card. So I can get a 20% discount, right?

M Normally, yes. But today is a holiday, so the discount is only 10%.

W Oh, really? When is the next train?

M Two o'clock. Regular seats are $40. But the train makes two extra stops.

W How much longer will it take?

M An extra 35 minutes.

W That's fine. I'll take a regular seat and use my membership card.

M Alright, here you are. Have a good trip.

여 괜찮아요, 전 이 멤버십 카드를 가지고 있어요. 그럼 20% 할인 받을 수 있죠, 맞나요?

남 보통은 그렇습니다. 하지만 오늘은 휴일이라서 10%만 할인됩니다.

여 아, 정말요? 다음 기차는 언제 있나요?

남 2시에 있습니다. 일반석은 40달러입니다. 하지만 그 기차는 두 정거장에 더 정차합니다.

여 얼마나 더 오래 걸릴까요?

남 35분 더 걸립니다.

여 괜찮아요. 일반석으로 하고 제 멤버십 카드를 사용할게요.

남 알겠습니다, 여기 있습니다. 즐거운 여행되십시오.

---

06 ③

해설 일인당 60달러인 6코스 메뉴를 7인분 주문하고 개인 공간을 대여하는 데 30달러가 추가되었는데 사전에 예약해서 총액의 10%를 할인 받으므로 지불할 금액은 405달러이다.

어휘 **raise** 인상하다, 올리다
private (장소가 남의 방해를 받지 않고) 혼자 있을 수 있는
in advance 사전에, 미리

W Hello, sir. How was your meal?

M It was great. I really enjoyed the main dish, a lamb steak.

W I'm glad you enjoyed it. So, you had the 6-course menu for seven people, correct?

M Yes, it costs $50 per person, right?

W Well, the price was raised to $60 last month.

M Wow, that's huge. And there must be a charge for reserving a private table.

W Yes, that costs an extra $30.

M Okay. Can I get a 10% discount for making a reservation in advance?

W Let me check. [pause] Yes, you can get a 10% discount from the total amount. Would you like to pay with your credit card?

M Yes, here you are.

여 안녕하세요, 손님. 식사는 어떠셨나요?

남 아주 좋았어요. 메인 요리인 양고기 스테이크가 정말 맛있었어요.

여 만족하셨다니 기쁩니다. 그러니까 6코스 메뉴를 7명분 주문하셨죠, 맞나요?

남 네, 그 메뉴가 일인당 50달러죠, 맞나요?

여 저, 지난달에 가격이 60달러로 인상되었어요.

남 와, 그건 크네요. 그리고 분명 개인 테이블 예약에 대한 비용이 있겠네요.

여 네, 그것에 대한 추가 30달러가 있습니다.

남 네, 사전에 예약한 것에 대한 10% 할인을 받을 수 있나요?

여 확인해보겠습니다. [잠시 후] 네, 총액에서 10% 할인 받으실 수 있습니다. 신용카드로 지불하시겠어요?

남 네, 여기 있습니다.

---

07 ④

해설 여자는 자동 스프링클러($60)를 구입하고 짧은 호스($10)도 구입하는데, 그 호스는 쿠폰을 사용하여 무료로 받기 때문에 여자가 지불해야 할 금액은 60달러이다.

어휘 **plant a garden** 정원[뜰]에 나무를 심다
sprinkler 스프링클러((물 뿌리는 장치))
automatic 자동의, 자동적인
come with ~이 딸려 있다
separately 별도로, 각각

M Hi, what can I do for you?

W Well, I'm thinking of planting a garden, but I don't know what kind of sprinkler to buy.

M We have several to choose from. This one here, for instance, is great for small gardens. It's $30.

W Hmm.... What about this one? It looks good.

M It's an automatic sprinkler. It uses a timer, and it costs $60.

W I travel a lot, so that's the one I want. Does it come with a hose?

M No, those are sold separately. A short hose is $10, and a longer one is $20.

W The shorter one should be fine. Oh, I also have this coupon I downloaded from the Internet. It's for a free hose. Can I use it?

M Certainly. It can be used for the hose you want.

W Great.

남 안녕하세요. 무엇을 도와드릴까요?

여 음, 정원에 나무를 심으려고 하는데요. 어떤 종류의 스프링클러를 사야 할지 모르겠어요.

남 고르실 수 있는 몇 가지가 있습니다. 예를 들어, 여기 있는 이것은 작은 정원에 좋습니다. 30달러예요.

여 음…. 이것은 어떤가요? 좋아 보이네요.

남 이 제품은 자동 스프링클러입니다. 타이머를 사용하고, 가격은 60달러입니다.

여 저는 여행을 자주 다녀서 그것이 제가 원하는 거네요. 호스도 딸려 오나요?

남 아뇨, 호스는 별도로 판매됩니다. 짧은 호스는 10달러이고, 더 긴 호스는 20달러입니다.

여 짧은 호스가 좋겠어요. 아, 인터넷에서 다운로드한 이 쿠폰도 가지고 있어요. 무료 호스 쿠폰이에요. 이걸 사용할 수 있을까요?

남 물론입니다. 손님께서 원하시는 호스에 사용하실 수 있습니다.

여 좋아요.

08 ②

해설 남자는 50달러인 월간 회원권의 3개월 치를 지불하겠다고 했는데 10% 학생 할인을 받을 수 있으므로 지불할 금액은 135달러이다.

어휘 sign up for ~을 가입하다, 신청하다
monthly 매달의; 월 1회의
yearly 매년의; 연 1회의
fee 요금
discount 할인
fill out ~을 작성하다, 기입하다

W Welcome to Paradise Fitness. How can I help you?
M Hi. I'd like to sign up for a membership.
W We offer monthly membership and yearly membership. Which one do you want?
M How much is the monthly membership?
W The fee is $50 per month. The yearly membership fee is $480, so it could save you $120.
M I'm a college student. Is there a discount for students?
W Yes. You can get a 10% discount for both memberships if you have a student ID.
M Okay. I'll pay for a monthly membership for three months. Here's my student ID.
W All right. Can you fill out this form?
M Sure.

여 파라다이스 피트니스에 오신 걸 환영합니다. 어떻게 도와드릴까요?
남 안녕하세요. 회원 가입을 하고 싶어요.
여 저희는 월간 회원권과 연간 회원권을 제공합니다. 어떤 걸 원하세요?
남 월간 회원권은 얼마인가요?
여 요금은 한 달에 50달러입니다. 연간 회원권은 480달러이니 120달러를 절약하실 수 있어요.
남 저는 대학생인데요. 학생 할인이 있나요?
여 네. 학생증이 있으시면 두 회원권 모두 10% 할인 받으실 수 있습니다.
남 좋아요. 월간 회원권 3개월치를 지불할게요. 여기 제 학생증이에요.
여 알겠습니다. 이 양식을 작성해주시겠어요?
남 물론이죠.

09 ③

해설 여자가 구매한 흰색 드레스는 50달러인데 20% 할인 중이므로 40달러이고 거기에 25달러짜리 샌들도 구입했으므로 지불할 금액은 65달러이다.

어휘 costume 의상, 복장
dress up 옷을 갖춰 입다, 변장을 하다
wing 날개
sandal 샌들
finishing touch 마무리, 마지막 손질

W Excuse me. I'm looking for a Halloween costume for my daughter.
M Come this way. How old is she?
W She's 7 years old and she wants to dress up like an angel.
M We have several angel costumes here. How about this white dress?
W It's pretty! How much is it?
M It was originally $50, but it's 20% off now.
W That sounds great. Wait, this dress doesn't have wings.
M It does. Look here! It has beautiful white wings on the back.
W Good, I'll take it. I also like these gold sandals.
M You made a good choice. The sandals will be the finishing touch for the dress, and they're only $25.
W Perfect. I'll take them as well. Here's my credit card.

여 실례합니다. 제 딸이 입을 핼러윈 의상을 찾고 있는데요.
남 이쪽으로 오세요. 따님이 몇 살인가요?
여 일곱 살이고 그 애는 천사처럼 차려 입고 싶어 해요.
남 여기 천사 의상이 몇 벌 있습니다. 이 흰색 드레스는 어때세요?
여 예쁘군요! 얼마인가요?
남 원래는 50달러였는데, 지금은 20% 할인 중입니다.
여 그거 좋은데요. 잠깐만요, 이 드레스에는 날개가 없네요.
남 있습니다. 여기 보세요! 등에 아름다운 하얀 날개가 있어요.
여 좋아요, 그걸 살게요. 이 금색 샌들도 마음에 들어요.
남 잘 선택하셨어요. 그 샌들은 드레스의 마무리가 될 텐데 25달러밖에 안 합니다.
여 완벽하군요. 그것도 살게요. 여기 제 신용카드요.

10 ②

해설 남자가 고른 은색 쟁반은 75달러로 검은색 쟁반보다 10달러 더 저렴하다고 했으므로 가격은 65달러이다. 거기에 포장비 4달러를 추가해야 하므로 지불할 금액은 69달러이다.

어휘 housewarming 집들이
hand-painted 손으로 그림을 그린
popular 인기 있는
tray 쟁반
gift-wrap 선물용으로 포장하다
charge 요금

W Hello. How can I help you?
M I'm looking for a nice gift for my friend. She just moved into a new house.
W You've come to the right place. We have a great collection of housewarming gifts.
M Those glasses look nice. How much are they?
W These hand-painted glasses are very popular these days. The set costs $150.
M It's too expensive. I'd like to stay under $80.
W Then I have something you'll like. How about this tray? It's $75.

여 안녕하세요. 어떻게 도와드릴까요?
남 친구에게 줄 멋진 선물을 찾고 있어요. 친구가 새 집으로 이사를 막 했거든요.
여 제대로 찾아오셨네요. 저희는 집들이 선물을 아주 많이 가지고 있습니다.
남 이 유리잔들이 멋져 보이네요. 그것들은 얼마인가요?
여 손으로 그림을 그린 이 유리잔들은 요즘 아주 인기가 많답니다. 세트가 150달러입니다.
남 너무 비싸군요. 저는 80달러 미만으로 유지하고 싶어요.
여 그러면 좋아하실 만한 게 있습니다. 이 쟁반은 어떤가요? 75달러입니다.

M	Hmm, I don't think she likes black. Is there a brighter color?	남	음, 제 친구가 검은색을 좋아하지 않는 것 같아서요. 더 밝은 색이 있나요?
W	We also have green and silver. The green tray is the same price as the black one, but the silver tray is $10 cheaper.	여	녹색과 은색도 있습니다. 녹색 쟁반은 검은색과 같은 가격이지만 은색 쟁반은 10달러 더 저렴합니다.
M	Perfect. I'll take a silver one. Could I have it gift-wrapped?	남	완벽해요. 은색 쟁반을 살게요. 선물용 포장을 해주실 수 있나요?
W	Yes, but there's a $4 charge for that. Is that alright with you?	여	네, 하지만 그것은 4달러 요금이 있습니다. 괜찮으세요?
M	No problem. Here's my credit card.	남	문제없어요. 여기 제 신용카드입니다.

 04 그림과 불일치하는 내용

✳✳ **기출 맛보기**

본문 p.51

01 ⑤

해설 달력 아래에 식물을 뒀다고 했으므로 그림 속의 웨딩 사진이 대화의 내용과 일치하지 않는다.

어휘 decorate 꾸미다, 장식하다
striped 줄무늬의
rug 깔개, 러그
bookshelf 책꽂이
calendar 달력
invite A over A를 집으로 초대하다
housewarming party 집들이

W	Hi, Harry. Congratulations on your wedding. Did you finish decorating the new house?	여	안녕, 해리. 결혼 축하해. 새집 꾸미는 건 다했어?
M	I just finished the living room. Look at this picture, Linda.	남	거실만 끝냈어. 이 사진 좀 봐, 린다.
W	Wow. I love the striped curtains on the window.	여	와. 창문에 있는 줄무늬 커튼이 너무 마음에 든다.
M	Thanks. Do you see those two cushions on the sofa? My sister made them as wedding gifts.	남	고마워. 소파 위에 쿠션 두 개 보여? 내 여동생이 결혼 선물로 만들어줬어.
W	That's lovely. Oh, you put a round table on the rug.	여	사랑스럽네. 아, 깔개 위에 원형 탁자를 뒀구나.
M	Yeah. We spend time reading books around the table. What do you think of the clock on the bookshelf?	남	응. 우리는 탁자에 둘러앉아 책 읽으며 시간을 보내거든. 책꽂이 위에 있는 시계는 어떤 것 같아?
W	It looks good in that room. By the way, is that a plant under the calendar?	여	방에 잘 어울리는 것 같아. 그건 그렇고, 달력 아래에 있는 게 식물이야?
M	Yes. I placed it there because the plant helps to clean the air.	남	맞아. 그 식물이 공기를 깨끗하게 해주기 때문에 거기에 뒀어.
W	You decorated your house really well.	여	집을 정말 잘 꾸몄구나.
M	Thanks. I'll invite you over when we have the housewarming party.	남	고마워. 집들이 할 때 초대할게.

STEP **1** · **2** Listen & Choose

본문 p.52

01 ⓒ **02** ⓑ **03** ⓐ **04** ⓑ **05** ⓒ **06** ⓐ **07** ⓑ **08** ⓒ **09** ⓑ **10** ⓒ

01 ⓒ

해설 여자는 물방울무늬인 것이 좋다고 했고, 남자는 체크무늬인 것이 더 좋다며 그것을 구입하기로 했다.

어휘 on sale 할인 판매 중인
polka dot 물방울무늬의
checkered 체크무늬의

M	These umbrellas are on sale! Which ones do you like?	남	이 우산들이 할인 판매 중이야! 넌 어느 것이 맘에 들어?
W	Well, I like the polka dot ones better than the plain ones. How about you?	여	음, 나는 무늬가 없는 것보다는 물방울무늬인 것이 좋아. 넌 어때?
M	I prefer the checkered ones. I'll take one of them.	남	나는 체크무늬인 것이 더 좋아. 그중에 하나를 사야겠어.

02 ⓑ

해설 여자는 뚜껑 있는 둥근 것이 좋다고 했고 그것은 뚜껑을 여는 페달도 있다고 했다.

어휘 trash can 쓰레기통
lid 뚜껑
make a good choice 잘 선택하다
pedal (자전거 등의) 페달

M There are several kinds of trash cans, ma'am. Do you want the square one with a lid or the round one without a lid?
W I don't like either. I want the round one with a lid.
M You made a good choice. It also has a pedal to open the lid.

남 손님, 쓰레기통이 몇 가지 종류가 있습니다. 뚜껑 있는 네모난 것을 원하세요, 아니면 뚜껑 없는 둥근 것을 원하세요?
여 둘 다 마음에 들지 않아요. 전 뚜껑 있는 둥근 것이 좋아요.
남 잘 선택하셨습니다. 그것은 뚜껑을 여는 페달도 있어요.

03 ⓐ

해설 the former가 가리키는 것이 무엇인지 주의한다. 여자가 하트 모양 접시와 사과 모양 접시를 말했으므로 전자는 하트 모양 접시이다.

어휘 either A or B A와 B 둘 중 하나
go with ~을 선택하다, 받아들이다
the former (둘 중에) 전자
(↔ the latter 후자)

M Honey, what about the teardrop-shaped plate? It has a heart pattern on it.
W I don't like the shape. I want to choose either the heart-shaped plate or the apple-shaped one. What do you think?
M In that case, I'll go with the former.

남 여보, 눈물 모양 접시 어때요? 이건 하트 무늬가 있어요.
여 모양이 마음에 들지 않아요. 하트 모양 접시와 사과 모양 접시 중에서 선택하고 싶어요. 어떻게 생각해요?
남 그렇다면 전자를 선택할게요.

04 ⓑ

해설 남자의 가방은 사각형 여행 가방으로, 이름표가 달려 있고 무늬가 없다고 했다.

어휘 suitcase 여행 가방

M Oh, no! One of my bags is missing.
W What does it look like? Is it a backpack?
M No, it's a suitcase. It has a name tag where my name and address are written. It's square without any pattern on it.

남 아, 이런! 내 가방 중 하나가 없어졌어요.
여 어떻게 생긴 거죠? 배낭인가요?
남 아니에요, 여행 가방이에요. 제 이름과 주소가 쓰여 있는 이름표가 있어요. 아무 무늬가 없는 사각형 모양이에요.

05 ⓒ

해설 마름모 모양이고 꼬리에 리본이 달린 연이 좋다고 했다.

어휘 look like ~처럼 보이다
quite 꽤
diamond shape 마름모 모양
tail 꼬리

M I think Bridget would love the kite that looks like a dragon.
W Well, I thought it looked quite scary.... How about the usual diamond shape?
M I think it's too simple. But the same shape with the ribbons on the tail would be good for her.
W I like that one, too. Let's get it.

남 브리짓은 용처럼 보이는 이 연을 좋아할 것 같아요.
여 음, 나는 그것이 꽤 무서워 보인다고 생각했어요…. 일반적인 마름모 모양은 어때요?
남 그건 너무 단순한 것 같아요. 그렇지만 꼬리에 리본이 달린 같은 모양은 그 애에게 적합할 거예요.
여 나도 그게 좋아요. 그걸로 사요.

06 ⓐ

해설 스피커 사이에 모니터가 있고, 전자 키보드가 책상 위에 올려져 있다고 했다.

어휘 monitor (컴퓨터) 모니터
crowded 꽉 찬; 복잡한
electric 전기의
convenient 편리한

M Grace, let me show you my new desk.
W Wow, Jake! It's so cool.
M Look at the monitor between the speakers. I changed my old monitor for this new one.
W Looks nice. But isn't your desk too crowded to put your electric keyboard on it?
M It's fine with me. I find it convenient there.

남 그레이스, 내 새 책상을 보여줄게.
여 와, 제이크! 정말 멋지다.
남 스피커 사이의 모니터를 봐. 나는 예전 모니터를 이 새 모니터로 바꿨어.
여 좋아 보이네. 하지만 네 책상은 전자 키보드를 올려놓기에 너무 꽉 차지 않아?
남 난 괜찮아. 난 거기가 편리하다고 생각해.

07 ⓑ

해설 바닥에 꽃무늬 매트가 있다고 했으므로 그림 속의 줄무늬 매트가 대화의 내용과 일치하지 않는다.

어휘 indoor 실내의

W Henry. I set up an exercise room in my house.
M Cool! The indoor bike under the clock looks nice.
W Thanks. What do you think of the mat with the flower pattern on the floor?

여 헨리. 나 집에 운동하는 방을 만들었어.
남 멋지네! 시계 밑에 있는 실내 자전거가 멋져 보여.
여 고마워. 바닥에 있는 꽃무늬 매트는 어떻게 생각해?

| mat 매트, 깔개
flower pattern 꽃무늬
hula-hoop 훌라후프 | M | Oh, it looks great! Is that a hula-hoop under the calendar? | 남 | 오, 좋아 보이는데! 달력 아래 그거 훌라후프야? |
| | W | Yes. I exercise with it every day. | 여 | 맞아. 난 그걸로 매일 운동하고 있어. |

08 ⓒ

해설 그네 앞에 시소가 있다고 했으 므로 그림 속 벤치가 대화의 내용과 일치하지 않는다. 어휘 community 지역 사회 slide 미끄럼틀 swing 그네 see-saw 시소	W	Honey, Sally sent me a picture of the new community park near her house.	여	여보, 샐리가 집 근처에 있는 새로운 지역 공원 사진을 내게 보내줬어요.
	M	Let me see it. Oh, I can see the elephant face at the top of the slide.	남	어디 봐요. 아, 미끄럼틀 맨 위에 코끼리 얼굴이 보이네요.
	W	Yeah, there are also swings next to it. Our son would like this park, too.	여	네, 그것 옆에 그네도 있어요. 우리 아들도 이 공원을 좋아할 것 같아요.
	M	He sure would. Oh, and there is a see-saw in front of the swings, too.	남	분명 그럴 거예요. 아, 그리고 그네 앞에 시소도 있네요.
	W	Wow, this park has everything a child could want.	여	와, 이 공원은 아이가 원하는 모든 것들이 있네요.

09 ⓑ

해설 네모난 탁자 대신 둥근 탁자 위 에 모자를 놓았다고 했으므로 그림 속 네모난 탁자가 대화의 내용과 일 치하지 않는다. 어휘 eye-catching 눈길을 끄는 instead of ~ 대신에 suggest 제안하다 magician 마술사 stick 지팡이	W	Austin, there have been some changes on our poster.	여	오스틴, 우리 포스터에 약간의 변화가 생겼어.
	M	Okay. Let me take a look.	남	응. 내가 한번 볼게.
	W	First of all, I wrote the date and the time under the title, Magic Show.	여	우선, 난 '마술 쇼'라는 제목 아래에 날짜와 시간을 적었어.
	M	Nice choice. It's more eye-catching. Oh, you put the hat on the round table, instead of the square one.	남	좋은 선택이야. 이게 더 눈길을 끄네. 아, 네모난 탁자 대신 둥근 탁자 위에 모자를 놓았구나.
	W	Yes. And as you suggested, I drew a magician holding a magic stick.	여	응. 그리고 네가 제안한 대로 마술 지팡이를 들고 있는 마술사를 그렸어.
	M	Nice. I think it's perfect now.	남	좋아. 이제 완벽한 것 같아.

10 ⓒ

해설 벽에 세 개의 사진이 있다고 했 으므로 그림 속 두 개의 사진이 대화 의 내용과 일치하지 않는다. 어휘 flower pot 화분 wall 벽	M	Mom, this is a picture from Science Day.	남	엄마, 이건 과학의 날 사진이에요.
	W	Let me see. The woman wearing glasses must be your science teacher.	여	어디 보자. 안경을 쓴 여성분이 틀림없이 너의 과학 선생님이겠구나.
	M	Yes, she is. Do you see the rocket next to the flower pot? I made it myself.	남	네, 맞아요. 화분 옆에 로켓 보이세요? 제가 직접 만들었어요.
	W	Oh, it looks fantastic! Good job. By the way, what are the three pictures on the wall?	여	오, 정말 멋져 보여! 잘했구나. 그런데, 벽에 있는 사진 세 개는 뭐니?
	M	They are pictures of great scientists.	남	그건 위대한 과학자들의 사진이에요.

STEP ③ · ④ Listen & Answer   본문 p.56

01 ③   **02** ④   **03** ⑤   **04** ②   **05** ⑤   **06** ④   **07** ⑤   **08** ⑤   **09** ⑤   **10** ⑤

01 ③

해설 남자가 물방울무늬 넥타이를 찾지 못해 대신 체크무늬를 골랐다 고 했으므로 그림 속의 넥타이가 대 화의 내용과 일치하지 않는다. 어휘 dress shirt 와이셔츠 high-top (발목을 덮는) 하이 톱의 sneakers 운동화 charger 충전기	W	Honey, did you finish packing your suitcase for your business trip?	여	여보. 당신 출장을 위한 여행 가방은 다 쌌나요?
	M	Yes, I put in the striped dress shirt you bought me for my birthday.	남	네, 당신이 내 생일에 사준 줄무늬 와이셔츠를 넣었어요.
	W	Good. You'll also need a pair of socks since you'll stay overnight.	여	잘했어요. 하룻밤 묵을 거니까 양말 한 켤레도 필요할 거예요.
	M	I've already packed a pair of plain socks.	남	이미 무늬 없는 양말 한 켤레를 챙겼어요.
	W	What about your tie? Did you find the one with polka dots?	여	넥타이는요? 물방울무늬가 있는 것을 찾았나요?

M	No, I looked everywhere but I couldn't find it. I chose a checkered one instead.	남	아뇨, 모든 곳을 봤지만 찾지 못했어요. 대신 체크 무늬 넥타이를 골랐어요.
W	All right. Oh, I think you'd better take extra shoes just in case.	여	좋아요. 아, 만약을 위해 여분의 신발을 가져가는 게 좋을 것 같아요.
M	Yeah, I'm taking my high-top sneakers with me.	남	네, 목이 긴 운동화를 가져갈 거예요.
W	Okay. And you didn't forget the charger for your cell phone, did you?	여	알겠어요. 그리고 당신 휴대 전화 충전기를 잊지 않았죠, 그렇죠?
M	Of course not. It's in my suitcase.	남	물론 잊지 않았어요. 그건 내 여행 가방 안에 있어요.
W	Good. I think you're ready. Travel safe.	여	좋아요. 준비가 다 된 것 같네요. 조심히 다녀와요.
M	Thanks.	남	고마워요.

02 ④

해설 오른쪽 구석에 큰 곰 인형이 있다고 했으므로 그림 속의 기린 인형이 대화의 내용과 일치하지 않는다.

어휘 air balloon 열기구
ceiling 천장
check out 확인하다
you bet! 바로 그거야!, 물론이지!

M	Rachel, what are you looking at?	남	레이첼, 뭐 보고 있어요?
W	It's a photo of the new kids' cafe that opened up last month. I'm going to take James there.	여	지난달에 문을 연 새 키즈 카페 사진이에요. 제임스를 거기 데려가려고요.
M	He must be excited. Wow! Look at the hot air balloon hanging from the ceiling.	남	그 애가 신나겠군요. 와! 천장에 매달려 있는 열기구 좀 봐요.
W	Isn't it fantastic? Also, check out the ball pool on the left.	여	환상적이지 않나요? 또, 왼쪽에 있는 볼풀을 확인해보세요.
M	It's quite big and it even has a slide that's shaped like a train.	남	그건 꽤 크고 기차처럼 생긴 미끄럼틀도 있네요.
W	Yeah, James loves trains, so he'll probably enjoy sliding down there.	여	네, 제임스는 기차를 좋아하니 아마 거기서 미끄럼틀 타는 걸 즐길 거예요.
M	I'm sure he will. There's also a giant teddy bear standing in the right corner.	남	분명 그럴 거예요. 오른쪽 구석에 서 있는 거대한 곰 인형도 있군요.
W	Yes, it's a great place for kids. I really like the square table on the right of the photo.	여	네, 아이들에게 아주 좋은 곳이에요. 난 사진 오른쪽에 있는 네모난 테이블이 정말 마음에 들어요.
M	I know why. You can rest there while watching James play.	남	왜 그런지 알죠. 제임스가 노는 것을 보는 동안 거기서 쉴 수 있으니까요.
W	You bet! And we can also have a cup of tea and chat.	여	바로 그거예요! 그리고 우리는 차 한 잔 마시며 이야기도 나눌 수 있어요.
M	That sounds good.	남	좋네요.

03 ⑤

해설 대화에서 그림에 풍선 세 개가 그려져 있다고 언급하고 있음에 유의한다. 남자가 풍선이 다섯 개가 있는 게 어떠냐고 물었지만 여자가 수정할 수 없다고 했으므로 그림 속의 풍선의 수가 대화의 내용과 일치하지 않는다.

어휘 download 다운로드하다
swing 그네
square 정사각형의
turn (어떤 나이·시기가) 되다
frame 틀, 테; 액자
location 장소
slide 미끄럼틀

W	Honey, I downloaded a free invitation card for Chloe's birthday party.	여	여보, 클로에의 생일 파티를 위한 무료 초대장을 다운로드했어요.
M	Wow! I can't believe it's free. There's a smiling sun in the upper right corner.	남	와! 이게 무료라니 믿을 수가 없군요. 오른쪽 상단에 웃고 있는 태양이 있군요.
W	Look at the swing below it. There's a little bird sitting on the swing.	여	그것 아래의 그네를 보세요. 그네 위에 앉아 있는 작은 새 한 마리가 있어요.
M	How cute! And you wrote the message "Chloe is turning 5!" in the square frame.	남	귀여워라! 그리고 '클로에가 다섯 살이 됩니다!'라는 메시지를 네모난 틀 안에 적었군요.
W	Yes. And I also wrote the date and location of the party there.	여	네. 그리고 거기에 파티 날짜와 장소도 적었어요.
M	Good job. I also like the slide on the left. I'm sure Chloe will love it.	남	잘했어요. 난 왼쪽에 있는 미끄럼틀도 좋아요. 클로에가 좋아할 게 확실해요.
W	Can you see the three balloons hanging from the slide?	여	미끄럼틀에 매달린 풍선 세 개가 보이나요?
M	Well, since Chloe will be turning 5, how about having 5 balloons?	남	음, 클로에가 다섯 살이 되니까 풍선 다섯 개가 있는 게 어떨까요?
W	I'd love to, but I cannot change those. I can only change or add the things in the box.	여	나도 그러고 싶지만 그건 바꿀 수가 없어요. 이 상자 안에 있는 것들만 변경하거나 추가할 수 있거든요.
M	Okay. Then, let's print it like this.	남	알겠어요. 그럼 이렇게 인쇄를 합시다.

04 ②

해설 남자가 의자를 탁자 주위에 빙둘러놓았다고 했으므로 그림 속의 쌓여 있는 의자가 대화의 내용과 일치하지 않는다.

어휘 set up ~을 준비하다, 놓다
laptop 노트북 컴퓨터
somewhere 어떤 곳
coat stand (길게 세워 놓는) 코트걸이

W Hi, Tom. Have you prepared everything for the meeting?
M I think so, Ms. Stuart. First of all, I hung a whiteboard on the wall as you asked.
W Good. And I'm sure you set up some chairs.
M Yes, they're around the table.
W Oh, did you get a round table?
M Yes, I put it in the middle of the room.
W Great. And I hope you remembered the laptop we use for meetings.
M Of course. I placed it on the table.
W Perfect. We also need somewhere to hang coats.
M I set a coat stand next to the table.
W All right. Thanks, Tom.

여 안녕하세요, 톰. 회의 준비 다했나요?
남 그런 것 같습니다, 스튜어트 씨. 우선, 요청하셨던 대로 벽에 화이트보드를 걸었습니다.
여 좋아요. 그리고 분명 의자들을 준비하셨겠죠.
남 네, 탁자 주위에 빙 둘러 있습니다.
여 아, 둥근 탁자를 구했나요?
남 네, 회의실 가운데에 놓았습니다.
여 잘했어요. 그리고 우리가 회의 때 사용하는 노트북 컴퓨터를 잊지 않았길 바라요.
남 물론입니다. 탁자 위에 올려놓았습니다.
여 완벽해요. 우리는 코트를 걸 공간도 필요해요.
남 제가 탁자 옆에 코트 걸이를 놓았습니다.
여 알겠어요. 고마워요, 톰.

05 ⑤

해설 여자가 오른쪽 쟁반이 펜을 놓기 위한 것이냐고 묻자 남자가 그럴 예정이라고 했으므로 이미 펜이 놓여 있는 그림 속의 쟁반이 대화의 내용과 일치하지 않는다.

어휘 organize 정리하다, 체계화하다
right-handed 오른손잡이의
avoid 피하다
annoying 성가신, 짜증스러운
decorative 장식의
touch 마무리, 손질
mouse pad 마우스 패드
previous 이전의
messy 어질러진
brilliant 멋진, 훌륭한

M Mom! I organized my desk just like you asked me to. Look at this!
W Wow! Good job! You placed a lamp on the left side. Since you're right-handed, this will help you avoid annoying shadows.
M Thanks, but it was your idea.
W I can see you also put a picture frame next to the lamp. It adds a decorative touch to your desk.
M Also, Mom, look at my new mouse pad.
W It's shaped like a soccer field. The previous one looked like a soccer ball, right?
M Yeah! You have a really good memory.
W There is a nice cup near your monitor. Is it for your pens?
M No, I'm going to put some flowers in it. Can you see the tray on the right side?
W Oh, you are going to lay all your pens on it! Am I right?
M Yes. That way I will be able to find them easily, but they won't be messy.
W What a brilliant idea!

남 엄마! 엄마가 제게 하라고 요청하신 대로 책상을 정리했어요. 이것 보세요!
여 와! 잘했구나! 넌 왼쪽에 램프를 놓아두었구나. 넌 오른손잡이니까 이렇게 하면 네가 성가신 그림자를 피하는 데 도움이 되겠는걸.
남 고마워요, 하지만 그건 엄마 아이디어였어요.
여 램프 옆에 사진 액자를 둔 것도 보이는구나. 그게 네 책상에 장식적 마무리를 더해주는구나.
남 그리고 엄마, 새 마우스 패드를 보세요.
여 축구장 같은 모양이구나. 이전 것은 축구공처럼 생겼었지, 맞지?
남 그래요! 엄마 정말 기억력이 좋으세요.
여 네 모니터 근처에 멋진 컵이 있구나. 펜을 위한 거니?
남 아니요, 전 거기에 꽃을 꽂을 거예요. 오른쪽에 쟁반 보이세요?
여 아, 그 위에 모든 펜들을 둘 거구나! 내 말이 맞니?
남 네. 그래야 제가 그것들을 쉽게 찾을 수 있으면서도 지저분하지 않을 거예요.
여 정말 멋진 생각이야!

06 ④

해설 한라산을 배경으로 찍은 가족사진 대신에 해변에서 찍은 사진을 골랐다고 했으므로 그림 속의 가족사진이 대화의 내용과 일치하지 않는다.

어휘 border 가장자리; 경계
arch 아치형(의)
headline (신문 기사의) 표제
column (인쇄된 페이지의) 세로 단

W Dad, I've finally finished my homework. It's a newspaper article about our family trip to Jeju Island.
M OK. Let me have a look at it. [pause] Wow, I love these stars on the border.
W Thanks. I put the newspaper's name, "My Family News," in an arch across the top.
M It looks good. And the headline under it, "The Emersons Travel in Style!" sounds wonderful.
W What about our family picture on the beach? I chose it instead of the picture at Mt. Halla.
M Good choice. And I see that the article is in two columns on the right of the picture.

여 아빠, 드디어 숙제를 끝냈어요. 제주도 가족 여행에 관한 신문 기사예요.
남 그래. 어디 한번 보자. [잠시 후] 와, 가장자리에 있는 이 별들이 마음에 드는구나.
여 감사해요. 신문 이름인 '우리 가족 뉴스'를 윗부분에 가로질러 아치형으로 넣었어요.
남 보기 좋구나. 그리고 그 아래에 있는 '에머슨 가족이 아주 멋지게 여행하다!'라는 표제가 멋지구나.
여 해변에서 찍은 가족사진은 어떠세요? 한라산에서 찍은 사진 대신에 이걸 골랐어요.
남 잘 선택했다. 그리고 사진 오른쪽에 2단 기사가 보이는구나.

W	Yes, I wrote about the first day of our trip. Can you check it for me?	여 네, 여행 첫날에 대해 썼어요. 확인해주실래요?
M	I'd be happy to.	남 기꺼이 그러마.

07 ⑤

해설 남자의 책상에 리본이 달린 상자가 있다고 했으므로 그림 속의 리본 달린 머그잔이 대화의 내용과 일치하지 않는다.

어휘 senior 선임, 선배
manager 부장, 관리자
job interview 취업 면접
mug 머그잔, 손잡이가 있는 컵
laptop 노트북 컴퓨터

W	Welcome to the Starplus publishing company. I'm Monica, your senior.	여 스타플러스 출판사에 온 것을 환영해요. 나는 선임인 모니카예요.
M	Oh, hello. I'm Sean. It's a pleasure to work with you.	남 아, 안녕하세요. 저는 션입니다. 함께 일하게 되어 기쁩니다.
W	Me, too. I'd like to show you around.	여 나도 그래요. 내가 안내해드릴게요.
M	Thanks. I can see a round table by the window.	남 고맙습니다. 창가에 둥근 테이블이 보이네요.
W	That's for our meetings. And the man who is sitting on a chair near the table is our sales manager, Steve.	여 그건 우리 회의용이에요. 그리고 테이블 근처 의자에 앉아 있는 남자는 우리 영업 부장인 스티브예요.
M	You mean the man who is talking on the phone? I met him at my job interview.	남 전화 통화하고 있는 남자분 말씀이죠? 면접에서 그분을 만났어요.
W	Good. And the woman standing next to the plant pot is Alice.	여 좋아요. 그리고 화분 옆에 서있는 여자분은 앨리스예요.
M	The woman holding a coffee mug? I also met her at my interview.	남 커피 머그잔을 들고 있는 여자분이요? 그분도 면접에서 만났어요.
W	Great. Did you meet Simon, who is working on a laptop at the desk?	여 잘됐네요. 책상에서 노트북으로 작업하고 있는 사이몬은 만났나요?
M	No, I didn't.	남 아니요, 만나지 않았어요.
W	Your desk is next to his. Can you see the box with a ribbon on it? That's a welcome gift for you.	여 당신 책상은 그의 책상 옆이에요. 리본이 달린 상자가 보이나요? 그건 당신을 위한 환영 선물이에요.
M	Wow! Thanks a lot.	남 와! 정말 감사합니다.

08 ⑤

해설 오른쪽에 의자 두 개를 두었다고 했으므로 그림 속의 의자 한 개가 대화의 내용과 일치하지 않는다.

어휘 set up 설치하다, 세우다
microphone 마이크
banner 현수막
eye-catching 눈에 띄는
request 요청하다
be all set 준비가 다 되다

W	Ethan, how's it going with the preparation for our Jazz Night?	여 에단, 우리 '재즈의 밤' 준비는 어떻게 돼가니?
M	I'm all finished. This is a picture of the stage I set up.	남 다 끝냈어요. 이게 제가 설치한 무대 사진이에요.
W	Let me see. You set up a microphone on the left side as I asked.	여 어디 보자. 내가 부탁한 대로 왼쪽에 마이크를 설치했구나.
M	Yes. And I placed a grand piano and its chair behind it.	남 네. 그리고 마이크 뒤에 그랜드 피아노와 의자를 두었어요.
W	Great. I like the banner that says "Jazz Night" on the wall. It's really eye-catching.	여 아주 좋구나. 나는 벽에 있는 '재즈의 밤'이라고 쓰인 현수막이 마음에 들어. 정말 눈에 띈다.
M	Thanks. What do you think of the drums under the banner?	남 감사합니다. 현수막 아래에 있는 드럼은 어떤가요?
W	I think they look good.	여 좋은 것 같아.
M	And as you requested, I put two chairs on the right. Are they for the singers?	남 그리고 요청하신 대로, 오른쪽에 의자 두 개를 놓았어요. 그것들은 가수들을 위한 건가요?
W	No, those are for the guitarists. I think we're all set for the show. Nice work!	여 아니, 그것들은 기타리스트들을 위한 거야. 공연을 위한 준비가 다 된 것 같아. 잘했어!
M	Thank you.	남 감사합니다.

09 ⑤

해설 남자가 집 앞에 있는 나무에 전구를 그렸다고 했으므로 그림 속의 나무가 대화의 내용과 일치하지 않는다.

M	Grandma, come and see what I drew in art class. It's a picture of your house on Christmas!	남 할머니, 제가 미술 시간에 그린 것을 오셔서 좀 보세요. 크리스마스의 할머니 댁을 그린 그림이에요!
W	Oh, it's wonderful! There's a snowman wearing a striped muffler in the front yard.	여 아, 훌륭하구나! 앞마당에 줄무늬 목도리를 한 눈사람이 있네.
M	I drew a sled beside the snowman, too. What do you think of the house?	남 눈사람 옆에 썰매도 그렸어요. 집은 어떻게 생각하세요?

어휘 **muffler** 목도리
front yard 앞마당
sled 썰매
beside ~ 옆에
light 전구

W I love the two bells on my front door.
M Good. And then I put a sign that says "Merry Christmas" in front of the house.
W Great. Oh, I see a tree beside the sign.
M Yes, just like in your yard. I drew lights on it, too! Aren't they beautiful?
W They are!
M I'm so glad you think so, Grandma, because it's for you!

여 현관문에 있는 종 두 개가 마음에 드는구나.
남 다행이에요. 그러고 나서 집 앞에 '메리 크리스마스'라고 쓰여 있는 팻말을 세웠어요.
여 멋지네. 아, 팻말 옆에 나무가 보이는구나.
남 네, 할머니 댁 마당에 있는 것과 같아요. 나무에 전구도 그렸어요! 아름답지 않나요?
여 그렇구나!
남 할머니, 그렇게 생각해주시니 기뻐요. 이 그림은 할머니를 위한 거니까요!

10 ⑤

해설 서랍장 위에 꽃 그림이 있는 꽃병을 놓았다고 했으므로 줄무늬가 있는 그림 속의 꽃병이 대화의 내용과 일치하지 않는다.

어휘 **contrast with** ~와 대조를 이루다
turn into ~이 되다, ~으로 변하다
solo 혼자서 하는, 단독의
focus on ~에 중점을 두다
turn out (결과가 특정 방식으로) 되다; 나타나다

M Before the play begins, why don't you check the stage?
W Okay. [pause] It looks good! Especially the poster on the wall.
M I agree. The woman's smiling face will contrast nicely with her loneliness.
W How about the window? Shouldn't it show a full moon?
M No, it's supposed to be a half-moon. It turns into a full moon later in the play, but it doesn't start out like that.
W Now I remember. Well, the bed below the poster is perfect.
M Yes, it's good to have it on the left side of the stage.
W And there's a chair beside the table. I remember you prepared two chairs before.
M Since it's a solo performance that is focusing on loneliness, a single chair will be better.
W Good idea. Oh, and is that the flower-printed vase we ordered on top of the drawers?
M Yes, it turned out well.

남 연극이 시작되기 전에 무대를 확인하는 게 어때?
여 그래. [잠시 후] 근사해 보이는데! 특히 벽에 있는 포스터가 멋져.
남 나도 그렇게 생각해. 저 여자의 미소 짓는 얼굴이 그녀의 외로움과 잘 대조될 거야.
여 창문은 어때? 보름달이 보여야 하지 않아?
남 아냐, 반달이어야 해. 연극 후반부에서는 보름달로 변하지만, 그렇게 시작하지는 않아.
여 이제 기억난다. 음, 포스터 아래에 있는 침대도 완벽하구나.
남 그래, 침대를 무대 왼편에 두니까 좋다.
여 그리고 테이블 옆에 의자도 하나 있어. 전에 네가 의자 두 개를 준비했던 걸로 기억하는데.
남 외로움에 중점을 두는 일인극이니까, 의자 하나가 더 좋을 거야.
여 좋은 생각이야. 아, 그리고 서랍장 위에 있는 거 우리가 주문한 꽃 그림이 있는 꽃병이야?
남 응, 꽃병이 잘 나왔어.

05 유형 표의 내용

✳✳ 기출 맛보기

본문 p.63

01 ③

해설 가격은 30달러 미만이고, 배터리가 8시간 넘게 지속되며, 선풍기 속도가 3단계이고, 접을 수 있는 휴대용 선풍기를 고른다.

어휘 **handheld** 휴대용인; 손에 들고 쓰는; (손에 들고 조작할 수 있을 정도의) 소형 기기
last 지속되다
recommend 추천하다
foldable 접을 수 있는, 접히는
cf. **fold** 접다
fit into ~에 꼭 들어맞다
convenient 편리한

M Julie, what are you looking at?
W I'm thinking of buying a new handheld fan. Can you help me pick one?
M Sure. Hmm, how about this one?
W It looks good, but I don't want to spend more than $30.
M Okay. And I think you should get one with a battery that lasts more than 8 hours.
W I think so, too. I usually spend more than 8 hours outside.
M What about the fan speed levels? Do you need a fan with four levels?

남 줄리, 뭘 보고 있어?
여 새 휴대용 선풍기를 살까 생각 중이야. 고르는 것 좀 도와줄래?
남 물론이지. 음, 이건 어때?
여 좋아 보이지만, 난 30달러 넘게 쓰고 싶지 않아.
남 알겠어. 그리고 배터리가 8시간 넘게 지속되는 걸 사야 할 거야.
여 나도 그렇게 생각해. 나는 보통 밖에서 8시간 넘게 보내거든.
남 선풍기 속도 단계는? 4단계 선풍기가 필요하니?

W	No. Three levels will be enough for me.	여	아니. 3단계면 나한테 충분할 거야.
M	Then you have two models left. I recommend the foldable one.	남	그럼 두 가지 모델이 남았네. 나는 접을 수 있는 걸 추천해.
W	What's special about it?	여	그게 뭐가 특별한데?
M	If you fold the handle, it'll easily fit into your handbag. It can also stand up on your desk.	남	손잡이를 접으면 네 손가방에 쉽게 들어갈 거야. 그건 책상 위에 세울 수도 있어.
W	That sounds convenient. I'll buy that one.	여	편리한 것 같네. 그걸로 살게.

STEP ❶·❷ Listen & Choose

01 ⓒ **02** ⓑ **03** ⓑ **04** ⓒ **05** ⓑ **06** ⓒ **07** ⓑ **08** ⓐ **09** ⓐ **10** ⓑ

01 ⓒ

해설 현재 시각인 8시 5분에 방영되고 있는 프로그램 중에 남자가 패션에는 관심이 없다고 했으므로 <뱀파이어>를 고른다.

어휘 soap opera 연속극, 드라마

M	It's 8:05. What's on TV?	남	8시 5분이야. TV에서 뭐 하니?
W	The documentary *The History of Gold* has finished, and a fashion program and the soap opera *The Vampire* are on.	여	다큐멘터리인 <금의 역사>는 끝났고, 패션 프로그램과 연속극 <뱀파이어>가 방영 중이야.
M	Well, I'm not interested in fashion.	남	음, 난 패션에는 관심이 없어.
W	Then, let's watch the other one.	여	그러면 다른 것을 보자.

02 ⓑ

해설 씨사이드 캠핑장을 제외한 나머지 두 곳 중에서 하룻밤에 80달러를 넘지 않는 캠핑장을 고른다.

어휘 campsite 캠핑장
per ~당
reserve 예약하다

M	Honey, how about going to one of the campsites on the list next week?	남	여보, 다음 주에 이 목록에 있는 캠핑장 중 한 곳에 가는 게 어때요?
W	Sounds great. There are three different campsites.	여	좋아요. 세 개의 다른 캠핑장이 있네요.
M	Yeah. Since we went to Seaside campsite last time, let's choose between the other two.	남	네. 씨사이드 캠핑장은 지난번에 갔으니까 나머지 둘 중에 골라봅시다.
W	Good. Hmm, I don't want to spend more than $80 per night. It's too expensive.	여	좋아요. 음, 전 하룻밤에 80달러 넘게 쓰고 싶지 않아요. 너무 비싸요.
M	I agree with that. I'll reserve this one right now.	남	나도 동의해요. 지금 바로 여기를 예약할게요.

03 ⓑ

해설 두께가 5mm 이상이고, 미끄럼 방지 기능이 있는 매트를 고른다.

어휘 home training 홈 트레이닝 ((가정에서 할 수 있는 간단한 운동))
non-slip 미끄럼을 방지하는
surface 표면
keep A from v-ing A가 v하지 못하게 하다
slide 미끄러지다

W	Excuse me. Are thicker mats better for home training?	여	실례합니다. 두꺼운 매트가 홈 트레이닝에 더 좋은가요?
M	Not really. But I think a mat should be at least 5 mm for home trainers.	남	그렇지는 않아요. 하지만 홈 트레이너용으로 적어도 5mm는 되어야 한다고 봐요.
W	I see. Then I have to choose between these two.	여	그렇군요. 그럼 이 둘 중에 골라야겠네요.
M	Right. I'd recommend this model with a non-slip surface. It keeps you from sliding around.	남	네. 저는 미끄럼 방지 표면이 있는 이 제품을 추천해 드려요. 이건 미끄러지지 않게 해줘요.
W	Okay. Safety is important. I'll take it.	여	알겠어요. 안전이 중요하죠. 그걸로 살게요.

04 ⓒ

해설 바다 전망이면서 조식이 포함되지 않은 방을 고른다.

어휘 book 예약하다
have A in mind A를 염두에 두다

W	Let's book a hotel room for our vacation.	여	우리 휴가를 위해 호텔 방을 예약하죠.
M	Okay. Which room do you have in mind?	남	좋아요. 어느 객실을 염두에 두고 있나요?
W	I was hoping to get a room with an ocean view.	여	난 바다 전망의 방을 잡길 바라고 있었어요.
M	Me too. Shall we have breakfast in the hotel?	남	나도요. 우리 호텔에서 아침 먹을까요?
W	I don't think we need to. I heard there are some good restaurants near the hotel.	여	그럴 필요 없을 것 같아요. 호텔 근처에 괜찮은 식당이 몇 개 있다고 들었거든요.

05 ⓑ

해설 2시 15분 이후에 시작하고 파티 시작 시각인 5시보다 최소 20분 전에 끝나는 영화를 고른다.

어휘 on one's way (to) (~로 가[오]는) 도중에
quarter 15분; 4분의 1

M Jeff's party will begin at 5 o'clock. What shall we do before the party?
W We can see a movie on our way to the party. Here, look at this listing.
M Well, if we leave now, we can get to the cinema around a quarter past two.
W It will take us about twenty minutes to get to Jeff's house, so that leaves only one choice.

남 제프의 파티가 5시에 시작될 거야. 파티 전에 우리 뭘 할까?
여 파티에 가는 길에 영화를 한 편 볼 수 있어. 여기, 이 목록 좀 봐.
남 음, 지금 출발하면 2시 15분쯤 극장에 도착할 수 있겠는데.
여 제프 집에 가는 데 20분 정도 걸릴 테니까 선택할 수 있는 게 딱 하나 남네.

06 ⓒ

해설 무게가 200그램이 넘지 않고, 블루투스 리모컨이 있는 셀카봉을 고른다.

어휘 selfie stick 셀카봉
prefer 선호하다
light 가벼운
remote control 리모컨

M Hello, I'm looking for a selfie stick. And I'd prefer a light one.
W Then I don't recommend a selfie stick over 200 grams.
M Okay. I also want a bluetooth remote control. I heard they're convenient to use.

남 안녕하세요, 셀카봉을 찾고 있는데요. 저는 가벼운 걸 선호해요.
여 그럼 200그램이 넘는 셀카봉은 추천드리지 않습니다.
남 네. 그리고 블루투스 리모컨도 원해요. 그게 사용하기 편리하다고 들었거든요.

07 ⓑ

해설 보증 기간이 1년이 넘는 것 중에서 더 저렴한 스마트 워치를 고른다.

어휘 warranty (품질 등의) 보증, 품질보증서
option 선택(권)
advice 조언

W Do you think a one-year warranty is too short for a smartwatch?
M Yes. I recommend one that has a warranty longer than one year.
W Okay. That leaves me with these two options.
M I'd get the cheaper one because it's as good as the other one.
W Okay. I'll take your advice.

여 스마트 워치에 1년 보증은 너무 짧을까?
남 응. 난 보증 기간이 1년 이상인 것을 추천해.
여 알겠어. 그럼 이 두 개의 선택권이 남네.
남 나라면 저렴한 것이 다른 것만큼 좋으니 더 저렴한 것을 살 것 같아.
여 좋아. 너의 조언을 따를게.

08 ⓐ

해설 남자는 평일 및 오후 5시 이후에는 일할 수 없다고 했다.

어휘 weekday 평일

W Working at the information desk seems easy, doesn't it?
M Yeah, but I can't work on the weekdays.
W I see. Then, how about this job?
M The pay is pretty good, but I can't work after 5 p.m. I need some time to do my homework.
W Then, that leaves you just one option.

여 안내 데스크에서 일하는 건 쉬울 것 같아, 그렇지 않니?
남 응, 그렇지만 난 평일에는 일할 수 없어.
여 그렇구나. 그럼 이 일자리는 어때?
남 급여가 꽤 괜찮긴 하지만, 오후 5시 이후에는 일할 수 없어. 숙제할 시간이 좀 필요하거든.
여 그럼 딱 한 가지 선택지만 남네.

09 ⓐ

해설 수채화 그림물감을 제외하고, 30가지 넘는 색상이 있는 미술용품을 고른다.

어휘 art supply 미술용품
watercolor 수채화 그림물감; 수채화
brush 붓
express 표현하다

W I'm searching for an art supplies set for children.
M Let me see. Watercolors might not be very convenient. The kids would need extra things like brushes.
W I agree. How about the number of colors?
M They'll need more than thirty colors to express what they want.

여 아동용 미술용품 세트를 찾고 있어요.
남 한번 볼게요. 수채화 그림물감은 그리 편리하지 않을 거예요. 아이들은 붓 같은 다른 것들이 필요할 거예요.
여 맞아요. 색상 수는 어떤가요?
남 아이들이 원하는 것을 표현하기 위해서는 30가지 넘는 색이 필요할 거예요.

10 ⓑ

해설 수요일에는 강좌를 들을 수 없고 요가보다 더 활동적인 것을 원하므로 태권도를 선택할 것이다.

어휘 would rather v 오히려 v하고 싶다
except ~을 제외하고

W Lucas, why don't we try a class at the health center this week?
M I have to work after school on Wednesday.
W How about taking the yoga class then?
M I'd rather take a more active class.
W Then, we have no choice except one.

여 루카스, 이번 주에 헬스 센터에서 강좌를 하나 수강하는 게 어때?
남 난 수요일에는 방과 후에 일해야 해.
여 그럼 요가 강좌를 수강하는 게 어때?
남 난 더 활동적인 강좌를 수강하고 싶어.
여 그럼 우린 하나 빼고 선택의 여지가 없네.

STEP ❸·❹ Listen & Answer

본문 p.68

01 ④ **02** ③ **03** ② **04** ③ **05** ④ **06** ③ **07** ④ **08** ② **09** ④ **10** ③

---

01 ④

해설 제일 먼저 콘서트를 제외한 후, 목요일 저녁과 평일 오후에 있는 프로그램도 제외하고 남은 것 중 더 저렴한 것을 고른다.

어휘 participate 참여하다
into ~에 관심을 가지고, ~에 열중하여
got it 알았습니다
appointment 약속
client 고객
cool 훌륭한, 멋진
sign up for ~을 신청하다
[선택지 어휘] postcard 우편엽서
decorate 장식하다
self-portrait 자화상

W Honey, our kids want to participate in one of the Family Arts Festival programs next week.
M Great! It will be nice to spend time together as a family.
W Let's decide which program to take from this list.
M Let me see. Our kids will like everything except for the concert. They're not that into music.
W Got it. This seems interesting and it's on Thursday evening.
M It seems good, but I have an appointment with my client at that time.
W I see. Since we both work during the day, we should pick something in the evening or on Saturdays.
M Yeah, we can't attend programs on weekday afternoons. That leaves us with these two options. How about this one?
W That sounds cool but it's the most expensive one. I don't want to spend that much money on a program.
M Okay. Let's sign up for this one, then. I think it'll be a lot of fun.

여 여보, 우리 아이들이 다음 주에 가족 예술 축제 프로그램 중 하나에 참여하고 싶어 해요.
남 잘됐네요! 가족으로 함께 시간을 보내는 것은 좋을 거예요.
여 이 목록에서 어떤 프로그램을 택할지 결정해요.
남 어디 봐요. 우리 아이들은 콘서트 빼고는 다 좋아할 거예요. 음악에 별로 관심이 없잖아요.
여 알겠어요. 이게 흥미로울 것 같은데 목요일 저녁에 있어요.
남 좋아 보이지만, 난 그 시간에 고객과 약속이 있어요.
여 그렇군요. 우리 둘 다 낮 동안은 일을 하기 때문에 저녁이나 토요일의 것을 골라야 하네요.
남 네, 우리는 평일 오후에는 프로그램에 참가할 수가 없죠. 그럼 이 두 가지 선택지가 남는군요. 이건 어때요?
여 멋질 것 같긴 한데, 그게 가장 비싸네요. 나는 프로그램에 그렇게 많은 돈을 쓰고 싶지 않아요.
남 좋아요. 그러면 이걸 신청합시다. 정말 재미있을 것 같아요.

---

02 ③

해설 직장에서 먼 동부를 제외하고 침실이 두 개이며, 월세가 1,000달러 이하인 곳은 아파트 C와 D이다. 이 중 경비원이 있는 아파트 C를 고른다.

어휘 narrow A down to B A를 B로 좁히다, 줄이다
inconvenient 불편한
can't afford to-v v할 여유가 없다
budget 예산, 경비
security guard 경비원, 보안요원
settle 결정하다; 정착하다
set up ~을 정하다; ~을 설치하다
view (집을 사거나 빌리기 위해) 둘러보다

M I see you are still looking for apartments. Can't find anything you like?
W I've narrowed it down to five, but it's still confusing.
M Do you care about the location?
W I don't want to be too far from work. That would be inconvenient.
M Okay, so not the east side. And you want two bedrooms, right?
W I really do, but I just can't afford to pay more than $1,000 a month.
M Well, that only leaves two. The cheaper one would be better for your budget. What do you think?
W That's important, but I also need a security guard for safety.
M Then I guess it's settled.

남 아직 아파트를 알아보고 있구나. 네가 원하는 걸 찾을 수가 없니?
여 다섯 군데로 좁히긴 했는데, 아직도 잘 모르겠어.
남 너는 위치를 신경 쓰니?
여 직장에서 너무 멀리 있는 것은 원치 않아. 그건 불편할 거야.
남 그래, 그럼 동부는 안 되겠구나. 그리고 너는 침실 두 개를 원하지, 맞지?
여 정말 그렇긴 한데, 난 한 달에 1,000달러 넘게 지불할 여유가 없어.
남 음, 그럼 두 군데만 남네. 더 저렴한 곳이 네 예산에 더 나을 거야. 어떻게 생각해?
여 그것도 중요하지만, 난 안전을 위해 경비원도 필요해.
남 그렇다면 결정된 것 같네.

W I think you're right. I'll call and set up a time to view that one.	여 네 말이 맞아. 전화해서 그 아파트를 둘러볼 시간을 정할게.

03 ②

해설 플라스틱 재질이고 용량은 2리터에서 3리터 사이이며, 가격은 20달러 이하인 빨간색 물뿌리개를 고른다.

어휘 watering can 물뿌리개
material 재질
metal 금속
durable 튼튼한, 내구성이 있는
[선택지 어휘] capacity 수용량

W Felix, we need to get a watering can for the garden.	여 펠릭스, 우리는 정원용 물뿌리개를 사야 해요.
M Why don't we buy one online? Look at this website.	남 온라인으로 하나 사는 건 어때요? 이 웹사이트를 봐요.
W Let me see. *[pause]* First, we have to consider the material.	여 어디 봐요. *[잠시 후]* 우선 우리는 재질을 고려해야 해요.
M How about the metal one? It looks more durable.	남 금속으로 된 건 어때요? 그게 더 튼튼해 보여요.
W I think plastic would be better since it's much lighter.	여 내 생각에는 플라스틱이 훨씬 더 가볍기 때문에 더 좋을 것 같아요.
M You're right. And which size of can do you want?	남 당신 말이 맞아요. 그리고 어떤 크기의 물뿌리개를 원해요?
W Between 2 to 3 liters would be enough.	여 2리터에서 3리터 사이면 충분할 것 같아요.
M Okay. What about the price?	남 알겠어요. 가격은요?
W I'd prefer not to spend more than $20.	여 20달러 넘게 쓰지 않는 게 좋겠어요.
M Then it's between these two. Which color do you prefer?	남 그러면 이 둘 중에 있네요. 어떤 색이 더 좋아요?
W I like the red one better.	여 나는 빨간색이 더 좋아요.
M Good choice. I'll order it now.	남 잘 선택했어요. 그걸로 지금 주문할게요.

04 ③

해설 유급이고 주(州) 내에서 할 수 있으며, 6월 이후에 시작해 9월 전에 끝나는 인턴직을 고른다.

어휘 ideally 이상적으로는
related to ~와 관련된
financial 재정(상)의, 금융의
location 위치, 장소
mind 상관하다, 언짢아하다
apply 지원하다
[선택지 어휘] receptionist (호텔, 병원 등의) 접수 담당자

W Hi, John. What are you doing?	여 안녕, 존. 뭐 하고 있어?
M I'm choosing an internship for the summer.	남 난 여름 인턴직을 고르고 있어.
W Can I look at your options?	여 내가 선택 사항을 좀 봐도 될까?
M Sure. Ideally I want to do something related to computer science.	남 물론이지. 이상적으로는 컴퓨터 공학과 관련된 일을 하고 싶어.
W So, one of these two then?	여 그럼 이 둘 중의 하나가 되겠네?
M Right. But they aren't paid. I can't take a position that isn't paid because of my financial situation.	남 맞아. 그런데 그 일들은 무급이야. 내 재정 상황 때문에 무급인 일은 할 수가 없어.
W I understand. Do you care about the location?	여 이해해. 너는 위치를 신경 쓰니?
M I would prefer to stay in this state.	남 나는 이 주(州)에 있는 게 더 좋아.
W And what about the start date? Some start sooner than others.	여 그리고 시작일은 어떠니? 몇 개는 다른 것보다 더 일찍 시작해.
M I can't start until June. And I need to be back in school in September.	남 난 6월이 되기까지는 시작할 수 없어. 그리고 9월에 학교로 돌아가야 해.
W Well, there is still one that could work for you. Are you okay with working part-time?	여 음, 네게 맞는 하나가 아직 있어. 시간제로 일하는 것도 괜찮니?
M I wouldn't mind. I'll apply for that one.	남 난 상관없어. 그것에 지원할래.

05 ④

해설 가죽 재질과 검정색을 제외한 후, 20달러 이하인 것 중에서 더 비싸더라도 고객 평가가 더 높은 것을 고른다.

어휘 care 신경 쓰다
leather 가죽
definitely 분명히
rating 평점, 평가

W Oliver, I'm thinking of buying one of these smartphone cases. Can you help me choose one?	여 올리버, 난 이 스마트폰 케이스들 중 하나를 살까 생각 중이야. 하나 고르는 것을 도와줄래?
M Sure. What do you think of this leather case? This is the one I have.	남 물론이지. 이 가죽 케이스는 어떻게 생각해? 이건 내가 가지고 있는 거야.
W Well, I don't care much about the material, but I think leather is hard to clean.	여 글쎄, 난 재질은 크게 신경 안 쓰지만, 가죽은 닦기가 힘든 것 같아.
M Okay. What about the color?	남 알았어. 색상은 어때?
W It's difficult to choose, but I definitely don't like black.	여 고르기는 어렵지만, 확실히 검은색은 좋아하지 않아.
M How much are you planning to spend on it?	남 그것에 얼마를 쓸 계획이니?
W No more than 20 dollars.	여 20달러 미만이야.

M	Then you have to choose from these two. How about the cheaper one?	남	그러면 이 둘 중에서 골라야 해. 더 저렴한 게 어때?
W	Actually, I'll choose the other one. It's more expensive, but it has a higher rating.	여	실은 난 다른 걸 고를래. 이게 더 비싸지만 평점이 더 높아.
M	Good choice.	남	잘 선택했어.

06 ③

해설 여행 기간이 20일 이내이고 출발일은 토요일이며 가이드 없이 더 많은 나라를 여행할 수 있는 여행 상품을 고른다.

어휘 honeymoon 신혼여행
destination 행선지, 목적지
brochure (안내, 광고용) 책자
allow A to-v A가 v하도록 허락하다
explore 탐험하다; 탐구하다

M	Honey, we should decide on our honeymoon destination. Do you have a place in mind?	남	자기야, 우리 신혼여행 행선지를 결정해야 해. 생각해둔 곳 있어?
W	I want to visit Europe. Here is a brochure about tour packages. Let's pick one.	여	난 유럽을 가보고 싶어. 여기 패키지여행 상품에 대한 책자가 있어. 하나 골라보자.
M	Okay. Let's see.... My work schedule won't allow me to take more than 20 days of leave.	남	알겠어. 어디 보자…. 나는 업무 일정상 20일 넘는 휴가는 쓸 수가 없어.
W	Oh, that's right. Maybe we should try one of these four.	여	아, 맞아. 아마도 우리는 이 넷 중에 하나를 해야겠네.
M	Well, our wedding is on Friday afternoon, so it would be better to leave the next day.	남	음, 우리 결혼식이 금요일 오후이니까, 그 다음 날 출발하는 게 나을 거야.
W	Okay, then do you think we need a guide?	여	좋아, 그럼 우리에게 가이드가 필요하다고 생각해?
M	I would prefer to explore by ourselves. Wouldn't you?	남	난 우리끼리 다니는 게 더 좋은데. 그렇지 않아?
W	That does sound like more fun. And I want to see as many countries as possible.	여	그게 정말 더 재밌을 것 같아. 그리고 난 가능한 한 많은 나라들을 보고 싶어.
M	Then I think we have made our choice.	남	그럼 우리 마음에 드는 것을 고른 것 같아.

07 ④

해설 스틱형 청소기 중에 가격이 500달러 이하이고, 가동 시간이 40분 이상이며, 보조 배터리가 있는 것을 고른다. 남자가 가동 시간이 더 긴 것을 고르려고 하다가 여자의 만류로 보조 배터리가 있는 것을 선택했음에 유의한다.

어휘 cordless 무선의
vacuum cleaner 진공청소기
stick 막대기
common 일반적인
as a rule of thumb 경험으로 보건대, 일반적으로
run time 가동[실행] 시간
second 보조의
extend 연장하다
moreover 게다가, 더욱이

M	I need a cordless vacuum cleaner. Can you help me choose a good one?	남	난 무선 진공청소기가 필요해. 좋은 걸 고르는 것을 도와줄 수 있니?
W	Sure. First, we have to choose either a handheld or a stick model. Which one do you want?	여	그래. 우선, 소형 모델과 스틱 모델 중 하나를 선택해야 해. 넌 어떤 걸 원해?
M	I'd prefer a stick one since it's the most common type.	남	스틱 모델이 가장 일반적인 종류이기 때문에 스틱 모델이 더 좋아.
W	Next, how much can you spend on it?	여	다음으로, 그것에 얼마를 쓸 수 있니?
M	I'd better not spend more than 500 dollars. What else should I consider?	남	난 500달러 넘게는 쓰지 않는 게 좋겠어. 내가 또 무엇을 고려해야 할까?
W	As a rule of thumb, battery life is the most important. I think its run time should be at least 40 minutes.	여	경험으로 보면 배터리 수명이 가장 중요해. 그것의 가동 시간이 적어도 40분은 돼야 한다고 생각해.
M	I see. Then, it looks like I have two choices left. I'll choose the one with longer run time.	남	그렇구나. 그러면 두 개의 선택지가 남는 것 같네. 가동 시간이 더 긴 것을 고를래.
W	Wait a minute! The other one includes a second battery. If I were you, I'd get this one.	여	잠깐만! 다른 하나는 보조 배터리를 포함하고 있어. 내가 너라면 이걸 살 거야.
M	Right, its second battery can extend its run time.	남	맞아, 보조 배터리가 가동 시간을 연장할 수 있잖아.
W	Definitely. Moreover, the difference in run time between these two is only 10 minutes.	여	그렇고말고. 게다가, 이 둘 사이의 가동 시간 차이는 겨우 10분이야.
M	Got it! I'll take it.	남	알았어! 그걸로 살게.

08 ②

해설 지역 도서관들에서 제공하는 수업 중 컬러링 북 수업은 이미 수강해서 제외하고, 딸의 연령인 6세를 대상으로 하는 수업 중에 오전에 진행하는 것은 제외한다. 남은 두 개의 선택지 중 거리가 더 가까운 곳을 고른다.

W	Honey, I want to sign Anna up for a library program.	여	여보, 안나를 도서관 프로그램에 등록시키고 싶어요.
M	What kind of program?	남	어떤 프로그램이요?
W	Take a look at this site. Local libraries are offering free classes for children.	여	이 사이트를 봐요. 지역 도서관들이 어린이를 위한 무료 수업을 제공하고 있어요.

어휘 local 지역의
kindergarten 유치원
exactly (맞장구치는 말로) 맞아, 바로 그거야

M They look great. One of them offers a coloring book class. Anna already took the class last year, didn't she?

W Yes, so I don't think she needs to take it again.

M Okay. Since Anna is 6 years old, <u>she won't be able to take this class.</u>

W That's right. A morning class is also not possible since she comes home from kindergarten at 1 p.m.

M Then, we have two choices left.

W I think this library is <u>too far from our house.</u> Anna won't be happy if she has to be in the car for a long time.

M Exactly. It'd be better to choose the library <u>that's closer to our house.</u>

W I hope Anna will enjoy this class!

남 좋아 보이네요. 그 중 하나가 컬러링 북 수업을 제공하는군요. 안나는 작년에 이미 그 수업을 들었죠, 그렇죠?

여 네, 그래서 다시 들을 필요는 없을 것 같아요.

남 알겠어요. 안나가 여섯 살이기 때문에 이 수업은 수강할 수 없겠군요.

여 맞아요. 그 애가 유치원에서 집으로 오후 1시에 오기 때문에 오전 수업도 불가능해요.

남 그러면, 두 가지 선택지가 남았네요.

여 이 도서관은 우리 집에서 너무 먼 것 같아요. 오랫동안 차 안에 있어야 한다면 안나는 좋아하지 않을 거예요.

남 맞아요. 우리 집에서 더 가까운 도서관을 선택하는 게 좋겠어요.

여 안나가 이 수업을 재미있어 하길 바라요!

09 ④

해설 15세가 들을 수 있는 수업 중에서 방과 후 배구 연습이 있는 목요일은 제외해야 한다. 한 달 수강료가 80달러 미만인 힙합과 케이팝 중에 학생 수가 더 적은 수업을 고른다.

어휘 brochure 팸플릿
limit 제한
volleyball 배구
practice 연습
budget 예산
price range 가격대
crowded 붐비는, 복잡한

M Penny, you said you wanted to take a dance class, right? I've brought the brochure of Astrid Dance Studio here.

W How nice of you! Let me see.... I'd like to take this class.

M I don't think you can. Its age limit is seventeen, and you're only fifteen.

W Oh, you're right. And I have volleyball practice after school every Thursday.

M Then you <u>can't take this class either.</u> What does your budget look like?

W Well, <u>I can't spend more than $80 a month.</u>

M You have these two classes in that price range. Which class are you interested in?

W They both sound good, but I prefer the class <u>that has fewer students.</u>

M That's a good idea. The studio <u>will be less crowded.</u>

W Yes, I'll sign up for it.

남 페니, 댄스 강좌를 수강하고 싶다고 했잖아, 맞지? 내가 아스트리드 댄스 스튜디오 팸플릿을 가져왔어.

여 정말 친절하구나! 어디 보자…. 난 이 수업을 듣고 싶어.

남 넌 그럴 수 없을 것 같아. 연령 제한이 열일곱 살인데, 넌 겨우 열다섯 살이잖아.

여 아, 네 말이 맞아. 그리고 나는 매주 목요일 방과 후에 배구 연습이 있어.

남 그러면 넌 이 수업도 들을 수 없겠다. 네 예산은 어떻게 되니?

여 음, 난 한 달에 80달러 넘게 쓸 수 없어.

남 그 가격대에는 이 두 강좌가 있어. 어떤 강좌에 관심이 있니?

여 둘 다 좋은 것 같지만, 나는 학생이 더 적은 강좌가 더 좋아.

남 좋은 생각이야. 스튜디오가 덜 붐빌 거야.

여 맞아, 그걸로 신청해야겠다.

10 ③

해설 우선 가격이 500달러가 넘는 것은 제외하고, 화면 크기가 10인치 이상이며 배터리 수명이 8시간 이상인 것 중에서 무게가 더 가벼운 것을 고른다.

어휘 tablet 태블릿 ((터치스크린이 있는 작은 컴퓨터))
be willing to-v 흔쾌히 v하다
have no idea 전혀 모르다
recommend 추천하다
definitely 그럼, 그렇고말고
continuous 연속적인, 계속적인
consider 고려하다
suit 잘 맞다, 편리하다
carry around 들고 다니다, 휴대하다

M Layla. Can you help me? I'm looking for a tablet online.

W Sure. How much <u>would you be willing to spend?</u>

M I'd prefer not to spend more than $500.

W Okay. What screen size would you like? There are many different sizes.

M I have no idea. What do you think?

W I recommend a screen size of 10 inches or more if you want to use it for online classes.

M All right. And I should get a tablet with a long battery life, right?

W Definitely. The battery life should be <u>at least 8 hours of continuous use.</u>

M Now I have two options left. What else should I consider?

남 라일라. 날 좀 도와 줄 수 있니? 난 온라인으로 태블릿을 찾아보고 있어.

여 물론이지. 얼마를 쓸 의향이 있니?

남 500달러 넘게 쓰고 싶지 않아.

여 알았어. 화면 크기는 어떤 걸 원해? 다양한 크기가 있어.

남 전혀 모르겠어. 넌 어떻게 생각하니?

여 네가 그걸 온라인 수업을 위해 사용하고 싶다면 10인치 이상의 화면 크기를 추천해.

남 좋아. 그리고 배터리 수명이 긴 태블릿을 사야겠지, 맞지?

여 그럼. 배터리 수명은 연속 사용 시 최소 8시간이어야 해.

남 이제 두 가지 선택지가 남았어. 내가 또 무엇을 고려해야 할까?

W Well, they're both good tablets. This one is lighter but more expensive. Which one do you think suits you better?	여 음, 그것들 둘 다 좋은 태블릿이야. 이게 더 가볍지만 가격이 더 비싸. 어떤 것이 네게 더 잘 맞는다고 생각하니?
M Since I'll carry the tablet around a lot, I'll go with the lighter one. Thanks, Layla.	남 난 태블릿을 자주 들고 다닐 테니까 좀 더 가벼운 거로 할게. 고마워, 라일라.

06 유형 언급되지 않은 내용·불일치하는 내용

☀☀ 기출 맛보기 본문 p.75

01 ④

해설 해석 참조

어휘 hold (행사 등을) 개최하다, 열다
take place 개최되다, 열리다
entrance fee 입장료
activity 활동

M What are you doing, Laura?

W Hi, Tim. I'm looking for winter festivals to visit during vacation.

M Is there anything good?

W Yes, look at this. There is a new local event called the Winter Lake Festival.

M Awesome. When does it start?

W It starts on December 18th, and it'll be held for two weeks.

M Cool. Oh, it'll take place in Stevenson Park.

W Great. It's near our school. If you don't have any plans during vacation, let's go together.

M Of course. Is there an entrance fee?

W Yes. Here, it says $3. It's not expensive.

M Good. Look! There are so many kinds of activities to enjoy.

W Yeah, there is ice skating, ice fishing, and a snowball fight.

M They all sound exciting. Let's have fun there.

남 뭐해, 로라?

여 안녕, 팀. 나는 방학 동안 방문할 겨울 축제를 찾아보고 있어.

남 뭐 좋은 거 있어?

여 응, 이것 좀 봐. 겨울 호수 축제라고 불리는 새로운 지역 행사가 있어.

남 멋진데. 언제 시작해?

여 **12월 18일에 시작하고 2주간 열릴 예정이야(① 기간)**.

남 근사한데. 아, **스티븐슨 공원에서 열리네(② 장소)**.

여 잘됐다. 우리 학교 근처잖아. 방학 동안 아무 계획 없으면 같이 가자.

남 당연하지. 입장료 있어?

여 응. 여기, **3달러(③ 입장료)**라고 적혀 있어. 비싸지 않네.

남 좋다. 봐! 즐길 수 있는 활동의 종류가 정말 많아.

여 응, **아이스 스케이팅, 얼음낚시, 눈싸움이 있어(⑤ 활동 종류)**.

남 모두 재밌어 보여. 거기서 재밌게 놀자.

02 ④

해설 올해는 100명의 학생들에게 장학금을 지급했다고 했다.

어휘 movement (사회적·정치적) 운동
donate 기부하다
cf. donation 기부
encourage 장려하다; 격려하다
scholarship 장학금
celebrate 기념[축하]하다
anniversary 기념일
make a difference 변화를 가져오다

W Good afternoon, listeners. Why don't you join the Sharing Friday Movement and donate two dollars to our fund every Friday? This movement started in 2001 in Finland as an idea to encourage people to do good. Since then, this idea has grown into a global movement. Most of the donations go to poor areas across the world and help people get clean water. This year, scholarships were given to 100 students in these areas to celebrate our 20th anniversary. Please join us, and help make a difference. If you want to get more information, visit our homepage.

여 청취자 여러분, 안녕하세요. **금요일 나눔 운동에 동참하셔서 매주 금요일에 2달러씩 저희 기금에 기부하는 건 어떠신가요(①)?** 이 운동은 사람들이 좋은 일을 하도록 장려하기 위한 아이디어로 **2001년 핀란드에서 시작됐습니다(②)**. 그 이후로, 이 아이디어는 세계적인 운동으로 커졌습니다. **기부금의 대부분은 전 세계의 가난한 지역으로 전해져서 사람들이 깨끗한 물을 얻도록 돕습니다(③)**. 올해는 저희의 20주년을 기념하기 위해 이 지역 **100명의 학생들에게 장학금을 지급했습니다(④)**. 저희와 함께 해주시고, 변화를 가져오는 것을 도와주세요. **더 많은 정보를 원하시면 저희 홈페이지를 방문해주세요(⑤)**.

01 ⓒ **02** ⓐ **03** ⓑ **04** ⓑ **05** ⓒ **06** ⓒ **07** ⓑ **08** ⓒ **09** ⓐ **10** ⓒ

01 ⓒ

해설 해석 참조

어휘 **caviar** 캐비아 ((어류, 특히 철갑상어 알을 소금에 절인 것))
strong (냄새가) 강한
probably 아마도
possibility 가능성

M	Have you tried the caviar over there?
W	Not yet, but I've seen it. Aren't there two colors?
M	Yeah, red and black. The black is usually expensive and strong.
W	Really? Then I'll try the black caviar. Do you know where it is from?
M	Probably Russia, but there are other possibilities.

남 저쪽에 있는 캐비아 먹어봤니?
여 아직, 그런데 보긴 했어. 두 가지 색깔이 있지 않니?
남 응, **빨간색과 검은색**(ⓐ 색깔). 검은 것이 보통 비싸고 향이 강해.
여 그래? 그러면 검은 캐비아를 먹어볼래. 캐비아의 원산지가 어딘지 아니?
남 **아마도 러시아일 텐데**(ⓑ 원산지), 다른 곳일 가능성도 있어.

02 ⓐ

해설 해석 참조

어휘 **native** 고유의

W	Tom, you've been to Madagascar, haven't you? I heard that the island is huge.
M	Right. It's the fourth largest island in the world.
W	Wow! I didn't know that. What language do people speak there?
M	They speak both French and Madagascar's native language.

여 톰, 너는 마다가스카르에 가본 적이 있지, 그렇지 않니? 그 섬이 아주 크다고 들었어.
남 맞아. 그건 세계에서 네 번째로 큰 섬이야(ⓑ 크기).
여 와! 그건 몰랐어. 그곳 사람들은 어떤 언어를 사용하니?
남 그들은 프랑스어와 마다가스카르 고유 언어 둘 다 사용해(ⓒ 사용 언어).

03 ⓑ

해설 해석 참조

어휘 **historical** 역사적인, 역사(상)의
impressive 인상적인
represent 나타내다

M	Welcome to Madison House. This historical building was built in 1780.
W	Wow, the ceilings are amazing! And the furniture is very impressive.
M	The furniture that you see represents the highest quality available at the time.
W	It certainly looks great.

남 매디슨 하우스에 오신 것을 환영합니다. **이 역사적인 건물은 1780년에 지어졌습니다**(ⓐ 건축 시기).
여 와, 천장이 멋지군요! 그리고 가구들이 아주 인상적이에요.
남 여러분께서 보고 계신 가구는 그 당시에 가능했던 **최고의 품질을 나타냅니다**(ⓒ 가구 품질).
여 정말 멋져 보이네요.

04 ⓑ

해설 해석 참조

어휘 **name** 이름을 지어주다
walk (동물을) 산책시키다
toilet train 배변 훈련을 시키다
responsibility 책임(감)

W	Dad, I want to have a puppy. I will name my puppy Toby.
M	Okay. But will you walk Toby every day?
W	That'll be easy.
M	Also, you'll have to toilet train Toby, too.
W	Really? Hmm... Dad, you'll help me, right?
M	Sometimes. But remember having a dog is a big responsibility.

여 아빠, 저는 강아지를 키우고 싶어요. 저는 강아지에게 토비라는 이름을 지어줄 거예요.
남 그래. 그런데 네가 매일 **토비를 산책시킬 거니**(ⓐ 산책시키기)?
여 그건 쉬울 거예요.
남 또, 넌 토비에게 **배변 훈련을 시켜야 해**(ⓒ 배변 훈련시키기).
여 정말요? 음… 아빠, 도와주실 거죠, 그렇죠?
남 가끔. 하지만 강아지를 키우는 건 큰 책임이 따른다는 것을 명심하렴.

05 ⓒ

해설 해석 참조

어휘 **exhibition** 전시회
run 열리다, 진행되다
admission fee 입장료

W	There will be a World Dinosaur Exhibition this Saturday. Why don't we take the kids?
M	That sounds great! What time shall we go?

여 이번 주 토요일에 '세계 공룡 전시회'가 열릴 거예요. 애들을 데려가는 게 어때요?
남 좋아요! 우리 몇 시에 갈까요?

W Since the exhibition runs from 10 a.m. to 5 p.m., how about going there in the afternoon?

M Okay. How much is the admission fee?

W It's $10 for an adult and $5 for a child.

여 전시회가 오전 10시부터 오후 5시까지 여니까(ⓐ 운영 시간) 오후에 가는 건 어때요?

남 그래요. 입장료는 얼마인가요?

여 어른은 10달러, 어린이는 5달러예요(ⓑ 입장료).

06 ⓒ

해설 행사장 근처에 주차장이 없으므로 대중교통을 이용해야 한다.

어휘 throughout ~내내
related to ~와 관련된
theme 주제
parking lot 주차장
nearby 근처에, 인근에
public transportation 대중교통

W Hello, listeners! Are you excited for the Greenville Animation Film Festival? This year, it'll start on December 5th and continue for one week. Throughout the festival, visitors can watch different animation movies related to the theme of this year, friendship, every night. Remember, there's no parking lot nearby. So, please use public transportation.

여 청취자 여러분, 안녕하세요! 그린빌 애니메이션 영화제가 기대되시나요? 올해는 12월 5일에 시작해서 일주일 동안 계속됩니다(ⓐ). 축제 기간 내내 방문객들은 매일 밤 올해의 주제인 우정(ⓑ)과 관련된 다양한 애니메이션 영화를 볼 수 있습니다. 근처에 주차장이 없다는 것을 명심하세요(ⓒ). 그러니 대중교통을 이용해주세요.

07 ⓑ

해설 참가자는 올해의 프로젝트 주제인 '우주 탐험'에 대한 과학 프로젝트를 만들어야 한다.

어휘 annual 매년의; 연간의
competition 대회, 시합; 경쟁
deadline 기한, 마감 시간[일자]
application 신청[지원](서); 적용, 응용

M Are you full of creative thoughts? Then our annual science contest, Show Me Your Creativity, is the perfect place for you to show your talents. This competition is open to all high school and university students. Students that wish to participate need to create a science project about this year's theme of space exploration. The deadline for applications is June 30th.

남 여러분은 창의적인 생각으로 가득 차 있나요? 그렇다면 저희의 연례 과학 경시 대회인 '당신의 창의력을 보여주세요'가 여러분의 재능을 선보일 완벽한 곳입니다. 이 대회는 모든 고등학생과 대학생에게 열려 있습니다(ⓐ). 참가를 원하는 학생들은 올해의 주제인 우주 탐험에 대한 과학 프로젝트를 만들어야 합니다(ⓑ). 신청 마감일은 6월 30일입니다(ⓒ).

08 ⓒ

해설 사전에 등록해야 하며, 현장 등록은 받지 않는다.

어휘 flashlight 손전등
adventure 모험
complete 완료된
planet 행성
register 등록하다
cf. registration 등록
in advance 사전에
on-site 현장의
accept 받다, 수락하다

W We are starting a special program — Family Night at the Museum. When the regular museum hours are over, you and your children get to walk around the museum with a flashlight. After your adventure is complete, you will sleep under the amazing models of planets and stars. All those who want to join must register in advance. On-site registration is not accepted.

여 저희는 '박물관에서의 가족의 밤'이라는 특별한 프로그램을 시작합니다. 정규 박물관 시간이 끝나면 여러분과 여러분의 아이들은 손전등을 들고 박물관 주변을 걸을 것입니다(ⓐ). 모험이 완료되고 나면, 여러분은 행성과 별의 놀라운 모형 아래에서 잠을 잘 것입니다(ⓑ). 참가를 원하시는 분들은 모두 사전에 등록해야 합니다(ⓒ). 현장 등록은 받지 않습니다.

09 ⓐ

해설 10월이 아닌 9월 한 달간 사진을 올릴 수 있다.

어휘 participate in ~에 참여하다
eco-friendly 친환경의
tag 태그를 붙이다
automatically 자동으로
post 게시하다

M Why don't you join our Green Action Photo Contest? From September 1st until September 30th, you can upload photos of your participating in eco-friendly activities on social media. By tagging your photos with the hash tag #GreenAction, you can automatically participate in our contest. The winning photos will be posted on the town's website until the end of this year.

남 저희의 그린 액션 사진 콘테스트에 참여하는 게 어떠신가요? 9월 1일부터 9월 30일까지(ⓐ) 소셜 미디어에 본인이 친환경 활동에 참여하는 사진을 올리면 됩니다. 해시태그 #GreenAction으로 사진에 태그를 붙임으로써 자동으로 대회에 참가할 수 있습니다(ⓑ). 우승 사진은 올해 말까지 마을 웹사이트에 게시될 예정입니다(ⓒ).

10 ⓒ

해설 오늘 미술관을 방문하는 사람들은 공연 관람이 무료이다.

W May I have your attention, please? As manager of Fantasia Gallery, I am pleased to announce that we

여 주목해주시겠습니까? 판타지아 미술관의 관리자로서, 저희의 개관을 기념하는 미술 쇼를 개최할

어휘 pleased to-v v하여 기쁜
free of charge 무료의, 공짜의

are holding a Magic Show to celebrate our grand opening. John Potter, who is famous for his card magic, will perform in the show. The show is free of charge for everyone visiting our gallery today. Seats are limited!

것임을(ⓐ) 알려드리게 되어 기쁩니다. 카드 마술로 유명한 존 포터가 공연할 것입니다(ⓑ). 공연은 오늘 미술관을 방문하시는 모든 분께 무료입니다(ⓒ). 좌석은 제한되어 있습니다!

STEP ③ · ④ Listen & Answer

본문 p.79

01 ④ **02** ⑤ **03** ③ **04** ③ **05** ② **06** ② **07** ③ **08** ② **09** ② **10** ④

01 ④

해설 해석 참조

어휘 Bollywood 발리우드 ((인도 뭄바이의 인기 있는 영화 산업))
combination 조합, 결합
depend on ~에 달려 있다

M I want to watch a movie. What about you?
W Me too. There's a new one from Bollywood that you might like.
M What's Bollywood?
W It's the Indian film industry, which is based in Mumbai. Mumbai used to be called Bombay, so it's a combination of Bombay and Hollywood.
M Oh, then I think *3 Idiots* is a well-known Bollywood movie.
W Right. That's one of its most famous movies. They produce nearly a thousand films each year, and billions of people watch them.
M That's amazing. What are Bollywood films like?
W There is a lot of singing and dancing, so a film's success often depends on the quality of the songs.

남 난 영화를 보고 싶어. 너는?
여 나도 그래. 네가 좋아할 만한 발리우드의 신작이 있어.
남 발리우드가 뭐야?
여 인도의 영화 산업인데, **뭄바이를 근거지로 하고 있어**(① 제작 지역). 뭄바이는 한때 봄베이로 불렸고, 그래서 발리우드는 봄베이와 할리우드를 합친 말이야.
남 아, 그럼 '세 얼간이'가 잘 알려진 발리우드 영화 같은데(② 대표작).
여 맞아. 그게 발리우드의 가장 유명한 영화 중 하나야. 발리우드는 **일 년에 천 편 정도의 영화를 제작하고**(③ 연간 제작 편 수), 수억 명의 사람이 그 영화들을 관람해.
남 엄청나구나. 발리우드 영화의 특징이 뭐야?
여 노래와 춤이 많이 나와, 그래서 **영화의 성공이 보통 노래의 질에 달려 있어**(⑤ 흥행 조건).

02 ⑤

해설 해석 참조

어휘 brochure (안내, 광고용) 책자
horseback riding 승마
hectare 헥타르 ((땅 면적의 단위. 1만 제곱미터 또는 약 2.5에이커))
can't wait to-v 어서 빨리 v하고 싶다
wildlife 야생 동물
settled 정해진; 안정적인; 계산이 끝난

W Nick, did you get a chance to look at this brochure for Camp John Hay?
M I did, and it looks great! They have a fitness gym, a golf course, and horses for horseback riding.
W Look, they have a big forest that reaches 246 hectares.
M Yes. There are over 250,000 pine trees. It sounds beautiful.
W The trees also help to keep temperatures cool during the summer there, between 15 to 23 degrees. I just wish it wasn't so far away.
M Yes, it's located in Baguio City. That's a long way from here, but I think the trip would be fun.
W Yeah, let's take our car. I can't wait to see the wildlife in the forest.
M All right, then it's settled. We're going.

여 닉, 캠프 존 헤이에 관한 이 책자를 볼 기회가 있었어요?
남 네, 그리고 아주 멋진 것 같아요! **거기엔 헬스장, 골프장, 그리고 승마용 말들도 있어요**(① 보유 시설).
여 봐요, 246헥타르에 달하는 큰 숲이 있대요(② 숲의 면적).
남 맞아요. 25만 그루가 넘는 소나무가 있어요. 아름다울 것 같아요.
여 그 나무들은 **여름 동안 그곳의 온도를 15도에서 23도 사이로 시원하게 유지**(③ 여름 기온)하는 데에도 도움이 돼요. 너무 멀지만 않으면 좋겠어요.
남 그래요, **바기오시(市)에 있네요**(④ 위치). 여기에서 거리가 멀지만, 여행은 재미있을 것 같아요.
여 네, 우리 차를 타고 가요. 숲속의 야생 동물을 어서 빨리 보고 싶어요.
남 좋아요, 그럼 정해졌어요. 우리 가는 거예요.

03 ③

해설 해석 참조

어휘 vendor 상인, 물건을 파는 사람
profit 수익(금), 이익
as usual 평소대로

W James, would you like to go to the Arendal Annual Flea Market with me?

M I'm not sure. It opens this Saturday, right?

W Yes. It is held in the parking lot of Arendal High School.

M I wonder how big it will be this time. There was not much to look around last year.

W It will be a lot bigger than the last time. I heard about 250 vendors registered this year.

M Oh, really? I might be able to find the board games I've been looking for.

W Probably. And the profits will be used for student scholarships and activities as usual.

M That's great. Then I'd like to join you.

W Okay. Let's go together.

여 제임스, 나랑 같이 아렌달 연례 벼룩시장에 갈래?

남 잘 모르겠어. 이번 주 토요일에 여는 거 맞지(① 개최 요일)?

여 응. 아렌달 고등학교 주차장에서 열려(② 개최 장소).

남 이번에는 얼마나 클지 궁금해. 작년에는 구경할 것이 별로 없었거든.

여 지난번보다 훨씬 클 거야. 올해 250명 정도의 상인들이 등록했다고(④ 판매 참가자 수) 들었거든.

남 아, 정말? 내가 찾던 보드게임을 구할 수 있을지도 모르겠다.

여 아마도. 그리고 수익금은 평소대로 학생 장학금과 활동에 사용될 거야(⑤ 수익금 용도).

남 잘됐네. 그럼 너랑 같이 가고 싶어.

여 좋아. 같이 가자.

04 ③

해설 해석 참조

어휘 on display 전시된, 진열된
be full of ~로 가득 차다
drama 극적 효과; 드라마
recently 최근에
auction 경매

M Diane, did you hear about the Maria Arroyo-Diamond exhibition?

W I did! Most of her work is on display. We should go together.

M I was hoping you would say that. She's one of my favorite artists.

W She's from Mexico, isn't she?

M Right. She moved to Italy after marrying her husband five years ago, but I think Mexico is where she developed her painting style.

W Her work is full of color and drama. I could see that coming from Mexican culture.

M Right, and she's become quite famous in Italy.

W Oh, I know. One of her artworks was recently sold for $80,000 in an auction.

M Wow! I think she'll be even more popular in the future.

남 다이앤, 마리아 아로요 다이아몬드의 전시회에 대해 들었니?

여 들었어! 그녀의 작품 대부분이 전시 중이야. 우리 같이 보러 가자.

남 네가 그렇게 말해주길 바라고 있었어. 내가 가장 좋아하는 예술가 중 한 명이거든.

여 그녀는 멕시코 출신이지(① 출신 국가), 그렇지 않니?

남 맞아. 5년 전에 남편과 결혼한 후(② 결혼 시기) 이탈리아로 이주했지만 나는 그녀가 자신의 화풍을 발전시킨 곳은 바로 멕시코라고 생각해.

여 그녀의 작품은 색채와 극적 요소로 가득 차 있지(④ 화풍). 난 그게 멕시코 문화에서 비롯된 것임을 알 수 있어.

남 맞아, 그리고 그녀는 이탈리아에서 꽤 유명해졌어.

여 아, 알고 있어. 그녀의 작품 중 하나가 최근 경매에서 8만 달러에 팔렸어(⑤ 작품 가격).

남 와! 난 그녀가 앞으로 훨씬 더 인기 있을 거라고 생각해.

05 ②

해설 해석 참조

어휘 immigration (다른 나라에 살러 오는) 이민, 이주
cf. immigrant 이민자, 이주민
in operation 사용 중인, 가동 중인
shut down (공장, 가게 등이) 문을 닫다
entirely 완전히
tourist attraction 관광 명소

M Welcome to Ellis Island! I'll be your guide for today. This island was used as an immigration station. Please look around.

W How long was it in operation?

M Good question. For more than sixty years.

W I see, did it shut down entirely?

M Unfortunately, yes. It opened in 1892 and closed in 1954. Now it's a popular tourist attraction, as you can see.

W Then how many immigrants did it receive during its history?

M Because of its location, New York City, and the fact that travel by ship was the main way to get from Europe to America, it received millions of immigrants.

W That's interesting. It has such a rich history.

남 엘리스 아일랜드에 오신 것을 환영합니다! 제가 오늘 여러분의 안내원이 될 것입니다. 이 섬은 이민국으로 쓰였습니다(① 용도). 둘러보세요.

여 얼마나 오래 (이민국으로) 사용되었나요?

남 좋은 질문이네요. 60년이 넘습니다(③ 시설 사용 기간).

여 그렇군요, 완전히 문을 닫았나요?

남 안타깝게도 그렇습니다. 1892년에 개관해서(④ 시설 개관 시기) 1954년에 폐관되었습니다. 지금은 보시다시피 인기 있는 관광 명소지요.

여 그러면 그동안은 얼마나 많은 이민자를 받았나요?

남 뉴욕시에 있다는 위치(⑤ 위치)와 유럽에서 미국으로 오는 주된 방법이 항해였다는 사실 때문에 수백만 명의 이민자를 받았습니다.

여 흥미롭네요. 역사가 참 깊군요.

06 ②

해설 반은 수영 실력이 아닌 연령에 따라 나뉜다.

어휘 application 신청[지원](서)
be scheduled to-v v할 예정이다
swimming goggles 물안경
suit 알맞다; (옷 등이) 어울리다

M Good afternoon, Oak Ridge residents! If you can't swim, or just want to improve your technique, Spring Swim Lesson Program is the chance you've been waiting for. Applications are now being accepted for the program, which is scheduled to begin in April, at the Community Center. There are separate classes for ages 8 to 12, ages 13 to 18, and ages over 18. Classes are offered in eight-week sessions. The cost is $80 per class, which includes swimming goggles and a cap. Classes are offered on weekday afternoons and Saturday mornings, so you can choose a time that suits you. For more information please contact the Community Center at 786-7110.

남 안녕하세요, 오크 릿지 주민 여러분! 여러분이 만약 수영을 못하신다면, 또는 단지 기술을 향상시키고 싶으시다면, 봄철 수영 강습 프로그램은 여러분이 기다려오신 기회입니다. 프로그램을 위한 신청서가 현재 접수되고 있는데, **이 프로그램은 커뮤니티 센터에서 4월에 시작될 예정입니다**(①). 8세에서 12세, 13세에서 18세, 그리고 18세 이상을 위한 별개의 반이 있습니다(②). 수업은 8주간의 과정으로 제공됩니다(③). 비용은 한 수업당 80달러인데, **이 가격에는 물안경과 수영모가 포함되어 있습니다**(④). 수업은 평일 오후와 토요일 오전에 제공되므로(⑤), 여러분에게 알맞은 시간을 선택하실 수 있습니다. 정보를 더 원하시면 786-7110으로 커뮤니티 센터에 연락하시길 바랍니다.

07 ③

해설 입장료는 무료이지만 놀이 기구의 표는 구입해야 한다.

어휘 original 최초의; 독창적인
recreation 오락, 레크리에이션
retail 소매(의)
year-round 일 년 내내
ride 놀이 기구; 타다
separate A into B A를 B로 분할하다
namely 즉, 다시 말해
fascinating 매력적인, 매우 흥미로운
world-class 세계 최상급의
complex (건물) 단지, 복합 건물

W Hello, visitors! Welcome to the Wharf Amusement Park. It is Macau's first theme park and offers recreation, retail stores, a convention center, hotels, and more, all in one place. Opened in December 2005, the park is locally managed. It opens year-round with no admission fee, but you must purchase tickets for the rides. The park is separated into 3 themed sections, namely Dynasty Wharf, East Meets West, and Legend Wharf. Also, you can enjoy many fine restaurants serving wonderful dishes from all over the world. Whether your travel is for business or pleasure, you are sure to enjoy your trip to this fascinating world-class amusement complex.

여 안녕하세요, 방문객 여러분! 와프 놀이공원에 오신 것을 환영합니다. 이곳은 **마카오 최초의 테마 공원이며**(①). 오락, 소매점, 컨벤션 센터, 호텔 등 모든 시설을 한곳에서 제공합니다. **2005년 12월에 개장한**(②) 이 공원은 지역에서 운영합니다. 입장료 없이 일 년 내내 문을 열지만, **놀이 기구의 표는 구입하셔야 합니다**(③). 공원은 세 가지 테마 구역으로 나뉘어 있는데(④), 즉 다이너스티 와프, 이스트 미츠 웨스트, 그리고 레전드 와프입니다. 또한, 여러분은 **전 세계의 훌륭한 요리를 제공하는 많은 멋진 레스토랑을 즐기실 수 있습니다**(⑤). 여러분의 여행이 용무를 위해서든 즐거움을 위해서든, 여러분은 분명히 이 매력적인 세계 최상급의 오락 단지로의 여행을 즐기실 것입니다.

08 ②

해설 관련 업무 경력이 보너스 요소가 되기는 하나 필수는 아니라고 했다.

어휘 enthusiastic 열렬한, 열광적인
relevant 관련 있는
regardless of ~에 상관없이
academic background 학력
document 서류, 문서
recruiter 신입 모집자

M Are you looking for an exciting job opportunity? Carson Electronics is now inviting applications for enthusiastic sales people for our Dallas office. Relevant work experience is a bonus, but it is not required. We are accepting all applications regardless of academic background. Please note that we will only accept applications that are complete. The application form is available on our website, www.carsonelectronics.com, and applications in other formats will not be accepted. All documents must be sent to our recruiter, David Johnson, by September 16th. Thank you for your interest in Carson Electronics!

남 흥미로운 취업 기회를 찾고 계신가요? 카슨 일렉트로닉스는 현재 **댈러스 지점**에서 일할 열정적인 **판매사원의 지원을 구하고 있습니다**(①). **관련 업무 경력은 보너스가 되지만, 필수는 아닙니다**(②). **학력에 상관없이 모든 지원서를 받고 있습니다**(③). 빠짐없이 작성된 지원서만 받을 것이라는 점에 주의하시기 바랍니다. **지원서 양식은 저희 웹사이트 www.carsonelectronics.com에서 구할 수 있으며**(④), 다른 형식의 지원서는 접수되지 않을 것입니다. **모든 서류는 반드시 9월 16일까지**(⑤) 신입 모집 담당자인 데이비드 존슨에게 보내져야 합니다. 카슨 일렉트로닉스에 관심을 가져주셔서 감사합니다!

09 ②

해설 여성 전용 걷기 행사라고 했다.

어휘 take place 개최되다; 일어나다
raise funds 기금을 모으다
raise awareness 인식을 높이다
participant 참가자
stroller 유모차
warm-up 준비 운동, 워밍업
take part 참가[참여]하다

W Hello, supporters! The Great Welsh Walk will take place next month on Sunday, October 9th. The Walk is a women-only walking event over a 5 km, 10 km, or half-marathon distance. The goal of the event is to help raise funds and awareness for the fight against breast cancer. Participants are welcome to walk with dogs or babies in strollers. The event will start at the Llanelli Discovery Center, and all who take part will be able to join a special aerobics warm-up session. Why not take part and encourage those around you to do the same?

여 서포터즈 여러분, 안녕하세요! 그레이트 웰시 워크가 다음 달 10월 9일, 일요일에 개최될 것입니다(①). 워크는 5km, 10km 또는 하프 마라톤 거리를 걷는, 여성 전용 걷기 행사입니다(②). 행사의 목적은 유방암 퇴치를 위한 기금을 모으고(③) 인식을 높이는 것을 돕기 위함입니다. 참가자들은 개와 함께 걷거나(④) 아기를 유모차에 태우고 함께 걸으셔도 좋습니다. 행사는 라넬리 디스커버리 센터에서 시작할 것이며, 참가하는 모든 분은 특별한 에어로빅 준비 운동 시간에 참여하실 수 있습니다(⑤). 참가하시고 여러분 주변 분들도 참가하도록 권해보시지 않겠습니까?

10 ④

해설 첫해가 아닌 그 다음해에 만여 개의 작품이 출품되었다.

어휘 humorous 재미있는
sponsor ~을 후원하다
crown 왕관을 씌우다; 왕관
in honor of ~에 경의를 표하여, ~을 기념하여
quoted 인용된
entry 출품[응모]작; 입장
subcategory 하위 범주

M The Bulwer-Lytton Fiction Contest is a humorous annual event sponsored by the English Department of San José State University. Participants are given the chance to write the worst possible opening line to a novel, and the most awful is crowned the winner. The contest is named in honor of English writer Edward George Bulwer-Lytton, author of the much-quoted first line "It was a dark and stormy night." The first year of the competition attracted just three entries from on campus, but it was widely advertised the next year and attracted around 10,000 entries. There are also now several subcategories including fiction, romance novels, and others.

남 불워 리턴 픽션 콘테스트는 산호세 주립 대학 영문학과가 후원하는(①) 재미있는 연례행사입니다. 참가자들은 가능한 한 최악의 소설 첫머리를 쓰는 기회가 주어지며(②), 가장 끔찍한 것이 우승자의 왕관을 쓰게 됩니다. 콘테스트는 영국인 작가 에드워드 조지 불워 리턴에 경의를 표하여 이름이 지어졌는데(③), 그는 정말 많이 인용된 첫 문장인 '어둡고 폭풍우가 몰아치는 밤이었다.'를 쓴 작가입니다. 대회의 첫해에는 교내에서 단 세 개의 출품작을 끌어모았으나(④), 그 다음해에는 널리 광고되어 만여 개의 출품작을 끌어모았습니다. 이제는 소설, 로맨스 소설 등을 포함하는 몇몇 하위 항목들도 있습니다(⑤).

유형 07 화자의 관계

☀☀ 기출 맛보기

본문 p.87

01 ②

해설 여자는 키패드에 문제가 생겨 집에 들어가지 못해 남자에게 전화했고, 남자가 방문하여 수리할 예정이므로 열쇠 수리공과 집주인의 관계임을 알 수 있다.

어휘 be locked out of (문이 잠겨) ~에 못 들어가다
respond 반응하다
electric 전기의
cost (비용이) 들다
including ~을 포함하여
service charge 서비스 비용
extra 추가 요금; 추가의
additional 추가적인

[Telephone rings.]
M Hello. This is G-Solution. How may I help you?
W Hello. I'm locked out of my home. The keypad on my door isn't responding.
M It might be an electric problem. It's probably a simple fix and it won't cost much.
W How much is it?
M It's 30 dollars including the service charge. But you'll have to pay extra if there are any additional problems.
W I got it. Can you come over right away?
M I'm afraid not. I'm doing a job at the Capital Bank.
W How long will it take you to finish?

[전화벨이 울린다.]
남 안녕하세요 지 솔루션입니다. 어떻게 도와드릴까요?
여 안녕하세요. 문이 잠겨 집에 들어갈 수 없어요. 제 현관 키패드가 반응이 없어요.
남 그건 전기 문제일 수 있습니다. 아마 간단한 수리일 것이고 비용도 많이 들지 않을 겁니다.
여 얼마인가요?
남 서비스 비용을 포함하여 30달러입니다. 하지만 추가적인 문제가 있으면 추가 요금을 내셔야 합니다.
여 알겠어요. 지금 바로 오실 수 있나요?
남 안 될 것 같습니다. 저는 캐피털 은행에서 작업 중이거든요.
여 끝내는 데 얼마나 걸리실까요?

M	Just one hour. I'll call you as soon as I'm done. Address, please?	남 한 시간이면 됩니다. 끝나는 대로 전화드리겠습니다. 주소를 알려주시겠어요?
W	705 Cozy Street near Lee's Dental Clinic.	여 리 치과 근처의 코지가(街) 705번지에요.
M	Okay. See you soon.	남 알겠습니다. 이따 뵙겠습니다.

STEP ① · ② Listen & Choose

본문 p.88

01 ⓒ **02** ⓑ **03** ⓐ **04** ⓑ **05** ⓑ **06** ⓐ **07** ⓑ **08** ⓑ **09** ⓒ **10** ⓐ

01 ⓒ

해설 check out, bill, room service로 보아 호텔에서 체크아웃하는 상황이므로 투숙객과 호텔 프런트 직원의 관계임을 알 수 있다.

어휘 check out (계산을 치르고) 호텔에서 나오다, 체크아웃하다 (↔ check in)
bill 청구서, 계산서
charge 비용, 요금; (값을) 청구하다

W	I'd like to check out. My name is Monica Scott.	여 체크아웃하고 싶은데요. 제 이름은 모니카 스콧입니다.
M	Ms. Scott? Here's your final bill.	남 스콧 씨요? 여기 최종 청구서입니다.
W	Hmm.... This is strange. I didn't order anything from room service.	여 음⋯. 이거 이상하군요. 전 룸서비스로 아무것도 주문하지 않았는데요.
M	Really? Let me check. *[clicking sound]* I'm so sorry, there was a mistake. I'll cancel that charge right away.	남 그렇습니까? 제가 확인해보겠습니다. *[클릭하는 소리]* 대단히 죄송합니다, 착오가 있었습니다. 그 요금은 바로 취소하겠습니다.

02 ⓑ

해설 남자의 소설을 여자가 영화로 만들고자 하는 상황이므로, 소설가와 영화감독의 관계임을 알 수 있다.

어휘 proposal 제안
turn A into B A를 B로 만들다
direct 감독하다
honor 영광

W	Hello, Mr. Johnson. Have you thought about my proposal?	여 존슨 씨, 안녕하세요. 제 제안에 대해 생각해 보셨나요?
M	Yes. You said you wanted to turn my novel into a movie, right?	남 네. 제 소설을 영화로 만들고 싶다고 하셨죠?
W	That's right. I loved your novel, and it would make a great movie.	여 맞아요. 전 당신의 소설이 너무 좋았고, 그건 훌륭한 영화가 될 거예요.
M	I'm glad to hear that. And if you directed the movie, it would be a great honor for me.	남 그 말을 들으니 기쁘군요. 그리고 당신이 그 영화를 감독한다면, 저에게 큰 영광이 될 거예요.

03 ⓐ

해설 send this package, delivered, Express Mail Service로 보아 우체국 직원과 손님의 관계임을 알 수 있다.

어휘 package 소포
scale 저울; 규모
within ~이내
Express Mail Service 특급우편 서비스

M	Hello. What can I do for you?	남 안녕하세요. 무엇을 도와드릴까요?
W	Hi, I'd like to send this package to Seoul, South Korea.	여 안녕하세요, 이 소포를 대한민국, 서울로 보내고 싶어요.
M	Put it on the scale, please. *[pause]* All right. You can have it delivered within a week using Express Mail Service for $15.	남 그걸 저울에 올려주세요. *[잠시 후]* 좋습니다. 15달러로 특급우편 서비스를 이용하시면 일주일 이내에 배달되도록 하실 수 있습니다.
W	That sounds good. I'll use that service.	여 그거 좋네요. 그 서비스를 이용할게요.

04 ⓑ

해설 남자가 캠핑 박람회 표, 코너 위치 등에 대해 묻고 여자는 질문에 답하고 있으므로 박람회장 안내원과 방문객의 관계임을 알 수 있다.

어휘 entrance 입구
whole 전체의, 모든
expo 박람회

M	Hi, I made an online reservation. Do I get the tickets here?	남 안녕하세요, 저는 온라인 예약을 했는데요. 여기서 표를 받으면 되나요?
W	You don't have to get tickets if you have a reservation number. Just show it at the entrance and you can enjoy the whole camping expo.	여 예약 번호가 있으면 표를 받지 않으셔도 됩니다. 입구에서 예약 번호를 보여주기만 하면 캠핑 박람회 전체를 즐기실 수 있습니다.
M	That's great. I heard there is a section for camping tables and chairs. Where can I find it?	남 잘됐네요. 캠핑 테이블과 의자 코너가 있다고 들었어요. 어디서 찾을 수 있나요?
W	When you go inside, you'll see it on your right.	여 안쪽으로 들어가시면 오른쪽에 보일 겁니다.

05 ⓑ

해설 writer like you, reading your books로 보아 독자와 작가의 관계임을 알 수 있다.

어휘 **world-famous** 세계적으로 유명한
in person 직접
autograph (유명인의) 사인

W I think I have seen you on TV. Aren't you Brad Johnson?
M Yes, I am.
W Wow! I never thought I'd meet a world-famous writer like you in person. I really enjoy reading your books. Could I get your autograph?
M Certainly.

여 당신을 TV에서 본 일이 있는 것 같아요. 브래드 존슨 씨 아니신가요?
남 네, 맞습니다.
여 와! 제가 당신처럼 세계적으로 유명한 작가를 직접 만날 거라고는 생각지도 못했어요. 저는 당신의 책들을 정말 즐겨 읽어요. 사인을 받을 수 있을까요?
남 물론이죠.

06 ⓐ

해설 return the car, have to pay an additional charge로 보아 남자는 차를 빌리는 고객이고 여자는 렌터카 직원임을 알 수 있다.

어휘 **fill up** ~을 가득 채우다
be supposed to-v v하도록 되어 있다
on time 정각에, 시간을 어기지 않고

M Should I fill up the tank before I return the car?
W Yes, you should.
M I see. And I'm supposed to return it on Saturday by 11 a.m., right?
W Yes. Please bring it back on time, or you'll have to pay an additional charge.

남 차를 반납하기 전에 연료 통을 가득 채워야 합니까?
여 네, 그렇게 하셔야 합니다.
남 알겠습니다. 그리고 토요일 오전 11시까지 차를 반납해야 하는 거죠, 맞죠?
여 네. 차를 정시에 돌려주십시오, 그렇지 않으면 추가 비용을 지불하셔야 합니다.

07 ⓑ

해설 햇볕에 화상을 입은 남자가 여자에게 진료받는 상황이므로 피부과 의사와 환자의 관계임을 알 수 있다.

어휘 **sunburn** 햇볕으로 입은 화상
symptom 증상
prescribe 처방을 내리다

W Hello, Mr. Cooper. You came here last week because of a sunburn. How are the symptoms now?
M Much better.
W Great. Let me look at the sunburn. [pause] The redness is almost gone.
M Yeah. The cream you prescribed was really helpful.

여 쿠퍼 씨, 안녕하세요. 지난주에 햇볕에 화상을 입어 이곳에 오셨었네요. 지금 증상은 좀 어떤가요?
남 훨씬 좋아졌어요.
여 다행이네요. 햇볕에 화상 입은 곳을 볼게요. [잠시 후] 붉은 기가 거의 없어졌네요.
남 네. 처방해주신 연고가 큰 도움이 됐어요.

08 ⓑ

해설 I made the dresses, any special pose, on the runway로 보아 남자는 드레스를 만든 의상 디자이너이고 여자는 패션모델임을 알 수 있다.

어휘 **gorgeous** 멋진
material 소재, 재료
emphasize 강조하다

M I'm honored to have you on my stage.
M My pleasure. The dresses you made are gorgeous.
M Thank you. The theme of today's show is "Nature", so I made the dresses with only natural materials.
W I see. Is there any special pose I should use on the runway?
M I asked the other models to walk slowly to emphasize the soft lines of the dress.

남 제 무대에 당신을 세우게 되어 영광입니다.
여 천만에요. 당신이 만든 드레스는 정말 멋지네요.
남 고마워요. 오늘 무대의 주제가 '자연'이어서 천연 소재만으로 드레스를 만들었어요.
여 그렇군요. 런웨이에서 제가 해야 할 특별한 포즈가 있나요?
남 저는 다른 모델들에게 드레스의 부드러운 라인을 강조하기 위해 천천히 걸어달라고 요청했어요.

09 ⓒ

해설 the sound effects you added, your voice acting으로 보아 남자는 오디오북에 음향 효과를 추가하는 녹음 기사이고, 여자는 목소리 연기를 하는 성우임을 알 수 있다.

어휘 **sound effects** 음향 효과
alive 살아 있는
various 다양한
role 역할

W Did you hear about one of the audio books we recorded in this studio last year?
M You mean "The Dreaming Tree?" I heard it was the bestselling audio book of the year.
W It was. The sound effects you added made the story feel alive.
M Thank you. Most of all, your voice acting was great in the various roles.

여 작년에 이 스튜디오에서 저희가 녹음한 오디오북 중 하나에 대해 들었나요?
남 '꿈꾸는 나무'를 말하는 건가요? 그해 가장 많이 팔린 오디오북이라고 들었어요.
여 맞아요. 당신이 추가한 음향 효과가 이야기를 생동감 있게 만들었어요.
남 고마워요. 무엇보다도, 다양한 역할에서 당신의 목소리 연기가 훌륭했어요.

10 ⓐ

해설 여자가 남자의 파티 음식을 맡기로 한 상황이므로 두 사람은 파티 주최자와 요리사의 관계임을 알 수 있다.

어휘 take charge of ~을 떠맡다, ~의 책임을 지다
take care of ~을 (책임지고) 맡다
from start to finish 처음부터 끝까지

M Welcome, Ms. Jones. Mr. Harvey told me you're coming.
W Thanks. I hear that you're holding a party at your house in two weeks.
M That's right. I'm hoping you could take charge of the food for my party.
W Sure. I'll be taking care of the party food from start to finish.

남 존스 씨 환영해요. 하비 씨가 제게 당신이 올 거라고 했어요.
여 감사합니다. 2주 후에 당신의 집에서 파티를 연다고 들었습니다.
남 맞아요. 당신이 제 파티 음식을 맡아주셨으면 합니다.
여 물론이죠. 파티 음식은 제가 처음부터 끝까지 맡겠습니다.

STEP 3 · 4 Listen & Answer

본문 p.91

01 ②   02 ⑤   03 ②   04 ④   05 ④   06 ⑤   07 ①   08 ③   09 ①   10 ②

---

01 ②

해설 a new brand of chocolate, Why don't you taste it?, this promotion week로 보아 신제품을 홍보하는 판매원과 손님의 관계임을 알 수 있다.

어휘 filling (음식물의) 속; 채움
be covered with ~로 덮이다
unusual 특이한, 드문
absolutely 매우, 절대적으로
promotion 홍보[판촉] (활동); 승진
pack 팩, 포장 용기; 꾸러미

W This is a new brand of chocolate. It's called *Moira*.
M *Moira*?
W Yes, the filling is made out of fresh cream and it's covered with dark chocolate.
M Well, it looks beautiful. It's a very unusual shape.
W Yes, this chocolate looks beautiful and also tastes wonderful. Why don't you taste it?
M Mmm.... Oh, it's wonderful... absolutely delicious.
W If you buy *Moira* during this promotion week, you can get two packs for the price of one.
M OK. I'll buy two packs.

여 이것은 새로 나온 초콜릿 제품입니다. '모이라'라고 하죠.
남 '모이라'요?
여 네. 속은 생크림으로 만들어졌고, 다크 초콜릿으로 덮여 있습니다.
남 음, 아름답네요. 아주 특이한 모양이에요.
여 네, 이 초콜릿은 보기에 아름답고 맛도 훌륭합니다. 맛을 한번 보시죠?
남 음…. 오, 놀랍군요… 매우 맛있어요.
여 이 홍보 주간 동안 '모이라'를 사시면, 한 팩 가격으로 두 팩을 사실 수 있습니다.
남 좋아요. 두 팩 사겠습니다.

---

02 ⑤

해설 남자는 여자의 집을 둘러보며 이삿짐을 옮기는 법을 이야기하고 여자는 이사할 예정이므로 이삿짐센터 직원과 고객의 관계임을 알 수 있다.

어휘 residence 거처, 거주지
handle 처리하다, 다루다
appropriate 적절한
padded 패드를 넣은, 푹신한
wrapping 포장지
cf. wrap 포장하다, 싸다
furniture 가구

M Hello, Ms. Palmer.
W Hi, Mr. Watts! Come on in.
M Thanks. Well, you said your new residence is in Fairfax County.
W Yes, it's 3481 Green Street.
M It takes an hour to get there from here. Can I look around the rooms and kitchen?
W Go ahead. Oh, I have a piano. How will it be handled?
M We have movers who are trained to handle all kinds of pianos. We use the appropriate padded wrapping to protect them.
W Good. Do you also wrap furniture with blankets?
M Sure. When are you planning to move?
W November 4th.
M Okay. I think a 5-ton truck will be enough for you.

남 안녕하세요, 파머 씨.
여 안녕하세요, 왓츠! 어서 들어오세요.
남 감사합니다. 음, 새 거처가 페어팩스 카운티에 있다고 하셨죠.
여 네, 그린가(街) 3481번지예요.
남 여기서 거기까지 가는 데 한 시간 걸리네요. 방과 부엌을 둘러볼 수 있을까요?
여 그러세요. 아, 저는 피아노가 있어요. 이건 어떻게 처리될까요?
남 저희는 모든 종류의 피아노를 다룰 수 있도록 훈련된 이삿짐 운반 직원들이 있습니다. 저희는 적절한 패드 포장지를 사용하여 피아노를 보호합니다.
여 좋아요. 가구도 천으로 싸주시나요?
남 물론이죠. 언제 이사하실 예정이시죠?
여 11월 4일이요.
남 알겠습니다. 5톤 트럭이면 충분할 것 같아요.

---

03 ②

해설 Aidan's mother, recovery room, surgery, prescribe, following my instructions 등으로

W Hello, I'm Erin Taylor, Aidan's mother.
M Oh, hello, Mrs. Taylor. Everything went well.

여 안녕하세요, 저는 에린 테일러입니다, 에이단의 엄마예요.
남 아, 안녕하세요, 테일러 씨. 다 잘됐습니다.

보아 환자 보호자와 의사가 환자에 대해 이야기하고 있는 상황임을 알 수 있다.

어휘 recovery room 회복실
cf. recover 회복하다
relief 안심, 안도
surgery 수술
prescribe (a) medicine 약을 처방하다
instruction ((보통 복수형)) 지시, 설명(서)

W Thanks. How's Aidan?
M He is in the recovery room, and he will recover soon.
W That's a relief. So will he be all right?
M Yes, it was a simple surgery. But <u>you should watch him closely</u> after he gets home.
W What should I do?
M I'll prescribe some medicine for him. Give him the medicine <u>following my instructions</u>.
W My son likes to play baseball. <u>When will he be able to play</u> again?
M Well, he can't play baseball for 3 months after the surgery. But after 3 months, it will be all right.
W I see. Thanks a lot.

여 감사드려요. 에이단은 어떤가요?
남 그는 회복실에 있는데, 곧 회복할 거예요.
여 다행이네요. 그럼 아이는 괜찮을까요?
남 네, 간단한 수술이었어요. 하지만 집으로 돌아간 후에는 그를 잘 지켜보셔야 해요.
여 제가 뭘 해야 할까요?
남 제가 그에게 약을 처방하겠습니다. 제 지시에 따라 그에게 약을 주세요.
여 제 아들은 야구하는 것을 좋아해요. 아이가 언제쯤 다시 경기를 할 수 있을까요?
남 음, 수술 후 3개월 동안은 야구를 할 수 없어요. 하지만 3개월 후에는 괜찮을 거예요.
여 그렇군요. 정말 감사합니다.

04 ④

해설 남자는 수업 시간에 졸았던 여자에게 처벌로 청소를 시켰으므로 교사와 학생의 관계임을 알 수 있다.

어휘 affect 영향을 미치다
grade 성적; 등급; 학년
have no choice but to-v v할 수밖에 없다
inform 알리다
punishment 처벌, 징계

M Monica, you seem very tired these days. What's the matter?
W Well, actually, I've been playing mobile games until late at night.
M That's not good. If you do that, then you <u>can't pay attention in class</u> the next day.
W I know. I'm sorry, Mr. Taylor.
M Your performance in class <u>will affect your grades</u>, and that can actually hurt your chances of going to university.
W Yes, you're right. I have to stop.
M If this happens again, I'll have no choice but to <u>inform your parents</u>.
W Yes, I understand.
M And you must stay after class to clean <u>as punishment</u> since you were sleeping during my lesson.
W Okay. I'm really sorry.

남 모니카, 요새 너무 피곤해 보이는구나. 무슨 일 있니?
여 저, 사실 밤늦게까지 모바일 게임을 하고 있어요.
남 그건 좋지 않아. 그러면 다음날 수업에 집중할 수 없잖니.
여 알고 있어요. 죄송해요, 테일러 선생님.
남 수업 시간에 너의 수행은 성적에 영향을 줄 것이고 그것은 실제로 네가 대학에 갈 기회를 망칠 수 있어.
여 네, 선생님 말씀이 옳아요. 그만해야겠어요.
남 이런 일이 다시 발생하면 너의 부모님께 알려드릴 수밖에 없단다.
여 네, 알겠습니다.
남 그리고 네가 내 수업 시간에 졸았기 때문에 처벌로 방과 후에 남아 청소를 해야 해.
여 알겠습니다. 정말 죄송합니다.

05 ④

해설 hire you, qualifications 등을 보아 구직 면접 상황임을 알 수 있다.

어휘 hire 고용하다
for one thing 우선
qualification 자격 요건, 자질
industry 업계, 산업
pay raise 임금 인상
fairly 공정[타당]하게

M Let's see. Your name is....
W Jennifer Winslot.
M So, why do you think <u>I should hire you</u>, Jennifer?
W Well, for one thing, I've got all the qualifications you mentioned in the ad.
M Oh, so do you have experience in the recording industry?
W Yes. I was a producer in a small recording company for three years.
M <u>Why did you leave the company?</u>
W Well, I worked on most of their major projects, but in the end they <u>wouldn't give me a pay raise</u>. So I decided <u>it was time to move on</u>.
M I see. We ensure that our employees are paid fairly.
W That's great.
M All right. I'll contact you in the next week.

남 어디 봅시다. 당신의 이름은….
여 제니퍼 윈슬롯입니다.
남 자, 제가 왜 당신을 고용해야 한다고 생각합니까, 제니퍼?
여 음, 우선 저는 광고에서 언급하신 자격 요건들을 전부 갖추었습니다.
남 아, 그러면 당신은 음반 업계에 경력이 있다는 거군요?
여 네, 작은 음반 회사에서 3년 동안 프로듀서로 있었습니다.
남 왜 그 회사를 그만뒀나요?
여 저, 대다수의 주요 프로젝트를 작업했습니다만, 결국 임금을 올려주려고 하지 않았습니다. 그래서 옮겨야 할 때라고 결심했습니다.
남 그렇군요. 저희는 직원들이 공정하게 급여를 받는 것을 보장합니다.
여 정말 좋군요.
남 좋습니다. 제가 다음 주에 연락드리겠습니다.

06 ⑤

해설 여자는 여행에 관한 정보를 문의하는 고객이고, 남자는 여행 예약 관련 사항을 안내하는 여행사 직원이다.

어휘 accommodation 숙박 시설
suit (~에게) 맞다; 어울리다
guarantee (that) (~을) 보장[약속]하다
wildlife 야생 생물
landscape 경치, 풍경
brochure 소책자, 팸플릿
be booked up (호텔 등) 예약이 다 차다

M Good morning, can I help you?
W Yes, please. I'd like some information about the special trips to the Amazon rain forest.
M Well, can you tell me more about <u>what you're looking for</u> first? When will you be going, and how long do you plan to stay?
W Well, I'd like to leave next month, and I'll be staying there for a week.
M OK. What kind of <u>accommodation</u> would you like?
W Oh, a good hotel. I don't like to be uncomfortable.
M Well, I think we have something here <u>that would suit you</u>. I guarantee, with this tour, you'll see plenty of wildlife and amazing landscapes.
W That sounds good. Thanks. I'll take that brochure and <u>have a look at it</u> tonight.
M After that, please contact us as soon as possible since these trips <u>are booked up quickly</u>.

남 안녕하세요, 도와드릴까요?
여 네. 아마존 열대 우림으로 가는 특별 여행에 관한 정보를 좀 얻고 싶어요.
남 음, 먼저 무엇을 찾고 계신지에 관해 더 말씀해주시겠어요? 언제 가시고 얼마나 머물 계획이신지요?
여 음, 다음 달에 출발하고 싶고, 거기서 1주일간 머물 예정입니다.
남 알겠습니다. 숙박 시설은 어떤 종류를 원하십니까?
여 아, 괜찮은 호텔로요. 불편한 것은 싫어요.
남 음, 여기 고객님께 맞는 것이 있는 것 같습니다. 이 투어에서 많은 야생 생물과 놀라운 경치를 보시게 될 것임을 보장합니다.
여 좋아요. 감사합니다. 그 소책자를 가져가서 오늘 밤에 한번 보겠습니다.
남 이 여행은 금방 예약이 다 차기 때문에 보시고 나서 가능한 한 빨리 저희에게 연락 주십시오.

07 ①

해설 남자의 첫 번째 말에서 뉴스 진행자가 허리케인이 임박한 곳에 있는 현지 기자와 생중계로 연결하여 뉴스를 진행하는 상황임을 알 수 있다.

어휘 approach 다가오다, 접근하다
southeastern 남동쪽의
cross 가로지르다; 엇갈리다
live 생중계로; 생중계의
high wind 강풍
pack up 짐을 꾸리다
extremely 몹시; 극단적으로
concerned 염려[걱정]하는

M Now, for the very latest on the hurricane which <u>is approaching</u> the southeastern United States, we cross live to Nancy Hilton in Miami. OK, Nancy. What's happening right now?
W Well, we're expecting hurricane Charlie in the next 24 hours. The state weather agency is warning people <u>to prepare for high winds</u>.
M What are people doing?
W Well, lots of people are leaving. The roads are full and others are packing up and getting ready to leave.
M Nancy, <u>how often do you get</u> these extremely strong hurricanes?
W Too often it seems this year! It's the third one.
M Well, good luck. <u>We're all concerned</u> about you.
W Thanks. We'll need it.
M And we'll hear more from Miami later this evening.

남 이제, 미국 남동부로 다가오고 있는 허리케인에 대한 가장 최신 소식을 알아보기 위해 마이애미에 있는 낸시 힐튼을 생중계로 연결해 보겠습니다. 자, 낸시. 지금 무슨 일이 일어나고 있죠?
여 음, 허리케인 찰리가 앞으로 24시간 후면 도착할 것으로 예상하고 있습니다. 기상청은 사람들에게 강풍에 대비하라고 경고하고 있습니다.
남 사람들은 무엇을 하고 있나요?
여 음, 많은 사람들이 떠나고 있습니다. 도로는 만원이며 다른 사람들은 짐을 꾸려서 떠날 준비를 하고 있습니다.
남 낸시, 이런 초강력 허리케인들이 얼마나 자주 옵니까?
여 올해는 너무 자주 오는 것 같습니다! 이번이 세 번째입니다.
남 저, 행운을 빕니다. 우리 모두 여러분들을 염려하고 있어요.
여 감사합니다. 우리는 행운이 필요할 겁니다.
남 그러면 오늘 저녁 늦게 마이애미로부터 좀 더 소식을 들어보도록 하겠습니다.

08 ③

해설 임대할 아파트를 찾는 여자에게 남자가 조건에 맞는 집을 소개하는 상황이므로 두 사람의 관계는 부동산 중개인과 고객이다.

어휘 rent 임대하다; 빌리다; 집세
available 이용할 수 있는; 시간이 있는
current 현재의
lease (토지, 건물 등의) 임대차 (계약)
expire 만기가 되다, 만료되다
budget 예산, 경비

M Can I help you?
W Yes, <u>I read your ad</u> in the paper. I'd like to rent the advertised apartment on Square Garden Road.
M Oh, I'm sorry. That one's <u>not available anymore</u>.
W Umm. My current lease expires next month. I want to move into a new place by the end of next month.
M OK, <u>what's your budget like</u>? I mean, how much do you want to spend on rent?
W About $750 a month, if possible.
M Ah, there is another apartment at that price <u>in the same neighborhood</u>.

남 도와드릴까요?
여 네, 신문에서 당신의 광고를 읽었어요. 광고에 난 스퀘어 가든가의 아파트를 임대하고 싶은데요.
남 아, 죄송합니다. 그곳은 이미 나갔습니다.
여 음. 현재 저의 임대차 계약이 다음 달로 만기가 돼요. 다음 달 말까지 새로운 곳으로 이사하고 싶어요.
남 알겠습니다, 예산이 얼마나 되시나요? 제 말은 집세로 얼마나 쓰시길 원하시나요?
여 가능하다면, 한 달에 750달러 정도입니다.
남 아, 같은 동네에 그 가격의 또 다른 아파트가 있습니다.

W	Is it on Square Garden Road?	여	스퀘어 가든가에 있나요?
M	Yes. It has two bedrooms, a living room, and a kitchen. Would you like to see it?	남	네. 침실 두 개, 거실과 주방이 있습니다. 둘러보시겠어요?
W	Yeah, I would.	여	네, 그러죠.

09 ①

해설 남자는 대사를 말하면서 연기를 하는 배우이고, 여자는 남자의 연기를 지도하면서 등장인물에 대해 설명해주는 감독임을 알 수 있다.

어휘 line ((보통 복수형)) 대사
tone 어조, 말투; (글의) 분위기
comfort 위로하다; 위로; 안락
have a hard time (in) v-ing
v하는 데 어려움이 있다
express 표현하다
cf. expression 표정; 표현
exactly 바로 그거야, 맞아; 정확히
indifferent 무관심한
be good at ~을 잘하다
shoot 촬영하다

M "Here, sit down for a cup of tea. I'm sorry about what happened."
W That was good. Just remember to pull out a seat for her as you say the line.
M Should I say it in a more friendly tone, since I'm trying to comfort her?
W No. Your character has a hard time expressing emotions.
M So... I care, but I'm not showing that I care?
W Exactly. It's hard, but you're doing a great job so far.
M Thanks. Should I have an indifferent expression for the next few lines?
W Perfect. You're really good at getting into character. We'll start shooting in 5 minutes.

남 "여기, 앉아서 차 한잔 해요. 일어난 일은 유감이에요."
여 그거 좋았어요. 그 대사를 말하면서 여자를 위해 의자를 빼주는 것만 기억하세요.
남 제가 그녀를 위로하려고 하는 거니까 좀 더 친근한 말투로 말해야 할까요?
여 아니요. 당신이 맡은 인물은 감정을 표현하는 데 어려움이 있어요.
남 그래서… 신경은 쓰지만, 신경 쓰는 것을 드러내지 않는다는 거죠?
여 바로 그거예요. 어렵지만 지금까지 아주 잘하고 있어요.
남 감사해요. 다음 대사 몇 줄에서 무관심한 표정을 지어야 할까요?
여 완벽해요. 맡은 인물에 정말 몰입을 잘하네요. 5분 후에 촬영을 시작할게요.

10 ②

해설 남자가 공항에서 승객을 태웠다고 했으므로 남자는 택시 운전사이며, 여자는 뒷좌석에 핸드폰을 두고 내린 휴대폰 주인이다.

어휘 own 소유하다
passenger 승객
pick up ~을 차에 태우다
arrange to-v v하도록 준비하다, 조정하다

[Cell phone rings.]
M Hello, Peter Jones speaking.
W Hi, umm, this is Erica Lee.
M Are you the person who owns this cell phone?
W Yes, I am! I lost it last night, but I couldn't try calling until this morning.
M Well, a passenger I picked up at the airport found it on my back seat.
W Really? I thought I lost it somewhere in the airport.
M Where are you calling from? I'm driving down Burwood Street. I can bring it to you if you are somewhere around here.
W Actually, I'm in Sydney now, and I won't be back in Melbourne until next week.
M I see. Just call again when you get back, and I'll arrange to have it delivered to you.
W You are so kind! Thank you!

[휴대전화벨이 울린다.]
남 여보세요, 피터 존스입니다.
여 안녕하세요, 음, 저는 에리카 리입니다.
남 이 핸드폰 주인이세요?
여 네, 맞아요! 어젯밤에 잃어버렸는데, 오늘 아침이 돼서야 전화할 수 있었어요.
남 저, 공항에서 태운 승객이 제 차 뒷좌석에서 발견했어요.
여 그래요? 전 공항 어딘가에서 잃어버린 줄 알았어요.
남 지금 어디서 전화하시는 건가요? 저는 버우드가(街)를 따라 운전하고 있어요. 이 근처에 계시다면 가져다 드릴 수 있어요.
여 사실, 저는 지금 시드니에 있고, 멜버른에는 다음 주에야 돌아갈 예정이에요.
남 그렇군요. 그럼 돌아와서 다시 전화하시면 핸드폰을 받으실 수 있도록 준비할게요.
여 정말 친절하시군요! 감사드려요!

본문 p.97

✳✳ 기출 맛보기

01 ④

해설 학교 주변의 과속 관련 민원에 따른 제한 속도 준수를 독려하고 있다.

어휘 citizen 시민
mayor 시장
ensure 확실하게 하다
request 요청하다
enforce 시행하다
speed limit 속도 제한
in response to ~에 응하여
complaint 항의, 불평
regarding ~에 대하여
excessive 과도한
obey (법을) 준수하다
cooperation 협조, 협동

M Hello, citizens of Portland. This is Jerry Wilson, your Mayor. As you know, Port Elementary School has opened, and it is so nice to hear the kids playing. To ensure the safety of the students at the school, we've been communicating with the New Jersey State Police and requested that they enforce speed limits in the area around the school. This is in response to the many complaints City Hall has received regarding excessive speeding, especially in front of the school. Please obey the speed limits for the safety of the kids and your fellow citizens. Thank you for your cooperation. Stay safe and healthy.

남 안녕하세요, 포틀랜드 시민 여러분. 저는 시장인 제리 윌슨입니다. 여러분도 아시다시피, 포트 초등학교가 개교하였고, 아이들이 뛰노는 소리를 듣는 게 정말 좋습니다. 학교 학생들의 안전을 위해 저희는 뉴저지주 경찰과 소통하면서 학교 주변 지역에 속도 제한을 시행할 것을 요청했습니다. 이것은 특히 학교 앞 과속과 관련해 시청에 많은 민원이 접수된 데에 따른 조치입니다. 어린이들과 다른 시민분들의 안전을 위해 제한 속도를 준수해주십시오. 협조해주시면 감사하겠습니다. 안전하고 건강하게 지내시길 바랍니다.

STEP ①·② Listen & Choose

본문 p.98

01 ⓐ　**02** ⓒ　**03** ⓒ　**04** ⓑ　**05** ⓒ　**06** ⓐ　**07** ⓐ　**08** ⓑ　**09** ⓒ　**10** ⓑ

01 ⓐ

해설 emergency, leave the building immediately 등을 통해 비상 대피 안내 방송임을 알 수 있다.

어휘 break out 발생하다
proceed to ~로 나아가다, 이동하다
stairway 계단

M Attention please. This is Brandon Harrison, the manager of this building. There has been a report of an emergency. A fire broke out in the restaurant on the seventh floor. Proceed calmly to the nearest exit and leave the building immediately. Do not use the elevators. Use the stairways.

남 주목해주십시오. 저는 이 건물의 관리자인 브랜든 해리슨입니다. 비상사태 신고가 있었습니다. 7층에 있는 식당에서 화재가 발생했습니다. 침착하게 가장 가까운 출구로 가셔서 즉시 건물을 나가십시오. 엘리베이터는 이용하지 마십시오. 계단을 이용하십시오.

02 ⓒ

해설 마지막 문장에 지진 피해자들을 위해 기부를 요청하는 내용이 잘 드러나 있다.

어휘 as a result of ~의 결과로서
in need 어려움에 처한
donate 기부하다
victim 피해자, 이재민

W Hello. I'm Angela, leader of World Peace Unity. As a result of the terrible earthquake in Chile last week, hundreds of people have died and over 20,000 people are now homeless. Now it's time for us to help those who are in need. Please donate your money for the victims.

여 안녕하세요. 저는 세계 평화 통합의 대표 안젤라입니다. 지난주 칠레에 일어난 심각한 지진의 결과로, 수백 명의 사람이 죽고 2만 명 넘는 사람들이 지금 집을 잃었습니다. 이제 저희가 어려움에 처한 사람들을 도울 때입니다. 피해자들을 위해 여러분의 돈을 기부해주십시오.

03 ⓒ

해설 마지막 문장에 쓰레기를 버리지 말라고 당부하는 내용이 잘 드러나 있다.

어휘 tidy 깔끔한, 잘 정돈된
pavement 보도, 인도
lawn 잔디(밭)

M Hello, everyone. Thank you for visiting Rainbow Zoo. It's a great place to meet your new friends in the animal kingdom, and we know you will have a great time visiting them. Please help us keep their home clean and tidy. We urge you not to leave garbage around the cages, on the pavement, or on the lawn.

남 안녕하세요, 여러분. 레인보우 동물원에 방문해주셔서 감사합니다. 동물원은 동물의 왕국에서 여러분의 새로운 친구들을 만나기에 훌륭한 장소이며, 저희는 여러분이 그들을 보러 가면서 즐거운 시간을 보내실 것을 알고 있습니다. 저희가 그들의 집을 깨끗하고 깔끔하게 유지하도록 도와주십시오. 우리 주변이나 보도 위, 또는 잔디 위에 쓰레기를 버리지 마시길 권고드립니다.

04 ⓑ

해설 독감을 예방하기 위해 학생들에게 예방 접종을 권장하는 내용이다.

어휘 **seasonal** 계절적인
influenza 독감(= **flu**)
shot 주사
protect A from v-ing A가 v하는 것을 막다
come down with (병에) 걸리다

W Hello, students. This is Alisa, your school nurse. Many students get sick with seasonal influenza, so I would <u>recommend you get a flu vaccine</u>. A flu shot can <u>protect you from coming down with flu</u>. Please get a flu shot offered in doctors' offices or health departments by the end of this month. Thank you.

여 학생 여러분, 안녕하세요. 저는 여러분의 보건 교사 알리사입니다. 계절성 독감에 걸리는 학생들이 많으니 독감 백신을 맞을 것을 권장합니다. 독감 주사는 여러분이 독감에 걸리는 것을 막아줄 수 있습니다. 병원이나 보건소에서 제공하는 독감 주사를 이번 달 말까지 맞으시길 바랍니다. 감사합니다.

05 ⓒ

해설 차량 훼손의 목격자가 있으면 경찰에 신고해달라고 요청하는 내용이다.

어휘 **tenant** 주민, 세입자
severely 심하게
damage 손상을 주다; 손상, 피해
overnight 밤사이에
report A to B A를 B에 신고[보고]하다
investigation 조사
underway 진행 중인

M Good afternoon. This is Adam Smith from the security office. This morning in the parking lot, one of our tenants found that her car <u>had been severely damaged</u> overnight. We reported the damage to the police and an investigation is underway. If there's anyone <u>who saw something unusual</u> last night, <u>please report it</u> to the police.

남 안녕하세요. 저는 경비실의 아담 스미스입니다. 오늘 아침 주차장에서, 주민 중 한 분이 자신의 차가 밤사이에 심하게 손상된 것을 발견하셨습니다. 우리는 피해를 경찰에 신고했으며 조사가 진행 중입니다. 어젯밤 뭔가 이상한 것을 보신 분이 계시면, 경찰에 신고해주시길 바랍니다.

06 ⓐ

해설 도시 내 행사로 지하철 운행 시간이 연장될 것이라고 안내하는 내용이다.

어휘 **announcement** 안내, 알림
international 국제적인
extended 연장된, 길어진

[Chime bell rings.]
W Hello, passengers. I'm Jane Walker from the Greenville Subway System. This is an announcement that we <u>will provide longer subway service hours</u> since an international film festival <u>will be held</u> in our city next month. You can easily check <u>the extended service schedules</u> using the Greenville Subway App. Thank you.

[차임벨이 울린다.]
여 안녕하세요, 승객 여러분. 저는 그린빌 지하철의 제인 워커입니다. 다음 달에 저희 도시에서 국제 영화제가 열리게 되어 지하철 운행 시간이 연장될 것이라는 안내 말씀드립니다. 그린빌 지하철 앱을 이용하시면 연장 운행 일정을 쉽게 확인하실 수 있습니다. 감사합니다.

07 ⓐ

해설 발표에 앞서 청중의 질의 방식을 안내하는 내용이다.

어휘 **host** 사회자
presentation 발표
audience 청중, 관객
hold 기다리다
so that ~하도록, ~하기 위해

M Hello, everyone. I'm the host of this seminar, Eric Bolton. Before we <u>begin our presentations</u>, let me say that we welcome questions from the audience. But we kindly request that <u>you hold your questions</u> until all speakers have finished their presentations. Then, please step to the microphone in the center of the room so that everyone <u>may hear your question</u>.

남 안녕하세요, 여러분. 저는 이 세미나의 사회자인 에릭 볼튼입니다. 발표를 시작하기 전에, 청중의 질의를 환영한다는 점을 말씀드리겠습니다. 단, 모든 발표자가 자신들의 발표를 끝낼 때까지 질의를 보류해주시길 정중히 부탁드립니다. 그런 다음, 여러분의 질문을 모두가 들을 수 있도록 회의장 가운데에 있는 마이크로 나와주십시오.

08 ⓑ

해설 Please make sure에 이어지는 부분이 요청 내용이다.

어휘 **moderate** (날씨가) 심하지 않은, 보통의, 중간의
turbulence (대기의) 난기류; 혼란
make sure (that) (~을) 분명히 하다, 확인하다
securely 안전하게
fasten 매다, 채우다
upright 똑바른; 수직의

W Attention, please. This is captain Amy Johnson. Please notice that <u>the seat belt sign has been turned on</u>. We expect to experience moderate turbulence for about 5 or 10 minutes. Please make sure that your seat belts <u>are securely fastened</u> and that your seats <u>are in the upright position</u>. Thank you.

여 주목해주십시오. 저는 기장 에이미 존슨입니다. 안전벨트 표시등이 켜졌음에 유의해주십시오. 약 5분이나 10분 동안 심하지 않은 난기류를 겪을 것으로 예상됩니다. 안전벨트가 안전하게 채워져 있는지 그리고 좌석이 똑바로 세워져 있는지 확인해주십시오. 감사합니다.

09 ⓒ

해설 어젯밤의 폭풍우로 미끄러워진 교내의 바닥을 걸을 때 조심할 것을 당부하는 내용이다.

어휘 administration 행정, 관리
rainstorm 폭풍우
hallway 복도
central 중앙의
stairway 계단
slippery 미끄러운
cf. slip 미끄러지다

M Good morning, students. This is Mr. Lewis from the school administration office. Last night's heavy rainstorm left the first floor hallway and the central stairway slippery. Please be extra careful when you walk through these areas. You could get seriously hurt if you slip on the wet floor.

남 학생 여러분, 안녕하세요. 저는 학교 행정실의 루이스입니다. 어젯밤의 심한 폭풍우로 1층 복도와 중앙 계단이 미끄럽습니다. 이 구간을 지날 때 각별히 주의하기 바랍니다. 젖은 바닥에서 미끄러지면 크게 다칠 수 있습니다.

10 ⓑ

해설 주말에 사물함을 교체할 예정이므로 금요일까지 사물함을 비워야 한다고 공지하는 내용이다.

어휘 vice principal 교감
replace 교체하다
empty 비우다; 빈

W Hello, students. This is your vice principal, Rachel Brown. As the student lockers are getting old, we've decided to replace the lockers over the weekend. We ask that you empty your lockers by this Friday. Make sure to take all the items from your lockers and leave nothing behind.

여 안녕하세요, 학생 여러분. 저는 교감 레이첼 브라운입니다. 학생 사물함이 오래된 관계로 주말 동안 사물함을 교체하기로 했습니다. 이번 주 금요일까지 사물함을 비워주시기 바랍니다. 사물함에서 물건을 모두 꺼내고 아무것도 남기지 않도록 확실히 하십시오.

STEP ③·④ Listen & Answer

본문 p.101

01 ②	02 ④	03 ⑤	04 ⑤	05 ⑤	06 ①	07 ②	08 ④	09 ②	10 ④

01 ②

해설 서점에서 열릴 작가 초청 행사를 홍보하는 내용이다.

어휘 pleased 기쁜, 만족해하는
in person 직접
incredible 놀라운
followed by 뒤이어, 잇달아
session (활동의) 시간, 기간
signing 사인, 서명; 계약

W Attention, please. This is the store manager of Blackwell Books. We are very pleased to announce that the best-selling author, Veronica Keys, will be coming to our bookstore this Saturday. Fans of the *Never-ending Wizardry* series will be given the incredible opportunity to meet Ms. Keys in person. She will do a short reading followed by a question-and-answer session, and then a book signing. As you may know, Ms. Keys has announced that her latest book will be the final novel in this series. So we are very lucky to have this event in our bookstore, and we'd like as many people as possible to attend.

여 주목해주시기 바랍니다. 저는 블랙웰 북스의 매니저입니다. 저희는 베스트셀러 작가인 베로니카 키스 씨가 이번 주 토요일 저희 서점에 오시는 것을 알리게 되어 매우 기쁩니다. <끝없는 마술> 시리즈의 팬들은 키스 씨를 직접 만나는 놀라운 기회를 얻을 것입니다. 그녀는 짧은 낭독을 하고 이어서 질의응답 시간을 가진 후에 책 사인회를 할 것입니다. 아시다시피 키스 씨는 자신의 최신작이 이 시리즈의 마지막 소설이 될 것이라고 발표했습니다. 따라서 이 행사를 저희 서점에서 하게 되어 정말 행운이며 가능한 한 많은 분들이 참석해주셨으면 합니다.

02 ④

해설 인기 휴양지의 특징과 그곳에서 즐길 수 있는 활동을 소개하고 있다.

어휘 destination (여행 등의) 목적지, 도착지
trail 산길, 오솔길; 자국, 흔적
magnificent 장대한, 참으로 아름다운, 감명 깊은
formation ((지질)) (암)층; 형성(물)
shady 그늘진, 그늘이 많은

M Hello, listeners! I'm Paul Larson from Sunny Tours. Have you been dreaming of the perfect vacation? With over 300 sunny days a year and many outdoor activities, Colorado Springs is a popular camping and family destination. Trails that pass through magnificent rock formations and shady mountain forests are perfect for hiking, biking, and horseback riding. Or you could try something different: a hot air balloon ride up into the big Colorado sky, or a historic train ride through Cripple Creek, or a visit to the

남 안녕하세요, 청취자 여러분! 저는 써니 투어의 폴 라슨입니다. 완벽한 휴가를 꿈꿔 오고 계십니까? 일 년에 300일 이상의 화창한 날씨와 많은 야외 활동 때문에 콜로라도 스프링스는 인기 있는 야영지 및 가족 여행지입니다. 장대한 암반층과 그늘진 산악림을 통과하는 산길은 하이킹, 자전거 타기, 승마에 안성맞춤입니다. 아니면 다른 것을 해보실 수도 있습니다. 열기구를 타고 콜로라도의 드넓은 하늘 위로 올라가 보거나, 역사가 깊은 기차를 타고 크리플 크리크를 통과하거나, 콜로라도

Colorado Springs Arts Center. There is something for everyone. Come see for yourself!

스프링스 예술회관에 방문하실 수 있습니다. 모든 사람을 위한 무언가가 있습니다. 직접 오셔서 확인해보세요!

03 ⑤

해설 시에서 후원하는 디자인 공모전에 참가하도록 독려하는 내용이다.

어휘 citywide 전 도시[시민]의
sponsor 후원하다; 후원자, 스폰서
mascot (행운의) 마스코트
submit 제출하다
gift certificate 상품권
take advantage of (기회 등을) 활용[이용]하다

W Good morning, students. This is your art teacher, Ms. Woods. This is an announcement about a wonderful opportunity available now. Our school is participating in a citywide design contest sponsored by the city government. The goal is to create a new town mascot in a fresh style. I encourage all students to participate. If you are interested, please submit your ideas to your homeroom teacher by the end of the month. The winner will get gift certificates. I hope that all of you will take advantage of this. Good luck!

여 안녕하십니까, 학생 여러분. 저는 여러분의 미술 교사 우즈입니다. 이 안내 방송은 지금 이용 가능한 굉장한 기회에 관한 것입니다. 우리 학교는 시(市) 정부에서 후원하는 시 디자인 공모전에 참가할 것입니다. 목표는 참신한 스타일의 새로운 시 마스코트를 만들어내는 것입니다. 모든 학생이 참가하기를 장려합니다. 만약 관심이 있다면 여러분의 아이디어를 담임 선생님께 월말까지 제출해주십시오. 우승자는 상품권을 받을 것입니다. 여러분 모두가 이 기회를 활용하길 바랍니다. 행운을 빕니다!

04 ⑤

해설 올바른 쓰레기 처리에 대한 협조를 요청하는 내용의 안내 방송이다.

어휘 concern 관련되다, 영향을 미치다; 걱정시키다
resident 주민, 거주자
complex 복합 건물, (건물) 단지
disposal 처리, 처분
cf. dispose of ~을 없애다, 처리하다
misplace 잘못 두다
mess 난잡해진[어질러 놓은] 것
remind A that A에게 ~라고 상기시키다, 다시 말해주다
improper 부적절한

M May I have your attention, please? This message concerns all residents of this apartment complex. Recently, there has been an increase in garbage around the waste disposal area. Many people are using incorrect garbage bags, misplacing their garbage, and generally creating an unpleasant mess. This is a huge inconvenience for the staff and other residents. Please be careful with your waste. Take the time to dispose of it correctly. We thank those of you who already do this, and remind those who are not careful that there are fines for improper waste disposal. Thank you.

남 주목해주시겠습니까? 이 메시지는 이 아파트 단지의 주민 모두와 관련이 있습니다. 최근, 쓰레기 처리장 주변에 쓰레기가 늘어 왔습니다. 많은 사람이 잘못된 쓰레기봉투를 사용하고, 쓰레기를 잘못 두어 대체로 불쾌한 혼잡을 만들고 있습니다. 이것은 직원과 다른 주민들에게 엄청난 불편입니다. 여러분의 쓰레기에 유의해주십시오. 시간을 들여 그것을 제대로 처리해주십시오. 이미 그렇게 하시는 분들께 감사를 표하며, 주의를 기울이시지 않는 분들께는 부적절한 쓰레기 처리에 대해 벌금이 있음을 다시 한 번 알려드립니다. 감사합니다.

05 ⑤

해설 축제 자원봉사자들에게 여러 가지 근무 유의 사항을 안내하는 내용이다.

어휘 apply 지원하다
essential 매우 중요한, 필수적인
serve as ~의 역할을 하다
assistant 보조
merchandise 상품
prior to ~에 앞서
scheduled 예정된
shift 교대 근무 (시간)
sign in (출근 시간을) 기록하다
must 필수품
participant 참가자

W Hello! Thank you for applying to help us! You are essential to the Churchill Book Festival's success this year. You will serve as author assistants, festival guides, and sales assistants in the merchandise area. Please arrive at least 20 minutes prior to your scheduled shift. This will give you enough time to sign in and get ready. You need to be prepared to stand or walk since there will be limited places to sit. Due to this, comfortable shoes are a must. Also, you're required to wear a volunteer's T-shirt. We'll give you the T-shirts after the orientation. Thanks again and please be polite and helpful to all participants.

여 안녕하세요! 저희를 돕기 위해 지원해주셔서 감사합니다! 여러분은 올해 처칠 도서 축제의 성공에 있어 매우 중요합니다. 여러분은 작가 보조, 축제 가이드, 그리고 상품 구역에서 판매 보조로 일하게 될 것입니다. 적어도 예정된 교대 시간 20분 전에 도착해주세요. 이것은 여러분이 출근 시간을 기록하고 준비할 충분한 시간을 줄 것입니다. 앉을 수 있는 공간이 한정되어 있어서 서 있거나 걸을 준비가 되어야 합니다. 이것 때문에 편한 신발은 필수품입니다. 또한, 여러분은 자원봉사 티셔츠를 입어야 합니다. 티셔츠는 오리엔테이션이 끝난 후에 드리겠습니다. 다시 한 번 감사드리며, 모든 참가자들에게 친절하고 도움이 돼 주시길 바랍니다.

06 ①

해설 First로 시작되는 문장부터 인터넷 범죄를 예방할 수 있는 구체적인 방법들을 알려주고 있다.

M Hello, listeners. This is Michael Andrews from the Cyber Crime Investigation Unit. Internet usage continues to increase, and so does Internet crime. However, if you are a little more careful in your daily

남 안녕하세요, 청취자 여러분. 저는 사이버 범죄 수사대의 마이클 앤드류스입니다. 인터넷 사용이 계속 증가하면서 인터넷 범죄도 증가하고 있습니다. 그러나 여러분이 일상적인 인터넷 사용에 조금 더

어휘 **crime** 범죄
investigation 수사, 조사
usage 사용(량); (단어의) 용법
increase 늘다, 증가하다
(↔ **decrease**)
risk 위험(요소)
victim 피해자, 희생자
absolutely 절대적으로, 완전히
minimum 최소한도, 최저; 최소한의
social networking site 소셜 네트
워킹 사이트(= **SNS**)
repeatedly 되풀이해서, 여러 차례
too good to be true 너무 좋아서
믿어지지 않는

Internet use, you can decrease your risk of becoming a victim. Here are a few simple steps that you can take to protect yourself. First, don't give more information than is absolutely necessary. Keep your personal details to a minimum, even on social networking sites. Second, change your passwords regularly. Don't use the same password repeatedly, and don't pick something simple like your birthday. Finally, try to remember that if an advertisement sounds too good to be true, it probably is (too good to be true).

주의한다면, 피해자가 될 위험을 줄일 수 있습니다. 여기 여러분이 자기 자신을 보호하기 위해 취할 수 있는 몇 가지 간단한 방법이 있습니다. 첫째, 꼭 필요한 것보다 많은 정보를 제공하지 마십시오. 소셜 네트워킹 사이트에서조차도 개인 정보를 최소한도로 유지하십시오. 둘째, 비밀번호를 주기적으로 변경하십시오. 똑같은 비밀번호를 되풀이해서 사용하지 마시고 생일처럼 간단한 것을 택하지 마십시오. 마지막으로, 어떤 광고가 너무 좋아서 믿어지지 않는다면 아마도 그럴 것(믿을 만하지 않은 것)임을 기억하도록 하십시오.

07 ②

해설 캠핑장에서의 화재 예방을 위한 주의 사항을 알려주며 협조를 당부하고 있다.

어휘 **campground** 야영장, 캠프장
(= **campsite**)
spark 불꽃, 불똥
approved 승인된, 허가된
location 장소, 위치
make sure (that) (~을) 확인하다;
반드시 ~하도록 하다
completely 완전히
violate 위반하다, 어기다
major 주요한, 중대한; 전공의

W Good afternoon, campers. This announcement is from the management office of Hancock Campground. Summer is here once again. It's a great time to go camping and enjoy nature. But, just like every other year, the summer sun has dried out the forests and killed the grass. This means that even the smallest spark can start a huge forest fire. So please build campfires in the approved locations and avoid building them near tents, vehicles, or trees. Make sure that all fires are completely out before leaving your campsite. And report anyone who violates these rules. If we all work together, we may be able to avoid having any major fires this year. We appreciate your cooperation.

여 안녕하세요, 야영객 여러분. 핸콕 야영장의 관리 사무소에서 안내 말씀 드리겠습니다. 또다시 여름이 왔습니다. 캠핑을 가서 자연을 즐기기에 좋을 때입니다. 그러나 다른 모든 해와 마찬가지로, 여름 태양은 숲을 메마르게 하고 풀을 말라죽게 했습니다. 이는 아무리 작은 불꽃이라도 큰 산불을 일으킬 수 있다는 뜻입니다. 그러니 부디 승인된 장소에서 모닥불을 피우고 텐트, 차량, 나무 근처에서 불을 피우는 것을 피해주십시오. 야영지를 떠나시기 전에 모든 불이 완전히 꺼졌는지를 반드시 확인하십시오. 그리고 누구든지 이 규정을 어기는 사람은 신고해주십시오. 우리 모두가 함께 노력한다면 올해 어떤 큰 화재도 피할 수 있을 것입니다. 협조해주시면 감사하겠습니다.

08 ④

해설 최근 들어 보행 중 스마트폰 사용으로 인한 사고가 다수 발생하고 있다는 사실을 알리며 그 위험성을 경고하고 있다.

어휘 **recently** 최근에
injury 부상
manhole 맨홀
stare at ~을 응시하다, 쳐다보다
matter 중요하다
response 답장, 응답
traffic 차량들, 교통(량)
keep A in mind A를 명심하다

M Hello, listeners. This is Dr. Michael Davis from the Fogville Health Center. I've been working as a doctor in this town for many years now, and recently I've started to see a new type of injury. Each year, more and more people are getting hurt when using a smartphone while walking. Several people have been hit by cars, and one unlucky woman even fell into an open manhole. It may sound highly unlikely to happen, but the fact is that walking while staring at a screen is really dangerous. It doesn't matter who you're texting. You should stop for a moment to type a response. Please pay attention to traffic and other people instead of your phone. I hope you keep this in mind and stay safe.

남 안녕하세요, 청취자 여러분. 저는 포그빌 의료 센터의 의사 마이클 데이비스입니다. 저는 이 동네에서 수년간 의사로 일해왔는데, 최근에 새로운 종류의 부상을 보기 시작했습니다. 매년, 보행 중 스마트폰을 사용하다가 점점 더 많은 사람들이 다치고 있습니다. 여러 명이 차에 치였고, 운이 없던 한 여성은 열린 맨홀에 빠지기도 했습니다. 아주 가능성이 적은 일처럼 들릴지 모르지만, (휴대폰) 화면을 응시하며 걷는 것이 정말 위험하다는 것은 사실입니다. 누구에게 문자를 보내는 것인지는 중요하지 않습니다. 답장을 보내기 위해서는 잠시 멈춰야 합니다. 휴대폰 대신 차량들과 다른 사람에게 주의를 기울여주십시오. 저는 여러분이 이것을 명심하시고 안전하게 지내시길 바랍니다.

09 ②

해설 hosts, studio, show 등의 어구를 통해 TV 프로그램의 새 사회자가 시청자들에게 인사하고 있음을 알 수 있다.

W Good evening, everyone! I'm Mindy Kang, and I just want to start by saying how honored I feel to have this opportunity. There is such a long and wonderful history here, and so many great hosts have sat in this chair before me. It's truly amazing to be in this studio working alongside the Emmy Award winning Mark

여 여러분, 안녕하세요! 저는 민디 강이고, 제가 이 기회를 얻게 되어 얼마나 영광인지 말씀드리는 것으로 시작하고 싶습니다. 이곳에는 아주 길고 아름다운 역사가 있으며, 저 이전에 수많은 훌륭한 진행자들께서 이 자리에 앉으셨습니다. 에미상 수상자인 마크 존슨 씨와 이 스튜디오에서 함께 일하

어휘 host 진행자
alongside ~와 함께; ~ 옆에
Emmy Award 에미상 ((미국의 텔레비전 우수 프로, 연기자 등에게 매년 1회 수여되는 상))
cover 다루다, 포함시키다
delight 매우 기쁘게 하다
entertain 즐겁게 하다; 대접하다

Johnson, who I spent so much time watching as a child. To be honest, I'm a bit nervous, but I know that we are going to have a lot of fun and cover some amazing stories that will delight and entertain you. Please support us and enjoy our show.

고 있다는 것이 정말 놀랍습니다. 제가 어릴 때 시청하면서 아주 많은 시간을 보냈던 분인데 말이죠. 솔직하게 말해서 약간 긴장되지만, 저희가 아주 즐거울 것이고 여러분을 매우 기쁘게 하고 즐겁게 할 몇몇 놀라운 이야기를 다룰 것임을 알고 있습니다. 저희 쇼를 많이 사랑해주시고 즐겨주시기 바랍니다.

10 ④

해설 주차장을 이용할 때 주의해야 할 사항들을 열거하고 있다.

어휘 interrupt 방해하다, 중단시키다
remind A that A에게 ~라고 상기시키다, 다시 말해주다
considerate 사려 깊은, 배려하는
urge A to-v A에게 v하라고 강력히 권고하다, 충고하다
respect 준수하다; 존경하다

M Attention please. I'm Paul Larson, your building manager. We are sorry to interrupt you, but there have been several recent complaints about the use of the parking lot. So, we have several requests. First, we would like to remind everyone that the use of the parking lot is for residents only. Visitors must park in the nearby lot. Second, please be considerate. Do not park in front of the exits or block another car, even if it is only for a few minutes. Finally, we strongly urge everyone to respect the parking lot's speed limit. Many children live here, and this is a huge safety issue. Thank you for your cooperation.

남 주목해주십시오. 저는 건물 관리인 폴 라슨입니다. 방해드려서 죄송합니다만, 최근 주차장 이용에 관한 몇 가지 항의가 있어 왔습니다. 따라서 몇 가지 요청 사항이 있습니다. 첫째, 모든 분께 주차장 이용이 거주자만을 위한 것임을 다시 알려드리고 싶습니다. 방문객들께서는 인근 주차장에 주차하셔야 합니다. 둘째, 배려해주시기 바랍니다. 아주 잠깐일지라도 출구 앞에 주차하시거나 다른 차를 가로막지 마십시오. 마지막으로, 모든 분께 주차장 제한 속도를 준수해주시기를 강력히 권고드립니다. 많은 어린이가 이곳에 살고 있어 이것은 큰 안전 문제입니다. 협조해주시면 감사하겠습니다.

09 세트형 문항

✳✳ 기출 맛보기

본문 p.107

01 ④   02 ⑤

해설 **01** 그늘에서도 자라는 식물들에 관한 내용이다.
① 식물 병해를 예방하는 방법들
② 식물 성장에 영향을 미치는 요소들
③ 집에서 식물을 기르는 것의 이점들
④ 그늘에서 자랄 수 있는 식물들
⑤ 그늘에서 식물이 자라도록 돕는 물질들

02 해석 참조

어휘 previously 이전에
gardening 원예
front yard 앞마당
shade 그늘
survive 살아남다
ultimate 최고의; 궁극적인
conditions 환경, 상황
pot 화분
indoors 실내에서
partial 부분적인
protection 보호
fascinating 대단히 흥미로운

W Hello, students. Previously, we discussed why gardening is a great hobby. But not everyone has a sunny front yard. So, today we'll learn about plants that grow even in shade. First, lemon balm survives in full shade. So if your place is sunless, it's the plant you should choose. Next, ivy is the ultimate shade-loving plant. Its ability to grow in shade makes it survive under trees where most plants can't. Also, there's mint. It lives well under low-light conditions, so you can grow it in a small pot indoors. Lastly, camellia grows better in partial shade. Especially when it's a young plant, it needs protection from the sun. Many plants like these can live even in the shade. Isn't it fascinating? Now, let's watch a video clip about how to grow these plants.

여 안녕하세요, 학생 여러분. 앞서, 우리는 왜 정원 가꾸기가 좋은 취미인지에 대해 이야기를 나눴습니다. 하지만 모든 사람이 햇빛이 잘 드는 앞마당을 가지고 있는 것은 아닙니다. 그래서 오늘 우리는 그늘에서도 자라는 식물에 대해 배워볼 것입니다. 첫째, **레몬밤**(① lemon balm)은 완전한 그늘에서 살아남습니다. 그래서 만약 여러분의 집에 햇빛이 들지 않는다면, 그것이 바로 여러분이 선택해야 하는 식물입니다. 다음으로, **담쟁이덩굴**(② ivy)은 가장 그늘을 좋아하는 식물입니다. 그늘에서 자랄 수 있는 그것의 능력은 대부분의 식물들이 살 수 없는 나무 아래에서 살아남게 합니다. 또한, **민트**(③ mint)도 있습니다. 그것은 조도가 낮은 환경에서도 잘 살기 때문에 실내에서 작은 화분에 재배할 수 있습니다. 마지막으로, **동백**(④ camellia)은 부분적으로 그늘진 곳에서 더 잘 자랍니다. 특히 어린 식물일 때는 태양으로부터 보호가 필요합니다. 이와 같은 많은 식물들이 그늘에서도 살 수 있습니다. 정말 흥미롭지 않나요? 이제, 이 식물들을 기르는 방법에 대한 동영상을 보도록 합시다.

01 ⓐ   **02** ⓑ   **03** ⓑ   **04** ⓒ   **05** ⓐ   **06** ⓐ   **07** ⓒ   **08** ⓑ   **09** ⓐ   **10** ⓐ

01 ⓐ   02 ⓑ

해설 **01** LED가 우리의 삶을 어떻게 더 좋게 만드는지에 관한 내용이다.
ⓐ LED를 사용하는 것의 이점
ⓑ LED가 어떻게 발명되었는가
ⓒ LED 기술을 발전시킬 방법들

[선택지 어휘] **advance** 발전시키다, 개선하다

02 해석 참조

어휘 **technology** 기술
advantage 장점
lifespan 수명
last 지속되다
device 장치, 기구
function 기능
visible (눈에) 보이는

W Hello, class! Last time we learned about LED technology. I hope all of you have a clear idea of what an LED is now. Today, I'll talk about how LEDs make our lives better. First, one of the advantages of LEDs is the long lifespan. LED bulbs are used in lamps and last for over 17 years before you need to change them. Also, thanks to their small size, LEDs can be used in almost any small devices. Any light you see on a computer keyboard is an LED light, and they can be used to show functions or make buttons more visible in low-light environments. Now, let's think about other products that use LEDs.

여 안녕하세요, 여러분! 지난 시간에 우리는 LED 기술에 대해 배웠습니다. 여러분 모두가 이제 LED가 무엇인지 분명히 알고 있기를 바랍니다. 오늘은 LED가 우리의 삶을 어떻게 더 좋게 만드는지에 대해 이야기하도록 하겠습니다. 첫째로, LED의 장점 중 하나는 긴 수명입니다. LED 전구는 램프(ⓐ lamps)에 사용되며 교체해야 하기까지 17년 넘게 지속됩니다. 또한, 작은 크기 덕분에 LED는 거의 모든 작은 장치에서 사용될 수 있습니다. **컴퓨터 키보드**(ⓒ a computer keyboard)에 보이는 모든 조명은 LED 조명으로, 그것들은 조도가 낮은 환경에서 기능을 표시하거나 버튼을 더 잘 보이게 하는 데 사용될 수 있습니다. 이제 LED를 사용하는 다른 제품들에 대해 생각해봅시다.

03 ⓑ   04 ⓒ

해설 **03** 허리 통증 완화에 효과적인 운동을 소개하는 내용이다.
ⓐ 살을 빼기 위한 다양한 유산소 운동들
ⓑ 허리 통증을 줄이는 데 효과적인 운동들
ⓒ 몸을 유연하게 만드는 활동들

[선택지 어휘] **aerobic** 유산소의
flexible 유연한

04 해석 참조

어휘 **suffer from** ~로 고통 받다
stretch (근육을) 당기다, 늘이다
strengthen 강화시키다
appropriate 적절한
relieve (고통 등을) 덜어주다, 완화하다
cf. **relief** 경감, 완화
tightness 긴장
spine 척추
activate 활성화하다

M Good morning, listeners. This is Dr. Cooper of Daily Health Line Radio. These days, you can see many people around you who suffer from back pain. Any incorrect positioning of your body or lifting of heavy objects may cause it. So, today, I'll share some useful types of exercise to help reduce your own back pain. As you probably know, yoga is a helpful way to stretch safely and strengthen your back. Doing the appropriate poses for even a few minutes a day can help relieve tightness and give your back some relief. Also, walking is the easiest exercise to keep your spine in a natural position to avoid back pain. When you walk, your back muscles are activated and stretched. I hope this will be helpful information for you and allow you to be fit again.

남 안녕하세요, 청취자 여러분. 데일리 헬스 라인 라디오의 쿠퍼 박사입니다. 요즘, 허리 통증으로 고통 받는 사람들을 주변에서 많이 볼 수 있습니다. 자세를 잘못 잡거나 무거운 물건을 드는 것이 그것을 유발할 수 있습니다. 그래서 오늘 저는 여러분의 허리 통증을 줄이는 데 도움이 되는 몇 가지 유용한 운동 종류를 공유하려고 합니다. 여러분이 아마 알고 있듯이, **요가**(ⓐ yoga)는 안전하게 스트레칭을 하고 허리를 강화하는 데 도움이 되는 방법입니다. 하루에 몇 분이라도 적절한 자세를 취하는 것은 긴장을 완화하고 허리를 풀어주는 데 도움이 될 수 있습니다. 또한, **걷기**(ⓑ walking)는 척추를 허리 통증을 피하는 자연스러운 자세로 유지해주는 가장 쉬운 운동입니다. 걸을 때 여러분의 허리 근육이 활성화되고 늘어나게 됩니다. 이것이 여러분에게 도움이 되는 정보가 되어 여러분이 다시 건강해질 수 있기를 바랍니다.

05 ⓐ   06 ⓐ

해설 **05** 먹을수록 살이 빠진다고 알려진 마이너스 칼로리 음식에 대한 잘못된 통념을 알리는 내용이다.
ⓐ 마이너스 칼로리 음식에 대한 진실
ⓑ 신체에 미치는 다이어트 식품의 영향
ⓒ 다양한 마이너스 칼로리 음식의 차이점들

W Today I'd like to talk about a dieting myth. Some people say certain foods require more energy to be digested than they provide. These foods are called "negative-calorie foods." In theory, the more of them that we eat, the more weight we will lose. These "negative-calorie foods" are mainly fruits and vegetables. Among them, celery is perhaps the most famous for burning lots of calories, but in fact, only about 10% of its calories are burned during digestion.

여 오늘 저는 다이어트에 관한 잘못된 통념 하나에 관해 이야기해보려고 합니다. 몇몇 사람들이 말하길 어떤 음식들은 공급하는 에너지보다 더 많은 에너지를 소화에 필요로 한다고 합니다. 이러한 음식은 '마이너스 칼로리 음식'이라고 불립니다. 이론적으로는, 우리가 그 음식을 더 많이 먹을수록 우리는 체중이 더 많이 줄어들게 됩니다. 이 '마이너스 칼로리 음식'은 주로 과일과 채소입니다. 그중에서도, **셀러리**(ⓑ celery)는 아마도 많은

06 해석 참조

어휘 myth (근거 없는) 통념; 신화
digest 소화하다
cf. digestion 소화
shortcut 지름길
moderation 적당함

Just like with other foods, the more celery that we eat, the more weight we will gain. Another example is an apple. It can promote fullness because it's high in water and fiber. But even with these qualities, there's no way we can lose weight by eating one because only about 5% of its calories are burned in the process of digestion. In reality, there are no shortcuts for dieting, and everything must be eaten in moderation.

칼로리를 소모하는 것으로 가장 유명할 테지만, 사실 셀러리가 가진 칼로리의 10% 정도만 소화 과정에서 소모됩니다. 다른 음식들과 마찬가지로, 셀러리를 더 많이 먹을수록, 더 체중이 늘 것입니다. 또 다른 예는 **사과**(ⓒ an apple)입니다. 사과는 수분과 섬유질의 함유량이 높기 때문에 포만감을 촉진할 수 있습니다. 하지만 이러한 특성들에도, 소화 과정에서 칼로리의 5% 정도만 연소되기 때문에 우리는 사과를 먹음으로써 체중을 감량할 수는 없습니다. 사실, 다이어트에 지름길이란 없으며 모든 음식은 적당히 먹어야 합니다.

---

07 ⓒ   08 ⓑ

해설 **07** 외래 씨앗의 유입으로 남극 생태계가 위험에 처했다는 내용이다.
ⓐ 남극에서 식물이 살고 자라는 방법
ⓑ 남극을 도울 이로운 씨앗들
ⓒ 남극 생태계가 위협받고 있는 이유

08 해석 참조

어휘 Antarctica 남극대륙
cf. the Antarctic 남극의
free from ~이 없는
ecosystem 생태계
exotic 외래의; 이국적인
it turns out (that) ~인 것으로 드러나다
accidentally 뜻하지 않게, 우연히; 잘못하여
dominate 지배하다; 우세하다

M Some of you may already know that there is a small amount of plant life in Antarctica. Only 1% of Antarctica is free from ice, but plants do grow there. Unfortunately, there is growing concern that the Antarctic ecosystem may be in danger. This is mostly due to the introduction of exotic plants, which come to Antarctica in various ways. First, plant seeds can arrive naturally, carried by wind, water, or birds. Next, more and more people are visiting Antarctica for tourism and to do scientific research, and some seeds can stick to their socks or backpacks. It turns out that each person that visits Antarctica accidentally carries an average of nine seeds with them. Efforts should be made to remove non-native seeds before they dominate the native ecosystem of Antarctica. Now, let's watch a video that explains this in detail.

남 여러분 중 몇몇은 남극대륙에 약간의 식물이 있다는 것을 이미 알고 계실지도 모릅니다. 남극대륙 중 겨우 1%만 얼음이 없지만, 식물이 정말로 그곳에서 자랍니다. 안타깝게도, 남극 생태계가 위험에 처했을지도 모른다는 우려가 커지고 있습니다. 이는 대체로 외래 식물들의 도입에 의한 것인데, 그것들은 남극대륙에 다양한 방법으로 들어옵니다. 먼저, 식물의 씨앗들은 **바람**(ⓐ wind), 물, 또는 새들에 의해 실려 자연스럽게 도달할 수 있습니다. 다음으로, 점점 더 많은 **사람들**(ⓒ people)이 관광과 과학 연구를 하려고 남극대륙을 방문하는데, 몇몇 씨앗은 그들의 양말이나 배낭에 붙을 수 있습니다. 남극대륙을 방문하는 개인은 뜻하지 않게 평균 9개의 씨앗을 지니고 오는 것으로 드러났습니다. 외래 씨앗들이 남극대륙의 천연 생태계를 지배하기 전에 그것들을 제거하려는 노력이 기울여져야 합니다. 이제, 이를 상세히 설명하는 영상을 봅시다.

---

09 ⓐ   10 ⓐ

해설 **09** 존중되어야 할 동물 복지에 관한 내용이다.
ⓐ 동물 복지를 존중하는 방법들
ⓑ 세계의 멸종 위기에 처한 동물들
ⓒ 동물 보호소 설립의 필요성

10 해석 참조

어휘 well-being 복지, 행복
suffering 고통
crucial 중요한
have access to ~에 접근하다
freedom from ~이 없음; ~로부터의 해방
discomfort 불편(하게 하는 것)
suitable 적절한
come up with 생각하다

W Before we start, I want to thank everyone for attending this class on the well-being of animals. Like people, animals have the right to be happy and healthy. Today, I'd like to talk about how we can treat animals with respect. This is mainly about protecting them from unnecessary suffering. First of all, there is the issue of hunger and thirst. It is crucial that animals always have access to fresh water and food that keeps them healthy. Also, freedom from discomfort is important. We should provide animals with an appropriate environment to live in. This includes a comfortable resting area that has suitable bedding, low noise levels, and natural light. Now I'd like you to come up with other examples of animal rights.

여 시작하기 전에 동물 복지에 대한 본 강좌에 참석해주신 모든 분께 감사드리고 싶습니다. 사람과 마찬가지로 동물은 행복하고 건강할 권리를 가지고 있습니다. 오늘, 저는 우리가 어떻게 동물을 존중하며 대할 수 있는지에 관해 이야기하려 합니다. 이는 주로 동물들을 불필요한 고통으로부터 보호하는 것에 관한 것입니다. 무엇보다도, **굶주림**(ⓑ hunger)과 목마름에 관한 문제가 있습니다. 건강하도록 유지해주는 신선한 물과 음식에 동물들이 항상 접근할 수 있는 것이 중요합니다. 또한, **불편함**(ⓒ discomfort)이 없는 것도 중요합니다. 우리는 동물들에게 살아갈 적합한 환경을 제공해야 합니다. 이것은 적절한 잠자리, 낮은 소음 수준과 자연광이 있는 편한 휴식 공간을 포함합니다. 이제 여러분이 동물 권리의 다른 예들을 생각해보시길 바랍니다.

01 ④ **02** ⑤ **03** ⑤ **04** ④ **05** ④ **06** ③ **07** ④ **08** ⑤ **09** ① **10** ④

01 ④ 02 ⑤

해설 01 불필요한 섭식의 원인을 파악하여 이를 예방하는 방법에 관한 내용이다.
① 목록을 만드는 것의 중요성
② 건강한 간식의 긍정적인 영향들
③ 살을 빼는 데 효과적인 활동들
④ 불필요한 섭식을 예방하는 방법
⑤ 식습관에 미치는 TV의 해로운 영향

02 해석 참조

어휘 trick A into v-ing A를 속여서 v하게 하다
aroma 냄새, 향기
commercial 광고 (방송); 상업의
distracting 주의를 딴 데로 돌리는
take up (취미로) 시작하다, 배우다
knitting 뜨개질
boredom 지루함, 따분함
alternate 대체 가능한, 대안이 되는; 번갈아 하다
sensible 현명한; 분별 있는

M What is hunger? Hunger is the natural feeling you experience about four or five hours after a meal. But even when you're not hungry, many things can trick you into thinking you are — the aroma of food, the sight of a favorite dish, or a commercial on television. Recognizing what makes you hungry is the first step in controlling your eating. To start with, keeping a food diary can help you notice when you feel hungry. If you find that sitting in front of the television makes you hungry, plan a distracting activity. Take up knitting or write letters when you are watching television. On the other hand, if boredom causes you to eat, make a list of alternate activities to do instead, such as talking to a friend or washing a car. The key is to learn what makes you hungry and then to set up an action plan to help you avoid eating. Any healthy eating plan must include ways to deal with hunger in a sensible manner. Now, let's talk about how to plan a healthy diet.

남 허기는 무엇인가요? 허기는 식사 후 약 네다섯 시간에 겪는 자연스러운 느낌입니다. 하지만 당신이 배고프지 않을 때조차, 많은 것들이 당신을 속여서 배고프다고 생각하게 할 수 있습니다. 이를테면 음식의 냄새, 가장 좋아하는 음식을 보는 것, 혹은 TV 광고 같은 것들이 그렇습니다. 무엇이 당신을 배고프게 하는지 알아내는 것은 당신의 섭식을 조절하는 첫 단계입니다. 가장 먼저, 음식 일지를 작성하는 것은 당신이 언제 배고픔을 느끼는지 알아내는 데 도움이 될 수 있습니다. 만약 텔레비전 앞에 앉아있는 게 당신을 배고프게 만든다는 것을 알아낸다면, 주의를 딴 데로 돌리는 활동을 계획하세요. 텔레비전을 시청할 때, **뜨개질**(① knitting)을 시작하거나 **편지를 쓰세요**(② writing letters). 반면에, 지루함 때문에 당신이 먹게 된다면, **친구와 말하기**(③ talking to a friend) 혹은 **세차하기**(④ washing a car)와 같은 대신 할 대체 활동들의 목록을 작성하세요. 중요한 것은 무엇이 당신을 배고프게 하는지 알아낸 다음 당신이 섭식을 피하도록 도움을 줄 수 있는 행동 계획을 수립하는 것입니다. 어떠한 건강한 섭식 계획이든 현명한 방식으로 배고픔에 대처하는 방법들을 포함해야 합니다. 이제 건강한 식단을 계획하는 방법에 대해 이야기해봅시다.

03 ⑤ 04 ④

해설 03 사막 환경에 적응한 여러 종류의 식물들에 대한 내용이다.
① 식물이 햇빛을 필요로 하는 이유들
② 건강한 성장을 위해 식물에 물을 주는 방법
③ 식물들에 위협을 가하는 다양한 요소들
④ 사막 환경에 있는 멸종 위기에 처한 종들
⑤ 사막에서 생존하는 식물의 여러 종류들

[선택지 어휘] **pose a threat** 위협을 가하다

04 해석 참조

어휘 cactus 선인장
spine 가시, 바늘
shade 그늘지게 하다
be equipped with ~을 갖추다
fleshy (잎이) 두껍고 부드러운; 뚱뚱한
volume 양
shed (잎을) 떨어뜨리다; 버리다
incredible 놀라운; 믿을 수 없는

W Hello, students. Last class, we learned about different kinds of animals that live in the desert. Today, we'll talk about desert plants that have amazingly adapted themselves to their environment. First, cactuses have sharp spines to shade them from the sun, keeping them cool. Next, some plants are equipped with fleshy leaves that contain much of their water supply. For example, aloes store large volumes of water with thick leaves which are covered with a waterproof coating. Also, plants such as acacias can change their leaves seasonally to lose less water. They shed their leaves during the hot season and grow them back as soon as the weather improves. Finally, there are plants with light-colored leaves which allow them to lose less water by reflecting sunlight. A good example of this is sagebrushes which have very light green to almost white leaves. Now, we'll look at some photos of these incredible plants.

여 안녕하세요, 학생 여러분. 지난 시간에, 우리는 사막에서 사는 여러 종류의 동물에 대해 배웠습니다. 오늘, 우리는 자신의 환경에 놀랄 만큼 적응한 사막 식물들에 대해 이야기할 겁니다. 먼저, **선인장**(① cactuses)은 햇빛으로부터 자신을 그늘지게 해서 시원한 상태를 유지하기 위한 날카로운 가시가 있습니다. 다음으로, 몇몇 식물들은 물 공급의 많은 양을 함유하는 두껍고 부드러운 잎을 갖추고 있습니다. 예를 들어, **알로에**(② aloes)는 방수 코팅으로 덮인 두꺼운 잎으로 많은 양의 물을 저장합니다. 또한, **아카시아**(③ acacias) 같은 식물들은 수분 손실을 더 적게 하도록 계절에 따라 잎을 바꿀 수 있습니다. 그것들은 더운 계절에 잎을 떨어뜨리고 날씨가 개선되면 바로 다시 자라게 합니다. 마지막으로, 햇빛을 반사함으로써 수분 손실을 더 적게 하도록 해주는 밝은 색의 잎을 가진 식물들이 있습니다. 이것의 좋은 예는 아주 밝은 녹색에서 거의 하얀색의 잎이 있는 **세이지브러시**(⑤ sagebrushes)입니다. 이제, 우리는 이 놀라운 식물들의 사진들을 보겠습니다.

05 ④   06 ③

해설 **05** 동물과 인간의 언어의 차이점에 대한 설명이다.
① 동물 언어에서 우리가 배울 수 있는 것
② 인간과 동물에서 언어가 어떻게 진화했는가
③ 동물 언어의 문법을 이해하는 것의 어려움
④ 인간과 동물 언어의 차이점
⑤ 인간 언어가 계속 발전하는 방법

06 해석 참조

어휘 evolution 진화
cf. evolve 진화하다
species (생물) 종(種)
visual 시각의
feather 깃털
possess 지니다, 소유하다
pattern (정형화된) 양식, 패턴; 무늬
enable A to-v A에게 v할 수 있게 하다

M   Good afternoon, class! What do you think is the greatest achievement of human evolution? Most of you would say it is language. Of course, all animal species have evolved systems of communication. Some monkeys, for example, use alarm calls to warn one another against dangers. Other natural forms of animal communication include scents for wolves marking their areas, visual signals like male peacocks showing their feathers to attract mates, and touch like cats rubbing heads with other cats to greet. Yet, animal communication doesn't have the one thing that every human language possesses. That thing is grammar, the fixed patterns and rules of word order that enable speakers of the same language to understand each other. Furthermore, human language is able to change easily. And its speed is incredible. During normal speech, humans can produce as many as 25 different sounds per second. And listeners can understand all of those signals immediately. Now, let's search the Internet for information on how human language evolved.

남   안녕하세요, 학생 여러분! 인간 진화에 있어서 가장 위대한 성취는 무엇이라고 생각하나요? 여러분들 중 대부분은 그것이 언어라고 말할 것입니다. 물론 모든 동물의 종들이 의사소통 체계를 진화시켜왔습니다. 예를 들어, 어떤 **원숭이**(① monkeys)는 서로에게 위험을 경고해주는 경고음을 사용합니다. 동물 의사소통의 다른 자연적 형태로는 **늑대**(② wolves)가 자신의 영역을 표시하는 냄새, 수컷 **공작새**(④ peacocks)가 짝을 유혹하기 위해 깃털을 보여주는 것과 같은 시각적 신호, 그리고 **고양이**(⑤ cats)가 다른 고양이에게 머리를 비비며 인사하는 것과 같은 촉감이 포함됩니다. 그러나 동물의 의사소통에는 모든 인간 언어가 지니고 있는 한 가지가 없습니다. 그것은 문법으로, 같은 언어를 가진 화자들이 서로 이해할 수 있게 해주는, 어순의 정해진 양식과 규칙입니다. 게다가, 인간의 언어는 쉽게 변화할 수 있습니다. 그리고 그 속도는 믿을 수 없을 정도입니다. 보통 속도로 말을 하는 동안, 인간은 1초에 각기 다른 25가지 소리를 낼 수 있습니다. 그리고 청자들은 즉시 그 모든 신호를 이해할 수 있습니다. 자 이제 인간의 언어가 어떻게 진화했는지에 대한 정보를 인터넷에 검색해봅시다.

07 ④   08 ⑤

해설 **07** 적절한 음악을 들으며 운동을 하는 것이 더욱 효과적이라는 내용이다.
① 규칙적인 운동의 장점
② 인간 정신에 미치는 음악의 영향
③ 신체 피로를 회복하는 방법
④ 효과적인 운동을 위한 음악의 사용
⑤ 개인을 위한 적절한 운동을 선택하기

08 해석 참조

어휘 go hand in hand 관련되다; 함께 가다
distract (주의를) 딴 데로 돌리다, 전환시키다
conduct 수행하다; 행동하다; 지휘하다
endurance 지구력; 인내
treadmill 트레드밀 ((회전식 벨트 위를 달리는 운동 기구))
selection 선발, (신중한) 선택
cf. select 선발[선택]하다
pace 속도; 걸음
findings ((주로 복수형)) (조사의) 결과
enhance 향상시키다, 높이다
beneficial 유익한, 이로운
appropriate 적절한
efficiently 효율적으로, 능률적으로
stick to ~을 계속하다
desired 바랐던, 희망했던
burnout 극도의 피로

W   Hello, everyone. Today, I want to talk about how music affects people doing exercise. Music and exercise go hand in hand, just like chocolate and peanut butter. Music does more than simply distract you from the pain of a workout. Research conducted at Brunel University has confirmed that listening to music while you exercise increases endurance. In the experiment, thirty participants exercised on a treadmill while listening to a selection of music. They were asked to maintain pace with the music. The findings show that when carefully selected, music can enhance endurance by 15% and improve the 'feeling states' of exercisers. The most interesting point is that exercise is much more beneficial when working out with music whose tempo is appropriate. For instance, the right tempo can help your body move more efficiently. If you are just walking, the tempo of hip hop can help you stick to your desired pace. Likewise, rock music may be good for running. The relaxing tempo of classical music and jazz can also help increase endurance levels during exercise. Music leads to less physical burnout, more time spent exercising, and more calories burned.

여   안녕하세요, 여러분. 오늘은 음악이 운동을 하는 사람들에게 어떤 영향을 미치는지에 대해 이야기하려고 합니다. 음악과 운동은 마치 초콜릿과 땅콩버터의 관계처럼 관련되어 있습니다. 음악은 단지 운동의 고통으로부터 당신의 주의를 다른 곳으로 돌리는 것 이상의 일을 합니다. 브루넬 대학에서 실시된 연구는 운동하면서 음악을 듣는 것은 지구력을 향상시킬 수 있다는 것을 확인했습니다. 그 실험에서, 서른 명의 참가자가 선정된 음악을 들으며 트레드밀 위에서 운동했습니다. 참가자들은 음악에 맞춰 운동하는 속도를 유지하라는 요구를 받았습니다. 실험 결과는 음악이 주의 깊게 선정되면 지구력을 15% 향상시키고 운동하는 사람들의 '감정 상태'를 개선할 수 있다는 것을 보여줍니다. 가장 흥미로운 점은 박자가 적절한 음악을 들으며 운동할 때 운동이 훨씬 더 이롭다는 점입니다. 예컨대, 적절한 박자는 당신의 몸이 더욱 능률적으로 움직이도록 도와줍니다. 당신이 그저 걷고 있다면, **힙합**(① hip hop) 박자가 당신이 원하는 걸음 속도로 계속 걷게 해줄 수 있습니다. 마찬가지로, **록 음악**(② rock music)은 달리기에 효과적일 수도 있습니다. **고전 음악**(③ classical music)과 **재즈**(④ jazz)의 느긋한 박자 역시 운동 중에 지구력을 늘리는 데 도움을 줄 수 있습니다. 음악은 신체를 덜 피로하게 하고, 운동에 더 많은 시간을 쏟게 하며, 더 많은 칼로리를 연소시킵니다.

해설 09 어린이들이 야외에서 활동할 때 얻는 건강상의 이점에 대한 내용이다.

① 아이들을 위한 야외 활동의 건강상의 이점
② 비만을 치료하는 데 효과적인 신체 활동
③ 아이들을 위한 다양한 종류의 야외 오락
④ 야외 활동 공간을 넓히는 것의 필요성
⑤ 적절한 야외 장소를 선택할 때 고려사항들

[선택지 어휘] **expand** 확대[확장]하다
consideration 고려(사항)

10 해석 참조

어휘 reveal 밝히다; 드러내다
significantly 상당히, 두드러지게
aerobic 유산소의, 호기성의
immune system 면역 체계
obesity 비만
remedy 해결책; 치료(법)

M Hello, listeners. This is Mike Wilson and I'm here to talk about the health of your children. Children who participate in outdoor activities are active and have lots of fun. Playing outside is a great idea, and it has a lot to offer. A recent study revealed that children who participate in outdoor play for several hours daily had significantly lower rates of eye trouble, like sore eyes, than those who spent shorter periods of time outdoors. Outdoor recreation such as hiking or rafting offers various physical benefits, like muscular and aerobic fitness. Health experts believe that children who explore and play outside are more likely to have a strong immune system. In addition, outdoor play gives children a great opportunity to exercise their bodies in an enjoyable way. With the increase in obesity among the young generation, outdoor play, like jogging, biking, or swimming, offers a good remedy for this issue. Children who take part in outdoor play also laugh a lot, which reduces blood pressure and stress. Now, how about taking your children outside for some fun in the sun?

남 안녕하세요, 청취자 여러분. 마이크 윌슨입니다. 저는 여러분 자녀의 건강에 대해 이야기하러 왔습니다. 야외 활동에 참여하는 아이들은 활달하고 즐거운 시간을 보냅니다. 야외에서 활동하는 것은 좋은 생각이며 제공하는 것이 많습니다. 최근 한 연구가 매일 몇 시간 동안 야외 활동에 참여하는 아이들이 야외에서 더 적은 시간을 보내는 아이들보다 눈병과 같은 안과 질환 발병률이 상당히 더 낮다고 밝혔습니다. **하이킹**(① hiking)이나 **뗏목타기**(② rafting)와 같은 야외 오락은 근력 및 유산소성 체력과 같은 다양한 신체적 이익을 제공합니다. 건강 전문가들은 야외에서 탐구하고 노는 아이들이 강한 면역 체계를 가질 가능성이 더 크다고 생각합니다. 게다가, 야외 활동은 즐거운 방식으로 신체를 단련할 수 있는 좋은 기회를 줍니다. 젊은 세대의 비만이 증가하면서, **조깅**(③ jogging), **자전거 타기**(⑤ biking), 또는 수영과 같은 야외 활동은 이런 문제에 좋은 해결책을 제공합니다. 야외 활동에 참여하는 아이들은 또한 많이 웃게 되는데, 이는 혈압과 스트레스를 낮춥니다. 이제 햇볕을 쬐며 즐기도록 아이들을 밖으로 데려가는 게 어떻습니까?

10 짧은 대화에 이어질 응답

✳✳ 기출 맛보기

본문 p.119

01 ⑤

해설 남자가 좋아하는 작가의 책 사인회에 여자가 같이 갈지 물었으므로 이에 긍정적으로 응답하는 것이 가장 적절하다.

① 정말? 내가 그녀를 봤어야 했는데.
② 말도 안 돼. 난 네가 많이 그리울 거야.
③ 아니. 난 그날 서점에 가지 않았어.
④ 미안해. 난 그녀의 글에 흥미가 없어.

어휘 hold (행사 등을) 열다[개최하다]
book signing event 책 사인회

W Did you hear that Golden Bookstore will hold a book signing event for Lora Johnson?
M Oh, she is one of my favorite writers. I've read all of her novels. When is it?
W This Sunday afternoon. Do you want to come with me?
M Yes. I can't believe I'm going to see her in person.

여 골든 서점이 로라 존슨의 책 사인회를 열 것이라는 것 들었니?
남 아, 그녀는 내가 가장 좋아하는 작가들 중 하나야. 난 그녀의 모든 소설들을 읽었어. 그건 언제야?
여 이번 일요일 오후야. 나랑 같이 갈래?
남 응. 내가 그녀를 직접 만난다니 믿기지 않아.

02 ②

해설 남자가 밤의 추운 날씨에 대비하는 게 좋겠다고 했으므로 따뜻한 재킷을 가져가겠다는 응답이 가장 적절하다.

M Have you finished packing your bags for your trip to Mount Jiri?
W I think so. Look! What else do I need?
M You'd better prepare for the cold weather at night.
W You're right. I'll take a warm jacket.

남 지리산 여행을 위해 짐 싸는 것을 끝냈니?
여 그런 것 같아. 봐! 이 외에 뭐가 필요할까?
남 밤에 추운 날씨를 대비하는 것이 좋을 거야.
여 네 말이 맞아. 따뜻한 재킷을 가져갈게.

① 또? 넌 가방을 두 번 잃어버렸어.

③ 왜? 난 네가 추운 날씨를 좋아하는 것을 알아.

④ 뭐라고? 난 널 위한 선물을 포장하는 것을 끝냈어.

⑤ 미안해. 하지만 넌 이 시점에 여행에 참여할 수는 없어.

어휘 pack (짐을) 싸다
had better+동사원형 ~하는 것이 좋을 것이다, ~해야 한다
prepare for ~을 대비하다

STEP 1·2 Listen & Choose

본문 p.120

01 ⓒ **02** ⓐ **03** ⓑ **04** ⓑ **05** ⓐ **06** ⓑ **07** ⓐ **08** ⓒ **09** ⓒ **10** ⓑ

01 ⓒ

해설 브라질에 간다는 남자에게 비행시간이 너무 길지 않느냐고 물었으므로 길지만 괜찮다는 응답이 가장 적절하다.

ⓐ 아니, 난 비행기 타는 것이 여전히 무서워.

ⓑ 응, 브라질은 날씨가 따뜻할 거야.

어휘 bother 신경 쓰이게 하다; 괴롭히다

W Nick, what are you going to do for Christmas?
M I'm going to Brazil to stay with my grandma.
W Wow, isn't the flight too long?
M I guess, but it doesn't bother me.

여 닉, 크리스마스에 뭐 할 거니?
남 할머니 댁에 머무르러 브라질에 갈 거야.
여 와, 비행시간이 너무 길지 않니?
남 아마 그렇겠지만, 난 그게 신경 쓰이지 않아.

02 ⓐ

해설 남자가 소풍에 가져갈 과일과 음료를 챙기겠다고 했으므로 다른 먹을 것인 샌드위치를 만들겠다는 응답이 가장 적절하다.

ⓑ 나는 어제 완벽한 소풍을 다녀왔어요.

ⓒ 그 공원은 여기서 가까워요.

어휘 You can say that again.
정말 그렇다.

M Honey, it's great weather outside today.
W You can say that again! How about going on a picnic to the Richmond Park?
M Good idea. I'll pack some fruits and drinks.
W Great. Then, I'll make some sandwiches.

남 여보, 오늘 바깥 날씨가 참 좋네요.
여 정말 그래요! 리치몬드 공원으로 소풍 가는 게 어때요?
남 좋은 생각이에요. 내가 과일과 음료를 좀 챙길게요.
여 좋아요. 그럼 나는 샌드위치를 좀 만들게요.

03 ⓑ

해설 지금 도서관에 가려는 남자에게 같이 가도 되는지를 물었으므로 이에 승낙하는 응답이 가장 적절하다.

ⓐ 도서관은 오늘 쉬는 날이야.

ⓒ 내일 독서 클럽에 가입하자.

W Liam, do you want to go to the library with me tomorrow?
M Actually, Jessica and I are going there right now.
W Then would you mind if I joined you?
M Of course not. Let's go together.

여 리암, 내일 나랑 도서관에 갈래?
남 실은, 제시카랑 나는 지금 거기에 갈 거야.
여 그럼 내가 너희와 함께 가도 괜찮을까?
남 물론이지. 같이 가자.

04 ⓑ

해설 새로 산 셔츠에 단추가 하나 없다고 했으므로 교환해야겠다는 응답이 가장 적절하다.

M Blair, how did your shopping go?
W It was good, Dad. I got this shirt at a good price.

남 블레어, 쇼핑은 어땠니?
여 좋았어요, 아빠. 좋은 가격에 이 셔츠를 샀어요.

ⓐ 물론이죠. 제가 아빠를 위해 셔츠를 주문해드릴게요.
ⓒ 저, 그건 제게 너무 비싸요.

어휘 missing 없어진

M It looks nice. Wait! It's missing a button.
W Oh, I should get it exchanged.

남 좋아 보이는구나. 잠깐! 그거 단추가 하나 없구나.
여 아, 교환해야겠네요.

---

05 ⓐ

해설 셸리가 어디가 아픈지 아느냐고 물었으므로 배탈이 났다고 알려주는 응답이 가장 적절하다.
ⓑ 너는 병원에 가야 해.
ⓒ 집에서 쉬고 나서 그녀는 괜찮아졌어.

[선택지 어휘] **have an upset stomach** 배탈이 나다

W Where is Shelly? I haven't seen her today.
M She's really sick, so she's resting at home.
W Do you know what's wrong with her?
M She has an upset stomach.

여 셸리는 어디 있어? 오늘 못 봤는데.
남 많이 아파서 집에서 쉬고 있어.
여 어디가 아픈지 알고 있니?
남 그녀는 배탈이 났어.

---

06 ⓑ

해설 스피커를 여자의 차에 두었다는 말을 듣고 남자는 그것들이 내일 필요하다고 했으므로 가져다주겠다는 응답이 가장 적절하다.
ⓐ 물론이죠. 내 텐트를 빌려도 돼요.
ⓒ 문제없어요. 당신 차는 수리되었어요.

M Honey, where are the speakers we used when we went camping?
W Oh, I just left them in my car.
M Really? I need to use them tomorrow.
W Okay. I'll bring you the speakers now.

남 여보, 우리가 캠핑 갔을 때 사용했던 스피커들이 어디 있나요?
여 아, 그냥 내 차에 뒀어요.
남 정말요? 내일 내가 그것들을 써야 해요.
여 알겠어요. 지금 스피커들을 가져다줄게요.

---

07 ⓐ

해설 새로 이사한 사무실까지 얼마나 걸리는지 물었으므로 소요 시간을 알려주는 응답이 가장 적절하다.
ⓑ 넌 집에서 더 일찍 나왔어야 해.
ⓒ 회사는 지난달에 이사했어.

어휘 except ~을 제외하고

W I heard your company moved to a new office. How is it?
M It's all good except one thing. It's far from my house.
W Oh, really? How long does it take to get there?
M It takes an hour by bus.

여 너희 회사가 새 사무실로 이사 갔다고 들었어. 거긴 어때?
남 한 가지 빼고 모두 좋아. 우리 집에서 멀어.
여 아, 정말? 거기에 가는 데 얼마나 걸리는데?
남 버스로 한 시간 걸려.

---

08 ⓒ

해설 회의가 있어 저녁 외식을 할 수 없다고 했으므로 식당 예약을 취소하겠다는 응답이 가장 적절하다.
ⓐ 좋아요. 내가 여섯 시에 다섯 명 예약할게요.
ⓑ 알겠어요. 내가 회의 장소와 시간을 정할게요.

M Honey, we can't eat out this evening.
W Why not? I've already booked a table at the restaurant.
M I'm sorry. I have an important business meeting at that time.
W Sorry to hear that. I'll cancel the reservation now.

남 여보, 우리 오늘 저녁에 외식할 수 없어요.
여 왜요? 내가 이미 식당에 예약했는데요.
남 미안해요. 그 시간에 중요한 업무 회의가 있어요.
여 유감이네요. 지금 예약을 취소할게요.

---

09 ⓒ

해설 여자가 읽지 않는 책을 어디에 기부해야 할지 물었으므로 기부 장소를 알려주는 응답이 가장 적절하다.
ⓐ 넌 책을 더 많이 읽어야 해.
ⓑ 내가 오늘 아침에 책들을 버렸어.

어휘 donate 기부하다

W I think I'm going to throw out these books. I don't read them any more.
M Really? Wait! How about donating them?
W Oh, that's a great idea. Where should I take them?
M I heard the city library collects them.

여 이 책들을 버릴 생각이야. 더는 읽지 않거든.
남 정말? 잠깐만! 그것들을 기부하는 건 어때?
여 아, 좋은 생각이야. 어디로 가져가야 할까?
남 시립 도서관이 책을 모은다고 들었어.

10 ⓑ

해설 남자는 여자가 수업 시간에 준 유인물을 잃어버렸다고 했으므로 복사본을 만들어주겠다는 응답이 가장 적절하다.

ⓐ 사실, 네 에세이를 찾지 못했어.
ⓒ 안타깝네. 나는 마감일이 기억나지 않아.

어휘 edit 교정하다; 편집하다
handout 유인물

M Mrs. Smith, can you give me advice on how to edit my essay?
W Sure. First, take a look at the handout I gave you last class. It has helpful examples.
M Really? Oh, I'm sorry. I'm afraid I lost it.
W Don't worry. I can make a copy for you.

남 스미스 선생님, 제 에세이를 교정하는 방법에 대해 조언해주실 수 있나요?
여 그럼. 먼저, 지난 수업 시간에 준 유인물을 살펴보렴. 도움이 되는 예시들이 있단다.
남 정말요? 아, 죄송해요. 제가 그걸 잃어버렸어요.
여 걱정 마렴. 복사본을 하나 만들어줄게.

STEP 3·4 Listen & Answer

본문 p.123

01 ①   **02** ③   **03** ②   **04** ①   **05** ④   **06** ③   **07** ⑤   **08** ⑤   **09** ②   **10** ⑤

01 ①

해설 교실에 두고 온 스웨터를 가져다 달라고 부탁하는 남자에게 어디에 뒀는지 물었으므로 스웨터의 위치를 알려주는 응답이 가장 적절하다.

② 수업 끝나고 만나자.
③ 3시에 거기서 출발했어.
④ 왼쪽에서 세 번째 방이야.
⑤ 내 스웨터는 갈색과 붉은색이야.

W Jake, Mr. Harrison asked me to take these books to the classroom. Will you wait here for me?
M Sure. Actually, I left my sweater there. Could you get it for me?
W No problem. Where did you leave it?
M It's hung on my chair.

여 제이크, 해리슨 선생님께서 내게 이 책들을 교실로 가져가라고 부탁하셨어. 여기서 날 기다려줄래?
남 물론이지. 사실, 나 거기에 내 스웨터를 두고 왔어. 가져다줄 수 있니?
여 문제없어. 어디에 뒀는데?
남 내 의자에 걸려 있어.

02 ③

해설 남자는 내일 수업에 여자가 빌려간 공책이 필요하다고 했으므로 내일 꼭 가져오겠다는 응답이 가장 적절하다.

① 네 공책은 아주 도움이 됐어.
② 내가 끝내자마자 알려줄게.
④ 내일 역사 시험이 있어.
⑤ 내가 공책 찾는 걸 도와줄게.

M Tonya, are you finished with my history notebook?
W Yeah, but I forgot to bring it.
M That's okay, but I need it for the history class tomorrow.
W Sorry, I'll make sure to bring it tomorrow.

남 토냐, 내 역사 공책 다 봤니?
여 응, 그런데 가져오는 걸 잊어버렸어.
남 괜찮아, 하지만 내일 역사 수업에 필요해.
여 미안해, 내일 꼭 가져올게.

03 ②

해설 여자가 캠프 등록 기간이 지난 게 아니냐고 물었으므로 아직 시간이 충분히 있다는 응답이 가장 적절하다.

① 걱정하지 마, 그렇게 비싸지 않아.
③ 우리 친구들 전부 그곳에 있을 거야.
④ 작년 캠프는 대단했어.
⑤ 어떻게 신청하는지 알려줄게.

어휘 sign up 등록하다, 참가하다

W I don't know what to do this summer vacation. Do you have any plans?
M Sure. I'm going to soccer camp. Why don't you sign up, too?
W That's an idea. But the deadline has already passed, hasn't it?
M I think there's still plenty of time.

여 이번 여름 방학 때 무엇을 해야 할지 모르겠어. 너는 계획이 있니?
남 그럼. 나는 축구 캠프에 갈 거야. 너도 등록하는 게 어때?
여 괜찮은 생각이야. 그런데 등록 기한이 이미 지났잖아, 그렇지 않니?
남 아직 시간이 충분한 것 같아.

04 ①

해설 콘서트에 갈 때 택시를 함께 타자고 제안하는 말에 승낙하는 응답이 가장 적절하다.
② 여기서 정말 멀구나.
③ 다음 버스를 기다리자.
④ 그 콘서트는 너무 늦은 밤에 해.
⑤ 그 먼 거리를 태워주다니 고마워.

M Are you going to the concert tonight?
W Of course, but I'm not sure how to get there.
M Steve and I are planning to share a taxi. You're welcome to join us if you like.
W That would be great.

남 오늘 밤 콘서트에 갈 거니?
여 물론이지, 하지만 어떻게 가야 할지 모르겠어.
남 스티브와 나는 택시를 같이 탈 생각이야. 원한다면 우리와 함께 가도 좋아.
여 그게 좋겠다.

05 ④

해설 여자는 남자에게 10분 후에 도착하는 막차를 타기 위해 서둘러야 하지 않는지 물었으므로 버스 정류장이 가까워서 그러지 않아도 된다는 응답이 가장 적절하다.
① 버스가 이미 떠났어요.
② 저는 여기서 버스를 타는 게 더 좋아요.
③ 네, 저는 6시부터 여기에 있었어요.
⑤ 그건 20분 후에 출발해요.

W Sam, why haven't you left yet? It's so late.
M I am about to leave to catch the last bus. It comes at 11:30.
W Really? It's 11:20 now! Don't you have to hurry?
M No, the bus stop is really close.

여 샘, 왜 아직 가지 않았나요? 많이 늦었어요.
남 마지막 버스를 타려고 지금 막 가려던 참이에요. 11시 30분에 오거든요.
여 정말요? 지금 11시 20분이에요! 서둘러야 하지 않나요?
남 아뇨, 버스 정류장이 정말 가까워요.

06 ③

해설 코미디와 액션 영화 중 하나를 선택해야 하는 상황이므로 코미디가 더 재미있겠다는 응답이 가장 적절하다.
① 그 액션 영화는 재미있었어.
② 시내 영화관에 가자.
④ 어제 온라인으로 표를 예매했어.
⑤ 영화 볼 시간이 없을 것 같아.

어휘 currently 현재, 지금

M Why don't we watch a movie tonight?
W Sounds good. What movies are playing now?
M A comedy and an action movie are currently playing.
W A comedy sounds like more fun to me.

남 오늘 밤에 영화 보지 않을래?
여 좋아. 지금 어떤 영화가 상영 중이지?
남 코미디랑 액션 영화가 현재 상영 중이야.
여 나는 코미디가 더 재미있을 것 같아.

07 ⑤

해설 여자가 남자에게 왜 보고서를 기한 내에 끝내지 못했는지 물었으므로 이유를 설명하는 응답이 가장 적절하다.
① 보고서를 집에 두고 왔어요.
② 보고서를 기한 내에 제출할게요.
③ 일주일 내내 보고서에 전념했어요.
④ 마감일은 다음 주 수요일이에요.

어휘 due 만기가 된; ~하기로 되어 있는
cf. due date 마감일
take a while 시간이 좀 걸리다
[선택지 어휘] turn in ~을 제출하다

W Eden, your report is due today. Do you have it?
M I'm sorry, Ms. Taylor, but I'm not finished yet. Can I have more time?
W Oh, why couldn't you finish it?
M It took me a while to pick a topic.

여 이든, 보고서 제출이 오늘까지야. 가져왔니?
남 테일러 선생님, 죄송하지만 아직 못 끝냈어요. 시간을 더 주실 수 있을까요?
여 아, 왜 끝내지 못했니?
남 주제를 정하는 데 시간이 좀 걸렸어요.

08 ⑤

해설 식당에 예약 없이 온 상황에서 4명이 앉을 자리가 있는지 여자가 확인해주는 상황이므로 20분 정도 기다려야 된다는 응답이 가장 적절하다.
① 저는 현지 요리를 좀 먹고 싶어요.
② 저희는 토요일에 파티를 열 거예요.
③ 물론이죠. 제가 그들과 금방 올게요.
④ 좋습니다. 예약되셨습니다.

어휘 **party** 일행, 무리; 정당; 모임

M I don't have a reservation. Do you have any free tables now?
W How many are there in your party?
M There are four of us.
W I think you'll have to wait for about 20 minutes.

남 전 예약을 하지 않았는데요. 지금 빈 테이블이 있나요?
여 일행이 몇 분이신가요?
남 저희는 4명이에요.
여 20분 정도 기다리셔야 할 것 같습니다.

09 ②

해설 남자가 가장 좋아하는 후보가 오디션 프로그램에서 우승할 것 같은지 물었으므로 당연히 그럴 만하다고 긍정하는 응답이 가장 적절하다.
① 이건 내가 제일 좋아하는 노래야.
③ 네가 좋아하는 가수는 이미 떨어졌어.
④ 오디션 참가자들이 많네.
⑤ 이 노래를 들으면 행복해져.

어휘 **candidate** 후보(자), 지원자
[선택지 어휘] **deserve** (마땅히) ~할 [받을] 만하다
participant 참가자

W Hey, what are you watching?
M It's a TV audition show. My favorite candidate is singing right now.
W Wow, he's really good. Do you think he'll win?
M He certainly deserves to.

여 얘, 뭐 보고 있니?
남 TV 오디션 프로그램이야. 내가 가장 좋아하는 후보가 바로 지금 노래하고 있어.
여 와, 정말 잘한다. 그가 우승할 거라고 생각하니?
남 그는 당연히 그럴 만해.

10 ⑤

해설 보고서를 같이 할 사람을 찾아야 하는 여자에게 남자가 케빈도 같이 할 사람을 찾고 있다고 알려줬으므로 케빈에게 물어봐야겠다는 응답이 가장 적절하다.
① 우리는 이 보고서를 끝내야 해.
② 난 너를 내 친구들에게 소개해줄 수 있어.
③ 나 혼자서는 보고서를 완성할 수 없었어.
④ 너는 책임감 있는 파트너가 되어야 해.
[선택지 어휘] **complete** 완성하다, 끝마치다; 완전한
responsible 책임감 있는; 책임이 있는

M Cindy, are you going to do your report with Danny?
W No, I worked with him last time. I have to pick someone else.
M I think Kevin is looking for a partner, too.
W Good. I should go and ask him right away.

남 신디, 대니랑 같이 보고서 작성할 거니?
여 아니, 지난번에 대니랑 했어. 난 다른 사람을 선택해야 해.
남 케빈도 같이 할 사람을 찾고 있는 것 같은데.
여 잘됐네. 지금 당장 가서 그 애에게 물어봐야겠다.

11 긴 대화에 이어질 응답

✳✳ 기출 맛보기

본문 p.127

01 ①

해설 폭풍으로 피해를 입은 남자에게 여자가 도와줄 것이 있는지 묻자, 지하실이 침수되어 엉망이라고 했으므로 정리하는 것을 도와줄 수 있다는 응답이 가장 적절하다.
② 걱정하지 마. 누구나 결정을 내리기 위해 시간이 필요해.
③ 알겠어. 우리가 위험한 상태라면 지하실에 가면 돼.
④ 응. 나무에 물을 좀 더 자주 주는 것은 어때?
⑤ 미안해. 나는 전구를 가는 방법을 몰라.

어휘 intense 강렬한
thunderstorm 폭풍우, 뇌우
throughout ~동안 죽
fallen 쓰러진
block 막다
electricity 전기
go out (불·전기 등이) 나가다
electronic device 전자기기
frustrating 답답하게 하는, 불만스러운
basement 지하실
mess 엉망인 상태

W Hi, James. Is everything okay? I heard there was a huge storm in your area last night.
M Yeah, we had some really intense thunderstorms throughout the night. There was some damage.
W Did anyone get hurt?
M Thankfully, no, but there were a lot of fallen trees, and the roads were blocked.
W Oh, my! That must have been scary!
M Yeah, it was. Then the electricity went out while the roads were being cleared.
W So, you didn't have any power last night?
M No, I couldn't turn on any lights or use any electronic devices, but it's okay now.
W That must have been so frustrating. Is there anything you need help with?
M Well, my basement is a mess. The water is up to my knees and all of my stuff down there is wet.
W Oh, no! I can come over today to help you clear it out.

여 안녕, 제임스. 괜찮아? 지난밤에 너희 지역에 큰 폭풍이 있었다고 들었어.
남 응, 밤새 정말 강렬한 폭풍우가 있었어. 피해도 좀 있었고.
여 다친 사람이 있니?
남 다행히 없지만, 쓰러진 나무가 많아서 도로가 막혔어.
여 오, 저런! 무서웠겠다!
남 응, 맞아. 그리고 도로가 치워지는 동안 전기가 나갔어.
여 그럼, 지난밤에 전기가 전혀 안 들어왔어?
남 응, 전등을 켜거나 전자기기를 사용할 수 없었지만 이제는 괜찮아.
여 정말 답답했겠다. 도움이 필요한 거라도 있니?
남 저, 지하실이 엉망이야. 물이 무릎까지 차서 거기에 있는 모든 내 물건들이 젖었거든.
여 아, 저런! 내가 오늘 가서 정리하는 걸 도와줄 수 있어.

STEP ①·② Listen & Choose

본문 p.128

01 ⓒ **02** ⓑ **03** ⓑ **04** ⓑ **05** ⓑ **06** ⓒ **07** ⓒ **08** ⓐ **09** ⓑ **10** ⓒ

01 ⓒ

해설 대출하려는 책을 언제까지 반납해야 하는지 물었으므로 기간을 알려주는 응답이 가장 적절하다.
ⓐ 전 이 책을 읽을 시간이 없어요.
ⓑ 누가 이미 그걸 대출했어요.

어휘 check out (책을) 대출하다

W I want to check these two books out, please.
M You can borrow this one, but that English dictionary can't be checked out.
W Oh, I didn't know that. When do I have to return this book?
M It must be returned two weeks from today.

여 이 두 권의 책을 대출하고 싶습니다.
남 이 책은 대출하실 수 있지만, 저 영어 사전은 대출이 안 됩니다.
여 아, 그건 몰랐네요. 이 책은 언제 반납해야 하죠?
남 오늘부터 2주 후에 반납되어야 합니다.

---

02 ⓑ

해설 구매한 물건에 문제가 있어 찾아온 손님이 영수증이 없다고 했으므로 영수증을 꼭 보관했어야 한다는 응답이 가장 적절하다.
ⓐ 죄송합니다만, 그 모델은 다 팔렸습니다.

M I bought this hair dryer here yesterday, but it doesn't work.
W Let me see. [pause] Oh, there seems to be a problem with the wire. May I see your receipt?
M I don't have it. I must have thrown it away.
W Oh dear. You really ought to have kept it.

남 어제 제가 여기서 이 헤어드라이어를 샀는데 작동하지 않아요.
여 한번 볼게요. [잠시 후] 아, 전선에 문제가 있는 것 같습니다. 영수증을 볼 수 있을까요?
남 영수증이 없는데요. 제가 버린 게 분명해요.
여 아, 저런. 그것을 꼭 보관하고 계셨어야 하는데요.

ⓒ 이상하군요. 그 헤어드라이어는
   잘 작동했는데요.

어휘 **receipt** 영수증
must have p.p. ~했음이 틀림없다
throw away ~을 버리다, 없애다
[선택지 어휘] **ought to have p.p.**
~했어야 하는 데 (하지 않았다)

---

03 ⓑ

해설 취업 기회를 놓치지 말라고 조
언했으므로 한 번 더 고려하겠다는
응답이 가장 적절하다.
ⓐ 음, 그러면 행운을 빌게.
ⓒ 너의 진심 어린 환대를 고맙게 생
   각해.

어휘 **afford to-v** v할 여유가 있다
pass up (기회 등을) 놓치다; ~을 간과
하다
have a lot on one's mind 고민
이 많다
advise A to-v A에게 v하라고 조언
[충고]하다
[선택지 어휘] **sincere** 진심 어린, 진실된
hospitality 환대

W Hey, Jack. I don't think you can afford to <u>pass up a</u>
    <u>job opportunity</u> to work abroad.
M Maybe you're right, but I've got a lot on my mind.
W I <u>advise you to take it</u>. Then, later, you can always
    move back home if you don't like it.
M OK, I'll consider it once more.

여 이봐, 잭. 내 생각엔 네가 해외에서 일할 취업 기회
   를 놓칠 여유가 없을 것 같아.
남 네 말이 맞을지도 모르지만 나는 고민이 많아.
여 난 그 기회를 받아들이라고 조언해. 그런 다음 나
   중에 그 일이 마음에 들지 않으면, 너는 언제든지
   집으로 돌아올 수 있어.
남 좋아, 한 번 더 고려해볼게.

---

04 ⓑ

해설 스카프의 할인율을 듣고 자신
도 하나 사고 싶다고 했으므로 서두
르라는 응답이 가장 적절하다.
ⓐ 죄송합니다, 판촉 행사는 어제 끝
   났어요.
ⓒ 잘 샀어. 스카프가 네게 잘 어울려.

어휘 **a good buy** 싸게 잘 산 물건

M What do you want to buy <u>at the sale</u>?
W A scarf. I saw a good one last week. It was <u>$50</u>, but
    we can save 25% today.
M Wow! 25% off! That's a really good buy. I'd like <u>to get</u>
    <u>one</u> for my mom, too.
W You'd better hurry. They'll be gone soon.

남 할인 판매에서 무엇을 사고 싶니?
여 스카프. 지난주에 멋진 걸 하나 봤어. 50달러였는
   데 오늘은 25%를 절약할 수 있어.
남 와! 25% 할인이라고! 정말 싸게 잘 사는 거네. 나
   도 엄마를 위해 하나 사고 싶어.
여 서두르는 게 좋을 거야. 곧 다 팔릴 거거든.

---

05 ⓑ

해설 자전거를 같이 타기로 한 여자
가 헬멧이 없다고 했으므로 안전을
위해 꼭 필요하다는 응답이 가장 적
절하다.
ⓐ 나는 새 자전거를 살 만큼 충분한
   돈이 있어.
ⓒ 다행히도, 난 사고에서 다치지 않
   았어.

어휘 **be good at** ~을 잘하다
[선택지 어휘] **safety** 안전

M Kathy! Let's ride our bikes to school together.
W Sounds nice. But <u>I'm not very good at biking</u>.
M It's okay. We can go slowly. Also, <u>remember to wear</u>
    your helmet.
W But I don't have a helmet yet.
M You really need one for your own safety.

남 캐시! 학교까지 같이 자전거 타고 가자.
여 좋아. 그런데 난 자전거를 아주 잘 타진 못해.
남 괜찮아. 천천히 가면 돼. 또, 헬멧 쓰는 것 기억해.
여 그렇지만 나는 아직 헬멧이 없어.
남 너 자신의 안전을 위해 하나가 정말 필요해.

---

06 ⓒ

해설 지갑을 찾고 있는 여자에게 남
자가 카운터에서 확인해보겠다고 했으
므로 그러면 큰 도움이 될 거라는 응
답이 가장 적절하다.

W Excuse me. After I left the restaurant, <u>did you see a</u>
    <u>wallet</u> on the table?
M Do you remember where you sat?

여 실례합니다. 제가 식당을 떠난 후에, 테이블에서
   지갑 하나를 보셨나요?
남 어디에 앉으셨는지 기억하시나요?

ⓐ 아니요, 괜찮습니다. 제가 이미 찾았습니다.
ⓑ 제 지갑을 보관해주시다니 정말 친절하시군요.

W Yes, it was the table right next to the mirror.
M I've just cleaned up that table, but I didn't see anything. Let me ask at the counter.
W Would you? That would be a great help.

여 네, 거울 바로 옆 테이블이었어요.
남 그 테이블을 막 치웠는데 아무것도 못 봤어요. 카운터에 물어볼게요.
여 그렇게 해주시겠어요? 그러면 정말 큰 도움이 될 거예요.

07 ⓒ

해설 보고서를 뒤늦게 내도 될지 문의했으므로 늦은 제출에 대한 불이익은 있을 것이라는 응답이 가장 적절하다.
ⓐ 서두르지 말아요. 마감은 다음 주 월요일 오전까지예요.
ⓑ 음, 당신은 완벽해지기 위해 더 열심히 연습해야 해요.

어휘 hand in 제출하다(= turn in)
due date 마감일
[선택지 어휘] penalty 불이익; 처벌
submission 제출

W Professor Jones, I'm sorry I didn't hand in my reports on time.
M Did you have any problems? You never miss due dates.
W I was recovering from the flu yesterday, so I'm wondering if I could turn them in now.
M Sure, but there will be a penalty for late submission.

여 존스 교수님, 제때 보고서를 제출하지 못해 죄송합니다.
남 무슨 문제라도 있었나요? 학생은 절대 마감일을 놓치지 않잖아요.
여 어제 제가 독감에서 회복하는 중이었어요, 지금 보고서를 제출해도 될지 궁금합니다.
남 그럼요, 그렇지만 늦은 제출에 대한 불이익이 있을 거예요.

08 ⓐ

해설 청소를 하지 않는 룸메이트에게 그 문제에 대해 이야기해봤는지 물었으므로 해봤지만 심각하게 여기지 않았다는 응답이 가장 적절하다.
ⓑ 걱정 마. 나는 그 애와 어떤 문제도 없어.
ⓒ 미안해. 나 아파트에서 이사 나가는 것을 연기했어.

어휘 share 함께 쓰다, 공유하다
get along (well) with ~와 잘 지내다
messy 지저분한
[선택지 어휘] take (it) seriously 심각하게 여기다
delay 연기하다, 미루다

M Alice, aren't you sharing an apartment with Jane?
W Yeah, but I'm thinking about moving out.
M Why? I thought you two get along well with each other.
W There have been a lot of problems between us. Actually, she never cleans up. The kitchen and the bathroom are always messy.
M That's awful. Have you talked about this issue with her?
W I have, but she didn't take it seriously.

남 앨리스, 너 제인이랑 아파트를 함께 쓰지 않니?
여 응, 그런데 나는 이사 가려고 생각 중이야.
남 왜? 난 너희 둘이 서로 잘 지낸다고 생각했는데.
여 우리 사이에는 많은 문제들이 있어 왔어. 사실 제인이 절대 청소를 안 하거든. 부엌이랑 욕실이 항상 지저분해.
남 끔찍하다. 이 문제에 대해 그 애와 이야기해봤어?
여 해봤지만 그 애는 심각하게 여기질 않더라.

09 ⓑ

해설 남자가 중고물품을 거래하는 앱을 설명하자 여자는 자신도 팔 물건이 많다고 했으므로 앱을 사용해 판매하라는 응답이 가장 적절하다.
ⓐ 음, 너는 새 옷을 사는 게 좋을 거야.
ⓒ 좋아. 시장에서 스웨터를 하나 사자.

W Paul, what are you doing?
M I'm trying to sell my old sweater using the Local Market app.
W Interesting! How do you use it?
M If I upload pictures of my sweater, somebody who needs a sweater will see and buy it.
W That's great. I also have a lot of things to sell.
M Then, you should sell them using this app.

여 폴, 뭐 하고 있어?
남 지역 마켓 앱을 사용해서 내 오래된 스웨터를 팔려고 해.
여 흥미로운데! 그걸 어떻게 사용하는 거야?
남 내가 내 스웨터 사진을 업로드하면 스웨터를 필요로 하는 누군가가 보고 구매하는 거야.
여 멋지다. 나도 판매할 많은 물건들이 있어.
남 그럼, 이 앱을 사용해서 그것들을 판매해.

10 ⓒ

해설 시험 때문에 수업에 빠질 수 없다고 했으므로 걱정하지 말라고 하며 필기를 빌려주겠다는 응답이 가장 적절하다.

W Chris, you don't look well. Why don't you go home early?
M I'd like to, but I don't want to miss biology class. The exam is only a few days away.

여 크리스, 너 몸이 안 좋아 보여. 집에 일찍 가는 게 어때?
남 그러고 싶지만, 생물학 수업에 빠지고 싶지 않아. 시험이 며칠밖에 안 남았잖아.

ⓐ 네 말이 맞아. 병원에 가야 할 것 같아.

ⓑ 그래서 그 선생님의 수업에 다시는 빠지지 말라고 말하는 거야.

어휘 lecture 강의
[선택지 어휘] **take notes** 필기하다

W But you need to get better first.
M I know, but a lot of the questions on the exam are from the lectures.
W Don't worry. I'll take good notes and lend them to you.

여 하지만 먼저 몸이 좋아져야 해.
남 알아, 그렇지만 많은 시험 문제가 강의에서 나오잖아.
여 걱정하지 마. 내가 필기를 잘해서 네게 빌려줄게.

STEP ③·④ Listen & Answer

본문 p.132

01 ① **02** ③ **03** ⑤ **04** ② **05** ⑤ **06** ③ **07** ② **08** ⑤ **09** ② **10** ⑤

01 ①

해설 보고서 제출에 대해 남자가 우려하고 있으므로 이를 진정시키는 응답이 가장 적절하다.

② 어리석게 굴지 마. 넌 다음번에 더 잘할 거야.
③ 나도 마찬가지야. 나도 두 과목에서 거의 낙제할 뻔했어.
④ 좋은 생각이 있어. 다시 한 번 해보면 어떨까?
⑤ 미안하지만 난 이번 주에 보고서를 끝낼 수가 없어.

어휘 term 학기, 기간; 용어; 조항
including ~을 포함하여
be in trouble 곤란을 겪다
[선택지 어휘] let down ~을 실망시키다

M Susan, did you finish the survey?
W Sorry, not yet.
M You told me it would be ready on Wednesday, but it's now Friday and you still haven't finished it.
W Well, I'm sorry, but there has been a lot of other work to finish this week. You know it's the end of the term.
M But you did promise. Look, the point is that the deadline for our team's report is in three days' time and if the survey isn't ready, we can't finish the report.
W I'm really sorry. It'll be in your hands first thing tomorrow. I promise.
M Please don't forget. If we can't hand the report in, four of us, including you and me, will be in big trouble.
W I know. Trust me. I won't let you down.

남 수잔, 표본 조사 끝냈어?
여 미안하지만, 아직 못 끝냈어.
남 수요일에 준비될 거라고 네가 말했는데, 지금 금요일이고, 넌 아직도 끝내지 못했네.
여 음, 미안해, 하지만 이번 주에 끝내야 할 다른 일들이 많았어. 너도 알다시피 학기 말이잖아.
남 하지만 넌 약속을 했잖아. 봐, 요점은 우리 팀 보고서의 제출 기한이 3일 후라는 거고 표본 조사가 준비되지 않으면, 우리는 보고서를 끝낼 수가 없어.
여 정말 미안해. 표본 조사가 내일 무엇보다도 먼저 네 손에 있을 거야. 약속해.
남 제발 잊지 마. 우리가 보고서를 제출하지 못하면, 너와 나를 포함해서 우리 네 사람은 큰 곤란을 겪을 거야.
여 알아. 나를 믿어. 널 실망시키지 않을게.

02 ③

해설 콘서트 표를 두 장 예매했지만, 매표소 기록상에는 한 장만 예매가 되어 있고 잔여 좌석도 없는 상황이므로 관리자와 이야기하고 싶다는 응답이 가장 적절하다.

① 괜찮습니다. 여기 표 값을 결제할 신용카드가 있습니다.
② 괜찮습니다. 안 좋은 좌석이라도 주십시오.
④ 회원 카드로 할인받을 수 있나요?
⑤ 이런, 좌석을 좀 더 일찍 예약했어야 했는데.

어휘 reservation 예약
sort 종류, 유형
available 이용 가능한
[선택지 어휘] unacceptable 받아들일 수 없는

W Welcome. May I help you?
M Yes, I made a reservation online, and I'd like to pick up my tickets.
W What sort of reservation was it?
M It was for today's 7 p.m. concert.
W And what is your name?
M Brown... John Brown.
W Yes, Mr. Brown. Here's your ticket.
M But I ordered two tickets. I'm going with my wife.
W Are you sure you ordered two?
M Of course. It was just yesterday. I clearly remember ordering two.
W I'm terribly sorry, but our records show a reservation for one, and the concert is now sold out. I'm afraid there are no other available seats.
M This is unacceptable! I want to speak to your manager.

여 어서 오세요. 도와드릴까요?
남 네, 온라인으로 예매를 했는데 표를 받고 싶어요.
여 어떤 종류의 예매였나요?
남 오늘 오후 7시 콘서트요.
여 성함이 어떻게 되십니까?
남 브라운… 존 브라운입니다.
여 네, 브라운 씨. 여기 손님의 표가 있습니다.
남 하지만 전 표 두 장을 주문했어요. 아내와 함께 가려고요.
여 분명 두 장을 주문하셨습니까?
남 물론입니다. 바로 어제인걸요. 두 장을 주문했던 것을 분명히 기억하고 있습니다.
여 대단히 죄송합니다만, 저희 기록상으로는 한 장 예매되어 있고 그 콘서트는 지금 매진되었습니다. 유감스럽게도 이용 가능한 다른 좌석이 남아 있지 않습니다.
남 이건 받아들일 수가 없군요! 관리자와 이야기를 하고 싶습니다.

03 ⑤

해설 남자는 저녁 모임에 갈 때가 아니라 돌아올 때 여자가 차에 태워주기를 원하므로 거기서 보자는 응답이 가장 적절하다.

① 응, 그래. 우리는 내 차로 갈 수 있어.
② 알겠어. 여기서 30분 뒤에 출발하자.
③ 우리 선물을 함께 사는 게 어때?
④ 미안하지만, 난 오늘 밤 파티에 못 가.

어휘 plenty 풍부한 양; 많이
starve 몹시 배고프다, 굶주리다
serve (음식을) 내다, 제공하다
give A a ride A를 차에 태워주다
[선택지 어휘] make it to (장소에) 이르다, 도착하다

M I hope there'll be plenty to eat for dinner at Pat's house. I'm starving.
W Don't worry about that. Pat always prepares a lot of food. I bought some chocolates for her. What are you bringing?
M A bottle of white wine.
W Why did you get white wine? Do you know what she's serving?
M I think she said she was going to cook fish.
W Oh, that sounds good. Let's see. Do you want me to pick you up later?
M Well, what time did she say the dinner was, six-thirty or seven o'clock?
W Seven.
M Then I have time to walk, so let's just meet at her house. But could you give me a ride home after dinner?
W No problem. See you there in the evening, then.

남 팻 집에서의 저녁 식사에 먹을 게 많으면 좋겠어. 배가 많이 고프거든.
여 그건 걱정하지 마. 팻은 항상 음식을 많이 준비해. 나는 그녀를 위해서 초콜릿을 좀 샀어. 너는 뭘 가져갈 거야?
남 화이트 와인 한 병.
여 왜 화이트 와인을 샀니? 그녀가 어떤 음식을 낼지 알고 있어?
남 그녀가 생선 요리를 할 거라고 말한 것 같아.
여 아, 잘됐다. 참, 내가 나중에 널 태우러 갈까?
남 글쎄, 그녀가 저녁 식사가 언제라고 했지, 6시 반이든가 7시든가?
여 7시.
남 그럼 걸어갈 시간이 있으니까, 그냥 그녀의 집에서 만나자. 하지만 저녁 식사 후에는 집까지 태워다 줄 수 있니?
여 물론이지. 그럼 저녁에 거기서 보자.

---

04 ②

해설 함께 운동하러 가자는 제안에 동의하며 빨리 준비해서 나오겠다고 했으므로 천천히 하라며 기다리겠다는 응답이 가장 적절하다.

① 오늘은 조깅하고 싶지 않아.
③ 좋아, 그리고 넌 언제 운동을 할지 선택할 수 있어.
④ 서두르지 마. 천천히 그리고 꾸준히 하면 이길 수 있어.
⑤ 그러고 싶은데, 지금 바로 사무실에 가봐야 해.

어휘 be into v-ing v하는 것에 열중하다
get rid of ~을 없애다
put on weight 체중이 늘다
can hardly+동사원형 거의 ~할 수가 없다
[선택지 어휘] take one's time 천천히 하다, 서두르지 않다

W Hi, Jason. Going out for a run?
M Yes.
W I see you're really into exercising these days.
M I'm trying to get rid of a few extra kilograms.
W Well, you have put on just a little weight over the last year.
M A little? Three years ago, I was 10 kilograms lighter than I am now.
W Oh, really?
M Yeah. I can't fit into the pants I bought last year.
W That's nothing to complain about. I got these pants only last month. At that time, they were very comfortable to wear. Now, they're so tight that I can hardly breathe.
M Then you should be getting some exercise, too. Why don't you join me?
W Great idea. I'll go and change my clothes quickly and be right back.
M Take your time. I'll wait for you.

여 안녕, 제이슨. 달리기하러 나가는 거야?
남 응.
여 너 요즘 운동에 아주 열중해 있는 것 같아.
남 몇 킬로그램 늘어난 체중을 빼려고 애쓰고 있어.
여 음, 작년에 너는 살이 아주 조금 찌긴 했어.
남 조금이라고? 3년 전에는 지금보다 10킬로그램 덜 나갔어.
여 오, 정말?
남 그래. 작년에 산 바지가 들어가질 않아.
여 그건 불평할 게 못 돼. 난 이 바지를 겨우 지난달에 샀어. 그 당시엔 입기 아주 편했지. 지금은 아주 꽉 끼어서 숨을 쉴 수가 없을 정도야.
남 그러면 너도 운동을 좀 해야겠다. 나와 함께 하는 게 어때?
여 좋은 생각이야. 빨리 옷 갈아입고 바로 돌아올게.
남 천천히 해. 기다리고 있을게.

---

05 ⑤

해설 자전거 타는 것과 같다며 제트 스키를 타러 가자는 제안에 자신은 자전거도 못 탄다며 거절하는 응답이 가장 적절하다.

① 네가 부러워. 넌 뭐든 잘하잖아.
② 응, 나는 제트 스키가 위험하다고 생각하지 않아.
③ 좋은 생각이야. 나는 이번 주에 수영을 배워야 해.
④ 아니, 그렇지 않아. 대신 이번 주말에 제트 스키를 타러 가자.

W Hey, Alan, what are you going to do this Saturday?
M I'm going jet-skiing on the Han River.
W Jet-skiing?
M Yeah. Have you ever tried it?
W No. How long have you been jet-skiing?
M About a month. It is really exciting.
W But jet-skiing looks very difficult to learn.
M Absolutely not. Anyone can learn it easily.
W Isn't it scary?
M No, not at all. It's just like riding a bike. You'll get the hang of it in no time. Do you want to come along?

여 이봐, 앨런, 이번 토요일에 무엇을 할 생각이야?
남 한강에 제트 스키를 타러 갈 거야.
여 제트 스키?
남 응. 타 본 적 있어?
여 아니. 제트 스키를 탄 지는 얼마나 됐니?
남 한 달쯤 됐어. 정말 신나.
여 하지만 제트 스키는 배우기가 아주 어려워 보여.
남 전혀 그렇지 않아. 누구든 쉽게 배울 수 있어.
여 무섭지 않니?
남 아니, 전혀. 마치 자전거를 타는 것과 같아. 너는 금방 요령을 터득할 거야. 함께 갈래?

어휘 **absolutely** (부정을 강조하여) 전혀; 절대적으로

get the hang of ~의 요령을 터득 하다

in no time 금방, 곧

come along 함께 가다; 나타내다

[선택지 어휘] **envy** 부러워하다

had better+동사원형 ~하는 편이 낫다

W No, I'd better not. I don't even know how to ride a bike.

여 아니, 안 가는 게 좋겠어. 난 자전거도 탈 줄 몰라.

---

06 ③

해설 남자는 친구 집에 가서 경기를 보려 했지만 눈보라가 온다는 어머니의 만류에 기상 예보를 확인하고 동의했으므로 친구에게 가지 않기로 알리겠다는 응답이 가장 적절하다.

① 정말 좋은 생각이네요! 알려줘서 고마워요.

② 저는 저녁 6시까지 일해서 거기에 7시까지 갈 수가 없어요.

④ 제가 오늘 밤 갈 수 있을지 잘 모르 겠지만 한 번 시도해볼게요.

⑤ 전 지금 떠나야만 해요. 내일 일찍 일어나야 되거든요.

어휘 **snow storm** 눈보라

[선택지 어휘] **give it a try** 시도하다, 한번 해보다

W Where are you going at this late hour?

M Mom, some friends and I are going to watch the Super Bowl at Bill's house.

W Why don't you just watch the game here?

M It's more fun to watch it together.

W Isn't Bill's house on Cedar Street?

M Yes. It's not that far.

W Well, you'll need to take the car anyway. I don't think it's a good idea to go at this time of night.

M Why not? I'll drive safely.

W I heard there's a big snow storm coming in tonight. The streets will be covered in snow when you're on your way back.

M Really? Let me check the weather forecast. [pause] Oh, you're right.

W Yes. Look at the sky. It's very cloudy.

M Then I'll call and let them know that I'm not coming.

여 이 늦은 시간에 넌 어디를 가는 거니?

남 엄마, 몇몇 친구들과 빌의 집에서 슈퍼볼 경기를 볼 거예요.

여 그냥 여기서 경기를 보지 그러니?

남 다 같이 보면 더 재미있어요.

여 빌의 집은 시더가(街)에 있지 않니?

남 맞아요. 그렇게 멀지 않아요.

여 음, 어쨌든 네가 차를 타야 하잖니. 이 밤 시간에 가는 건 좋은 생각이 아닌 것 같아.

남 왜 안돼요? 조심히 운전할 거예요.

여 오늘 밤에 엄청난 눈보라가 올 거라고 들었어. 네가 돌아올 때쯤 거리는 눈으로 뒤덮일 거야.

남 정말요? 기상 예보를 확인해볼게요. [잠시 후] 아, 엄마 말씀이 맞네요.

여 그래. 하늘을 봐. 매우 흐리잖니.

남 그럼 전화해서 친구들에게 전 못 간다고 알릴게요.

---

07 ②

해설 일자리를 잃고 오늘 본 면접에서도 거절당했다고 했으므로 격려의 말이 응답으로 가장 적절하다.

① 나는 둘 중 어느 회사에서도 일하고 싶지 않아요.

③ 말도 안돼요! 나는 당신이 누구보다 자격이 있다고 생각해요.

④ 그 말을 들으니 유감이지만 기회를 줘서 고마워요.

⑤ 어리석은 소리 마세요. 당신은 지금 그대로도 멋져요.

어휘 **out of work** 실직한 (= unemployed)

lecturer 강사

sociology 사회학

turn down ~을 거절[거부]하다

overqualified 필요 이상의 자격 [경력]을 갖춘

W Lucas, what did you say you do for a living?

M Well, I'm currently out of work.

W Oh, are you?

M Yes. Only last week I had two jobs, but now I'm unemployed.

W What did you do?

M I was a part-time lecturer at two different universities, but both universities said they didn't need me next year.

W What subject do you teach?

M Sociology. But it's really hard to get full-time university teaching jobs.

W Are you looking for other jobs?

M Yes. I had two different interviews today, but they both turned me down. They said I was overqualified.

W Oh, that's too bad. I hope you'll get a good job soon.

여 루카스, 무슨 일을 한다고 하셨죠?

남 저, 전 현재 실직 상태입니다.

여 아, 그래요?

남 네. 지난주만 해도 직장이 둘이나 있었는데, 지금은 실직 상태죠.

여 무슨 일을 하셨는데요?

남 대학 두 곳에서 시간 강사를 했는데, 두 대학 모두 내년에 제가 필요하지 않다고 했어요.

여 무슨 과목을 가르치시는데요?

남 사회학입니다. 하지만 대학 전임 강사직은 정말 구하기가 어렵네요.

여 다른 일자리를 찾고 계신가요?

남 네. 오늘 회사 두 곳에서 면접을 봤는데, 양쪽 모두 저를 거절하더군요. 저의 자격이 과하다면서요.

여 아, 안됐군요. 곧 좋은 일자리를 구하시길 바라요.

---

08 ⑤

해설 남자의 개가 밤새 짖는 바람에 잠을 잘 수 없어 출근하지 못할 뻔했다고 했으므로 사과의 말이 응답으로 가장 적절하다.

M Hi, Hailey. I haven't seen you around for a while, even though we live next door to each other.

W Hi, Andy. Actually, I'm here to ask you something.

M What is it?

남 안녕하세요, 헤일리. 서로 옆집에 살고 있는데도 한동안 못 봤네요.

여 안녕하세요, 앤디. 실은 뭐 좀 물어보려고 왔어요.

남 뭔가요?

① 우리 옆집에 사는 이웃사람이 안 쓰러워요.

② 저는 부모님과 아주 좋은 시간을 보냈어요.

③ 당신 덕분에 제 개가 이제 나아졌어요.

④ 당신은 지각하는 것에 대해 내게 전화했어야 해요.

어휘 bark 짖다
[선택지 어휘] **thanks to** ~ 덕분에, 때문에
make sure (that) 반드시 ~하도록 하다

W Well, I want to know what happened last night.
M What do you mean?
W Your dog was barking all night long. I thought something had happened.
M Sorry about that. I wasn't at home last night. I spent the night at my parent's house.
W I could hear him very clearly from my house! Why did you leave him alone?
M Because my parents don't like dogs, and I thought he would be okay.
W Well, I wasn't able to get any sleep, and I almost missed work this morning.
M I'm terribly sorry. I'll make sure that never happens again.

여 저, 지난밤에 무슨 일이 있었는지 알고 싶어서요.
남 무슨 말씀이신지요?
여 당신의 개가 밤새도록 짖었어요. 저는 무슨 일이 생겼다고 생각했죠.
남 죄송해요. 저는 지난밤에 집에 없었어요. 부모님 댁에서 밤을 보냈거든요.
여 개의 소리를 우리 집에서 아주 또렷하게 들을 수 있었어요! 왜 개를 혼자 내버려 두었나요?
남 부모님이 개를 좋아하지 않으시고, 전 개가 괜찮을 거라고 생각했어요.
여 글쎄요, 저는 잠을 한숨도 잘 수 없었고 오늘 아침에 출근을 못 할 뻔했어요.
남 정말 죄송합니다. 다시는 그런 일이 일어나지 않도록 할게요.

09 ②

해설 음악 취향이 다른데 영화 취향도 다르다는 것을 알 수 있으므로 공통점이 전혀 없다는 응답이 가장 적절하다.

① 이번 주말에 코미디 영화 보러 가자.
③ 너는 나와 같은 종류의 영화에 관심이 많구나.
④ 널 울게 만든 로맨스 영화가 뭐야?
⑤ 나도. 난 사랑 이야기를 읽는 데 많은 시간을 보내.

어휘 **be into** ~에 관심이 많다, ~을 좋아하다
mainly 주로
chase 추격; 뒤쫓다, 추적하다
predictable 너무 뻔한; 예측할 수 있는
[선택지 어휘] **have A in common** A를 공통으로 지니다

W So what do you feel like doing tonight? Any ideas?
M Well, I'd like to see a film or maybe see if there are any good bands playing around town, if you're into music.
W Yes, that's a good idea. What kind of music do you like, then?
M Oh, all sorts really, you know, but mainly I like blues and jazz.
W Oh, really? I'm more into dance music myself, so maybe....
M Well, we could always go and see a film. I really like movies. And I especially like action movies, you know, car chases, guns, bombs, anything that's fast and exciting.
W Oh, right. To be honest with you, I'm not really into violent films. I like romantic comedies better. Do you like that kind of movie?
M I don't like predictable love stories. They are so boring.
W Well, we don't have anything in common.

여 그래, 오늘 저녁에 뭘 하고 싶니? 무슨 아이디어라도 있어?
남 음, 나는 영화를 보거나 아니면 네가 음악에 관심이 있다면 시내에 괜찮은 밴드가 공연하는지 알아보고 싶어.
여 응, 괜찮은 아이디어야. 그래서 넌 어떤 종류의 음악을 좋아하니?
남 아, 그러니까 온갖 종류를 정말 다 좋아하는데, 주로 블루스와 재즈를 좋아해.
여 아, 정말? 난 댄스 음악에 더 관심이 많아, 그럼 아마도…
남 음, 우리는 언제든지 영화를 보러 갈 수 있잖아. 난 영화를 정말 좋아해. 특히 액션 영화를 좋아하지. 자동차 추격, 총, 폭탄, 뭐든 속도감 있고 흥미진진한 것들 말이야.
여 아, 그렇구나. 솔직히 말하면, 난 폭력적인 영화는 별로 안 좋아해. 로맨틱 코미디가 더 좋아. 그런 종류의 영화 좋아하니?
남 난 너무 뻔한 사랑 이야기는 안 좋아해. 너무 지루해.
여 음, 우리는 공통점이 전혀 없구나.

10 ⑤

해설 여러 프로젝트 중 교통 문제 개선책에 대해 들었으므로 다른 프로젝트에 대해서도 궁금증을 드러내는 질문을 하는 것이 가장 적절하다.

① 정말? 너의 카풀에 동참하고 싶어.
② 아, 안됐다. 교통이 악화되기만 할 거야.
③ 잘됐다. 대중교통이 더 저렴해진다니 기뻐.
④ 알겠어. 집에 차를 두고 왔으면 내가 태워다 줄게.

어휘 **mayor** 시장
association 협회, 조합
improve 개선하다

M Hi, April! What a pleasant surprise. How are you and your family?
W We're all fine, thanks. And you?
M I'm fine too. I haven't seen you in ages. What have you been up to?
W I've been busy. I've been getting advice from the mayor's office on a project.
M What kind of project?
W We're starting a neighborhood association to try to improve life in this community.
M This is the first I've heard of it. Is it a lot of work?
W Yeah, but it's also interesting.
M Well, I wish someone would do something about the traffic, especially during rush hour.

남 안녕, 에이프릴! 뜻밖에 만나게 되어 정말 기뻐. 너와 가족들은 어떻게 지내니?
여 우리는 모두 잘 지내, 고마워. 넌?
남 나도 잘 지내. 널 못 본 지 오래됐네. 어떻게 지냈니?
여 바빴어. 시장님의 사무실에서 프로젝트에 관한 조언을 얻고 있어.
남 어떤 종류의 프로젝트인데?
여 우린 이 지역 생활을 개선하려고 노력하는 지역 협회를 시작할 거야.
남 난 처음 듣는 얘기인데. 일이 많니?
여 응, 하지만 재미있기도 해.
남 음, 누군가 교통 문제를 어떻게 좀 해주면 좋겠어, 특히 출퇴근 시간에 말이야.

encourage A to-v A가 v하도록 장려[격려]하다
transport 교통수단; 수송[운송]하다
cf. transportation 교통수단, 수송, 운송

W Actually, that's one of our projects. We're encouraging people to leave their cars at home and to use public transport.
M That's good to hear. What else are you guys doing?

여 실은 그것도 우리 프로젝트 중 하나야. 우리는 사람들이 차를 집에 두고 대중교통을 이용하도록 장려하고 있어.
남 그 얘기 들으니 반갑다. 그밖에 너희들이 하고 있는 일이 뭐야?

---

12 유형 담화 상황에 적절한 표현

본문 p.139

※※ 기출 맛보기

01 ③

해설 포스터의 글자 크기를 키우는 것을 제안하고 싶어 하므로 글자 크기를 키우는 것이 가능한지 묻는 말이 가장 적절하다.
① 포스터에 다양한 색깔의 글자체를 사용하는 게 어때?
② 네 친구들에게 콘서트를 알리는 게 좋을 것 같아.
③ 포스터에 있는 글자 크기를 더 크게 만들 수 있니?
④ 학교 축제에서 콘서트를 여는 게 어때?
⑤ 포스터에 중요한 정보를 넣어야 해.

어휘 hold (행사 등을) 열다
in charge of ~을 담당하는
complete 완성하다
necessary 필수적인
notice 알아차리다
suggest 제안하다
increase 늘리다, 증가시키다

W Amy is the leader of a high school band and Terry is one of the band members. The band is going to hold a mini concert in the school festival, and Terry is in charge of making a concert poster. When he completes the poster, he shows it to the band members. Even though the poster has all the necessary information, it's hard to read it because the size of the letters is too small. Amy thinks if Terry changes the font size to a larger one, it could be easier to notice. So, Amy wants to suggest that Terry increase the size of the letters on the poster. In this situation, what would Amy most likely say to Terry?

여 에이미는 고등학교 음악 밴드의 리더이고 테리는 밴드 멤버들 중 한 명이다. 그 밴드는 학교 축제에서 미니 콘서트를 열 예정이고, 테리가 콘서트 포스터를 만드는 것을 담당하고 있다. 그는 포스터를 완성하자 그것을 밴드 멤버들에게 보여준다. 포스터에는 모든 필수적인 정보가 있기는 하지만 글자 크기가 너무 작아서 읽기가 어렵다. 에이미는 테리가 글자체의 크기를 더 큰 것으로 바꾸면 알아차리기 더 쉬울 수 있다고 생각한다. 그래서 에이미는 테리가 포스터에 있는 글자의 크기를 키워야 한다고 제안하고 싶어 한다. 이 상황에서, 에이미가 테리에게 할 말로 가장 적절한 것은 무엇인가?

STEP ❶·❷ Listen & Choose

본문 p.140

01 ⓐ **02** ⓒ **03** ⓒ **04** ⓑ **05** ⓐ **06** ⓒ **07** ⓑ **08** ⓑ **09** ⓐ **10** ⓐ

01 ⓐ

해설 결시를 원하지 않아서 대안이 있는지 여쭤보기로 했으므로 다른 날에 시험을 볼 수 있을지 묻는 말이 가장 적절하다.
ⓐ 제가 다른 날에 시험을 보는 게 가능할까요?
ⓑ 제가 시험에서 뭘 잘못했는지 말씀해주시겠어요?
ⓒ 저희 팀이 댄스 대회에서 더 잘했으면 좋을 텐데요.

M Yumi is a member of her college dance team. Her team is scheduled to participate in the city dance competition. However, there is a midterm exam on the day of the competition. She does not want to miss the exam. Thus, she decides to ask her professor if there are any alternatives. In this situation, what would Yumi most likely say to her professor?

남 유미는 자신이 다니는 대학의 댄스 팀 일원이다. 그녀의 댄스 팀은 시(市) 댄스 대회에 참가할 예정이다. 그러나 대회 당일에 중간고사가 있다. 그녀는 그 시험을 놓치는 것을 원하지 않는다. 그래서 그녀는 대안이 있는지 교수님께 여쭤보기로 한다. 이 상황에서, 유미가 교수님에게 할 말로 가장 적절한 것은 무엇인가?

어휘 be scheduled to-v v할 예
정이다

participate in ~에 참가하다
competition 대회; 경쟁
alternative 대안, 선택 가능한 것

02 ⓒ

해설 허리가 아픈 브라이언에게 요
가를 시작하라고 제안하고 싶어 하
므로 요가를 해볼 것을 권하는 말이
가장 적절하다.

ⓐ 너는 방과 후에 더 연습해야 해.

ⓑ 너는 의사의 지시를 따를 필요가
있어.

ⓒ 허리 통증을 위해 요가를 해보는
게 어때?

어휘 upcoming 다가오는
[선택지 어휘] **instruction** ((주로 복
수형)) 지시

W Cathy and Brian are members of the same orchestra. Sitting for a long time preparing for the upcoming concert, Brian gets back pain. Cathy had the same problem last year, but her pain disappeared after starting yoga. Therefore, she wants to suggest to Brian that he start yoga. In this situation, what would Cathy most likely say to Brian?

여 캐시와 브라이언은 같은 오케스트라의 단원이다. 다가오는 콘서트를 준비하면서 오랜 시간 앉아있었기 때문에 브라이언은 허리가 아프다. 캐시는 작년에 같은 문제가 있었지만 그녀의 통증은 요가를 시작한 후로 사라졌다. 그래서 그녀는 브라이언에게 요가를 시작하라고 제안하고 싶어 한다. 이 상황에서, 캐시가 브라이언에게 할 말로 가장 적절한 것은 무엇인가?

03 ⓒ

해설 프로젝트를 도와준 제시카에
게 저녁을 사주려고 하므로 자신이
대접하겠다는 말이 가장 적절하다.

ⓐ 계산서에 잘못된 것이 있어.

ⓑ 오늘은 각자 내자.

ⓒ 이번에는 내가 대접할게.

어휘 co-worker 동료
bill 계산서, 청구서; 지폐; 법안
[선택지 어휘] **separately** 각자, 따로
따로

treat 대접하다, 한턱내다; 다루다

M When Tony was given a new project by his manager, his co-worker Jessica helped him with it. Today he wants to buy Jessica a nice dinner, so he takes her to a famous restaurant in town. After dinner, Jessica is about to pay the bill, but Tony doesn't want her to. In this situation, what would Tony most likely say to Jessica?

남 토니가 관리자에게 새 프로젝트를 받았을 때, 동료인 제시카가 그 프로젝트를 도와주었다. 오늘 그는 제시카에게 근사한 저녁을 사주고 싶어서, 시내에 있는 유명한 레스토랑에 그녀를 데리고 간다. 식사 후, 제시카가 막 계산하려고 하지만 토니는 그녀가 계산하길 원하지 않는다. 이 상황에서, 토니가 제시카에게 할 말로 가장 적절한 것은 무엇인가?

04 ⓑ

해설 메리에게 리드 싱어가 되어달
라고 말하고 싶어 하므로 메리가 리
드 싱어가 되어야 한다고 생각한다
는 말이 가장 적절하다.

ⓐ 이번에는 다른 노래를 연주하자.

ⓑ 나는 네가 우리의 리드 싱어가 되
어야 한다고 생각해.

ⓒ 우리가 연습이 더 필요하다고 생
각하지 않니?

어휘 amazed 놀란
[선택지 어휘] **lead singer** 리드 싱어
[보컬]

W Jasper and Mary are trying to form a rock band. Since they don't have a singer yet, the guitarist Mary sings instead in their first practice. Hearing her sing, everyone is amazed that she has a perfect voice for rock music! So, Jasper wants to tell Mary to be the lead singer for their band. In this situation, what would Jasper most likely say to Mary?

여 재스퍼와 메리는 록 밴드를 만들려고 하고 있다. 그들은 노래할 사람이 아직 없기 때문에, 첫 연습에서 기타리스트인 메리가 대신 노래한다. 그녀가 노래하는 것을 듣자 모두는 그녀가 록 음악에 완벽한 목소리를 가졌다는 것에 놀란다! 그래서 재스퍼는 메리에게 밴드의 리드 싱어가 되어달라고 말하고 싶어 한다. 이 상황에서, 재스퍼가 메리에게 할 말로 가장 적절한 것은 무엇인가?

05 ⓐ

해설 이사 가서도 계속 긴밀한 연락
을 할 것을 제안하고 싶어 하므로 헤
어지더라도 연락하고 지내자는 말이
가장 적절하다.

M Alex and Emma have been close friends since they were children. One day, Alex tells Emma that his family is going to move to another city. But he really

남 알렉스와 엠마는 어렸을 때부터 친한 친구였다. 어느 날, 알렉스는 엠마에게 그의 가족이 다른 도시로 이사 갈 것이라고 말한다. 그러나 그는 그녀

ⓐ 헤어지더라도 연락하고 지내자.
ⓑ 새 도시에 익숙해지길 바라.
ⓒ 너의 친절한 말에 깊이 감명 받았어.

어휘 remain 계속 ~이다
in close touch (with) (~와) 긴밀한
연락을 하는
[선택지 어휘] get used to ~에 익숙
해지다

hopes to keep his friendship with her. So, Alex wants to suggest that they remain in close touch even after he leaves the city. In this situation, what would Alex most likely say to Emma?

와의 우정을 지키길 매우 바란다. 그래서 알렉스는 그가 도시를 떠난 후에도 계속 긴밀한 연락을 할 것을 제안하고 싶어 한다. 이 상황에서, 알렉스가 엠마에게 할 말로 가장 적절한 것은 무엇인가?

---

06 ⓒ

해설 바지를 반품하고 돈을 돌려받기로 결정했으므로 반송하고 환불받고 싶다는 말이 가장 적절하다.
ⓐ 다른 바지로 교환할 수 있나요?
ⓑ 내일까지 바지를 배송해줄 수 있을까요?
ⓒ 바지를 반송하고 환불받고 싶어요.

어휘 uncomfortable 불편한
[선택지 어휘] get a refund 환불받다

W Olivia ordered a pair of pants from an online shopping mall. When they are delivered, she finds out that the pants are uncomfortable. So, she decides to call the customer service center to return the pants and get her money back. In this situation, what would Olivia most likely say to the customer service employee?

여 올리비아는 온라인 쇼핑몰에서 바지 한 벌을 주문했다. 그것이 배송되자 그녀는 바지가 불편하다는 것을 알게 된다. 그래서 그녀는 고객 서비스 센터에 전화해서 바지를 반품하고 돈을 돌려받기로 결정한다. 이 상황에서, 올리비아가 고객 서비스 직원에게 할 말로 가장 적절한 것은 무엇인가?

---

07 ⓑ

해설 표지판을 읽는 것을 돕고 싶어 하므로 도움이 필요한지와 목적지를 묻는 말이 가장 적절하다.
ⓐ 저를 꼭 붙잡고 계세요. 제가 안내해 드릴게요.
ⓑ 도와드릴까요? 어디로 가고 싶으세요?
ⓒ 목적지가 어디세요? 제가 거기까지 태워다 드릴 수 있어요.

어휘 have difficulty (in) v-ing
v하는 데 어려움을 겪다
[선택지 어휘] hold on to ~을 꼭 잡다
destination 목적지, 도착지

M While Sophia is waiting for the bus, she sees an old man at the bus stop. He's looking at the information on the bus stop sign. He seems to be having difficulty reading the sign. So, she wants to help him read it. In this situation, what would Sophia most likely say to the old man?

남 소피아가 버스를 기다리는 동안, 버스 정류장에 있는 어떤 노인이 보인다. 그는 버스 정류장 표지판의 정보를 보고 있다. 그는 표지판을 읽는 데 어려움을 겪고 있는 것처럼 보인다. 그래서 그녀는 그가 그것을 읽는 것을 돕고 싶어 한다. 이 상황에서, 소피아가 노인에게 할 말로 가장 적절한 것은 무엇인가?

---

08 ⓑ

해설 케빈이 완전히 회복되지 않았다고 생각해서 외출을 막고 싶어 하므로 외출을 금지하는 말이 가장 적절하다.
ⓐ 네가 경주에서 우승해 아주 자랑스럽구나.
ⓑ 완전히 낫기 전에는 외출하면 안돼.
ⓒ 운동회에 네 친구들을 초대하는 게 어떠니?

어휘 be supposed to-v v하기로 되어 있다
representative 대표(자), 대리인
sprain (발목 등을) 접질리다, 삐다
recover (건강을) 회복하다; 되찾다
[선택지 어휘] heal 낫게 하다, 치유하다

W Kevin is supposed to run as the class representative on the school sports day. But he sprained his ankle, so he needed to be careful for a couple of weeks. One week later, Kevin decides to go practice for the race. However, his mother thinks he is not fully recovered yet and wants to stop him. In this situation, what would Kevin's mother most likely say to Kevin?

여 케빈은 학교 운동회에서 반 대표로 달리기를 하기로 되어 있다. 하지만 그는 발목을 접질려서 몇 주 동안 조심해야 했다. 일주일 후 케빈은 달리기 연습을 가기로 한다. 그러나 그의 어머니는 그가 아직 완전히 회복되지 않았다고 생각해서 그를 막고 싶어 한다. 이 상황에서, 케빈의 어머니가 케빈에게 할 말로 가장 적절한 것은 무엇인가?

09 ⓐ

해설 해당 캠프 기간 동안 가족 휴가가 있어서 다른 캠프를 찾아보는 것을 제안하고 싶어 하므로 다른 날짜에 진행하는 캠프를 찾아보자고 제안하는 말이 가장 적절하다.

ⓐ 다른 날짜에 하는 캠프를 찾아보는 게 어때?

ⓑ 너는 먼저 이 전단지에 있는 캠프 날짜를 확인해야 해.

ⓒ 너는 캠프에 참가하려면 부모님의 허락이 필요해.

어휘 flyer 전단지
[선택지 어휘] permission 허락

M Today Clara gets a flyer for an interesting camp and asks Becky to sign up for the camp together. However, Becky has a family vacation during that period. So, Becky wants to suggest to Clara that they look for another camp. In this situation, what would Becky most likely say to Clara?

남 오늘 클라라는 흥미로운 캠프 전단지를 받고 베키에게 함께 캠프에 등록하자고 한다. 그러나 베키는 그 기간 동안 가족 휴가가 있다. 그래서 베키는 클라라에게 다른 캠프를 찾아보는 것을 제안하고 싶어 한다. 이 상황에서, 베키가 클라라에게 할 말로 가장 적절한 것은 무엇인가?

10 ⓐ

해설 산책로로 걸어 올라가기 위해 차를 세워 달라고 부탁하고 싶어 하므로 여기서 내려달라는 말이 가장 적절하다.

ⓐ 여기서 내릴 수 있을까요?

ⓑ 시장까지 가는 데 시간이 얼마나 걸리나요?

ⓒ 서울에서 갈 만한 곳을 추천해주실래요?

어휘 view 경치, 전망; 견해
entire 전체의
trail 오솔길, 산길; 자국, 흔적
feel like v-ing v하고 싶다
on foot 걸어서
pull over (차를) 한쪽으로 대다
[선택지 어휘] let off (차에서) ~을 내려주다

W Amy is visiting Seoul for the first time. Today, she wants to go to a place where she can see a view of the entire city. She takes a taxi to go to N Seoul Tower. As the taxi gets near the destination, she sees some people walking along a beautiful trail leading up to the tower. She suddenly feels like following the trail on foot. So, she wants to ask the driver to pull over. In this situation, what would Amy most likely say to the taxi driver?

여 에이미는 서울을 처음으로 방문하는 중이다. 오늘, 그녀는 도시 전경을 볼 수 있는 장소에 가고 싶다. 그녀는 택시를 타고 N 서울타워로 간다. 택시가 목적지에 가까워지자 그녀는 몇몇 사람들이 타워로 이어지는 아름다운 산책로를 따라 걷고 있는 것을 본다. 그녀는 갑자기 산책로를 걸어서 가고 싶다. 그래서 그녀는 택시 운전사에게 차를 세워 달라고 부탁하고 싶어 한다. 이 상황에서, 에이미가 택시 운전사에게 할 말로 가장 적절한 것은 무엇인가?

STEP ③·④ Listen & Answer

본문 p.144

01 ⑤ **02** ⑤ **03** ④ **04** ④ **05** ③ **06** ③ **07** ⑤ **08** ④ **09** ④ **10** ③

01 ⑤

해설 음식이 잘못 제공되었으므로 손님의 주문대로 스테이크를 더 익혀달라고 부탁하는 말이 가장 적절하다.

① 이렇게 멋진 경험을 주셔서 감사해요.

② 이 시간에는 가능한 것이 없습니다.

③ 완전히 익힌 스테이크를 주문하고 싶어요. 너무 늦었나요?

④ 고객 한 분이 주문을 바꾸고 싶어 해요. 괜찮나요?

⑤ 죄송해요. 제가 이 주문을 잘못 받았어요. 더 익혀 주시겠어요?

M Michael started a new job as a waiter in a steak restaurant today. His first night as a waiter is almost over. It is nearly 10 o'clock and the last table has just been served. Michael is walking around the dining room and a customer calls him over. The customer says the steak which Michael brought her is rare, but she had ordered it well-done. So, Michael says sorry and takes the steak off the table and walks into the kitchen. He wants to ask the chef to cook it to well-done. In this situation, what would Michael most likely say to the chef?

남 마이클은 오늘 스테이크 레스토랑에서 웨이터로 새 일을 시작했다. 웨이터로서 첫날 밤이 거의 끝나간다. 10시가 거의 다 되었고, 마지막 테이블에 식사가 방금 제공되었다. 마이클이 식당을 돌아다니고 있는데 한 손님이 그를 부른다. 그 손님은 마이클이 자신에게 가져다준 스테이크가 덜 익었는데, 자신은 완전히 익힌 것을 주문했다고 말한다. 그래서 마이클은 죄송하다고 하며 그 스테이크를 테이블에서 집어 들고 주방으로 걸어 들어간다. 그는 요리사에게 그것을 완전히 익힌 것으로 조리해 달라고 부탁하고 싶다. 이 상황에서, 마이클이 요리사에게 할 말로 가장 적절한 것은 무엇인가?

어휘 *rare* (고기가) 덜 익은
well-done (고기가) 완전히 익은

---

02 ⑤

해설 대학에서 컴퓨터 공학을 공부하길 원하는 존에게 학업을 소홀히 하지 않도록 설득하고 싶어 하므로 공부를 더 열심히 해야 한다는 말이 가장 적절하다.

① 걱정하지 마. 연습이 완벽함을 만드는 거야.

② 그건 전적으로 너에게 달렸어. 난 전혀 신경 쓰지 않아.

③ 필요한 것이 있다면, 망설이지 말고 물어보렴.

④ 넌 지금까지 잘 해내고 있구나. 네가 무척 자랑스러워.

⑤ 나중에 원하는 것을 공부하기 위해 넌 더 열심히 해야 해.

어휘 **computer science** 컴퓨터 공학

department 학과; 부서

neglect 소홀히 하다; 무시하다

[선택지 어휘] **entirely** 전적으로, 완전히

hesitate 망설이다, 주저하다

W John is a high-school student. He took a math exam last week but didn't do very well. Since his math grade was bad, his math teacher, Ms. Thompson, asks him what's going on with him these days. John says he couldn't study much because he is a member of the school dance club and was very busy practicing for a contest before the test. She asks John what he wants to do after high school. John says he wants to study computer science in college. Ms. Thompson knows that he needs a high grade in math to get into the computer science department. So, Ms. Thompson wants to persuade John not to neglect his studies. In this situation, what would Ms. Thompson most likely say to John?

여 존은 고등학생이다. 그는 지난주에 수학 시험을 보았는데 별로 잘 보지 못했다. 그의 수학 성적이 나빠서, 수학 교사인 톰슨 선생님이 그에게 요즘 무슨 일이 있는지 묻는다. 존은 그가 교내 댄스 동아리의 구성원이고 시험 전에 공연을 위해 연습하느라 무척 바빠서 공부를 많이 할 수 없었다고 말한다. 선생님은 존에게 고등학교 졸업 후 무엇을 하고 싶은지 묻는다. 존은 대학에서 컴퓨터 공학을 공부하고 싶다고 말한다. 톰슨 선생님은 컴퓨터 공학과에 들어가려면 그에게 높은 수학 성적이 필요하다는 것을 안다. 그래서 톰슨 선생님은 존이 학업을 소홀히 하지 않도록 설득하고 싶어 한다. 이 상황에서, 톰슨 선생님이 존에게 할 말로 가장 적절한 것은 무엇인가?

---

03 ④

해설 의심한 것에 대해 사과하고 싶어 하므로 믿었어야 했다며 사과하는 말이 가장 적절하다.

① 미안하지만 그가 누구인지 너에게 알려줄 수 없어.

② 너는 마지막으로 남은 우유를 언제 마셨니?

③ 내가 우유를 살 차례라는 걸 잊어버렸어.

④ 정말 미안해, 너를 믿었어야 했는데.

⑤ 다시는 그런 일이 없을 거라고 네가 약속했잖아.

어휘 **belong to** ~ 소유이다; ~에 속하다

insist (that) (~라고) 주장하다

doubt 의심하다

[선택지 어휘] **A's turn to-v** A가 v할 차례

M David and Mark are roommates. Last week, Mark ate a sandwich that belonged to David. When David talked to Mark about this, Mark promised that it wouldn't happen again. However, this morning David finds that the milk he bought yesterday is empty. David asks Mark if he finished it, but Mark insists that it wasn't him. He says that actually one of David's friends drank the milk. David doesn't believe him and leaves angrily. A few hours later, David runs into that friend and learns that Mark was telling the truth. So David wants to apologize to Mark for doubting him. In this situation, what would David most likely say to Mark?

남 데이비드와 마크는 룸메이트이다. 지난주, 마크는 데이비드 것인 샌드위치를 먹었다. 데이비드가 이에 관해 마크에게 이야기했을 때, 마크는 다시는 그런 일이 없을 거라고 약속했다. 그러나 오늘 아침 데이비드는 어제 산 우유가 비어 있는 것을 발견한다. 데이비드는 마크에게 우유를 다 마셨냐고 물어보지만, 마크는 자신이 그런 게 아니라고 주장한다. 그는 실은 데이비드의 친구들 중 한 명이 우유를 마셨다고 말한다. 데이비드는 그를 믿지 않고 화내며 자리를 떠난다. 몇 시간 후, 데이비드는 그 친구와 마주쳐서 마크가 사실을 말하고 있었던 것임을 알게 된다. 그래서 데이비드는 마크에게 의심한 것에 대해 사과하고 싶어 한다. 이 상황에서, 데이비드가 마크에게 할 말로 가장 적절한 것은 무엇인가?

---

04 ④

해설 좋아하는 재즈곡을 듣고, 비슷한 재즈곡들을 추천해줄 수 있는지 알고 싶어 하므로, 비슷한 다른 재즈곡들을 아는지 물어보는 말이 가장 적절하다.

W Theresa and Hena are sisters. While Hena enjoys listening to jazz music, Theresa doesn't like it much. She considers jazz too complicated. One day, Theresa hears a jazz song at a coffee shop while waiting for a friend. Unlike the jazz songs she has heard before, she finds the song calm and relaxing.

여 테레사와 헤나는 자매이다. 헤나는 재즈 음악을 듣는 것을 즐기는 반면, 테레사는 별로 좋아하지 않는다. 그녀는 재즈 음악이 너무 복잡하다고 생각한다. 어느 날, 테레사는 친구를 기다리면서 커피숍에서 어떤 재즈곡을 듣는다. 그녀는 자신이 전에 들어봤던 재즈곡들과 달리 그 곡이 차분하

① 소리를 좀 줄여줄 수 있니?
② 이 곡 제목을 찾는 것을 도와줘.
③ 내가 재즈 클럽에 가입할 방법이 있을까?
④ 이것과 비슷한 다른 재즈곡들을 아니?
⑤ 나와 함께 재즈 콘서트에 갈래?

어휘 complicated 복잡한
relaxing 편안한, 느긋한

After arriving home, she listens to the song again with Hena. Hena says it is one of her favorite jazz songs, too. Now, Theresa wants to know if Hena can recommend any similar jazz songs. In this situation, what would Theresa most likely say to Hena?

고 편안하다고 생각한다. 집에 도착한 후, 그녀는 그 곡을 헤나와 함께 다시 듣는다. 헤나는 그것이 자신도 가장 좋아하는 재즈곡들 중 하나라고 말한다. 이제, 테레사는 헤나가 비슷한 재즈곡들을 추천해줄 수 있는지 알고 싶어 한다. 이 상황에서, 테레사가 헤나에게 할 말로 가장 적절한 것은 무엇인가?

---

05 ③

해설 가게에서 실수했다고 생각하며 찰리가 바로잡기를 원하므로 돌아가서 거스름돈을 잘못 줬는지 알아보라는 말이 가장 적절하다.
① 우유 사는 걸 잊었네. 가서 좀 사다 줄래?
② 고맙다, 찰리! 거스름돈은 가져도 돼!
③ 돌아가서 가게에서 실수하지 않으셨는지 여쭤봄.
④ 그 물품들은 어제까지 세일 중이었어.
⑤ 왜 그렇게 돈을 많이 썼니?

어휘 emphasize 강조하다
tolerate 너그럽게 봐주다; 참다
strict 엄격한
when it comes to ~에 관해서라면
moral 도덕(상)의
errand 심부름

M Marie, the mother of two teenage boys, has always emphasized the importance of honesty to her sons. She absolutely will not tolerate lying or stealing and has taught these values to her children since they were little boys. She's a loving and kind mother, but very strict when it comes to moral issues. One day she gave Charlie, her youngest son, 20 dollars to go on a shopping errand for her. She knows that the items she needs — milk, butter, eggs, flour, and salt — cost around 15 dollars. Charlie comes back from the shop and hands his mom 10 dollars in change, which is a lot more than she expected. She thinks the cashier made a mistake and wants Charlie to make it right. In this situation, what would Charlie's mother most likely say to Charlie?

남 두 십 대 소년의 어머니인 마리는 아들들에게 정직의 중요성을 항상 강조해왔다. 그녀는 거짓말이나 도둑질을 절대 너그럽게 봐주지 않을 것이며 어렸을 때부터 아이들에게 이러한 가치를 가르쳐왔다. 그녀는 사랑이 많고 다정한 어머니이지만, 도덕적인 문제에 관해서라면 매우 엄격하다. 어느 날 그녀는 막내아들인 찰리에게 20달러를 주면서 장보기 심부름을 보냈다. 그녀는 필요한 물건인 우유, 버터, 달걀, 밀가루와 소금의 가격이 약 15달러라는 것을 알고 있다. 찰리는 가게에서 돌아와 엄마에게 거스름돈으로 10달러를 건네는데, 이것은 그녀가 예상했던 것보다 훨씬 많은 돈이다. 그녀는 계산원이 실수를 했다고 생각하고 찰리가 이를 바로잡길 원한다. 이 상황에서, 찰리의 어머니가 찰리에게 할 말로 가장 적절한 것은 무엇인가?

---

06 ③

해설 가게 방침상 불가능한데도 이번에만 교환을 해주기로 결정했으므로 이번만 예외라고 당부하는 말이 가장 적절하다.
① 환불받도록 도울 수 있어서 기쁩니다.
② 죄송합니다. 방침을 위반할 수 없습니다.
③ 알겠습니다. 이번 한 번만 교환하게 해드릴게요.
④ 고맙습니다. 생각을 바꿔주셔서 감사해요.
⑤ 억지를 부리시는군요. 제가 도와드릴 수 있는 것은 없습니다.

어휘 policy 방침, 정책
pleading 애원; 변론, 항변
[선택지 어휘] violate 위반하다, 어기다
unreasonable 불합리한

W Last week Susan received a music CD by the singer MOA as a birthday present from her brother. She, unfortunately, already had the same one. Today she takes the CD to the music store where her brother bought it. She doesn't have the receipt. But she hopes the store will let her exchange it for one by the Lee Lee Band. After entering the store, she explains the situation to the store manager, Ben. He says the store's policy is no exchanges or refunds without a receipt. However, after a lot of pleading, Ben finally decides to accept her request just this time. In this situation, what would Ben most likely say to Susan?

여 지난주 수잔은 오빠에게 생일 선물로 가수 MOA의 음악 CD를 받았다. 안타깝게도 그녀는 같은 것을 이미 가지고 있었다. 오늘 그녀는 자신의 오빠가 CD를 샀던 음반 가게로 그것을 가져간다. 그녀는 영수증이 없다. 그러나 그녀는 가게에서 그것을 리리밴드의 CD로 바꿔주기를 바란다. 가게에 들어가서 그녀는 가게 매니저인 벤에게 상황을 설명한다. 그는 가게 방침 상 영수증이 없으면 교환이나 환불이 안 된다고 말한다. 하지만 여러 차례 부탁하자 벤은 결국 이번에만 그녀의 요청을 들어주기로 결정한다. 이 상황에서, 벤이 수잔에게 할 말로 가장 적절한 것은 무엇인가?

07 ⑤

해설 아무것도 하지 않는 스티브의 태도를 더는 간과할 수 없다고 말하기로 결심했으므로 그것을 지적하는 말이 가장 적절하다.

① 너는 왜 미리 내 도움을 요청하지 않았니?

② 우리는 프로젝트를 위해 다음에는 무엇을 해야 하지?

③ 이 프로젝트를 너와 함께 하게 되어 기뻐.

④ 네가 매우 아팠다고 들었어. 괜찮은 거야?

⑤ 더 이상은 참을 수 없어. 넌 네 몫을 해야 해!

어휘 **mind** 신경 쓰다; 마음에 꺼리다
overlook (잘못된 것을) 간과하다
careless 무심한; 부주의한
attitude 태도, 자세

M Lucy is working on an important group project with one of her classmates, Steven. Lucy has always been working harder than Steven, and recently she has discovered that Steven hardly cares about the project. Because they are friends, Lucy hasn't minded much. But when Lucy was sick last weekend, she asked Steven to do a few things for the project by Monday, and Steven promised that he would. However, when Monday comes, Lucy finds that nothing has been done. Now, Lucy decides to tell Steven that she can't overlook his careless attitude anymore. In this situation, what would Lucy most likely say to Steven?

남 루시는 반 친구 중 한 명인 스티븐과 함께 중요한 그룹 프로젝트를 진행하고 있다. 루시는 항상 스티븐보다 더 열심히 해왔고, 최근에 스티븐이 프로젝트에 거의 신경 쓰지 않는다는 것을 알게 되었다. 그들은 친구이기 때문에, 루시는 별로 개의치 않아왔다. 하지만 루시가 지난 주말에 아팠을 때, 그녀는 스티븐에게 프로젝트를 위해 몇 가지 일을 월요일까지 해달라고 부탁했고, 스티븐은 그러겠다고 약속했다. 그러나 월요일이 되었을 때 루시는 아무 일도 완성되지 않았다는 것을 알게 된다. 이제 루시는 스티븐의 무심한 태도를 더는 간과할 수 없다고 그에게 말하기로 결심한다. 이 상황에서, 루시가 스티븐에게 할 말로 가장 적절한 것은 무엇인가?

08 ④

해설 길거리 음식 축제에 가는 것으로 주말 계획을 바꾸자고 제안하고 싶어 하므로 축제에 가자는 말이 가장 적절하다.

① 우리 주말 동안 쉬는 게 좋겠어.

② 다음 주에 더 많은 고궁에 방문하는 게 어때?

③ 우리의 주말 계획을 잊지 말도록 해.

④ 우리 쇼핑은 생략하고 축제에 가는 게 어때?

⑤ 주말에 여러 축제가 있다고 들었어.

어휘 **generally** 보통, 대개
had better+동사원형 ~하는 게 낫다
[선택지 어휘] **be sure to-v** 꼭[반드시] v하다
skip 생략하다, 건너뛰다

W Linda and Beth are cousins, and they are on vacation together for the first time. They have similar interests and generally enjoy the same activities. This weekend they are planning to visit some palaces and do some shopping downtown. While surfing the Internet, Linda finds an advertisement for a street food festival. The festival will be held this weekend. She thinks that it will be something that they both would enjoy. So, Linda wants to suggest to Beth that they change their plans for the weekend. In this situation, what would Linda most likely say to Beth?

여 린다와 베스는 사촌지간으로, 처음으로 함께 휴가 중이다. 그들은 비슷한 관심사를 가지고 있으며 보통 같은 활동을 즐긴다. 이번 주말에 그들은 몇몇 고궁에 방문하고 시내에서 쇼핑을 좀 할 계획이다. 인터넷 서핑을 하다가 린다는 길거리 음식 축제 광고를 발견한다. 그 축제는 이번 주말에 열린다. 그녀는 그것이 그들 둘 다 즐길 거라고 생각한다. 그래서 린다는 주말 계획을 바꾸자고 베스에게 제안하고 싶다. 이 상황에서, 린다가 베스에게 할 말로 가장 적절한 것은 무엇인가?

09 ④

해설 가구점의 배송 서비스는 추가 요금을 내야 한다고 안내하는 말이 가장 적절하다.

① 죄송합니다만, 일요일 배송은 불가합니다.

② 맞습니다. 저희는 24시간 이내에 배달해드릴 것을 약속합니다.

③ 손님의 가구는 명시된 날짜에 배송될 것입니다.

④ 네, 하지만 배송료를 추가로 내셔야 합니다.

⑤ 가격은 세금을 포함하고 있어서 추가 요금이 붙지 않습니다.

M Alex works for a furniture store. Today, one woman visits the store to buy a table. She originally wants to buy only a table, but when she sees a beautiful antique dresser, she wants to buy it, too. She asks Alex about the price of the dresser. Alex says that there is a 10% off sale on all furniture. She decides to buy the dresser and the table. After paying for her things, she tries carrying them on her own. But her car is too small and they're too heavy to carry alone. She asks Alex if the store can deliver them to her house. The store's delivery service is available at an additional charge. So, Alex wants to explain to her that there is a delivery fee. In this situation, what would Alex most likely say to the customer?

남 알렉스는 가구점에서 일한다. 오늘, 한 여자가 탁자를 사기 위해 상점에 방문한다. 처음에 그녀는 탁자만 사고 싶었지만 예쁘고 고풍스러운 서랍장을 보자 그것도 사고 싶어 한다. 그녀는 알렉스에게 서랍장의 가격을 묻는다. 알렉스는 모든 가구가 10% 할인 판매 중이라고 말한다. 그녀는 서랍장과 탁자를 사기로 결정한다. 물건 값을 지불한 후에, 그녀는 혼자 힘으로 그것들을 옮겨 보려고 한다. 그러나 그녀의 차는 너무 작고 그것들은 혼자서 옮기기에 너무 무겁다. 그녀는 알렉스에게 상점에서 물건들을 그녀의 집으로 배달해줄 수 있는지 묻는다. 상점의 배달 서비스는 추가 요금을 내야 이용할 수 있다. 그래서 알렉스는 배달료가

있다고 그녀에게 설명하고 싶어 한다. 이 상황에서, 알렉스가 손님에게 할 말로 가장 적절한 것은 무엇인가?

---

10 ③

해설 자리를 조금 옮겨줄 수 있는지 물어보기로 했으므로 한 자리 옮겨 달라고 부탁할 것이다.

① 이 자리 주인 있습니까?
② 제가 앉아도 괜찮겠습니까?
③ 한 자리 옮겨주시는 게 가능할까요?
④ 곧 지하철에서 내리실 건가요?
⑤ 당신도 예술 센터에서 하는 전시회에 가시는 건가요?

어휘 head to ~로 향하다
exhibition 전시(회)
review 평론, 서평; 검토

W Dick and Jane have just gotten on the subway. They are heading to the Arts Center downtown to see a new exhibition. They are searching for a seat on the subway. On one of the benches there are two empty seats. But the two empty seats are not together. A man is sitting between the two empty seats. They stand in front of the man for a moment. The man is reading a review of the new exhibition at the Arts Center in the newspaper. Dick and Jane really want to sit together, so Dick decides to ask the man if he could move aside a bit. In this situation, what would Dick most likely say to the man?

여 딕과 제인은 방금 지하철을 탔다. 그들은 새 전시회를 보러 시내에 있는 예술 센터로 향하는 중이다. 그들은 지하철에서 자리를 찾고 있다. 긴 의자 중 하나에 두 개의 빈자리가 있다. 그러나 그 빈자리 두 개는 같이 붙어 있지 않다. 한 남자가 두 빈자리 사이에 앉아 있다. 둘은 그 남자 앞에 잠시 서 있다. 그 남자는 신문에서 예술 센터의 새 전시회에 관한 평론을 읽고 있다. 딕과 제인은 정말 함께 앉고 싶어서 딕은 그 남자에게 자리를 조금 옮겨줄 수 있는지 물어보기로 한다. 이 상황에서, 딕이 그 남자에게 할 말로 가장 적절한 것은 무엇인가?

어휘 antique 고풍스러운; 골동의
dresser 서랍장
additional 추가의
[선택지 어휘] specified 명시된

실전 모의고사 1회

본문 p.152

01 ⑤	02 ⑤	03 ②	04 ⑤	05 ①	06 ④	07 ④	08 ③	09 ②	10 ②
11 ③	12 ②	13 ③	14 ③	15 ③	16 ③	17 ④			

01 ⑤

해설 일부 주차장 폐쇄에 따른 조치로 새 주차 공간을 안내하고 대중교통 이용을 권장하는 내용이다.

어휘 previously 사전에, 미리
construction 건설, 건축; 구조
reserve (자리 등을) 따로 잡아 두다; 예약하다
advise A to-v A가 v하도록 권고[충고]하다
encourage A to-v A가 v하도록 권장[장려]하다
inconvenience 불편
make good use of ~을 유용하게 이용하다

W Attention, please. This is Ellie Clark from the administration office. As it was previously announced, the north parking lot will be closed from November due to the construction of the new library. Those of you who have reserved spaces in the north parking lot will be given new spaces in the east parking lot. Anyone who is not given a new space is advised to park off campus. Finally, due to the limited number of parking spaces, we encourage you to ride the bus or subway. We apologize for the inconvenience and hope that everyone will make good use of the new library.

여 주목해주시길 부탁드립니다. 저는 행정실의 엘리 클락입니다. 사전에 안내된 것과 같이, 새 도서관 건립으로 인해 북쪽 주차장이 11월부터 폐쇄될 것입니다. 북쪽 주차장에 공간을 보유하신 분들은 동쪽 주차장에 새로운 공간을 배정받으실 것입니다. 새 공간을 받지 못한 모든 분은 캠퍼스 밖에 주차하시길 권고합니다. 마지막으로, 한정된 주차 공간 수로 인해, 저희는 여러분께 버스나 지하철을 이용하시길 권장합니다. 불편을 끼쳐 죄송하며 모두 새 도서관을 잘 이용하시길 바랍니다.

02 ⑤

해설 남자는 원어로만 진행되는 수업에 참여하면 억지로라도 그 언어를 말하게 되므로 말하기 능력 향상에 도움이 된다고 말하고 있다.

어휘 entirely 완전히, 전부
assignment 과제, 임무
lecture 강의
force (어쩔 수 없이) ~하게 만들다
sign up for ~을 신청하다

W Peter, you're taking Spanish next semester, right?
M Yes, I'm taking it from Ms. Garcia.
W And the class will be taught entirely in Spanish?
M Yes, all assignments, discussions, and lectures are entirely in Spanish. Why?
W I'm trying to decide between that class and the one taught in English by Mr. Berk.
M If you want to improve your speaking ability, Ms. Garcia's class will be more helpful than Mr. Berk's.
W Maybe you're right. I really just want to reach a conversational level for traveling.
M Me, too. That's why I chose Ms. Garcia. I want to be forced to speak in Spanish as much as possible. If that sounds good, you should also take her class.
W Okay, I think I'll sign up for her class. Thanks.

여 피터, 너 다음 학기에 스페인어 수업 들을 거지?
남 응, 가르시아 선생님의 수업을 들을 거야.
여 그리고 그 수업은 전부 스페인어로만 배우는 거니?
남 응, 모든 과제, 토론, 강의 전부 스페인어로 해. 왜?
여 그 수업과 버크 선생님께서 영어로 가르치시는 수업 중에 결정하려고 하는 중이거든.
남 말하기 능력을 향상하고 싶다면, 가르시아 교수님의 수업이 버크 선생님 것보다 더 도움이 될 거야.
여 네 말이 맞는 것 같아. 난 정말 여행에 필요한 회화 수준에만 도달하고 싶어.
남 나도. 그게 내가 가르시아 선생님을 선택한 이유야. 난 억지로라도 가능한 한 많이 스페인어로 말하기를 원해. 그게 좋으면 너도 그분 수업을 듣도록 해.
여 그래, 그분 수업을 신청해야겠어. 고마워.

03 ②

해설 팩스를 보낸 비용을 방에 달아 달라고 하고 객실 번호를 말하는 것으로 보아 호텔 직원과 투숙객 사이의 대화임을 알 수 있다.

어휘 charge (외상으로) 달아 놓다; 청구하다; 요금
make an appointment 예약하다; 약속을 잡다

W Good afternoon. May I help you?
M Yes, please. Can you fax these documents for me?
W Sure. Where to?
M One to Shanghai, and the other one to London. Here are the numbers. Can you charge these to my room?
W What's your name and room number?
M Owen Brooks, Room 1512.

여 안녕하세요. 도와드릴까요?
남 네, 부탁드려요. 이 서류들을 팩스로 보내주실 수 있나요?
여 물론입니다. 어디로 보내십니까?
남 하나는 상하이로, 다른 하나는 런던으로요. 여기 번호요. 비용은 제 방에 달아주시겠어요?
여 성함과 객실 번호가 어떻게 되시죠?
남 오웬 브룩스이고 1512호실입니다.

fill out ~을 작성하다

W There isn't any charge. Because you are a VIP, they will be free.	여 지불하실 비용은 없으십니다. VIP이시기 때문에 무료입니다.
M That's great. <u>Are there any messages</u> for me?	남 잘됐네요. 저에게 온 메시지가 있나요?
W Yes, there's one. Here you are.	여 네, 하나 있습니다. 여기요.
M Thanks. And <u>can I make an appointment to use the meeting room</u> on Tuesday at 10 a.m.?	남 고맙습니다. 그리고 화요일 오전 10시에 회의실 사용을 예약할 수 있을까요?
W Yes, you can. Could you fill out this form please?	여 네, 가능합니다. 이 양식을 작성해 주시겠습니까?
M Sure.	남 물론이죠.

04 ⑤

해설 책을 보관할 공간이 더 필요해서 4단 책장이 아닌 5단 책장을 새로 놓았다고 했으므로 그림의 4단 책장이 이 대화의 내용과 일치하지 않는다.

어휘 **redecoration** 다시 꾸밈
study 서재
rug 깔개
tidy 깔끔한, 잘 정돈된
stripe-patterned 줄무늬의
bookcase 책장
space 공간
match 어울리다; 맞먹다

M Janice, how's the redecoration of your study going?
W It was just finished last week. Look at this picture, Eric.
M Wow, what a change! Look at the floor. There's no rug any more.
W Yeah, I think <u>it is tidier without a rug</u>. What do you think about the stripe-patterned walls?
M Hmm, well... I prefer how they were before. But I like the curtains. <u>The flowers on the curtains are lovely.</u>
W Me too. And I placed the sofa <u>under the window.</u> I love to read books there.
M Cool. By the way, is that <u>a new bookcase against the wall?</u> I remember there was a 4-shelf bookcase, not a 5-shelf one.
W You're right. I needed <u>more space to keep books.</u>
M Great. I think it matches your study quite well.

남 제니스, 서재를 다시 꾸미는 것은 어떻게 되고 있어?
여 그건 지난주에 막 끝났어. 이 사진을 봐, 에릭.
남 와, 확 바뀌었네! 바닥을 좀 봐. 이제는 깔개가 없어.
여 응, 난 깔개가 없는 게 더 깔끔하다고 생각해. 줄무늬 벽은 어떻게 생각해?
남 음, 글쎄… 난 이전 것이 더 좋아. 하지만 커튼은 마음에 들어. 커튼의 꽃들이 사랑스러워.
여 나도 그래. 그리고 나는 소파를 창문 밑에 뒀어. 나는 거기서 책 읽는 걸 좋아해.
남 멋지다. 그런데, 벽에 있는 것은 새 책장이야? 내가 기억하기에 5단 책장이 아니라 4단 책장이 있었거든.
여 맞아. 나는 책을 보관할 더 많은 공간이 필요했거든.
남 좋다. 내 생각에 책장이 네 서재에 꽤 잘 어울리는 것 같아.

05 ①

해설 남자가 기다릴 시간이 없어 택시를 타야겠다고 하자 여자가 택시를 불러주겠다고 했다.

어휘 **attendant** 안내원; 시중드는 사람
in a hurry 바쁜; 서둘러[급히]
van 화물차, 밴
wait around[about] (특별히 하는 일 없이) 그냥 기다리다

M Excuse me. Do you work here?
W I'm the parking attendant. How can I help you?
M I'm really in a hurry, but <u>my car is blocked behind a delivery van.</u>
W I'm sorry. I'm sure the driver <u>would be happy to move</u> if you ask him. I will come with you.
M I didn't see anyone with the van. Oh, I'm going to be late!
W Again, I'm very sorry. I will try to find the driver and <u>have him move the van</u> as soon as possible.
M I don't have time to wait around. Maybe I should take a taxi.
W I will call one for you. <u>It will only take a minute.</u>
M Would you? That would be great. Thanks so much.

남 실례합니다. 여기서 일하시나요?
여 저는 주차 관리원입니다. 무엇을 도와드릴까요?
남 제가 지금 아주 급한데, 제 차가 어떤 운송 화물차에 막혔어요.
여 죄송합니다. 그 운전자분께 요청하시면 분명 기꺼이 차를 빼주실 겁니다. 제가 함께 가겠습니다.
남 그 화물차에는 아무도 없었어요. 아, 저 이러다 늦겠어요!
여 다시 한 번, 정말 죄송합니다. 제가 운전자를 찾아서 그분이 가능한 한 빨리 화물차를 이동하시도록 해보겠습니다.
남 전 기다리고 있을 시간이 없어요. 택시를 타야 할까 봐요.
여 제가 택시를 불러 드리죠. 단 1분이면 됩니다.
남 그래 주시겠어요? 그래 주시면 좋겠군요. 정말 감사합니다.

06 ④

해설 컴퓨터 할인가 650달러, 회원 카드 발급비 20달러, 무선 마우스 50달러를 모두 합해 지불할 금액은 720달러이다.

W Can I help you find something?
M Yes, I'm looking for the computer from your advertisement.
W That's <u>a very popular choice</u> and a good decision. It's <u>$750</u> or <u>$650</u> with a membership card.

여 찾으시는 것을 도와드릴까요?
남 네, 광고에 나온 컴퓨터를 찾고 있어요.
여 그 제품은 아주 인기 있는 품목이고, 탁월한 선택이십니다. 그것은 750달러인데 회원 카드가 있으면 650달러입니다.

<table>
<tr><td>

어휘 membership 회원 자격, 회원임

enrollment fee 입회비

wired 유선의 (↔ wireless 무선의)

sure thing ((구어)) 물론이죠, 그럼요

</td><td>

M Well, I don't have a membership card. Can I get one today?

W Of course, but there is a one-time enrollment fee of $20.

M OK, and then I can get the discount, right?

W Yes.

M Oh, and I would like to purchase a mouse, too.

W Sure. It'll be $20 for a wired mouse, and $50 for a wireless one.

M I'll take a wireless one, please.

W Sure thing. Will that be all?

M Yes. Here's my credit card.

</td><td>

남 음, 저는 회원 카드가 없어요. 오늘 하나 만들 수 있나요?

여 물론입니다, 그런데 1회 입회비 20달러가 있습니다.

남 괜찮아요, 그러면 할인을 받을 수 있죠, 그렇죠?

여 그렇습니다.

남 아, 그리고 마우스도 하나 사고 싶어요.

여 알겠습니다. 유선 마우스는 20달러이고 무선 마우스는 50달러입니다.

남 무선 마우스로 살게요.

여 좋습니다. 그렇게만 하면 될까요?

남 네. 여기 제 신용카드요.

</td></tr>
</table>

07 ④

<table>
<tr><td>

해설 여자는 아들이 아픈데 남편이 출장 중이어서 어머니가 오기 전까지 자신이 돌봐야 한다고 말했다.

어휘 stuck in traffic 교통 체증으로 꼼짝 못하는

take care of ~을 돌보다

(= look after)

handle 처리하다

</td><td>

[Cell phone rings.]

M Hello?

W Bob, it's Jane.

M Hi. You're late. Are you stuck in traffic?

W No, I haven't left home yet. I'm planning to be there after lunch, so please take all my phone calls until then.

M Sure. But what's wrong? Are you sick?

W No, I'm okay. But my son has a cold and he can't go to school today. My husband is out of town on a business trip, so I'm taking care of him.

M Then you'll be at home all day taking care of him. You won't be in after lunch.

W I will. My mom's coming over to look after him. But she can't get here until noon.

M OK. No problem. I'll handle everything until you get here.

W Thanks.

</td><td>

[휴대전화벨이 울린다.]

남 여보세요?

여 밥, 저 제인이에요.

남 안녕하세요. 늦으시네요. 교통 체증 때문에 꼼짝 못하고 있나요?

여 아니요, 집에서 아직 못 나갔어요. 점심 후에 가려고 하니 그때까지 저한테 오는 전화를 다 받아주세요.

남 그럴게요. 그런데 무슨 일이에요? 아프세요?

여 아뇨, 전 괜찮아요. 그런데 제 아들이 감기에 걸려서 오늘 학교에 갈 수가 없어요. 남편은 시외로 출장 중이라 제가 아들을 돌보고 있거든요.

남 그러면 집에서 하루 종일 아들을 돌봐야 하잖아요. 점심 이후에도 못 오겠는데요.

여 갈 거예요. 저희 어머니가 아들을 돌보러 와주실 거예요. 그런데 정오까지는 여기 오실 수가 없으시요.

남 알겠어요. 괜찮아요. 당신이 올 때까지 제가 다 처리할게요.

여 감사해요.

</td></tr>
</table>

08 ③

<table>
<tr><td>

해설 해석 참조

어휘 exhibit 전시(하다)

tepee 티피 ((과거 북미 원주민의 원뿔형 천막))

must have p.p. ~했음이 틀림없다

put up ~을 세우다

take down 해체하다

buffalo 버팔로, 물소

plain 밋밋한, 무늬가 없는

religious ceremony 종교의식

</td><td>

W The next exhibit shows several different types of Native American tepees.

M They look like tents. Were they really used as living spaces?

W Yes, many Native Americans lived in tepees. And they brought these tepees with them when they traveled.

M That must have been very difficult.

W Actually, it was easy to put up and take down a tepee because of the simple construction. Two people could put up a tepee in under an hour.

M What are they made from?

W All of the tepees you see here are covered with buffalo skin.

M That one is really colorful! I thought tepees would be more plain.

</td><td>

여 다음 전시는 북미 원주민 티피의 몇 가지 다양한 종류를 보여주고 있어요.

남 텐트처럼 생겼는데요. 정말 주거 공간으로 사용됐나요?

여 네, **많은 북미 원주민이 티피 안에서 살았어요(①** 용도). 그리고 이동할 때 이 티피들을 가지고 다녔지요.

남 그건 분명 매우 힘들었겠네요.

여 사실, 간단한 구조 때문에 티피를 세우고 해체하는 게 쉬웠어요. **두 사람이 한 시간 이내로 티피를 세울 수 있었거든요(②** 설치 소요 시간).

남 티피는 무엇으로 만들어졌나요?

여 **여기 보시는 모든 티피는 물소 가죽으로 덮여 있어요(④** 소재).

남 저건 정말 화려하네요! 티피는 더 밋밋할 거라고 생각했어요.

</td></tr>
</table>

W Most tepees were plain. But some tepees used for religious ceremonies were painted with different images, such as pictures of animals.

M Oh, I see.

여 티피 대부분은 무늬가 없었어요. **하지만 종교 의식에 사용된 몇몇 티피는 동물 그림과 같은 다양한 그림이 그려져 있었어요**(⑤ 그림 장식).

남 아, 그렇군요.

09 ②

해설 고등학교 시절 인기 축구 선수였다고 했다.

어휘 subscriber 구독자
rather than ~보다는
pursue 추구하다
career 경력; 직업
enroll in ~에 입학하다, 등록하다
make[earn] a living 생계를 꾸리다
establish 설립하다; 확립하다

M Hello, subscribers! Francis Rivera was chosen as the Person of the Year by News Weekly. Francis Rivera traveled throughout his life. Born in Puerto Rico, he had lived in Mexico, Texas, California, and Colorado by the time he was fourteen. At high school in Colorado he was a star football player. But rather than pursuing a career in sports, he enrolled in medical school. In order to make his living while at college, he had to work two part-time jobs. Despite this, he graduated at the top of his class. For the next twenty years, Francis traveled with little money, but established free medical programs in many poor countries.

남 안녕하세요, 구독자 여러분! 프랜시스 리베라가 <뉴스 주간지>에서 올해의 인물로 선정되었습니다. 프랜시스 리베라는 일생 동안 여행을 했습니다. **푸에르토리코에서 태어난**(①) 그는 열네 살 때까지 멕시코, 텍사스, 캘리포니아, 콜로라도에서 살았습니다. 콜로라도에서 고등학교 시절에 **그는 인기 축구 선수였습니다**(②). 하지만 그는 스포츠 경력을 추구하기보다 **의과 대학에 입학했습니다**(③). 대학에 다니는 동안 생계를 꾸리기 위해, **그는 아르바이트 두 개를 해야 했습니다**(④). 이런 상황에도 불구하고 그는 수석으로 졸업했습니다. 그 후 20년 동안 프랜시스는 거의 무일푼으로 여행했으나, 많은 가난한 나라에 **무료 의료 프로그램을 만들었습니다**(⑤).

10 ②

해설 장비를 대여해야 하고, 강습은 필요 없으며, 야간에도 스키를 타고 작은 사물함을 빌리기로 했다.

어휘 as much as possible 되도록 많이
settled 결정된, 정해진; 안정된

M Here we are! I can't wait to start skiing.

W Me too. I can't remember the last time we came here.

M I know. Let's get our tickets and go have fun.

W You know, we need to rent the equipment. Maybe we should get one of these packages.

M Sounds good. It's been a while, but I don't think I need a lesson.

W Me neither. What about night skiing?

M I came to ski as much as possible!

W Hmm.... I've never tried night skiing before, but it sounds more fun!

M Absolutely. Lastly, do we need a large locker?

W I think a small one will be big enough to keep our shoes in.

M OK then, it's settled. I'll pay for that package.

남 도착했어! 어서 빨리 스키를 타고 싶어.

여 나도 그래. 우리가 마지막으로 여기 왔던 게 언제였는지 기억도 안 나.

남 맞아. 우리 표 끊고 가서 재미있게 놀자.

여 있잖아, 우리 장비를 대여해야 해. 아마도 이 패키지 중 하나를 골라야 할 것 같아.

남 좋은 생각이야. 오랜만이긴 하지만 난 강습은 필요 없을 것 같아.

여 나도 그래. 야간 스키는 어때?

남 난 가능한 한 스키를 많이 타려고 왔어!

여 음…. 나는 한 번도 야간 스키를 타본 적이 없지만 더 재미있을 것 같아!

남 당연하지. 마지막으로 우리 큰 사물함이 필요할까?

여 내 생각에 우리 신발을 보관하는 데는 작은 사물함으로도 크기가 충분할 거야.

남 좋아 그럼, 결정됐어. 저 패키지로 계산할게.

11 ③

해설 유선 방송 서비스를 이전하려는 여자에게 남자가 이사 가는 곳을 물어봤으므로 위치를 알려주는 응답이 가장 적절하다.
① 물론이죠. 전 다음 주에 이사 가요.
② 유선 방송이 설치되기를 기대하고 있어요.
④ 해약금이 있는지 궁금해요.
⑤ 이사를 도와주셔서 정말 감사해요.

[Telephone rings.]

M Hello. This is Cable Center. How may I help you?

W Hi. I'm calling to transfer my cable service because I'm moving houses.

M I think I can help you. Could you let me know where you are moving to?

W Just across town, near Central Park.

[전화벨이 울린다.]

남 안녕하세요. 케이블 센터입니다. 어떻게 도와드릴까요?

여 안녕하세요. 제가 이사를 할 거라서 유선 방송 서비스를 이전하려고 전화했어요.

남 제가 도와드릴 수 있을 것 같습니다. 어디로 이사 가시는지 알려주시겠어요?

여 바로 시내 반대편, 센트럴 파크 근처예요.

12 ②

해설 남자가 만나기로 한 날에 휴가를 낼 수 없다고 하자 여자가 다른 날에는 시간이 없다고 했다. 따라서 밤늦게 만나면 된다는 응답이 가장 적절하다.

① 응, 상사가 회의를 취소했어.
③ 아니, 난 네 사무실 근처에서 기다리고 있어.
④ 잘됐네! 난 내일 너와 같이 점심 먹을 수 있어.
⑤ 나는 더 많은 휴가를 요청할 필요가 있어.

어휘 take a day off 하루 휴가를 내다
available 시간이 있는
[선택지 어휘] time off 휴가

[Cell phone rings.]
W Hi, Philip. It's me. Are we still meeting tomorrow?
M My boss wouldn't let me take the day off. We're too busy.
W Oh, no! I'm not available on other days this week.
M Well, we could still meet later at night.

[휴대전화벨이 울린다.]
여 안녕, 필립. 나야. 우리 여전히 내일 만나는 거지?
남 상사가 휴가를 못 내게 해. 너무 바쁘거든.
여 아, 이런! 나는 이번 주에 다른 날에는 시간이 안 되는데.
남 음, 밤늦게라도 만나면 되지.

13 ③

해설 사라의 생일 파티에 참석하게 해주면 경기를 보러 가겠다고 했으므로 생일 당사자인 사라에게 물어보겠다는 응답이 가장 적절하다.

① 너 오기 싫은 게 확실하니?
② 난 농구만큼 축구를 좋아하지 않아.
④ 신디와 마크는 생일이 지난달에 있었어.
⑤ 더 많은 우리 반 아이들과 친구가 되고 싶어.

어휘 run into ~와 우연히 만나다
cheer on ~을 응원하다
not a big fan of ~을 좋아하지 않는
afterward (그) 후에, 나중에

W Jim! I'm so glad to have run into you here.
M Hi, Karen. What's new?
W You know I'm playing on the soccer team this year. I was actually hoping that you would cheer me on this Saturday.
M Oh, you know I'm not a big fan of sports.
W I remember. But this game is really important to me. And some of our classmates are coming.
M Really? Who?
W John, Cindy, Mark, Jeff, Dan, and Sara.
M Oh, Sara? Is she really coming? Because she said this Saturday is her birthday.
W Right, after the game we will go to her birthday party.
M I would be happy to come to the game if I could join her party afterward.
W You would? Great! I'll ask Sara right away.

여 짐! 여기서 우연히 만나다니 정말 반가워.
남 안녕, 캐런. 뭐 새로운 일이라도 있니?
여 너도 알다시피 나는 올해 축구팀에서 뛰고 있잖아. 사실은 이번 토요일에 네가 나를 응원해주길 바라고 있었어.
남 아, 내가 운동 경기를 좋아하지 않는 거 알잖아.
여 기억해. 하지만 이 경기는 내게 정말 중요해. 그리고 우리 반 친구들도 몇 명 올 거야.
남 진짜? 누구?
여 존, 신디, 마크, 제프, 댄, 그리고 사라.
남 어, 사라? 그 애가 진짜 와? 이번 토요일이 자기 생일이라고 했거든.
여 맞아, 경기 후에 우린 그 애의 생일 파티에 갈 거야.
남 그 후에 나도 파티에 참석할 수 있다면 기꺼이 경기를 보러 갈게.
여 그럴래? 잘됐다! 내가 사라한테 바로 물어볼게.

14 ③

해설 안 입는 옷을 버리지 말고 자선단체에 기부하라는 여자의 권유에 가장 적절한 응답을 고른다.

① 이 모든 옷들을 처리하는 걸 도와줄게.
② 그 기관에 연락하는 방법을 알려줄 수 있어.
④ 네 흥미를 끌지도 모르는 자선단체가 많이 있어.
⑤ 넌 다음번에 옷을 살 땐 두 번 생각해야 해.

W Sean, why are all of your clothes in boxes?
M That's just some of my old stuff that I never wear anymore. I'm throwing all of it out.
W Some of these are as good as new! You are really throwing them away?
M Well, I don't need them anymore, and just keeping them is wasting space.
W Have you thought about donating them to Helping Hand?
M Helping Hand? I don't know what that is.
W It's a place that accepts old clothes and things.

여 션, 왜 네 옷이 모두 상자 안에 들어 있니?
남 더 이상 입지 않는 오래된 것 중 일부일 뿐이야. 전부 버리려고 해.
여 이 중 몇 벌은 새것처럼 좋은걸! 정말 버릴 거야?
남 음, 난 그 옷들이 더 이상 필요 없고, 그냥 가지고만 있는 건 공간 낭비야.
여 헬핑 핸드에 기부하는 건 생각해봤니?
남 헬핑 핸드? 난 그게 뭔지 모르겠어.
여 오래된 옷이나 물건을 받는 곳이야.

어휘 stuff (막연히) 일[것], 물건
throw out[away] ~을 버리다
donate 기부하다
sort 분류하다, 구분하다
give away ~을 거저 주다, 선물로 주다
needy (경제적으로) 어려운, 궁핍한
[선택지 어휘] get rid of ~을 처리하다,
없애다
charity 자선[구호]단체
appeal (to) (~의) 관심[흥미]을 끌다

M What happens to the clothes?
W They will be cleaned and sorted, and then given away to needy families.
M Great. Then it will be the perfect place for these.

남 그 옷들이 어떻게 되는 건데?
여 세탁하고 분류된 후에 어려운 가정에 나눠질 거야.
남 잘됐다. 그럼 그곳이 이 옷들을 위한 완벽한 곳일 거야.

---

15 ③

해설 어머니가 혼잡한 백화점에서 아이를 잃어버리지 않으려고 손을 꼭 잡고 있는 상황에서 할 말로 가장 적절한 것을 고른다.
① 그건 네게 잘 어울려.
② 여기서 뛰면 안 돼.
③ 내 손을 놓지 마라.
④ 저쪽에 있는 가게로 가자.
⑤ 다음 주가 네 이모의 결혼식이야.

어휘 crowd 인파, 군중
[선택지 어휘] let go of (쥐고 있던 것을) 놓다; ~에서 손을 놓다

W Matilda is a six-year-old girl. Matilda and her mother will be attending her cousin's wedding next Saturday. Matilda's mother would like to buy Matilda a pretty pink dress for the wedding. So today, Matilda's mother goes shopping at a department store with Matilda. Since it is near the holiday season, there are a lot of people at the department store. Matilda's mother holds her daughter's hand very tightly. She doesn't want to lose her daughter in the crowd. In this situation, what would Matilda's mother most likely say to Matilda?

여 마틸다는 여섯 살 소녀이다. 마틸다와 그녀의 어머니는 다음 주 토요일 사촌의 결혼식에 참석할 예정이다. 마틸다의 어머니는 결혼식을 위해 마틸다에게 예쁜 분홍색 드레스를 사주고 싶다. 그래서 오늘, 마틸다의 어머니는 마틸다와 함께 백화점에 쇼핑을 하러 간다. 휴가 시즌이 가까운 때여서 백화점에 많은 사람이 있다. 마틸다의 어머니는 딸의 손을 매우 꼭 잡는다. 그녀는 많은 인파 속에서 딸을 잃어버리고 싶지 않다. 이 상황에서, 마틸다의 어머니가 마틸다에게 할 말로 가장 적절한 것은 무엇인가?

---

16 ③   17 ④

해설 16 정원 일을 하는 것이 심리적인 이점을 준다는 내용이다.
① 정신 건강을 위한 다양한 취미들
② 감정을 표현하는 것의 장점들
③ 정원 가꾸기의 심리적 이점들
④ 채소밭을 건강하게 유지하는 방법들
⑤ 당신의 채소밭을 위한 수익성 있는 작물들

[선택지 어휘] profitable 수익성이 있는

17 해석 참조

어휘 disability 장애
boundary 경계[한계](선)
significance 중요성, 중대성
convince 납득시키다
weed 잡초를 뽑다; 잡초
loosen the soil 굳은 땅을 부드럽게 고르다

M The term "gardening" itself brings to our mind feelings that relax the body and mind. If the word alone can give us peace of mind, imagine the benefits from participation in the activity. Did you know that a few minutes of gardening every day can not only relax your body but also cure mental disabilities? This is just the beginning. The benefits that gardening can bring are beyond boundaries. Various mental health organizations, over the last few years, have proven the significance of gardening to mental health. Are you convinced, but not sure how to start? Try planting vegetables in an attractive design which will add interest to your landscape. Plant seeds for carrots and cucumbers early in the spring. After that, complete your garden with some flowers, like sunflowers, red roses, or tulips. Then add in some strawberry or watermelon seeds. As you water, weed, and loosen the soil in your garden each day, you will come to see its relaxing and stress-relieving benefits.

남 '정원 가꾸기'란 용어는 그 자체로 우리 마음에 몸과 마음을 편안하게 하는 느낌을 가져다줍니다. 만약 이 단어 하나만으로 우리에게 마음의 평화를 줄 수 있다면, 그 활동에 참여함으로써 받을 수 있는 이로움을 생각해 보십시오. 당신은 매일 몇 분의 정원 가꾸기가 당신 몸의 긴장을 풀게 할 뿐만 아니라 정신적 장애를 치료할 수 있다는 것을 아셨나요? 이것은 그저 시작에 불과합니다. 정원 가꾸기가 가져올 수 있는 혜택은 경계를 넘어섭니다. 많은 정신 건강 기관에서 지난 몇 년간 정신 건강에 대한 정원 가꾸기의 중요성을 입증해왔습니다. 납득되시지만 어떻게 시작해야 할지 모르시겠습니까? 당신의 풍경에 흥미를 더할 수 있는 매력적인 방식으로 채소를 한번 심어보십시오. 당근(① carrots)과 오이(② cucumbers) 씨앗을 초봄에 심으십시오. 그 후에, 당신의 정원을 해바라기, 붉은 장미, 튤립과 같은 몇몇 꽃으로 완성하십시오. 그러고 나서 딸기(③ strawberry) 또는 수박(⑤ watermelon)의 씨앗을 더하십시오. 매일 정원에 물을 주고, 잡초를 뽑고, 굳은 땅을 부드럽게 고르면서, 당신은 우리 마음을 느긋하게 해주고, 스트레스를 덜어주는 정원의 효과를 보게 될 것입니다.

01 ③	02 ⑤	03 ⑤	04 ③	05 ①	06 ⑤	07 ②	08 ③	09 ④	10 ①
11 ①	12 ②	13 ④	14 ④	15 ②	16 ⑤	17 ④			

01 ③

해설 친구에게 추천받기, 독서회 가입하기, 베스트셀러 목록 살펴보기 등 책을 고르는 데 도움이 되는 방법들을 소개하고 있다.

어휘 select 고르다
recommendation 추천[서]
consist of ~로 구성되다
previous 이전의
currently 현재(는)

M How many times has this happened to you? You plan a trip to the library or bookstore, but once there, you can't decide on a book. You know you can't read every book that comes out. So, how can we choose one? Let me suggest a few ways to select a book. First, look at what your friends are reading. Ask them for recommendations. Next, join a book club. Book clubs usually consist of people who get together to discuss books. Each week, they choose a new book and discuss the previous book. Third, find bestseller lists. Many online bookstores have lists of the currently best-selling books. Finally, when you find a book online, you will be given recommendations for other books you might like.

남 몇 번이나 당신에게 이런 일이 일어났던가요? 당신은 도서관이나 서점에 가기로 계획하지만, 일단 거기에 가면, 책을 결정할 수가 없습니다. 당신은 출간되는 도서를 전부 읽을 수는 없다는 것을 알고 있습니다. 그렇다면 우리는 어떻게 책을 고를 수 있을까요? 제가 책을 고르는 몇 가지 방법을 추천해드리겠습니다. 먼저, 친구들이 무엇을 읽고 있는지 살펴보세요. 그들에게 추천해달라고 요청하세요. 다음으로, 독서회에 가입하세요. 독서회는 보통 책에 관해 토론하기 위해 한데 모인 사람들로 구성되어 있습니다. 매주, 그들은 새 책을 선정하고 이전의 책에 관해 토론합니다. 세 번째로, 베스트셀러 목록을 찾아보세요. 여러 온라인 서점은 현재 가장 잘 팔리는 책들의 목록이 있습니다. 마지막으로, 당신이 온라인을 통해 책을 찾아보면, 당신이 마음에 들어 할지도 모르는 다른 책들을 추천받게 될 것입니다.

02 ⑤

해설 여자는 받는 사람의 마음에 들지 않을 수도 있는 선물을 하는 것보다 기프트 카드를 선물해 받는 사람이 원하는 것을 직접 고르도록 하는 것이 좋다고 했다.

어휘 gift card 기프트 카드 ((상품권의 기능과 신용카드의 편리함을 합친 선불카드))
focus on ~에 초점을 맞추다; 집중하다
attach 붙이다, 첨부하다
personal 직접[몸소] ~한; 개인적인

M Okay, the last thing to buy is a gift for your mother.
W I've already decided to give her a gift card.
M But a gift card doesn't show that we care.
W With a gift card, she can choose anything she wants. What could be better than that?
M Choosing a gift shows we cared enough to spend time thinking about her.
W I do care. I just don't want to waste money on something that she might not like.
M You shouldn't focus on money. The important thing is your mother's happiness.
W I agree. That's why I want her to have exactly what she wants.
M Alright, but let's at least attach a personal message.

남 자, 마지막으로 살 것은 당신 어머님을 위한 선물이에요.
여 난 어머니께 기프트 카드를 드리기로 이미 결정했어요.
남 하지만 기프트 카드는 우리가 마음 쓴다는 것을 보여주지 않아요.
여 기프트 카드로 어머니께서는 원하는 것을 무엇이든 고르실 수 있어요. 그보다 뭐가 더 좋을 수 있겠어요?
남 선물을 고른다는 건 우리가 어머님을 생각하면서 시간을 보낼 만큼 충분히 신경 썼다는 것을 보여줘요.
여 난 정말 신경 쓰고 있어요. 어머니께서 좋아하시지 않을 수도 있는 것에 돈을 낭비하고 싶지 않을 뿐이에요.
남 돈에 초점을 맞춰서는 안 돼요. 중요한 건 어머님의 행복이에요.
여 동의해요. 그게 내가 어머니께서 꼭 원하시는 걸 갖길 바라는 이유예요.
남 알겠어요, 하지만 적어도 직접 쓴 메시지를 붙여서 드리자고요.

03 ⑤

해설 our show, ask the hard questions, TV interview 등을 통해 프로듀서와 쇼 진행자의 관계임을 알 수 있다.

어휘 make an appearance 출연하다
involvement 연루, 관련
politics 정치, 정치적인 문제들
be willing to-v 기꺼이 v하다
give it a try 시도하다, 한번 해보다
cure 치료제[법]; 치료하다

W This week Anderson Smith will make an appearance on our show. Remember, your job is to ask the hard questions our viewers want answered.
M Don't worry. I've prepared a list of difficult questions.
W Which topics will you discuss?
M Mainly, the future of his company, but also his involvement in politics.
W I don't know if he'll be willing to talk about that, but you should give it a try.
M Of course.
W And next week you'll be interviewing Dr. Romney.
M Isn't he the doctor who found a new cure for heart disease?
W Yes. It will be his first TV interview, so be well prepared.
M I always am.

여 이번 주에 앤더슨 스미스가 우리 쇼에 출연할 거예요. 명심하세요, 당신의 일은 우리 시청자들이 답변받기를 원하는 어려운 질문들을 하는 거예요.
남 걱정하지 마세요. 제가 어려운 질문들의 목록을 준비했어요.
여 어떤 주제들을 토론할 건가요?
남 주로, 그의 회사의 미래에 관한 것인데, 그의 정치적 연루에 관해서도 할 거예요.
여 그가 그것에 대해 이야기하려고 할지는 모르겠지만, 당신이 시도는 해봐야죠.
남 물론이에요.
여 그리고 다음 주에 당신은 롬니 박사를 인터뷰할 거예요.
남 새로운 심장병 치료제를 발견하신 그 의사 선생님 아니신가요?
여 맞아요. 그게 그의 첫 텔레비전 인터뷰가 될 테니 준비 잘 해주세요.
남 전 항상 준비되어 있어요.

04 ③

해설 계산대 위에 식물을 두었다고 했으므로 그림 속의 램프가 대화의 내용과 일치하지 않는다.

어휘 cozy 아늑한, 포근한
water purifier 정수기
compact 작은, 소형의

M Madison, congratulations on the opening of your hair salon.
W Thank you! So, what do you think?
M It looks great! The interior design is very cozy.
W Due to the small space, I was only able to place three mirrors on one wall.
M I also like these two long sofas that are opposite the mirrors.
W So do I! My parents bought them for me as a gift.
M Cool! Oh, there's a counter by the door.
W Yes, I put a plant on it. It helps clean the air.
M It looks great there! Is that a cabinet you made on the left side of the door?
W Yes, I made it so I could put a water purifier there. I didn't make it very high because I had to place the TV on it.
M Well done! It's very compact and well-designed.

남 매디슨, 미용실 개업을 축하해.
여 고마워! 그래서 어떻게 생각해?
남 좋아 보이는걸! 실내 디자인이 매우 아늑하네.
여 공간이 작아서 벽 하나에 거울 세 개만 놓을 수 있었어.
남 난 거울들 반대편에 있는 두 개의 긴 소파도 마음에 들어.
여 나도 그래! 우리 부모님께서 선물로 사주셨어.
남 멋진걸! 아, 문 옆에 계산대가 있구나.
여 응, 그 위에 식물을 뒀어. 그게 공기를 깨끗하게 해줘.
남 거기에 놓으니 좋네! 문 왼쪽에 있는 캐비닛은 네가 만든 거야?
여 응, 정수기를 거기 놓으려고 내가 만들었어. 텔레비전을 그 위에 두어야 해서 너무 높게 만들진 않았어.
남 잘했네! 캐비닛이 작으면서도 잘 설계되었어.

05 ①

해설 남자는 여자에게 소금을 사다 달라고 부탁했다.
① 소금 사오기
② 엄마에게 전화하기
③ 요리하는 것 돕기
④ 감기약 찾기
⑤ 엄마에게 음식 가져다주기

어휘 a couple of 둘의, 두서너 개의
be out of ~이 떨어지다, 바닥나다
bill 지폐; 계산서; 법안
change 잔돈, 거스름돈

W Dad, I'm home!
M Hi, Emma. Did you talk to your mother today?
W No, not yet. Is everything okay?
M I talked to her on the phone a couple of hours ago, and she's not feeling well.
W What's wrong with her?
M It sounds like she has the flu, and she hasn't eaten anything yet. So, I made some chicken noodle soup.
W That's so sweet of you. I could take some to her office after I change clothes.
M Oh, thanks, but I'll do that. Could you buy some salt instead? I need more salt, but we're almost out of it.

여 아빠, 저 집에 왔어요!
남 어서 오렴, 엠마. 오늘 엄마랑 얘기했니?
여 아뇨, 아직 못했어요. 무슨 일이 있나요?
남 네 엄마랑 두어 시간 전에 통화했는데, 몸 상태가 안 좋다고 해서 말이야.
여 무슨 문제예요?
남 감기에 걸린 것 같더구나, 그리고 아직 아무것도 못 먹었어. 그래서 내가 국수를 넣은 닭고기 수프를 좀 만들었지.
여 아빠는 정말 자상하세요. 옷 갈아입고 제가 엄마 사무실까지 가져다드릴 수 있어요.
남 아, 고맙지만 그건 내가 하마. 대신 소금 좀 사다 줄래? 소금이 더 필요한데, 거의 다 떨어졌구나.

W	Sure. Can I have some money?	여	물론이죠. 돈 좀 주시겠어요?
M	Here's a five-dollar bill. You can keep the change.	남	5달러짜리 여기 있다. 잔돈은 가져도 된단다.

06 ⑤

해설 5킬로그램의 소포를 속달 우편(킬로당 $15)을 이용해서 보낼 것이고, 박스 가격($3)도 추가로 지불해야 하므로 지불할 금액은 78달러이다.

어휘 **in time for** ~에 시간 맞춰, 늦지 않게
working day 영업일
(= business day)
guarantee 보증[약속]하다
extra 추가의, 여분의
parcel 소포
weigh 무게가 ~이다

W	Hello, I want to send these presents to Australia in time for Christmas.	여	안녕하세요, 저는 크리스마스에 맞춰 이 선물들을 호주로 보내고 싶어요.
M	It's $7 per kilogram for ordinary airmail service. It takes five to seven working days.	남	일반 항공 우편은 킬로그램당 7달러입니다. 영업일 기준으로 5일에서 7일이 걸립니다.
W	Oh, no. Christmas is only four days away. Can't it be delivered any faster?	여	아, 이런. 크리스마스는 4일밖에 남지 않았는데요. 좀 더 빨리 배달될 수는 없나요?
M	There is a faster service. Express Post takes a maximum of three days, guaranteed.	남	더 빠른 서비스가 있습니다. 속달 우편은 최대 3일 이내 배달을 보장해드립니다.
W	Great. How much does that cost?	여	좋아요. 그건 비용이 얼마죠?
M	It's a bit expensive: $15 per kilogram. And you'll need a size 3 box, which is an extra $3.	남	조금 비쌉니다. 킬로그램당 15달러입니다. 그리고 손님은 3 사이즈의 박스가 필요한데, 그건 추가로 3달러입니다.
W	I see, and my parcel weighs 5 kilograms. That's going to be really expensive!	여	그렇군요, 그리고 제 소포는 무게가 5킬로그램이네요. 이거 정말 비싸겠군요!
M	I'm afraid there's no other way to get the presents to Australia by Christmas Day.	남	유감스럽게도 크리스마스까지 호주로 선물을 보낼 다른 방법은 없을 것 같습니다.
W	Okay. I'll go with Express Post. Here's my credit card.	여	알겠습니다. 속달 우편으로 할게요. 여기 제 신용카드요.

07 ②

해설 남자는 아픈 여동생을 돌봐야 해서 모임에 참석하지 못한다고 했다. 전반부에 피곤하다고 했지만 그것이 독서 클럽 모임에 가지 못하는 이유는 아님에 유의한다.

어휘 **make it** 참석하다, 가다
housework 집안일
take care of 돌보다
get well 병이 나아지다

M	Hi, Lucy. Can you talk?	남	안녕, 루시. 얘기할 수 있니?
W	Sure. Are you all right? You don't look good.	여	물론이지. 너 괜찮아? 안색이 안 좋아 보인다.
M	I'm just tired. I had a math test this morning, so I studied late last night.	남	그냥 피곤한 거야. 오늘 오전에 수학 시험이 있어서 어젯밤 늦게까지 공부했거든.
W	You must be tired. Did you read the book for our book club meeting?	여	피곤하겠구나. 우리 독서 클럽 모임의 책은 읽었니?
M	Of course. But it looks like I can't make it to the meeting today.	남	물론이지. 하지만 난 오늘 모임에 참석할 수 없을 것 같아.
W	What's wrong? Do you have more exams to prepare for?	여	무슨 일이야? 준비해야 할 시험이 더 있니?
M	No, I don't. My mom just called and told me to come home early today.	남	아니, 그렇지는 않아. 엄마가 방금 전화하셔서 오늘 집에 일찍 오라고 말씀하셨어.
W	Why? Do you need to help her with housework?	여	왜? 집안일을 도와드려야 하니?
M	No, actually my little sister has a bad cold, but my mom won't be home until late tonight.	남	아니, 사실 내 여동생이 심한 감기에 걸렸는데 엄마가 오늘 밤 늦게까지 집에 못 오셔.
W	Oh, you have to take care of her, then.	여	아, 그러면 네가 동생을 돌봐야겠구나.
M	Yeah. I won't miss the meeting next time.	남	응. 다음에는 모임에 빠지지 않을게.
W	I understand. I hope she gets well soon.	여	이해해. 네 동생이 빨리 나아지기를 바라.

08 ③

해설 해석 참조

어휘 **annual** 연례의, 매년의
welcome to-v ((비격식)) 자유로이 v할 수 있는
prepare 준비하다
provide 제공하다
would rather+동사원형 (than) (~하기 보다는 차라리) v하겠다

M	Hi, Rachel, are you coming to the annual company trip?	남	안녕하세요, 레이첼, 연례 회사 야유회에 오시나요?
W	Hi, Kyle. Yes, I heard we will be hiking up Mt. Cornwall this year.	여	안녕하세요, 카일. 네, 올해에는 콘월산을 등산할 거라 들었어요.
M	Oh, is your family coming? You know, family is welcome to join the trip.	남	아, 가족들도 오시나요? 그러니까, **야유회에 가족이 참가할 수 있잖아요**(① 가족 동반 가능 여부).
W	Sure, my husband and son will be there. It's being held this Saturday, May 18th, right?	여	네, 제 남편과 아들이 갈 거예요. **이번 토요일인 5월 18일에 열리죠**(② 날짜), 맞나요?

M	Yes. Do we need to prepare anything?	남	네. 우리가 뭐라도 준비할 필요가 있을까요?
W	I don't think so. They will provide water, snacks, and lunch.	여	그렇진 않을 거예요. **회사에서 물, 간식, 그리고 점심을 제공해줄 거거든요**(④ 식사 제공 여부).
M	Excellent. Are you taking the shuttle bus from the office?	남	좋네요. 사무실에서 셔틀버스를 타고 가시나요?
W	I'd rather drive with my family. I'll meet you there.	여	저는 가족들과 운전해서 가려고요. 거기서 뵐게요.
M	Okay, we are meeting in the parking lot at 9 a.m. Make sure to be there on time.	남	그래요, **오전 9시에 주차장에서 모일 거예요**(⑤ 모이는 장소). 시간 맞춰 오세요.
W	I will.	여	그럴게요.

09 ④

해설 추천서 제출은 의무 사항이다.

어휘 outstanding 우수한, 눈에 띄는
scholarship 장학금
award A B A에게 B를 수여하다
tuition 등록금, 수업료
school expenses 학비
candidate 지원자; 후보자
pursue 수행하다, 추구하다
apply for ~을 신청하다, ~에 지원하다
cf. application 지원서
cf. applicant 지원자
detail 상세히 알리다[열거하다]
a letter of recommendation 추천서

| W | Good afternoon, students. This is professor Angela Hawkins. Today, I'm glad to introduce the Outstanding Achievement Scholarship to you. This is a scholarship given to students who work to improve the lives of children. Those who are awarded this scholarship will get $10,000 to be used for tuition and school expenses. Candidates must pursue a major in the field of education and maintain excellent grades. All students applying for this scholarship must send in an application form by February 16th. Applicants must write an essay of around 5 pages, detailing their work with children. A letter of recommendation should also be included in the application. Results will be announced in May. Good luck! | 여 | 안녕하세요, 학생 여러분. 저는 안젤라 호킨스 교수입니다. 오늘 '우수 성과 장학금'을 소개하게 되어 기쁩니다. 이것은 아이들의 삶이 나아지도록 노력하는 학생들에게 주어지는 장학금입니다. 이 장학금을 받는 학생들은 등록금과 학비로 사용될 **1만 달러를 받을 것입니다**(①). 지원자들은 **교육 분야를 전공해야 하며**(②), 우수한 성적을 유지해야 합니다. 이 장학금을 신청하는 모든 학생들은 **지원서 양식을 2월 16일까지 제출해야 합니다**(③). 지원자들은 아이들과의 일을 상술하는 5페이지 가량의 에세이를 써야 합니다. **또한 추천서도 지원서에 포함되어야 합니다**(④). **결과는 5월 중에 발표될 것입니다**(⑤). 행운을 빕니다! |

10 ①

해설 가족 휴가인 8월 5~10일과 겹치지 않고 물놀이를 포함하며 350달러 이하인 캠프를 선택한다.

어휘 beg 애원[간청]하다
avoid 피하다
disappointed 실망한
afford to-v v할 여유가 있다

W	Honey, the kids have been begging to go to summer camp this year. I think we should send them.	여	여보, 아이들이 올해 여름 캠프에 보내 달라고 애원하고 있어요. 애들을 보내줘야 할 것 같아요.
M	I agree. Let's look at some of the options.	남	동의해요. 선택 사항 중에 몇 개를 봅시다.
W	Firstly, we need to avoid August 5th to 10th because of our family vacation.	여	먼저, 우리 가족 휴가 때문에 8월 5일부터 10일까지는 피할 필요가 있어요.
M	Oh, that's right. Hmm.... This one looks nice. They offer hiking.	남	아, 맞아요. 음…. 이것이 좋아 보이네요. 하이킹을 제공해요.
W	Well, the kids would be disappointed without water activities.	여	저, 물놀이가 없으면 아이들이 실망할 것 같아요.
M	Right. Then, what about this one? They offer both.	남	맞아요. 그럼, 이건 어때요? 둘 다 제공하네요.
W	It's also the most expensive. We can't afford to spend over $350.	여	제일 비싸기도 하네요. 우린 350달러 넘게 지출할 여유가 없어요.
M	Then, I guess we're left with this camp.	남	그러면 이 캠프가 남은 것 같네요.
W	Yeah, let's sign up for this one.	여	네, 이것으로 등록하죠.

11 ①

해설 자외선 차단제를 바르지 않았냐고 물어보는 남자의 말에 가져오는 것조차 잊어버렸다는 응답이 가장 적절하다.
② 응, 나 햇볕에 꽤 심하게 탔어.
③ 아무래도 우리 실내로 돌아가야겠어.
④ 아니, 날 위해 그럴 필요는 없어.
⑤ 응, 모래에 앉아 있고 싶지 않아.

M	Look at the sandy beach! It's so beautiful.	남	저 모래사장 좀 봐! 정말 아름답다.
W	Yeah, but the sun is so strong that I might get a sunburn.	여	그래, 하지만 햇볕이 너무 강해서 심하게 탈 것 같아.
M	Don't worry. You put on sunscreen, didn't you?	남	걱정하지 마. 너 자외선 차단제 발랐잖아, 그렇지 않니?
W	No, I even forgot to bring it.	여	아니, 자외선 차단제 가져오는 것도 잊어버렸어.

12 ②

해설 전화 연결 상태가 좋지 않아 소리가 잘 들리지 않는다는 여자의 말에 끊고 다시 전화하겠다는 응답이 가장 적절하다.
① 내가 방금 해봤는데, 통화 중이었어.
③ 이 일로 널 또 귀찮게 해서 미안해.
④ 전화 잘못 거신 게 분명해요.
⑤ 그것에 대해 생각해보고 다시 전화할게.

어휘 barely 거의 ~ 않다; 간신히
[선택지 어휘] hang up 전화를 끊다

[Cell phone rings.]
W Hello? Adam?
M Hi, Debbie! I've been trying to call you all morning.
W Hello? Adam? Can you hear me? Hello? I can barely hear you. I think the connection is very bad.
M Oh, okay. I'll hang up and call again.

[휴대전화벨이 울린다.]
여 여보세요? 아담?
남 안녕, 데비! 오전 내내 너에게 전화하려 했어.
여 여보세요? 아담? 내 말 들리니? 여보세요? 네 말이 거의 안 들리는데. 연결 상태가 매우 안 좋은 것 같아.
남 아, 알겠어. 끊고 다시 전화할게.

13 ④

해설 문제의 원인을 모르는 상황에서 전문가가 곧 도착한다고 했으므로 원인을 곧 찾아낼 수 있겠다는 말이 가장 적절하다.
① 이 지역 수질은 좋아.
② 물고기가 전부 죽은 것이 내 잘못이라고는 생각하지 않아.
③ 그게 바로 물고기에게 먹이를 더 자주 줘야 한다고 내가 주장했던 이유야.
⑤ 넌 인터넷 어디에서도 그런 정보를 찾을 수가 없어.

어휘 be in trouble 곤란을 겪다, 어려움에 처하다
could have p.p. ~일 수도 있었다
a number of 다수의
chemical 화학 물질; 화학의
investigate 조사[연구]하다
[선택지 어휘] insist 주장하다

M I can't believe all of our fish died. Our business is really in trouble now.
W Do you think it could have been the food we gave them? Or maybe it was the way we cleaned the tanks.
M It's hard to know at this point. It could have been a number of things.
W Maybe it was the water quality?
M What do you mean?
W Well, certain chemicals in the water can affect the fish.
M I don't know, but I've called an expert. He will come and investigate what happened. Hopefully we can fix this situation soon.
W When is he coming?
M He'll be here in an hour.
W I guess we'll find out what the cause was soon enough.

남 우리 물고기가 모두 죽었다는 걸 믿을 수가 없어. 우리 사업은 이제 정말 곤란해졌어.
여 넌 그게 우리가 준 먹이 때문이었을 수도 있다고 생각하니? 아니면 아마도 우리가 수조를 청소한 방식 때문이었을지도 몰라.
남 현시점에서는 알기 어려워. 그건 여러 가지 때문이었을 수도 있어.
여 아마도 수질 때문이었을까?
남 무슨 말이야?
여 음, 물속에 있는 특정 화학 물질들이 물고기들에게 영향을 끼칠 수 있어.
남 모르겠어, 하지만 내가 전문가에게 전화했어. 그가 와서 무슨 일이 있었는지 조사할 거야. 바라건대, 우리가 이 상황을 곧 수습할 수 있으면 좋겠어.
여 그가 언제 오는데?
남 한 시간 후에 도착할 거야.
여 원인이 무엇이었는지 곧 찾아낼 수 있겠어.

14 ④

해설 조언을 구하는 여자의 말에 책을 읽고 교환학생으로 가기로 결심한 남자가 책을 빌려주겠다는 응답이 가장 적절하다.
① 내가 올바른 직업을 선택했는지 확신이 없어.
② 넌 할 수 있어. 너의 새로운 삶에 행운을 빌어.
③ 나도 교환학생이 되는 것에 지원할 생각이야.
⑤ 실망하지 않으려면 빨리 예약하는 것을 추천해.

어휘 the same old 흔히 있는, 예전 그대로의

M What have you been up to, Tammy?
W Oh, the same old stuff. What about you, Simon?
M I'm planning to live abroad for a while as an exchange student in Germany.
W Really? How did you decide to do that?
M I read a book, which provided me with a newly found appreciation for different cultures, people, and places.
W Can you speak German?
M A little, but I'm studying it so hard now.
W Wow... you've made up your mind. I don't know if I could do it.
M I know it's going to be hard, but I think it will be a great opportunity for me.

남 뭐 하고 지냈니, 태미?
여 아, 늘 똑같지 뭐. 넌 어때, 사이먼?
남 난 독일에 교환학생으로 한동안 나가서 살 생각이야.
여 정말? 어떻게 그러기로 결심했니?
남 내가 책을 한 권 읽었는데, 그 책이 내게 다른 문화와 사람들, 그리고 장소들에 대한 새롭게 발견된 인식을 줬어.
여 너는 독일어를 할 수 있니?
남 약간, 하지만 난 지금 정말 열심히 공부하고 있어.
여 와… 너 결심했구나. 난 내가 그런 걸 할 수 있을지 모르겠어.
남 어려울 것이라는 건 알지만, 그건 내게 좋은 기회가 될 것 같아.

provide A with B A에게 B를 제공하다 (= **provide B for A**)
appreciation 인식; 감상; 감사
make up one's mind 결심하다

W What's your secret? I want to be as brave as you are.
M I'll lend you my book. You can find some ideas in it.

여 비결이 뭐야? 나도 너처럼 용감해지고 싶어.
남 내 책을 빌려줄게. 그 속에서 몇 가지 아이디어를 찾을 수 있을 거야.

---

15 ②

해설 자료가 사라진 상황이므로 복사본을 보내줄 수 있는지를 묻는 것이 가장 자연스럽다.
① 너는 컴퓨터 수리를 받았니?
② 너의 자료 복사본을 나에게 보내줄 수 있니?
③ 보고서가 사라져서 우리는 다시 시작해야만 해.
④ 우리가 보고서를 제시간에 끝낼 수 있을 것 같지가 않아.
⑤ 미안해. 내가 컴퓨터를 끄지 말았어야 하는데.

어휘 **lab** 실험실 (= **laboratory**)
shut off (기계 등이) 꺼지다, 멈추다
along with ~와 함께
[선택지 어휘] **start over** 다시 시작하다
shouldn't have p.p. ~하지 말았어야 하는데 (했다)

M Jacob is in the lab finishing a report that he and his partner, David, worked very hard to complete. Suddenly the computer shuts off. When Jacob turns it on again, he finds that most of the report, along with much of the data, is gone. He wouldn't finish it on time if he started from the beginning. He is worried, but then remembers that David has a copy of the data on his computer. So, Jacob wants to ask David if he could email the data. Jacob calls David and he answers on the phone. In this situation, what would Jacob most likely say to David?

남 제이콥은 실험실에서 그와 그의 파트너 데이비드가 완성하기 위해 아주 열심히 작업했던 보고서를 마무리하고 있다. 갑자기 컴퓨터가 꺼진다. 제이콥이 그것을 다시 켰을 때, 그는 많은 자료와 함께 보고서의 대부분이 사라졌음을 알게 된다. 처음부터 시작한다면 그는 제때에 마치지 못할 것이다. 그는 걱정하지만, 그때 데이비드가 그의 컴퓨터에 자료 복사본을 가지고 있는 것을 기억해낸다. 그래서 제이콥은 데이비드에게 그 자료를 이메일로 보내줄 수 있는지 물어보고 싶어 한다. 제이콥은 데이비드에게 전화하고 그가 전화를 받는다. 이 상황에서, 제이콥이 데이비드에게 할 말로 가장 적절한 것은 무엇인가?

---

16 ⑤   17 ④

해설 16 노인들이 독립적인 삶을 살기 위해 이용할 수 있는 공동체 시설과 생활을 소개하며 권하고 있다.
① 자립 생활 공동체의 장단점
② 독립적으로 사는 노인들의 체력의 중요성
③ 노인들이 자녀들과 건강한 삶을 살 수 있는 방법
④ 혼자 사는 노인 수 증가의 문제점
⑤ 노인들이 자립 생활 공동체로 이주해야 하는 이유

17 해석 참조

어휘 **independently** 독립적으로
force A to-v A가 (어쩔 수 없이) v하게 만들다
assistance 도움, 원조
a wide range of 다양한, 광범위한
facility ((보통 복수형)) 시설, 설비
miniature 아주 작은, 축소된
around ~에 맞춰, ~에 대하여
adopt (특정한 방식을) 취하다; 채택하다
balanced 균형 잡힌, 안정된

W Today I'd like to introduce a solution for seniors who would like to live independently. Many seniors are forced to live with their children when they need assistance in their daily lives. If you are in this position, I have some good news for you. Simply by moving to an independent living community, you can receive the care that you need. At an independent living community, there are a wide range of facilities and activities for you to enjoy. There are walking paths, biking areas, miniature golf courses, swimming pools, and much more. Plus, independent living communities are designed around healthy living for seniors. You can remain in good health by adopting an active life. Wake up early, take long lazy walks, eat a balanced diet, and avoid stress. These things will help you live a healthy life. If you are finding it difficult to lead an active life in your home, consider moving to one of the many independent living communities near you.

여 오늘 저는 독립적으로 살고 싶은 노인들을 위한 해결책 하나를 소개하고자 합니다. 많은 노인들은 일상생활에서 도움이 필요할 때, 자녀들과 함께 살 수밖에 없습니다. 만약 여러분이 이런 입장이라면, 여러분을 위한 좋은 소식이 있습니다. 단순히 자립 생활 공동체로 이주함으로써, 여러분은 필요한 보살핌을 받을 수 있습니다. 자립 생활 공동체에는 즐길 만한 다양한 시설과 활동이 있습니다. 산책로, 자전거 구역, 소형 골프장, 수영장과 그 밖의 많은 시설이 있습니다. 게다가, 자립 생활 공동체는 노인들의 건강한 생활에 맞춰 설계되었습니다. 활동적인 삶을 취함으로써 여러분은 계속해서 건강할 수 있습니다. **일찍 일어나고(①), 느긋이 오랫동안 산책하고(②), 균형 잡힌 식사를 하며(③) 스트레스를 피하세요(⑤)**. 이렇게 하면 건강한 삶을 사는 데 도움이 될 것입니다. 여러분이 집에서 활동적인 생활을 영위하기 어렵다면, 주위에 있는 많은 자립 생활 공동체 중 한 군데로 이사하는 것을 고려해 보십시오.

01 ④	**02** ②	**03** ④	**04** ④	**05** ②	**06** ②	**07** ⑤	**08** ⑤	**09** ②	**10** ②
11 ②	**12** ⑤	**13** ②	**14** ③	**15** ②	**16** ②	**17** ③			

01 ④

해설 let me tell you how to play this game에서 알 수 있듯이 게임 방법을 설명하고 있다.

어휘 total 합계를 내다; 합계, 총수
announce 발표하다, 알리다
straw 빨대

W Hello, students. This is Kayla Wood, your P.E. teacher. Now, we're ready for the final game. After this game the points will be totaled and the winner announced. So, let me tell you how to play this game. All the members of your team put straws in their mouths. And the boy at the end of the line puts one of these snacks called an onion ring on his straw. The onion ring must be passed from straw to straw down the line. When the boy at the other end of the line has the onion ring on his straw, his team will be asked a quiz question. If the team gets it right, it gets one point. Dropping the onion ring means your team is out. Now, are you ready to start?

여 안녕하세요, 학생 여러분. 체육 교사 카일라 우드 입니다. 이제 마지막 게임 준비가 되었습니다. 이번 게임 후에 점수가 합산되어 우승자가 발표될 것입니다. 그럼, 이 게임을 하는 방법을 알려드리겠습니다. 여러분 팀의 모든 팀원은 입에 빨대를 뭅니다. 그리고 줄의 끝에 있는 학생은 양파링이라고 불리는 이 과자 하나를 자신의 빨대에 끼워주세요. 양파링은 (사람들의) 줄을 따라 빨대에서 빨대로 전해져야 합니다. 그 줄의 반대쪽 끝에 있는 학생이 자신의 빨대에 양파링을 전달받으면 그 팀에게 퀴즈 문제가 주어질 것입니다. 그 팀이 문제를 맞히면 1점을 얻습니다. 양파링을 떨어뜨리면 탈락입니다. 이제 시작할 준비가 됐나요?

02 ②

해설 남자는 컴퓨터 부품의 재활용 방법을 찾아서 환경 오염을 막아야 한다고 말하고 있다.

어휘 dump 버리다
landfill 쓰레기 매립지
manufacturer 제조 회사[업자]
recycle 재활용하다
prevent 예방하다, 막다

W It seems that no one can live without computers these days.
M Very true. Unfortunately, we have a high price to pay for that.
W What do you mean?
M Because so many people want the latest computers, used computers are being thrown away every day.
W That's a problem.
M About 12 million computers are dumped into the landfills every year in America.
W There must be something we can do.
M I think the manufacturers need to rethink the way they build computers.
W In what way?
M They need to find ways to recycle all the computer parts.
W Oh, right. Isn't that called electronic recycling? I read about it somewhere.
M Yes, by recycling the parts, we can prevent environmental pollution in a big way.
W I agree.

여 요즘에는 아무도 컴퓨터 없이는 살 수 없는 것처럼 보여.
남 맞는 말이야. 안타깝게도, 우린 그것 때문에 치러야 할 큰 대가가 있어.
여 무슨 말이야?
남 매우 많은 사람들이 최신 컴퓨터를 원하기 때문에 중고 컴퓨터가 매일 버려지고 있어.
여 그거 문제네.
남 미국에서는 매년 약 천이백만 대의 컴퓨터가 쓰레기 매립지에 버려지고 있어.
여 우리가 할 수 있는 뭔가가 틀림없이 있을 거야.
남 내 생각엔 제조 회사들이 컴퓨터를 생산하는 방식을 재고해볼 필요가 있어.
여 어떤 방식으로?
남 그들이 모든 컴퓨터 부품을 재활용하는 방법을 찾을 필요가 있어.
여 아, 맞아. 그건 전자제품 재활용이라고 불리지 않아? 어딘가에서 그것에 대해 읽었어.
남 응, 부품을 재활용함으로써 환경 오염을 많이 예방할 수 있어.
여 나도 그렇게 생각해.

03 ④

해설 남자가 사고가 난 차를 your car라고 했으므로 여자가 운전자임을 알 수 있고, 남자는 차를 수리하고 도색한다고 했으므로 정비공임을 알 수 있다.

W The accident wasn't my fault. The light was green.
M Uh-huh.
W The guy in the other car tried to make a left turn when he shouldn't have.

여 사고는 제 잘못이 아니었어요. 신호등은 초록색이었어요.
남 네.
여 그러지 말았어야 하는 때에 다른 차량에 있던 남자가 좌회전을 시도했지 뭐예요.

어휘 should not have p.p.
~하지 않았어야 하는데 (그렇게 했다)
damage 손상을 입히다; 손상, 피해
barely 거의 ~ 않다
scratch 긁힌 상처; 긁다, 할퀴다
insurance 보험(금)
claim (보상금 등에 대한) 청구, 신청; 주장

M That's too bad. But your car isn't badly damaged.
W And his car barely has a scratch. So he suggested we avoid the insurance company.
M So you're not making an insurance claim?
W No. We didn't call the police either. I just want you to tell me how much it'll cost to fix my front bumper.
M OK. Well, after I repair it, I will have to repaint the whole bumper.
W I know that. But the other driver will be paying for it. So just tell me the cost.
M Just a minute.

남 그것 참 유감이네요. 하지만 손님의 차는 심하게 손상되지는 않았어요.
여 그리고 그 사람 차는 거의 긁히지도 않았어요. 그래서 그 사람이 보험 처리를 하지 말자고 제안했고요.
남 그럼 보험금 청구는 안 하세요?
여 네. 우리는 경찰도 부르지 않았어요. 앞 범퍼를 수리하는 데 비용이 얼마나 들지만 알려주세요.
남 알겠습니다. 음, 수리한 후에 범퍼 전체를 다시 도색해야겠는데요.
여 알아요. 하지만 상대편 운전자가 비용을 지불할 거예요. 그러니 비용만 알려주세요.
남 잠시만요.

04 ④

해설 초 두 개짜리 촛대를 찾았느냐는 남자의 질문에 여자가 yes로 대답하고 테이블 위에 놓았다고 했으므로 그림 속의 촛대가 대화의 내용과 일치하지 않는다.

어휘 set up ~을 설치하다
portrait 초상화, 인물 사진
candlestick 촛대

[Cell phone rings.]
W Hello?
M Hi, Jenny. It's me. I just called to see how setting up the stage is going.
W It's almost done. First of all, I hung the curtains with the leaf pattern for the window.
M Great. Did you find a heart-shaped picture frame?
W Yes, and I put a portrait of a woman in it.
M What about the coffee table?
W I placed a round one on the left side as you said.
M Good. And did you find that two-armed candlestick I was talking about?
W Yes, I put it on the table. It seems to be much better than the three-armed one. And I placed a striped sofa in the middle of the stage.
M Then it sounds like everything's ready!

[휴대전화벨이 울린다.]
여 여보세요?
남 안녕, 제니. 나야. 무대 설치가 어떻게 되어가고 있는지 알아보려고 전화했어.
여 거의 다 됐어. 우선, 나뭇잎 무늬가 있는 커튼을 창문에 달았어.
남 잘했어. 하트 모양 액자는 찾았니?
여 응, 그리고 그 안에 여자 초상화를 넣었어.
남 커피 테이블은 어떻게 됐어?
여 네가 말했던 대로 둥근 것을 왼쪽에 배치했어.
남 좋아. 그리고 내가 이야기했던 초 두 개짜리 촛대는 찾았니?
여 응, 테이블 위에 놓았어. 초 세 개짜리 촛대보다 훨씬 더 괜찮은 것 같아. 그리고 무대 중앙에 줄무늬 소파를 놓았어.
남 그럼 다 준비된 것 같아!

05 ②

해설 남자와 여자가 할 일을 잘 구분해야 한다. 남자는 대사를 외우겠다고 했고 여자는 남자가 야구 연습을 빠질 수 있도록 코치에게 이야기하겠다고 했다.

어휘 rehearsal 리허설, 예행연습
costume (무대) 의상
line ((복수형)) (연극, 영화의) 대사
punish 벌주다

W Brad, how did you feel about the rehearsal today?
M Um, pretty good. And the costume went well with my character.
W Yeah, it looked nice. How about the lines?
M Well, I couldn't remember some of my lines.
W I know Shakespeare is difficult, but you are Hamlet and you must memorize all your lines.
M I know.
W Final rehearsal is Friday night. Until then you are to spend every minute practicing your lines.
M But what about my baseball practice? Our coach will punish me if I don't go.
W I'll talk to him. Don't worry.
M Okay, then I'll do it.

여 브래드, 오늘 리허설이 어땠다고 생각하니?
남 음, 꽤 좋았어요. 그리고 의상도 제 배역과 잘 맞았어요.
여 그래, 멋져 보이더구나. 대사는 어땠니?
남 저, 제 대사 중 몇 줄을 기억하지 못했어요.
여 셰익스피어 작품이 어렵다는 것은 알지만, 네가 햄릿 역을 맡았으니 네 대사를 모두 외워야만 해.
남 알고 있어요.
여 최종 리허설은 금요일 밤이야. 그때까지 넌 대사를 연습하는 데 모든 시간을 할애해야 해.
남 그렇지만 제 야구 연습은 어떡하죠? 연습하러 가지 않으면 우리 코치님이 제게 벌을 주실 거예요.
여 코치님께는 내가 얘기할게. 걱정하지 마.
남 네, 그럼 그렇게 할게요.

06 ②

해설 남자가 구입하기로 한 것은 가격이 더 저렴한 샴푸($12)와 헤어 마스크($15)이다. 컨디셔너는 사지 않기로 했음에 유의한다. 따라서 지불할 총 금액은 27달러이다.

어휘 dye 염색하다
hydrating 보습의

W Good Morning. How can I help you?

M Hello. I'm looking for some shampoo for dry hair.

W How about this? It coats your hair, leaving it silky smooth.

M Sounds good. How much is it?

W It's $26.

M That's very expensive. How is this 12-dollar shampoo?

W That's good, too. But if you color your hair, I recommend the other shampoo.

M I don't dye my hair, so I'll take the cheaper one. What conditioners do you have?

W I have a nice conditioner for $7 and a deep hydrating hair mask for $15.

M I'll take both of them. My hair tends to be very dry.

W If you use the hair mask, you won't need the conditioner. Would you still like both?

M Oh, really? Then I'll just take the hair mask. Here's my credit card.

여 안녕하세요. 어떻게 도와드릴까요?

남 안녕하세요. 건조한 모발을 위한 샴푸를 좀 찾고 있어요.

여 이건 어떠세요? 머리카락을 코팅해서 매끈하고 부드럽게 해줍니다.

남 좋은데요. 얼마인가요?

여 26달러입니다.

남 너무 비싸네요. 이 12달러짜리 샴푸는 어떤가요?

여 그것도 좋아요. 하지만 머리를 염색하신다면, 다른 샴푸를 권해드려요.

남 전 염색하지 않으니, 더 저렴한 걸로 할게요. 컨디셔너는 어떤 게 있나요?

여 7달러짜리 괜찮은 컨디셔너와 15달러짜리 강한 보습용 헤어 마스크가 있습니다.

남 둘 다 살게요. 제 머리카락은 매우 건조한 편이거든요.

여 헤어 마스크를 사용하시면 컨디셔너는 필요 없을 거예요. 그래도 둘 다 원하시나요?

남 아, 정말요? 그럼 헤어 마스크만 할게요. 여기 제 신용카드요.

07 ⑤

해설 여자는 릴리의 선생님과의 면담 때문에 남자를 태우러 공항에 갈 수 없다고 했다. 식사 준비는 공항 마중과는 상관없는 언급임에 유의한다.

어휘 pick A up A를 (차에) 태우러 가다
appointment 약속, 예약
cancel 취소하다
seafood 해산물

[Cell phone rings.]

W Oh, honey. I was waiting for your phone call. How was your business trip?

M It was a success. Everything went well.

W That's great. When are you coming home?

M I'll be home tomorrow. Do you think you can pick me up at 3 p.m. at the airport?

W 3 p.m.? I'm afraid I can't.

M Oh, is that because you have a doctor's appointment tomorrow?

W No, that's next week. Actually, I have a parent-teacher meeting with Lily's teacher at that time.

M Did something happen to Lily?

W No, everything is fine. But I'm afraid I can't cancel the appointment.

M That's okay. I'll just take a taxi home.

W I'm sorry. I'll make your favorite seafood dish tomorrow.

M That'd be great. See you at home.

[휴대전화벨이 울린다.]

여 아, 여보. 당신 전화를 기다리고 있었어요. 출장은 어땠어요?

남 성공적이었어요. 모든 게 잘되었어요.

여 잘됐네요. 언제 집에 오나요?

남 내일 집에 갈 거예요. 오후 3시에 공항으로 태우러 올 수 있어요?

여 오후 3시요? 안 될 것 같은데요.

남 아, 내일 병원 예약이 있기 때문이에요?

여 아니요, 그건 다음 주예요. 사실은 그 시간에 릴리의 선생님과 학부모-교사 면담이 있어요.

남 릴리에게 무슨 일이 있었나요?

여 아니요, 모든 게 좋아요. 하지만 그 약속을 취소할 수는 없을 것 같아요.

남 괜찮아요. 그냥 집에 택시를 타고 갈게요.

여 미안해요. 내일 당신이 좋아하는 해산물 요리를 만들어 놓을게요.

남 그거 좋죠. 집에서 봐요.

08 ⑤

해설 해석 참조

어휘 technically 엄밀히 말하면; 기술적으로
on average 평균적으로
cf. average 평균의
lay (알을) 낳다; 놓다
hatch 부화하다
height 키[신장]; 높이

W Welcome to the San Diego Zoo. I'm your guide, Mary.

M Mary, is that a flamingo on the pond?

W Yes. Technically, it is a Greater Flamingo. They are found in Africa, Asia, and Europe.

M I heard they live for twenty years on average.

W That's true. And they usually live longer when cared for by humans.

여 샌디에이고 동물원에 오신 것을 환영합니다. 저는 여러분의 가이드인 메리입니다.

남 메리, 연못에 있는 저것이 홍학인가요?

여 맞습니다. 엄밀히 말하면, 그것은 대홍학입니다. **그것들은 아프리카, 아시아와 유럽에서 발견됩니다(① 서식지)**.

남 전 **대홍학이 평균 20년 동안 살 수 있다(② 평균 수명)**고 들었어요.

여 사실입니다. 그리고 인간의 보살핌을 받으면 보통 더 오래 살죠.

M Oh, I see. How many eggs do they lay?	남 아, 그렇군요. 알은 몇 개 낳나요?
W They lay only one egg at a time, and the eggs take about thirty days to hatch.	여 한 번에 한 개만 낳고, **알이 부화하는 데는 약 30 일이 걸립니다**(③ 알의 부화 기간).
M I didn't know that. So that one is an adult?	남 그건 몰랐네요. 그럼 저건 다 자란 건가요?
W Yes, it's about 120 centimeters tall, which is the average height for an adult.	여 네, **키가 약 120센티미터인데**(④ 키), 그것은 다 자란 홍학의 평균 키입니다.
M It sure is beautiful.	남 정말 아름답네요.

09 ②

해설 코코넛밀크가 신선할 때는 향이 강하지 않다고 했다.

어휘 liquid 액체
contain 포함하다, 들어있다
ingredient (특히 요리 등의) 재료, 성분
tropical 열대 (지방)의
sweeten (설탕 등을 넣어) 달게 하다
by itself 그것만으로; 단독으로
frozen (식품이) 냉동된

M Coconut milk is a liquid that comes from coconut fruit. As the name suggests, it is white and has the rich taste of milk. The color and taste are due to the high amount of oil it contains. Coconut milk has a very unique smell, but when it's fresh, the smell is not strong. It is a common ingredient in the dishes of many tropical regions, such as the curries of Southeast Asia. To make these curry sauces, the milk is first cooked over high heat to separate the cream from the oil. In southern China, sweetened coconut milk is served by itself as a drink. In all cases, unused coconut milk is usually stored frozen, as this makes it last longer.

남 코코넛밀크는 코코넛 열매에서 나오는 액체입니다. 이름에서 알 수 있듯이, 이것은 흰색이고 우유 맛이 진하게 납니다. 이 색과 맛은 **코코넛밀크에 함유된 많은 양의 기름 때문입니다**(①). **코코넛밀크는 매우 독특한 향이 있지만, 신선할 때는 향이 강하지 않습니다**(②). 코코넛밀크는 동남아시아의 카레와 같은 **많은 열대 지방 요리의 흔한 재료입니다**(③). 이 카레 소스를 만들려면, **기름에서 크림을 분리하기 위해 코코넛 밀크가 우선 센 불에 조리되어야 합니다**(④). 중국 남부 지방에서는 **달콤하게 만든 코코넛밀크 자체가 음료로 제공됩니다**(⑤). 모든 경우에, 사용되지 않은 코코넛밀크는 주로 냉동해서 보관되는데, 이렇게 하면 더 오래 가기 때문입니다.

10 ②

해설 록 음악을 제외하고 천 달러 예산을 넘지 않는 주말 밴드 중에서 가수가 없는 것을 고른다. 밴드가 필요한 토요일이 주말이라는 점에 주의한다.

어휘 mood 분위기; 기분
budget 예산, 경비
obviously 확실히, 분명히
vocalist 가수, 보컬리스트

M Planning this event has been really difficult!
W Yes, but now we only need to make a final choice about the band.
M Right. I like rock, but I'm not sure if it will set the right mood.
W I agree. Jazz or blues would be better. What do you think?
M You're right. We also have to consider that our budget is $1,000.
W Okay, and we obviously need them for 3 hours on Saturday night.
M Do you think it would be better to have a singer?
W I think a band without a vocalist would be nice, since we only need background music during the event.
M I agree. And, if we really need a singer, you will jump on stage, right?
W You must be kidding! Okay, then I guess we've decided.

남 이 행사 준비는 진짜 힘들었어!
여 응, 그래도 이제 마지막으로 밴드 선택만 하면 돼.
남 그래. 난 록 음악이 좋지만, 그게 적절한 분위기를 조성할지 모르겠어.
여 나도 동의해. 재즈 음악이나 블루스가 더 좋을 것 같아. 어떻게 생각하니?
남 네 말이 맞아. 우리 예산이 1,000달러라는 것도 고려해야만 해.
여 알겠어, 그리고 토요일 밤에 3시간 동안 확실히 그들이 필요해.
남 너는 가수가 있는 게 더 나을 거라고 생각하니?
여 행사 동안 단지 배경 음악이 필요한 거니까 가수 없는 밴드가 좋을 것 같아.
남 나도 동의해. 그리고 만약 가수가 정말 필요하다면, 네가 무대 위에 올라갈 거잖아, 그렇지?
여 너 농담하는 거지! 그래, 그럼 결정이 난 것 같아.

11 ②

해설 시험 결과를 걱정하는 여자가 지난번에 만점을 받았으니 걱정할 필요가 없을 것 같다는 남자에게 할 말로 가장 적절한 응답을 고른다.
① 난 내가 낙제할 걸 알았어.
③ 시험이 취소되어서 안심했어.
④ 맞아, 너는 점수를 걱정해서는 안 돼.

M Kate, did you hear that the exam results came out already?
W Really? Oh, I'm really concerned about mine.
M I don't think you need to worry. You got full marks in the last exam.
W I'm afraid it won't be like the last time.

남 케이트, 시험 결과가 벌써 나왔다는 것 들었니?
여 정말? 아, 내 결과가 정말 걱정돼.
남 걱정할 필요 없을 것 같은데. 너 지난 시험에서 만점 받았잖아.
여 이번에는 지난번과 같지 않을 것 같아.

⑤ 시험 결과를 보는 게 기대돼.

어휘 full marks (시험에서) 만점

---

12 ⑤

해설 제니가 왜 캐나다로 이주하는지 물었으므로 이유를 설명하는 응답이 가장 적절하다.
① 그녀의 마지막 근무일이거든.
② 지난달에 결정됐어.
③ 송별회 때문이야.
④ 난 캐나다로 여행 가고 싶어.

어휘 farewell party 송별회

W Jim, what are you doing after work today?
M I'm going to Jenny's farewell party. She's moving to Canada.
W Oh, really? Why is she moving to Canada?
M She's going to live with her parents.

여 짐, 오늘 퇴근 후에 뭐 할 거니?
남 제니의 송별회에 갈 거야. 그녀가 캐나다로 이주하거든.
여 아, 정말? 왜 캐나다로 이주하는데?
남 부모님과 함께 살 거래.

---

13 ②

해설 여자는 현재 룸메이트를 바꾸는 것도, 예전에 함께 살았던 스미스 씨 가족에게 돌아가는 것도 불가능하므로 그러한 상황에 대한 아쉬움을 표현하는 응답이 적절하다.
① 전 혼자 사는 게 정말 좋아요.
③ 하지만 세레나는 최근에 더 깨끗해졌어요.
④ 이사 가게 해 주신 것에 대해 감사드리고 싶어요.
⑤ 스미스 씨 가족이 제 홈스테이 가정이 된다니 정말 기뻐요.

어휘 vacuum 진공청소기로 청소하다; 진공
[선택지 어휘] by oneself 혼자
should have p.p. ~했어야 했는데 (하지 않았다)

M Hyunjeong, I'm really sorry you're not happy with your roommate. But I can't do much about the problem now.
W But Serena is too dirty. She doesn't wash her dishes and never vacuums the floor.
M I talked to her and she promised to try to clean up.
W She hasn't changed.
M I'll talk to her again.
W Can I move back in with the Smiths, the homestay family I had when I first came to America?
M No, someone else is staying with them now.
W That's too bad. Can't you find me a new roommate?
M I don't have any new students coming over for another 4 months.
W I should have stayed with the Smiths.

남 현정 씨, 룸메이트가 마음에 들지 않아서 정말 유감이에요. 하지만 그 문제에 대해 지금 해줄 수 있는 게 별로 없어요.
여 그렇지만 세레나는 너무 지저분해요. 설거지를 안 하고 절대 바닥을 진공청소기로 청소하지도 않아요.
남 제가 세레나에게 얘기를 했고 그녀는 깨끗이 하겠다고 약속했어요.
여 그 애는 달라진 게 없어요.
남 제가 다시 얘기할게요.
여 제가 미국에 처음 왔을 때 홈스테이 가정이었던 스미스 씨 댁으로 다시 들어갈 수 있을까요?
남 안 돼요, 지금은 다른 학생이 머물고 있어요.
여 정말 곤란하네요. 새 룸메이트를 찾아주실 수는 없나요?
남 앞으로 4개월간은 새로 오는 학생이 없어요.
여 스미스 씨 댁에 머물렀어야 했네요.

---

14 ③

해설 여자가 축제에서 할 공연에 대해 구체적인 제안을 해야 한다고 했으므로 좀 더 생각해보겠다는 응답이 가장 적절하다.
① 그것에 대해서 이미 너무 많이 생각해봤어.
② 아, 이런. 아직 결정이 안 됐다면 좋을 텐데.
④ 응, 네 제안에 전적으로 동의해.
⑤ 물론이지, 난 다른 반들처럼 노래하고 싶어.

어휘 can't carry a tune 음치이다
short play 토막극
specific 구체적인, 명확한
suggestion 제안, 제의
cf. make[offer] a suggestion 제안[제의]하다

W Jinho, have you thought about the performance our class should do for the school festival?
M Let's do a play.
W I'd rather do a dance. Many classes are doing special dances.
M I know everyone loves to dance. But not me!
W Well, how about singing a song?
M No, I don't like that either. I can't carry a tune. But I do like to act. I want to do a short play.
W About what? What's the title?
M Hmm... I don't know.
W Well, you have to make a specific suggestion to the class. Subin has suggested doing a Nanta-style drumming show.
M Really?
W And Sue has suggested doing card magic tricks.
M Well, then I'll put some more thought into it.

여 진호야, 학교 축제에서 우리 반이 해야 할 공연에 대해 생각해봤니?
남 연극을 하자.
여 나는 차라리 춤을 추겠어. 많은 반들이 특별한 춤을 출 거야.
남 다들 춤추고 싶어 한다는 걸 알아. 하지만 나는 아니야!
여 음, 노래하는 건 어때?
남 아니, 그것도 싫어. 난 음치야. 하지만 연기하는 것은 정말 좋아해. 토막극을 하고 싶어.
여 무엇에 대해서 말이니? 제목이 뭐야?
남 음… 모르겠어.
여 음, 네가 반 아이들에게 구체적인 제안을 해야 해. 수빈이는 난타 방식의 드럼 연주 쇼를 하자고 제안했어.
남 정말?
여 그리고 수는 카드 마술을 하는 것을 제안했어.
남 음, 그렇다면 좀 더 생각해볼게.

15 ②

해설 부모님의 노고에 대해 감사를 전하고 싶어 하므로 모든 지원에 감사드린다는 말이 가장 적절하다.

① 제가 그것을 계산할게요.
② 모든 지원에 감사드려요.
③ 이 졸업 파티는 멋지네요.
④ 제가 도와드릴 수 있어서 정말 기뻐요.
⑤ 가게를 정말 잘 단장하셨네요.

어휘 convenience store 편의점
run 운영하다
[선택지 어휘] fix up 단장하다, 수리하다

W Tim graduated from law school and got a job in New York City. He is successful, but so busy that he can't visit his parents very often. This Sunday, however, he is free. So he drives his new car to his hometown. He parks and walks into the small convenience store his parents run. When he was a child, the store seemed special. Now he realizes it's tiny and simple. He watches his parents for a minute. They look old and tired. He feels more grateful than ever for their efforts to help him graduate. Thus, Tim would like to tell them how thankful he is for everything. In this situation, what would Tim most likely say to his parents?

여 팀은 법학 전문 대학원을 졸업하고 뉴욕시에 일자리를 얻었다. 그는 성공했지만 너무 바빠서 부모님을 자주 찾아뵙지 못한다. 그러나 이번 일요일은 한가하다. 그래서 그는 새로 구입한 차를 운전해서 고향에 간다. 그는 차를 주차하고 부모님께서 운영하시는 작은 편의점으로 걸어 들어간다. 그가 어렸을 때, 그 가게는 특별해 보였다. 그는 이제 가게가 자그마하고 간소하다는 것을 깨닫는다. 그는 부모님을 잠시 바라본다. 부모님은 늙고 지쳐 보인다. 그는 자신이 졸업할 수 있게 도와주신 부모님의 노고에 그 어느 때보다 더 감사함을 느낀다. 그래서 팀은 모든 것에 대해 자신이 얼마나 감사하고 있는지 부모님께 말하고 싶어 한다. 이 상황에서, 팀이 부모님께 할 말로 가장 적절한 것은 무엇인가?

16 ②   17 ③

해설 16 예술이 건강을 유지하는 것과 밀접하게 관련되어 있다는 내용이다.

① 예술을 치료 목적으로 이용하는 방법
② 예술이 건강에 미치는 긍정적인 영향
③ 사람들이 예술을 창조하는 이유
④ 환자들을 위한 다양한 종류의 예술 수업들
⑤ 그림과 음악 사이의 관계

[선택지 어휘] therapy 치료(법)
positive 긍정적인

17 해석 참조

어휘 broadcast 방송
have to do with ~와 관계가 있다, 관련되다
dramatically 크게, 급격히; 극적으로
blood pressure 혈압
comfort 위안, 위로; 편안함
sculpture 조각품, 조소
promote 촉진하다, 조장하다
sign up for ~에 등록하다
wander 거닐다, 돌아다니다

M Hello, everyone. Today, I want to talk about art. "Wait a minute," you might say, "this is a broadcast about health. What does that have to do with art?" Let me explain. The fact is that art is closely connected to staying healthy. Do you know that just by listening to Mozart for 10 minutes, you can improve your health? It can dramatically lower your blood pressure. You can gain the same benefits by watching ballet. Additionally, art simply makes you feel better. Reading a poem or classic novel takes you to another world. Those activities can provide comfort during periods of stress. Furthermore, art helps your mind to be active. Exploring an art gallery with paintings and sculptures promotes creativity and critical thinking, which help to keep your brain healthy. Lastly, studies have also shown that art can help sick people get well. That's why some doctors advise their patients to draw or paint. So find your joy through the arts. Join dance lessons or sign up for a photography course; let your mind wander into the creative space.

남 안녕하세요, 여러분. 오늘 저는 예술에 대해 이야기하려고 합니다. 여러분은 "잠깐만요, 이건 건강에 관한 방송이에요. 그게 예술과 무슨 관계가 있죠?"라고 말할지도 모르겠군요. 제가 설명해 드릴게요. 예술은 건강을 유지하는 것과 밀접하게 관련되어 있는 것이 사실입니다. 모차르트 음악을 10분 동안 듣는 것만으로 건강을 증진시킬 수 있다는 것을 알고 있나요? 그것은 여러분의 혈압을 크게 낮출 수 있습니다. 여러분은 **발레**(① ballet)를 관람함으로써 같은 이로움을 얻을 수 있습니다. 게다가, 예술은 간단하게 여러분의 기분이 좋아지게 합니다. **시**(② poem)나 고전 소설을 읽는 것은 여러분을 다른 세상으로 데려갑니다. 그러한 활동들은 스트레스를 받는 시기에 위안을 줄 수 있습니다. 더구나, 예술은 여러분의 마음이 활동적이게 되도록 돕습니다. 그림과 **조각품**(④ sculpture)이 있는 미술관을 탐방하는 것은 창의성과 비판적 사고를 촉진하는데, 이것들은 여러분의 뇌를 건강하게 유지하는 데 도움을 줍니다. 마지막으로, 연구들 또한 예술이 아픈 사람들이 회복하는 데 도움이 될 수 있다는 것을 보여주었습니다. 그것이 바로 몇몇 의사들이 자신의 환자들에게 그림을 그리거나 색칠을 하라고 조언하는 이유입니다. 그러니 예술을 통해 여러분의 즐거움을 찾으세요. 춤 강좌에 참여하거나 **사진 촬영**(⑤ photography) 수업에 등록하세요. 여러분의 마음이 창의적인 공간을 거닐도록 하세요.

| 01 ② | 02 ③ | 03 ⑤ | 04 ④ | 05 ④ | 06 ④ | 07 ② | 08 ③ | 09 ④ | 10 ③ |
| 11 ④ | 12 ① | 13 ③ | 14 ④ | 15 ④ | 16 ② | 17 ⑤ | | | |

01 ②

해설 라디오 프로그램에서 제공할 세금 관련 상담 프로그램을 소개하고 청취와 전화 연락을 독려하며 홍보하고 있다.

어휘 announcement 소식, 발표
file for ~을 신고하다, 제출하다
consultation 상담, 자문
expert 전문가
tune in 주파수[채널]를 ~에 맞추다
toll-free (기관, 회사에 거는 전화가) 무료의

M You're listening to KLOS radio, and we have a special announcement. It's the time of year when we must all file for taxes. If you're afraid of having to pay more tax, worry no more. That's because we're offering our listeners a free consultation with Mr. Stephen Collins, an expert tax lawyer at Barnes Law Firm. He'll be at our studio for any questions from 2 p.m. to 4 p.m. tomorrow. He'll also give you useful tips to help you file your own taxes and tell you ways to save money. So if there's anything you'd like to know about taxes, tune in and give us a call. We're sure you'll greatly benefit from this consultation, so join us tomorrow. Our toll-free number is 1-800-552-8255.

남 여러분은 KLOS 라디오를 듣고 계시며 특별한 소식이 있습니다. 지금은 일 년 중 우리 모두 세금을 신고해야 하는 때입니다. 더 많은 세금을 내야 하는 게 두려우시다면, 더 이상 걱정하지 마십시오. 왜냐하면 저희가 청취자분들께 반즈 법률 사무소의 전문 세법(稅法) 변호사이신 스티븐 콜린스 씨와 함께 무료 상담을 해드리기 때문입니다. 그분은 내일 오후 2시부터 4시까지 그 어떤 질문에도 답해주시기 위해 저희 스튜디오에 나오실 겁니다. 그분은 또한 여러분이 세금을 신고하는 것을 돕는 유용한 조언을 해드릴 것이며 돈을 절약할 수 있는 방법을 알려드릴 것입니다. 그러니 세금에 관해 알고 싶은 게 있으시다면 주파수를 맞추고 저희에게 전화해주십시오. 여러분은 분명히 이 상담에서 큰 도움을 받으실 수 있으니 내일 저희와 함께하세요. 저희의 수신자 부담 전화번호는 1-800-552-8255입니다.

02 ③

해설 남자가 새로 전학 온 친구가 무서워 보인다고 하자 여자는 겉모습으로 사람을 판단해서는 안 된다고 말하고 있다.

어휘 cafeteria 구내식당, 카페테리아
wear make-up 화장하다
taste 취향, 기호; 맛
used to+동사원형 (과거에) v하곤 했다
misunderstand 오해하다
judge 판단하다
appearance 겉모습
regret 후회하다

M Hey, Catherine. Where have you been?
W I was in the cafeteria talking to Karen. She has great stories from when she lived in Germany.
M Karen? You mean that new girl? Well, she looks a little scary.
W What do you mean? She's really nice.
M She always dresses in dark clothing and she wears so much make-up.
W But, that's a matter of personal taste, isn't it?
M Hmm... I suppose you're right. On second thought, I used to be misunderstood because people thought I looked unkind.
W Yeah, it was hard to start talking to you at first. I think we shouldn't judge people by their clothing or appearance.
M Right. I kind of regret what I said now.
W Don't worry about it. Come with me and I'll introduce you to her.

남 야, 캐서린. 어디 있었어?
여 구내식당에서 캐런과 이야기하고 있었어. 그 애가 독일에서 살았을 때의 재밌는 이야기가 있거든.
남 캐런? 새로 온 그 여자애 말하는 거야? 음, 좀 무서워 보이던데.
여 그게 무슨 뜻이야? 그 애는 정말 친절해.
남 그 애는 항상 어두운 옷을 입고 화장을 너무 짙게 하잖아.
여 그렇지만 그건 개인의 취향 문제야, 그렇지 않니?
남 음... 네 말이 맞는 것 같아. 다시 생각해보니 사람들은 내가 불친절해 보인다고 생각해서 나는 오해를 받곤 했어.
여 그래, 처음엔 너에게 말을 걸기가 어려웠지. 난 옷이나 겉모습으로 사람을 판단해서는 안 된다고 생각해.
남 맞아. 내가 한 말이 지금 좀 후회돼.
여 걱정하지 마. 나와 함께 가면 그 애에게 널 소개해줄게.

03 ⑤

해설 여자는 신발이 불편해 왈츠가 잘 되지 않는다고 하고, 남자는 살사와 맘보 스텝을 보여주겠다고 하는 것으로 보아 수강생과 댄스 강사의 관계임을 알 수 있다.

W Carlos? Do you mind if we stop for a little while? I just can't get these steps right.
M Sure. Your rhythm and timing weren't so good in the partner waltz today. What's the matter?

여 카를로스? 우리 잠시 좀 멈춰도 될까요? 난 이 스텝을 제대로 할 수가 없어요.
남 그래요. 오늘 파트너 왈츠에서 당신의 리듬과 타이밍이 별로 좋지 않았어요. 무슨 일 있어요?

어휘		
brand new 완전 새것인		

어휘 brand new 완전 새것인
blister 물집
Band-Aid ((상표명)) 반창고

W Actually, my shoes are brand new. They've given me blisters.

M I'll get some Band-Aids for you. Do you have another pair of shoes?

W Only the sandals I had on when I came to the studio.

M They'll be fine today.

W OK. I'll go and get them.

M I'm going to show you some basic salsa and mambo steps next. Don't worry. I won't push you too hard.

W I don't mind. I love the Latin style. If I change my shoes, the pain won't be that bad.

여 사실, 제 신발이 완전 새것이라서요. 신발 때문에 물집이 생겼어요.

남 반창고 좀 갖다 드릴게요. 다른 신발이 있나요?

여 연습실에 올 때 신고 온 샌들밖에 없어요.

남 오늘은 그걸 신으셔도 괜찮아요.

여 알겠어요. 가서 가져올게요.

남 다음으로 살사와 맘보의 기본 스텝을 보여드릴게요. 걱정하진 마세요. 당신을 그리 심하게 몰아붙이지 않을게요.

여 전 괜찮아요. 라틴 스타일을 좋아하거든요. 신발을 갈아 신으면, 통증이 그리 심하지 않을 거예요.

04 ④

해설 여자가 포스터의 캠핑카를 자전거로 바꿀 것을 제안하고 있는 상황이므로 그림 속의 자전거가 대화의 내용과 일치하지 않는다.

어휘 location 장소, 위치
stand out 눈에 띄다; 뛰어나다
native American 미국 원주민
campfire 모닥불
enjoyable 즐거운, 재미있는
absolutely 정말 그렇다, 그렇고 말고
half moon 반달
go well with ~와 잘 어울리다

M Ann, I finished designing the poster for this year's summer camp. What do you think?

W It looks great. You put the date and location under the title, Elm High School Summer Camp.

M Yes. I want them to stand out.

W They really do. I can see two native American tents on the left. I love them.

M I'm glad you like them.

W I also like the campfire between the tents. Sitting around a campfire is an enjoyable part of the camping experience.

M Absolutely! And I put a camping car on the right side.

W Well, since it's a school camp, how about changing the camping car into a bicycle?

M You're right. I'll make the change right away. What do you think about a half moon above the mountains?

W It goes well with everything else. Good job!

남 앤, 제가 올해 여름 캠프의 포스터 디자인을 끝냈어요. 어떻게 생각하시나요?

여 멋져 보이네요. '엘름 고등학교 여름 캠프'라는 제목 아래 날짜와 장소를 넣었군요.

남 네, 그것들이 눈에 띄길 원해서요.

여 정말 그렇네요. 왼쪽에 미국 원주민 텐트 두 개가 보여요. 정말 마음에 들어요.

남 마음에 드신다니 기뻐요.

여 텐트 사이에 있는 모닥불도 좋아요. 모닥불 주변에 둘러앉는 것은 캠핑 경험의 즐거운 부분이죠.

남 정말 그래요! 그리고 저는 오른쪽에 캠핑카를 두었어요.

여 음, 이건 학교 캠프니까 캠핑카를 자전거로 바꾸는 건 어때요?

남 그 말이 맞네요. 바로 수정할게요. 산 위의 반달에 대해서는 어떻게 생각하세요?

여 다른 모든 것들과 잘 어울려요. 훌륭해요!

05 ④

해설 남자는 여자에게 친구인 밥이 오면 공책을 전해주라고 부탁했다.
① 선생님께 전화하기
② 즉시 밥에게 전화하기
③ 숙제 가져다주기
④ 밥에게 숙제 전해주기
⑤ 책상에 공책 올려두기

어휘 drop by 잠깐 들르다
in time 제시간에
way 아주; 훨씬

[Telephone rings.]

W Hello?

M Hi, Mom. It's Jerry.

W Hi. Are you OK? Is something wrong?

M I left my homework at home.

W Do you want me to bring it to you?

M No, you don't need to.

W Will your teacher let you bring it tomorrow?

M No. I phoned my friend Bob. He hasn't left for school yet.

W Bob?

M Yes. I asked Bob to drop by our apartment and get it. Can you give him the blue notebook on my desk?

W OK. Won't Bob be late for school?

M He'll be here in time. I came here way too early today.

[전화벨이 울린다.]

여 여보세요?

남 안녕, 엄마. 제리예요.

여 그래. 너 괜찮아? 무슨 일 있니?

남 집에 숙제를 두고 왔어요.

여 숙제를 가져다줄까?

남 아니요, 그러실 필요 없어요.

여 선생님께서 내일 가져오도록 하신 거니?

남 아니요. 제가 친구 밥에게 전화했어요. 아직 학교로 출발하지 않았대요.

여 밥이라고?

남 네. 밥에게 우리 아파트에 들러서 숙제를 가져다 달라고 부탁했어요. 제 책상 위에 있는 파란색 공책을 그에게 전해주시겠어요?

여 그래. 밥이 학교에 늦지는 않을까?

남 시간 내에 올 거예요. 오늘 제가 여기 너무 일찍 온 거라서요.

06 ④

해설 앞쪽의 좋은 좌석($90) 두 개를 예매하는데 학생 할인 10%가 두 좌석 모두가 아니라 한 좌석에만 적용된다는 점에 유의한다. 따라서 지불할 금액은 171달러이다.

어휘 section 부분, 구획
identification 신분증 (= ID);
신분증명
bill 지폐; 계산서; 법안
change 잔돈

W Do you still have tickets to the Dream Concert?
M We have a couple of seats left in the front section and a few in the back.
W How much are the seats in the front?
M Those are $90 per seat. They're the best seats we have.
W And the ones in the back?
M Those are $50 per seat.
W Okay, then I'll buy two tickets for the good seats. Also, are you offering student discounts?
M Yes. We offer 10% off if you show your student identification.
W Okay, here's my ID and two one-hundred-dollar bills.
M Actually, we only offer the discount to people who have an identification card.
W Oh, if I had known that, I would have brought my friend's. But I understand.
M Thank you, and here's your change.

여 아직 드림 콘서트 표가 있나요?
남 앞부분에 두어 좌석과 뒤쪽에 몇 개가 남아 있습니다.
여 앞쪽 좌석은 얼마인가요?
남 그것들은 좌석당 90달러입니다. 저희가 가진 최고의 좌석입니다.
여 그리고 뒤쪽 좌석은요?
남 그것들은 좌석당 50달러입니다.
여 알겠어요, 그럼 좋은 좌석으로 두 장 살게요. 학생 할인도 해주시나요?
남 그렇습니다. 학생증을 보여주시면 10퍼센트 할인을 해드립니다.
여 알겠어요, 여기 제 학생증과 백 달러짜리 지폐 두 장이요.
남 사실, 저희는 학생증을 가지고 계신 분께만 할인을 해드립니다.
여 아, 그걸 알았다면, 친구 것도 가져왔을 텐데. 그렇지만 괜찮아요.
남 감사합니다, 그리고 여기 잔돈입니다.

07 ②

해설 남자가 일주일짜리 요리 강좌를 신청해서 여행을 연장하려 한다고 했다.

어휘 amazing 굉장한
explore 답사하다, 탐험하다
pretty much 거의
sign up for ~을 신청하다, 등록하다
take care of ~을 처리하다

[Cell phone rings.]
M Mom! It's me, Jacob.
W Jacob! How is your trip going?
M Rome is just amazing! There's so much to do and see.
W I wish I was there with you. So, you are coming home next Monday, right?
M Well, I was thinking of staying for one more week.
W Really? Are you going to visit other cities in Italy?
M No, I'll stay in Rome for the rest of my trip.
W Then, do you have more places to explore in the city?
M No, I've been to pretty much every place in Rome. Actually, I signed up for a week-long cooking class here run by an Italian master chef.
W Good idea! Let me know if you need help to change your flight schedule.
M It's okay. I already took care of it.
W Alright. Always be safe and have fun!

[휴대전화벨이 울린다.]
남 엄마! 저 제이콥이에요.
여 제이콥! 여행은 어떻게 되어가고 있니?
남 로마는 정말 굉장해요! 할 것도 많고 볼 것도 많아요.
여 내가 너하고 거기 있으면 좋을 텐데. 그런데 다음 주 월요일에 집에 오는 거 맞지?
남 음, 일주일 더 머물까 생각 중이었어요.
여 그래? 이탈리아의 다른 도시들을 방문할 거니?
남 아니요, 남은 여행 기간 동안 로마에 머물 거예요.
여 그러면 그 도시에 더 답사할 곳이 있니?
남 아니요, 로마의 거의 모든 곳을 가봤어요. 사실, 전 이탈리아 주방장이 운영하는 일주일짜리 이곳 요리 강좌를 신청했어요.
여 좋은 생각이야! 네 비행기 시간을 변경하는데 도움이 필요하면 알려다오.
남 괜찮아요. 제가 벌써 처리했어요.
여 알겠다. 언제나 안전하고 즐겁게 보내렴!

08 ③

해설 해석 참조

어휘 as long as ~이기만 하면; ~하는 한
junior (4년제 대학의) 3학년 학생, (고등학교의) 2학년 학생
senior 마지막 학년[졸업반] 학생; 연장자
recommendation letter 추천서
application 지원[신청](서)
due ~하기로 되어 있는, 예정된

M Sally, have you heard about the National Student Leadership Conference?
W Yes, I heard it's pretty amazing.
M Then, let's go together this year. They're holding it at Heritage Oak University.
W When's the conference?
M From July 18th to the 23rd.
W I would love to, but isn't it hard to get accepted?
M Yeah, but you can apply as long as you're a junior or a senior in college, and have a recommendation letter.

남 샐리, 너 전국 학생 리더십 학회에 대해 들어본 적 있어?
여 응, 그거 아주 굉장하다고 들었어.
남 그럼, 올해에 같이 가자. **헤리티지 오크 대학에서 개최할 거래**(① 개최 장소).
여 학회는 언제야?
남 **7월 18일부터 23일까지야**(② 개최 기간).
여 가고는 싶은데, 참여 허가를 받기 어렵지 않아?
남 응, 하지만 **대학교 3학년이거나 졸업반이고, 추천서만 있으면 지원할 수 있어**(④ 지원 자격).

W I guess we could try. When are applications due?
M They're due on the 25th of next month. And since today's only the beginning of May, we still have time to get one of the 50 spaces.
W Okay, let's go for it.

여 한번 시도해볼 수는 있겠다. 지원서는 기한이 언제까지야?
남 다음 달 25일이 마감이야. 그리고 오늘이 5월 초일 뿐이니까, 우리는 **50개의 자리**(⑤ 모집 인원) 중 하나를 차지할 시간이 아직 있어.
여 그래, 우리 한번 해보자.

09 ④

해설 모든 수업은 오전에 진행한다.

어휘 local 지역의
be in charge of ~을 담당하다
string (악기의) 현[줄]
recreational 오락의
enroll 등록하다 (= sign up)
limit 한정[제한]하다

W The Beethoven Summer Music Camp is offering a variety of music programs to keep your kids busy this summer. The camp will provide a wonderful opportunity for children aged 7 to 15 to receive classical music education. We have some of the best music teachers in the local area, and each of them will be in charge of up to 10 children. Our camp includes voice, string, and piano lessons. All classes will be held in the morning so that students are free to enjoy various recreational activities in the afternoon. You can enroll your child in a one-week program to a four-week program. The tuition cost for each week is $400. Space is limited, so please sign up today.

여 베토벤 여름 음악 캠프는 이번 여름 여러분의 자녀들을 계속 바쁘게 할 다양한 음악 프로그램을 제공하고 있습니다. 캠프는 7세에서 15세 아이들에게(①) 고전 음악 교육을 받을 수 있는 멋진 기회를 제공할 것입니다. 저희는 지역의 가장 우수한 몇몇 음악 교사들이 있고 **각각의 교사가 아이들을 10명까지 담당할 것입니다**(②). 저희 캠프는 성악, 현악, 그리고 피아노 교습을 포함합니다(③). 학생들이 오후에 다양한 오락 활동을 자유롭게 즐길 수 있도록 **모든 수업은 오전에 열릴 것입니다**(④). 1주에서 4주 프로그램에 자녀를 등록하실 수 있습니다. **매 주별 수업료는 400달러입니다**(⑤). 정원이 한정되어 있으니, 오늘 등록하십시오.

10 ③

해설 수요일이나 금요일에 진행하고, 참가 최대 인원이 12명 이상이고, 권장 연령이 10~11세를 포함하며, 단체 할인을 해주는 곳을 선택한다.

어휘
reserve 예약하다
field trip 현장 학습, 견학
available 이용 가능한
go with 고르다, 받아들이다
qualify 자격을 주다
discount 할인
[선택지 어휘] maximum 최대; 최대의
participant 참가자

M Clara, I have to reserve a museum field trip for our school students. I made a list of museums around here. Could you help me choose?
W Sure. Let me see. Firstly, when are you planning to go on the trip?
M Anytime Wednesday or Friday is available.
W Okay. How many students are you going to take there?
M I'll take 12 students there.
W You have these three options. Oh, there is an age recommendation. How old are your students?
M Most of them are 10 years old, but some are 11 years old.
W Then I guess that leaves these two. Which one would you like?
M Well, I'd go with this one. It qualifies us for a group discount.
W That's good. Have a nice field trip!
M Thanks for helping me.

남 클라라, 내가 우리 학교 학생들을 위해 박물관 현장 학습을 예약해야 해서요. 이 근처의 박물관 목록을 만들었거든요. 고르는 것을 좀 도와주겠어요?
여 물론이죠. 어디 봐요. 첫째로, 언제 현장 학습을 갈 계획인가요?
남 수요일이나 금요일 아무 때나 가능해요.
여 좋아요. 거기 얼마나 많은 학생들을 데려갈 건가요?
남 열두 명의 학생을 거기 데려갈 거예요.
여 이 세 가지 선택지가 있네요. 아, 연령 권장이 있네요. 학생들이 몇 살인가요?
남 대부분은 열 살이지만 일부는 열한 살이에요.
여 그러면 이 두 개가 남는 것 같군요. 어떤 게 좋아요?
남 음, 저는 이걸로 할게요. 거기선 우리에게 단체 할인 자격을 주거든요.
여 잘됐네요. 즐거운 현장 학습 되세요!
남 도와줘서 고마워요.

11 ④

해설 아델의 전화번호를 갖고 있지 않다고 했으므로 번호를 보내주겠다는 응답이 가장 적절하다.
① 내가 그녀에게 곧 알려줄게.
② 아, 그녀의 결혼식은 멋졌어.
③ 아델은 아름다운 신부가 될 거야.
⑤ 내가 어딘가에 적어둔 날짜가 있어.

어휘 definitely 분명히, 확실히

W Mark, do you know the date of Kelly's wedding?
M I'm not sure, but Adele definitely knows. Why don't you give her a call?
W Good idea, but I don't have her number.
M Really? I'll send it to your phone, then.

여 마크, 켈리의 결혼식 날짜 아니?
남 난 잘 모르지만, 아델은 분명 알 거야. 그녀에게 전화해보는 게 어때?
여 좋은 생각이지만 난 그녀의 전화번호가 없어.
남 정말? 그럼 내가 네 전화로 번호를 보내줄게.

12 ①

해설 남자가 여자에게 가고 싶은 식당이 있는지 물었으므로 원하는 장소를 말하는 응답이 가장 적절하다.
② 그건 우리 집에서 세 블록 떨어져 있어.
③ 다음번에는 너와 같이 점심 먹을게.
④ 최근에 피자를 너무 많이 먹었어.
⑤ 2시에 만나자.

M Vanessa, do you want to <u>have lunch with me</u> at Pizza King?
W I'd love to, but I had pizza last night. <u>How about a different place?</u>
M That's fine with me. Where would you like to go?
W I want to try the new Chinese restaurant.

남 바네사, 피자 킹에서 함께 점심 먹을래?
여 그러고 싶긴 한데, 어젯밤에 피자를 먹었어. 다른 곳은 어때?
남 나는 괜찮아. 어디 가고 싶니?
여 새로 생긴 중국 음식점에 가보고 싶어.

13 ③

해설 집에서 가장 가까운 수리점의 위치를 알려주었으므로 고장 난 카메라를 그곳으로 가져가겠다는 응답이 가장 적절하다.
① 당신의 관리자와 이야기할 수 있을까요?
② 칩 가격으로는 비싼 것 같네요.
④ 일회용 사진기는 어디서 살 수 있습니까?
⑤ 수리점은 바로 모퉁이를 돌면 있습니다.

어휘 blink 깜박거리다
chip (전자) 칩; 조각
loose 헐거운, 풀린
screwdriver 드라이버
extension (전화의) 내선; 연장
[선택지 어휘] supervisor 관리자; 감독관
disposable 일회용의, 사용 후 버릴 수 있는

[Telephone rings.]
W Thank you for calling Camera World. What can I do for you?
M My digital camera's screen is blinking and the shutter doesn't work.
W Alright. <u>That sounds like a problem</u> with the main chip.
M What do you mean?
W The chip inside your camera <u>may have come loose</u>.
M Let me see. <u>I can't get the camera open</u> without a small screwdriver.
W When you find a tool, call back and ask for extension 51.
M I don't know much about cameras. I don't think <u>I should open it up myself</u>.
W Well, we have five locations in the city you can visit for a repair.
M <u>Which one is closest</u> to my place? I live on King's Road.
W We have one on Third Street. It probably takes about ten minutes to get there from your place.
M I'll bring it in right away, thank you.

[전화벨이 울린다.]
여 카메라 월드에 전화 주셔서 감사합니다. 무엇을 도와드릴까요?
남 제 디지털카메라 화면이 깜박거리고 셔터가 작동하지 않아요.
여 네. 메인 칩에 문제가 있는 것 같습니다.
남 무슨 뜻이죠?
여 카메라 안에 있는 칩이 헐거워졌을 수 있습니다.
남 한번 보죠. 소형 드라이버 없이는 카메라를 열 수가 없어요.
여 연장을 찾으시면, 다시 전화를 주시고 내선 51번을 요청하세요.
남 저는 카메라에 대해서는 잘 몰라요. 제가 직접 열면 안 될 것 같네요.
여 음, 수리를 위해 방문 가능한 지점이 시내에 다섯 군데 있습니다.
남 어느 곳이 우리 집과 가장 가까운가요? 저는 킹스 가에 살아요.
여 3번가에 하나 있습니다. 고객님 댁에서 거기까지 가는 데 아마 약 10분 정도 걸릴 것입니다.
남 제가 바로 가지고 갈게요, 감사합니다.

14 ④

해설 드라이클리닝 비용이 많이 든다며 다음에 옷을 살 때 세탁기로 세탁 가능한 옷을 구매하라고 했으므로 옷을 살 때 그 점을 명심하겠다는 응답이 가장 적절하다.
① 당신은 그 옷들을 세탁기로 세탁할 수 있어요.
② 세탁하기 전에 지시사항이 적힌 표를 먼저 읽어보세요.
③ 당신은 세탁바구니에 세탁물을 넣어 두어야 해요.
⑤ 맞아요. 새 세탁기를 하나 사는 게 좋겠어요.

어휘 dry clean 드라이클리닝하다
ruin 망치다, 엉망으로 만들다
machine wash 세탁기로 빨다
insist 주장하다; 고집하다

W Andy, don't put those clothes in the washing machine.
M Why? I think we can wash these clothes in the washing machine.
W No, we can't. These are 100% silk. We <u>should have them dry cleaned</u>.
M How much does it cost to dry clean a shirt?
W A shirt costs $10.
M Really? It's very expensive.
W Well, <u>it's better than ruining our clothes</u> by machine washing them. It's cheaper in the end.
M Why did you buy clothes that <u>can't be machine washed</u>? Think about the money we spend to dry clean them.
W So are you <u>insisting that I put these</u> in the machine?

여 앤디, 그 옷들은 세탁기에 넣지 마요.
남 왜요? 이 옷들은 세탁기에 넣고 세탁할 수 있을 것 같은데요.
여 아니요, 할 수 없어요. 이건 100% 실크예요. 이것들은 드라이클리닝해야 해요.
남 셔츠를 드라이클리닝하는 데 비용이 얼마나 들죠?
여 셔츠는 10달러예요.
남 정말요? 매우 비싸군요.
여 음, 그렇게 하는 게 옷을 세탁기로 세탁해서 망치는 것보다 낫잖아요. 결국 더 싼 거예요.
남 당신은 왜 세탁기로 세탁할 수 없는 옷을 샀나요? 그것들을 드라이클리닝하기 위해 우리가 쓰는 돈을 생각해봐요.
여 그럼 당신은 내가 이 옷들을 세탁기에 넣어야 한다고 주장하는 건가요?

[선택지 어휘] **instruction** 설명; 지시
laundering 세탁
cf. **laundry** 세탁물; 세탁(소)
keep A in mind A를 명심하다

M No, but you should buy clothes that can be machine washed next time.

W All right. I'll keep that in mind when I buy clothes.

남 아니요, 그렇지만 당신은 다음번엔 세탁기로 세탁할 수 있는 옷을 사야 해요.

여 알겠어요. 옷을 살 때 그 점을 명심할게요.

---

15 ④

해설 회의 시간이 앞당겨져 주문한 아침 식사를 할 수 없으므로 주문을 취소해달라는 말이 가장 적절하다.
① 제가 준비하는 동안 택시를 한 대 불러주세요.
② 발표를 위해 노트북을 대여할 수 있을까요?
③ 오믈렛이 아닌 스크램블드에그를 받았어요.
④ 제가 전에 주문한 아침 식사를 취소하고 싶어요.
⑤ 목적지까지 가는 가장 빠른 길을 좀 알려주시겠어요?

어휘 **hang up** 전화를 끊다
urgent 긴급한, 다급한
forward 더 일찍; 앞으로
destination 목적지, 도착지

M Emily is staying at a hotel on a business trip. She has an important presentation this afternoon and wants to start the day with a nice breakfast. Emily calls for room service and orders an omelet and toast. However, soon after she hangs up, Emily receives an urgent call telling her that the time of the meeting has been moved forward. She leaves immediately, and takes a taxi to her destination. On the way, Emily suddenly remembers the room service she ordered. So, Emily is going to call the hotel to cancel it. In this situation, what would Emily most likely say to the hotel staff?

남 에밀리는 출장차 한 호텔에 머무르고 있다. 그녀는 오늘 오후에 중요한 발표가 있어 맛있는 아침 식사로 하루를 시작하고자 한다. 에밀리는 룸서비스를 이용하기 위해 전화해 오믈렛과 토스트를 주문한다. 그러나 전화를 끊고 얼마 지나지 않아, 에밀리는 회의 시간이 앞당겨졌다는 긴급한 전화를 받는다. 그녀는 즉시 나가서 택시를 타고 목적지까지 간다. 가는 길에 에밀리는 갑자기 자신이 주문한 룸서비스가 기억난다. 그래서 에밀리는 그것을 취소하기 위해 호텔로 전화를 걸려고 한다. 이 상황에서, 에밀리가 호텔 직원에게 할 말로 가장 적절한 것은 무엇인가?

---

16 ②   17 ⑤

해설 16 집을 정돈하는 방법을 소개하는 내용이다.
① 오래된 물건을 재활용할 필요성
② 집을 정돈하는 방법
③ 관리가 잘 된 집의 장단점
④ 계획되지 않은 지출을 방지하는 방법
⑤ 가정용품을 살 때 고려해야 할 것

[선택지 어휘] **necessity** 필요(성)
recycle 재활용하다
organize 정리하다
pros and cons 장단점
well-kept 관리가 잘 된
prevent 예방하다
household goods 가정용품

17 해석 참조

어휘 **clear out** ~을 없애고 청소하다
extra 여분의
tidy 잘 정돈된, 깔끔한
closet 벽장
let go 버리다, 놓다
throw out 버리다
keep in order 정리해 두다, 질서를 바로잡아 두다

W Hello, everyone. Do you feel you have too many things in your house? Sometimes, it's a good idea to clear out extra things. Today, I'd like to share some tips to make your home tidy. Firstly, every month, take a good look at your closet. When did you wear that T-shirt last? If it's been hanging in your closet for over a year without being worn, it's a sign to let it go. You may think you will wear it someday. I can tell you, you won't. Say goodbye. Keep your closet only 80 percent full, and always put your things back in the same place. Another idea is to think hard before you buy something. Ask yourself, "Do I really need this vase or do I just want it?" Also, think carefully about where you place new things in your house. For example, suppose you want a coffee table, but you don't have a good place for it. Then you don't need it. Lastly, when you do buy something new, throw out something old. If a chair is too old, buy a new one and throw the old one out. Free yourself from too many things, and keep your house in order.

여 안녕하세요, 여러분. 여러분은 집에 물건이 너무 많다고 느끼시나요? 때때로 여분의 물건들을 치우는 것은 좋은 아이디어입니다. 오늘 저는 여러분의 집을 정돈하는 몇 가지 조언을 공유하려고 합니다. 우선, 매달 여러분의 옷장을 잘 살펴보세요. 저 **티셔츠**(① T-shirt)를 마지막으로 입은 게 언제인가요? 일 년 넘게 안 입은 채로 옷장에 걸려 있었다면 그것은 버리라는 신호입니다. 여러분은 그걸 언젠가 입을 거라고 생각할 수도 있습니다. 제가 말씀드리죠, 안 입을 겁니다. 작별인사를 하십시오. 옷장은 80퍼센트만 채워놓고, 여러분의 물건을 항상 같은 곳에 다시 갖다 놓으세요. 또 하나의 아이디어는 무언가 살 때 골똘히 생각해보는 것입니다. "내가 정말 이 **화병**(② vase)이 필요한가, 아니면 그냥 원하는 것인가?"라고 스스로에게 질문하십시오. 또한 집에 새로운 물건을 어디에 둘지에 대해서도 주의 깊게 생각하십시오. 예를 들어, 여러분이 **커피 테이블**(③ coffee table)을 원한다고 가정해봅시다. 하지만 당신은 그것을 놓을 좋은 장소가 없습니다. 그렇다면 여러분은 그게 필요 없습니다. 마지막으로, 새로운 것을 사면 오래된 것은 버리세요. 만일 **의자**(④ chair)가 너무 낡았으면 새로운 걸 사고 오래된 건 버리세요. 너무 많은 물건들에서 벗어나 여러분의 집을 정돈하십시오.

| 01 ③ | 02 ② | 03 ⑤ | 04 ③ | 05 ④ | 06 ⑤ | 07 ⑤ | 08 ② | 09 ④ | 10 ④ |
| 11 ① | 12 ⑤ | 13 ⑤ | 14 ④ | 15 ⑤ | 16 ① | 17 ③ | | | |

01 ③

해설 가족을 부양할 수 없게 되었을 때에 대비한 보험 가입의 필요성을 언급한 뒤 마지막에 보험 상담을 받기 위해 전화 달라고 했으므로 보험 상품에 가입하도록 권유하려는 것이 목적이다.

어휘 comfortably 편안하게, 부족함 없이
shelter 주거; 피난처
adequately 적절히, 충분히
cf. adequate 적절한, 충분한
insure 보험에 들다; 보증하다
cf. insurance 보험
provider 공급자
analyze 분석하다
requirement 요건, 조건

W If suddenly you could not support your family, would they continue to live comfortably? Would they have the money for food, shelter, clothing, and education? If you aren't adequately insured, they will be in a big trouble. But most people don't know how much insurance is adequate. That is why Acme Insurance Co. is the right insurance provider for you. We will analyze your current spending habits and lifestyle, and your family's needs, such as university costs for your children. Call us to make an appointment to discuss your insurance requirements today.

여 만약 당신이 갑자기 가족을 부양할 수 없게 된다면 당신의 가족이 계속 편안하게 살 수 있을까요? 그들에게 음식, 주거, 의복 그리고 교육을 위한 돈이 있을까요? 당신이 만약 적절히 보험에 들어 있지 않다면 그들은 큰 곤경에 빠질 것입니다. 하지만 대부분의 사람들이 어느 정도의 보험이 적당한지 모릅니다. 그것이 애크미 보험사가 당신에게 적절한 보험 회사인 이유입니다. 저희는 귀하의 현재 소비 습관과 생활방식 그리고 자녀들의 대학 학비와 같은 가족의 필요 경비를 분석해드릴 것입니다. 보험 요건을 논의하시려면 오늘 바로 전화하셔서 약속을 잡아주세요.

02 ②

해설 남자는 아이들의 과도한 TV 시청을 지적하면서, 부모가 아이들의 TV 시청을 감독해야 한다고 말하고 있다.

어휘 take steps 조치를 취하다
addicted to ~에 중독된
monitor 감독[감시]하다
randomly 무작위로, 닥치는 대로

M Honey, our kids are watching too much television these days. Some steps must be taken.
W I know. They are addicted to TV, and sometimes watch things that they shouldn't.
M Right. I think parents need to monitor what they watch.
W Can you tell me more about it?
M It is about letting kids watch certain programs rather than randomly watching anything. My friend, Matthew, is a great example of this.
W What does he do?
M Every Sunday, he sits down with the kids and decides which programs the kids can watch.
W I see. That's a great idea.
M They can turn on the TV when it's time to watch the program. After the end of the program, the TV is turned off.
W That sounds good. Let's give it a try.

남 여보, 애들이 요즘 TV를 너무 많이 보고 있어요. 조치가 취해져야 해요.
여 알고 있어요. 아이들이 TV에 중독되었고 가끔 보지 말아야 할 것을 보더라고요.
남 맞아요. 나는 부모가 애들이 보는 것을 감독할 필요가 있다고 생각해요.
여 그것에 대해 더 말해줄래요?
남 애들이 무작위로 아무거나 시청하게 하기보다는 특정한 프로그램들을 시청하게 하는 거예요. 내 친구 매튜가 이 일의 훌륭한 본보기예요.
여 그가 무엇을 하는데요?
남 매주 일요일에, 그는 아이들과 함께 앉아 그 애들이 어느 프로그램을 시청할 수 있는지 정해줘요.
여 그렇군요. 좋은 생각이네요.
남 그 애들은 그 프로그램을 볼 시간이 되면 TV를 켤 수 있어요. 프로그램이 끝난 후에는 TV가 꺼지죠.
여 그거 좋네요. 우리 한번 시도해 봐요.

03 ⑤

해설 아이를 수준에 맞는 반으로 옮겨야 한다는 남자는 교사이며, 남편과 상의한 후 아들에게 잘 말해보겠다는 여자는 학부모이다.

어휘 be aware of ~을 알아차리다, 깨닫다

M Billy has been having a hard time in class.
W I wasn't aware of that. He never said a thing about it.
M That's why I wanted you to come in here. We need to consider moving him into a lower level class.
W Oh my. That would really break Billy's heart.

남 빌리가 수업을 힘들어하고 있습니다.
여 저는 그걸 몰랐어요. 아이는 그것에 대해서 말한 적이 없거든요.
남 그것이 어머니가 여기로 오시길 바란 이유입니다. 빌리를 수준이 더 낮은 반으로 옮기는 것을 고려해야 합니다.
여 오, 이런. 그러면 빌리가 정말 상심할 거예요.

break one's heart ~을 상심하게 만들다
motivate A to-v A가 v하도록 동기를 부여하다
sensitive 예민한, 민감한
update ~에게 가장 최근의 정보를 알려주다
progress 진척, 발전

M It may also motivate him to work harder so he can move back into this class.
W Well, if this is what you think is best, I'll tell my husband and we will explain it to our son.
M Thank you. This is really the best thing for him.
W I know it is. I'm just worried about Billy. He is very sensitive.
M I will keep you updated on his progress.
W Thank you.

남 그것이 또한 이 반으로 돌아오기 위해 빌리가 더 열심히 하도록 동기를 부여할 수도 있습니다.
여 음, 이것이 선생님께서 최선이라고 생각하시는 거라면, 남편과 의논한 후 아들에게 설명하도록 하겠습니다.
남 감사합니다. 이것은 정말 빌리에게 최선의 조치입니다.
여 알아요. 다만 저는 빌리가 걱정될 뿐이에요. 매우 예민하거든요.
남 빌리의 진척 상황에 대해서 계속 알려드리겠습니다.
여 감사합니다.

---

04 ③

해설 여동생이 의자에 앉아서 기타를 연주하고 있다고 했으므로 매트 위에서 기타를 치고 있는 여자가 대화의 내용과 일치하지 않는다.

어휘 checkered-patterned 체크무늬의
duck 오리
stream 개울, 시내
recognize 알아보다

M Hey, Sally. What are you looking at?
W Hi, Harry. It's a photo I took at the picnic I went on with my family.
M You're a good photographer. Oh, I like that checkered-patterned mat.
W Thanks. It was a free gift I got from the ice cream store.
M It seems perfect for a picnic. Oh, there're three ducks in the stream. They are so cute!
W I agree. And do you recognize my sister, Amelia? She is sitting on a chair playing the guitar.
M Yes, I remember her. By the way, who is the boy wearing a T-shirt with a soccer ball on it?
W He is my brother, Daniel.
M And these people playing badminton must be your parents, right?
W Yes, we all enjoyed our picnic.
M I'm sure your family had a wonderful time.

남 안녕, 샐리. 뭘 보고 있니?
여 안녕, 해리. 가족과 함께 갔던 소풍에서 내가 찍은 사진이야.
남 너 사진 잘 찍는구나. 아, 나는 저 체크무늬 매트가 마음에 들어.
여 고마워. 그건 내가 아이스크림 가게에서 받은 사은품이야.
남 소풍에 딱 좋은 것 같아. 아, 개울에 오리 세 마리가 있네. 너무 귀엽다!
여 나도 그렇게 생각해. 그리고 너 내 여동생 아멜리아 알아보겠어? 그 애는 의자에 앉아서 기타를 연주하고 있어.
남 아, 기억하지. 그런데 축구공이 그려진 티셔츠를 입은 남자아이는 누구니?
여 그 애는 내 남동생 다니엘이야.
남 그리고 배드민턴 치는 이 분들은 네 부모님이겠네, 맞아?
여 응, 우리는 모두 소풍을 즐겼어.
남 가족들이 분명 즐거운 시간을 보냈겠어.

---

05 ④

해설 여자가 가족의 호수 별장에 갈 것을 제안하고 부모님께 여쭤보겠다고 했다.

어휘 hang out 놀다, 어울리다
be supposed to-v v하기로 되어 있다
cool off 더위를 식히다; 서늘해지다
rent 빌리다
find out ~을 알아내다

M Amy, some of my friends from college are visiting this weekend. Let's hang out together.
W Sounds great! Oh, isn't it supposed to rain over the weekend?
M No, I've already checked the weather, and it is going to be sunny.
W Great. So, what shall we do this weekend?
M I know a great place to hike.
W That would be nice, but if it's hot, we should go somewhere to cool off.
M Do you have any place in mind?
W How about going to my family's lake house? Then we could go hiking and swimming there!
M That sounds like a great idea. We can rent a car over the weekend.
W Good. I'll find out if it's OK with my parents.
M Let me know. I'll call the guys and tell them about our idea.

남 에이미, 이번 주말에 내 대학 친구 몇 명이 올 거야. 같이 놀자.
여 좋아! 아, 주말 동안 비가 온다고 하지 않았어?
남 아니, 내가 이미 날씨를 확인했는데 화창할 거야.
여 잘됐다. 그래서 이번 주말에 우리 뭐 할까?
남 나 하이킹할 좋은 곳을 알고 있어.
여 괜찮을 것 같긴 한데, 날씨가 더우면 더위를 식힐 수 있는 장소로 가야 하잖아.
남 염두에 둔 장소라도 있니?
여 우리 가족의 호수 별장으로 가면 어때? 그럼 하이킹을 하고 거기서 수영도 할 수 있잖아!
남 정말 괜찮은 생각인 것 같아. 주말 동안 차를 빌리면 되겠다.
여 좋아. 부모님께 그래도 되는지 여쭤볼게.
남 내게 알려줘. 애들한테 전화해서 우리 생각을 말할게.

---

06 ⑤

해설 두 사람은 모두 햄 치즈 샌드위치($7)와 아메리카노($4)를 주문할 것이므로 남자가 지불할 금액은 22 달러이다.

어휘 **classic** 전형적인, 표준적인
treat 한턱내기, 대접
promotion 승진; 촉진, 장려; 홍보[판촉] (활동)
cf. **promote** 승진시키다; 촉진하다; 홍보하다
raise 급여 인상

W	What kind of sandwich do you want?
M	I think I'll get a ham and cheese sandwich.
W	Okay, I think I'll just have a classic one. I only have $5. A ham and cheese sandwich costs $7.
M	It's my treat today. We're celebrating!
W	Celebrating what? Did you get the promotion?
M	Yes, plus I got a bigger raise than I expected. Eat and drink whatever you want.
W	Wow, that's great! Congratulations! I guess I will have the same thing as you. And I'll order an americano. I can pay for that. It's only $4.
M	No way. Anything you want is on me. I'll also have an americano.
W	Thanks. You should get promoted more often.
M	My pleasure. Let's order now.

여	어떤 종류의 샌드위치로 할 거야?
남	나는 햄 치즈 샌드위치로 하려고 해.
여	그래, 나는 그냥 기본 샌드위치로 할까 해. 5달러밖에 없거든. 햄 치즈 샌드위치는 7달러네.
남	오늘은 내가 낼게. 우리 축하하는 거야!
여	무엇을 축하하는 건데? 승진한 거야?
남	맞아, 게다가 기대했던 것보다 더 많은 급여 인상을 받았어. 네가 원하는 무엇이든 먹고 마셔.
여	와, 잘됐다! 축하해! 나도 너랑 같은 것으로 할게. 그리고 아메리카노도 주문할래. 그건 내가 낼 수 있어. 겨우 4달러거든.
남	아니야. 네가 원하는 것은 뭐든지 내가 낼게. 나도 아메리카노를 마실래.
여	고마워. 너 더 자주 승진해야겠다.
남	천만에. 이제 주문하자.

07 ⑤

해설 여자는 가게에 연어가 있었지만 스테이크가 할인 중인 것을 보고 마음이 바뀌었다고 했다.

어휘 **salmon** 연어
barbecue (고기 등을) 불에 직접 굽다, 숯불 위에 그릴을 얹고 굽다

M	Here, Annie. Let me help you with those shopping bags.
W	Thanks.
M	*[pause]* I think we're ready to make a baked salmon dish. You bought salmon, didn't you?
W	Actually, I didn't get any salmon.
M	Was the store out of fish?
W	No, they had some.
M	Then, did they look bad?
W	No, they looked fresh. But then I saw that steaks were on sale, so I changed my mind. Maybe we can have salmon another time.
M	OK. Then, let's barbecue the steaks in the yard. I'll fire up the grill.
W	Thanks. I'll get the salad and potatoes ready.

남	이리 줘, 애니. 그 쇼핑백들 드는 걸 도와줄게.
여	고마워.
남	*[잠시 후]* 구운 연어 요리를 만들 준비가 다 된 것 같아. 연어 사왔지, 그렇지 않아?
여	사실, 나는 연어를 사지 않았어.
남	가게에 연어가 다 떨어졌니?
여	아니야, 몇 개 있었어.
남	그럼 연어가 안 좋아 보였어?
여	아니, 신선해 보였어. 그런데 그때 스테이크가 할인 중인 것을 보고 마음이 바뀌었어. 연어는 다음번에 먹어도 될 것 같아.
남	좋아. 그럼 마당에서 스테이크를 구워 먹자. 내가 석쇠에 불을 붙일게.
여	고마워. 나는 샐러드와 감자를 준비할게.

08 ②

해설 해석 참조

어휘 **diaper** 기저귀
on (the) air 방송 중인
toddler 유아(용의)

	[Telephone rings.]
M	Plus Home Shopping. How can I help you?
W	I'd like to ask you about the diapers you are selling on the air.
M	Okay, you're talking about the Baby Love Diapers, right?
W	Yes. Is it silky? My baby has a sensitive skin.
M	Certainly. It is made with 100% cotton.
W	Right. How many diapers are in one pack?
M	Hold on, please. *[pause]* There are fifty in a pack.
W	If I order now, can I receive them by this week?
M	Of course. As soon as you purchase them, we'll send them out the next working day.
W	Okay. Can I pay with my credit card?
M	Certainly. And if you buy more than 5 packs, we'll give you a toddler's toy for free.
W	Great. I'd like to order 10 packs.

	[전화벨이 울린다.]
남	플러스 홈쇼핑입니다. 어떻게 도와드릴까요?
여	방송에서 팔고 있는 기저귀에 대해 여쭤보고 싶은데요.
남	네, '아기 사랑 기저귀'를 말씀하시는 거죠, 맞나요?
여	네. 그건 부드럽나요? 제 아기가 민감한 피부여서요.
남	물론이죠. **그것은 100% 면으로 만들어졌습니다**(① 재질).
여	그렇군요. 한 묶음에 몇 개의 기저귀가 들었나요?
남	잠시만요. *[잠시 후]* **한 팩에 오십 개가 들어 있습니다**(③ 묶음당 수량).
여	지금 주문하면, 이번 주까지 받을 수 있나요?
남	그럼요. 손님께서 구매하시자마자, **바로 다음 영업일에 발송해드릴 겁니다**(④ 발송 예정일).
여	네. 신용카드로 결제할 수 있나요?
남	물론입니다. 그리고 5팩 이상 구매하시면, **유아용 장난감을 무료로 드립니다**(⑤ 사은품).
여	잘됐네요. 10팩 주문할게요.

09 ④

해설 월요일에는 식당 메뉴의 모든 품목이 10% 할인된다.

어휘 relaxing 마음을 느긋하게 해 주는
scenery 경치, 풍경
throughout ~동안, ~내내

M Hello, visitors! Welcome to Crystal Lake Park in Urbana. Please come and enjoy the beautiful and relaxing scenery here. We offer boat rentals, such as rowboats and canoes, from Monday to Friday from 1 p.m. to 8 p.m., and Saturday and Sunday from 10 a.m. to 8 p.m. If you have one of our coupons, you can get a $3 discount on a boat rental. For any boat rental, at least one member of the group must be age 20 or older. You can also relax at our cafe and enjoy your choice of sandwiches, salads, and snacks. We offer a 10% discount on all menu items on Mondays. Our doors will be open from June 1 all throughout summer and into fall until October 31. So please stop by for a tasty sandwich or a lovely boat ride on the lake.

남 안녕하세요, 방문객 여러분! 어배너에 있는 크리스탈 호수 공원에 오신 것을 환영합니다. 오셔서 이곳에서 아름다우면서도 한가로운 경치를 즐기세요. 저희는 **월요일에서 금요일 오후 1시부터 8시, 토요일과 일요일 오전 10시부터 오후 8시까지**(①) 노 젓는 보트, 카누와 같은 보트를 대여해드립니다. 저희의 쿠폰 중 한 장을 가지고 계시면, 보트 대여료에서 3달러를 할인받으실 수 있습니다(②). 보트를 대여하시려면, **적어도 일행 중 한 분은 20세 이상이어야 합니다**(③). 여러분은 카페에서 휴식도 취하실 수 있으며 샌드위치, 샐러드, 그리고 가볍게 드실 수 있는 음식을 선택해서 즐기실 수 있습니다. **월요일에는 메뉴의 모든 품목에 10%의 할인을 제공해드립니다**(④). 공원은 6월 1일부터 여름 내내, 그리고 10월 31일로 이어지는 가을까지 개장합니다(⑤). 그러니 맛있는 샌드위치나 호수에서의 멋진 보트 타기를 위해 잠시 들르시길 바랍니다.

10 ④

해설 여자가 9월까지는 일정이 꽉 찼다고 했으므로 9월까지만 운영하는 캠핑장을 제외하고 해변이나 호수인 곳 중에 무료 와이파이가 있으며 반려동물이 허용되는 곳을 고른다.

어휘 make a reservation 예약을 하다
camping site 캠핑장, 야영지
(= campsite)
a full schedule 꽉 찬 일정
leave out 빼다
connection 연결
option 선택(권)

M Honey, I want to talk to you about our camping trip this autumn.
W I almost forgot about it. Did you make a reservation?
M Not yet, but I made a list of camping sites. Let's choose one together.
W Good! Oh, we can't choose this one because I have a full schedule until September.
M Okay. Let's leave this one out.
W Since we usually go camping in the mountains, I want to go camping on the beach or a lake this time.
M I'd also like that.
W We'd better choose a campsite with a free WiFi connection. We probably need to get Internet while camping.
M That's right. Now we have only two options left.
W Oh, we forgot the most important thing! We have to bring our dog, Max.
M Right! Let's choose this one.

남 여보, 이번 가을 우리 캠핑 여행에 대해 얘기하고 싶어요.
여 거의 잊고 있었네요. 당신이 예약을 했나요?
남 아직이요, 하지만 캠핑장 목록을 작성했어요. 우리 같이 골라봐요.
여 좋아요! 아, 난 9월까지 일정이 꽉 차기 때문에 이건 선택할 수 없어요.
남 알았어요. 이건 빼죠.
여 우리가 보통 산으로 캠핑을 가기 때문에, 이번에는 해변이나 호수로 캠핑을 가고 싶어요.
남 나도 그게 좋겠어요.
여 무료 와이파이 연결이 되는 캠핑장을 선택하는 게 좋겠어요. 우리는 아마 캠핑하는 동안 인터넷을 해야 할 거예요.
남 맞아요. 이제 두 가지 선택지만 남았군요.
여 오, 우리가 가장 중요한 것을 잊었어요! 우리 개 맥스를 데려가야 하잖아요.
남 맞아요! 이걸로 고릅시다.

11 ①

해설 여자가 언제 시간이 되는지 확실하지 않은 상황에서 남자가 나중에 전화하면 될지 물었으므로 자신이 내일 아침에 전화하겠다는 응답이 가장 적절하다.
② 우리가 함께 하면 끝낼 수 있어.
③ 우린 오늘 밤에 만나서 그것을 할 거야.
④ 꼭 제시간에 갈게.
⑤ 우리 프로젝트 마감일이 거의 다 되었어.

M We need to work on our project soon. When do you want to meet?
W I think I'll have some time tomorrow, but I'm not sure when.
M Should I give you a call later?
W Let me call you tomorrow morning.

남 우리 프로젝트를 곧 시작해야 해. 언제 만날래?
여 내일 시간이 있을 것 같긴 한데 언제인지 확실하지 않아.
남 내가 나중에 전화할까?
여 내일 아침에 내가 전화할게.

12 ⑤

해설 오늘로 예정되었던 시험을 걱정하는 남자에게 시험이 월요일로 연기됐음을 알려주었으므로 주말에 공부할 수 있겠다는 응답이 가장 적절하다.
① 들었지만, 그다지 신경 안 써.
② 그래, 시간이 얼마 남지 않았어.
③ 아니, 그 소식을 어제 들었어.
④ 월요일 시험은 평소보다 더 어려웠어.

W What's wrong, Chris? You look really stressed out.
M I'm worried that I'm going to fail today's test. I didn't get to study at all.
W Didn't you hear the news? The test has been delayed until Monday.
M That means I can study over the weekend.

여 무슨 일이야, 크리스? 너 스트레스가 정말 심해 보여.
남 오늘 시험에 불합격할까 봐 걱정돼. 공부를 하나도 못했거든.
여 소식 못 들었니? 시험이 월요일로 연기됐어.
남 그럼 내가 주말 동안 공부할 수 있다는 거네.

13 ⑤

해설 남자의 음식이 잘못 나와서 원래 주문한 것으로 달라고 요청한 상황이므로 이 문제를 빨리 해결해 주겠다는 응답이 가장 적절하다.
① 죄송합니다, 저희는 감자튀김이 다 떨어졌습니다.
② 준비되시면 주문을 받겠습니다.
③ 좋은 제안이군요. 그것으로 하겠습니다.
④ 물론입니다. 저희는 세트 메뉴에 할인을 제공합니다.

어휘 overcook 너무 오래 익히다
for starters 우선
well-done (고기가) 잘 익은[구워진]

M Excuse me! Can you come here, please?
W What seems to be the problem here, sir? You don't look very happy.
M Well, for starters, my steak is overcooked. And I asked for a baked potato, but you gave me french fries.
W I am sorry, sir. That is what a well-done steak looks like at our restaurant.
M But I asked for medium.
W I wrote down your order on my pad here. Let me take a look.
M Yes, please check.
W [pause] Yes, sir. I actually wrote down an "M" for medium. I think there was a mistake with your order in the kitchen.
M So, I would like to have my original order. Is that OK?
W Certainly. I will take care of the problem right away.

남 저기요! 여기 좀 와주시겠어요?
여 여기 무슨 문제가 있습니까, 손님? 매우 언짢아 보이시는군요.
남 음, 우선 제 스테이크가 너무 익혀졌어요. 그리고 전 구운 감자를 주문했는데 감자튀김을 주셨고요.
여 죄송합니다, 손님. 저희 레스토랑의 잘 구워진 스테이크는 그렇게 보입니다.
남 하지만 저는 중간 정도로 구워진 것을 주문했어요.
여 제가 여기 주문서에 손님의 주문을 적었습니다. 한번 살펴보겠습니다.
남 네, 확인해주세요.
여 [잠시 후] 네, 손님. 제가 중간 정도로 구워진 것을 의미하는 'M'을 실제로 적어 놨네요. 주방에서 손님 주문에 실수가 있었던 것 같습니다.
남 그렇다면 제가 원래 주문한 것을 받고 싶습니다. 괜찮을까요?
여 물론입니다. 문제를 바로 처리해 드리겠습니다.

14 ④

해설 여자가 과제 때문에 함께 갈 수 없는 신디를 어떻게 설득할지 물었으므로 (신디의) 과제를 도와주겠다고 약속해보겠다는 응답이 가장 적절하다.
① 알다시피, 난 설득력 있는 사람이 아니야.
② 나중에 더 많은 사람이 합류할 테니 걱정하지 마.
③ 네가 대신 가고 싶어 한다고 그녀에게 말할게.
⑤ 음, 우리 계획에 대해 내가 그녀에게 얘기해야 한다고 생각하니?

어휘 worth v-ing v할 가치가 있는, v해볼 만한
even number 짝수
(↔ odd number 홀수)
persuade A to-v A가 v하도록 설득하다
cf. persuasive 설득력 있는
convince 설득하다; 확신[납득]시키다

M So how far away is the amusement park we're going to tomorrow?
W It's about two and a half hours away.
M Wow! That's really far. Is it worth visiting?
W Trust me. This new place is supposed to be truly amazing.
M I hope so.
W Anyway, it would be nice to have an even number of people going tomorrow. Then nobody would have to sit alone on a ride.
M Well, there'll be five including the two of us.
W I wish Cindy could join us. It's too bad she's busy with her assignment.
M You're right. Hmm.... Why don't I try to persuade her to come with us to the amusement park?
W Really? What will you say to convince her?
M What if I promise to help with her assignment?

남 그래서 우리가 내일 가는 그 놀이동산이 얼마나 멀리 떨어져 있니?
여 약 2시간 반 정도 떨어진 곳에 있어.
남 와! 정말 멀다. 갈 만한 가치가 있을까?
여 날 믿어봐. 이 새로운 장소는 정말로 놀라울 거야.
남 나도 그랬으면 해.
여 어쨌든, 내일 가는 사람들의 수가 짝수면 좋을 텐데. 그럼 아무도 놀이 기구에 혼자 앉지 않아도 될 텐데.
남 음, 우리 둘을 포함해서 5명일 거야.
여 신디도 우리와 함께 갈 수 있으면 좋을 텐데. 과제 때문에 바쁘다니 너무 아쉬워.
남 네 말이 맞아. 흠…. 우리와 함께 놀이동산에 가자고 내가 그녀를 설득해보면 어때?
여 정말? 그녀를 설득하기 위해 뭐라고 말할 거니?
남 내가 과제를 도와주겠다고 약속하면 어떨까?

15 ⑤

해설 토니는 자신의 물건을 빌려 가고 소중히 다루지도 않는 캘빈의 무례한 행동을 더 이상 참을 수 없으므로 그에 대한 경고의 말을 할 것이다.
① 언제 새 모자를 사줄 거니?
② 내게 그것과 어울리는 장갑이 있어.
③ 네 친구들에게 네 옷을 빌려주지 마.
④ 네 가죽 재킷을 내일 내가 빌릴 수 있을까?
⑤ 묻지 않고 내 물건을 가져가지 말아줘.

어휘 permission 허락, 허가
damage 손상시키다
be about to-v 막 v하려 하다
stand 참다, 견디다
[선택지 어휘] **match** 어울리다

W Tony's best friend, Calvin, always borrows his things without first asking for permission. Sometimes, when Calvin returns what he has borrowed, it is broken or damaged. One time, he even lost Tony's favorite baseball cap. Although he said he was sorry for losing the hat, he didn't offer to pay for it. Now, Calvin is about to leave Tony's house, and he is wearing Tony's new leather jacket. Tony can't stand this any longer. So, Tony decides to tell Calvin that he should ask for his permission before using his stuff. In this situation, what would Tony most likely say to Calvin?

여 토니의 가장 친한 친구인 캘빈은 항상 허락을 먼저 구하지 않고 그의 것을 빌려간다. 때때로 캘빈이 빌려갔던 것을 돌려줄 때 그것은 부서졌거나 손상되어 있다. 한 번은 토니가 가장 좋아하는 야구 모자를 잃어버린 일도 있다. 그는 모자를 잃어버려 미안하다고 말했지만 모자 값을 내겠다고는 제의하지 않았다. 지금, 캘빈은 막 토니의 집을 나서려고 하는데, 그는 토니의 새 가죽 재킷을 입고 있다. 토니는 더 이상 이것을 참을 수 없다. 그래서 토니는 캘빈에게 그의 물건을 쓰기 전에 허락을 구해야 한다고 말하기로 결심한다. 이 상황에서, 토니가 캘빈에게 할 말로 가장 적절한 것은 무엇인가?

---

16 ①   17 ③

해설 16 훌륭한 코치가 갖춰야 할 지식과 필요한 노력에 대해서 설명하는 내용이다.
① 훌륭한 코치의 요소
② 좋은 코칭 이면의 과학
③ 스포츠 코치의 다양한 역할
④ 개인 훈련의 중요성
⑤ 현대의 코치들이 직면한 어려움

17 해석 참조

어휘 fitness 신체 단련, 건강; 적합함
art 기술; 예술
A as well as B B뿐만 아니라 A도
athlete 운동선수
a great deal 다량; 많이
up-to-date (정보가) 최신의
clinic 강습, 교습; 병원
seek out ~을 구하다, 찾아내다

M Hello, everyone. Today, I want to talk a bit about sports. In my opinion, all sports are good. But the truth is that good coaches are needed to make a sport truly great. Sports and fitness coaching is an art as well as a science. First of all, coaches must have an understanding of the sport. Coaches must plan for the season, know the rules, and provide a good environment for athletes to succeed. While most coaches already know a great deal about a sport, they must also continue to learn and develop new training techniques. For example, staying up-to-date on new research, as well as attending coaching clinics, and seeking out tips from other coaches are all good methods. Also, watching videos and reading books can also be helpful. Finally, attending university classes is a great idea for any coach who wants to grow and improve.

남 안녕하세요, 여러분. 오늘 저는 스포츠에 대해 조금 이야기하고자 합니다. 제 생각에 모든 스포츠는 유익합니다. 하지만 사실은, 스포츠를 정말로 아주 유용하게 만들려면 훌륭한 코치가 필요합니다. 스포츠와 체력 훈련을 지도하는 것은 과학일 뿐만 아니라 기술입니다. 우선, 코치라면 스포츠에 대한 이해가 있어야 합니다. 코치는 시즌 계획을 세우고, 규칙을 알고, 운동선수들이 성공할 수 있는 좋은 환경을 제공해야 합니다. 대부분의 코치들은 스포츠에 대해 이미 많은 것을 알고 있겠지만, 계속 배우고 새로운 훈련 기법을 개발하기도 해야 합니다. 예를 들면, **코칭 강습에 참여(②)**할 뿐만 아니라 **새로운 연구에 대해 최신 동향을 파악(①)**하고 있고, **다른 코치들로부터 조언을 구하는 것(④)**은 모두 좋은 방법입니다. 또한 영상을 보거나 책을 읽는 것 역시 도움이 될 수 있습니다. 마지막으로, 성장하고 (능력을) 향상하고 싶은 코치라면 **대학교 수업을 수강(⑤)**하는 것도 좋은 생각입니다.

| 01 ③ | 02 ③ | 03 ① | 04 ③ | 05 ① | 06 ② | 07 ④ | 08 ② | 09 ③ | 10 ⑤ |
| 11 ⑤ | 12 ③ | 13 ⑤ | 14 ⑤ | 15 ② | 16 ⑤ | 17 ① | | | |

01 ③

해설 However로 시작하는 문장이 결정적 단서로, 뒤에 콜레스테롤 신약의 부작용에 대한 구체적인 내용이 이어지고 있다.

어휘 cholesterol 콜레스테롤
prescription 처방전
medication 약, 약물
allergic 알레르기성의, 알레르기가 있는
reaction 반응
overlook 간과하다
side effect 부작용
dizziness 현기증
rash 발진, 뾰루지

M Hello. Welcome back to my channel, *Dr. Harris' office*. Today we are going to talk about a recently developed drug named Lenochol. It is designed for people who have high cholesterol. According to its instructions, it helps to reduce cholesterol levels if used daily. However, before you take this prescription medication, there are a few things you need to consider. You may experience unexplained muscle pain or weakness while you're on it, and in that case call your doctor right away. Any allergic reaction to this medication should also not be overlooked. Common side effects include sleepiness, dizziness, and rashes on the skin.

남 안녕하세요. '해리스 의사의 진료실' 채널에 돌아오신 것을 환영합니다. 오늘 우리는 최근에 개발된 레노콜이라는 이름의 약에 대해 이야기하려고 합니다. 이 약은 콜레스테롤 수치가 높은 사람들을 위해 고안되었습니다. 설명서에 따르면, 그것은 매일 사용된다면, 콜레스테롤 수치를 낮추는 것을 도울 수 있습니다. 그러나 이 처방 약을 복용하기 전에, 고려해야 할 몇 가지 사항이 있습니다. 그것을 복용하는 동안, 이유 없는 근육통이나 무기력함을 느낄지도 모르는데, 그런 경우에는 즉시 주치의에게 연락하십시오. 이 약에 대한 어떤 알레르기 반응 또한 간과되어서는 안 됩니다. 일반적인 부작용은 졸음, 현기증, 피부 발진을 포함합니다.

02 ③

해설 여자는 더 이상 입지 않는 옷들을 재사용해서 앞치마나 가방과 같은 다른 물건을 만드는 것이 환경을 돕는 방법이라고 말하고 있다.

어휘 anymore 이제는
throw away 버리다
condition 상태
give away 기부하다, 선물로 주다
reuse 재사용하다, 다시 이용하다
environment 환경
apron 앞치마
give it a try 한번 해보다

W Elliot, what are all these clothes in this box?
M They're old clothes I don't wear anymore, so I want to throw them away.
W Why? Some of them are in good condition.
M They're not good enough to sell or give away. And I haven't worn them in a year.
W Why don't you reuse these clothes? We should think about the environment.
M Then what can I do with the clothes I don't wear anymore?
W You can make an apron out of your old shirt. Look! I made this bag out of my old jeans.
M It looks great! But I don't think I can do that.
W You can learn how to make things from old clothes online. This is a great way to help the environment.
M Okay. I'll give it a try.

여 엘리엇, 이 상자 안에 있는 이 옷들은 다 뭐야?
남 이제는 안 입는 오래된 옷들이라서 버리고 싶어.
여 왜? 그것들 중 몇몇은 상태가 좋은데.
남 그것들은 팔거나 기부할 만큼 좋지는 않아. 그리고 난 그것들을 일 년 동안 안 입었어.
여 이 옷들을 재사용하는 게 어떠니? 우리는 환경을 생각해야 하잖아.
남 그러면 더 이상 입지 않는 옷들로 내가 뭘 할 수 있는데?
여 넌 낡은 셔츠로 앞치마를 만들 수 있어. 봐! 난 이 가방을 낡은 청바지로 만들었어.
남 멋지다! 하지만 나는 그렇게 할 수 없을 것 같아.
여 온라인에서 헌 옷으로 물건들을 만드는 방법을 배울 수 있어. 이건 환경을 돕는 좋은 방법이야.
남 알았어. 한번 해볼게.

03 ①

해설 자동차를 좋은 가격에 살 수 있도록 하겠다고 하고 더 생각해보겠다는 것으로 보아 시험 운전을 해본 뒤에 자동차 판매원과 고객이 나누는 대화임을 알 수 있다.

어휘 interior 내부(의); 실내 장식
frankly 솔직히 (말하면)
afford ~할[살] 여유가 되다
make sure 반드시 ~하도록 하다, 확실히 하다
think over ~을 심사숙고하다
business card 명함

M If you go straight and then make a right at the light, we will be back at the lot.
W You mean this light?
M Yes. That's it. And then you can park anywhere you like.
W Okay.
M *[pause]* Great. So, what do you think?
W Well, I like the way it drives, and the interior is very nice. I like it a lot, but frankly, I'm not sure if I can afford it.
M I'll make sure you get a good deal.
W Even so, I'd like to think it over a bit more.

남 직진하신 후 신호등에서 우회전하시면, 우리는 주차장에 돌아가게 됩니다.
여 이 신호등 말씀이시죠?
남 네. 그것입니다. 그리고 나서 원하시는 곳 어디든지 주차하시면 됩니다.
여 알겠습니다.
남 *[잠시 후]* 좋습니다. 자, 어떻게 생각하십니까?
여 글쎄요, 차가 달리는 방식이 마음에 들고 차 내부도 아주 좋아요. 상당히 마음에 들긴 하는데, 솔직히 살 여유가 있는지는 모르겠어요.
남 확실히 좋은 가격에 사실 수 있도록 하겠습니다.
여 그렇다 해도, 좀 더 심사숙고하고 싶어요.

M Here's my business card. When you're ready, please give me a call.

W I will. Thanks for all your help today.

남 여기 제 명함입니다. 준비되시면, 전화해주세요.

여 그럴게요. 오늘 도와주셔서 감사합니다.

04 ③

해설 새끼 새 세 마리가 나뭇가지 위에서 노래를 부르고 있다고 했으므로 그림 속의 날고 있는 새 세 마리가 대화의 내용과 일치하지 않는다.

어휘 striped 줄무늬가 있는
chick 새끼 새
branch 나뭇가지
cling to ~에 달라붙다; ~을 고수하다
squirrel 다람쥐
furry 털로 덮인
stick out ~을 내밀다

M Rachel, you don't need me to read the book for you?

W It's okay, Daddy. I already know the story. It's about a small mouse that's looking for a home.

M Hmm.... You're talking about the mouse that's wearing a striped sweater, right?

W Yes, and the mother bird sitting in the nest is asking the mouse if she wants to live there.

M Oh, you really do know the story. How many chicks does the mother bird have?

W Three. They are sitting on the branch and singing.

M I see. What's this clinging to the left side of the tree?

W That's a squirrel. He has a long furry tail.

M Oh, you're right. What's sticking its head out from the hole in the tree?

W It's an owl. He asks the mouse if she wants to live in there.

M You really impress me, Rachel. Shall we turn to the next page?

남 레이첼, 내가 책을 읽어줄 필요가 없는 거니?

여 괜찮아요, 아빠. 이미 줄거리를 알고 있어요. 이건 집을 찾는 작은 쥐에 관한 이야기예요.

남 음···. 줄무늬 스웨터를 입고 있는 쥐에 관해 말하고 있는 거지, 그렇지?

여 네, 그리고 둥지에 앉아 있는 어미 새가 쥐에게 그곳에 살고 싶은지 묻고 있어요.

남 아, 너 정말 이야기를 알고 있구나. 어미 새에게는 몇 마리의 새끼 새가 있니?

여 세 마리요. 새끼 새들은 나뭇가지에 앉아서 노래를 부르고 있어요.

남 그렇구나. 나무 왼편에 달라붙어 있는 이건 뭐니?

여 다람쥐예요. 길고 털이 많은 꼬리가 있어요.

남 오, 네 말이 맞아. 무엇이 나무의 구멍 밖으로 머리를 내밀고 있지?

여 올빼미예요. 그가 쥐에게 구멍 안에서 살고 싶은지 물어봐요.

남 정말 대단하구나, 레이첼. 다음 페이지로 넘어갈까?

05 ①

해설 남자의 개가 아파서 병원에 데려가야 하므로 딸을 돌봐달라고 부탁하고 있다.

어휘 do the laundry 빨래를 하다
ill 아픈, 병 든
rush 서두르다; 급히 수송하다[보내다]
look after ~을 돌보다

[Cell phone rings.]

M Laura, it's me, Noah, your next-door neighbor.

W Oh, hi, Noah.

M Sorry to bother you, but are you busy?

W No, not really. I was about to do the laundry. What's up?

M Well, I think my dog, Rocky, is ill.

W What happened to him?

M I think he ate something he shouldn't. I need to rush him to the hospital.

W Oh, dear. Do you want a ride to the hospital?

M No, but I was wondering if you could look after my little daughter, Claire.

W Don't worry. I'll come over right now.

M Thank you so much. I may be late.

W Not a problem. What are neighbors for?

[휴대전화벨이 울린다.]

남 로라, 저예요, 옆집에 사는 이웃 노아예요.

여 아, 안녕하세요, 노아.

남 방해해서 죄송한데, 바쁘신가요?

여 아니요, 별로요. 빨래하려던 참이었어요. 무슨 일이세요?

남 음, 저희 집 개 로키가 아픈 것 같아요.

여 로키에게 무슨 일이 있었나요?

남 제 생각에 로키가 먹으면 안 되는 것을 먹은 것 같아요. 로키를 병원에 빨리 데려가야 해요.

여 오, 이런. 병원까지 태워다 드릴까요?

남 아니요, 그렇지만 제 어린 딸 클레어를 돌봐주실 수 있는지 궁금했어요.

여 걱정하지 마세요. 제가 지금 당장 갈게요.

남 정말 고마워요. 제가 늦을지도 몰라요.

여 괜찮아요. 이웃 좋다는 게 뭐겠어요?

06 ②

해설 커피 머신($200)은 10% 할인을 받고 에스프레소 캡슐(한 팩당 $10)은 기본 할인 10%에 추가 10% 할인을 더해 20% 할인을 받는다. 따라서 여자가 지불할 금액은 220달러이다.

M Good morning. May I help you?

W I noticed the sale sign outside. Is everything really 10% off?

M Yes. We're having a moving sale.

W That's great. Do you still have the Norman 8 Coffee Machine?

M Let me check.... [pause] No, I'm afraid we don't carry that brand anymore.

남 안녕하세요. 도와드릴까요?

여 밖에 있는 할인 판매 표시를 봤어요. 정말로 모든 게 10% 할인되나요?

남 네, 저희는 가게 이전 세일을 하고 있습니다.

여 잘됐군요. 노르만 8 커피 머신이 아직 있나요?

남 확인해볼게요···. [잠시 후] 아니요, 유감이지만 저희는 더 이상 그 브랜드를 취급하지 않습니다.

어휘 moving sale 이전 세일
carry (가게에서 품목을) 취급하다;
소지하다; 나르다
discount on ~에 대한 할인
special deal 특가 상품
additional 추가의

W I see. Then how much is this one?
M It's normally $200, but today you can get a 10% discount on everything here.
W Okay, I'll take it. Do you have any special deals on espresso capsules?
M Well, normally, a pack of 20 capsules costs $10. But I can give you an additional 10% discount on each pack.
W Then I'll take 5 packs. Here's my credit card.

여 알겠습니다. 그럼 이건 얼마인가요?
남 보통 때는 200달러인데, 오늘은 여기 있는 모든 것에 대해 10% 할인받으실 수 있습니다.
여 좋아요, 그것을 사겠습니다. 에스프레소 캡슐에 대해서는 특가 상품이 있나요?
남 음, 일반적으로 캡슐 20개가 들어있는 한 팩은 10달러입니다. 하지만 손님께 각 팩에 10%를 추가로 할인해드릴 수 있습니다.
여 그렇다면 다섯 팩을 살게요. 여기 제 신용카드요.

07 ④

해설 남자는 소개받은 아파트가 북향이라 햇빛이 거의 들지 않아서 다른 아파트를 보고 싶다고 했다.

어휘 make up one's mind 결심하다
electricity 전기
reasonable 적당한
face 향하다
arrange 준비하다, 주선하다

[Cell phone rings.]
M Hello, I'm David Nelson. You showed me an apartment yesterday.
W Hello, Mr. Nelson. I was waiting for you to call. Did you make up your mind?
M Well, I loved the apartment, but I decided not to rent it.
W You asked for an apartment with two bedrooms and a large kitchen. Is that correct?
M Yes, the apartment was perfect for my needs.
W Then, you didn't like the neighborhood?
M No, I quite liked the neighborhood. It's quiet and safe.
W Was the rent too high to afford?
M No, I thought $1,200 a month including water and electricity was reasonable.
W Then, what seems to be the problem?
M Actually, the apartment gets little sunlight because it faces north.
W Oh, I get that. Shall I arrange some other apartments to show you then?
M Yes, please.

[휴대전화벨이 울린다.]
남 여보세요, 데이비드 넬슨입니다. 어제 제게 아파트를 보여주셨죠.
여 안녕하세요, 넬슨 씨. 손님 전화를 기다리고 있었어요. 결정하셨습니까?
남 음, 그 아파트가 좋지만 임대하지 않기로 결정했어요.
여 침실 두 개와 큰 부엌이 있는 아파트를 원하셨잖아요. 그게 맞나요?
남 네, 그 아파트는 제 필요에 딱 맞았어요.
여 그러면 동네가 마음에 안 드셨나요?
남 아뇨, 동네도 꽤 좋았어요. 조용하고 안전해서요.
여 집세가 감당하기에 너무 비쌌나요?
남 아뇨. 수도와 전기 포함해서 한 달에 1,200달러면 적당하다고 생각했어요.
여 그러면 뭐가 문제인 것 같나요?
남 사실 그 아파트가 북쪽을 향해 있기 때문에 햇빛이 거의 들지 않더군요.
여 아, 알겠습니다. 그럼 다른 아파트를 보시도록 준비해드릴까요?
남 네, 부탁드려요.

08 ②

해설 해석 참조

어휘 compete 경쟁하다, 겨루다
cf. competitor (시합) 참가자
according to ~에 따라
theme 주제, 테마
I bet 틀림없이
award 상; 수여하다
crown A B A에게 B의 영예를 지니게 하다
episode (프로그램의) 1회 방송분; (재미있는) 사건, 에피소드

W I can't wait to watch the TV show, The Greatest Cake Master.
M Is it the TV program you mentioned before?
W Yes. 20 cake masters from around the world will compete against each other.
M That sounds interesting. How will they choose the winner?
W Well, competitors make a cake according to the theme of the week and judges will remove the weakest one until there is only one baker remaining.
M I bet the winner will receive a special award.
W Right. The winner will be crowned The Greatest Cake Master, and receive a grand prize of $50,000.
M Wow, that's huge. I think it is going to be very popular.
W Let's watch the first episode together. It will be on this Thursday at 8 p.m.

여 '최고의 케이크 명인' TV 쇼를 어서 보고 싶어.
남 그거 네가 전에 말했던 TV 프로그램이야?
여 응. **전 세계의 스무 명의 케이크 명인들이 서로 경쟁할 거야(① 참가자 수).**
남 흥미로운데. 우승자는 어떻게 선택하는 거야?
여 음, **참가자들은 그 주의 주제에 따라 케이크를 만들고 심사위원들은 단 한 명의 제빵사가 남을 때까지 가장 못한 사람을 탈락시켜(③ 경연 방식).**
남 우승자는 분명 특별한 상을 받겠네.
여 맞아. **우승자는 '최고의 케이크 명인'의 영예를 얻고 대상 상금 5만 달러를 받게 돼.(④ 우승 혜택).**
남 와, 상금이 크네. 내 생각에 그 프로그램은 아주 인기를 끌 것 같아.
여 첫 회 같이 보자. **이번 목요일 오후 8시에 방송될 거야(⑤ 첫 회 방영일).**

09 ③

해설 온수 욕조는 야외에 있다.

어휘 construction 건설, 건축
Celsius 섭씨의
on average 평균적으로
heated 난방을 한
washroom 화장실, 세면장
hot tub 온수 욕조

W Good afternoon, listeners. Why don't you plan a visit to the Ice Hotel in Quebec this winter? It is North America's first ice hotel. The hotel is made from 400 tons of ice that is specially produced for construction. Temperatures inside the hotel stay around minus 4 degrees Celsius on average, and guests sleep in special sleeping bags on beds made of snow and ice. However, there are heated washrooms and outdoor hot tubs for guests to warm up in. Each year, thousands of families come to tour the hotel, which even has a fun ice slide for kids. Tours are available in French or English, seven days a week.

여 안녕하세요, 청취자 여러분. 올겨울 퀘벡에 있는 얼음 호텔 방문을 계획해보시면 어떨까요? 그것은 북미의 첫 번째 얼음 호텔입니다. **그 호텔은 건설용으로 특수 제작된 얼음 400톤으로 지어졌습니다(①).** 호텔 내부 온도는 평균 섭씨 영하 4도 정도로 유지되며(②), 투숙객들은 눈과 얼음으로 만들어진 침대 위에 있는 특수 침낭에서 잠을 잡니다. 하지만 투숙객들이 들어가서 몸을 덥힐 수 있는, **난방을 한 화장실과 야외 온수 욕조가 있습니다(③).** 매년 수많은 가족이 이 호텔을 관광하러 오며, **이곳에는 아이들을 위한 재미있는 얼음 미끄럼틀도 있습니다(④).** 투어는 일주일 내내 불어 혹은 영어로 이용할 수 있습니다(⑤).

10 ⑤

해설 폭과 높이가 50센티미터 이하이면서 햇볕이 완전히 들지 않아도 살 수 있고 매주 물을 주지 않아도 되는 식물을 고른다.

어휘 wide 폭이 ~인
cf. width 폭, 너비
fit (어떤 장소에 들어가기에) 맞다
high 높이가 ~인
cf. height 높이, 키
[선택지 어휘] scindapsus 스킨답서스
lily 백합
hydrangea 수국
succulent 다육식물

M Hazel, could you help me choose a plant for the space under the window?
W Sure, what are you looking at?
M I have this list of five plants. How about this one?
W The space is only 50 cm wide. It won't fit.
M Then, what about this plant? It's only 24 cm wide.
W Hmm... wait. Isn't it too tall? It would cover part of the window.
M You're right, then it should be under 50 cm high.
W Yes, and there won't be much sun. It has to be able to live with less than full sunlight.
M Then that leaves us with these two.
W You know, we sometimes forget to water the plants. With this one, we don't have to water it every week.
M Okay. Then let's get it.

남 헤이즐, 창문 아래 공간에 놓을 식물 고르는 것 좀 도와줄래요?
여 그럼요, 뭘 보고 있어요?
남 식물 다섯 개의 목록이 있어요. 이건 어때요?
여 그 공간은 폭이 겨우 50센티미터예요. 안 들어갈 거예요.
남 그럼, 이 식물은 어때요? 폭이 겨우 24센티미터예요.
여 음… 잠시만요. 너무 키가 크지 않나요? 창문의 일부를 가릴지도 몰라요.
남 당신 말이 맞아요, 그럼 높이가 50센티미터 아래여야 하네요.
여 네, 그리고 거긴 햇볕이 많이 들지 않을 거예요. 햇볕이 완전히 들지 않아도 살 수 있는 것이어야 해요.
남 그럼 이 두 개가 남는군요.
여 저기, 우리가 식물에 물주는 걸 가끔 잊어버리잖아요. 이 식물이라면 우리가 매주 물을 주지 않아도 돼요.
남 알겠어요. 그럼 그걸로 사요.

11 ⑤

해설 여자는 열쇠를 잃어버린 남자에게 마지막으로 사용한 시기를 묻고 있다. 따라서 아침에 사용했다는 응답이 가장 적절하다.
① 빨간 열쇠고리에 달려 있어.
② 난 오늘 밤에 열쇠가 필요할 거야.
③ 유감이지만 그게 내가 가지고 있는 마지막 여분의 열쇠야.
④ 네 사물함을 확인해보는 게 좋겠어.

[선택지 어휘] spare 여분의, 예비용의

W What's wrong, Jack? Did you lose something?
M Yeah, I lost my keys. I've looked everywhere, but I can't find them.
W I'll help you look. When was the last time you used them?
M I locked my house this morning with them.

여 무슨 문제 있니, 잭? 뭐 잃어버렸니?
남 응, 열쇠를 잃어버렸어. 전부 다 찾아봤지만, 찾을 수가 없어.
여 찾는 거 도와줄게. 마지막으로 열쇠를 사용했을 때가 언제였니?
남 오늘 아침에 우리 집 현관을 열쇠로 잠갔어.

12 ③

해설 남자가 몸이 괜찮아진 여자에게 파티에 오라고 했으므로 참석 여부를 말하는 응답이 가장 적절하다.
① 아쉽다. 나 동네에 없었어.
② 그런 것 같아. 좋은 시간 보내길 바라.
④ 오늘 와줘서 고마워. 파티를 즐겨.
⑤ 넌 감기약을 좀 먹었어야 했어.

어휘 get over (병 등에서) 회복하다; ~을 극복하다

[Cell phone rings.]
M Hi, Karen. It's me. Are you feeling better today?
W Yes, I got over my cold and I'm feeling much better.
M Oh, then you should come to the party tonight.
W Sorry. I think I'd better stay in bed today.

[휴대전화벨이 울린다.]
남 안녕, 캐런. 나야. 오늘 몸은 좀 괜찮아졌어?
여 응, 감기가 다 나아서 훨씬 괜찮아졌어.
남 아, 그럼 오늘 밤 파티에 와.
여 미안해. 오늘은 침대에 누워 있는 게 나을 것 같아.

13 ⑤

해설 파티에서 남은 음식을 먹는 것에 질려서 오늘 저녁 외식하자는 여자의 제안에 대한 적절한 응답을 고른다.
① 전혀요. 음식에 까다롭지 않거든요.
② 알겠어요. 내가 좋은 태국 음식점을 찾아볼게요.
③ 그러면 고맙겠어요. 다음 번 저녁은 내가 살게요.
④ 초대해주셔서 감사합니다. 정말 기대하고 있어요.

어휘 leftover (식사 후의) 남은 음식
frankly 솔직히
feel like v-ing v하고 싶다
[선택지 어휘] picky 까다로운
look forward to ~을 고대하다

W I'm a bit hungry. What should we have for dinner?
M We have a lot of leftovers from the party. Let's eat those.
W I'm tired of the leftovers. We had them for dinner last night and breakfast this morning.
M Well, I can make you pasta if you want.
W Hmm, I don't feel like having pasta now. Do you remember that Thai food we had with Lillian?
M Oh, are you talking about the shrimp and seafood dish at the Thai Market?
W Yes, it was pretty great. How about going there for dinner tonight?
M What about the leftovers?
W We'll have them tomorrow.
M Okay. Frankly, I didn't feel like having leftovers, either.

여 난 좀 배고파요. 저녁으로 무엇을 먹을까요?
남 우리에게는 파티에서 남은 음식이 많이 있어요. 그것들을 먹죠.
여 난 남은 음식이 질려요. 우린 어제 저녁과 오늘 아침으로 그것들을 먹었어요.
남 음, 당신이 원한다면 내가 파스타를 만들게요.
여 음, 지금 파스타를 먹고 싶지 않아요. 우리가 릴리안과 함께 먹었던 태국 음식을 기억해요?
남 아, 타이 마켓에서 먹었던 새우와 해산물 요리 말하는 건가요?
여 맞아요, 그건 매우 훌륭했어요. 오늘 밤에 저녁 식사하러 거기에 가는 게 어때요?
남 남은 음식들은 어떻게 하고요?
여 우리가 내일 먹겠죠.
남 좋아요. 솔직히 나도 남은 음식을 먹고 싶지 않았어요.

14 ⑤

해설 경기에 참가할 수 있도록 말다툼을 한 친구들을 설득해보겠다고 했으므로 좋은 생각이라며 상황을 해결하면 좋겠다는 응답이 가장 적절하다.
① 확실해? 난 그 경기가 이번 주라고 생각했어.
② 너는 당장 그 애들과 화해하는 게 좋겠어.
③ 네 말이 맞아. 그렇게 좋은 친구들이 있는 네가 부러워.
④ 그거 훌륭한 생각이네. 아마도 코치님께서 네 말을 들어주실 거야.

어휘 get into an argument (with) (~와) 말다툼[논쟁]을 하다
work out (일이) 잘 풀리다; 운동하다
overhear 우연히 듣다
make up (with) (~와) 화해하다
(= make peace with)

W Max, have you heard? There was a problem during practice while you were gone.
M What happened?
W George and Travis got into an argument. It was so bad that practice was cancelled.
M I hope things work out for them soon. There's a soccer game next week.
W Well, I overheard the coach saying that unless George and Travis make up, he won't let them in the game.
M So, they might not be able to play next week? But they're the best players on the team!
W I know, but what can we do?
M I know both of them well, so I'll go and talk to them.
W Good thinking! I hope you can solve this situation.

여 맥스, 너 들었니? 네가 없는 동안 연습 중에 문제가 있었어.
남 무슨 일이 있었는데?
여 조지와 트래비스가 말다툼을 했어. 너무 심해서 연습이 취소되었어.
남 그 애들이 곧 잘 풀면 좋겠는데. 다음 주에 축구 경기가 있잖아.
여 글쎄, 코치님께서 말씀하시는 것을 우연히 들었는데, 조지와 트래비스가 화해하지 않으면 경기에 내보내지 않으실 거야.
남 그럼, 다음 주에 그 애들이 경기를 뛰지 못할지도 모른다는 거야? 그렇지만 그 애들은 팀 내 최고의 선수들이잖아!
여 나도 알지만, 우리가 뭘 할 수 있겠어?
남 내가 그 애들을 둘 다 잘 아니까, 내가 가서 얘기해볼게.
여 좋은 생각이야! 네가 이 상황을 해결할 수 있으면 좋겠어.

15 ②

해설 옆 테이블의 요리를 보고 같은 것을 먹고 싶어 하므로 옆 테이블에서 먹는 것을 달라는 말이 가장 적절하다.

① 파스타를 조리하는 데 얼마나 걸리나요?

② 옆 테이블에 계신 분이 드시는 것으로 할 수 있을까요?

③ 제 친구도 제가 시키는 것으로 주세요.

④ 오늘의 주방장 특별 요리가 무엇인지 말씀해주시겠어요?

⑤ 당신의 식당에 대한 아주 좋은 평을 읽었어요.

어휘 signal 신호를 보내다; 신호 [선택지 어휘] review 평가, 리뷰; 재검토

M Sally is at a restaurant with her friend Oliver. The two have met to try a new restaurant that Sally has read about. After looking at the menu, Sally decides on a pasta dish, and she signals the waiter. The waiter comes to take their order. However, just then she looks over at the next table, and notices the dish a man is eating. She doesn't know what it is but it looks delicious, and she wants to have it instead of the pasta. In this situation, what would Sally most likely say to the waiter?

남 샐리는 친구 올리버와 함께 한 식당에 있다. 그 둘은 샐리가 (식당에 대한 평을) 읽어본 적이 있는 새로운 식당에 가보기 위해 만났다. 메뉴를 본 후, 샐리는 파스타 요리로 결정하고 웨이터에게 신호를 보낸다. 종업원이 주문을 받으러 온다. 그러나 바로 그때, 그녀는 옆 테이블을 살펴보고 한 남자가 먹고 있는 요리가 눈에 들어온다. 그녀는 그것이 무엇인지는 모르지만 맛있어 보여서, 파스타 대신 그것을 먹고 싶어 한다. 이 상황에서, 샐리가 종업원에게 할 말로 가장 적절한 것은 무엇인가?

---

16 ⑤   17 ①

해설 16 체육을 통해 기대할 수 있는 여러 가지 긍정적인 사항들을 나열하며 체육 교육의 중요성을 설명하고 있다.

① 학교에서 팀워크 가르치기

② 팀 스포츠를 하는 것의 장점

③ 학생들의 건강이 향상된 이유

④ 균형 잡힌 교육의 필요성

⑤ 학교 체육의 중요성

17 해설 참조

어휘 Physical Education (P.E.) 체육

possibility 가능성

scholarship 장학금

career 직업; 경력

attitude 태도, 자세

encourage A to-v A가 v하도록 장려[격려]하다

institution 기관, 시설; (사회) 제도

endure 오래가다, 지속되다; 견디다

W Hello, everyone. I'm Mavis Clark, a P.E. teacher at Arlington High School. People sometimes think that Physical Education, or P.E., costs too much money. So I want to explain to you what P.E. is all about. An education is about creating opportunities to try new things and discover gifts. If it were not for P.E., many people wouldn't find out that they have a talent for a sport, or even that they enjoy it. Once experienced, sport can be enjoyed for life. For some it will provide the possibility of a college scholarship or even a career. Furthermore, playing team sports has lots of advantages. It builds positive attitudes and encourages students to use teamwork in order to win. It also builds a strong school spirit through competition with other institutions. It is often the experience of playing on a team together that builds the strongest friendships at school. And many of those friendships endure for years afterwards.

여 안녕하세요, 여러분. 저는 알링턴 고등학교의 체육 교사 메이비스 클락입니다. 사람들은 가끔 체육에 돈이 너무 많이 든다고 생각합니다. 그래서 저는 여러분께 체육의 모든 것에 대해 설명하려고 합니다. 교육은 새로운 것들을 시도하고 재능을 발견할 기회를 만들어내는 것입니다. 체육이 없다면, 많은 사람은 자신이 스포츠에 재능이 있다는 사실이나, 스포츠를 좋아한다는 사실조차 알아낼 수 없을 것입니다. 스포츠는 일단 한번 경험하면 평생 즐길 수 있습니다. 어떤 사람들에게는 체육이 대학 장학금이나 심지어 직업을 얻을 가능성을 제공해줄 것입니다. 게다가, 팀 스포츠를 하는 것에는 많은 장점이 있습니다. 팀 스포츠는 **긍정적인 태도**(② positive attitude)를 길러주고 학생들이 이기기 위해 **팀워크**(③ teamwork)를 사용하도록 장려합니다. 또한, 다른 단체와의 시합을 통해 강한 **애교심**(④ school spirit)을 길러줍니다. 대개 학교에서 가장 끈끈한 **우정**(⑤ friendship)을 쌓게 하는 것은 바로 한 팀에서 함께 경기하는 경험입니다. 그리고 그런 우정은 대부분 그 후로도 오래 지속됩니다.

01 ②   **02** ①   **03** ④   **04** ③   **05** ①   **06** ②   **07** ④   **08** ④   **09** ③   **10** ②

11 ②   **12** ②   **13** ①   **14** ⑤   **15** ②   **16** ①   **17** ④

01 ②

해설 새로 나온 제품의 특징을 설명하고 무료 샘플 시식을 홍보하는 내용이다.

어휘 microwavable 전자레인지로 조리할 수 있는
flavor 맛, 풍미
roasted 구운
guarantee 보장[약속]하다
unwrap (포장지 등을) 벗기다, 뜯다
be priced at 가격이 ~이다
give out ~을 나눠 주다

W Shoppers, may I have your attention please? If you haven't decided what to have for dinner this evening, how about trying these delicious new microwavable dinners? They come in three flavors: Roasted Garlic, Spicy Barbecue, and Creamy Italian. I guarantee that you will love all these flavors, but the best part is how easy they are to prepare. Simply unwrap them, microwave them for 5 minutes, and then mix in the special sauce that is included. They are priced at $8 each, but today we are giving out coupons for 50% off. If you are interested, please come up and try a free sample.

여 쇼핑객 여러분, 주목해주시겠습니까? 오늘 저녁 식사로 무엇을 드실지 결정하지 못하셨다면 이 맛있고 새로운 전자레인지로 조리할 수 있는 저녁 식사는 어떠신가요? 구운 마늘, 매콤한 바비큐, 크림이 듬뿍 든 이탈리아식을 포함해 세 가지 맛이 있습니다. 저는 여러분이 이 모든 맛을 좋아하시리라 확신합니다만, 가장 좋은 점은 그것들을 준비하기가 얼마나 쉬운가 하는 것입니다. 포장을 벗기고 전자레인지에 5분간 돌린 다음, 들어 있는 특제 소스에 섞어 주기만 하면 됩니다. 개당 8달러이지만, 오늘은 50퍼센트 할인 쿠폰을 나눠 드리고 있습니다. 관심 있으시면 오셔서 무료 샘플을 시식해보세요.

02 ①

해설 규모가 작은 학원에 만족하는 남자의 경험을 바탕으로 소규모 학원이 지닌 장점에 관해 이야기하고 있다.

어휘 advantage 이점, 장점
highly regarded 높이 평가받는
cf. regard 평가하다, 존중하다; ~으로 여기다
relatively 비교적
supportive (사람을) 지원하는, 격려하는

W Andy, are you doing well at your academy?
M Yes, I'm very satisfied with it.
W That's good. You were once very worried about choosing between a larger academy and a smaller one.
M Yes, but now I'm sure that a smaller one has more advantages.
W What do you think is the biggest advantage?
M I think they have a better learning environment.
W What's so good about it?
M Well, in big, highly regarded academies, the class sizes are very large. So the teachers usually don't have enough time to have a close relationship with their students.
W It does sound better for students who want a relatively close relationship with their teachers to attend smaller academies.
M Sure. And students can study in a more supportive environment.

여 앤디, 학원에서 잘하고 있니?
남 응, 나는 아주 만족해.
여 잘됐네. 한때 규모가 큰 학원과 작은 학원 중에서 결정하는 것을 매우 고민했잖아.
남 그랬지, 하지만 지금은 더 작은 학원이 이점이 더 많다고 확신해.
여 가장 큰 장점이 뭐라고 생각해?
남 학습 환경이 더 좋은 것 같아.
여 어떤 점이 그렇게 좋은데?
남 음, 규모가 크고 높이 평가받는 학원은 학급 크기가 매우 커. 그래서 선생님들은 학생들과 친밀한 관계를 맺을 충분한 시간이 없지.
여 선생님들과 비교적 친밀한 관계를 원하는 학생은 더 작은 학원에 다니는 게 정말 더 좋을 것 같네.
남 물론이야. 그리고 학생들은 (서로) 더 힘이 되어주는 환경에서 공부할 수 있어.

03 ④

해설 뱃멀미 때문에 그룹 관광에 참여할 수 없는 남자 관광객에게 여자가 다른 구경거리를 소개해주는 것으로 보아 여자의 직업은 여행 가이드임을 알 수 있다.

어휘 seasick 뱃멀미가 난, 뱃멀미의
throw up 토하다, 게우다
sightseeing 관광, 구경

M I noticed that you have a boat ride scheduled for tomorrow, but I don't think I can go.
W Why not?
M I get really seasick. The last time I was on a boat, I was throwing up the whole time. I don't want to try again.
W Have you tried taking medicine for it?
M Yes, but it didn't help.
W That's too bad. The island is one of the best parts of the tour.

남 보트 타기를 내일로 잡으신 걸로 아는데, 전 못 갈 것 같아요.
여 왜요?
남 뱃멀미가 심해서요. 지난번에 보트를 탔을 때, 내내 토했어요. 다시는 시도하고 싶지 않아요.
여 멀미약은 드셔 보셨어요?
남 네, 하지만 도움이 안 됐어요.
여 그것 참 안됐네요. 그 섬은 우리 관광에서 최고의 부분 중 하나거든요.

attraction (사람을 끄는) 명소[명물];
매력
brochure (안내, 광고용) 책자

M	What can I do instead?
W	You can come with us in the morning. There are a lot of sightseeing attractions nearby. I'll give you a brochure.
M	Thanks. When will the group return?
W	We'll be back around noon.

남 그 대신에 저는 뭘 할 수 있을까요?
여 아침에 저희와 함께 가시면 돼요. 근처에 관광 명소가 많이 있거든요. 제가 책자를 드릴게요.
남 고맙습니다. 사람들은 언제 돌아오나요?
여 정오경에 돌아올 거예요.

---

04 ③

해설 현관 계단 옆에 우체통이 있다고 했으므로 그림 속 작은 칠판은 대화의 내용과 일치하지 않는다.

어휘 swing 그네
porch 현관
relax 편하게 하다, 쉬게 하다
ceiling 천장
welcoming 따뜻이 맞이하는; 안락해 보이는
mail box 우체통

W	Here we are. This is my house.
M	It looks wonderful! There's a swing chair hung on the left side of the porch.
W	That's my favorite part of the house. It's nice to sit on it and relax.
M	Sounds great! You hung two plant baskets on the ceiling.
W	Yes. I think they make the home feel more welcoming.
M	Right. Look! There's a mail box by the porch stairs.
W	I made it myself. I wrote our address, "384 Scott Street," on it.
M	Lovely! Oh, I like the bench below the window.
W	My husband and I love to sit there and drink tea. That's why we put a small round table in front of it.
M	It looks romantic!

여 여깁니다. 이게 우리 집이에요.
남 멋져 보여요! 현관 왼쪽에 그네 의자가 걸려 있군요.
여 그게 제가 집에서 제일 좋아하는 부분이에요. 그것에 앉아 휴식을 취하는 것이 좋아요.
남 좋겠군요! 천장에 두 개의 식물 바구니를 걸었네요.
여 네. 그것들이 집에 더 따뜻이 맞이하는 느낌을 주는 것 같아요.
남 맞아요. 봐요! 현관 계단 옆에 우체통이 있군요.
여 제가 직접 만들었어요. 거기에 우리 집 주소 '스콧가 384번지'를 적었죠.
남 멋지네요! 아, 창문 아래 벤치가 마음에 드는군요.
여 제 남편과 저는 거기 앉아서 차 마시는 것을 좋아해요. 그게 우리가 그것 앞에 작은 원형 테이블을 놓은 이유예요.
남 낭만적인 것 같네요!

---

05 ①

해설 여자는 구직 중인 남자에게 직원을 모집하려는 박물관 관리자를 소개해주겠다고 했다.

어휘 recognize 알아보다; 인정하다
law firm 법률 회사[사무소]
suitable 적당한, 알맞은
stable 안정적인, 안정된
recruit (신입을) 모집하다

M	May I take your order?
W	A large coffee, please. [pause] Oh, is that you George? It's me, Laurie!
M	Laurie? I almost didn't recognize you! How have you been?
W	Pretty good. I'm working for a law firm now.
M	I always knew you would do well.
W	Thanks. So, what are you up to these days?
M	I graduated about six months ago, but it's been hard to find a suitable job. So I'm working here part-time until I can find something more stable.
W	What was your major?
M	History.
W	Really? I know the manager of a museum downtown. He's planning to recruit more staff. I can introduce you to him if you'd like.
M	Really? You would do that for me?
W	Of course. Just text me your information. Here's my number.

남 주문하시겠어요?
여 커피 큰 걸로 주세요. [잠시 후] 어, 너 조지니? 나야, 로리!
남 로리? 못 알아볼 뻔했어! 어떻게 지냈니?
여 아주 잘 지냈어. 난 지금 법률 회사에서 일하고 있어.
남 난 항상 네가 잘해낼 걸 알고 있었어.
여 고마워. 그런데 넌 요즘 뭐 하고 지내니?
남 난 6개월 전쯤에 졸업했는데, 적당한 일을 찾기가 어려웠어. 그래서 좀 더 안정적인 일을 찾을 수 있을 때까지 여기서 시간제로 일하고 있어.
여 네 전공이 뭐였지?
남 역사야.
여 정말? 내가 시내에 있는 한 박물관의 관리자를 알아. 그는 더 많은 직원을 모집하려고 계획 중이야. 너만 좋다면 그분께 널 소개해줄 수 있어.
남 정말? 날 위해 그렇게 해줄래?
여 물론이지. 네 정보를 나에게 문자로 좀 보내줘. 여기 내 번호야.

---

06 ②

해설 남자는 80달러짜리 재킷을 50% 할인한 가격에 구입하고, 50달러인 스웨터 두 벌을 구매하면서 하나는 반값만 내면 되므로 남자가 지불할 금액은 115달러이다.

W	Hello. May I help you?
M	Yes, I like this blue sweater very much. Is this a new arrival?
W	Yes. The regular price on this sweater is $50, but...
M	Oh, sorry to interrupt, but this black jacket is nice, too.

여 안녕하세요, 도와드릴까요?
남 네, 이 파란색 스웨터가 매우 마음에 들어요. 신상품인가요?
여 네, 이 스웨터의 정상 가격은 50달러입니다만…
남 아, 말씀 도중에 미안하지만, 이 검은색 재킷도 좋네요.

어휘 new arrival 신상품
interrupt 방해하다

W	It's the most popular one in our store. It's $80. But all the jackets are 50% off this week.
M	Hmm... it's a great deal. I'll get one.
W	Okay. And I was going to tell you that if you buy two sweaters of the same type, you'll get the second one at half price.
M	Oh, really? Blue and green are my favorite colors. I'll get those two then.
W	All right. Is that all?
M	Yes. Here is my credit card.

여	그건 저희 매장에서 가장 인기 있는 것입니다. 가격은 80달러이고요. 하지만 이번 주에 재킷은 모두 50% 할인입니다.
남	음… 아주 좋은 가격이네요. 하나 살게요.
여	네. 그리고 같은 종류의 스웨터를 두 벌 구매하시면 두 번째 것은 반값에 가져가신다는 말씀을 드리려고 했습니다.
남	아, 정말이요? 파란색이랑 녹색이 제가 가장 좋아하는 색이에요. 그럼 저 두 개를 살게요.
여	알겠습니다. 그게 전부인가요?
남	네. 여기 제 신용카드입니다.

07 ④

해설 여자는 토요일마다 봉사 활동을 하러 동물 보호소에 가야 해서 바이올린 강좌를 들을 수 없다고 했다.

어휘 catalogue 카탈로그, 목록
tuition fee 수업료
animal shelter 동물 보호소
do volunteer work 자원 봉사를 하다

W	Hi, John, what are you looking at?
M	Hi, Scarlett. It's a catalogue of classes at the community center. I'm thinking of taking a violin class on Saturdays.
W	Cool! I took violin lessons when I was little, but now I can't play at all.
M	Really? Then why don't we take the class together? The tuition fee is only $80 a month.
W	Oh, that's a good price, but I can't.
M	Why not? Is it because the community center is too far from your place?
W	No, it only takes half an hour by bus.
M	Then, maybe you don't have a violin to practice with?
W	No, actually, I visit an animal shelter every Saturday to do volunteer work.
M	Oh, I see. Well, I'll play the violin for you when I finish the course.
W	That sounds nice! I'm already looking forward to it.

여	안녕, 존, 뭘 보고 있니?
남	안녕, 스칼렛. 커뮤니티 센터에서 하는 수업 카탈로그야. 난 토요일마다 바이올린 수업을 듣는 것을 생각 중이야.
여	멋진데! 나는 어릴 때 바이올린 수업을 들었는데 지금은 전혀 연주하지 못해.
남	정말? 그럼 같이 수업을 듣는 게 어때? 수업료가 한 달에 80달러밖에 안 해.
여	아, 가격이 괜찮긴 한데 난 못할 것 같아.
남	왜 안 되는데? 너희 집에서 커뮤니티 센터가 너무 멀어서 그래?
여	아니, 버스로 30분밖에 안 걸려.
남	그럼, 혹시 연습할 바이올린이 없어서야?
여	아니, 사실 난 자원 봉사를 하러 매주 토요일에 동물 보호소에 가.
남	아, 그렇구나. 음, 강좌를 수료하면 내가 널 위해 바이올린을 연주해줄게.
여	좋아! 벌써 기대된다.

08 ④

해설 해석 참조

어휘 apparently 듣자[보아] 하니; 분명히
upcoming 다가오는, 곧 있을
apply 지원하다
cf. application 지원[신청]서
qualified 자격이 있는
cf. qualify 자격이 있다
permission 허락, 허가
prove 보여주다; 입증[증명]하다
trial ((주로 복수형)) 선수 선발전; 시험; 재판
submit 제출하다

M	Hello, Ms. Green. Did you want to see me?
W	Yes, Jonathan. You've heard about Diamond Valley Baseball Team, haven't you?
M	Of course I have.
W	Apparently, they are looking for 5 new players for the upcoming season. Why don't you apply to the team?
M	Oh, I'd love to. But I'm not sure I'm qualified.
W	It requires you to have at least a B average and get permission from your parents.
M	That won't be a problem.
W	Good. If you qualify, you will have the chance to prove your baseball skills. Trials will be held on May 16th.
M	I got it. How can I apply then?
W	You need to submit your application to Mr. Thomas' office, which is located in the gym.
M	Okay. Thank you for telling me, Ms. Green.

남	안녕하세요, 그린 선생님. 절 보길 원하셨나요?
여	그래, 조나단. 다이아몬드 밸리 야구팀에 대해 들어봤을 거야, 그렇지 않니?
남	물론이죠, 들어봤어요.
여	듣자 하니, 다가오는 시즌을 위해 **다섯 명의 새로운 선수들을 찾고 있다는구나**(① 선발 인원). 그 팀에 지원해보지 않겠니?
남	아, 그리고 싶어요. 하지만 제가 자격이 있는지 모르겠어요.
여	**야구팀은 네가 최소 평균 B 학점이고 부모님의 허락을 받을 것을 요구한단다**(② 지원 자격).
남	그건 문제없을 거예요.
여	좋아. 네가 자격이 있으면 네 야구 실력을 보여줄 기회가 주어질 거야. **선수 선발전은 5월 16일에 열려**(③ 선발전 날짜).
남	알겠어요. 그럼 어떻게 지원할 수 있죠?
여	**토마스 코치의 사무실로 지원서를 제출해야 하는데, 그건 체육관 안에 있어**(⑤ 지원 방법).
남	알겠습니다. 알려주셔서 감사합니다, 그린 선생님.

09 ③

해설 참가비는 무료이고 점심도 무료로 제공된다.

어휘 invaluable 매우 귀중한
limit 제한하다
free of charge 무료의
enrollment 등록
cf. enroll 등록하다
on a first-come, first-served basis 선착순으로, 순번대로

M I'm happy to inform you of Crestmont's Summer Safety Program. This is an invaluable class for anyone who wants to prepare for possible accidents over the summer. The course will be held from 10 a.m. to 4 p.m. on June 9th and 10th. And it will be limited to students between the ages 12 and 17. The course is free of charge and will include a free lunch. The class will hold up to 30 students, and enrollment will be on a first come, first served basis. You can stop by the Crestmont Fire Department to enroll or do it online. Our website address is www.crestmontfire.com.

남 저는 크레스트몬트 여름 안전 프로그램에 대해 알려드리게 돼서 기쁩니다. 이것은 여름 동안에 발생 가능한 사고에 대비하려는 학생들을 위한 매우 귀중한 수업입니다. 이 강좌는 **6월 9일과 10일에** (①) 오전 10시부터 오후 4시까지 열립니다. 그리고 **12세에서 17세 사이의 학생들로 제한됩니다** (②). 이 강좌는 무료이며 무료 점심이 포함될 것입니다(③). 수업은 30명 정원이며, 등록은 선착순입니다(④). 등록하기 위해 크레스트몬트 소방서에 방문하시거나 온라인으로 하실 수 있습니다 (⑤). 저희 웹사이트 주소는 www.crestmontfire.com입니다.

10 ②

해설 아침 9시 이후에 출발하여 오후 11시 전에 도착하며 직항편이 아닌 항공편을 고른다. 직항편을 선택하려다 예산 때문에 경유하는 항공편으로 변경한 것에 유의한다.

어휘 way 매우; 아주 멀리
operate 운영하다; 작동하다
indirect 우회하는; 간접적인
(↔ direct 직항[직행]의; 직접적인)
budget 예산
may as well+동사원형 ~하는 편이 낫다
go with ~을 선택하다, 받아들이다

W Honey, have you searched for our plane tickets to Orlando?
M Yeah, the cheapest one leaves at 5 a.m.
W That's way too early. I think it's better to take the plane which leaves after 9 a.m.
M Okay. Does the hotel's shuttle bus run 24 hours a day?
W No, it operates from 7 a.m. to 11 p.m. So, we need to arrive before 11 p.m.
M Right. And are you okay to take an indirect flight?
W Not really. I prefer to take a direct flight.
M Then, there are two options left, and both are over $600.
W Oh, that's over our budget.
M You know, an indirect flight won't be that bad.
W Alright.... Since we're already spending $650 on the hotel, I guess we may as well save on the plane tickets.
M Okay, then we're going with that one.

여 여보, 올랜도로 가는 항공권 알아봤어요?
남 네, 제일 싼 게 오전 5시에 출발해요.
여 그건 매우 많이 일러요. 오전 9시 이후에 떠나는 비행기를 타는 게 더 좋을 것 같아요.
남 알겠어요. 호텔 셔틀 버스는 24시간 운행하나요?
여 아니요, 오전 7시에서 오후 11시까지 운영해요. 그러니 우리는 오후 11시 전에 도착해야 해요.
남 그렇군요. 그리고 당신 경유하는 항공편을 타도 괜찮아요?
여 별로요. 나는 직항편을 타는 게 더 좋아요.
남 그럼, 두 개의 선택이 남는데 둘 다 600달러가 넘어요.
여 아, 그건 우리 예산을 초과하네요.
남 있잖아요, 경유하는 항공편이 그렇게 나쁘진 않을 거예요.
여 알겠어요…. 호텔에 이미 650달러를 쓰기로 했으니, 비행기 표는 아끼는 편이 나을 것 같아요.
남 좋아요, 그럼 우리 저걸로 선택해요.

11 ②

해설 등산 중에 여자가 얼마나 더 가야 하는지 물었으므로, 남은 거리를 알려주는 응답이 가장 적절하다.
① 난 이렇게 멀리 하이킹하는 데 익숙하지 않아.
③ 가능한 한 빨리 집에 가자.
④ 이 산은 여름에 가장 좋아.
⑤ 산 정상이 정말 기대돼.

어휘 farther (공간, 시간상으로) 더 멀리
[선택지 어휘] be used to v-ing v하는 데 익숙하다
peak (산의) 정상

W Nick, are you planning to climb the whole mountain without a break?
M Yeah, I'd prefer to keep moving. Do you want to rest?
W Actually, I really do. How much farther do we need to go?
M It's less than a kilometer to the top.

여 닉, 쉬지 않고 산을 끝까지 등반할 계획이니?
남 응, 계속 이동하는 게 더 좋아. 넌 쉬고 싶니?
여 사실은, 정말 그래. 우리 얼마나 더 멀리 가야 하니?
남 정상까지 1킬로미터도 채 안 남았어.

12 ②

해설 빌려준 지우개를 바로 돌려주겠다고 했으므로 서두를 필요 없다는 응답이 가장 적절하다.
① 마음껏 먹어! 많이 남았어.
③ 아니, 괜찮아. 내가 스스로 가져올 수 있어.
④ 도와줘서 정말 고마워.
⑤ 당연하지. 기꺼이 그럴게.

[선택지 어휘] **Help yourself** (음식을) 마음껏 드세요
take one's time 천천히 하다

M Do you happen to have an eraser you could lend me?
W Sure, I do. Here it is.
M Thanks a lot. I'll return it right away.
W Take your time. There's no hurry.

남 혹시 나한테 빌려줄 지우개 하나 있니?
여 그럼, 있어. 자, 여기 있어.
남 정말 고마워. 바로 돌려줄게.
여 천천히 해. 서두를 필요 없어.

---

13 ①

해설 타이어를 교체하는 데 필요한 도구를 트렁크에서 빼버렸다고 했으므로 정비공을 부르는 수밖에 없다는 응답이 가장 적절하다.
② 트렁크가 잠겨 있어서 열 수가 없어.
③ 여행 가방 꺼내는 걸 도와줄게.
④ 고마워. 네가 없었다면 난 그것을 할 수 없었을 거야.
⑤ 설명서는 앞좌석 아래에 있어.

어휘 **flat** (타이어가) 바람이 빠진; 평평한
auto mechanic's shop 자동차 정비소
cf. **mechanic** 정비공
make it (장소에) 이르다, 도착하다
instruction manual 취급 설명서
suitcase 여행 가방

W There's something wrong with our car. I think we have a flat tire.
M There's an auto mechanic's shop a couple of miles down the road. Can we make it there?
W I don't think we can go any farther. Maybe I can fix it by myself.
M Have you changed a tire before?
W I've watched my father do it a few times. I think I know what to do.
M OK. I'll help you. What do we do first?
W We need to find a tool to remove the tire.
M Check the trunk. I'll find the instruction manual.
W OK. *[pause]* Oh, I took out the tools to make room for the suitcases.
M Then we'll just have to call a mechanic.

여 우리 차에 이상이 있어. 타이어가 바람이 빠진 것 같아.
남 이 길에서 몇 마일 아래에 자동차 정비소가 하나 있어. 거기까지 갈 수 있을까?
여 더 못 갈 것 같은데. 내가 혼자 고칠 수 있을 것 같아.
남 전에 타이어를 갈아본 적 있니?
여 아버지께서 하시는 걸 몇 번 봤어. 뭘 해야 할지 알 것 같아.
남 좋아. 내가 도와줄게. 먼저 무엇을 하지?
여 타이어를 뺄 도구를 찾아야 해.
남 트렁크를 확인해 봐. 나는 설명서를 찾아볼게.
여 알겠어. *[잠시 후]* 아, 내가 여행 가방을 넣을 공간을 만드느라 도구들을 빼 버렸어.
남 그럼 우리는 정비공을 부르는 수밖에 없겠네.

---

14 ⑤

해설 이미 가지고 있는 운동 기구도 사용하지 않으면서 새로운 것을 또 사고 싶어 하므로 구입에 반대하는 의견을 제시하는 것이 가장 적절하다.
① 당신이 그것을 또 샀다니 믿을 수 없어요!
② 당신은 밤늦게 운동하면 안 돼요.
③ 훌륭해요. 정말 좋은 운동 방법이네요!
④ 그게 바로 신모델일수록 더 좋은 이유죠.

어휘 **be about to-v** 막 v하려고 하다
brand-new 신품의, 아주 새로운
strengthen 강화시키다, 더 튼튼하게 하다
core 중심부의; 핵심적인
transform 변형시키다
[선택지 어휘] **work out** 운동하다

W Can you change the channel, please? My favorite TV show is about to start.
M Oh, wait. I want to watch this program.
W What is it about?
M They're introducing their brand-new model. It really strengthens your core muscles.
W Not this again!
M That guy was able to transform his body in just 2 weeks by using it.
W Don't you already have something similar?
M Yes, but this is the newest model. If I use this, I'll be able to have stronger muscles.
W You've only used the one you have now a few times!
M I know, but I'm pretty sure I'm going to use this one every day.
W Well, I don't think you should buy it.

여 채널 좀 바꿔 줄래요? 내가 제일 좋아하는 TV쇼가 막 시작하려고 해요.
남 어, 잠깐만요. 난 이 프로그램을 보고 싶어요.
여 그게 무엇에 관한 건데요?
남 신모델을 소개하고 있어요. 그게 중심부 근육들을 정말로 강화시켜 준대요.
여 이번에는 안 돼요!
남 저 남자는 그걸 사용해서 단 2주 만에 몸을 바꿀 수 있었어요.
여 당신은 이미 비슷한 것을 가지고 있지 않나요?
남 그렇긴 하지만 이건 최신 모델이에요. 내가 이걸 사용하면, 더 튼튼한 근육을 가질 수 있을 거예요.
여 당신은 지금 가지고 있는 것도 몇 번밖에 안 썼잖아요!
남 알아요, 하지만 난 이것은 매일 사용할 거라고 아주 확신해요.
여 저, 나는 당신이 그것을 사면 안 될 것 같아요.

15 ②

해설 우승하는 데 도움이 될 새로운 방법을 제안하고 싶어 하는 상황이므로 다른 방법을 시도해보자는 말이 가장 적절하다.

① 우리 함께 축하하는 게 어때?
② 우리가 우승하려면 다른 방법을 시도해야 할 것 같아.
③ 우린 정말 잘하고 있어. 계속 이렇게 하자!
④ 우리가 올해 대회에서 우승했다니 믿을 수가 없어.
⑤ 우리 오늘 모임을 취소하고 내일 만나도 될까?

어휘 be made up of ~으로 구성되어 있다 (= consist of)
yearly 매년의, 해마다 있는
aim to-v v하는 것을 목표로 하다
upcoming 다가오는, 곧 있을
ineffective 효과적이지 못한; 무능한
[선택지 어휘] keep up ~을 계속하다, 유지하다

W Ian is part of a school club called the Science Buzz. It is made up of 15 members who meet to discuss scientific topics and, most importantly, practice for the yearly National Science Competition. The Science Buzz was able to come in third place last year. This year, they are aiming to win first place. The members have been practicing daily for the upcoming competition, but Ian feels that their current practice method is ineffective. He has already thought of a better method that might help them win. So, he wants to suggest to club members that they use the new method. In this situation, what would Ian most likely say to his club members?

여 이언은 사이언스 버즈라는 학교 동아리의 일원이다. 그것은 과학적 주제에 대해 토론하기 위해, 또 가장 중요하게는 매년 열리는 전국 과학 경진 대회를 대비한 연습을 하기 위해 모이는 15명의 회원들로 이루어져 있다. 사이언스 버즈는 작년에 3위를 차지할 수 있었다. 올해, 그들은 1위를 하는 것을 목표로 하고 있다. 회원들은 다가오는 대회를 위해 매일 연습을 해오고 있지만, 이언은 자신들의 현재 연습 방법이 효과적이지 않다고 느낀다. 그는 우승하는 데 도움이 될 만한 더 좋은 방법을 이미 생각해냈다. 그래서 그는 동아리 회원들에게 새로운 방법을 사용할 것을 제안하고 싶어 한다. 이 상황에서, 이언이 동아리 회원들에게 할 말로 가장 적절한 것은 무엇인가?

16 ①   17 ④

해설 **16** 자연에서 발견되는 구조를 반영한 건축물들에 대해 설명하고 있다.

① 자연에서 영감받은 건축물
② 자연을 이용하는 건축의 원칙들
③ 건물을 환경 친화적으로 만드는 방법들
④ 건축물이 환경에 미치는 영향
⑤ 자연에서 발견되는 모양들이 예술적인 이유

[선택지 어휘] inspire 영감을 주다

17 해석 참조

어휘 eco-friendly 환경 친화적인
architecture 건축물
cf. architectural 건축(상)의
impact 영향
masterpiece 걸작, 명작
reflect 반영하다; 반사하다
resemble ~와 닮다 (= look like)
cathedral 대성당
skyscraper 고층 건물
model after ~을 본떠서 만들다
symbolize 상징하다
beehive 벌집
glow 빛나다; 불빛

M Good morning, class! Previously, we learned about eco-friendly architecture around the world. Those structures focus on minimizing the negative environmental impact. Today, we are going to learn about architectural masterpieces that reflect structures found in nature. First, the national stadium in Beijing, which hosted numerous sports events during the Beijing Olympics in 2008, resembles a bird's nest. Next, a cathedral in Barcelona, La Sagrada Familia, was designed to look like a forest. Also, Taipei 101, the 101-story skyscraper opened in Taipei in 2004, was modeled after bamboo, which symbolizes learning and growth. Lastly, a museum of modern art in Cape Town has windows that look like a beehive at night when they glow with a warm yellow light. Now, let's search for other examples of this kind of architecture on the Internet.

남 안녕하세요, 여러분! 이전에 우리는 세계의 친환경 건축물에 대해 배웠습니다. 그 구조물들은 환경에 부정적인 영향을 최소화하는 데 중점을 둡니다. 오늘, 우리는 자연에서 발견되는 구조를 반영한 건축 걸작들에 대해 배워보겠습니다. 첫째, **베이징**(① Beijing)에 있는 국립 경기장은 2008년 베이징 올림픽 동안 수많은 스포츠 경기를 열었는데, 새의 둥지를 닮아 있죠. 다음으로, **바르셀로나**(② Barcelona)에 있는 대성당인 라 사그라다 파밀리아는 숲과 같이 보이도록 설계되었습니다. 또한, 2004년 **타이베이**(③ Taipei)에 문을 연 101층짜리 고층 건물인 타이베이 101은 대나무를 본떠서 만들었는데, 대나무는 배움과 성장을 상징합니다. 마지막으로 **케이프타운**(⑤ Cape Town)에 있는 현대미술관은 밤에 따뜻한 노란 불빛으로 빛날 때 벌집처럼 보이는 창문이 있습니다. 이제 인터넷으로 이러한 종류의 건축물들의 다른 예들을 찾아봅시다.

| 01 ① | 02 ② | 03 ⑤ | 04 ② | 05 ⑤ | 06 ③ | 07 ③ | 08 ② | 09 ⑤ | 10 ④ |
| 11 ⑤ | 12 ④ | 13 ③ | 14 ③ | 15 ⑤ | 16 ④ | 17 ② | | | |

01 ①

해설 학생들에게 양로원에 방문해서 노인분들과 함께 시간을 보내는 자원봉사에 참여하도록 권하고 있다.

어휘 committee 위원회
senior citizen 노령자, 어르신
nursing home (작은 사설) 양로원
host (행사를) 주최하다; (손님을 초대한) 주인
Thanksgiving 추수 감사절
pair (둘씩) 짝을 짓다
assistance 도움, 원조

M Attention, students. This is your vice principal, Liam Moore. Our school has formed a committee to find volunteers to visit senior citizens. Volunteers will go to the local nursing home on November 18th. We will host a Thanksgiving party there from 3 p.m. to 8 p.m. People who volunteer will be paired with seniors to have conversations with them and provide assistance throughout the party. Many of the elderly living at the nursing home often do not have visitors, so I'd like to encourage you to come and spend some time with them.

남 학생 여러분, 주목해주세요. 저는 교감인 리암 무어입니다. 우리 학교는 노인분들을 방문할 자원봉사자들을 찾기 위해 위원회를 구성했습니다. 자원봉사자들은 11월 18일에 지역 양로원에 갈 것입니다. 우리는 오후 3시부터 8시까지 그곳에서 추수감사절 파티를 주최할 겁니다. 자원봉사 할 사람들은 노인분들과 짝을 지어서 그분들과 대화를 나누고 파티 내내 도움을 제공할 것입니다. 양로원에 살고 계시는 노인분들 중 많은 분께서 방문자들이 없는 경우가 흔하니, 여러분이 와서 그분들과 함께 시간을 보내길 권합니다.

02 ②

해설 가까운 식료품점에 차로 가려는 아들에게 어머니가 걸어서 갈만한 거리를 차로 가는 것은 건강에 좋지 않다고 말하고 있다.

어휘 be out of ~이 떨어지다
grocery store 식료품점
distance 거리
regularly 정기적으로
exercise 운동을 하다
go on a diet 다이어트를 하나

W Felix, we're out of butter. Can you get some at the grocery store?
M Butter? Are you baking cookies?
W Yes, I'm going to make your favorite chocolate chip cookies.
M Okay, I'll go right now. Where is the car key, Mom?
W Why don't you just walk? It only takes about 15 minutes.
M But it will take less than 5 minutes by car.
W You usually drive everywhere even if it's within walking distance. That isn't good for your health.
M I regularly go to the gym and exercise.
W You don't need to go on a diet or join a gym when you walk a lot. Walking is a free and easy way to lose weight and become healthier.
M Got it. I'm going to walk to places that are nearby.
W Great! Here's the card.

여 펠릭스, 버터가 떨어졌구나. 식료품점에서 좀 사다 줄 수 있니?
남 버터요? 쿠키를 구우실 거예요?
여 그래, 네가 가장 좋아하는 초콜릿 칩 쿠키를 만들 거야.
남 알았어요, 지금 바로 갈게요. 엄마, 차 열쇠는 어디있어요?
여 그냥 걸어가는 게 어떠니? 15분 정도밖에 안 걸리잖니.
남 하지만 차로는 5분도 안 걸릴 거예요.
여 너는 보통 걸어서 갈 수 있는 거리라 하더라도 어디든 운전을 하잖니. 그건 건강에 좋지 않아.
남 전 정기적으로 체육관에 가서 운동을 해요.
여 많이 걸으면 다이어트를 하거나 체육관에 가입할 필요가 없단다. 걷기는 체중을 줄이고 더 건강해지는 무료이면서 쉬운 방법이야.
남 알았어요. 가까운 곳은 걸어서 갈게요.
여 아주 좋아! 카드 여기 있다.

03 ⑤

해설 여자가 남자의 판정에 항의하자 남자가 벤치로 돌아가라고 하는 것으로 보아 스포츠팀 감독과 심판의 관계임을 알 수 있다.

어휘 ridiculous 말도 안 되는, 터무니없는
object 반대하다; 물건; 목적
disrupt 방해하다, 지장을 주다
call 외치다; (심판의) 판정
land (땅에) 떨어지다; 내려앉다; 착륙시키다
have no say 발언권이 없다

W Wait a minute! This is ridiculous. I object! Ashley and Melanie from our team clearly blocked that ball.
M Please don't disrupt the game.
W How could you call "out" when the ball was blocked and landed on the other side of the court?
M That's for me to decide, not you.
W This is so unfair. I can't believe this!
M You have no say in this matter. I will not stand for this kind of behavior. Now, get back to the bench.
W This is not the first time you've made a wrong call. I'm going to report this to the association.

여 잠시만요! 이건 말도 안 돼요. 이의 있습니다! 우리 팀의 애슐리와 멜라니가 분명 그 공을 막았어요.
남 경기를 방해하지 마세요.
여 공이 막아져서 코트의 반대쪽에 떨어졌는데 어떻게 '아웃'을 외칠 수 있습니까?
남 그건 당신이 아니라 제가 결정하는 거예요.
여 이건 정말 불공평합니다. 믿을 수가 없군요!
남 당신은 이 일에 관해서 발언할 권리가 없어요. 전 이러한 행동을 참지 않을 겁니다. 이제, 벤치로 돌아가주세요.
여 당신이 잘못된 판정을 한 게 이번이 처음이 아니잖아요. 이 일을 협회에 보고하겠어요.

association 협회

M This is my final warning to you.	남 이건 당신에게 드리는 제 마지막 경고입니다.
W Fine! I'm going to do something about this. You wait and see.	여 좋아요! 전 이 일에 관해 뭐라도 할 겁니다. 두고 보십시오.
M Final warning!	남 마지막 경고예요!

04 ②

해설 위쪽 무대 양옆에 두 개의 큰 바위가 있다고 했으므로 그림 속의 선인장이 대화의 내용과 일치하지 않는다.

어휘 puppet show 인형극
symbol 상징
palm tree 야자수
folk tale 민간 설화

W Let's talk about some stage details for our puppet show.

M Okay. I brought a picture of a puppet show that I was part of. Take a look.

W Hmm.... The stage is divided into two levels.

M Isn't that a good idea? Look at the sun on top, in the middle. We should do that, too.

W Sure. Let's also place two huge rocks on both sides of the top stage.

M Yes, they are important symbols in this puppet show.

W Right. And there's a nice palm tree in the middle of the top stage.

M Yeah. What do you think about the house on the left side of the lower stage?

W I think it's cool. Do you see that the bottom stage has a large sunflower on each side?

M Aren't they beautiful? I heard this puppet show is based on a Mexican folk tale.

W Oh, I see.

여 우리 인형극의 무대 세부 사항에 관해 얘기 좀 하자.

남 그래. 내가 참여했던 인형극 사진을 가져왔어. 한번 보렴.

여 음…. 무대가 두 개의 단으로 나누어져 있네.

남 좋은 생각 아니야? 맨 위 중앙에 있는 태양을 봐. 우리도 저렇게 해야 해.

여 물론이지. 우리도 마찬가지로 위쪽 무대의 양옆에 큰 바위 두 개를 두자.

남 그래, 바위는 이 인형극에서 중요한 상징이야.

여 맞아. 그리고 위쪽 무대의 중앙에는 멋진 야자수 한 그루가 있네.

남 응. 아래쪽 무대의 왼쪽에 있는 집은 어때?

여 멋지다고 생각해. 아래쪽 무대에는 양쪽에 큰 해바라기가 있는 거 보여?

남 아름답지 않니? 난 이 인형극이 멕시코 민간 설화를 기반으로 한다고 들었어.

여 아, 그렇구나.

05 ⑤

해설 여자가 남자에게 하드 드라이브 포맷을 권하자 남자는 어떻게 하는지 보여달라고 부탁했다.
① 남자가 과제 끝내는 것 돕기
② 바이러스 퇴치 프로그램 설치하기
③ 여자의 컴퓨터에 남자의 데이터 저장하기
④ 남자의 컴퓨터를 수리할 사람 부르기
⑤ 남자에게 하드 드라이브 포맷하는 방법 보여주기

어휘 paper (학생의) 과제물, 리포트
repair 수리하다 (= fix)
external 외부의
speed things up 작업을 빨리하다
come over 들르다
rest (어떤 것의) 나머지; 휴식

W Hey Justin, did you finish your paper?

M No, I need to call someone to repair my computer first.

W What's wrong with it?

M It keeps turning off.

W Did you try fixing it yourself?

M I'm not very good with computers.

W Maybe you just need to reformat your hard drive. Just don't forget to save all the data first on an external drive.

M Could you please show me how? I don't think I can do it by myself.

W Sure. But could you save all the data first? It will speed things up.

M Okay, I can do that.

W Then, I'll come over around six today and help you with the rest.

M Thanks so much.

여 저기 저스틴, 과제 다 끝냈니?

남 아니, 먼저 내 컴퓨터를 고치기 위해서 누군가를 불러야 해.

여 뭐가 잘못됐는데?

남 컴퓨터 전원이 계속 꺼져.

여 직접 고치려고 해봤니?

남 나는 컴퓨터를 별로 잘 다루지 못해.

여 아마 하드 드라이브를 재포맷만 하면 될 거야. 먼저 외장 하드에 모든 데이터를 저장하는 것 잊지 말고.

남 어떻게 하는지 네가 좀 보여줄래? 나 혼자서는 못 할 것 같아.

여 물론이야. 그런데 먼저 모든 데이터를 저장해줄래? 그러면 작업을 더 빨리할 수 있을 거야.

남 알겠어, 그건 할 수 있어.

여 그럼, 내가 오늘 6시쯤 들러서 나머지를 도와줄게.

남 정말 고마워.

06 ③

해설 잡지를 2년 구독하면 한 권당 정가 10달러에서 60퍼센트 할인된 4달러에 받아볼 수 있으므로 여자가 지불할 금액은 96달러이다.
($4×24권=$96)

[Telephone rings.]

W Hello?

M Hello. This is Tom Ford calling from World Geographic. I was wondering if you'd be interested in subscribing to our magazine.

W Well, I do read your magazine regularly.

[전화벨이 울린다.]

여 여보세요?

남 안녕하세요. 월드 지오그래픽의 톰 포드라고 합니다. 저희 잡지를 구독하시는 데 관심이 있으신지 궁금해서요.

여 글쎄요, 그 잡지를 정기적으로 읽긴 해요.

어휘 subscribe to ~을 구독하다, 가입하다

cf. subscription 구독(료)

currently 지금, 현재

sign up for ~을 신청하다, 가입하다

M Great, because we are currently offering a one-year subscription, that's 12 magazines, for only $72.

W That sounds okay.

M Actually, it's a great deal! That's 40% off the regular price of $10 per magazine. And the two-year subscription is even cheaper.

W How much is that?

M You can get 24 magazines at 60% off the regular price.

W 60% off the regular price? That's $4 per magazine.

M Exactly. You'll be able to save a lot of money if you read our magazine regularly.

W I'll sign up for the two-year subscription then.

남 잘됐네요, 지금 저희가 12권, 1년 정기 구독을 단 72달러에 제공하고 있거든요.

여 괜찮은 것 같네요.

남 사실, 그건 정말 싼 겁니다! 잡지 한 권당 정가 10달러에서 40퍼센트 할인된 겁니다. 그리고 2년 구독은 훨씬 더 저렴합니다.

여 그건 얼만가요?

남 24권의 잡지를 정가에서 60퍼센트 할인된 가격으로 받아보실 수 있습니다.

여 정가에서 60퍼센트 할인이요? 잡지당 4달러인 셈이군요.

남 맞습니다. 저희 잡지를 정기적으로 보신다면, 많은 돈을 절약하실 수 있을 겁니다.

여 그럼 2년 구독을 신청할게요.

---

07 ③

해설 남자는 아르바이트 시간과 겹쳐서 생물학 수업을 들을 수 없다고 대답했다.

어휘 definitely 분명히 (= certainly)

biology 생물(학)

registration 등록, 신청

conflict with ~와 상충하다, 대립하다

require 필요하다

cf. requirement 필요(조건)

science (과학으로서의) 이과

determined 굳게 결심한

support oneself (재정적 도움 없이) 자립하다

W Hey, Mark. I just bought my textbooks, and I'm definitely going to need your help with biology.

M Oh, I'm sorry to tell you this, but I'm not able to take biology this semester.

W Why not? Was the course already full? You didn't miss the registration, did you?

M No, it conflicts with my part-time job. I didn't have a choice.

W But biology is required for all science majors. What are you going to do?

M Well, I think I can still take it next year.

W It certainly won't be easy to take several requirements at once.

M I know, but I'm still determined to support myself at university.

W That's good. Well, I'm sure you will do well.

여 안녕, 마크. 나 방금 교재 샀는데, 내가 생물학을 공부하는 데는 분명 네 도움이 필요할 거야.

남 아, 이런 말을 해서 미안한데, 난 이번 학기에 생물학을 들을 수 없어.

여 왜 못 들어? 수강 인원이 이미 다 찼니? 네가 등록 기간을 놓친 건 아니지, 그렇지?

남 응, 아르바이트 시간과 겹치거든. 선택의 여지가 없었어.

여 하지만 생물학은 모든 이과 전공에 필수잖아. 어떻게 할 거니?

남 음, 내년에 들을 수 있을 것 같아.

여 여러 필수 과목을 한꺼번에 듣는 건 분명 쉽지 않을 거야.

남 알아, 그렇지만 난 대학을 다니며 자립하기로 여전히 굳게 결심했어.

여 좋다. 뭐, 난 네가 잘할 거라고 확신해.

---

08 ②

해설 해석 참조

어휘 coral reef 산호초

marine 해양의, 바다의

polyp 폴립 ((산호류 같은 원통형 해양 고착 생물))

attach 들러붙다; 붙이다

calcium 칼슘

M Clara, how was your trip to Jeju Island?

W Great! I saw some amazing coral reefs!

M Sounds exciting. You know, I was surprised to learn that coral reefs are actually made of the bodies of tiny marine animals.

W Right. They are called polyps. It takes hundreds of years for them to make a coral reef.

M Wow, that's quite long. Does a coral reef keep growing?

W Sure. It gets bigger as new polyps are born and attach themselves to the coral reef.

M Interesting. It's also strange that coral reefs are so hard. They're the bodies of animals!

W I heard it's because polyps make a kind of stone from calcium that they find in the water.

M That's really amazing.

남 클라라, 제주도 여행은 어땠니?

여 아주 좋았어! 굉장한 산호초를 봤거든!

남 재미있었겠다. 있잖아, 난 산호초가 사실 **아주 작은 해양 생물의 몸체로 만들어진다**(① 구성 물질)는 것을 알고 놀랐어.

여 맞아. 그건 폴립이라고 해. 그것들이 **산호초 하나를 만드는 데는 수백 년이 걸려**(③ 생성되는 기간).

남 와, 상당히 오래 걸리네. 산호초는 계속 자라니?

여 물론이야. **새로운 폴립이 태어나서 산호초에 스스로 들러붙으면서 산호초는 더 커져**(④ 성장 원리).

남 흥미롭네. 산호초가 매우 단단한 것도 신기해. 동물의 몸체잖아!

여 그건 **폴립이 물속에서 얻는 칼슘에서 일종의 돌을 만들어내기 때문**(⑤ 단단한 이유)이라고 들었어.

남 그거 정말 놀라운데.

09 ⑤

해설 파워 냅은 오후 3시가 지나면 효과가 떨어진다.

어휘 refresh 원기를 회복시키다, 기운 나게 하다
power nap 기력을 회복하기 위한 낮잠
alternative 대안, 선택 가능한 것
term 용어, 말; 학기
define 정의하다
demonstrate 분명히 보여주다, 증명하다
practice 실천하다; 연습하다

W Hello, listeners! I'm Susan Cruz from Austin Sleeping Clinic. Drinking a cup of coffee is a common way to refresh yourself, but a power nap <u>can be a nice alternative</u>. The term "power nap" was created by James Maas. It is defined as a nap taken during the day of less than thirty minutes. Many studies demonstrate that power naps <u>improve creativity and performance</u>. There are several examples of famous people who have practiced power napping regularly, including John F. Kennedy and Albert Einstein. But power napping <u>becomes less effective later in the day</u>, especially past three o'clock in the afternoon.

여 안녕하세요, 청취자 여러분! 저는 오스틴 수면 클리닉의 수잔 크루즈입니다. 커피 한 잔을 마시는 것은 원기를 회복할 수 있는 흔한 방법입니다만, 파워 냅이 좋은 대안이 될 수 있습니다. **'파워 냅'이라는 용어는 제임스 마스에 의해 만들어졌습니다**(①). 그것은 **낮 동안 취하는 30분 이내의 낮잠으로 정의됩니다**(②). 많은 연구는 파워 냅이 창의력과 수행력을 향상시킨다(③)는 것을 보여줍니다. 존 에프 케네디와 알베르트 아인슈타인을 포함해, **파워 냅을 규칙적으로 실천한 여러 유명인의 사례가 있습니다**(④). 그러나 **파워 냅은 하루 중 늦은 때에는 효과가 덜해지는데, 특히 오후 3시가 지나면 그렇습니다**(⑤).

---

10 ④

해설 인원이 세 명이어서 소형 (compact)차를 제외했고 전기차는 충전 시간이 오래 걸려 선택하지 않았다. 비용이 하루 70달러 이하인 것 중에서 내비게이션이 있는 것을 고른다.

어휘 rental 임대의
compact 소형인
suitable 적당한
recharge 다시 충전하다
budget 예산, 경비
be down to ~밖에 남지 않다
GPS (= Global Positioning System) 전(全)지구 위치 파악 시스템
navigation 운항, 주행지시
must-have 필수품
[선택지 어휘] fuel 연료

W Hello, Luke. What are you doing?
M I'm looking at a rental car website. I want to rent a car for my trip to San Francisco, but I'm not sure which one to choose from this list.
W Let me help you. First, <u>how many people will you travel with</u>?
M I'll be traveling with my two friends, so the total number of people is three.
W Then I don't think a compact car <u>is suitable</u>. You need a larger car.
M I see. What do you think of this electric car? It's the newest model.
W I don't recommend it because <u>it needs a lot of time to fully recharge</u>.
M Oh, I didn't think about that.
W Do you have a budget for the rental?
M I'd like to stay under $70 a day.
W Now <u>you're down to these two</u>. Would you like a GPS navigation system?
M Definitely. It's my first visit to San Francisco, so GPS is a must-have. I'll reserve this one now.

여 안녕, 루크. 뭐하고 있니?
남 렌터카 사이트를 보고 있어. 샌프란시스코 여행을 위해 차를 빌리고 싶은데 이 목록에서 어떤 차를 골라야 할지 모르겠어.
여 내가 도와줄게. 먼저, 몇 명과 함께 여행할 거니?
남 친구 두 명과 여행할 거니까 총 사람 수는 세 명이야.
여 그러면 소형차는 적당하지 않을 것 같아. 넌 더 큰 차가 필요해.
남 알겠어. 이 전기차는 어떻게 생각하니? 최신 모델이야.
여 그건 완전히 다시 충전하려면 시간이 오래 걸리기 때문에 추천하지 않아.
남 아, 그 생각을 안 했네.
여 렌트를 위한 예산은 있니?
남 하루에 70달러 아래로 있고 싶어.
여 이제 이 둘 밖에 남지 않았어. GPS 내비게이션을 원하니?
남 물론이지. 샌프란시스코는 처음 방문이라서 GPS는 필수품이야. 지금 이걸 예약할게.

---

11 ⑤

해설 물을 주는 주기를 묻고 있으므로 일주일에 두 번이 좋다는 응답이 가장 적절하다.
① 매주 전화할게.
② 난 두 달 후에 돌아올 거야.
③ 짐 싸는 걸 도와주다니 친절하구나.
④ 우리 집에는 식물 다섯 개가 있어.

어휘 water (화초 등에) 물을 주다

W I bet you are excited about your trip! Are you all packed?
M Yes, I'm almost ready. But <u>I don't know what to do about my plants</u>.
W <u>I'd be happy to care for them</u> while you are gone. How often should I water them?
M About twice a week would be perfect.

여 너 분명 여행 때문에 신나겠구나! 짐 다 쌌니?
남 응, 거의 준비됐어. 하지만 내 식물들을 어떻게 해야 좋을지 모르겠어.
여 네가 없는 동안 내가 기꺼이 돌봐줄게. 물을 얼마나 자주 줘야 하니?
남 일주일에 두 번 정도가 딱 좋아.

---

12 ④

해설 남자가 이집트 역사에 대한 조사를 어디서부터 시작할지 모르겠다

M Mrs. Gardner, I'm not sure <u>what to write my paper about</u>.

남 가드너 선생님, 보고서를 무엇에 관해 써야 할지 잘 모르겠어요.

고 했으므로 도움이 될 도서 목록을 주겠다는 응답이 가장 적절하다.
① 네 보고서는 금요일까지란다.
② 미안하지만, 이건 용납할 수 없어.
③ 이번 여름에 이집트를 방문할 계획이란다.
⑤ 제출하기 전에 네 보고서를 점검해라.

[선택지 어휘] unacceptable 용납할 수 없는
go over 점검[검토]하다

W Well, what about the history of Egypt? It's very interesting.
M I think that's good. But I don't know where to start my research.
W I'll give you a list of some helpful books.

여 음, 이집트의 역사는 어떠니? 아주 흥미롭단다.
남 그거 좋은 것 같네요. 그런데 어디서부터 조사를 시작해야 할지 모르겠어요.
여 도움이 될 만한 도서 목록을 줄게.

13 ③

해설 남자는 졸업 후에 여행할 계획이므로 최근 여행을 마치고 돌아온 여자에게 좋았던 곳을 알려달라는 응답이 가장 적절하다.
① 난 휴학을 하고 싶어.
② 우리 간단히 먹으러 가야겠다.
④ 난 대학 등록 사무실에 가봐야 해.
⑤ 정말 집만 한 곳은 없어, 그렇지 않니?

어휘 overseas 해외로
backpack 배낭여행하다
cf. backpacker 배낭여행객
enroll 등록하다
cf. enrollment 등록, 입학
destination 목적지, 도착지
[선택지 어휘] grab a bite to eat 간단히 먹다

M Soyeon! Long time no see! What have you been up to?
W Actually I just got back to Korea last week.
M Really? How long were you away?
W I was away for almost a year.
M Were you studying overseas?
W No, I was backpacking all over the world.
M That's awesome. But I thought you were studying to be a doctor.
W I took a year off from school. I'm re-enrolling today. That's why I'm here.
M My parents wouldn't let me do that. So, I plan to travel after I graduate.
W Really? That's great. Have you thought about a destination?
M Can you tell me the places you liked best, first?

남 소연아! 오랜만이다! 어떻게 지냈니?
여 실은 지난주에 한국에 돌아왔어.
남 정말? 얼마나 오랫동안 한국을 떠나 있었는데?
여 거의 일 년 정도 나가 있었어.
남 유학하고 있었니?
여 아니, 전 세계를 배낭여행하고 있었어.
남 멋지다. 하지만 난 네가 의사가 되기 위해 공부하고 있다고 생각했어.
여 일 년 휴학했었어. 오늘 재등록할 거야. 그래서 여기 있는 거야.
남 우리 부모님은 내가 그렇게 하는 걸 허락하지 않으실 거야. 그래서 나는 졸업 후에 여행할 계획이야.
여 정말? 멋지다. 목적지는 생각해봤니?
남 네가 가장 좋았던 곳부터 말해줄래?

14 ③

해설 응원하는 팀이 큰 점수 차로 지고 있음에도 여자는 승리할 수 있다고 생각하고 있다. 남자는 여자에게 어떻게 그렇게 긍정적일 수 있는지 물었으므로 자신이 항상 긍정적인 면을 본다는 응답이 가장 적절하다.
① 그저 내가 아주 열심히 연습했기 때문이야.
② 너는 게임의 규칙을 배워야 해.
④ 너와 함께 하게 해줘서 고맙다고 말하고 싶었어.
⑤ 네 말이 맞아. 이번엔 우리가 포기하는 편이 나을 것 같아.

어휘 go downhill 내리막길로 접어들다, 악화되다
positive 긍정하는; 확신적인
[선택지 어휘] look on the bright side 긍정적[낙관적]으로 보다

W Hi, Jake. I just got here. So, how's the game going?
M Not so good. We were doing well until halftime, but after that, it went downhill.
W What happened?
M The players made a lot of mistakes. I'm sure even you would have gotten mad if you had seen it.
W Well, I'm positive that we'll win this time.
M That's what you said last time, but we lost. Remember?
W Yes, but I have a good feeling today.
M Our team needs to score at least ten points in the next five minutes to win.
W I know, but I still think we can win.
M Seriously, I wonder how you can stay so positive.
W Well, you know I always look on the bright side.

여 안녕, 제이크. 나 방금 도착했어. 그래, 경기는 어떻게 돼가고 있어?
남 그리 좋지 않아. 우리 팀이 전반전까지는 잘하고 있었는데, 그 이후에는 내리막길로 접어들었어.
여 무슨 일이 있었는데?
남 선수들이 실수를 많이 했어. 네가 봤다면, 분명 너라도 화가 났을 거야.
여 글쎄, 나는 이번에 우리 팀이 이길 거라고 확신해.
남 그건 네가 지난번에도 했던 말이었는데, 우리 졌잖아. 기억나?
여 응, 하지만 오늘은 느낌이 좋아.
남 우리 팀이 이기려면 앞으로 5분 내에 최소 10점은 점수를 내야 해.
여 알아, 그렇지만 나는 여전히 우리가 이길 수 있다고 생각해.
남 진심으로, 너는 어쩌면 그렇게 긍정적일 수 있는지 궁금해.
여 글쎄, 내가 항상 긍정적인 면을 본다는 거 너도 알잖아.

15 ⑤

해설 알렉스는 전 집주인에게 부엌의 누수를 고쳐주겠다고 한 약속을 지키지 않은 이유를 물어볼 것이다.

① 우리가 이사 들어오기 전에 모든 게 수리되면 좋겠습니다.

② 우리가 곧 이사 들어올 수 있다고 생각하시나요?

③ 배관공의 전화번호를 알려주시겠습니까?

④ 이미 집을 수리해놓으신 것에 감사드립니다.

⑤ 당신이 왜 약속을 지키지 않았는지 알고 싶습니다.

어휘 in need of ~이 필요한
cracked 금이 간, 갈라진
leak (액체, 기체가) 새는 곳[틈]; (액체, 기체가) 새다
move in 이사 (들어)오다
[선택지 어휘] anytime soon ((부정문, 의문문에서)) 곧
plumber 배관공
keep one's promise 약속을 지키다

M Alex has recently purchased a house that is a little old and in need of repairs. Some of the repairs that he will immediately have to work on are a broken door, a cracked wall, and a leak in the kitchen sink. Fortunately, when he first purchased the house, the previous owner had promised him that she would fix the leak in the kitchen before Alex and his family moved in. On the day of the move, however, he finds that the sink is still leaking. So, Alex calls the previous owner and she picks up. He wants to ask her why the sink hasn't been repaired. In this situation, what would Alex most likely say to her?

남 알렉스는 최근 약간 낡아서 수리가 필요한 집을 샀다. 그가 즉시 착수해야 할 수리 중 몇몇은 부서진 문, 금이 간 벽, 그리고 부엌 싱크대의 누수이다. 다행히도, 그가 처음 그 집을 샀을 때, 전 집주인은 알렉스와 그의 가족이 이사 들어오기 전에 부엌의 누수를 고쳐주겠다고 약속했다. 그러나 이삿날, 그는 싱크대에서 여전히 물이 새고 있는 것을 발견한다. 그래서 알렉스는 전 집주인에게 전화를 걸고 집주인이 전화를 받는다. 그는 왜 싱크대가 수리되지 않았는지 묻고 싶다. 이 상황에서, 알렉스가 전 집주인에게 할 말로 가장 적절한 것은 무엇인가?

---

16 ④   17 ②

해설 16 기내 수하물의 최소화, 베개, 음식, 오락거리 준비, 시차증의 예방 등을 설명하면서 장거리 비행 경험을 개선시키는 방법을 말하고 있다.

① 시차증의 흔한 증상들

② 장거리 비행에 챙겨갈 것들

③ 모두가 장거리 비행을 싫어하는 이유

④ 장거리 비행 경험을 개선시킬 조언들

⑤ 장거리 비행을 짧게 해줄 활동들

17 해석 참조

어휘 ruin 망치다
carry-on (가방, 짐 등이) 기내에 반입할 수 있는
entertain 즐겁게 하다
A as well as B B뿐만 아니라 A도
jet lag 시차증 ((비행기를 이용한 장거리 여행 시 시차로 인한 피로감))
fatigue 피로
mild 가벼운, 약한
depression 우울증
time zone 표준 시간대
adapt to (상황에) 적응하다
accordingly 그에 맞춰
exposure to ~에의 노출

W Hello, listeners. A long flight can often ruin a pleasant holiday or business trip. So, what can you do to make your travel time comfortable? First of all, reduce your carry-on luggage as much as possible. One small backpack is good for the plane because it can easily be placed under your seat. If you plan on trying to sleep, bring a travel pillow. Also, consider bringing something to entertain yourself with, as well as your own food. Finally, remember that most travelers suffer from jet lag after a long flight. The symptoms of jet lag may include headaches, fatigue, irregular sleep patterns, and mild depression. To minimize the effects of jet lag, try matching your sleeping hours on the plane with your destination's time zone. Drink a lot of water and do as much stretching as you can. Upon arrival, adapt to the local time and eat accordingly. Also, it helps to get exposure to sunlight if possible.

여 안녕하세요, 청취자 여러분. 장거리 비행은 즐거운 휴가나 출장을 종종 망쳐버릴 수 있습니다. 그러면 이동 시간을 편안히 보내기 위해 무엇을 할 수 있을까요? 우선, 기내 수하물을 가능한 한 줄이세요. 기내에는 작은 배낭 하나가 적당한데, 좌석 아래에 쉽게 놓일 수 있기 때문입니다. (이동 중) 잠을 잘 계획이라면 여행용 베개를 챙겨가세요. 또한, 음식뿐만 아니라 오락거리도 챙겨갈 것을 고려하세요. 마지막으로, 여행자 대부분이 장거리 여행 후 시차증으로 고생한다는 것을 기억하세요. 시차증의 증세는 두통, 피로감, 불규칙한 수면 패턴과 가벼운 우울증을 포함할 수도 있습니다. 시차증의 영향을 최소화하려면 기내에서의 수면 시간을 목적지의 표준 시간대와 맞추어보세요. **물을 많이 마시고(①)** 할 수 있는 한 많이 **스트레칭 하세요(③).** (목적지에) 도착하자마자 **현지 시간에 적응하고 그에 맞춰 식사하세요(④).** 또한, 가능하면 **햇볕을 쬐는 게(⑤)** 도움이 됩니다.

| 01 ③ | 02 ③ | 03 ⑤ | 04 ④ | 05 ③ | 06 ④ | 07 ④ | 08 ③ | 09 ⑤ | 10 ⑤ |
| 11 ③ | 12 ① | 13 ④ | 14 ① | 15 ④ | 16 ② | 17 ② | | | |

01 ③

해설 학부모들에게 학교에서 최근 시작한 사이버 괴롭힘 반대 캠페인 활동에 대해 설명하고 있다.

어휘 campaign against ~에 반대하는 캠페인
bullying (약자를) 괴롭히기
cf. bully (약자를) 괴롭히다
display 전시하다
increase[raise] awareness of ~에 대한 의식을 높이다
victim 피해자, 희생자

W Welcome, parents. Thank you for making the time to come for this meeting. As you may know, our school has recently started a campaign against cyber-bullying. Students have been creating posters to display around the school. They will have messages written on them meant to increase awareness of this growing problem. Our main goal is to make everyone in the community aware, and to let victims know that they are not alone. We also want to let students know that bullying online is wrong. We hope this campaign can help reduce and prevent cyber-bullying problems in our school. Thank you again for coming this evening.

여 학부모 여러분, 환영합니다. 이 회의에 오실 시간을 내주셔서 감사드립니다. 아시는 분도 계시겠지만, 우리 학교는 최근 사이버 괴롭힘에 반대하는 캠페인을 시작했습니다. 학생들은 학교 주변에 전시하기 위한 포스터들을 만들어왔습니다. 포스터에는 증가하고 있는 이 문제점에 대한 의식을 높이려는 메시지들이 적힐 것입니다. 우리의 주된 목적은 공동체에 있는 모든 사람이 인식하게 하는 것이며, 피해자들에게 자신이 혼자가 아니라는 것을 알리려는 것입니다. 우리는 또한 학생들에게 사이버 괴롭힘이 잘못된 것임을 알리고 싶습니다. 우리는 이 캠페인이 우리 학교의 사이버 괴롭힘 문제를 줄이고 예방하는 데 도움이 될 수 있길 바랍니다. 오늘 저녁 참석해주셔서 다시 한 번 감사드립니다.

02 ③

해설 여자는 아들이 모바일 게임을 너무 많이 하는 것 같다고 걱정하지만, 남자는 게임에서 배울 수 있는 것이 있고, 적당한 놀이는 성장기 두뇌에 좋다고 했다.

어휘 focus on ~에 집중하다, 초점을 맞추다
judge 비판하다, 평가하다
appeal to ~의 흥미를 끌다, ~의 마음에 들다; ~에 호소하다
fairly 꽤, 상당히
advanced 고도의, 고급의
moderate 적당한; 중도의

W Honey, where's our son?
M Darren is in his room playing mobile games.
W Again? He plays mobile games too much these days. I'm worried about him.
M Half an hour a day is not that much. Also, playing games is natural at his age.
W I know most children want to play them, but they are just for fun. Darren needs to focus on what is more important.
M Maybe you should try some of the games that Darren plays before you judge them.
W Why would I want to play them?
M They might not appeal to you, but they require some fairly advanced skills. They teach creativity.
W He may be learning something, but it can't be as useful as studying.
M Actually, a moderate amount of play is perfect for a growing brain.

여 여보, 우리 아들 어디 있어요?
남 대런은 자기 방에서 모바일 게임을 하고 있어요.
여 또요? 요즘 모바일 게임을 너무 많이 하네요. 그애가 걱정돼요.
남 하루 30분은 그렇게 많지 않아요. 게다가, 게임을 하는 건 그 나이에 당연한 거예요.
여 아이들 대부분이 게임을 하고 싶어 하는 건 알지만, 그건 재미 삼아 하는 것뿐이잖아요. 대런은 더 중요한 것에 집중해야 해요.
남 대런이 하는 게임을 비판하기 전에 당신이 그중 몇 가지를 해보는 게 좋겠어요.
여 내가 왜 그 게임들이 하고 싶겠어요?
남 당신에겐 흥미롭지 않을 수도 있지만, 그 게임들은 꽤 고도의 기술이 필요해요. 창의성을 가르쳐줘요.
여 대런이 뭔가 배우고 있을 수도 있지만, 공부하는 것만큼 도움이 될 리 없어요.
남 사실, 적당한 양의 놀이는 성장기 두뇌에 아주 좋아요.

03 ⑤

해설 남자가 외출하기 전에 여자에게 아이를 돌볼 때의 주의사항을 일러주고 있으므로 남자는 부모이고 여자는 베이비시터임을 알 수 있다.

M Penelope's already asleep, so just listen in case she cries.
W Okay, no problem.
M She was sick last week. I think she is fine now, but if she starts crying, please check for a fever.
W Of course. I'll remember to do that.

남 퍼넬로페는 이미 잠들었어요, 혹시 울지도 모르니 귀 기울여 주시기만 하면 돼요.
여 네, 문제없어요.
남 그 애는 지난주에 아팠어요. 지금은 괜찮은 것 같지만, 만약 울기 시작하면 열을 확인해주세요.
여 물론입니다. 그렇게 하는 걸 기억할게요.

어휘 in case (~할) 경우에 대비해서
fever 열

M And here's a list of emergency contact numbers just in case.

W Is this the number of your family doctor?

M Yes. Do you have any questions before we leave?

W Just one. Is there anything I can do to help Penelope if she can't sleep?

M You can read her this book. It's her favorite.

W Okay. Enjoy yourselves and don't worry about anything.

M Thank you. We'll be back by ten o'clock.

남 그리고 만약을 위해서 비상 연락처의 목록이 여기 있어요.

여 이건 가족 주치의의 전화번호인가요?

남 그래요. 우리가 나가기 전에 궁금하신 것 있나요?

여 한 가지 있어요. 만약 퍼넬로페가 잠을 못 자면 제가 도울 수 있는 게 있나요?

남 이 책을 읽어주시면 돼요. 그 애가 가장 좋아하는 책이거든요.

여 알겠습니다. 재미있게 보내시고 아무것도 걱정하지 마세요.

남 고마워요. 우리는 10시까지 돌아올게요.

04 ④

해설 여자가 사진 속 세 명이 좋아 보인다고 했으므로 그림 속 분수 앞에 있는 남자 두 명이 대화의 내용과 일치하지 않는다.

어휘 field trip 현장 학습, 견학 여행
space center 우주 센터
huge 거대한
spaceman 우주 비행사, 우주인
fountain 분수

M Mom, come take a look! This is a picture from our field trip to the Space Center.

W Nice picture. There is a huge rocket at the back. Is it a real rocket?

M No, it's just a model. But I was told that it's half the size of the real one.

W Oh, there is a spaceman next to the rocket. Is it a model as well?

M No, he is a real person. He walks around the center and guides visitors.

W I see. And there's a fountain in the center. It looks like the earth.

M It's a popular photo spot. My friends and I waited for a long time to take a picture there.

W The three of you look great! And there is a table with a striped parasol on the right side.

M Yes, we had our lunch there. Your sandwich was so delicious. Thanks, Mom.

W I'm glad you had a great time!

남 엄마, 오셔서 좀 보세요! 이건 우주 센터로 현장 학습을 갔을 때 찍은 사진이에요.

여 사진이 멋지구나. 뒤쪽에 거대한 로켓이 있네. 진짜 로켓이니?

남 아니요, 이것은 그냥 모형이에요. 하지만 진짜 로켓의 절반 크기라고 들었어요.

여 아, 로켓 옆에 우주 비행사가 있구나. 이것도 모형이니?

남 아뇨, 진짜 사람이에요. 그 사람은 센터를 돌아다니며 방문객들을 안내해줘요.

여 그렇구나. 그리고 중앙에 분수가 있구나. 그건 지구처럼 보여.

남 그것은 인기 있는 사진 촬영지예요. 저와 제 친구들은 거기서 사진을 찍으려고 오래 기다렸어요.

여 너희 셋이 좋아 보이는구나! 그리고 오른편에 줄무늬 파라솔이 있는 테이블이 있네.

남 네, 저희는 거기서 점심을 먹었어요. 엄마가 만들어주신 샌드위치가 아주 맛있었어요. 고마워요, 엄마.

여 아주 좋은 시간을 보냈다니 기쁘구나!

05 ③

해설 자발적 제안의 표현인 <Why don't I ~?>가 포함된 여자의 말에 주목한다.

어휘 decoration 장식(품)
have a hard time v-ing v하는 데 어려움을 겪다
a couple of 둘의, 두 사람의
direction 방향, 위치

W Wow! You did an amazing job with these decorations.

M I'm glad you think so. Did you just arrive?

W Yes. Is everyone already here?

M No, I'm still waiting for David and Sue. They're having a hard time finding the place.

W Where are they now?

M They're only a couple of blocks away, but the restaurant's kind of difficult to see from the main street.

W I'll give them a call with the directions.

M You don't have to. I just talked to them.

W Then, why don't I go out and meet them?

M That would be wonderful. While you do that, I'll order the food.

W Sounds good. I'll be back soon.

M Thanks, Kayla.

여 와! 너 이 장식품들로 놀랍게 잘했구나.

남 그렇게 생각한다니 기쁜걸. 방금 도착한 거야?

여 응. 모두들 이미 여기 다 모인 거야?

남 아니, 아직 데이비드랑 수를 기다리는 중이야. 그 애들은 장소를 찾는 데 어려움을 겪고 있어.

여 지금 어디 있는데?

남 겨우 두 블록 떨어진 곳에 있는데, 레스토랑이 큰 길에서 약간 잘 보이지 않아.

여 내가 그 애들에게 전화해서 방향을 알려줄게.

남 그러지 않아도 돼. 내가 방금 말해줬어.

여 그럼, 내가 밖에 나가서 마중하는 게 어떨까?

남 그래 주면 아주 좋지. 네가 그러는 동안, 나는 음식을 주문할게.

여 좋아. 금방 돌아올게.

남 고마워, 케일라.

06 ④

해설 2달러짜리 화분 30개를 사고
5달러 할인을 받아 55달러이며, 15
달러짜리 바구니 2개를 샀으므로
30달러를 더하면 지불할 금액은 85
달러이다.

어휘 flowerpot 화분
windowsill 창틀

M How much are these flowerpots? They're beautiful and lovely.
W They're $2 each.
M One would look pretty on a windowsill.
W Absolutely. It would also look nice if you put a few of these in a basket and hung it by a window.
M I'd like to get about thirty of them. Can you give me a little discount?
W If you buy thirty, I'll give you five dollars off.
M Okay, I'll take them. How much is this basket?
W It's $15.
M I'll take two baskets, please. Can I get a discount on these, too?
W I'm sorry, but I'm afraid not.
M That's okay. I'll take them. Here's my card.

남 이 화분들은 얼마예요? 예쁘고 사랑스럽네요.
여 각각 2달러씩입니다.
남 하나를 창틀에 두면 예쁘겠어요.
여 물론이죠. 이것을 바구니에 몇 개 담아서 창문 옆에 걸어두어도 멋질 겁니다.
남 30개정도 사고 싶어요. 할인을 좀 해주실 수 있나요?
여 30개를 사신다면, 5달러를 할인해드릴게요.
남 좋아요, 그것들을 살게요. 이 바구니는 얼마죠?
여 15달러입니다.
남 바구니는 두 개 살게요. 이것도 할인받을 수 있나요?
여 죄송하지만, 안 될 것 같습니다.
남 괜찮아요. 그렇게 살게요. 여기 카드요.

07 ④

해설 여자는 할머니를 뵈러 뉴욕에
가야 해서 도울 수 없다고 했다.

어휘 take care of 책임을 지고 떠
맡다; 돌보다
quit 그만두다
project (연구) 과제; 계획
on holiday 휴가 중에, 휴가를 얻어

W How is your preparation for International Student Night this Saturday going?
M It's harder than I thought. I don't have many friends to help me out.
W That's too bad. What do you need help with?
M We need people to take care of the food. Can you help?
W Oh, I'd love to, but I can't.
M Why not? Is it because of your part-time job at the restaurant?
W No, that's not it. I quit that job last month.
M Then do you have a group project to finish?
W No. Actually, I'm going to New York this Friday. I'll come back in a week.
M Oh, are you going to New York on holiday?
W No, I'm visiting my grandmother. It's her 70th birthday.
M I see. I hope you have a good time.

여 이번 토요일 국제 학생의 밤 준비는 어떻게 되어 가고 있니?
남 생각했던 것보다 더 어려워. 나를 도와줄 친구가 별로 없어.
여 정말 안됐구나. 어떤 도움이 필요하니?
남 우리는 음식을 책임지고 맡아줄 사람들이 필요해. 네가 도와줄 수 있니?
여 아, 그러고 싶지만 할 수 없어.
남 왜 안 돼? 식당에서 하는 아르바이트 때문인 거니?
여 아니, 그건 아니야. 난 지난달에 그 일을 그만뒀어.
남 그러면 끝내야 할 그룹 과제가 있는 거야?
여 아니야. 사실은 내가 이번 금요일에 뉴욕에 가. 일 수일 후에 놀아올 거야.
남 아, 휴가를 보내러 뉴욕에 가는 거니?
여 아니, 할머니를 뵈러 가. 할머니의 70세 생신이시 거든.
남 그렇구나. 좋은 시간 보내길 바라.

08 ③

해설 해석 참조

어휘 historic 역사적인, 역사적으로
중요한
feature ~을 특징으로 삼다
rebuild 재건축하다
consist of ~로 구성되다
site (중요한 일 등이 있었던) 땅, 유적
지; (건설) 현장, 부지
name 지정하다; 이름을 지어주다
explore 답사[탐험]하다

W I'm so excited about our trip to New York City this weekend!
M Me, too. What do you want to do first, honey?
W I want to go to Historic Richmond Town in Staten Island.
M Oh, that's the historic village that features real buildings from the past.
W Yes. They haven't been rebuilt. All of the buildings are original.
M That sounds interesting. How many buildings are there?
W The town consists of over 30 historic buildings and sites. The oldest building is nearly 350 years old.
M Wow, I really want to see that one. By the way, do you know when Historic Richmond Town was named as a historic site?

여 이번 주말 뉴욕시 여행에 난 정말 설레요!
남 나도요. 가장 먼저 뭘 하고 싶어요, 여보?
여 스태튼섬에 있는(① 소재지) 리치먼드 역사 마을에 가고 싶어요.
남 아, 거긴 옛날부터 있었던 실제 건물들이 특징인 역사 마을이죠.
여 네. 그 건물들은 재건축된 적이 없어요(② 건물의 재건축 여부). 모든 건물이 원래 있던 그대로예요.
남 흥미롭군요. 건물이 몇 채 있나요?
여 그 마을은 30채가 넘는 역사적인 건물들(④ 건물 수)과 유적지로 이루어져 있어요. 가장 오래된 건물은 350년 가까이 되었어요.
남 와, 그 건물을 정말 보고 싶네요. 그건 그렇고, 리치먼드 역사 마을이 언제 사적지로 지정되었는지 알아요?

W	I heard that happened in 1958.
M	I'm excited to explore the lives of Americans from the past.

여 1958년에 되었다고(⑤ 사적지로 지정된 연도) 들었어요.

남 과거 미국인들의 생활을 답사할 생각에 신나요.

09 ⑤

해설 호텔 숙박료는 등록비에 포함되어 있다.

어휘 competition (경연) 대회, 시합
cf. competitor (시합) 참가자; 경쟁자
cf. compete 경쟁하다, 겨루다
annual 연례의, 매년의; 한 해의
restriction 제한, 규제, 제약
application 지원(서), 신청(서)
category 부문, 범주
belong to ~에 속하다; ~의 소유이다
accommodation 숙박 (시설)
registration fee 등록비

M Hello, listeners. I'm Eric Bolton, the organizer of the AFB Chess Tournament. I'm pleased to announce that the 15th AFB Chess Tournament will be at the Midway Hotel. This competition is an annual event which has been held since 2009. There are no age restrictions on applications. The competition will be divided into three categories. Category A will consist of competitors who are under 15. Those between the ages of 15 and 20 will belong to Category B, and competitors 21 and older will belong to Category C. Category winners will receive $5,000 and the chance to compete for the grand prize of $15,000. Hotel accommodations are included in the registration fee of $250.

남 안녕하세요, 청취자 여러분. 저는 AFB 체스 선수권 대회의 조직위원인 에릭 볼튼입니다. 저는 제15회 AFB 체스 선수권 대회가 미드웨이 호텔에서 개최됨을 알리게 되어 기쁩니다. **이 대회는 2009년부터 열린 연례행사입니다(①). 지원에는 나이 제한이 없습니다(②). 대회는 세 부문으로 나뉠 것입니다(③). A 부문은 15세 미만의 참가자들로 구성될 것입니다. 15세에서 20세 사이의 참가자들은 B 부문에 속할 것이며, 21세 이상의 참가자들은 C 부문에 속할 것입니다. 부문별 우승자들은 5천 달러는 받고 만 5천 달러의 대상을 두고 경쟁할 기회도 받게 될 것입니다(④). 호텔 숙박은 등록비 250달러에 포함되어 있습니다(⑤).**

10 ⑤

해설 우선 오전 9시에 출발하는 투어와 시간이 3시간을 초과하는 것을 제외하고 전기 자전거가 아닌 것 중에서 가격이 더 저렴한 것을 선택한다.

어휘 flyer 광고 전단지
remaining 남은
maximum 최대, 최대한
exhausted 진이 다 빠진
go with 고르다, 받아들이다
book 예약하다
[선택지 어휘] duration (지속되는) 기간; 지속

W Owen, look at this flyer. It's about bike tours in the city. Why don't we go on one of these tomorrow?

M Great idea. Hmm, 9 a.m. seems too early to start a tour.

W I agree. Let's choose one of the remaining four tours.

M Okay. How much time can we spend on the tour?

W 3 hours is the maximum for me. If we ride more than that, I'll get exhausted.

M Okay. Which type of bike do you think we should choose, city or electric?

W I don't like electric bicycles. I've never ridden one and they're too fast.

M Then there are two choices left. Which one do you want?

W I'd like to go with the cheaper one.

M Sounds good. Let's book this tour.

여 오웬, 이 전단지 좀 봐. 도시의 자전거 투어에 관한 거야. 내일 이것들 중 하나를 가는 게 어때?

남 좋은 생각이야. 음, 오전 9시는 투어를 시작하기에 너무 이른 것 같아.

여 동의해. 남은 네 개의 투어 중 하나를 선택하자.

남 좋아. 우리가 투어에 얼마나 많은 시간을 쓸 수 있니?

여 내게는 3시간이 최대야. 그것보다 더 많이 타면 나는 완전히 지칠 거야.

남 알았어. 도시형 (자전거)하고 전기 (자전거) 중 우리가 어떤 종류의 자전거를 선택해야 한다고 생각하니?

여 나는 전기 자전거는 별로야. 한 번도 타본 적이 없는 데다 그건 너무 빨라.

남 그러면 두 가지 선택이 남았어. 어떤 걸 원하니?

여 더 싼 걸로 고르고 싶어.

남 좋아. 이 투어를 예약하자.

11 ③

해설 상자를 트렁크에 넣어야겠다는 여자의 말에 뒷좌석에 놓을 것을 제안하는 응답이 가장 적절하다.
① 내가 트렁크를 닫아도 괜찮아?
② 여기에 주차할 수 있는지 아니?
④ 다행히 네 차는 넓은 트렁크가 있구나.
⑤ 다음 교통 신호를 기다리는 게 어때?

[선택지 어휘] spacious 넓은, 널찍한

W Hi, James! Here!

M Hi, Debbie! Get in the car! Parking is not allowed here.

W Okay, but first I need to put this box in the trunk.

M Why don't you put it in the back seat?

여 안녕, 제임스! 여기야!

남 안녕, 데비! 차에 타! 여기에는 주차할 수 없어.

여 알았어, 그런데 먼저 이 상자를 트렁크에 넣어야 해.

남 뒷좌석에 놓지 그래?

12 ①

해설 남자가 어느 것이 할인 중인지 묻고 있으므로, 할인 대상 품목을 알려주는 응답이 가장 적절하다.

② 10퍼센트 할인받으실 겁니다.
③ 할인 판매는 다음 주 화요일에 끝납니다.
④ 주문하신 상품이 발송되었습니다.
⑤ 현금과 신용카드 모두 가능합니다.

어휘 currently 현재, 지금
[선택지 어휘] tag (표시하기 위해 붙인) 꼬리표, 태그

M I'd like to buy these five shirts. They are $100 at a discount, right?
W I'm sorry, but these items aren't currently on sale.
M Oh, I didn't know that. Then which ones are on sale?
W Anything with a yellow tag.

남 이 셔츠 다섯 장 살게요. 할인해서 100달러 맞죠?
여 죄송합니다만, 이 품목들은 현재 할인 중이 아닙니다.
남 아, 그건 몰랐네요. 그럼 어느 것이 할인 중이죠?
여 노란색 꼬리표가 붙어 있는 것입니다.

13 ④

해설 남자가 자신이 고른 벽의 페인트 색깔을 바꾸고 싶어 하므로 그 색이 새 가구와 잘 어울리지 않는다는 응답이 가장 적절하다.

① 바라건대, 모든 게 내일까지 완료되면 좋겠어요.
② 흰색과 검은색은 서로 아주 잘 보완해줘요.
③ 책상은 저쪽 창가에 두면 정말 보기 좋겠어요.
⑤ 새 책장의 크기가 만족스럽지 않아요.

[선택지 어휘] hopefully ((구어)) 바라건대; 희망을 갖고
complement 보완[보충]하다
go well with ~와 잘 어울리다

M I'm so excited about having our own home library.
W Me too. We just need to move in the new furniture.
M Great! Did the desk and bookcases arrive?
W Yes. I chose black instead of white. What do you think?
M Hmm... I like them. I think you made a great choice.
W I'm glad. I was afraid you wouldn't like them.
M Well, I do. And have the walls been painted?
W Open the door and take a look. [pause] What do you think?
M Oh, I don't think I like it. I'm afraid we're going to have to paint the whole room again.
W But you're the one who wanted this color.
M I'm sorry, but it doesn't go well with the new furniture.

남 우리만의 가정 도서관이 생긴다니 아주 신이 나요.
여 나도 그래요. 우리는 새 가구를 들이기만 하면 돼요.
남 잘됐어요! 책상이랑 책장이 도착했나요?
여 네. 내가 흰색 대신 검은색으로 골랐어요. 어떻게 생각해요?
남 음… 마음에 들어요. 당신이 잘 선택한 것 같아요.
여 다행이에요. 당신이 마음에 들어 하지 않을까봐 걱정했거든요.
남 음, 마음에 들어요. 그리고 벽은 페인트칠 됐어요?
여 문 열고 한번 봐요. [잠시 후] 어때요?
남 아, 마음에 안 드는 것 같아요. 우리 방 전체를 다시 페인트칠해야 할 것 같아요.
여 하지만 이 색깔을 원했던 건 바로 당신이잖아요.
남 미안해요, 하지만 그 색이 새 가구와 잘 어울리지 않아요.

14 ①

해설 지금 하는 선택이 가장 중요하다는 남자의 조언에 동의하며 더 열심히 하겠다는 응답이 가장 적절하다.

② 좋은 충고야. 나는 내 삶을 즐기기 시작할 거야.
③ 음, 나는 여름에 해변에 가는 편이 낫겠어.
④ 고마워. 나도 이번 5월에 졸업하는 것에 들떠 있어.
⑤ 정말 고마워. 네가 추천했던 수업이 정말로 도움이 됐어.

어휘 close to v-ing 거의[곧] v할 것 같은
manage to-v 용케 v하다
determined 단단히 결심한
cf. determination 결단력, 결심
have a long way to go (목표를 달성하려면) 아직 멀었다
matter 중요하다; 문제
[선택지 어휘] follow one's example ~을 본받다

W Congratulations, Evan! I heard you're graduating in May.
M Thanks. How about you? Are you close to finishing your studies?
W No. I have a lot more to do. How did you manage to graduate so fast?
M I was determined, so I took summer classes.
W Wow, I envy your determination.
M Well, you can always start now.
W True, but I have a long way to go. Two years ago I took some time off, but I now realize that was a mistake.
M I'm sure you did what was best.
W No, I wish I could go back and change my decision.
M Well, it's your choices now that matter the most.
W You're right. I'll follow your example and work harder.

여 축하해, 에반! 네가 5월에 졸업한다는 얘기 들었어.
남 고마워. 너는 어때? 공부가 거의 끝나가고 있니?
여 아니. 할 일이 아주 많아. 너는 어떻게 용케 그렇게 빨리 졸업할 수 있었니?
남 나는 굳게 결심했어서 여름 학기를 들었지.
여 와, 너의 결단력이 부러워.
남 글쎄, 너도 언제든지 바로 시작할 수 있어.
여 맞아, 하지만 나는 갈 길이 멀어. 2년 전에 휴학을 좀 했는데, 그게 실수였다는 걸 이제 깨달았어.
남 나는 네가 최선이었던 것을 했다고 확신해.
여 아니야, 과거로 돌아가서 내 결정을 바꿀 수 있다면 좋겠어.
남 음, 가장 중요한 건 바로 지금 하는 너의 선택이야.
여 네 말이 맞아. 너를 본받아서 더 열심히 할 거야.

15 ④

해설 마이클은 애셔에게 배달이 아닌 주문 접수를 맡기려 하므로 업무가 달라질 것이라고 말할 것이다.

① 당신은 고객들에게 사과드려야 합니다.

② 유감이지만, 당신을 해고해야 할 것 같습니다.

③ 당신은 이 소포를 잘못된 주소로 배달했어요.

④ 당신은 다른 직책에서 일하기 시작할 것입니다.

⑤ 저는 이 업종에 경력이 있는 사람을 고용하고 싶어요.

어휘 **by oneself** 혼자
concerned 걱정하는
[선택지 어휘] **let A go** A를 해고하다; A를 풀어주다, 석방하다

W Michael is the owner of a small delivery company. He started the business alone, taking care of both the office work and the deliveries by himself. Now, he has 10 employees working for him, and the business is continuing to grow. Recently, Michael has hired a new employee, Asher, to help with deliveries. Unfortunately, Asher hasn't been performing well, and has already delivered 6 packages to the wrong addresses. Michael is concerned, and finally decides to tell Asher to take orders instead of doing deliveries from now on. In this situation, what would Michael most likely say to Asher?

여 마이클은 작은 택배 회사의 사장이다. 그는 사무와 배달 업무 둘 다 혼자 처리하며 사업을 홀로 시작했다. 이제, 그는 그를 위해 일하는 10명의 직원이 있으며, 사업은 계속해서 성장하고 있다. 최근에, 마이클은 배달 업무를 도와줄 새 직원 애셔를 고용했다. 유감스럽게도, 애셔는 일을 잘 못하고 있으며, 이미 6개의 소포를 잘못된 주소로 배달했다. 마이클은 걱정하며 결국 애셔에게 이제부터는 배달을 하는 대신 주문을 받으라고 말하기로 결정을 내린다. 이 상황에서, 마이클이 애셔에게 할 말로 가장 적절한 것은 무엇인가?

16 ②   17 ②

해설 **16** 태양 에너지 사용에 몇 가지 단점이 있기는 하나 단점보다 장점이 더 많다는 점을 부각시켜 말하고 있다.

① 오늘과 미래의 태양 에너지

② 태양 에너지의 부정할 수 없는 장점들

③ 태양열 기술의 최근 발전들

④ 청정에너지에 대해 주의를 환기시키려는 이유

⑤ 태양 에너지가 어떻게 세상을 바꿨는가

[선택지 어휘] **call attention to** ~에 대해 주의를 환기시키다

해설 **17** 해석 참조

어휘 **source** (사물의) 원천, 근원
solar panel 태양 전지판
have an effect on ~에 영향을 미치다
efficiency 효율(성)
initial 초기의, 처음의
renewable 재생 가능한
be likely to-v v하기 쉽다
break down (기계, 차가) 고장 나다
make sense 타당하다, 말이 되다
switch to ~로 바꾸다, 전환하다

M Good afternoon, everyone! Today, we'll talk about saving the Earth with solar energy. Solar energy is a never ending source of energy. If you install solar panels on your roof, they will produce most of the electricity that your house needs. Of course, there are some disadvantages to using solar energy. Most solar panels need large areas of land. The silicon used in the panels is also very expensive. Air pollution and weather can have a large effect on their efficiency. Also, solar energy can only be gathered while the sun is shining. During the night, your expensive solar-energy equipment will be useless. Still, there are many more advantages than disadvantages of solar energy. The high initial cost can be recovered over time. Other renewable sources, wind and water power, are noisy, expensive and more likely to break down than solar-energy systems. Hence, economically, using solar energy still makes good sense. And most of all, it's the right thing to do. If no one switches to cleaner power sources, environmental problems will only get worse.

남 여러분 안녕하세요! 오늘 우리는 태양 에너지로 지구를 구하는 방법에 관해 이야기할 겁니다. 태양 에너지는 절대 고갈되지 않는 에너지원입니다. 지붕에 태양 전지판을 설치한다면, 태양 전지판은 당신의 주택이 필요로 하는 전기의 대부분을 생산할 것입니다. 물론, 태양 에너지를 사용하는 것에는 몇 가지 단점이 있습니다. **태양 전지판 대부분은 넓은 토지 면적을 필요로 합니다(①). 전지판에 사용되는 실리콘 또한 매우 비쌉니다(③). 대기 오염과 날씨는 전지판의 효율에 큰 영향을 미칠 수 있습니다(④). 또한, 태양 에너지는 햇빛이 비치고 있을 때에만 모을 수 있습니다(⑤).** 밤 동안에는 비싼 태양 에너지 장비들이 무용지물이 될 것입니다. 그렇지만, 태양 에너지는 단점보다 장점이 더 많습니다. 높은 초기 비용은 시간이 지나면 회복될 수 있습니다. 풍력, 수력과 같은 다른 재생 가능한 에너지는 소음이 심하고 비싸며 태양 에너지 시스템보다 고장 나기 더 쉽습니다. 따라서, 경제적인 측면에서, 태양 에너지를 사용하는 것은 여전히 합리적입니다. 그리고 무엇보다도, 그것은 옳은 일이기도 합니다. 더 깨끗한 동력 자원으로 아무도 바꾸지 않는다면, 환경 문제는 더 악화되기만 할 것입니다.

01 ⑤	02 ①	03 ⑤	04 ⑤	05 ③	06 ③	07 ⑤	08 ④	09 ④	10 ④
11 ③	12 ⑤	13 ①	14 ②	15 ⑤	16 ②	17 ③			

01 ⑤

해설 도미네이터라는 놀이 기구가 정기 안전 점검으로 운행이 중단될 것임을 알리고 있다.

어휘 due to ~ 때문에
routine 정기적인; 일상의 일
inspection 점검, 검사
ride 놀이 기구
give out (여러 사람에게) ~을 나눠주다
good for ~와 같은 가치를 지니는
sincerely 진심으로
take full advantage of ~을 최대한 이용하다
thrilling 스릴 넘치는, 아주 신이 나는
attraction 인기거리; 명소, 명물; 매력

M May I have your attention, please? The Dominator will be closed this afternoon due to a routine safety inspection. The last rides will be given at 3 p.m. If you are unable to get on the ride before then, we will be giving out tickets, good for one free ride, at the ticket office. These tickets can be used anytime before September. We sincerely apologize for any disappointment, and hope that you will take full advantage of the many other thrilling attractions available at Coaster City. Thank you.

남 주목해주시겠습니까? 도미네이터가 정기 안전 점검으로 오늘 오후에 폐쇄될 예정입니다. 마지막 탑승은 오후 3시에 있을 것입니다. 만약 그 전에 놀이 기구에 탑승하실 수 없다면, 매표소에서 놀이 기구 1회 무료 탑승권을 나눠드리도록 하겠습니다. 이 탑승권은 9월 전에 언제든지 사용하실 수 있습니다. 실망하시게 한 점 진심으로 사과드리며, 코스터 시티에서 이용하실 수 있는 다른 스릴 넘치는 많은 인기 놀이 기구들을 최대한 이용하시기 바랍니다. 감사합니다.

02 ①

해설 역기 들기로 근력만 기르는 남자에게 여자가 유산소 운동을 병행해야 한다고 조언하고 있다.

어휘 huff and puff (몹시 지쳐서) 헉헉거리다
catch one's breath 호흡을 가다듬다
out of breath 숨이 가쁜
combine 병행하다; 결합하다
cf. combination 결합(물)
aerobic 유산소 운동의
cycling 자전거 타기, 사이클링
tiring 피곤하게 만드는
sore 아픈, 쑤시는

W Ah! We missed the bus.
M [huffing and puffing] Hold on. I need to catch my breath. Why aren't you out of breath?
W Well, I'm combining two different kinds of exercises. I lift weights and go jogging.
M Two different kinds? Anyway, I lift weights every day, too.
W Then you are only building muscle strength. For your lungs and heart, you also need aerobic activities like cycling, running, or jumping rope.
M Hmm... so what do you suggest?
W I think you need a combination of aerobic exercise and weight lifting.
M Sounds tiring. My muscles are already sore after lifting weights.
W If you have sore muscles, you need to stretch, too. Stretching will help your muscles recover.
M All right. It'll be hard at first, but I'll try.

여 아! 버스를 놓쳤어.
남 [헉헉거리며] 기다려. 호흡을 가다듬어야겠어. 너는 왜 숨이 안 차니?
여 글쎄, 나는 다른 두 가지 종류의 운동을 병행하고 있어. 난 역기를 들고 조깅을 해.
남 두 가지 다른 종류라고? 어쨌든, 나도 매일 역기를 들어.
여 그럼 넌 근력만 기르고 있는 거야. 폐와 심장을 위해서는 자전거 타기, 달리기, 줄넘기 같은 유산소 운동도 필요해.
남 음… 그래서 어떻게 하면 좋겠다는 거야?
여 네가 유산소 운동과 역기 들기를 병행해야 한다고 생각해.
남 피곤할 것 같아. 역기 들기 후에 내 근육이 이미 쑤시거든.
여 근육이 쑤신다면 스트레칭도 해야 해. 스트레칭은 근육이 회복되는 것을 도울 거야.
남 그래. 처음에는 힘들겠지만, 노력해볼게.

03 ⑤

해설 남자가 쓴 소설 원고에 관해 논의하고 일부 문법적 오류를 수정했다는 것에서 남자는 작가이고 여자는 편집자임을 알 수 있다.

어휘 overall 전반적으로; 전반적인, 전체의
train conductor 기차 차장
cf. conductor (버스나 기차의) 승무원; 지휘자
fit 적절하다, 들어맞다

M What did you think about the work I emailed you?
W I liked it overall, except for a few details.
M Oh, like which ones?
W I didn't get why the train conductor suddenly changed clothes. It just didn't seem to fit.
M Actually, I'm glad you noticed that detail. It might be puzzling, but it's going to be related to a later crime.

남 제가 이메일로 드린 작품에 대해 어떻게 생각하셨나요?
여 전반적으로 좋았어요. 몇 가지 세부 사항들만 제외하면요.
남 아, 예를 들면 어떤 것이요?
여 저는 왜 기차 차장이 갑자기 옷을 갈아입는지 이해가 안 됐어요. 그건 좀 적절하지 않아 보였어요.
남 사실, 저는 당신이 그 세부 사항을 알아채주셔서 기뻐요. 그게 영문 모를 일일 수도 있지만, 이후의 범죄와 연관이 될 겁니다.

puzzling 영문 모를, 헷갈리게 하는
minor 사소한, 작은
grammatical 문법의

W So, we should keep it then?
M Yes. It's an important clue.
W I see. Also, I made <u>some minor grammatical changes</u> here and there.
M Okay. What did you think about the ending of the chapter?
W It was perfect. I think this is going to be a best seller.

여 그럼, 그대로 둬야 하나요?
남 네. 그것은 중요한 단서예요.
여 알겠어요. 또한, 제가 여기저기 사소한 문법적인 수정을 좀 했어요.
남 네. 챕터의 결말에 대해서는 어떻게 생각하셨어요?
여 완벽했어요. 제 생각에 이건 베스트셀러가 될 거예요.

---

04 ⑤

해설 창문의 하트무늬 커튼이 마음에 든다고 했으므로 그림 속 물방울 무늬 커튼이 대화의 내용과 일치하지 않는다.

어휘 stage setting 무대 장치
check out 확인하다
arched 아치형의
story line 줄거리

W Louis, how's the stage setting for the student drama going?
M It's finished, Ms. Wyatt. I've got a picture of the stage. Can you check it out?
W Okay. There is <u>a big arched door</u> on the left side of the stage.
M And I put a diamond-shaped clock on the wall next to the door.
W Good. And you placed a sofa <u>against the wall</u>. I like the two cushions on it.
M I'm glad you like them. Is <u>the lamp on the round table</u> okay with you?
W It looks perfect to me.
M What do you think about the windows on the right side?
W They're good. I especially like the heart-patterned curtains.
M Thanks. I chose them to <u>match the story line</u>.
W Good job!

여 루이스, 학생 연극 무대 장치는 어떻게 되어가고 있니?
남 그건 끝났어요, 와이어트 선생님. 제가 무대 사진을 갖고 있어요. 확인해주실 수 있나요?
여 그래. 무대 왼편에 큰 아치형의 문이 있구나.
남 그리고 문 옆의 벽에 마름모꼴의 시계를 달았어요.
여 좋아. 그리고 벽에 기대어 소파를 놓았구나. 소파 위의 쿠션 두 개가 마음에 들어.
남 마음에 드신다니 기뻐요. 원형 테이블 위의 램프는 괜찮나요?
여 내겐 완벽해 보이는구나.
남 오른편의 창문은 어떻게 생각하세요?
여 괜찮아. 난 특히 하트무늬의 커튼이 마음에 드는구나.
남 감사합니다. 줄거리에 맞추려고 그걸 선택했어요.
여 훌륭해!

---

05 ③

해설 남자는 여자에게 청소하는 사람들이 오면 자신의 사무실을 청소하도록 해달라고 부탁했다.
① 파일들이 어디에 있는지 남자에게 말해주기
② 계약서의 복사본을 만들어주기
③ 남자의 사무실이 청소되도록 하기
④ 내일 사용할 파일 준비를 마쳐 놓기
⑤ 남자가 돌아올 때까지 사무실에 남아 있기

어휘 take off (어떤 장소에서) 떠나다; (옷, 모자 등을) 벗다; 이륙하다
contract 계약(서)

M Helen, you're still here? Why haven't you left?
W I still have a lot of work to do.
M Well, <u>try not to stay too late</u>. I'm taking off.
W Oh, before you go, could you tell me <u>where I can find copies</u> of last year's contracts?
M The files are in the cabinet behind my desk.
W Thanks.
M By the way, are you staying until 9?
W Yeah, I think so.
M Sorry, but when the cleaning people come, could you make sure <u>they do my office</u>?
W Sure, no problem.
M Great. <u>They've missed it a couple of times recently.</u> It's a bit of a mess.
W OK. Don't worry. See you tomorrow!

남 헬렌, 아직 여기 있구나? 왜 퇴근 안 했어?
여 아직도 할 일이 많이 있거든.
남 음, 너무 늦게까지 있지 않도록 해. 나는 갈게.
여 아, 가기 전에 작년 계약서 복사본을 어디서 찾을 수 있는지 좀 알려줄래?
남 그 파일들은 내 책상 뒤에 있는 캐비닛 안에 있어.
여 고마워.
남 그런데 9시까지 남아 있을 거야?
여 응, 그럴 것 같아.
남 미안한데, 청소하는 분들이 오면, 내 사무실을 청소하게 해줄 수 있을까?
여 물론이야, 문제없어.
남 잘됐다. 그들이 최근에 두어 번 내 사무실 청소를 깜빡했거든. 사무실이 조금 지저분한 상태야.
여 알겠어. 걱정하지 마. 내일 봐!

---

06 ③

해설 두 사람의 여행 경비는 총 360달러이다($50×2+$80×2+$80+$20=$360). 마지막에 남자가 여자에게 총액의 반을 달라고 했으므로 여자가 지불할 금액은 180달러이다.

W Paul, <u>how much do I owe you</u> for the trip last week?
M Let's see... the car rental was <u>$50</u> per day.
W We only rented the car for two days, right?

여 폴, 지난주 여행에 대해 내가 너한테 얼마를 주면 될까?
남 어디 보자… 자동차 대여는 하루에 50달러였어.
여 우리는 이틀만 차를 대여했지, 맞니?

M Yes. And it cost $80 to fill up the tank. We drove about 450 miles, so we filled it up twice.

W What about food?

M I remember we only ate out for lunch and dinner.

W Right. Thanks to the free breakfast from the hotel, we didn't have to spend much money on food.

M Yeah. According to my credit card statement, we spent $80 in total for food.

W Oh, you need to add an extra $20 for snacks and coffee. You paid with cash at the convenience store.

M Right. I forgot about it. [pause] I think that's all. Please give me half of the total.

남 응. 그리고 휘발유를 가득 채우는데 80달러 들었어. 우리는 약 450마일을 운전했고 그래서 두 번 가득 채웠어.

여 음식은 어떻지?

남 우리는 점심과 저녁 식사만 외식한 것으로 기억해.

여 맞아. 호텔 무료 아침 식사 덕분에 우리는 음식에 많은 돈을 쓸 필요가 없었어.

남 그래. 내 신용카드 명세서에 따르면 우리는 음식에 통틀어 80달러를 썼어.

여 아, 간식이랑 커피에 대해 추가로 20달러를 더해야 해. 네가 편의점에서 현금으로 계산했잖아.

남 맞다. 그걸 잊었네. [잠시 후] 그게 다인 것 같아. 그 총액의 절반을 줘.

07 ⑤

해설 남동생이 깁스를 일주일 더 하고 있어야 하기 때문에 가족 여행을 취소해야 하는 상황이다.

어휘 time off 휴가, 휴식 시간

possibly ((특히 can't, couldn't 부정문에서)) 아무리 해도, 도저히

cast 깁스, 석고 붕대

be supposed to-v v하기로 되어 있다

indoor 실내의

skating rink (롤러) 스케이트장, 아이스링크 (= ice rink)

M Alright, Mom, I'm all packed for the hot springs tomorrow.

W I'm sorry, Benjamin, but we should cancel our family trip.

M Oh, no! I thought you had already gotten the time off from work.

W It's not that. It's your little brother.

M But it's spring break! He can't possibly have school work!

W Well, his doctor said he should keep his cast on for another week.

M So we're going to stay home? It's supposed to rain all week, and there's nothing to do!

W Actually, since you've always wanted to go skating, I am planning to take you to an indoor skating rink.

M Really? Can I bring my friend Kelly?

W Sure. Just check with her parents first.

남 자, 엄마, 내일 온천에 가기 위한 짐을 다 챙겼어요.

여 미안하지만, 벤자민, 우리 가족 여행을 취소해야 한단다.

남 안 돼요! 전 엄마가 이미 직장에 휴가를 내셨다고 생각했는데요.

여 그래서가 아니란다. 네 남동생 때문이야.

남 그렇지만 봄방학이잖아요! 그 애에게 학교 과제가 있을 리 없어요!

여 음, 의사 선생님 말씀이 깁스를 일주일 더 하고 있어야 한다는구나.

남 그럼 우리 집에 있는 거예요? 일주일 내내 비가 올 거고, 할 게 아무것도 없는 걸요!

여 사실, 네가 항상 스케이트를 타러 가고 싶어 해서, 널 실내 스케이트장에 데려갈 계획이란다.

남 정말요? 제 친구 켈리를 데려가도 되나요?

여 물론이지. 다만 그 애 부모님께 먼저 여쭤보렴.

08 ④

해설 해석 참조

어휘 entirely 전부, 완전히

generate (전기·열 등을) 만들어내다, 발생시키다

architect 건축가

art deco 아르 데코 ((1920~30년대에 유행한 장식 미술의 한 양식. 기하학적 무늬와 강렬한 색채가 특징))

distinctive 독특한; 구별되는

M Monica, look over there. It's the Hoover Dam.

W Oh, wow! It's even bigger than I'd imagined.

M Would you like to stop and take a look?

W That sounds fun. In fact, I was just reading about it this morning.

M I remember. You said it was almost entirely made of concrete and bigger than the Great Pyramid of Giza.

W That's right. And it generates more than 4 billion kWh per year.

M It sure is an impressive structure.

W That's the work of the architect, Gordon Kaufmann. He wanted the dam to make a powerful impression.

M He certainly succeeded. I've never seen anything like it.

W Kaufmann's work, including the Hoover Dam, was heavily influenced by the Art Deco movement of the 1930s. That's where it gets its distinctive style.

M I see. Let's take some pictures!

남 모니카 저기 좀 봐. 저건 후버댐이야.

여 어, 와! 내가 상상했던 것보다 훨씬 더 크네.

남 잠시 멈춰서 구경할래?

여 그게 재미있겠다. 사실, 오늘 아침에 그 댐에 관한 글을 읽고 있었어.

남 기억해. **그 댐의 거의 전체가 콘크리트로 만들어졌고(① 건축 자재)** 기자의 피라미드보다 더 크다고 네가 말했잖아.

여 맞아. 그리고 **연간 40억 킬로와트가 넘는 전력을 만들어내(② 발전량)**.

남 정말 굉장한 건축물이야.

여 **그건 건축가 고든 카우프만의 건축물이야(③ 설계자).** 그는 이 댐이 강렬한 인상을 주길 원했어.

남 그럼 확실히 성공했네. 난 이런 걸 본 적이 없어.

여 후버댐을 포함해 카우프만의 건축물은 **1930년대 아르 데코 운동에 크게 영향을 받았어(⑤ 건축 양식).** 거기서 바로 후버댐이 그런 독특한 양식을 가지게 된 거야.

남 그렇구나. 우리 사진 찍자!

09 ④

해설 버스는 30분 간격으로 운행한다.

어휘 memorial 기념관, 기념비
attraction 명소, 명물
run (버스 등이) 운행하다
pass 탑승권, 출입증; 합격; 통과, 지나감
board 탑승하다

W Welcome to the Discovery Tour Bus. Our first stop is the National Mall, where you can see the Lincoln and Jefferson Memorials. This tour bus will stop at a total of 9 tourist attractions including the White House and Georgetown. You may stay on this bus, or take a look around at any of the 9 stops and wait for the next bus. It is exactly 11:00 right now, and the buses run every half hour. Also, please remember to show your tour pass before boarding the bus. I hope you enjoy the tour and have a great day!

여 디스커버리 투어 버스에 탑승하신 것을 환영합니다. **첫 번째 정거장은 내셔널 몰이며**(①), 이곳에서 여러분은 링컨 기념관과 제퍼슨 기념관을 보실 수 있습니다. 이 투어 버스는 백악관과 조지타운을 포함해 **총 9곳의 관광 명소에서 정차할 것입니다**(②). 여러분은 버스에 그대로 계시거나, **9개의 정거장 중 어디든지 주변을 둘러보시고**(③) 다음 버스를 기다리시면 됩니다. 현재 시각은 11시 정각이며, **버스는 30분마다 운행합니다**(④). 또한, **버스에 탑승하시기 전에 관광 탑승권을 보여주시는 것을**(⑤) 기억해주시기 바랍니다. 관광을 즐기시고 좋은 하루 보내시길 바랍니다!

10 ④

해설 예산이 1,500달러 아래이고 층수가 5층 이하이며 화장실은 2개 이상인 것 중에서 더 새 것인 아파트를 선택한다.

어휘 budget 예산
floor (건물의) 층
frequently 자주, 빈번히
make an appointment 약속을 하다

W Hello, Mr. Cromwell. I'm Miranda Wilson. I called you yesterday about renting a 3-bedroom apartment.
M Hello, Ms. Wilson. Could you tell me what your budget is?
W I don't want to spend more than $1,500 a month.
M Is there anything else you want?
W I like lower floors since I frequently go out with my kids. I'd like it to be not higher than the 5th floor.
M Okay. How many bathrooms would you like?
W I need at least two bathrooms since we are a family of five.
M Now you can choose between these two. Which one do you prefer?
W I'll choose the newer one. I'm worried that an older apartment would have too many problems.
M All right. I'll make an appointment to see this apartment tomorrow.

여 안녕하세요, 크롬웰 씨. 저는 미란다 윌슨입니다. 어제 방 3개짜리 아파트 임대 때문에 전화를 드렸죠.
남 안녕하세요, 윌슨 씨. 예산이 어떻게 되시는지 말씀해주시겠어요?
여 한 달에 1,500달러 넘게 내고 싶지는 않아요.
남 뭐 더 원하시는 게 있으세요?
여 아이들과 자주 외출하기 때문에 낮은 층이 좋습니다. 5층보다 높지 않았으면 좋겠어요.
남 알겠습니다. 화장실은 몇 개를 원하세요?
여 저희 가족이 5명이니까 최소한 화장실 두 개는 필요해요.
남 그러면 이 둘 중에서 하나를 선택하실 수 있습니다. 어떤 게 더 좋으세요?
여 더 새 것으로 하겠습니다. 오래된 아파트는 문제가 너무 많을까봐 걱정이 돼요.
남 좋습니다. 내일 이 아파트를 볼 약속을 잡을게요.

11 ③

해설 남자가 새로 구매한 차의 장점을 나열하는 상황이므로 마치 광고하는 것 같다는 응답이 가장 적절하다.
① 내가 그걸 살 수 있을지 모르겠어.
② 널 위해 대기 중인 차가 한 대 있어.
④ 네가 차를 팔아야 한다니 유감이야.
⑤ 너희 아버지는 새 차를 구매하셔서 기쁘시겠구나.

어휘 compact 소형인; 빽빽한
economical 경제적인, 실속 있는
astonished 깜짝 놀란
fuel 연료

M You know, I bought a compact car. It runs well, and it's so easy to park.
W Is it much more economical than that larger model you used to have?
M Definitely. I was astonished at how much I'm saving on fuel. I really like the car. It's a pleasure to drive.
W You sound like an advertisement.

남 있잖아, 내가 소형차를 구매했어. 그건 잘 달리고, 주차하기도 매우 쉬워.
여 네가 갖고 있던 그 큰 차보다 훨씬 더 경제적이니?
남 물론이지. 내가 연료에 쓰는 돈을 얼마나 많이 절약하고 있는지 알고서 깜짝 놀랐어. 난 정말로 그 차가 마음에 들어. 운전하는 게 즐거워.
여 너 마치 광고하는 것 같아.

12 ⑤

해설 여자가 역사 동아리에 가입하려면 누구에게 말해야 하는지 물었으므로 담당 선생님을 알려주는 응답이 가장 적절하다.

W I heard Mary and Tom are going to the Folk Village this afternoon. It sounds like fun.
M Yes, they're in the history club. They go to many interesting places.

여 메리와 톰이 오늘 오후에 민속촌에 갈 거라고 들었어. 재미있을 것 같아.
남 응, 그 애들은 역사 동아리에 들었거든. 많은 흥미로운 장소를 다녀.

① 난 신청할 시간이 없어.
② 그 애들은 매달 여행을 떠나.
③ 우리만의 동아리를 시작해야 해.
④ 그 애들은 민속촌에 가는 것을 아주 좋아해.

어휘 sign up 가입하다, 신청하다
[선택지 어휘] in charge of ~을 맡고 있는, 담당의

---

13 ①

해설 재난에 대비하는 것이 너무 과하지 않냐는 말에 서운해하는 남자에게 이제부터는 준비를 돕겠다는 응답이 가장 적절하다.
② 그건 사실이 아니에요. 나는 통조림 식품 먹는 것을 정말 좋아해요.
③ 물론이죠. 우리 오늘 캠핑 용품을 사러 가요.
④ 진정해요. 당신은 내일 상점에 갈 수 있어요.
⑤ 내 말을 오해하지 마요. 나는 단지 미리 준비하고 싶을 뿐이에요.

어휘 canned 통조림으로 된
disaster 재난, 재해
whistle 호루라기; 휘파람
frustrated 불만스러워 하는, 좌절감을 느끼는
take A seriously A를 심각[진지]하게 받아들이다
[선택지 어휘] get A wrong A를 오해하다, 잘못 생각하다
in advance 미리

W I'd like to join them. Who should I talk to about signing up?
M Mr. Beckman is in charge of the club.

W Honey, what's all this canned food in the kitchen cabinet?
M I bought those yesterday for emergencies.
W Emergencies?
M Well, after the last earthquake, I realized that disasters can happen at any time.
W I guess it wouldn't hurt to be prepared.
M My thoughts exactly. So, I made a list of things to buy. We still need whistles, batteries, blankets, masks, and so on.
W Don't you think that's too much?
M Of course not! You just don't understand how important this is.
W Okay, okay. You don't have to get frustrated.
M Well, it feels like I'm the only one who is taking this seriously.
W Fine. I'll help you prepare from now on.

여 나도 그 애들과 함께하고 싶어. 가입에 관해 누구에게 말씀드려야 하지?
남 베크만 선생님께서 그 동아리를 담당하셔.

여 여보, 부엌 수납장에 있는 이 통조림 식품은 다 뭔가요?
남 비상사태에 대비해 내가 어제 사다 놓았어요.
여 비상사태요?
남 음, 지난번 지진 이후에 재난이 언제든 일어날 수 있다는 걸 깨달았어요.
여 준비해서 나쁠 건 없겠지요.
남 내 생각도 똑같아요. 그래서 내가 사야 할 물건들의 목록을 만들었어요. 우리는 아직도 호루라기, 건전지, 담요, 마스크 등이 필요해요.
여 그건 너무 과하다고 생각하지 않아요?
남 물론 아니죠! 당신은 이게 얼마나 중요한지 정말 이해를 못하는군요.
여 알겠어요, 알겠어. 불만스러워 할 것까진 없어요.
남 저, 내가 이걸 심각하게 받아들이고 있는 유일한 사람인 것처럼 느껴지네요.
여 좋아요. 이제부터는 내가 당신이 준비하는 걸 도울게요.

---

14 ②

해설 두 번째 조언 또한 기회에 관한 것이라고 했으므로, 찾고 있던 기회를 발견하면 꼭 붙잡아야 한다는 응답이 가장 적절하다.
① 성공은 종종 큰 희생으로 얻어집니다.
③ 제 조언은 당신의 건강에 초점을 맞추라는 것입니다.
④ 그것은 제게 일생에 한 번 있는 기회였습니다.
⑤ 당신이 기부에 그렇게 의욕적이시다니 기쁩니다.

어휘 generous 후한; 관대한
motivate 동기를 부여하다
cf. motivated 의욕을 가진
play a big role in ~에서 큰 역할을 하다
be looking to-v v할 길을 찾고 있다
succeed in ~에 성공하다
have to do with ~와 관계가 있다

W Thank you for agreeing to this interview, Mr. Johnson.
M It's my pleasure, Miss...?
W Smith, but you can call me Judy.
M It's nice to meet you, Judy. I often read your magazine.
W I'm glad to hear that. You know, I've read about your recent generous donation. What motivated you?
M I think my children played a big role in that.
W I see. And do you have any advice for those who are looking to succeed in business?
M I have two pieces of advice. First, always be looking for opportunities. People often miss what is right in front of them.
W Okay.
M My second piece of advice also has to do with opportunity.
W And what is that?
M When you find it, you need to seize it.

여 이 인터뷰에 응해주셔서 감사드립니다, 존슨 씨.
남 별말씀을요, 성함이…?
여 스미스입니다만, 주디라고 부르셔도 됩니다.
남 만나서 반가워요, 주디. 저는 종종 귀사의 잡지를 읽습니다.
여 그 말씀을 들으니 기쁘네요. 아시겠지만, 존슨 씨께서 최근에 하신 후한 기부에 대해 읽었습니다. 무엇이 존슨 씨에게 동기를 부여했나요?
남 제 아이들이 큰 역할을 한 것 같습니다.
여 그렇군요. 그리고 사업에서 성공할 길을 찾고 있는 사람들을 위해 해주실 조언이 있으신가요?
남 두 가지 조언이 있습니다. 첫째는, 항상 기회를 찾고 있으라는 것입니다. 사람들은 자주 자신들 바로 앞에 있는 기회들을 놓치지요.
여 네.
남 두 번째 조언 또한 기회와 관련이 있습니다.
여 그러면 그것은 무엇인가요?
남 기회를 발견하면, 그것을 꼭 붙잡아야 합니다.

[선택지 어휘] **at a great cost** 큰 희생을 치르고; 큰돈을 들여서
seize 꽉 붙잡다
once-in-a-lifetime 일생에 한 번의

15 ⑤

해설 요청하지도 않은 세차 비용이 추가로 청구된 이유를 물으며 항의할 것이다.

① 신용카드로 지불해도 괜찮나요?

② 무료 세차에 대해 제가 어느 분께 감사를 드려야 하나요?

③ 제 차를 수리하는 데 왜 이렇게 시간이 오래 걸렸나요?

④ 여기서 백화점까지 어떻게 가야 하나요?

⑤ 왜 제가 요청하지 않은 서비스에 대해 비용이 청구된 건가요?

어휘 **awful** 심한; 끔찍한
screech 삐걱삐걱[끽끽] 소리가 나다
pull into ~에 차를 세우다
[선택지 어휘] **charge for** ~에 대한 요금을 청구하다

M Juliet is driving to the department store when she hears an awful screeching noise coming from her car. Worried, she pulls into the nearest repair shop. They tell her that she needs to have the brakes fixed. About one hour later, her car comes out and she sees that they have not only fixed the brakes, but have even washed the car. Feeling satisfied with a free car wash, Juliet goes to pay. She reviews her bill, but sees an extra $10 charge for a car wash. Now, she wants to make a complaint about it. In this situation, what would Juliet most likely say to the employee?

남 줄리엣은 백화점으로 차를 몰고 가는 중에 차에서 심한 삐걱거리는 소리가 나는 것을 듣는다. 그녀는 걱정되어, 가장 가까운 정비소에 차를 세운다. 그들은 브레이크를 고쳐야 한다고 말한다. 한 시간쯤 뒤에, 그녀의 차가 나오고 그녀는 그들이 브레이크를 수리했을 뿐 아니라, 세차까지 해 놓은 것을 알게 된다. 무료 세차에 만족감을 느끼며, 줄리엣은 돈을 내러 간다. 그녀는 청구서를 자세히 살피는데, 세차비로 10달러가 추가로 청구된 것을 본다. 이제 그녀는 그것에 대해 항의를 제기하고 싶어 한다. 이 상황에서, 줄리엣이 직원에게 할 말로 가장 적절한 것은 무엇인가?

16 ②   17 ③

해설 **16** 운동을 신중하게 하기 위한 방안들에 대한 설명이다.

① 운동을 위한 준비 운동의 이점

② 운동하는 동안 안전하기 위한 조언들

③ 운동하고 신체적으로 활동적이어야 하는 이유들

④ 사람들을 건강하게 할 수 있는 운동의 종류

⑤ 올바른 운동 장비를 선택하는 방법

17 해석 참조

어휘 **frequent** 빈번한, 자주 있는
injury 부상
immediately 즉시
warm up 준비 운동을 하다
pad 보호대[패드, 완충재]
vulnerable 취약한, 상처를 입기 쉬운
keep in mind 명심하다, 기억해두다

W Good afternoon, everyone. We all know that frequent physical activity is good for us, and there are many activities to choose from. You can play hockey or baseball. You can take yoga classes. But no matter what you do, do it carefully. First of all, do not exercise if you are sick. If you do get an injury, stop what you are doing immediately. Wait until you are feeling better. Next, make sure to warm up. If you are swimming, start off slowly. Give your muscles a chance to move before working them too hard. Before playing a sport, do some easy jogging or walking, followed by stretching. Third, wear pads to protect vulnerable parts of your body for activities such as skateboarding. Also, wear footwear that is comfortable and gives you the necessary support. Finally, follow the rules of the game you are playing. They keep the game fair and protect the people playing. Likewise, follow the rules of the road if you are inline skating or riding your bike. Keep these in mind, and you can fully enjoy working out.

여 좋은 오후입니다, 여러분. 우리 모두 빈번한 신체 활동이 우리에게 좋다는 것을 알고 있고, 선택할 수 있는 많은 활동들이 있습니다. 여러분은 **하키**(① hockey)나 야구를 할 수 있습니다. 요가 수업을 들을 수도 있습니다. 하지만 여러분이 무엇을 하든, 그것을 신중하게 하세요. 우선, 아프면 운동하지 마세요. 만약 부상을 입으면, 하고 있는 것을 즉시 멈추세요. 나아질 때까지 기다리세요. 다음은, 반드시 준비 운동을 하세요. **수영**(② swimming)을 한다면, 천천히 시작하세요. 근육을 너무 힘껏 사용하기 전에 근육이 움직일 기회를 주세요. 운동을 하기 전에, 약간의 간단한 조깅이나 걷기를 하고, 이어서 스트레칭을 하세요. 세 번째로, **스케이트보드 타기**(④ skateboarding)와 같은 활동을 위해서는 신체의 취약한 부분을 보호하기 위한 보호대를 착용하세요. 또한, 편하고 여러분에게 필요한 지탱하는 힘을 주는 신발을 신으세요. 마지막으로, 여러분이 하는 경기의 규칙을 따르세요. 경기 규칙은 경기를 공정하게 유지하고 경기하는 사람들을 보호합니다. 마찬가지로, **인라인스케이트**(⑤ inline skating)를 타거나 자전거를 탄다면 도로의 규칙을 따르세요. 이것들을 명심하면 여러분은 운동을 충분히 즐길 수 있습니다.

MEMO

ANSWER PART II 실전편

01회

01 ⑤ 02 ⑤ 03 ② 04 ⑤ 05 ① 06 ④ 07 ④ 08 ③ 09 ② 10 ② 11 ③ 12 ② 13 ③ 14 ③ 15 ③ 16 ③ 17 ④

02회

01 ③ 02 ⑤ 03 ⑤ 04 ③ 05 ① 06 ⑤ 07 ② 08 ③ 09 ④ 10 ① 11 ① 12 ② 13 ④ 14 ④ 15 ② 16 ⑤ 17 ④

03회

01 ④ 02 ② 03 ④ 04 ④ 05 ② 06 ② 07 ⑤ 08 ⑤ 09 ② 10 ② 11 ② 12 ⑤ 13 ② 14 ③ 15 ② 16 ② 17 ③

04회

01 ② 02 ③ 03 ⑤ 04 ④ 05 ④ 06 ④ 07 ② 08 ③ 09 ④ 10 ⑤ 11 ④ 12 ① 13 ③ 14 ④ 15 ④ 16 ② 17 ⑤

05회

01 ③ 02 ② 03 ⑤ 04 ③ 05 ④ 06 ⑤ 07 ⑤ 08 ② 09 ④ 10 ④ 11 ① 12 ⑤ 13 ⑤ 14 ④ 15 ⑤ 16 ① 17 ③

06회

01 ③ 02 ③ 03 ① 04 ③ 05 ① 06 ② 07 ④ 08 ② 09 ③ 10 ⑤ 11 ⑤ 12 ③ 13 ⑤ 14 ⑤ 15 ② 16 ⑤ 17 ①

07회

01 ② 02 ① 03 ④ 04 ③ 05 ① 06 ② 07 ④ 08 ④ 09 ③ 10 ② 11 ② 12 ② 13 ① 14 ⑤ 15 ② 16 ① 17 ④

08회

01 ① 02 ② 03 ⑤ 04 ② 05 ⑤ 06 ③ 07 ③ 08 ② 09 ⑤ 10 ④ 11 ⑤ 12 ④ 13 ③ 14 ③ 15 ⑤ 16 ④ 17 ②

09회

01 ③ 02 ③ 03 ⑤ 04 ④ 05 ③ 06 ④ 07 ④ 08 ③ 09 ⑤ 10 ⑤ 11 ③ 12 ① 13 ④ 14 ① 15 ④ 16 ② 17 ②

10회

01 ⑤ 02 ① 03 ⑤ 04 ⑤ 05 ③ 06 ③ 07 ⑤ 08 ④ 09 ④ 10 ④ 11 ③ 12 ⑤ 13 ① 14 ② 15 ⑤ 16 ② 17 ③

첫단추 BUTTON ʓ